SOCIAL
PHILOSOPHY
& POLICY CENTER

MARKET EDUCATION

The Unknown History

Andrew J. Coulson

transaction

Transaction Publishers
New Brunswick (USA) and London (UK)

Published by the Social Philosophy and Policy Center and by Transaction
Publishers 1999

Library of Congress Cataloging-in-Publication Data

Coulson, Andrew J. (Joseph), 1967–
    Market education : the unknown history / by Andrew J. Coulson.
      p.   cm. — (Studies in social philosophy & policy ; no. 21)
    Includes bibliographical references and index.
    ISBN 1-56000-408-8 (hardcover). — ISBN 0-7658-0496-4 (softcover)
    1. Education—Aims and objectives—United States.   2. Education—
History.   3. Educational change—History.   4. Comparative education.
5. Public schools—United States—Evaluation.   6. Privatization in education—United States.   7. Educational accountability—United States.
8. Educational change—United States.   I. Title.   II. Series.
LA212.C68   1999
370'.973—dc21   98-44583
                                                          CIP

Cover Design: Kathy Horn
Cover Image copyright © 1999 PhotoDisc, Inc.

Photo Credits: The classroom photo that appears on page 177 was provided
courtesy of Emily Sachar, and is copyright © Emily Sachar 1988–89. The Ptole-
maic map photo, which appears on page 60, was provided courtesy of the Special Collections Division, University of Washington Libraries, negative number: UW#16667.

To Kay

Series Editor: Ellen Frankel Paul
Series Managing Editor: Harry Dolan

The Social Philosophy and Policy Center, founded in 1981, is an interdisciplinary research institution whose principal mission is the examination of public policy issues from a philosophical perspective. In pursuit of this objective, the Center supports the work of scholars in the fields of political science, philosophy, law, and economics. In addition to this book series, the Center hosts scholarly conferences and edits an interdisciplinary professional journal, *Social Philosophy & Policy.* For further information on the Center, write to: Social Philosophy and Policy Center, Bowling Green State University, Bowling Green, OH 43403.

Contents

viii   Contents

Acknowledgments

In the four years during which I researched and wrote *Market Education,* there were times when the task seemed truly daunting. It is due to the support and encouragement of my wife Kay, my family, and my friend and colleague Myron Lieberman that the manuscript was eventually completed.

Numerous hurdles exist, however, on the road between a manuscript and a published work. On occasions too numerous to mention, Myron Lieberman knocked down or brushed aside those hurdles, paving the way toward successful publication. I cannot thank him enough.

During the planning stages of *Market Education,* I benefited immensely from conversations with Shrikant Rangnekar, which led to many improvements in the structure of the book, and spurred me to dig even further into the historical evidence than I had originally intended.

I am also deeply grateful to Ellen Frankel Paul, for her excellent editorial insights, as well as to Harry Dolan and the rest of the extraordinarily capable staff of the Social Philosophy and Policy Center, Bowling Green State University.

Several people offered extensive comments on the manuscript itself or the ideas contained therein, for which I am indebted. These include Stephen Arons, David Boaz, Stewart Deuchar, Chester Finn, Herbert Gintis, Gene Glass, Norman Henchey, Paul Peterson, Lawrence Stedman, and Herbert Walberg. Kay's contributions to the organization and style of the book were of tremendous value. My parents also read rough drafts of many chapters, expurgating most of my offenses against the English language. Any remaining errors are, of course, my own.

Finally, I must thank the many other teachers, parents, and scholars with whom I have spoken and corresponded over the years, but who cannot all be mentioned here by name. I have been impressed by their passion and dedication to the ideals of public education, and hope that they will recognize in this book a similar commitment to educational excellence for all.

Introduction

> *Our public schools are afflicted with a host of troubles. Some of them*
> *are new, but many have been plaguing the schools for years, persisting in*
> *the face of countless attempts to solve them. Despite the unrelenting ef-*
> *forts of a generation of reformers, it is fair to say that we have gotten lost*
> *somewhere on the road to educational excellence. So we are faced with a*
> *choice: keep driving around until the education-reform bandwagon runs*
> *out of gas, or swallow our pride, pull over, and look at a map.*
>
> *The map in question is the history of education, and though it has been*
> *almost completely ignored in the modern debate over schooling, it is our*
> *best hope for finding solutions to our chronic educational woes.*

Over the past two decades, an enormous mass of research and rhetoric has
accumulated on the subject of school reform. While much of this work has been
constructive, its value has been undermined by an inexplicable omission: it has
lacked any sense of history. Virtually all of the problems identified by critics
have been treated as recent phenomena, and their prospective solutions have
been presented as original and untried. But ours is not the first generation to
seek an education for its children, and the educational challenges we face today
have in fact been fermenting for thousands of years.

That point is most sharply driven home in a letter from a prominent lawyer,
outlining his views on education. He was born in the early sixties in a small
town and lamented its lack of a high school, so he decided to found one him-

1

self. But rather than fully endowing the school, which he could easily have afforded to do, he decided to pay only a third of the necessary costs. He explained his decision in this way:

> I would promise the whole amount were I not afraid that someday my gift might be abused for someone's selfish purposes, as I see happen in many places where teachers' salaries are paid from public funds. There is only one remedy to meet this evil: if the appointment of teachers is left entirely to the parents, and they are conscientious about making a wise choice through their obligation to contribute to the cost. People who may be careless about another person's money are sure to be careful about their own, and they will see that only a suitable recipient shall be found for my money if he is also to have their own.[1]

The significance of this letter derives not so much from its content as from its context: as I mentioned, its author was born in the early sixties — not the early nineteen-sixties, or the early eighteen-sixties, *but the early sixties of the first century A.D.* History abounds with hard evidence on the same issues that plague our schools today, but it has been almost entirely overlooked by contemporary reformers. What we don't know is hurting us.

To bridge the history gap, this book brings together the hard-won lessons of both past and present. From the golden age of Greece to the young American republic, from the fall of Rome to the rise of public schooling, it reveals what worked, what didn't, and why. Armed with this knowledge, and with a clear understanding of the educational goals of families and the public at large, it sets out to find the most effective possible way to organize schooling. It does not simply point to a few good schools here or there, or to some redeeming qualities of schools, and then hope that they will magically be duplicated. Nor does it propound a single cookie-cutter definition of a "good" education. Instead, it offers a practical way of bringing responsive and innovative schools into being on a widespread basis — schools adapted to the specific needs of the families they serve, and accessible to all, not just the wealthy.

The first step in meeting the educational needs of families is to understand what those needs are. Consequently, Part I of this book, titled "What We Want," draws together the opinions and aspirations of parents and the general public on issues ranging from curriculum to classroom violence. In order to figure out whether our schools are in need of only minor tweaks or a major overhaul, this section also examines how well public schools are currently meeting people's educational goals.

Using the goals presented in Part I as a yardstick, Part II, titled "What's Been Tried," reveals which approaches to schooling have measured up, and which have not. It provides concrete examples of school systems from 500 B.C. to the late twentieth century, ranging from complete parental freedom to centralized government control. It answers a host of modern questions on the way schools have worked. How was the curriculum set? How quickly did it change to meet the changing demands of families? Who chose the teachers? How much autonomy were they given? How did they perform? For each approach, the successes and failures that resulted are explored, highlighting what students learned and how well they were able to apply that learning.

The last section, "What Works," distills the fundamental ingredients of effective, responsive schools from the evidence presented in Part II. It shows why some school systems have enjoyed continuous innovation and improvement, while others have stagnated or declined. In Chapter 10, the most talked-about school reform proposals, from charter schools to national curricula, are held under a microscope to see whether or not they satisfy the essential requirements for success. The concluding chapter presents a plan for applying the lessons of history and current research to the task of educating our children.

Part I

What We Want

1

Getting Used to Disappointment

In 1841, Horace Mann, the godfather of American public schooling, promised: "Let the Common School be expanded to its capabilities, let it be worked with the efficiency of which it is susceptible, and nine tenths of the crimes in the penal code would become obsolete; the long catalogue of human ills would be abridged."[1]

In 1998, the Los Angeles County School Board voted to arm its public school police with shotguns.[2]

Has public schooling failed?

Few people would be willing to write off the public schools simply because the predictions of a romantic nineteenth-century crusader turned out to be overly optimistic. But how *do* we decide whether public schooling is a success or a failure? Do public schools need to be reformed or replaced? If so, how and with what? These questions cannot be answered without first having a clear idea of our purposes for schooling. Until we know what we want, it is impossible to say whether or not we are getting it. This chapter is therefore dedicated to pulling together people's most broadly and deeply held educational goals, and to finding out how well those goals are being met.

What Parents Want for Their Own Children

The Bottom Line

There is significant agreement among parents as to the ultimate ends of schooling. In U.S. polls dating from the early seventies to the present, parents have repeatedly said that they send their children to school mainly to improve their career prospects and help them to lead richer and more satisfying lives.[3] The answers have been phrased in many different ways, such as "getting better jobs," learning to "get along better with people at all levels of society," "earning more money," becoming "more knowledgeable," and being "better prepared for life," but parents have consistently ranked finding a good job and enjoying a better life as the top priorities.

Comparing the opinions of parents between countries on this issue is more difficult, since few international surveys have specifically asked about people's fundamental educational goals; but the importance given to preparation for employment is clearly universal. More than 85 percent of citizens polled from a dozen industrialized countries ranked job skills as either "essential" or "very important" on a list of qualities they wanted students to develop.[4] This placed it second out of eight choices, coming in just behind self-confidence. The more specific the question, and the more directly it refers to the parents' own children, the clearer the results. A 1990 poll in Great Britain found that almost all parents of teenaged children wanted them to receive more career guidance, and the vast majority also sought increased vocational training for specific jobs.[5]

Much of this emphasis on employment is eminently practical—it is hard to have any kind of life at all without a decent income—but the intrinsic benefits of work cannot be discounted. The sense of satisfaction and achievement that comes from completing a worthy task is indisputable, whether or not it is accompanied by financial gain. One of the greatest hopes parents have is that their children will not only become financially successful, but happy in their work as well.

Knowledge

For their goals to be met, parents also agree that students must acquire the right balance of knowledge, skills, and values. When asked to rate the importance of a wide range of fields studied in elementary schools and high schools, most parents, regardless of nationality, place mathematics and their native language at the top of the scale.[6]

This emphasis makes the results of recent tests all the more disturbing. According to an international study released in December 1995, "one out of five

Americans surveyed did not understand the directions on an aspirin bottle; almost a quarter could not work out a newspaper weather chart."[7] While the United States had a disproportionate number of underachievers, roughly a fifth of the populations of all seven countries participating in the study were found to be barely literate—unable, for instance, to read and grasp a bus schedule.[8] Even a significant number of people with high levels of schooling performed at the lowest levels of literacy. At virtually the same time that these international results were released, calculators were banned in England on two national mathematics tests after serious weaknesses were found in students' understanding of basic arithmetic. Only one eleven-year-old in four was able to calculate 15 percent of 80.[9] While the poor performance of the United States on cross-national mathematics tests is well known—and is discussed later in this book—U.S. students perform poorly even by American standards. A recent nationwide assessment of math skills found that "only 14 percent of eighth graders scored at the seventh-grade level or above."[10]

Beyond the core studies of math and native language, the importance different families give to the various school subjects varies widely. Belgian and Finnish parents, for instance, place a very high priority on their children learning a foreign language, while those in the United States and the United Kingdom give it significantly less importance.[11] Such differences exist not only between countries, but within them as well. It is not uncommon for polls conducted at the state or city level to show almost as much variation in parents' priorities as international surveys do.

Despite the different weights parents give to different subjects, the fact remains that the vast majority want their children exposed to a broad range of interconnected knowledge from the sciences, humanities, and arts. When asked what courses college-bound students should take, a majority of Americans list mathematics, English, history/U.S. government, science, business, and a foreign language. Many parents also add geography, health/physical education, vocational training, art, and music. Vocational and business training are given significantly higher rankings when the question is asked regarding students not bound for college, but the other subjects still elicit strong support.[12] In summary, most parents want their children to understand the way things are, how they got that way, and how they have been described by the world's great writers. But are children really learning these facts and ideas?

When U.S. education secretary Richard Riley released the results of a national history test in the fall of 1995, he felt obliged to quote from the ballad "Wonderful World," saying: "It's clear, as the song says, students don't know much about history."[13] Remarkably, the majority of twelfth-graders failed to even reach the "basic" level of achievement, the test's lowest ranking. Only one student in ten was found to be "proficient." Maris Vinovskis, a professor of history at the University of Michigan, admitted that "[t]he results are deeply disturbing.

I was shocked, really. . . . We are facing a real crisis."[14] Students fared better on the national geography test, but even these results were not particularly encouraging. Almost one high-school senior in three lacked a "basic" understanding of geography, and only a quarter were considered "proficient." Only 10 percent of seniors correctly picked Canada as the United States' largest trading partner in a multiple-choice question, a result unlikely to please parents on either side of the border.[15]

Skills

Most parents hope that, in addition to becoming knowledgeable, their children will develop the skills necessary for success in life and work. As reflected in the popular "back to basics" movement, mastery in reading, writing, and arithmetic is widely viewed as an absolute necessity. Fully 96 percent of Americans believe that more emphasis should be put on teaching tougher, more challenging basic courses in reading, writing, math, and science.[16] This focus on elementary skills is sometimes interpreted as being at odds with more advanced learning, but when parents are asked to explain their stressing of the basics they most often point out that these skills are prerequisites to virtually all advanced studies. A Minneapolis father, for instance, explained:

> It seems to me that when I went to school, we started with the basics, with the basic building blocks. You didn't start writing compositions until you had all the grammar down. . . . Now, it's more like they get plopped down right in the middle and are told "Write us a story and if the spelling isn't right, we'll take care of that later." . . . It's backward.[17]

Parents also show their appreciation for more sophisticated skills when presented with a list of options and asked to rate their importance. A majority of parents I have talked with consider knowing how to research a topic and how to logically form opinions to be either important or very important skills. Parents do value these and other advanced studies—they simply want their children to be able to read and write proficiently before they are moved along to more complex assignments.

Unfortunately, but not surprisingly, students have an even poorer grasp of advanced thinking skills than they do of the basics. British academics complain loudly that even students entering the best universities "can't do algebra and don't understand [mathematics]." Professors at Leeds and Cambridge complain that students' higher-level skills have been declining in recent years and that entering freshmen "do not have a firm grasp of the conceptual base of mathematics—the centrality of proof."[18] But once again it is the United States leading the charge of the dull brigade. When American students were tested against children in China, Taiwan, and Japan on conceptual and visualization skills, they performed abysmally, falling further behind their Asian counterparts the longer they spent in school.[19] In the national tests of mathematics, history, and geography discussed thus far, all of which are part of the U.S. National Assessment of Educational Progress (or NAEP), only a tiny fraction of American students reach the "advanced" level of competence. Across grades and across subjects, few students demonstrate a true understanding and mastery of the subject matter they are supposed to have learned.

After academic training, such as it is, the development of social skills is often next in importance for parents. One mother even gave this as her primary concern, saying: "Academics and the interaction with other children, that's why I send him [her son] to school. In fact, if it weren't for the social aspects, I'd probably teach him at home."[20] Even parents who do choose to home-school their children value the teaching of interpersonal skills. Home-schoolers often arrange group activities among themselves to teach their children to get along and work with others.

Beyond these common priorities, the importance families accord to different skills varies significantly. For some, the nurturing of musical and artistic skills is profoundly important. These parents often seek additional training for their children outside of the traditional classroom, sending them to piano or dance instructors. Others stress athletics, coaching their children themselves or participating in local sports leagues. Still others put the emphasis on logical thinking, or creativity—and the list goes on.

Values

In the case of values and religion, as in the areas of knowledge and skills, there is some overlap between the goals of different families. Courtesy, love of learning, diligence, and—with at least one historical exception[21]—honesty, are all universally prized. But even these basic qualities are not accorded equal importance. Many parents stress love of learning as the central value they wish schools to instill in their children, while others give it only secondary consideration. A poll of two thousand German citizens found similar disparities when it asked respondents to choose the most important aim of education from the following list: Obedience/Submission, Order/Diligence, or Independence/Free will. Answers to this question varied greatly depending upon the age and level of education of the respondents.[22] Those over sixty and those with a low level of education ranked Order/Diligence and Independence/Free will approximately equally. Highly educated respondents and those under thirty years of age favored Independence/free will by a margin of more than three to one. Few parents named Obedience/Submission as their choice, but here the difference between subgroups was as high as five to one. Similar variations exist between nations as well, with almost nine tenths of American and Portuguese citizens polled ranking instruction in good citizenship as essential or very important, while fewer than six in ten French and Swiss respondents agreed.[23]

For sheer contentiousness, it is hard to find any schooling issue on a par with religion. Differences in dogma among various sects and faiths, and conflicts between religious and secular groups, have led to fierce battles over the content of public instruction around the world. In the United States, the kettle has been boiling for a century and a half. Just in the last eighty years, U.S. public schools have seen the struggle between proponents of evolutionary theory and the biblical creation story swing full circle. In the early 1920s, all reference to the theory of evolution had been expunged from the textbooks of Florida, Louisiana, Texas, and Kentucky.[24] By the end of the decade, after the famous Scopes "monkey" trial in which a teacher was prosecuted for and found guilty of teaching evolution, anti-evolution bills had been introduced in thirty-seven states.[25] Naturally, supporters of evolutionary theory cried foul. Today, the converse is true, with evangelical Christians mightily disgruntled over the exclusion of their beliefs on the origin of man from their children's classes. Recently, Tennessee legislators proposed a bill that would turn back the clock to the 1930s, by requiring the firing of any teacher who taught evolution as a fact.[26] The battle wages on.

Even when parents share the same religious beliefs, they do not always see eye to eye on the role of religion in the schools. For some parents, academics and religion are entirely separate issues, the first being mainly the responsibility of the school, and the second, that of the home. Others see the religious and scholarly education of their children as inseparable, insisting that they be provided in a thoroughly integrated manner. There are also those who would ideally like to see academics and religion taught together, but who nonetheless oppose the idea in practice. Their opposition stems from the fact that, at least in the case of government-run schools, it is impossible to do justice to one's own religion without impinging on the right of others to do the same. This last attitude has been reflected in public opinion polls, which indicate that a majority of U.S. citizens favor prayer at their local schools—unless some parents strongly object. In the case where there are objections, support for school prayer drops to a minority.[27]

Getting There Is Half the Problem

First and foremost, parents see the goals of education in terms of outcomes: Will my child know how to write with proper grammar and spelling? Will she be able to find a good job? Will he know how and why our country was founded? But they are also concerned with the conditions in which their children learn. Children spend nine to twelve years in the educational systems of most industrialized nations, and their school environment during that span of time is of great concern to most families. In addition to their ultimate goals for schooling, then, parents also have a variety of secondary concerns about their children's education. Some of these concerns are valued in and of themselves: school cleanliness and safety, for instance. Nobody wants to send their kids to a filthy school with knife fights in the cafeteria and gun-play on the playground, whether or not it has a good academic program. Other desires reflect what parents see as requirements for their more fundamental goals to be met. Most parents like to see orderly classrooms not because they are closet drill-sergeants, but because they don't believe it is possible to learn with books and papers flying through the air, and a constant din drowning out the teacher.

Discipline, drugs, violence, and declining standards

What are parents' main concerns about the conditions in their children's classrooms? Every year since 1969, U.S. pollsters have asked parents what they considered to be the most serious problems with their local public schools. At or near the top of the list of problems during this entire period was school discipline.[28] Recently, drugs and violence have pushed their way to the fore, as student behavioral problems have worsened, going from simple disorderliness to physical assault and even homicide.[29] A 1994 poll found that four out of five African-American parents with children in the public schools see drugs and violence as serious problems in their local schools.[30] A majority of white parents voiced similar fears. Even suburban middle-class neighborhoods are not immune to this hostile environment. During a group discussion in Danbury, Connecticut, conducted by the Public Agenda research organization, the generally positive mood of the participants darkened when the subject turned to safety:

> After some minutes of conversation, one father mentioned that his daughter routinely avoids using the restroom for fear of being accosted by a tough set of teenagers. The positive tone of the conversation quickly changed to one of anger and frustration, as more respondents shared stories about the fear and intimidation their children experienced.[31]

Beatings are unfortunately not the worst threat facing schoolchildren. The rash of mass murders at public schools in the fall of 1997 and spring of 1998 will not soon be forgotten. On the first of October, 1997, two Mississippi children were killed and seven others were shot, allegedly by a boy suspected of killing his mother that same morning. Exactly two months later, three students were gunned down during a pre-class prayer meeting at Kentucky's Heath High School. Five others were wounded. On March 21, 1998, four girls and a teacher were killed and eleven others were wounded when two camouflage-wearing Arkansas boys allegedly opened fire on their classmates at Westside Middle School in Jonesboro. The boys charged with the murders were eleven and thirteen years old.[32] Death came to small-town Pennsylvania on the night of April 26, 1998, when an eighth-grader shot teacher John Gillette to death and wounded two fellow students during a school dance. Springfield, a mill-town nestled in Oregon's Willamette Valley, added another chapter to this tale of horror when a Thurston High student let loose a hail of bullets in his school's cafeteria. Two children died and another twenty-three were wounded. The boy's parents were later found dead at their home.

These attacks represent only a fraction of the violent crime that takes place in schools every day. While mass-murders on school grounds make international news, assault, theft, and the like are too common to make it beyond local television and radio. Students who make bomb threats, or who actually build incendiary devices and bring them to school,[33] often fail to register on the radar screens of the national media. Fully 660,695 assaults took place on school grounds in the United States in 1992, making schools the second most likely place for such crimes to occur, according to the U.S. Bureau of the Census.[34]

Even when discipline problems do not erupt into violence, parents feel that these problems have a considerable impact on students' educational experiences. Parents see undisciplined classrooms as an impediment to the ability of teachers to do their jobs, eating away at the time and energy they might otherwise be able to devote to their pupils. With the teacher's attention focused on managing a handful of disruptive students, the others can easily be shortchanged. In the words of one pollster: "If school officials cannot keep students in line, then the school, in the eyes of the public, is a 'poor' one."[35]

The seriousness with which these views are held is beyond question, and parents overwhelmingly favor strong action to eliminate discipline problems. Seven parents in ten want teachers to be able to eject repeatedly disruptive students from the classroom,[36] and even more are in favor of expelling students for drug use and weapons possession. Virtually all parents believe that stronger penalties for possession of weapons by students would be very effective in reducing violence.[37] Lack of discipline is often given as one of the primary reasons for leaving the public system entirely, in favor of private schools.[38]

The prospects for safe public schools, however, are not looking up. Weapons offenses by juveniles actually doubled between 1985 and 1993, according to the U.S. Department of Justice, and the arrest rate for thirteen- and fourteen-year-old boys was found to be higher than for men between twenty-five and twenty-nine years old.[39] Much of this crime is taking place in or near the schools. In mid-

1995, the chancellor of New York City schools reported increases in assault, harassment, robbery, and larceny.[40] Nationwide, one U.S. student in three feels unsafe at school, and 42 percent avoid using the bathrooms out of fear. The reality of these worries is brought home by the fact that 100,000 students report having carried guns to school, according to *Time* and *Newsweek*.[41] In 1991 alone, 600,000 U.S. students were assaulted in school or on school grounds.[42]

While U.S. schools are among the world's most violent, no country is without its share of problems. Canadians are just as worried about the safety of their children,[43] and with good reason. Even that country's capital, despite its normally sedate atmosphere and small-town charm, is not a stranger to school violence. In March 1996, a thirty-student brawl at one Ottawa high school led to five arrests. Less than a week later, a child at a different school was stabbed in the chest and neck while eating in the cafeteria.[44] Sadly, there is much room for improvement in the safety of most countries' schools.

Ideally, parents want not only a safe school environment, with clean and well-maintained facilities, but also one that gives individual attention to their children. They generally prefer small schools in which students and teachers can get to know one another, to large impersonal ones with thousands of students and miles of hallways. Despite this desire for homey neighborhood schools, the trend in the U.S. public school system has been toward ever-larger centralized mega-schools. While only 3 percent of schools have fewer than two hundred students, fully one school in four has more than a thousand. At the high-school level, the majority of children attend institutions enrolling over a thousand students.[45]

Depending on the views of the parents and the character of their children, some favor a free atmosphere that lets students direct their own learning experiences, while others look for structure and guidance. High academic standards, however, are almost universally sought, with roughly three quarters of American parents favoring tougher grading and a greater willingness on the part of teachers to fail high-school students who don't learn their material. Well over 80 percent believe that high-school students should not be eligible for graduation unless they can demonstrate competence in writing and speaking.[46]

Public school officials have made the occasional foray into stricter standards in recent years, but their systems' policies are still virtually the opposite of what families want. Thanks to the ubiquitous practice known as "social promotion," in which children are promoted from grade to grade whether or not they have passed their courses, an untenable situation exists in most high schools. So many high-school seniors are so far behind the expectations for their grade level that strict graduation standards would decimate the ranks of those eligible to receive a degree. As NAEP tests have shown, fewer than half of twelfth-graders can do seventh-grade work in mathematics and only 5 percent can handle the precollege material many of them are expected to know.[47] The abysmal situation in high schools is the result of what can only be called compound disinterest: schools begin ignoring students' learning deficits at an early age, and the students' shortcomings are magnified with each passing grade. A recent New York state survey found that more than two thirds of elementary teachers had been pressured to promote students who were not ready academically to move to the next grade. Six out of ten of these teachers reported that "their elementary schools promoted students to middle or junior high school without requiring them to show that they were competent to move ahead."[48] Parents' longing for tougher standards is, for now at least, unrequited.

Control

Given the variation in preferences and values from family to family, and the concerns parents have for their children's safety, it is not surprising that they also want significant control over the educational process. Only two out of five parents in a 1987 poll thought that parents in general had enough control over the curriculum in their children's schools, while slightly more than half felt that they did not.[49] When asked about their own children, parents express an even greater desire for educational decision-making power. A clear trend emerges when parents are asked how much control they want over various aspects of their children's schooling, and how much control they actually feel they have. In the teaching of knowledge, skills, and particularly values, parents overwhelmingly wish for greater control. This is not to say that parents want to be responsible for determining how each minute of class time is spent, but rather that they want to be able to emphasize some areas, and sideline others. In essence, they want some degree of choice and influence over their children's curriculum, in order to meet their particular educational goals.

Many parents feel particularly powerless when it comes to effecting changes in their local schools. A common source of frustration is that they don't know to whom they should address their questions and complaints, or from whom they should expect satisfaction. In the words of one inner-city mother who transferred her child from the local public school to an independent Catholic school:

> [Public school] parents call me and say, "I've talked to the teachers, the principal, and get nowhere; they won't give me satisfactory answers." All I can do is refer them back to the school to try again because in a public setting, who do you go to? No one knows. Here [at my child's private school], you always know who to go to.[50]

This problem is not confined to the inner city. A recent New York state public opinion survey revealed widespread confusion and frustration. Respondents across the state simply had no idea whom to hold accountable for the problems they saw in their public schools.[51] A Minneapolis father from an "above average" suburban school district voiced similar complaints on a National Public Radio call-in show. In his case, however, the school had solicited parental input, only to ignore it:

> Every single parent committee that [my wife] has been on has been set up—to me, it seems—with the express purpose of giving ornery parents a place to park so they won't bother the school district. They have had committees for the latchkey program that gave recommendations that were ignored. There have been parent advisory committees on various other subjects that have given various bits of advice that were completely ignored, overlooked, or in other ways just basically brushed off.[52]

Across the United States, the overwhelming consensus is that parents have little or no control over their public schools. This fact was plainly illustrated by a 1990 Gallup poll that asked respondents how much control they felt parents actually had over six different aspects of their children's public school education. As shown in Figure 1, significant majorities said that parents had "very little" or "almost no" control over everything from curriculum and textbooks to teacher selection and salaries.[53]

Choice

The lack of control that parents have over their public schools has spawned a variety of reform proposals meant to alleviate the problem, including public school choice, charter schools, and tuition vouchers. Just under half of U.S. states allow parents some degree of choice from among their local public schools, instead of simply assigning them to one based on their place of residence, as do the other states.[54] Charter or "magnet" schools are an extension of the public school choice concept, with the added proviso that they are freed from some state regulations and are encouraged to specialize in a particular area such as science or the arts. Most charter and public school choice programs place restrictions on parents' choices. Some of these restrictions are the result of state codes of education, which might, for example, limit the number of schools eligible to participate. Other restrictions stem from court desegregation orders, which require schools to maintain racial balance quotas. Outside the U.S., Holland, Sweden, New Zealand, England, and even Russia, offer some form of school choice to parents.

As an indicator of the extent to which parents support choice, the most revealing reform proposal is the school voucher. Under voucher plans, govern-

Figure 1. U.S. Public Perception of the Level of Parental Control over the Public Schools

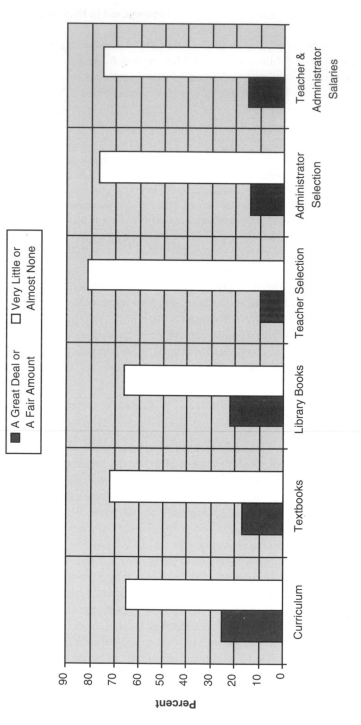

Data source: Stanley M. Elam, "The 22nd Annual Gallup Poll of the Public's Attitudes toward the Public Schools," *Phi Delta Kappan*, September 1990, 45.

ments or private organizations give low-income parents a certain amount of money which they can put toward the tuition at whatever school they decide is appropriate, be it public or private. Some voucher programs forbid parents from sending their children to religiously affiliated schools, while others give them the freedom to choose from any available institution. And though existing programs are restricted to low-income families, some proposals would allow all families to participate. On the whole, vouchers are the least restrictive of the three kinds of reforms, and so they are the most effective in highlighting both the positive and negative reactions families have toward choice in schooling.

It is possible to follow the development of U.S. public sentiment toward government-funded voucher programs thanks to a succession of polls that have investigated this issue for more than a decade. The particular question that has been asked over the years is as follows:

> In some nations, the government allots a certain amount of money for each child for his or her education. The parents can then send the child to any public, parochial, or private school they choose. This is called the "voucher system." Would you like to see such an idea adopted in this country?

The responses to this question (see Figure 2) indicate that parents with children in the public schools have been generally favorable to vouchers since 1983, with their support rising to an overwhelming majority (76 percent) by 1992. Parents with children in nonpublic schools are even stronger advocates of vouchers, supporting them by a margin of 84 percent to 15 percent.[55] The introduction of school vouchers as described in the above question is also favored by members of the general public who do not have school-aged children, but this is not the whole story. Support for parents' right to choose their children's school depends to a large extent on how choice would affect other important educational goals. Some parents, for example, feel that if a voucher program increased their level of choice and control at the expense of other children's education it would be unacceptable. Others worry that the cost of vouchers for students already enrolled in private schools, added to the cost of vouchers for public school students, would mean that overall education spending would rise dramatically. A few people also express hesitation about the inclusion of religious schools among the choices available to parents, due to the constitutional limitations on entanglement between church and state.

The impact of these concerns on people's attitudes is striking. When the wording of voucher questions is changed in such a way as to highlight cost considerations, possible negative side-effects, or government entanglement in religion, public support drops noticeably. In 1994, *Phi Delta Kappan,* an education magazine sponsoring yearly U.S. polls, changed the wording of its voucher

Figure 2. U.S. Public School Parents' Opinions on Vouchers

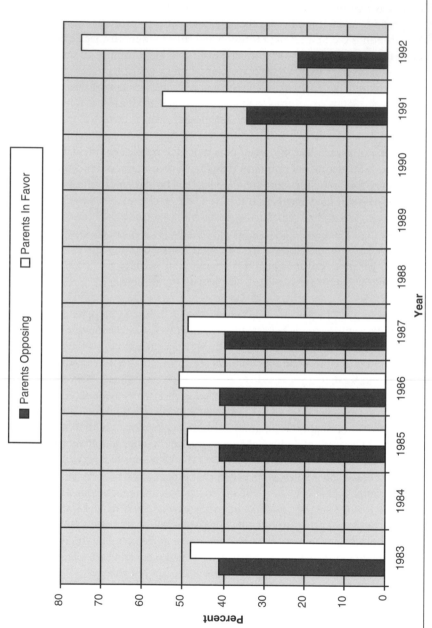

Data sources: Various authors, The 15th, 17th, 18th, 19th, and 23rd Annual Gallup Polls of the Public's Attitudes toward the Public Schools, *Phi Delta Kappan*, September 1983, 1985, 1986, 1987, 1991; and National Catholic Education Association (NCEA), *The People's Poll on Schools and School Choice: A New Gallup Survey* (Washington, DC: National Catholic Education Association, 1992), 16. (No figures are available for 1984, 1988, 1989, or 1990.)

question, removing the statement that some kinds of voucher programs are already in use in other countries, substituting the term "church-related" for "parochial," and emphasizing the fact that the government would subsidize tuition at nongovernment schools.[56] Respondents were not told that the government would continue to pay tuition costs for families choosing public schools. Together, these changes focused people's attention on the issues, risks, and concerns mentioned above, with the result that their support was greatly diminished. While parents with children in nonpublic schools continued to support the idea, public school parents were slightly opposed to it, 51 percent to 48 percent.[57]

Clearly, parents and the general public do not favor school vouchers unconditionally. Still, the desire of individual families for educational freedom is beyond question. When parents are asked if they would send their own children to a private school if they could afford it, majorities in the United States, the United Kingdom, and France all say yes.[58] The question of whether or not a funding plan can be devised which would meet this demand, while assuaging the aforementioned concerns, is taken up in the conclusion of this book.

Information

Central to all of the concerns discussed thus far is the issue of information. When asked whether or not they would like more detailed information about their schools, parents overwhelmingly answer yes.[59] What is especially unfortunate is that the particular kinds of information parents would like to have—what innovations are being introduced and why, what courses are being taught and how, college requirements, the school's ranking on national and international tests—are the areas most commonly neglected in school publications.

One of the most glaring indications of how poorly informed parents are comes from the discrepancy between the quality ratings they give to their own schools versus those of the nation at large. In 1995, for instance, only 20 percent of those polled gave the nation's schools a quality rating of A or B, while twice as many gave that rating to their local schools.[60] Many educators see this as an indication that the recent criticism of public schooling is misguided, since the schools with which people are presumably more familiar are given higher, if still mediocre, scores. Parents themselves say that the chief reason they rate their local schools better is because their schools place more emphasis on high academic achievement than those elsewhere. But are they right?

In 1992, education scholar Harold Stevenson published the results of a decade's worth of international studies comparing not only educational performance, but attitudes as well. In his studies, he looked at hundreds of classrooms and families in the U.S., China, Taiwan, and Japan. What he found was that

American parents were by far the most satisfied with their local schools, while their children had the worst performance overall. Though in the first grade they were only slightly behind their Asian counterparts in mathematics, by the fifth grade the *best* American schools had lower scores than the *worst* schools from all three other nations. Unaware of this fact, the American parents reported being quite pleased with the performance of their schools and their children.[61]

One possible explanation for this discrepancy is that Americans just have much lower standards than people in other countries, and are thankful for even the most meager successes of their children. But that fails to explain the preoccupation of U.S. citizens and news media with the middling to poor standing of their children on international tests. It seems more reasonable to think that U.S. parents rate the nation's schools poorly because they are familiar with the international test results, and that they rate their own schools more highly because they have no idea how they compare to others in the U.S. or abroad. To parents, it seems, no news is good news. Those who say that the discrepancy between parental ratings of local versus national schools are the result of lack of information appear to be right, but the information is lacking at the local rather than the national level. As George Gallup himself remarked more than twenty-five years ago: "Since [parents and the general public] have little or no basis for judging the quality of education in their local schools, pressures are obviously absent for improving the quality."[62]

A Chicago fifth-grade teacher expressed a similar view to author Jonathan Kozol, saying: "It's all a game. . . . Keep [the kids] in class for seven years and give them a diploma if they make it to eighth grade. They can't read, but give them the diploma. The parents don't know what's going on. They're satisfied."[63]

Another prime example of this situation recently played itself out in East Austin, Texas. Consistently greeted by A's and B's on their children's report cards, the parents of Zavala Elementary School had been lulled into complacency, believing that both the school and its students were performing well. In fact, Zavala was one of the worst schools in the district, and its students ranked near the bottom on statewide standardized tests. When a new principal took over the helm and requested that the statewide scores be read out at a PTA meeting, parents were dismayed by their children's abysmal showing, and furious with teachers and school officials for misleading them with inflated grades.[64]

Educating the Children of Others

Public Aims of Education

Interest in the education of children is not limited to the bond between parent and child. The desire of people around the world to educate all their nations' children can be measured, in part, by the level of financial support they are willing to dedicate to that end; and by this measure, support for education is strong. From the late 1980s through the early 1990s, Canadians have favored increased expenditures on public education.[65] Roughly half of U.S. citizens polled during the same period also supported higher spending on education.[66] In fact, education spending has gone up in virtually every industrialized country over the last decade, both per student and in the aggregate.[67] Whenever Americans are asked which part of their local and federal government budgets should be cut, education is among the least common responses, and the state of the schools often tops voters' lists of decisive issues at election time.[68]

School levies do often fail at the polls, but this can generally be traced, as noted below, to skepticism about the way that particular districts handle the funds they are given. When voters believe their education taxes are being squandered, support for levies evaporates. In principle, however, it is clear that the public places a high value on learning, for the children of others as well as their own. But why? And are they happy with the way public schools are handling the job?

Throughout history there have been two principal reasons that people have taken an interest in the education of their fellow citizens. The first is a benevolent desire to ensure that every child receives the training necessary to survive and thrive in the adult world. Often, this desire is interwoven with a strand of self-interest, based on the belief that well-educated children are more likely to become capable and productive members of society, benefiting not only themselves, but others around them as well. A second and quite different impulse has led some individuals to see education as a tool for indoctrinating and molding youths into the "right" kind of adults, with or without their parents' consent. Among the general public, the goal of simply improving the lot of children seems ever to have been the dominant one. Coercive and manipulative educational ideas have usually been restricted to politicians and demagogues, as will become clear from the tour of education history provided in the coming chapters. Certainly this trend seems to hold in the late twentieth century. It is not especially common to find private citizens advocating that government-run schools should impose a particular religion or culture on the children of others. In fact, a recent U.S. poll found that a majority of respondents favored granting individual parents more say over their children's curriculum and the allocation of their schools' budgets.[69]

For kids' sake

The safety and well-being of children is, to most people, an end in itself. In modern times, this natural impulse to protect the young has become inextricably linked to formal schooling. Without some basic skills and knowledge, children cannot hope to succeed in the modern world, and thus there is a strong desire on the part of many people to see that they get an education. Happily, there is very little difference between the fundamental things that people want for their own children and what they want for the children of others. Where parents are in agreement on the preeminent importance of instruction in mathematics and their native language, so too is the public at large.[70] As discussed in the previous section, citizens around the world, whether or not they are parents, usually place a high value on career guidance and job training for students.

Formalizing these preferences into a required curriculum, however, gets a decidedly uneven reception. Opinion on the merits of a uniform national curriculum has tended to be positive in theory and negative in practice. In both the United States and the United Kingdom, parents originally supported the idea of a core curriculum shared by schools across the nation, seeing it as a sort of guarantee that their local schools would measure up to recognized standards. A common curriculum also appeals to people who think it would minimize the problems of students who transfer between schools in different parts of the country—students who sometimes find they are ahead for their grade in some subjects, and behind in others. In U.S. polls of the late eighties and early nineties, almost 70 percent of respondents favored requiring their local schools to adopt a standardized national curriculum.[71] U.K. residents answered almost identically when polled in 1987.[72]

In practice, the response to increasing central government control over school curricula has been far less favorable. Beginning around 1990, Britain began an education-reform process centered around a national curriculum, with the provision for student testing at ages seven, eleven, and fourteen. Early signs of public skepticism appeared when an overwhelming majority of respondents in a national poll stated that they disapproved of the changes taking place in the educational system. By the time the new system was more or less in place in 1993, support for the general idea of a national curriculum had dropped to 58 percent, while the testing component received only 50 percent approval. Support ebbed still further when teachers opposed the government's national tests, claiming they were too complicated and time-consuming. By a three-to-one margin, the British public backed a national teachers' strike opposing the tests.[73] Support may once again be on the rise, but squabbling over specifics continues.

In the United States, the idea of a uniform curriculum met with tremendous approval as late as the summer of 1994,[74] but the mood quickly soured after the release, in the fall of the same year, of the voluntary federal history standards. Even before they were officially made public, the national history standards were criticized for bias, omissions, and excessive political correctness. Criticism of the standards continued to rage well into the next year, including a 99-

to-1 Senate vote condemning them.[75] The voluntary mathematics standards released in 1989 by the National Council of Teachers of Mathematics were not nearly as controversial, but they have nonetheless failed to be adopted on a widespread basis.[76]

By 1995, two thirds of U.S. citizens wanted the federal government to have *less* influence over education.[77] The public's longing for clear educational standards remains, but sentiment toward government involvement in such standards ranges from mixed to negative. According to a poll conducted for *U.S. News & World Report* in the spring of 1996, only one quarter of Americans favoring well-defined standards believe that they should be set by federal authorities. Four respondents in ten thought that standard setting should be left at the local level.[78] The increasingly skeptical climate of public opinion toward central government intervention in the curriculum has not been lost on politicians. Ramsay Selden, formerly of the Council of Chief State School Officers, observed: "There's absolutely no interest now in having any kind of activity on standards. . . . The whole issue has become like a political toxic-waste dump, and nobody wants to go near it."[79] The pendulum continues to swing, however, as national standards have once again become a hot concept in the second term of the Clinton presidency. In a U.S. poll released in the summer of 1997, two thirds of respondents felt that a national curriculum would improve academic achievement "quite a lot" or "a great deal."[80]

The ability of schools to prepare children for gainful employment receives a more constant verdict: Guilty. Those who must deal with the job skills of recent high-school graduates on a daily basis are the first to give public schooling a failing grade. The estimation of a high-school education's value is so low among business people that grades and other school-related factors are given the least weight in hiring decisions. Far more important are the candidate's previous work experience, communication skills, and general disposition.[81] This skepticism is amply justified. Echoing National Assessment of Educational Progress findings, Pacific Telesis discovered in 1992 that three out of five high-school graduates applying for jobs flunked a seventh-grade-level company exam. When Intel began interviewing applicants in 1996 for positions at a new Washington state plant, the results were equally dismal. Out of four hundred candidates tested on ninth-grade math, reading, and writing skills, only eighty received satisfactory grades.[82] Across the country, one third of American businesses report that their employees' poor learning skills are preventing them from reorganizing work responsibilities.[83]

A more visceral example of the gap in basic skills among entry-level job applicants can be found in the plight of a Brooklyn music store owner. Calling in to a National Public Radio talk show in the fall of 1995, "Jerry" lamented that he had noticed a constant reduction in the abilities of high-school graduates, adding: "I have a young lady that I hired last week who not only can't read but

I've had to draw pictures . . . for her to teach her how to use a very simple cash register!"[84]

Even more revealing than Jerry's predicament, and the fact that he claimed to have hired the best candidate available, was the response he received from Bruce Biddle and David Berliner, the show's guests. Berliner and Biddle are the authors of the controversial book *The Manufactured Crisis: Myths, Fraud, and the Attack on America's Public Schools,* which contends that the intense criticism to which public schooling has been subjected over the last decade is a misguided fabrication of conservative politicians and business leaders.[85] Biddle, the first to respond, asked Jerry to think about the fact that a higher percentage of American youth now graduate from high school, and that this was a "marvelous" achievement. How the higher graduation rate can be construed as marvelous if the additional graduates are illiterate was not adequately explained, but Biddle did have one piece of advice for the store owner in need of a cashier: "Perhaps in the long run you should be looking for some of our college graduates, rather than high-school graduates." Before Jerry could respond, Berliner interjected with the comment that he was "getting tired of business people telling [him] that they can't find qualified students," and that they should simply offer higher wages and benefits until they *can* find the "talented" individuals they're searching for.

Thus, according to public schooling's most vigorous defenders, employers looking for applicants with elementary-school qualifications must hire college graduates and offer them generous salary and benefit packages. A sobering thought . . . or perhaps one that will drive employers to drink.

Fringe benefits

Clearly, despite the dubious success of present efforts, there is great public support for helping children to reach their potential, and become happy, successful adults. It is too simplistic, though, to say that the public's educational views are entirely altruistic. As is only natural, a reasonable amount of self-interest is also present. In most cases, concerns of altruism and self-interest support rather than conflict with one another, explaining, perhaps, some of education's broad popularity. What, then, are the aspects of education that benefit not only the children themselves but also the citizenry at large? Responses to this question tend to be either political or economic. Central to the political issue is the widespread belief that democracy cannot survive unless the whole population enjoys at least a rudimentary level of education. In the felicitous expression of Thomas Jefferson: "If a nation expects to be both ignorant and free, it expects what never was and never will be." Most people seem to agree with this principle, and are willing to help ensure that their fellow citizens have the opportunity to become competent in reading and writing, and develop a basic familiarity with the central laws and ideals of their country. These basic competencies, along with the lessons of personal experience, allow individuals to fulfill the minimum requirements of citizenship, and lead the way to more meaningful participation in the political process. The educated person not only safeguards his or her own political interests, but adds to the strength of the democracy itself.

So, do public schools succeed in conveying a basic understanding of their nation's political documents and ideas? In the United States, the answer appears to be no. Mortimer J. Adler, author of the wonderful book *We Hold These Truths: Understanding the Ideas and Ideals of the Constitution,* conducted innumerable seminars on the subject in high schools around the country during the 1980s. In discussing the Declaration of Independence, professor Adler was dismayed to find that, almost without exception, students had *never before* read that document. He wrote:

> The discussions that followed revealed how little they understood the meaning of the Declaration's principal terms before the discussion began, and how much more remained to be done after the seminar was over to bring them to a level of understanding that, in my judgment, is the minimal requisite for intelligent citizenship in this country. The same can also be said with regard to the Constitution and the Gettysburg Address.[86]

A subject that has received far more attention than schools' failure to teach the basic rights and duties of citizenship has been their record on teaching values. Here, however, there is far less agreement among parents as to what should be taught. On the subject of values, the public is more cautious, drawing a distinction between the benefits of voluntarily sharing certain common values, and the harm of indoctrinating children with those values whether or not their families approve. The risk that such coercive power could be dangerously misused, and the fact that it strikes many people as a violation of freedom of thought and conscience, cause people in most countries to shy away from this use of schooling. When an opinion poll asked the Japanese public if their nation's Fundamental Education Law should be amended to include teaching "patriotic loyalty to Japan," for example, they rejected the idea.[87] Since the beginning of public schooling in the United States, the choice of values embodied in the curriculum has been hotly debated. Like parents, the general public seems to agree on a few basics such as honesty and tolerance of other ethnic and religious groups, but beyond these fundamentals, the universal imposition of an "approved" set of values garners little support.

But no education system can be truly value-neutral. All teaching relies on a particular approach to knowledge and truth, and different approaches often lead to different conclusions. A prime example, already discussed, is the case of evolution versus the biblical creation story. By themselves such differences can coexist peacefully, but when one view or the other is imposed by the government in the public schools, conflict is inevitable. In recent years, public outcries have arisen over such disparate issues as in-school condom distribution, mandatory public-service requirements for students, school prayer, and the interpretation of history. The present educational system is clearly failing to reflect the ideological diversity of the nation, at the cost of mounting social discord.

A Parting of the Ways

So far, we have looked at the public's opinions on the ultimate goals of education, but most people are also concerned with the ways in which their goals are pursued. Nonparents tend to have the same attitudes as parents regarding the approach schools should take to discipline problems and the like, and thus there is no need to raise those issues again here. But there are several other contentious issues regarding the delivery of education upon which we have not yet touched. A common thread tying these issues together is the extent to which school policy has diverged from the public's preferences.

Racial busing

Still one of the most highly charged issues in U.S. education is the practice of forcing students to be bused from one community to another for the purpose of racial integration. Many of its early advocates continue to view busing as a viable and appropriate means of improving the education of black children. A growing tide of opposition has nonetheless arisen over the last decade, among both blacks and whites. In a 1993 poll, Americans opposed busing by a margin of more than two to one.[88] It is doubtful that this opposition can be attributed primarily to racism since the same poll found that people of all colors would have no objection to voluntarily sending their own children to a mixed-race school. Other surveys of parental attitudes confirm this conclusion. In his 1995 book *Forced Justice: School Desegregation and the Law,* professor David Armor noted that attitude and opinion studies show

> [s]ubstantial and increasing white support for the concept of school integration in general, which includes willingness to send children to schools with up to one-half black or minority enrollments. The studies also show strong white parental support for various voluntary desegregation techniques such as magnet schools . . . and no significant opposition to increasing the minority enrollment in their

current schools. . . . [B]lacks not only strongly support the concept of school integration but also are more willing than whites to accept widely varying racial
compositions of schools.[89]

A more likely explanation for the opposition to mandatory busing is that priorities have shifted from counting white and black faces to ensuring that good
schools are available to all children. As Robert Robinson, head of the New
Jersey chapter of the National Association for the Advancement of Colored
People (NAACP), declared in November 1995:

> Racial balance is not the important factor here, equal and quality education is. . . .
> There are studies that show that an integrated school does not necessarily provide
> quality education. Equal and quality education in all schools, regardless of racial
> balance, should be our goal.[90]

Robinson was the second NAACP official in as many months to question or
criticize busing programs, despite the fact that the organization's official policy continues to favor them. The issue has become so prominent and controversial within the NAACP that it was formally debated during the organization's national meeting in the summer of 1997. Opposition to mandatory busing
has also come from black mayors across the country, including Freeman
Bosley, Jr. of St. Louis, Norm Rice of Seattle, and Michael White of Cleveland,
all of whom have begun efforts to replace mandatory busing with voluntary
programs.[91] Americans of Asian, African, and European descent have brought
suits in recent years to dismantle their communities' racial quotas and forced
busing programs. In the fall of 1995, cases were pending in California, Massachusetts, North Carolina, Maryland, and elsewhere. A recent lawsuit filed by a
group of both black and white families from Philadelphia contends that

> [i]n essence, the school district has turned *Brown v. Board of Education,* the Bill
> of Rights of the United States Constitution, and the federal Civil Rights Act up-
> side down by precluding white and minority children from attending the schools
> of their choice in order to impose arbitrary and illegal racial quotas.[92]

For one black family, the prospect of their daughter being kept out of her chosen public school because of her race is a bitter irony. Forty years earlier, the
girl's great-grandparents took legal action against a South Carolina district for
keeping blacks out of the white schools. That legal challenge played a part in
the Supreme Court's landmark decision on school desegregation, which in turn
led to the racial quotas presently keeping their great-granddaughter out of her
chosen school.[93] Much of the growing dissatisfaction with busing and racial
quotas is the result of such unintended consequences. The research referred to
by Robinson, which questions the educational value of forced integration, has

also contributed to the policy's negative perception. (This research is discussed in Chapter 4.)

Exclusively inclusive

Another controversial issue that has recently drawn public attention is the practice of placing children with sometimes severe emotional or learning problems in the same classes with other students. Inclusion, or mainstreaming, is based upon the belief that emotionally disturbed and mentally disabled children will gain more from their interactions in regular classrooms than they would from being placed in special classes. (The term "inclusion" also applies to physically handicapped students, but since the mainstreaming of the physically handicapped is widely accepted and rarely controversial[94] it is not discussed here.) Support for inclusion stems in part from the perception that the separate classes in which disabled students had historically been placed (if they were in school at all) delivered poor quality educational services.

In its most assertive form, known as *full* inclusion, even children with grave psychological disorders are now mainstreamed. Though inclusion is popular among many educational theorists and advocates for the disabled, both the general public and classroom teachers are less fond of the practice. When asked if they supported inclusion, only one quarter of the U.S. public polled in 1995 said yes.[95] Resistance to inclusion—particularly full inclusion—is high enough among classroom educators that the American Federation of Teachers has an official policy against it. The main reason for this opposition is the disruptive effect that such children can sometimes have on a class, and the fact that they can consume so much of the teacher's attention that she is not able to attend satisfactorily to her other pupils. Of course, not all learning-disabled children have a negative effect on the classroom atmosphere, and there seems to be much less opposition to inclusion in such relatively benign cases. The unfortunate fact, however, is that a good many cases are not benign, and some are intensely problematic, as can be seen from the following two teachers' comments that appeared in an on-line discussion group:

> I am currently working in a third grade inclusion classroom. The demands made of the regular classroom teacher are crazy. I have a third grade class with 8 SLD [Specific Learning Disability] students and 2 EH [Emotionally Handicapped] students as well as 20 regular students. . . . I have a special education teacher with me for two hours out of our seven hour day. My load of paper work is still the same, my regular students are on different levels. . . . I now have twice as much work as I did before and have to protect my class from two emotionally challenged students who have been violent at times. . . . The special education teacher who I work with is wonderful but her duties are for two hours a day in my class.

Any questions as to whether inclusion works or not? — Frustrated Teacher looking for a new career.

I have 18 LD [learning-disabled students] and 18 Low-average underachievers! Half a resource teacher 3 hours a week! To quote my colleagues—Inclusion S@%KS! Hopeless for regular teacher, detrimental to students.[96]

Despite these very pragmatic considerations, there is often little a school can do other than simply go along with troublesome inclusion placements, due to a U.S. federal law known as the Individuals with Disabilities Education Act (IDEA), passed in 1975. The IDEA states that disabled children must be educated in the least restrictive environment possible, which has been increasingly interpreted to mean that they should be placed in classrooms with nondisabled children as much as possible. School districts violating this law have been taken to court on a number of occasions over the years, leading administrators to lean heavily toward inclusion in order to avoid legal problems.

Special education spending

Another area in which public-school special education policy seems to have diverged from the aims and desires of the public is spending. Over the years, U.S. citizens have been polled on their attitude toward educational spending on children with learning problems. On the whole, the public's response to this question has been fairly evenly split between those who would like to see the same amount spent on these children as on other children, and those who would like to see more money spent. In the most recent poll, 48 percent favored higher spending on the learning disabled, while 45 percent favored equal spending.[97] In practice, the public schools spend roughly two-and-a-half times as much per child on the mentally and physically handicapped as they do on the nondisabled.[98] It is possible that this figure might be able to win majority support from the public, but it is only an average. In some cases, costs are far higher.

According to legal precedents set in the U.S. Supreme Court, and various lower courts around the country, "cost is not a proper consideration in determining the components of an appropriate education . . . for a specific child with disabilities."[99] In other words, public school districts must pay for an "appropriate" education for each handicapped child regardless of the cost. What is deemed appropriate for a given child is legally determined jointly by the child's parents and a panel of specialists. Not even a state legislature can reduce the spending on a special education placement once the panel has made its decision.

Many placements with annual costs ranging from $30,000 to $90,000 a year per child have been upheld by the courts. In 1995, a case came to light involving a twelve-year-old blind boy in New York state. Each week the boy is flown back and forth from his home in the northwestern tip of the state to a special school at the southeastern tip. The total transportation and schooling cost comes to $136,000 per year—an amount equivalent to the annual spending on an average class full of children. The boy's local school district has been required to pay this bill, despite the fact that there is a nearby regional school that draws blind and visually impaired students from several local communities. At $30,000 to $40,000 a year, the regional school's tuition is only a fraction of the cost of the child's current placement. Despite the fact that the local district is financially responsible, its administrators have no say in the matter, and no avenue of appeal.[100]

Of course, it is possible that the public would agree to such placements, and to the overall level of special education expenditure, if they were presented in a clear and concise way, complete with arguments pro and con. This has not happened. The American people are simply not aware of how much is being spent on special education, and, based on the polls, it is not clear whether or not they would approve if they were.

Never enough

The issue of school cost is, of course, much broader than the case of special education placements. Per-pupil spending in the public school system has ballooned over the past thirty years in the United States. Between 1959–60 and 1989–90, the average annual cost of educating a child in the public schools rose from $1,710 to $5,233, in constant 1990–91 dollars.[101] In other words, inflation-adjusted spending more than tripled. Given this increase, and the widespread perception that the quality of public education has either stagnated or declined over the same period, it should come as little surprise that the public does not think it is getting its money's worth from the public schools. Local school bond levies have been defeated with increasing regularity in the last decade, and opinion polls reveal growing public skepticism about the ability of public schools to spend money wisely. A 1995 survey found that three quarters of New York state residents do not believe that the public school system is giving them a good value for their money.[102]

People are thus of two minds on the issue of educational expenditures. Most support high education spending in the abstract (as discussed above), but many also lack confidence in the ability of their local public schools to spend their money wisely, and this makes them hesitant to vote for higher education taxes in practice. Finding a way out of this dilemma is a concern addressed throughout this book.

The Big Picture

The preceding sections make up both an education wish list and a status report—detailing the knowledge, skills, and values that parents and the public want children to learn, the environment in which they would like that learning to take place, and the extent to which their goals are being met. Putting the pieces of this puzzle together, three fundamental points emerge:

- Parents around the world share many of the same educational goals, particularly in the areas of basic academics and job skills. They differ, sometimes significantly, in their priorities for more advanced skills and subject areas, but their sharpest differences arise over moral, religious, and ideological issues.
- The public at large generally echoes the attitudes and goals that parents have for their own children, both in their areas of agreement and disagreement.
- At present, the most fundamental goals of both parents and the rest of the public are a long way from being met. Furthermore, people's differences frequently lead to conflict when the public schools defer to one view or segment of the population at the expense of all others.

The purpose of this chapter was to determine whether or not our schools are in need of change, based on how well they are fulfilling people's educational aspirations. By now, the answer to that question is clear. Across subjects, and across countries, public schools are failing to live up to the expectations many families have for them. What can be done about it?

It is tempting to just jump into the fray of education reform, attacking this or that aspect of the problem and hoping for the best. That, however, has been tried, and the results are not impressive. Education reform efforts begun more than a decade ago have produced little improvement in any of the areas described in this chapter. In our haste to treat the symptoms of public schooling's illness, too little effort has been expended on diagnosing its causes, and until those underlying causes are identified, the ministrations of reformers will continue to be, in the words of education researcher Chester Finn, Band-Aids for battle wounds.[103]

Using the goals discussed in this chapter as a yardstick, Part II goes beyond a superficial assessment of our educational problems, identifying the roots of both success and failure in schooling.

Part II

What's Been Tried

2

Right from the Beginning:
Classical Athens and Beyond

What if families could choose any school they wanted? What if there were no rules on what or how teachers taught? Would children learn more or less? Would society be drawn together or blown apart? These are treated as hypothetical questions in the modern debate over schooling, but the answers have been right behind us all along.

Why Bother with the History of Education?

Public schools have existed in most countries for over one hundred years. As the members of each new generation have attended public schools, and gone on to send their children to public schools, the institution's roots have grown a little deeper. To many, the terms "education" and "public schooling" have actually become synonymous. So long as we see public schools in this way, as timeless and immutable, it is impossible to seriously assess their performance or evaluate alternatives. There is no better way of overcoming this problem than to open our eyes to history.

Our ancestors have tried more and different ways of educating their children than most people would imagine, and the discovery of these varied approaches gives us a much broader perspective on our current situation. The history of schooling includes both frightening failures and delightful successes, and this is where it shows its greatest worth. By keeping in mind the purposes of education discussed in the previous chapter, and seeing how well the various historical approaches to schooling achieved them, we can find invaluable clues as to which modern reform proposals have merit and which do not. Of course, cultural and economic conditions have changed over time, but certain common refrains do emerge from the hum of the centuries when we listen carefully enough.

The following historical tour visits schools from ancient Greece to the medieval Arab empire, and from the Reformation to the rise of modern nations.[1] To make better sense of all these experiences, each period and place is looked at from two different angles: the conditions under which schooling took place, and the outcomes of that schooling. For each period, the section on conditions describes what schools were like, how they worked, and whether or not families got the education they were seeking. To determine how responsive schools were, the conditions section also looks at the amount of choice parents had, the range of offerings available to them, and the speed with which schools changed those offerings in response to changing demands. The lives of teachers are also investigated, to find out how much autonomy they enjoyed, the conditions under which they were hired, remunerated, and fired, and the extent to which they tried to improve their services through innovation. The outcomes section for each period reveals how much students actually benefited from their schooling, by showing what they learned and how well they were able to apply that learning. The question of how much a given school system contributed to its nation's overall harmony and economic prosperity is taken up in the outcomes section, as is the social impact of parental choice. Setting the stage for each historical period is a short introduction that aims to give the flavor of the time.

Classical Greece: History's Greatest Lesson in Schooling

What makes ancient Greece such an ideal starting point for our investigations is not just that it was one of the first places to see formal education spread beyond a tiny ruling elite, but also that Greek schooling developed along two very different and conflicting lines. This contrast, which pervaded every aspect of education from curriculum, to management, to the role of the parent, is an unparalleled showcase for the topics discussed in Chapter 1, and its best representatives were the city-states of Athens and Sparta. Before diving into the details, though, it is helpful to know how the great divide began.

During its golden age, Greek civilization was made up of semi-independent city-states scattered about the Mediterranean. Though it was eventually to become the most influential of these states, Athens was still a relative backwater around the year 590 B.C. Beset by petty, bickering dictators and seething social unrest, Athens teetered on the brink of civil war. A small number of families had taken control of all the arable land, paying starvation wages to the peasants who farmed it, and since the economy was almost entirely agrarian, few peasants could escape their fate by taking up other work. Chronic debtors were sold into slavery at home or abroad, and corrupt magistrates kept the poor from defending what few rights they had. Under this institutionalized oppression a peasant uprising seemed inevitable, and the aristocracy dug in its heels in anticipation. In the hope of averting the looming catastrophe, a popular merchant and poet named Solon was chosen by both rich and poor to take on the task of restoring social harmony and establishing a new constitution.

Though of noble birth and at least middle-class means, Solon criticized the city's aristocracy for its arrogance and abuse of power.[2] The wealthy pressured him to maintain the status quo by making only token concessions, but he knew that more would be required to avert bloodshed. Many of the poor called for a complete redistribution of the land, but since that too would have meant war, he did not consider it a viable option. Eschewing both extremes, Solon tried to follow a middle course, forbidding the use of people as collateral for loans, freeing and repatriating Athenians sold as slaves, encouraging economic diversification, and canceling both public and private debts, among other acts. Then he stepped down, and took a long trip to Egypt to escape the squabbling that ensued. Neither side was satisfied by his measures, but by and large they stuck, and Solon thus succeeded in forging a constitution on which the world's first democracy was eventually to be built.

In contrast to the troubled early years of Athens, Sparta was a comparatively stable town before the turn of the sixth century B.C. Her most famous poets wrote about love, revelry, and wine, with occasional sidebars on bravery and military spirit, and their words seem to have been taken to heart by the city's inhabitants. Citizens enjoyed a fair amount of personal freedom, foreigners were generally welcomed, and local products were freely exported. At the time, Sparta was particularly known for bronze and pottery as well as a few musical forms. All of this was about to change.

By the time Solon had begun to turn Athenian society around, a dramatic reversal was already under way in Sparta. Led by a much mythologized figure named Lycurgus,[3] Sparta took a sharp turn off the path of human liberty and put in place one of the most totalitarian governments in history. The central idea of the new Spartan regime was that individuals and families should not be left to make their own decisions in matters of importance such as marriage, employment, or education. Instead, Spartans were called upon to subordinate their own interests to the collective will of the people, as interpreted by their part-aristocratic, part-democratic government. Appointed and elected rulers controlled virtually every aspect of their lives down to the food they ate and the songs they sang. The city's borders were closed, travel was restricted, and all the energies of the people were directed toward creating a purely military society.

Education in Athens

A century and half after Solon's tenure, Athenian democracy was a reality, if still slightly rough around the edges. Government regulations were few, and with the exception of two years of mandatory military training, the state played no role in schooling.[4] According to Plato's dialogue "Protagoras," the common practice was for parents to teach their children whatever they could during the early years of life, after which point the children would be sent off to school.[5]

Anyone who wished could open a school, setting whatever curriculum and tuition he deemed appropriate. From among the available teachers, parents were free to choose whichever one taught the things they wanted their children to learn, at a price they could afford. Since the schools were run as private enterprises, they had to compete to attract students, and this kept prices relatively low. Even the poorest families apparently sent their sons to school for a few years despite the absence of state funding (sadly, girls rarely received formal education in Athens, as in so many cultures up to modern times). Tuition was generally paid month by month, and parents were careful to see that they got their money's worth. During one month in the Greek calendar filled with official holidays, many low-income families kept their children at home rather than paying the full monthly fee for only a couple of weeks worth of teaching.[6]

Elementary school

It was customary for parents to send their sons to school from the age of six or seven until they turned fourteen, though this varied according to individual circumstances. Wealthy parents likely sent their children to school earlier and kept them there for longer than did parents with limited means. This difference was due not only to the need to pay school fees, but also to the fact that poor and middle-class families could not afford to support their children indefinitely, and so had to ensure that they learned a trade or craft through apprenticeship, an experience distinct from schooling. Even in this time-honored tradition, the Athenians were innovators. When a child was apprenticed to a tradesman other than his father, his parents would draw up a statement indicating what they expected him to be taught, and the tradesman received payment only if he provided the stipulated training.[7]

At the elementary level, Athenian parents sought three general categories of education for their children: gymnastics, music, and literacy. Competence in each of these areas was of great practical importance. Stamina, strength, and agility meant the difference between life and death at a time when wars were a constant threat, and every able-bodied male citizen was expected to serve in the army. To understand the importance of musical instruction it must be remembered that Greek culture had been orally transmitted, largely in song, for centuries prior to the rise of Athens. Just as reading and a grasp of important works of literature are crucial to modern education, so was the knowledge and appreciation of epic poetry important in the fifth and fourth centuries B.C. The value Athenian citizens placed on music and poetry remained high, though the values embodied in the oral tradition were gradually formalized into written laws. Writing began to rise in significance in the fifth century, as a tool for improving the political and judicial systems, for accurately recording the works of scientists, playwrights, and philosophers, and for making economic transactions more reliable. In the minds of the city's more philosophically oriented citizens, this combination of physical, musical, and intellectual development also satisfied an appreciation for harmony and balance in the human character.

While music and reading were probably taught in the same school, the study of gymnastics was carried out at a special location, called a "palaestra," which consisted of changing rooms and an exercise field. The gymnastics teacher was expected to have an organized method of instruction which would improve stamina, strength, and agility, while keeping the risk of injury to a minimum. Physical trainers also seem to have provided their students with nutritional advice.[8] Children began their gymnastics training by performing aerobic exercise routines to build endurance and flexibility. As their bodies and skills developed, they were taught javelin and discus tossing, a variety of ball-games and other sports, and also wrestling and boxing.

At writing school, the child was first taught to recognize and write the letters of the alphabet. For the youngest children, this was done through song, and there is even a fragmentary play that survives from late in the fourth century B.C. in which the actors represented letters and formed syllables by pairing up with one another in the appropriate poses.[9] Once the child had learned his alphabet, he was taught to write on a folding wooden tablet covered with wax, into which he would etch letters with the pointed end of a stylus, and rub them out with the wide end. At first the writing teacher would lightly trace the letters, and the student would then scratch his pen over them in order to learn how to draw their shapes. Once he had mastered this step, the child would begin to write on his own.[10] Basic arithmetic was also taught at writing school.

Music lessons, and more advanced writing instruction, centered around the study of Homer's epics, the *Iliad* and the *Odyssey*. Sitting at benches, the students recited these works to the accompaniment of a small stringed instrument called a lyre. Homer's epics were used not only for their literary merit, but also because the values they espoused were deeply held by a great many Athenians. Still, musical training was probably the least widespread of the elementary disciplines, having less practical value than writing and physical conditioning. It was considered essential to a proper education only among the upper class, and on occasion not even there. This situation is nicely captured in a play by Aristophanes, in which a defendant accused of stealing pleads for acquittal on the grounds that he does not even know how to play the lyre. Unmoved, the judge replies that he hasn't learned the lyre either, so he has to be forgiven if he is so stupid as to condemn the accused.[11]

Enter the high school

As Athenian culture broadened and developed, the elementary school curriculum developed with it. Sculpture, painting, and architecture all flourished in the city's heyday, and more and more parents started to seek drawing and painting lessons for their children. By Aristotle's time—the mid 300s B.C.— this had become a common option. Several generations later, these arts were considered a fourth core subject area, being studied by virtually all pupils.[12]

Adaptation to the changing demands of parents and students was, in fact, a hallmark of Athenian education. Each step in the evolution of Athenian society was matched by a corresponding change or expansion in the offerings of educators. The philosophers and scientists of the day were continually advancing the frontiers of human understanding, establishing in their wake a demand for a deeper and more comprehensive level of education. At the same time, the democratic franchise was extended to an ever-larger segment of the population, and the powers of the people's assembly were growing apace. In order to win popular support in this vibrant democracy, it became necessary for would-be statesmen not only to offer compelling policies, but also to deliver them with clarity and elegance. Training in oratory was thus an important political asset. Together, the emerging educational demands of politics and science made higher-level teaching an economically viable endeavor. Athenians not only wanted higher education, they were willing to pay for it. This market niche was quickly filled by a new entrepreneurial class of teachers, known as sophists, anxious to earn a living from their scholarly pursuits.

At first, when the demand for higher learning was still limited in any one community, the sophists traveled from city to city, holding forth on whatever topic they felt confident to teach, and for which there were eager pupils. When the flow of students had ebbed at a given location, they would pack their bags and resume their journey. Recruiting new pupils was always an important task for the sophists, since their livelihoods depended on it. The most common technique they used was to give free public lectures in the town square, advertising their talents and whetting the intellectual appetites of prospective students. Fortunately for the sophists, the spread of learning served not to diminish but rather to increase the demand for their services. As more and more people became better educated, the value of an education increased. This trend was not lost on elementary school teachers who eventually began to diversify into the new secondary and higher education markets by offering advanced classes to adults and children over the age of fourteen. For many years, however, the bulk of higher education was still carried out by the wandering professors.

Rhetoric was no doubt the most common field taught by the sophists, but the range of subjects was astonishingly diverse. Curious students could choose from "mathematics (including arithmetic, geometry, and astronomy), grammar, etymology, geography, natural history [i.e., biology, horticulture, etc.], the laws of meter and rhythm, history, . . . politics, ethics, the criticism of religion, mnemonics, logic, tactics and strategy, music, drawing and painting, [and] scientific athletics."[13] Lectures were held in open spaces outdoors, in the homes of the teachers, and occasionally in buildings borrowed or leased for the purpose. There appear to have been no age restrictions on these lectures, so any student both interested in and capable of participating could do so.

Gradually, as the higher-education market matured, a few fixed schools were established in Athens. In addition to Plato's Academy and Aristotle's Lyceum, neither of which charged a fee due to the wealth and preferences of their founders, several for-profit secondary schools were in existence by the turn of the fourth century B.C. Only a few of these were sufficiently famous to come down to us by name, and of these the best known is the school of Isocrates. Contrary to Plato, Isocrates argued that knowledge without application was useless. He said, "I hold that man wise who can usually think out the best course to take and that man a philosopher who seeks to gain that insight."[14] Though reportedly too shy to become prominent in public life, Isocrates was extremely successful—both financially and by popular acclaim—in teaching the art of public speaking to others. This, coupled with his pragmatic lessons on applied philosophy and mathematics, attracted a significant body of students to his lectures—a larger group, it seems, than was to be found at the Academy.

Teachers in the open market

The pedagogical freedom and market pressures of Athens both allowed and encouraged educators to make great strides. The city's schools were the first to introduce games as a pedagogical tool, and to reduce the use of corporal punishment—ubiquitous in Egypt and Sparta—to the exception rather than the rule. Elementary schools altered their curricula to meet changing parental demands, and an entirely new educational institution, secondary schooling, was brought into being as a result of market forces. In the words of Adam Smith:

> The demand for such [higher] instruction produced, what it always produces, the talent for giving it; and the emulation which an unrestrained competition never fails to excite, appears to have brought that talent to a very high degree of perfection.[15]

In every respect, from fees charged to subjects taught, the goals of teachers were brought into line with those of students and their families. The sophists, like modern teachers, would no doubt have wanted to charge more for their services than they did, but the simple fact that there were others around who could undercut their prices kept tuition to the level students were willing to spend. This did not prevent good teachers, such as Isocrates, from earning an excellent living from their labors, but it no doubt sent their less competent colleagues packing. The sophists could teach whatever they wanted, however they wanted, so long as there were people interested in their material, and confident in their methods. Would-be teachers who either had nothing interesting to say, or who lacked the ability to communicate what they knew, were encouraged to find a different career by the simple expedient that they could not make a living teaching. One great virtue of this system was that as long as there were enough people interested in what a teacher had to say, it did not matter if the rest of the public was actively hostile to his work, he could still carry on. Aspasia's school was by far the best example of this fact.

Defying prejudices of the day, this foreign-born woman set up shop in Athens teaching philosophy and rhetoric, and unabashedly advocated the liberation and education of the city's women. According to Plato, her lectures attracted such towering figures as Socrates and Pericles, the latter of whom—one of Athens's greatest statesmen—eventually became her lover and lifelong companion. When asked (in Plato's dialogue "Menexenus") of his ability to improvise a speech, Socrates avowed that he was up to the task and, referring to Aspasia, added, "I have an excellent mistress in the art of rhetoric—she who has made so many good speakers."[16] In the same dialogue, Socrates goes on to suggest that one of the most famous speeches in ancient history, the funeral oration given by Pericles, was actually written by her. Though it would be next to impossible to substantiate this claim, it certainly implies a healthy respect for her abilities on the part of Plato.[17] Demonstrating the breadth of her appeal, Aspasia's school also attracted a large number of girls from well-to-do families, an emancipatory innovation that drew harsh criticism from many of the city's crusty conservatives.[18] What is perhaps most significant about her case is the fact that, despite the intensely sexist climate of the city, the majority was not able to prevent Aspasia from opening her school and reaching out to the disenfranchised female population.

Education in Sparta: Big Brother Goes to School

If Athenian education could have an opposite, that opposite was to be found in Sparta. Every aspect of child-rearing which in Athens was the right and responsibility of parents, was in Sparta the prerogative of the government. State rule, unmitigated by written laws, began before a child was even conceived, and ended only in death. Marriages tended to be arranged by the parents, though the proper age for this decision was laid down by the state.[19] To get the real flavor of the relationship between family and state in Sparta, it helps to know the views of the city's most acclaimed leader, Lycurgus, on reproduction. According to his biographer, Plutarch:

> First and foremost Lycurgus considered children to belong not privately to their fathers, but jointly to the city, so that he wanted citizens produced not from random partners, but from the best. Moreover he observed a good deal of stupidity and humbug in others' rules on these matters. Such people have their bitches and mares mounted by the finest dogs and stallions whose owners they can prevail upon for a favour or fee. But their wives they lock up and guard, claiming the right to produce their children exclusively.[20]

This bit of genetic engineering was followed up by a sort of government triage, in which newborn babies were brought before the city elders and inspected for defects. If they decided it was better for the state and for itself, the baby was dispatched to a cliff on nearby Mount Taygetus, from which it was thrown.[21]

At the age of seven, all the male children who had passed this test were separated from their families and taken to live in school dormitories—here again, the education of girls received less attention than that of boys.[22] The way in which students were treated was well-captured by the terms used to describe them. A class of boys was referred to as a "boua," the same word used for a herd of cattle, and from each herd, a dominant boy was chosen to act as herd-leader. With satisfying consistency, their head teacher was called "paidono-mus," or boy-herdsman. This individual was chosen from the aristocracy, and was granted the authority to train the boys, and to harshly discipline them if any failed to follow his instructions. In his efforts, he was assisted by two "floggers" armed with whips.[23] Parents had no direct say in the education or upbringing of their children, having to cede their responsibilities and desires to this single, monolithic state system.

Educational boot camp

The children were administered an education consisting almost exclusively of sports, endurance training, and fighting. When questions were posed to them, a prompt reply was expected, and those who failed to answer to the teacher's satisfaction were regarded as incompetent, and given a bite on the thumb or some similar punishment.[24] Arithmetic is not mentioned as a part of the curriculum by any of Sparta's chroniclers, and reading, if introduced at all, was given short shrift. Plutarch says that students were not exposed to letters any "more than was necessary,"[25] and since scrolls and written laws were virtually nonexistent in Sparta, this could not have been much at all. Speech and writing were further discouraged by an outright prohibition on learning rhetoric, the violation of which was a punishable offense.[26] Educational innovation, whether it involved additions to the curriculum or the adoption of new techniques in wrestling or military training, was shunned or forbidden.

Conditions in the schools were as harsh as the children could tolerate, so that they would become accustomed to the deprivation and discomfort of military campaigns. Each night the boys bedded down on mats made from reeds, and each day they went about their chores and training in bare feet and simple, uniform clothing. Anyone who saw a boy exhibiting cowardice or shirking his duties was permitted to beat him for the offense. It was also customary for men to incite fights between groups of boys to discover which were strongest and craftiest.

At dinner time, boys were fed simple, hearty meals, but were served deliberately small portions so that they would constantly be hungry if this were their only source of sustenance. To supplement this meager fare, children were encouraged to steal. The city's leaders seem to have believed that, if you want an army that thinks nothing of pillaging neighboring states, it is exceedingly helpful to have citizens accustomed to robbing their neighbors. While those caught stealing were severely punished, it was more for failing to get away with the crime than for attempting it in the first place. According to Isocrates, who admittedly was not a great admirer of Sparta, skill in theft was considered a noble accomplishment, paving the way to the highest political offices.[27] Of course, students were encouraged to steal primarily from the subjugated peasant and slave populations rather than from other citizens.

By the time they had reached the age of eighteen, Spartan youths were tough, fit, and ruthless, but also inexperienced. The missing element in their training was provided by an institution known as the "krypteia." Young men were gathered into bands and dispatched to the countryside where they would have to hunt and steal to survive. Their primary mission, however, was to attack their own peasant population whenever the opportunity arose, killing those who had the audacity to defend themselves.

By now it is probably obvious that Spartan teachers—or, more accurately, trainers—had virtually no say in what or how they taught. The state curriculum left no room for art, literature, science, or philosophy, and indeed anyone who strayed from the physical training mandated by law would surely have been beaten or exiled. Any deviation from accepted practice, in almost any field, was considered a reproach and a threat to the revered status quo.

Rather than being chosen by families, teachers were appointed by the state. So long as the city's generals and magistrates felt that the schools were producing capable warriors, their positions were secure. Any signs of leniency or failure to instill a proper attitude of submissiveness to state authority could result in teachers being ousted, however. This system seems to have undergone few changes during its two-hundred-year reign.

Outcomes of Athenian Schooling

Having described the different approaches to schooling in Athens and Sparta, we can look to the conditions of their people for a reflection of the effects of those systems. It would be unrealistic, of course, to attribute all of the differences between Athenian and Spartan civilizations to their schools, but formal education clearly played an influential role.

To the classical Greeks, Athens was the "school of Hellas" and the "metropolis of wisdom." Of the three most influential philosophers in Western antiquity—Socrates, Plato, and Aristotle—the first two were Athenian citizens, and the third a resident alien, studying and teaching in the city for much of his life. The greatest Western historian of the period, Thucydides, was Athenian, and his successor, Xenophon, though an ardent admirer of Spartan militancy, was born and raised just over fifteen miles from Athens. Sophocles, Euripides, and Aristophanes, from whose minds flowed the most profound tragedy and biting satire in the literature of ancient Greece, were also natives of the city of Athena.

But what of the public at large? One particularly useful indication of the general level of learning in the city is the proportion of citizens who were literate. A variety of techniques have been used to estimate Athenian literacy, primarily centering on the reading required for participation in public life, the archeological evidence of writing on pottery fragments and the like, and references to reading in contemporary plays and prose works. By all accounts, Athens was the most literate society in the Western world at that time. Most urban citizens could no doubt recognize the letters of the alphabet, and perhaps half of them could read and write with varying degrees of facility.[28] Written language was still young, however, and fluency was necessarily concentrated in those fields which required or directly benefited from it. In the same way that second or third languages we learn in school today sometimes atrophy for lack of use, the ability to read and write probably deteriorated among those Athenians who learned their letters in school but had only occasional cause to read and write in their daily lives. In rural areas, too, literacy was probably much more limited. Still, with the city's bustling economy, thriving public life, philosophers, poets, and historians, there was good cause for many citizens to keep their language skills honed.[29]

Athenian artistic and intellectual achievements went hand in hand with the spirit of freedom and community that pervaded the society. With little resort to government intervention or coercion,[30] Athens enjoyed not only an explosion of artistic, literary, and scientific work, but also a thriving economy. As more and more Athenians became educated, the economy grew in both size and diversity, benefiting both consumers and entrepreneurs. Isocrates observed that "the articles which it is difficult to get, one here, one there, from the rest of the world, all these it is easy to buy in Athens."[31] From the businessman's perspective, the increase in cultural sophistication and economic success of the population at large meant an increasing market for domestic and imported goods of all kinds. As economic historian Rondo Cameron points out:

> Some cities, such as Athens, concentrated a number of commercial and financial functions within their boundaries in much the same way as Antwerp, Amsterdam, London, and New York did in subsequent eras. Banking, insurance, joint-stock ventures, and a number of other economic institutions that are associated with later epochs already existed in embryonic form in classical Greece.[32]

The possibility of achieving financial success through craftsmanship or commerce was, in turn, a strong incentive for getting an education, and the availability of both academic schooling and skilled apprenticeships brought about a labor force of exceptional diversity. The mutually reinforcing relationship between growing prosperity and ever-wider access to education made possible an unprecedented advance in economic prosperity and quality of life. With its busy port and frenzied marketplace, Athens imported not only spices and copper, but people and ideas as well. Traders came from all over the world to do business in Athens, bringing with them their knowledge, views, and insights. Athenian prosperity also attracted artists and philosophers who found in the city a vast market for entertainment, learning, and all things of beauty.

The independent schools and apprenticeships of Athens not only helped to secure the economic gains described above, but also made political life accessible to a broader segment of the population. Tradesmen and businessmen, wage workers, and sailors began to assert themselves in the political scene, raising to leadership positions such people as "Cleon the tanner, Lysicles the sheep dealer, Eucrates the tow seller, Cleophon the harp manufacturer, and Hyperbolus the lampmaker."[33] Freedom of speech enjoyed greater respect and protection in classical Athens than it has in almost any other culture up to modern times. Because Athens was a direct democracy, in which all citizens were expected to participate as regularly as possible in the governing assembly and on court juries, the city's political life was vibrant—particularly by modern U.S. standards. Athenians knew that their collective decisions exerted a powerful influence on their lives, and they therefore shared a compelling interest in protecting the personal freedom and comparatively high standard of living that citizens enjoyed. Pericles, in his speech commemorating the first soldiers to fall in the Peloponnesian War, stated what they were fighting to preserve:

> Our constitution is called a democracy because power is in the hands not of a minority, but of the whole people. When it is a question of settling private disputes, everyone is equal before the law; when it is a question of putting one person before another in positions of public responsibility, what counts is not membership of a particular class, but the actual ability which the man possesses. No one, so long as he has it in him to be of service to the state, is kept in political obscurity because of poverty. And, just as our political life is free and open, so is our day to day life in our relations with each other.[34]

Of course, Athenian social and political life was plagued at times by many of the same flaws that confront us today and that we have battled against in our own recent past: slavery, sexism, and belligerent foreign policy among them. But the Athenians' ideals and the success with which they approached those ideals are truly astonishing when we remember that they were building their society virtually from scratch, whereas we have had two and a half thousand years of good and bad examples to learn from. It is hard to establish how much of their achievement can be attributed to their approach to schooling, but we can say this: Athenian parents had complete discretion over the content and manner of their children's education, and these children went on to create a culture responsible for some of the greatest advances in art, science, and human liberty in history.

Spartan Outcomes

The picture which comes down to us of Sparta in the fifth and fourth centuries B.C. is a very different one. With the exception of one or two historians who have attempted to show the existence of literacy among the common people in Sparta, the field is almost unanimous in finding the Spartans to be among the least literate people in ancient Greece, if not the ancient world as a whole. Apart from the kings and perhaps a few generals and magistrates, the Spartans were an illiterate people. Isocrates did not hesitate to observe that the Spartans "have fallen so far behind our common culture and learning that they do not even try to instruct themselves in letters."[35] Knowledge of arithmetic was equally limited, since it was not taught in the schools. Evidence such as we have for Athenian literacy is almost nonexistent for Sparta. There were no witty plays to attend, no written laws to read, no complex commercial transactions to complete, no reason, in other words, to become literate. Even if there had been, attendance at the state schools was compulsory and their whole mission was to produce men willing to die for their city, not to produce entrepreneurs or scholars.

Sparta had virtually no science or literature, and little art. Her legacy to modern times is negligible, apart from being a beacon to those advocating totalitarian systems of education during the French Revolution,[36] nineteenth-century America,[37] and the rise of Germany's National Socialist (Nazi) party.

Like the Athenians, the Spartans sought social stability, but their means were the exact opposites of those chosen in Athens. Government coercion and regulation were used pervasively to control the lives of the people. From birth to death, Spartans followed a prescribed lifestyle of subservience to the state, well characterized by Plutarch in the following passage:

> Altogether he [Lycurgus] accustomed citizens to have no desire for a private life, nor knowledge of one, but rather to be like bees, always attached to the community, swarming together around their leader, and almost ecstatic with fervent ambition to devote themselves entirely to their country.[38]

In order to prevent the Spartans from being distracted by material things and physical comforts, it is believed that Lycurgus used a tool of government still popular today: currency devaluation. By declaring iron to be the only legal currency and then devaluing it to the point where it would have taken cartloads of the stuff for even the smallest purchase, he succeeded in eliminating virtually all foreign trade. The same tactic affected teaching as well, as Plutarch tells us that "no teacher of rhetoric trod Laconian [Spartan] soil . . . [b]ecause there was no coined money."[39] The Spartan economy was basic, and far more dependent upon slave and serf labor than that of Athens, since Spartan citizens were allowed only to train for war in the state schools, and could neither acquire a broader learning nor apprentice themselves to skilled tradesmen. To keep up the production of basic necessities, Sparta subjugated the entire peasant population of its region. To keep its own people from rebelling, or from even finding out that there might be a reason to rebel, communication with the outside world was cut off. Without modern means of communication, withdrawing from the surrounding states was comparatively easy. Foreigners were generally refused entry, and Spartan citizens were forbidden to travel abroad without special permission from the government.[40]

The parallel with the Soviet Union prior to the fall of the Berlin Wall is hard to overlook, and indeed goes beyond the issues of travel and communication restrictions. As in the old Communist states,[41] the Spartan government sanctioned some forms of artistic expression and outlawed others. An Athenian orator remarked that "they care naught for the other poets . . . but for Turtaios they care so exceedingly that they made a law to summon every one to the king's tent, when they are on a campaign, to hear the poems of Turtaios, considering that this would make them most ready to die for their country."[42] Music that strayed too far from the military theme was punishable by law[43] — a far cry from the city's earlier days when frolicsome poems about love and wine were the norm.

Rome: The Decline and Fall of the Educational Market

The brutal, authoritarian educational system of the Spartans continued to churn out single-minded soldiers for hundreds of years, but beyond the battlefield its influence was negligible. Apart from the island of Crete, which is said to have been the inspiration for Lycurgus's statist vision, Greek education was Athenian in both its manner and content. By the time Isocrates had entered his nineties in the middle of the fourth century B.C., the Mediterranean coast was spotted with Hellenistic[44] cities whose streets hosted a daily morning pilgrimage of students on the way to school. The combined achievement of Greek philosophers and sophists had succeeded in giving their approach to education a foot in the door of Western civilization. Interestingly, it was none other than a pupil of Aristotle's who soon kicked this door off its hinges.

Aristotle's father had been physician to King Philip II of Macedon, a nation sharing both a border and a language with Greece, and when the King sought a tutor for his son, Aristotle was thought eminently suitable. The boy was a quick study, and by the age of fifteen he was appointed governor of Macedon and soon thereafter managed to quell a sedition.[45] This, however, was just a warm up. By his mid-twenties, Alexander the Great conquered Greece, Persia, Syria, Palestine, and Egypt, and marched almost to the Ganges River in India before his soldiers, tired of the grueling pace, staged a sit-down strike.[46] Evidence of the military buildup in Macedonia had been visible for some time, and the combined might of the Greeks might well have staved off or even prevented their ultimate downfall, but unite they could not. Sparta was always a law unto herself, and Athens had been losing friends for decades. Contrary to her domestic policy of limited government and equal rights for all citizens, Athens was belligerent and imperialistic toward her Greek allies, expecting from them the tributes of loyal subjects, rather than free exchange among peers. By the time Alexander was ready to bulldoze his way into the history books, the Athenians had managed to alienate or infuriate half of the Mediterranean. Divided, Greece fell.

Alexander set the world aflame, and though his empire died with him in 323 B.C., its ashes were fertile soil for the seeds of Hellenistic civilization. From southeastern Europe and northern Africa to the Middle East, his soldiers had carried not only spears and shields but ideas and institutions as well. Upon his death the lands he had conquered were divided up among his generals, most of whom actively fostered the spread of Greek traditions and language.

Roman Education

Two hundred years after the conquests of Alexander, a new order had engulfed the Mediterranean. From simple agrarian roots, Rome had risen to the status of a world power, acquiring along the way an appetite for learning and culture. A few early rumblings of this appetite can be traced to about 169 B.C., and one of history's least auspicious beginnings.

Dispatched as ambassador to Rome by the King of Pergamum,[47] the philosopher Crates was idling down a street in the Palatine quarter one night when he stumbled and fell into an open sewer. Having broken his leg in the fall, Crates remained in the city during his convalescence, and made the best of his stay by giving lectures on language and writing. His mishap was Rome's gain, for in addition to his diplomatic skills he was also head of the library at Pergamum—the second greatest storehouse of knowledge in the ancient world after the library of Alexandria in northern Egypt. The erudition displayed by Crates motivated a number of Romans to follow in his footsteps (albeit at a safe distance), and Rome soon enjoyed several schools of language.[48] More than anything else, these schools set a decisive precedent: they, like Crates, taught in Greek.

Under the Republic

While Crates brought higher literary studies to Rome, a rudimentary form of primary education had already existed there for at least a generation. In both levels of schooling, the role of the state was much as it had been in Athens. According to Cicero: "Our people have never wished to have any system of education for the free-born youth which is either definitely fixed by law, or officially established, or uniform in all cases."[49] Also as in Athens, the absence of government intervention did not prevent a network of schools, apprenticeships, and tutoring from developing. The health and growth of Roman education was compromised, however, by a combination of two factors: most of what the Romans wanted to learn, only the Greeks could teach; and in Rome, virtually all Greeks were slaves. In many cases Greek slaves were brought to Rome expressly for the purpose of teaching.

The combination of slavery and education produced less than stellar results. There was little incentive for teachers to innovate or apply themselves assiduously, since they could rarely enjoy the full fruit of their labor. Occasionally slave teachers were freed after many years of service, but in their day-to-day work this possibility must have seemed a dim light at the end of a very long tunnel. Teacher morale was often low, discipline was harsh, and the use of play in learning entirely disappeared. Counting and alphabet games that had amused and instructed Athenian schoolchildren hundreds of years before were unknown in Rome. The result of this barren educational environment was boredom and rebelliousness on the part of students.

In wealthy families education began with tutoring in the home, but for most children it started around the age of seven when they were sent off to elementary school. There, boys and sometimes girls learned reading, writing, simple counting skills, and bits of knowledge in other fields gleaned from the works used in language instruction. Elementary teachers were often fairly backward and poorly educated themselves, and in their attempts to maintain control of the classroom, were generous in meting out corporal punishment. Several blows of a ruler to the back of the hand could be expected for a minor offense, and more severe transgressions were cause for flogging. Beatings were such a common aspect of school life that they were frequently mentioned by contemporary writers. The poet Martial went so far as to compose a letter to the master of a noisy neighborhood school:

> What right have you to disturb me, abominable school-master, object abhorred alike by boys and girls? Before the crested cocks have broken silence, you begin to roar out your savage scoldings and blows. Not with louder noise does the metal resound on the struck anvil, when the workman is fitting a lawyer to a horse.[50] . . . Dismiss your scholars, brawler, and take as much for keeping quiet as you receive for making noise.[51]

While the drab and often cruel experience of primary school was shared by the majority of children, higher educational attainment was more limited. The need to acquire job training, together with the cost of tuition, meant that a refined liberal education was beyond the means of many families. Apprenticeship was again the most common secondary training for most youths and teenagers of lower and middle-class means. It was at this age, too, that girls tended to be discouraged from further study. Beginning as early as twelve or as late as fifteen, apprenticeships could last anywhere from six months to five years depending on the difficulty of the skills to be learned and the aptitude of the child.[52] To the greatest extent possible, though, manual labor was foisted upon members of the slave population (who were also apprenticed to trades), so that free craftsmen made up only a fraction of the manual labor force.

For those youths who would not immediately need to earn a living, more advanced language studies followed their elementary education, usually at around age twelve. In both content and method, schools of language mimicked their Hellenistic counterparts. Still at the center of the curriculum after hundreds of years were the epics of Homer. Since most "middle" schools taught Latin and Greek more or less simultaneously, it was not uncommon for children to learn Greek works both in the original language and in translation. There were also an increasing number of original texts available in Latin, but the *Iliad* and the *Odyssey* became, if anything, more entrenched with the passage of time.

At fifteen or sixteen, some students would progress from this intermediate literary instruction to the study of rhetoric, usually after a brief period of military service. Schools of rhetoric offered a systematic program of exercises, beginning with the paraphrasing of notable works, and progressing to original compositions defending a position, eulogizing a respected individual, or criticizing some unsavory act. This training was well suited to the law courts and the political life of the Republic, and it produced orators of great subtlety and inventiveness. Intelligence, forcefulness, and grace in public speaking could raise a man from relative anonymity to preeminence in government. Ironically, this education for statesmanship persisted long after even the pretense of democracy had faded from Roman society.

Schools fit for an emperor

Just as the Romans haltingly began to develop a literature and culture of their own, the Republic was thrown into chaos. In the turbulent years following the assassination of Julius Caesar in 44 B.C. and the rise of Emperor Augustus, Rome was transfigured. Over the ensuing decades, the vital and animated debates that had scorched the air of the senate were stripped of their meaning and substance by the emperor's increasing power. Where once critical decisions had been made, only suggestions were now offered. In a few short years, Rome ceased to be a republic, becoming instead an empire run by absolute rulers. Throughout this transformation, its educational system remained remarkably constant in some respects, while being altered substantially in others.

With politics closed to advancement on the basis of merit and public speaking ability, the study of rhetoric lost much of its usefulness, but it remained the focus of higher education well into Rome's decline. In the absence of any real-world significance, classroom exercises grew into a twisted parody of their earlier forms. While a youth growing up in the age of the Republic might have been asked to present an argument on some pressing political issue, assignments in the third and fourth centuries A.D. were often reduced to sheer fantasy. The need for rigorous and logical thinking was among the first casualties of this degeneration. Since a well-conceived argument was not expected to sway the emperor or his magistrates, style became all important. Poetic delivery and a mellifluous voice became the most praiseworthy qualities for a student of rhetoric.

One reason that rhetoric persisted, despite being reduced to a parody of its former self, was the influence and intervention of the government. Just as Spartan autocrats had seen education as a way of maintaining the loyalty of their citizens, so too did the Roman emperors. Both direct and indirect means were used by the emperors to ensure that schools cast them in a favorable light.

As far back as the late first century B.C. and early first century A.D., Emperor Augustus suppressed teachers and scholars critical of his regime, collecting and burning their tracts—a practice that remained popular under later emperors. Both Augustus and his successor, Tiberius, prosecuted educators of whose teachings they disapproved. Everything from historical writings favoring republicanism to discussions of birth control were vetoed by the state.[53] Going right to the heart of the matter, emperor Julian Augustus ordained in 362 A.D. that teachers must be officially certified, and went so far as to assume personal control over the final approval.[54] Dissenters were silenced simply by denying them certification. This policy was adopted by his successors as well, and Theodosius II reaffirmed it, ruling that those who were caught "unduly and insolently [usurping] the garb of philosophers," that is, teaching without a license, should be publicly condemned for their infamy and deported from the city in which they taught. As a concession to the emperor's wealthy and powerful supporters, private tutors were exempted from the certification process.[55] Nonetheless, it was illegal for private teachers to give lectures in the public schools, and vice versa.[56]

The regulation and suppression of education comprised only half of the carrot-and-stick approach adopted by Roman rulers. The second aspect was to offer teachers—who tended to be citizens rather than slaves during this period—special benefits, considerations, and funds in return for their faithful service. This largess grew with each successive government. The more teachers distorted the facts in favor of the emperor, the greater their rewards. Vespasian (9–79 A.D.) was the first of the emperors to place teachers on the payroll, issuing a state salary to Greek and Latin rhetoricians. He then expanded upon this legislation by exempting teachers from many of the laws and duties of citizenship.[57] After the year 74, it was illegal to harass or sue teachers, or to force them to have soldiers billeted in their homes.[58] By the fourth century, teachers and their families had been exempted from most taxes, and from all public and military service. These were general edicts, however, applying equally to teachers throughout the empire. Truly egregious bribery was reserved for those professors who praised the emperor directly, and in especially glowing terms.

Eventually, a custom developed in which teachers of rhetoric came from all over the empire into the presence of their nominally divine ruler. At such meetings, rhetoricians were expected to extol the virtues and achievements of their host in prepared speeches known as panegyrics. In one slavish example, the teacher Pacatus disingenuously confessed to his emperor that "in truth it is impossible to say whether it is your greatness that commends you to our hearts, or your face to our eyes."[59] Successful panegyrists did quite well in the bargain. For his flattery of Emperor Majorian, a man by the name of Sidonius was made a count, and when he turned his talents to successive rulers, was appointed prefect of Rome. Sidonius was under no illusions about his rise to power, noting in one of his writings that the prefecture had been obtained through a judicious use of the pen.[60] Extending beyond simple flattery, the lure of imperial patronage induced educators to distort historical fact.[61] Typically, panegyrists would downplay or omit the achievements of the emperor's rivals, and play up his own accomplishments beyond reason. Once made, these exaggerations and distortions could not easily (or safely) be retracted, and thus they no doubt corrupted the teaching of history itself.

Outcomes of Roman Education

While Roman civilization holds a special place in Western history thanks to its longevity, stability, and contributions to the spread of written law, it was not marked by significant scientific or cultural progress. Under the Republic, education limped along, maintaining some of the accomplishments of the Greeks, but rarely adding to them in any substantial way. Literacy in the city of Rome in the first century B.C. probably approached that of classical Athens, but Rome's literary and scientific contributions do not compare. While the Greeks had invented most of the major forms of Western literature from biography to tragedy, and had achieved greatness in many of them, the Roman corpus was more spare in both quality and originality.

The great feats of Roman engineering were also largely derivative. The Greeks, Assyrians, Babylonians, Persians, and Egyptians had all been building aqueducts long before the Romans. Roman military hardware, such as the catapult, was predominantly of Greek invention, and "her early naval vessels were timber-by-timber copies of those used by the Greeks and Carthaginians."[62] The whole eight-hundred-year period from 300 B.C. to 500 A.D. saw fewer technological and scientific advances than the two hundred years that preceded it. This lack of innovation has been chiefly ascribed to two causes: reliance on slave labor and bureaucracy. While classical Athenian trades, crafts, and schools had all been dominated by free citizens and foreign residents, the archeologist and historian of technology Henry Hodges writes that in Rome:

> The dirty end of production . . . was put entirely into the hands of slaves and increased output could be achieved only by one of two means: either by acquiring more slaves or by making those one had work harder. Since it is not in the nature of slaves either to invent new means of production or to exploit new materials, the possibility of any further technological development came to an abrupt end.[63]

Hodges also argues that many industrial, commercial, and agricultural enterprises came under government control during the Empire, managed by civil servants who had no personal stake in increasing the efficiency or profitability of their operations. So long as output was adequate, their jobs were secure and there was no incentive for them to strive for improvements. In practice, they simply maintained the status quo—a sharp contrast to the success of the Athenian economy under its government's laissez-faire policy.

The reason these economic facts are so important is that they mirrored the experience in education. Roman educational history is a chronicle of stagnation followed by collapse. Robbed not only of their professional but also their personal freedom, republican Rome's teachers had little incentive to find new and better ways of teaching or new subjects to teach, and so they didn't. Though free citizens started to displace slaves as teachers under the late Republic and the Empire, the state simultaneously began to impose restrictions on the profession itself and to suppress dissenting views; thus, teachers continued to be prevented from practicing according to their own judgment.

Where the Romans did innovate was in educational funding. Progressively, the source of teachers' salaries shifted away from the students and toward the state, with the teachers' attentions often following close behind. Even when the emperor took no personal interest in a teacher's actions, the incentive to satisfy the needs of students was largely erased by the fact that the teacher's salary was independent of his performance.

The effects of increasing government funding, state teacher certification, and the handing down of favors did not go unnoticed, even by those within the government itself. One such insider was Pliny the Younger. Having practiced law from the age of eighteen, Pliny distinguished himself in his successful prosecution of political corruption and extortion cases. He also had an abiding interest in education, and upon discovering that the town where he was born had no secondary school, he decided to found one himself. As indicated in the brief excerpt cited in the Introduction, Pliny decided to pay only one third of the total cost for the new school, explaining his decision this way:

> I would promise the whole amount were I not afraid that someday my gift might be abused for someone's selfish purposes, as I see happen in many places where teachers' salaries are paid from public funds. There is only one remedy to meet this evil: if the appointment of teachers is left entirely to the parents, and they are conscientious about making a wise choice through their obligation to contribute to the cost. People who may be careless about another person's money are sure to be careful about their own, and they will see that only a suitable recipient shall be found for my money if he is also to have their own. . . . I am leaving everything open for the parents: the decision and choice are to be theirs—all I want is to make the arrangements and pay my share.[64]

Rome's eventual collapse was not marked by any single cataclysmic event, but rather was the product of a gradual degeneration. Part of the problem was that the late Empire was a dictatorship backed by the army; in order to stay in power, it had to keep its soldiers well looked-after and well paid. But the steady income from military conquests had dried up, and new sources of revenue had to be found. At first, the emperors used inflation and heavy taxes on the rich, but soon they had devalued the currency to the point of worthlessness and all but emptied the coffers of the wealthy. Next they turned the tax system on the middle classes. Between inflation and these new confiscatory taxes, middle-class employment lost much of its luster. There was no longer any point in spending years in formal education or training, since highly educated citizens enjoyed fewer and fewer perks over subsistence farmers. Not surprisingly, the urban middle class began to shrink as a result.

By the fifth century, the Roman Empire was in a rapidly accelerating tailspin. According to economist Bruce Bartlett, some Romans actually began giving themselves as slaves to the few remaining wealthy landowners, for the simple reason that slaves paid no taxes.[65] By the time the "barbarians" finally took Rome, the Empire had already sacked itself. But history, like nature, abhors a vacuum, and it was not long before the Roman Empire's heir-apparent—the Catholic Church—stepped in to fill the void.

Darkness in the West, Dawn in the East

Once a small and persecuted sect, Christianity was officially established by Emperor Constantine in the year 325. This new-found authority, coupled with the Church's substantial wealth, allowed it to assert itself politically. Its intellectual leaders first learned from and eventually absorbed many of the Empire's administrative and legal functions. Saints Ambrose and Augustine both complained of their heavy judicial duties.[66] It was not long before Christianity's growing influence and sophistication made it an appealing refuge for the old aristocracy, and, as pagan nobles became Christian bishops, they brought with them not only their rank and leadership experience, but also their classical learning.[67]

For some of these new converts, the move from courtroom to pulpit did not diminish the appeal of rhetoric. By simply substituting biblical figures for Greek and Roman ones, they preserved the oratorical form with few alterations. But there was also a strong purist contingent within the Church trying to keep all pagan influences at bay. This view is well illustrated by the correspondence between a newly ordained priest named Paulinus and his former teacher of classical literature. Paulinus believed that true Christians must say no to Apollo and the Muses, writing: "New is the force and greater the god that now moves the soul, and he permits not leisure in work or play for the literature of fable."[68] Inevitably, disputes often arose within the Church over the proper role of pre-Christian learning.

These disputes were gradually overcome by temperate voices who saw a need to preserve the culture of the past. Augustine, for instance, is said to have smuggled "Plato into the (Christian) schools under his bishop's robe."[69] Methodically, Church Fathers sifted the secular corpus through Christianity, keeping everything they considered acceptable, or at least not blasphemous, and tossing back the rest. The compromise thus achieved established the limits of educational curricula in the West for a thousand years.

These limits were seldom even approached, however, for the schools of early Christianity served a very different purpose from those of antiquity. For the ancient Greeks, the ultimate goal of scholarship was to understand the world, and thereby learn how to lead a good, happy, and successful life. Greece's greatest thinkers studied and taught every subject imaginable: while generally remembered for his complex metaphysical discussions, Aristotle spent years making observations and writing essays in such fields as anatomy, biology, physics, and meteorology. Christianity replaced this search for worldly knowledge with a search to know God, and as a tool in that effort observation of the world was thought vastly inferior to the study of scripture. Thus, while monks transcribed and illuminated a variety of ancient secular books in the centuries to come, the methods and conclusions communicated by all but the most abstract works received little hearing in their schools.

The term "Dark Ages," used to describe the period of European history between the collapse of Rome and the fourteenth-century Renaissance, has fallen into disuse among historians. For many Christians, this trend is long overdue, for they consider the medieval rise of Christianity to have been a great boon to humanity. From the standpoint of mass education, however, the medieval era was indeed a dark age. Despite isolated pockets of learning concentrated around the monasteries of Europe, the overwhelming majority of the populace was uneducated and illiterate.

With the end of mass education and the loss of interest in the physical world, there began a long decline in scientific knowledge. A graphic example of this trend is depicted in Figures 1 and 2, which represent, respectively, the state of European geographical knowledge in the second and ninth centuries A.D. The more recent sketch—hardly resembling a map at all—is dramatically inferior to Ptolemy's work, which preceded it by seven hundred years.

The atrophy of learning in Western Europe touched every discipline. What limited medical wisdom had been accumulated by Greek and Roman physicians was supplanted by utter mysticism. Augustine himself believed that diseases were caused by demons, a great step backward from the work of the Greek physician Hippocrates in the fifth century B.C. Writing on epilepsy, which was called "the sacred disease," Hippocrates had stated: "It is not any more sacred than other diseases, but has a natural cause, and its supposed divine origin is due to man's inexperience."[70] Alcuin, teacher to Charlemagne,

Figure 1. Second-Century World Map

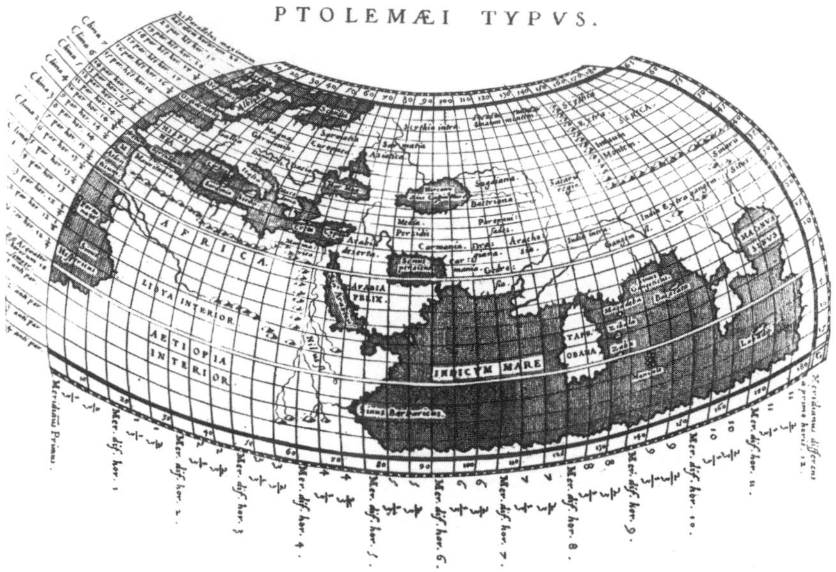

and one of the greatest scholars of the eighth century A.D., had a grasp of mathematics well below that of his ancient Greek predecessors.

In the year 529, the Roman Emperor Justinian formally closed all the schools of Athens that failed to teach orthodox Christianity, including Plato's Academy and Aristotle's Lyceum, founded nine centuries before.[71] At around the same time, members of the well-educated Nestorian Christian sect were also driven from Greece and Macedonia, taking with them the works of Aristotle and such other philosophers as they found conducive to their religious cause.[72] Together these scholars made their escape from Europe, seeking refuge in the dawning East.

Education in the Arab World

First under the Persians, and later under the Arabs, scholarship thrived. From the sixth through the eleventh centuries, when Western monarchs could barely sign their own names,[73] Muslims, Jews, and Christians preserved and advanced classical knowledge in intellectual centers across the Middle East. Initially, their efforts centered on translation—introducing the Greek philosophical and literary heritage to readers of Syriac and Arabic. The field of inquiry was soon broadened, however, with the integration of Hindu arithmetic and medicine. At its pinnacle in the tenth and eleventh centuries, Islamic scholarship was a rich mixture

Figure 2. Ninth-Century World Map

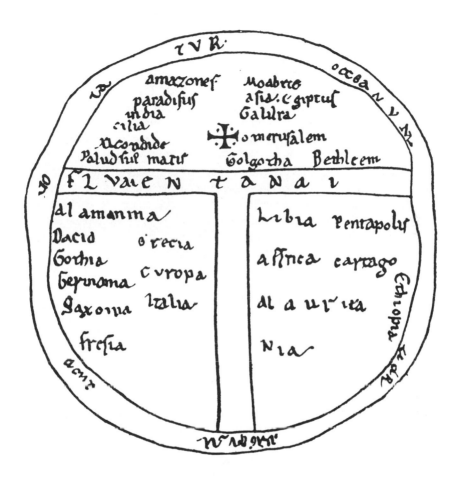

of Eastern and Western legacies combined with new work in mathematics, physics, and the life sciences. And while the caliphs governed their empire with monarchical powers, and were often ruthless toward their rivals, they refrained from systematically intervening in education until the eleventh century.

Before the birth of the prophet Mohammed around the year 570, many children in Persia (now Iran) were already attending elementary schools reminiscent of those of Athens. They learned basic grammar and arithmetic, usually in the teacher's home, and occasionally also poetry, horsemanship, or swimming. Once Islam took hold in the seventh century, however, a new form of elementary education grew up beside the first, a form in which the *Koran* became the central, sometimes the only, subject of instruction.[74] These two forms of elementary schooling continued to exist in parallel with one another, with many of the secular schools charging tuition, while others, along with virtually all of the religious institutions, were maintained by private charitable grants.[75]

In the mid eighth century, under Caliph Abu al-Abbas al-Saffah, the Islamic empire stretched from northwestern India to northwestern Africa and across the Mediterranean into Spain. As Muslim civilization spread and grew more sophisticated, so did its educational institutions. Two sorts of secondary schools were available to teenaged boys and sometimes girls. Private "circle" schools, so called because of the way pupils gathered around their teachers, offered lectures on an immense range of topics, though any single school would have taught only a few. Many branches of mathematics and the sciences were studied, along with medicine, philosophy, literature, jurisprudence, and a host of other disciplines.[76] Note-taking was encouraged due to the limited supply of texts, and discussion of the material was commonly encouraged. These schools spread rapidly as there were no legal restrictions on entering the teaching profession, and the demand for instruction was considerable. It was typical for students to sample many such "circles" seeking an appropriate and engaging teacher, and, in an interesting reversal of the sophist's itinerancy, many older students traveled from city to city seeking rather than professing knowledge.[77]

Mosques, the centers of so much community activity, provided a second avenue to higher education. Though focused on the *Koran,* mosque schools also held lectures in comparative and historical religions. Greater diversification followed, and while it is doubtful whether they ever achieved the range of circle schools, mosques did provide secular teaching in some areas.

Though it enjoyed vast powers and did not hesitate to use them in many areas of life, the medieval Islamic state initially played little role in education. Artists and scholars were sometimes generously patronized by the caliphs and lesser officials, but there was no systematic government funding or operation of schools. Just as it had in Athens and republican Rome, schooling flourished under these circumstances, and a fairly coherent educational system evolved. Education generally reached even the poorest children thanks to the religious and secular grant-maintained schools, and to the profound conviction of the time that every child should achieve at least basic literacy and a knowledge of scripture. One modern scholar of medieval Muslim education, presumably unfamiliar with the precedent set in Athens, has expressed surprise at the success of this decentralized educational market:

> The most astonishing fact about it is that it worked in spite of the lack of [government] organization. Even the rules and regulations were not uniform in most cases. However, the form of the classes and the methods of teaching were to a great extent the same throughout the Muslim world.[78]

Some of the consistency in techniques was no doubt the result of respect for tradition in what was a very traditional society, but the influence of competition and emulation were also key factors. Muslim scholars, like the sophists before them, strove to learn from each other's successes, copying the things that worked and abandoning those that didn't. They were driven by the same impetus that exists in any competitive market: the desire of consumers to reap the advantages of the latest techniques and discoveries. Those teachers who failed to keep pace with the advances in human knowledge taking place within the Arab world could not have prevented their students from finding other teachers who did.

This period of unfettered learning did not last. The power of education as a tool of political and religious indoctrination eventually proved too tempting, and around the middle of the eleventh century Nizam-al-Mulk established state-run schooling. Nizam, the chief minister of Sultan Malik Shah, was notable for his interventionist government policies and his religious intolerance. An orthodox follower of the Sunnite branch of Islam, he actively sought to suppress the competing Shi'ah branch, and looked askance on Jews and Christians. In keeping with his views, the state schools he founded were designed to inculcate Sunnite orthodoxy, and to promote his own partisan political aims.[79] Control over what was taught passed from the hands of the learners to the hands of the rulers.

Outcomes of Schooling under Islamic Rule

During its golden age in the eighth through the tenth centuries, the Muslim world enjoyed a level of literacy at least the equal of anything that had gone before. In poetry and philosophy it was hugely prolific, and in the sciences it led the world. Hundreds of years before Copernicus, Galileo, or Newton, the early eleventh-century Arab thinker al-Biruni took it for granted that the world was round, "noted 'the attraction of all things towards the center of the earth,' and remarked that astronomic data can be explained as well by supposing that the earth turns daily on its axis and annually around the sun, as by the reverse hypothesis" (i.e., that the sun orbits the earth).[80] Arab mathematicians broke new ground in complex calculations and trigonometry—the word "algebra" itself comes to us from Arabic. The physicist Alhazen made leaps in the understanding of optics, describing the behavior of lenses and mirrors, explaining rainbows, and giving the first accurate account of human sight. The *Canon of Medicine,* by the scientist and philosopher Avicenna (Ibn Sina), became the accepted medical reference text in Europe for several centuries.

A crucial factor in these advances was the existence and widespread tolerance of dissension among scholars. While religion was the driving force in Arab society, it was initially viewed as compatible with criticism and secular inquiry. A saying ascribed to Mohammed serves to illustrate the ideals of the early and middle stages of Arab civilization: The best among you are not those who neglect this world for the other, or the other world for this. They are the ones who work for both together.[81] So long as schooling and state were kept separate, skeptics and agnostics coexisted with orthodox Muslims, and both in turn were tolerant of the Hebrew and Christian scholars who contributed so much to the early work of translation and teaching. Education historian Abraham Blinderman writes:

> Perhaps few other periods in the tragic history of the Jewish people have been as meaningful to them as this period of Judaeo-Arabic communion. The renaissance of Jewish letters and science in Arab lands is a glorious testimonial to the cultural cosmopolitanism of the Arabs at a time when Jews in Europe were being burned as witches, plague-begetters, and ritualistic murderers.[82]

In Spain and along the coast of the Mediterranean, wherever Muslims and Europeans commingled, a vast accumulation of Arab and classical knowledge began to flow into Europe, rekindling interest in the physical world. The exchange was slow at first, but by the tenth and eleventh centuries, translators and scholars could be found crowding the libraries of Cordova, busily searching for some Aristotelian tome previously thought lost, or for a mathematician who could explain the Hindu-Arabic numeral system that much of the world continues to use to this day.

Though this transmission of existing knowledge continued for hundreds of years, the Muslim world's role as a source of new learning began to diminish from the late eleventh century onward. At that time, when the schools were seized by political leaders as a club with which to bludgeon their opponents, the freedom of thought and speech that had raised Islam to cultural preeminence was extinguished. What had been a vibrant and diverse intellectual society gradually began to calcify. The practical, research-oriented studies that had occupied so many Muslim physicists and physicians were swept away as revelation displaced inquiry and as tradition smothered innovation. Ironically, schools abounded during this period:

> As Islam began to decline after the end of the eleventh century, the number of its schools of higher learning increased and flourished. These colleges were, however, almost all denominational schools opened and supported by leaders of various Islamic religious factions. Each denominational college was open, with few exceptions, only to followers of a given sect. Religious and literary studies and Arabic language and grammar dominated the subject matter at the expense of philosophy, science, and social studies.[83]

And so it was that schooling, which at first had fed the intellectual life of the Muslim empire, eventually poisoned it. The living world, once considered an open book for all to study and interpret, was slammed shut.

Education and the Reformation in Germany and France

Fortunately, the withering of intellectual activity in Islam did not lead to the destruction of all that her people had preserved and created. As scientific and philosophical works made their way out of Spain, Sicily, and North Africa, they found an avid audience in Europe. Like a blast of oxygen they fueled Italy's intellectual and artistic Renaissance of the fourteenth century, and helped it to spread throughout the continent. Educationally, this reawakening manifested itself first in the fledgling universities of the time and the theoretical treatises of the humanists, leaving elementary levels of schooling largely untouched. The few exceptions, though sometimes admirably successful, were small in scale and had no direct effect on the education of the masses.

Over the centuries that followed, however, a combination of social and economic factors helped to broaden educational access. In a bustling German town around the year 1500, a public notice proclaimed: "Everybody now wants to read and to write."[84] Though this was still something of an exaggeration, it captured the spirit of the time. With the development of movable metal type, books became cheaper and more widespread, making literacy in the common languages of the people a practical and valuable skill for the first time (in Europe) in a thousand years. Literacy also came within reach of a larger segment of the population, thanks to the diversification of the economy and the appearance of a small but growing middle class that could afford both books and teachers' fees.

Due to the spread of printing and reading, ideas could be disseminated more quickly and to a larger audience than ever before. Combined with a growing public resentment of the Catholic Church, this information revolution had much the same effect as lighting a match in a dark room . . . filled with gunpowder.

To its critics, the Church appeared to have settled into an organized state of corruption similar to that of the decaying Roman Empire it had supplanted. In the Vatican, many alleged, the behavior preached as immoral one day a week was too frequently practiced on all the others, and the sale of divine forgiveness (called "indulgences") turned the pulpit into heaven's box office. The most notable of the Church's critics was a disaffected cleric named Martin Luther (1483–1546). At first, Luther was only mildly reproved by the Church hierarchy, but his criticisms eventually touched a nerve, sparking a war of words that polarized opinion throughout the German states.[85] While papal representatives fought back with Latin tracts directed to the clergy and nobility, Luther published his pamphlets in German, appealing to popular animosity toward abuses of Church power and the taxation of German citizens to support the Roman pontificate. Because the Catholic Church had been so intimately involved in schooling, the coming Reformation was to have a significant impact on education.

Conditions in Germany

In the years before Luther, two factors were already bringing changes in German education. The most notable was that an increasing number of citizens wished to learn German rather than Latin, and the existing church schools had little inclination to oblige them. As a result, entirely private schools began to spring up that introduced both children and adults to reading and writing in German, along with some arithmetic. These popular independent schools spread rapidly in the larger towns, but were less numerous in villages and rural areas. Even the rural population was not entirely without private instruction, however, as some scholars traveled the countryside teaching the rudiments of language to the local children for a fee. There were also a range of self-help books that allowed people to teach themselves to read, with titles such as: *A Most Useful Book of Sounds, Illustrated with Figures Giving the True Sound of Each Letter and Syllable, from Which Young Men, Husbands and Wives and Other Adults, Also Children, [Girls] as well as [Boys], Can Easily Learn to Read in as Little as 24 Hours*—a sort of sixteenth-century "Hooked on Phonics."[86]

The second cause of change in the provision of education was the public's desire for greater control over the church schools. As townspeople still favoring an education in Latin contributed more generously to their local parish educational funds, building new schools and retaining more teachers, they sought proportionately greater control over school staffing and curriculum. This did not sit at all well with the clerics who had until then been responsible for such decisions, and they often resisted any circumscription of their authority. Many considered it the fundamental right of the Church to control education. In the majority of cases, however, the citizens eventually won out, and city councils became the primary authorities over the schools formerly run by the clergy. Because clerics made up the vast majority of those capable of giving Latin instruction, most teachers in "city schools," as they came to be called, continued to be members of the clergy. Even in city secondary schools, however, there was growing interest in German-language instruction. School costs at these quasi-public institutions were paid for with a combination of tuition fees and taxes, broadening access, while still leaving some incentive for the students and their parents to ensure that they were receiving value for their money.

The new trends toward private schooling and local community control were derailed by one of the largest social upheavals in European history. The Reformation threw German schooling into chaos. Schools staffed or run by the clergy closed down as monks and nuns abandoned the life of the monastery and the convent in droves. The process was accelerated by the nobility, who seized the opportunity to close all the monasteries that remained, excepting those that had adopted Protestantism.

Finally, after several decades, new schools started to appear. Free-enterprise elementary schools, which had been the least affected by the turmoil, were the first to recover. The printing industry had been central to the success of Protestant reform, and the demand for elementary instruction in reading and writing was even greater in the wake of the Reformation than it had been before.

The efforts of private citizens to educate themselves and their children were once again cut short, however, by Luther and his close associate Melanchthon. Believing that the people could not be left to look after their own education, these two reformers called for the creation of a government-run school system. Though independent schools existed and were spreading, Luther wrote to the reigning political authorities: "It is to you, my lords, to take this task [education] in hand, for if we leave it to the parents, we will die a hundred times over before the thing would be done."[87]

The reformers' plans were largely successful, and soon the existing private elementary schools were joined by state-run institutions. Because they were paid for by taxes rather than tuition fees, the new schools tended to make private instruction financially burdensome. Parents were now faced with a choice between state schools that charged little or no tuition, and private schools that did. Furthermore, parents who preferred to continue educating their children at independent schools despite the tuition costs were required to pay the state education taxes regardless. Private schools were further discouraged by the attitudes and actions of the new state educational authorities, who derided and persecuted such schools.[88] Attempts were even made to legislate private instruction out of existence,[89] and in response private schools were sometimes forced to carry on their classes clandestinely.

Government attacks on independent schools were often met with resistance from local communities. In the municipality of Heidenheim, for instance, town leaders exchanged heated letters with the local Duke, who had summarily closed their local German school, replacing it with a tax-supported Latin one. They wrote:

> Our young people, most of whom have no aptitude for Latin and are growing up to be artisans, are better served by a German teacher than a Latin master, for they need to learn writing and reading, which is of great help to them in their work and livelihood.[90]

Melanchthon's vision for mass state-education was inspired by the guiding principle of the Reformation: the direct interpretation of the Bible by individuals. The practice, however, was substantially different from its inspiration. If scriptural analysis was left to laymen, so the argument went, "incorrect" interpretations might result. The definition of what was incorrect was, of course, established by the leaders of the Reformation. As a result, reading, writing, and religion were taught using a pair of German-language elementary catechisms composed by Luther. Luther's views on what constituted an acceptable education were narrow and authoritarian. He felt that secular schools would lead to moral bankruptcy, and believed that parents should be compelled to teach their children according to his own views. Once again, education became religious indoctrination, only this time it was legally mandated by the state. Fortunately for the majority of students who would not go on to a life in the clergy or government service, *elementary* instruction was, usually, given in their mother tongue.

The fate of Germany's semi-public secondary schools was much the same as that of its private elementary schools. Political authorities at the state level were only slightly less hostile to local government institutions than they were to private enterprises. Pushed and squeezed by state bureaucrats, city secondary schools found their curricula and attendance ever more limited. At the same time, new state-run institutions were created and given special privileges which the city schools did not enjoy, such as the right to send their graduates on to university or into particular professions. Occasionally, city schools were simply taken over by the states outright. Once under state control, the secondary school curriculum began turning away from the popular movement toward education in German and back to the classical languages so dear to the hearts of reformers. State regulations typically ordained that the new government secondary schools would teach in Latin, and that their curricula would culminate in the study of classical literature and scripture. Graduates were expected to converse fluently in Latin and have a passing acquaintance with Greek.

Whatever the reformers' intentions, all this government intervention in education eventually took the same course it had always taken. Through control of the schools and the press, state authorities sought to control the people. In the district of Würtemberg, for example, Duke Ulrich established a system of schools and scholarships for intellectually inclined poor children, but required them to swear allegiance to him and remain in his service. These students were all trained in Latin, the classics, and theology, and produced for the Duke a new generation of teachers who were ideologically and personally loyal. Eventually they were given the responsibility of censoring the presses of Würtemberg, choosing which books were theologically acceptable, and hence publishable, and which were not. There were also German-language elementary schools in the district, but their teaching, curriculum, and textbooks were all strictly regulated in order to inculcate loyalty and Protestant dogma.[91] Here and in other German territories, the public generally failed to beat a path to the new schoolhouse doors despite state subsidization. The next step, of course, was the gradual introduction of mandatory attendance laws, but even this apparently failed to sway most of the population, who resisted state schooling—and particularly the Latin curriculum—even after the widespread imposition of compulsory attendance in the eighteenth century.[92]

Conditions in France

The French were not a widely educated people in the centuries before and immediately after the Reformation. Vast tracts of countryside had yet to be touched by either printing or the division of labor, and as a result literacy was confined to a small fraction of the population. Despite this, France was crucial to the continued existence of the Catholic Church, as one of the few remaining bastions of Catholicism in Western Europe. Without a strong French clergy, capable of assuaging the Church's critics and addressing their concerns, the fall of Catholicism in the West was a real possibility. The task of producing such a clergy, and of providing a religious and classical education to any others who sought it, fell to the Society of Jesus. Founded in 1540 by Ignatius of Loyola, the Society of Jesus was an international monastic order pledged to educate the young and render unquestioning obedience to the papacy.

Within fifty years of its inception it had spread through Europe, the Americas, and the Far East, establishing hundreds of schools and colleges. In France it quickly became the preeminent source of formal education, catering to more than thirteen thousand students, and having no less than fourteen colleges in the city of Paris alone in 1627.[93] This astonishing growth resulted from a combination of profound dedication on the part of its members, a carefully designed management structure, and a pedagogical approach that is widely regarded as the most advanced of its time.

In running their schools the Jesuits followed a variety of study plans which culminated in the *Ratio Studiorum* of 1599. This document laid out in precise detail how and what students were to be taught, and how a college was to be administered. It was followed throughout the Society for hundreds of years, essentially without modification. Among its notable innovations were the creation of distinct grade levels within the grammar school, the use of group teaching, a much reduced recourse to corporal punishment, and the specialized instruction of future teachers.

Prior to the Jesuits, schooling had been comprised of three more-or-less distinct levels: elementary, grammar (secondary), and university. The frequent lack of subdivisions within these broad groupings meant that novice and advanced students would often sit side-by-side in the same classroom, making group lectures and discussions all but impossible. To circumvent the problem of teaching pupils with such disparate abilities, the Jesuits broke their curriculum into five grades. Rather than grouping the children by age, as is commonly done today, they were grouped according to their command of the course materials. Though a formal promotion ceremony was held yearly, each child was allowed to progress through the grades at his own pace and could be promoted at any time after completing a test.[94] Problems of excessively easy or difficult assignments were thus greatly reduced.

The impact of this innovation was dramatic. Apart from oral readings of the classics, which could be interpreted on many levels, there had previously been little group activity in the classroom. Though each teacher had presided over as many as two hundred children, the students came up to his or her desk one at a time to have work assigned or assessed, keeping the pace of instruction at a crawl. Suddenly, thanks to the introduction of performance-based grade levels, students could be systematically taught in groups. Ages varied by as much as three years in a single class, but the students' abilities were necessarily comparable since performance dictated their placement. The interactive discussions permitted by this new environment, coupled with a tailoring of the material to the students' level of understanding, also helped to ease the historical brutality of schooling.

Emancipated from their isolation and boredom, and released from the frustrations caused by incomprehensible coursework, children became less rebellious in the classroom. With the possibility that their interest in learning might actually be aroused rather than extinguished, they no longer needed to be beaten into studying. At the same time, the monastic order whose purpose it was to educate the young decided that hurting them might not be the ideal way to advance that goal. Under the Jesuits, corporal punishment became a relatively rare event, and was no longer administered by the instructor himself, being left instead to a brother specially charged with the task. Beatings, it was decided, should not enter into the teacher-student relationship.

To ensure that these and the other rules of the *Ratio Studiorum* were followed to the letter, the Society took great care in training its future educators. Every attempt was made to choose only the brightest and most professorially inclined students, and the solid reputation enjoyed by the Jesuits in their early days, even among religious adversaries, gives an indication of their success. From theological seminars to lectures in the classics, from frequent debates to practice teaching, Jesuit novices underwent the most elaborate and systematic teacher-training yet seen. Despite these worthy efforts, the process suffered from an insurmountable flaw: it stood still in a constantly changing world.

In a hundred different ways young Jesuits were encouraged, prodded, and forced to teach in precisely the same manner as their predecessors. The *Ratio Studiorum* specifically prohibited the use of "books or writings not in the usual course," as well as the introduction of "any new method of teaching or disputation."[95] Both the number of grades and their contents were fixed,[96] allowing little freedom to adapt to the ever-growing body of human knowledge. Even the Prefect General, who supervised the teachers, was forbidden to alter any "custom or precedent, or to introduce a new one," and was specifically directed to "take great care that new teachers carefully retain the method of teaching of their predecessors."[97] The fate of those unable or unwilling to follow the Order's many regulations was unequivocal: "If there are any too prone to innovations, or too liberal in their views, they shall certainly be removed from the responsibility of teaching."[98]

Outcomes in Germany and France

While German literacy continued to grow throughout most of the sixteenth century, this is more accurately seen as the continuation of a trend that began before the Reformation than one which was caused by it. Most of the attention and success of the reformers' schools was to be found in the creation of a literate, classically educated elite capable of running the expanding clerical and civil bureaucracies. As historian Gerald Strauss has concluded: "For our explanation of how literacy came to grow in the sixteenth century we must look to mundane pragmatic causes, not to the Lutheran Reformation."[99]

Just prior to the Reformation there had been significant overlap in the education of the nobility and the training of at least the more avid youngsters from the middle classes. Education had been in the mother tongue for all but the clergy, and literate families in the towns and villages could and did share in the prose of their countrymen. Legal proceedings had also been held in German, allowing citizens to participate directly in any court actions which affected them. Once the strictly Latin secondary school system of the reformers was imposed, however, German gradually disappeared as a language of law and culture.[100] This caused an ever-greater rift between the uneducated masses and the learned elite which persisted for hundreds of years.

In rolling back some of the Protestant gains in Europe, and in raising up a new generation of priests with theological loyalty and excellent organizational and debating skills, the Jesuits were successful. For the broader population, however, the education they offered was of steadily declining value. Carved in stone to the last detail, and focused narrowly on religious instruction, Jesuit schools and colleges could not respond to the changes that began at the turn of the eighteenth century. The Age of Reason reawakened and took to new heights an idea that had first come to light in Athens more than two thousand years before: that the world is a rational place, comprehensible by the human mind. Dogmas and preconceptions were increasingly cast aside in an effort to understand nature through reason and observation. Existing practices and institutions that did not share the new spirit of critical inquiry were simply left behind in the headlong rush to expand human knowledge. There were some Jesuits, contributors in the fields of mathematics and astronomy, who seemed to embrace the excitement of the new age, but the anchor of tradition kept them, and in particular their schools, from any but a token participation. What chance they may have had to cut loose from the past was extinguished when the Society of Jesus was suppressed by the papacy in 1773, after years of internal squabbling within the Church hierarchy.

Educational Liberty

Though separated by a thousand years and innumerable cultural differences, the two civilizations enjoying the greatest achievements in art, science, and literacy of their times relied on unregulated, family-driven school systems. Classical Athens and the early medieval Muslim empire left parents free to attend to their children's education in whatever way they saw fit. For the most part, this educational responsibility appears to have been discharged with care and wisdom, ensuring that the younger generation was well prepared for adult life and work.

More importantly, parental freedom and responsibility proved to be far more effective in achieving the ends outlined in Chapter 1 than did the monolithic state- and church-run systems of Sparta, Germany, and France. Independent Athenian and early Muslim schools competed with one another in an effort to serve the needs of their patrons, adapting their curricula and modes of instruction to keep pace with changing demands. Centralized bureaucratic institutions, on the other hand, generally imposed a fixed set of teachings on their students and failed to respond to advances in science and technology. Instruction in Latin, for example, frequently supplanted the increasingly popular study of native languages in post-Reformation educational systems, greatly reducing the value of schooling for the vast majority of Europeans.

Of the three bureaucratic school systems described in this chapter, only Sparta's was even remotely the product of democratic political choices,[101] so it could be argued that the failure of these systems was due to their dictatorial origins, not to the fact that they limited parental choice or prevented free and vigorous competition among schools. The following chapter puts this argument to the test, to see if government-run schools in more democratic nations enjoy a better record than the free-market educational systems of Athens and the early medieval Islamic world.

3

Revolutions:
The More Things Change . . .

> *Government schooling, under monarchies and empires, clearly has a grim history behind it, but what about modern democracies? How much could they really have in common with their autocratic predecessors?*

Much of the public's support for public schooling rests on two assumptions: that government education helped to unite people of diverse backgrounds and thus forged stronger communities and nations; and that it brought literacy and learning to a wider segment of the population than would otherwise have been possible. To determine whether or not these assumptions are justified, this chapter investigates the nineteenth-century origins of government schooling in three nations: the United States, England, and France.

An Establishment of Education:
The U.S. Embraces Government Schooling

Well before the turmoil of the Revolution, schooling was an established part of life in the American colonies. Although there was no single system of education, the needs of most citizens were catered to by one or another of the available options. In smaller towns and rural areas, "district" schools were formed on a neighborhood-by-neighborhood basis. These were semi-public institutions, financed by a combination of tuition charges and local taxes, which allowed some of the poorer students to attend for free while those who could afford to largely paid their own way. Parents enjoyed a great deal of control over district schools, with each family not only choosing but supplying its own textbooks, and participating in the selection of teachers. Since the teachers were often billeted in rotation in students' homes, they were a captive audience for parents' questions, criticisms, and praise.

In more populous areas, many schools were entirely independent. Teachers would simply hang out a shingle and solicit paying pupils through word of mouth and advertisements in the local press. Some of these establishments were modest affairs, conveying only the rudiments of the Three R's, while others offered intensive and specialized instruction in areas such as applied mathematics and accounting. Some teachers attempted to appeal to the widest possible clientele by offering a whole smorgasbord of classes for students of all ages. The following school advertisement, which appeared in the *Boston Gazette* in the spring of 1720, was fairly typical of urban areas:

> At the house formerly Sir Charles Hobby's are taught Grammar, Writing after a free and easy manner, in all the hands usually practiced, Arithmetick Vulgar and Decimal in a concise and practical Method, Merchants Accounts, Geometry, Algebra, Mensuration [i.e., the calculation of lengths, surfaces, and volumes], Geography, Trigonometry, Astronomy, Navigation and other parts of the Mathematicks, with the use of Globes and other Mathematical Instruments, by Samuel Grainger. They whose business won't permit 'em to attend the usual School Hours, shall be carefully attended and instructed in the Evenings.[1]

Educational Conditions in the New Republic

By the time the United States had won their independence,[2] literacy and numeracy were becoming valuable assets. Rising household incomes also permitted more families to forego their older children's earning potential, freeing them up for further studies. For these and other reasons, school enrollment increased significantly in the first fifty years of the nation's history, particularly among girls.[3] In 1831, the young Frenchman Alexis de Tocqueville remarked that it was rare to find a New Englander who had not had the benefit of an elementary education, and who was not familiar with the history and constitution of the United States. The further he traveled toward the South and West, the less this observation held true, but he noted that even the huts of Western pioneers were seldom without a few volumes of Shakespeare.[4]

Though memorization and repetition made up a greater part of the pedagogical method than is currently thought best, the nation's schools were generally considered effective. In his 1837 comparison of American and German education, Francis Grund concluded that the schools of the United States were superior in teaching reading and speaking, though they usually lacked the classical and philosophical content of German institutions.[5] For students wishing to pursue such studies, however, there existed private academies in many cities and towns that specialized in preparation for classical University programs.

Independent private schools catered to the majority of city dwellers during this period, but there were families who could not readily afford even the smallest tuition fees. To meet the educational needs of the very poor, free schools had been established by philanthropists and religious societies in much of the country. As urban populations swelled, and education grew in importance, these charitable efforts expanded as well. Local voluntary associations were formed to both finance and manage the free schools, precluding the need for government involvement. Women became particularly involved in organizing associations to help children and women in need, while other forms of mutual-aid societies sprang up around particular trades or religious denominations. The Quakers were especially active in such organizations, founding numerous schools for the children of black freedmen between 1770 and the first decades of the nineteenth century.[6]

In the U.S., thanks to the absence of an entrenched aristocracy, there was little of the opposition to mass education that was exhibited across Europe, where the nobility worried that an educated populace would demand an end to its privileged position. Rather than fearing an educated public, most U.S. political and social leaders believed that a minimum level of education for all citizens was necessary to maintain a stable democracy. Still, social and economic advancement was not high on the agendas of charity school organizations, which favored literacy and moral instruction as tools for combating the problems of crime and vice. Parents were often seen as adversaries in this context, for the reformers tended to equate poverty with apathy and immorality, and wished to isolate children from the presumed harmful influences of their families. During the 1820s and 1830s, urban centers in the East saw a significant influx of immigrants and freed slaves. These newcomers were welcomed by some, but many citizens, including many education reformers, feared the effects of cultural and racial mixing. As a result, charity schools were not always hospitable to members of ethnic and racial communities different from those of their founders.

African-American schooling

At the turn of the nineteenth century, decades before the great tides of European immigration would flood into the Northeast, the most striking conflicts arose over the education of black children. Racial tensions ran particularly high in Boston, despite the fact that it was well in advance of most cities in abandoning slavery. The climate was so hostile that African-American leaders felt it necessary to encourage members of their community to "bear up under the daily insults [they met] on the streets of Boston." The not uncommon tradition of relegating disruptive white students to the "nigger seat" at the back of the class must also have given black parents pause when deciding whether to send their sons and daughters to the public schools.[7]

Tax-supported public schooling had existed in Boston since 1635, though the public schools enrolled only a small fraction of the total student population at the end of the eighteenth century. African-American enrollment had remained particularly low, perhaps in part due to the apprehensions of parents. Convinced that their children could not obtain the support and attention they needed from the existing system, a group of black parents requested that a separate system be created for them. The petition was opposed from many sides, and it was soon rejected by the school committee. This did not stop the movement for segregated schools, however, and further petitions were made along with efforts to establish a privately funded black school. With contributions from parents and help from several white philanthropists, a free private school was eventually established in the home of Primus Hall, a prominent black resident. Its beginnings were shaky, but by 1806 the school had settled into a new location in a local church basement and had even managed to elicit a small financial contribution from the public school committee. This, however, was to prove a mixed blessing, for the committee soon demanded complete control over the school, despite the fact that it was subsidizing only a portion of its operating costs.[8]

The committee's attempt to gain control of the independent black school proved successful, and in 1818 it voted to dismiss the incumbent schoolmaster and appoint a new one of its own choosing. Over the next three decades enrollment among Boston's African-American children remained fairly low, and attendance uneven. One of the greatest impediments to higher enrollment was the limited practical benefit that education conferred on blacks in the antebellum period. Racism and tradition conspired to exclude blacks from virtually all white-collar employment, leaving educated blacks only slightly better off than their illiterate fellows. The frustration and resentment evoked by this reality can be clearly heard in the words of a young graduate of the New York African Free School:

> Am I arrived at the end of my education, just on the eve of setting out into the world, of commencing some honest pursuit, by which to earn a comfortable subsistence? What are my prospects? To what shall I turn my head? Shall I be a mechanic? No one will employ me; white boys won't work with me. Shall I be a merchant? No one will have me in his office; white clerks won't associate with me. Drudgery and servitude, then, are my prospective portion.[9]

Against this and other obstacles, many African Americans continued to push for better schools for their children. At times the Boston public school committee made some effort to address their concerns, adding new classes and constructing a new primary school building. Much of the funding for these undertakings was, however, drawn from a private endowment left to Boston's black community by philanthropist Abiel Smith, and held in trust by the school committee. On other occasions the committee responded only with apathy or intransigence. When a group led by Abiel's brother Barney petitioned for the creation of a black high school, the committee declined, declaring the project "inexpedient." Perhaps the most bitter and prolonged dispute between parents and the committee was over the schoolmaster William Bascom. Parents had repeatedly condemned Bascom as incompetent, but the committee ignored their complaints, refusing to replace him. The dispute finally boiled over in 1833 when parents charged Bascom with taking sexual liberties with the girls under his care. After a perfunctory investigation, the committee claimed that the girls in question were of "bad character" and that the allegations must therefore be false. Over the heated objections of parents, Bascom was retained as schoolmaster.[10]

Embittered by their lack of control over the segregated schools, African-American parents began to see them as a hindrance rather than a help in their quest for educational advancement. First in 1840 and again in 1844 and 1845, members of the African-American community petitioned the committee to end school segregation. In each case the issue was dismissed with little or no comment. It was not until a fourth petition was presented in 1846 that the committee saw fit to explain in full its continued refusal to integrate the public schools. In addition to questioning the mental capacities of blacks and impugning the validity of some signatures on the petition, the committee flatly denied the claim that segregated schools were in any way illegal, virtually daring the petitioners to take the matter up in court. After three more years of agitation, that is precisely what happened. Benjamin Roberts, in the name of his daughter Sarah, filed suit against the City of Boston, alleging that she was illegally refused admission to her neighborhood public school because of her color.[11]

Pleading the case for Sarah, attorney Charles Sumner observed that the Massachusetts constitution declared "all men, without distinction of race or color, [to be] equal before the law." Legally segregating students by race, he argued, was in clear violation of this provision. The presiding judge, Massachusetts Supreme Court Chief Justice Shaw, responded with a carefully contrived interpretation of the law, claiming that the constitutional guarantee meant only that all citizens had an equal responsibility to abide by the laws of their state, not that those laws had to treat all citizens equally. In his opinion, the school committee was free to assign children to schools in whatever manner it chose, and black students were required to heed its decisions. Dubious though it was, the Chief Justice's opinion became law in Massachusetts. Six years later, Shaw's legal handiwork was undone by the state legislature, but only after vigorous campaigning by black activists and white abolitionists.[12] The damage, however, had already been done. The original Massachusetts Supreme Court ruling provided a key legal precedent that was used by the U.S. Supreme Court in 1896 to rule in *Plessy v. Ferguson* that racial segregation was not a violation of the Fourteenth Amendment, which guarantees the equal protection of the law to all citizens.[13]

The experience of African Americans in Boston, however unpleasant, was infinitely more agreeable than that facing Southern slaves. Slave owners saw literacy and learning as threats to their control over their human property, and actively fought efforts by blacks and whites to set up schools for slaves. In the early 1830s, Georgia, Virginia, Alabama, South Carolina, and North Carolina all passed laws prohibiting anyone from teaching slaves to read.[14] Opponents of these measures appeared from time to time, but to no avail. Little would change in black education until the Civil War.

Politics and prejudice

Despite the widespread popularity of both tuition-charging and charitable private schools, as well as semi-public district schools, there were those who believed that control over education rightfully belonged to the state. One of the earliest proponents of this belief was James G. Carter, a Massachusetts congressman of the 1830s. In direct opposition to the central idea of the American Revolution—that power and responsibility should be left in the hands of the people—Carter argued that government should seize the reigns of education for its own self-preservation. He wrote: "The ignorant must be allured to learn, by every motive which can be offered to them. And if they will not thus be allured, they must be taken by the strong arm of government and brought out, willing or unwilling, and made to learn, at least, enough to make them peaceable and good citizens."[15] To some extent, Carter's position was based on his belief that the poor, particularly recent immigrants, remained in ignorance by choice, and not because of difficult circumstances. "The more ignorant and degraded people are," he claimed, "the less do they feel the want of instruction, and the less they will seek it."[16]

Carter's was not an isolated voice, being echoed most prominently by the soldier and politician Samuel Smith. Smith wrote that "it is the duty of a nation to superintend and even to coerce the education of children. . . . [H]igh considerations of expediency not only justify but dictate the establishment of a system which shall place under a control, *independent of and superior to parental authority,* the education of children."[17] Smith also provided for the case of recalcitrant parents, suggesting that it be made a crime to withhold one's children from the state schools (an idea taken up again by Oregonians in the early twentieth century).[18] If this sounds frighteningly reminiscent of the totalitarian systems of monarchs and emperors past, it is with good reason. Like the extremists among the French Revolutionaries before them, and the German Nazi party that was to rise up a century later, early state-schooling advocates in the U.S. held up ancient Sparta as their educational ideal. After praising what he saw as the "wisdom and energy" of Lycurgus's authoritarian education policy, Carter asked rhetorically: "If the Spartan could mold and transform a nation to suit his taste, by means of an early education, why may not the same be done at the present day?"[19]

Though popular in some circles—Smith won an essay contest held by the American Philosophical Society—broader public support for these ideas was lacking. Having only recently fought a war to break away from excessive government control, and still mindful of the perils of established religion, the prospect of an established education system had no great appeal to most Americans. This, however, was about to change. As immigration boomed in the mid nineteenth century, members of the Anglo-Saxon Protestant majority began to fear that the social homogeneity and cohesiveness they were accustomed to was in danger. The solution, they were told, was as close as the nearest public school. Typical of this new argument was an article from *The Massachusetts Teacher,* published in 1851, concerning itself with the Irish immigration "problem." In a twisted foreshadowing of the sonnet that would grace the Statue of Liberty, it stated that:

> The poor, the oppressed, and, worse than all, the *ignorant* of the old world, have found a rapid and almost a free passage to the new. . . . The constantly increasing influx of foreigners during the last ten years has been, and continues to be, a cause of serious alarm to the most intelligent of our own people. . . . Will it, like the muddy Missouri, as it pours its waters into the clear Mississippi and contaminates the whole united mass, spread ignorance and vice, crime and disease, through our native population? Or can we, by any process, not only preserve ourselves from the threatened demoralization but improve and purify and make valuable this new element which is thus forced upon us, and which we cannot shut out if we would?[20]

The answer to this rhetorical question was that not much could be done to salvage adult immigrants, irretrievably indolent and immoral as they allegedly were. Their children, however, could ostensibly be saved from the twin ailments of Irish birth and Catholic faith by the "great remedy" of Protestant public schooling:

> The rising generation must be taught as our own children are taught. We say *must be,* because in many cases this can only be accomplished by coercion. In too many instances the parents are unfit guardians of their own children. If left to their

direction the young will be brought up in idle, dissolute, vagrant habits, which
will make them worse members of society than their parents are. . . . Nothing can
operate effectually here but stringent legislation, thoroughly carried out by an efficient police;—the children must be gathered up and forced into school, and
those who resist or impede this plan, whether parents or *priests,* must be held accountable and punished.[21]

As wave after wave of new immigrants flooded into U.S. ports, the idea of a
legally mandated school system gained in popularity. In addition to the effects
of xenophobia and religious intolerance, many Americans were genuinely
moved by the noble promises of government schooling's advocates. The most
passionate and influential of these advocates was Horace Mann of Massachusetts, who was appointed secretary of the first state-level board of education in
1837 (a government body created by none other than state representative James
Carter). Though the powers of the board were initially quite limited, Mann
leveraged the high profile of his new position to disseminate his idealized view
of government-run education. He truly believed that mandatory government
schooling would end crime and poverty, and he preached this belief with elo-
quence and unrelenting determination. In 1841, he wrote the passage cited at
the beginning of Chapter 1: "Let the Common School be expanded to its capabilities, let it be worked with the efficiency of which it is susceptible, and nine
tenths of the crimes in the penal code would become obsolete; the long catalogue of human ills would be abridged."[22] Seven years later he was still less reserved in his vision of public schooling's potential, promising that

[w]hen [public schooling] shall be fully developed, when it shall be trained to
wield its mighty energies for the protection of society against the giant vices
which now invade and torment it;—against intemperance, avarice, war, slavery,
bigotry, the woes of want and the wickedness of waste,—then, there will not be
a height to which the enemies of the [human] race can escape, which it will not
scale, nor a Titan among them all, whom it will not slay.[23]

Looking back after one hundred and fifty years of public schooling in the
United States, it is clear that Mann was promising more than he could deliver,
but questioning these assertions at the time proved difficult. Those who opposed the expansion of public schooling were seen as opponents of progress
and promoters of immorality and destitution. Despite this fact, serious objections to the increasing state role in education were raised throughout the period.
Given the caution and distrust with which government intervention was
widely viewed, it is unsurprising that public schooling was seen by some as
a potential threat to liberty and a usurping of the responsibilities of parents
and local communities. Reporting on the issue, the education subcommittee
of the Massachusetts legislature concluded: "The establishment of the Board

of Education seems to be the commencement of a system of centralization and monopoly of power in a few hands, contrary, in every respect, to the true spirit of our democratical institutions; and which, unless speedily checked, may lead to unlooked-for and dangerous results."[24] The majority of this bipartisan committee feared that whatever the good intentions of present administrators, a government education bureaucracy would likely lose touch with the people it was meant to serve, and could easily become a tool of state control over the political and religious thought of citizens. In conclusion, the committee called for the abolition of the state board of education. When it came to a vote, this legislative measure was narrowly defeated, and Mann dismissed its supporters as "bigots and vandals."[25] Their fears, however, were soon realized.

God and Mann

The 1850s and 1860s saw tax-supported government schooling spread throughout much of the North and West. Cultural and religious tensions had worsened over the same period, and since the newly formed public schools were controlled by the native Anglo-Saxon Protestant majority, they became an extension of popular bigotry. Public-school textbooks routinely denigrated immigrants and Catholics, with one claiming that America was becoming "the common sewer of Ireland."[26] Immigrant communities in New York, Chicago, and elsewhere complained that the schools taught their children to feel ashamed of their faith and heritage. The treatment of religion in the public schools had, in fact, become a recurrent thorn in the side of Catholics, Jews, and even some Protestants. In order to minimize opposition from the many Protestant sects, Mann had assured them that the public schools would make regular use of the Protestant Bible, but that all particularities of dogma over which there was some debate among Protestants would be eliminated from the classroom. Mann was thus engaged in a difficult problem of religious arithmetic—one dealing with factions instead of fractions. His attempted solution, mirroring that of mathematics, was to find the lowest common denomination of all the Protestant sects. This attempt was not entirely successful. Orthodox Protestants, whose doctrines asserted a variety of absolute claims about God and the road to salvation, were offended that their profound beliefs were simply dispensed with in the name of expediency. Only among liberal Protestants, who found their faith reflected in the schools, did Mann's approach avoid opposition.

The stripped-down Protestantism of the government schools was also offensive to Catholics, who wished to use their own version of the Bible, and their own teachings. Catholic leaders had consistently asked that school boards either provide them with schools of their own, or remove all traces of Protestantism and bigotry from the existing institutions, but to little avail. The New York school board offered to remove any particular instances of religious slander from its textbooks that the Catholic Bishop cared to list, but there was no question of removing the Protestant Bible altogether. Finally, in Philadelphia, the Catholic version of the Bible was allowed into some schools. For many Protestants this proved unacceptable, and tensions escalated and finally exploded into the "Philadelphia Bible Riots" of 1844. In the process, thirteen people lost their lives and St. Augustine's Church was burned to the ground. Some school districts were more successful at making concessions and satisfying the needs of religious minorities, but frightful cases continued to occur. Catholic children were occasionally whipped or beaten by their teachers for refusing to read from the Protestant Bible, and legal actions against the teachers generally came to naught. In one case from the 1850s, the Supreme Court of Maine declared it legal for all students in the government schools to be compelled to read the Protestant Bible.[27] Though Jews were not as vigorous as Catholics in denouncing sectarian religious practices in the public schools, their opposition was constant. In court cases, letters to the editor, and magazine articles, Jewish citizens and community leaders strove to defend their right to religious freedom.[28]

Education without representation

Stretching through the religious, racial, and political conflicts that dogged the expansion of public schooling, was the question of whose right and responsibility it was to educate children. Most disputes had arisen when state authorities sought to control some aspect of instruction that had traditionally been the responsibility of parents or local communities. Throughout the second half of the nineteenth century, education reformers, bureaucrats, and teachers' organizations pushed to increase their powers. In his 1864 biennial report, California's State Superintendent of Public Instruction approvingly cited east-coast legal precedents, stating:

> The child should be taught to consider his instructor, in many respects, superior to the parent in point of authority. . . . [T]he vulgar impression that parents have a legal right to dictate to teachers is entirely erroneous.[29]

Even the right of parents to criticize government school teachers was vetoed by contemporary law. Section 654 of the Penal Code of California read: "Every parent, guardian, or other person, who upbraids, insults, or abuses any teacher of the public schools, in the presence or hearing of a pupil thereof, is guilty of a misdemeanor."[30] This special protection afforded to state educators was so strikingly similar to that enshrined in the law of Imperial Rome that it almost smacks of plagiarism.

The Wisconsin Teachers' Association, like many similar bodies, declared in 1865 that "children are the property of the state."[31] This sentiment was even more broadly framed a year later, by O. Hosford, the Michigan Superintendent of Public Instruction. Speaking at the eighth meeting of the National Teachers' Association—precursor to the National Education Association—Hosford proclaimed:

> Self-protection is the first law of governments as well as of individuals. . . . There is also the duty of self development which governments must observe, making themselves strong and effective in their various departments, and this too if need be at the expense of individual preferences or interests. The duties which a citizen owes to the government are prior to any personal or individual claims, and should be so esteemed; for public interest is far superior to private good.[32]

As a banner for the expansion of government schooling, the phrase "public interest" was often a bitter irony. Despite a petition with 100,000 signatures asking to preserve neighborhood control of schools, the mayor of New York signed into law an 1896 bill centralizing the control of education under a single citywide board. Anti-immigrant bias was a major motivation in this case, as in so many others, with a confidential report to the mayor stating that local control of schooling was a dangerous thing in a city "impregnated with foreign influences."[33]

Such undemocratic tactics were also rationalized on the grounds of efficiency. Centralization and government control, it was argued, were bound to bring education to a larger segment of the population and to do so at a lower cost. The fact was, however, that the expansion of public schooling simply pushed aside existing private schools without substantially raising overall enrollment rates. As tax-spending on the government system increased in the middle of the nineteenth century, more parents were drawn away from tuition-charging schools, but the percentage of the child population being educated remained essentially constant in all the cities for which adequate data have survived.[34] Increased state-level expenditures on the education of poor students also failed, at least initially, to have their intended effect. As state funding rose, individuals and communities curtailed their charitable spending, so the total amount of money available to the poor did not increase.[35] While there were few data on the effects of school centralization available at the time, recent research into late nineteenth and early twentieth century school-board consolidations points to decreasing, not increasing efficiency,[36] and highlights the passionate opposition of most small communities to consolidation.[37] Despite this local opposition, the rate of school-board consolidation only accelerated after the turn of the century.

Educational Outcomes in Nineteenth-Century America

Before independence was declared, reading was already a common feature of the cultural landscape. Thomas Paine's "Common Sense" sold 100,000 copies in the Colonies,[38] and each copy was probably read by (or at least read *to*) more than one person. By the time the U.S. Constitution was drafted in 1787, free male literacy was already at about 65 percent, and probably over 80 percent in New England.[39] Women lagged behind, discouraged from becoming educated by the still vigorous sexism that has plagued them, though with diminishing severity, for almost the entire history of civilization. During the nineteenth century, literacy advanced rapidly, and by 1850, only one in ten people identified themselves as illiterate on the U.S. census.[40] Allowing for the possibility that some people who could neither read nor write did not admit to their illiteracy, it is safe to say that between three quarters and four fifths of the population was already literate before public schooling as we know it had gotten off the ground.

Though literacy and (elementary) schooling were already enjoyed by the overwhelming majority of citizens,[41] advocates of government schools unanimously campaigned for mandatory attendance laws. In practice, these laws had no discernable effect on enrollment. Between 1852 and 1918, compulsory-education legislation was passed in all the states.[42] Despite the passage of such laws, school enrollment increased only 3.7 percent between 1890 and 1918.[43] The enrollment rate of white children actually dropped by 2.6 percent between 1850 and 1900, and the aggregate rate increased only because of the dramatic rise in black enrollment following the abolition of slavery—from 1.9 percent in 1860 to 31.1 percent in 1900.[44] It was only after 1920 that school enrollment began to increase at a faster rate, coinciding with the ever more rapid urbanization of the populace and growth of industry. These demographic and economic transformations combined to reduce the need for child labor on family farms, and increased the economic value of literacy and education generally.

The obvious upshot of these trends is that U.S. history lends no support to the idea that parents need to be forced to educate their children. In America, as elsewhere, the decision of families to enroll their children in school has been based on the most practical of concerns: Does formal instruction offer my children something of value, something worth paying for, at a price I can afford?

Prior to the introduction of "free" public schooling, apprenticeships, private schools, and semi-public district schools prepared American children for gainful employment and further study. Agricultural productivity increased significantly in the early nineteenth century, and more people were able to find work in areas other than farming. This led to a doubling in the real income of workers between the Revolution and the 1840s. By 1880, real income had doubled again.[45] Declining transportation costs over land allowed frontier farmers and settlers to widen trade between West and East. Since farmers and craftsmen were able to draw upon each other's strengths, both could devote their energies to improving the quality and volume of their own output, confident in the knowledge that there was a growing market to absorb any increases in their productivity.

The growth of long-distance trade increased the need for reliable communications, and this helped to increase the value of education—particularly literacy. An explosion of newspapers in the early 1800s—made possible by lower printing costs and higher per-capita incomes—also helped to spread reading and writing. In the twenty years following 1840, the amount of money spent on books tripled, as did the number of newspapers.[46]

Perhaps the most revealing aspect of nineteenth-century American education is the impact of public versus private schools on religious and ethnic relations. One of the central beliefs of modern educators is that public schooling has a unifying effect on American society, and that without it, the various racial, religious, and political groups that comprise that society would become polarized and antagonistic to one another. They would, in modern political jargon, be balkanized. Based on the experiences of the 1800s, this belief is not only wrong, it is exactly backward.

Prior to the government's involvement in education, there were nondenominational schools, Quaker schools and Lutheran schools, fundamentalist schools and more liberal Protestant schools, classical schools and technical schools, in accordance with the preferences of local communities. Some had homogeneous enrollments, others drew students from across ethnic and religious lines. In areas where schools of different sects coexisted, they and their patrons seldom came into conflict, since they did not try to foist their views on one another. They lived and let live in what were comparatively stable, though increasingly diverse, communities. It was only after the state began creating uniform institutions for all children that these families were thrown into conflict. Within public schools, many parents were faced with an unpleasant choice: accept that objectionable ideas would be forced on their children, or force their own ideas on everyone else's children by taking control of the system. It was this artificial choice between two evils that led to the Philadelphia Bible Riots, the beatings of Catholic children, the official denigration of immigrant values and lifestyles in public schools and textbooks, and laws—which would today be viewed as utterly unconstitutional—forcing the Protestant Bible on all families. The unpardonable treatment of black families by the government schools, which persisted for over a century, does nothing to lighten this grim picture.

Forgotten Lessons: Education in Nineteenth-Century England

After the religious civil wars of the mid seventeenth century, England was a country without a King. Puritan rebels snatched the reins of government from the monarchy, abolished the House of Lords, and withdrew the political powers of Anglican bishops. To cement their victory, they executed King Charles I, on the grounds that his continued existence might encourage royalist revolt.

They had little time to enjoy their newfound authority, however, as they were themselves deposed only eleven years later. In 1660 the monarchy was restored, and all its political and religious trappings with it. To forestall any further Puritan uprisings, a host of restrictive laws were put in place. The Corporation Act of 1661 restricted public office to Anglicans, and it was quickly followed by the broader Act of Uniformity.[47] Under this new legislation, educators at all levels were forced to sign a declaration of conformity to the Church of England's liturgy, and to give their oaths of allegiance to the Crown. Nonconformists—those who refused to adopt the state religion—were thus prohibited from teaching in public and private schools, and their ministers were forbidden from coming within five miles of where they had once preached.

Educational Conditions in England

As political winds shifted over the next hundred years, the repressive religious and education laws were at times ignored and at other times reasserted. Having been forced to retreat from public life, Puritans focused their energies on trade and commerce, expanding the middle class and thus the market for innovative schools. To satisfy this growing demand, a few private, fee-charging academies began to appear, founded illegally in many instances by nonconformist ministers who had been formally ejected from the teaching profession. In an effort to attract both dissenting (non-Anglican) and Anglican families, these schools offered an updated, predominantly secular curriculum with an emphasis on English, mathematics, and the natural sciences. One such school, operating in Tottenham in the 1670s, taught "geometry, arithmetic, astronomy and geography, with gardening, dancing, singing and music" in addition to English and some Latin.[48]

Traditional endowed grammar schools, supported by Church, government, or private grants, and thus assured of a steady income independent of their ability to attract students, continued to provide the same classical Latin training they had offered since the Middle Ages. The polarization of these two sorts of institutions, and their respective fates, clearly illustrates the role of market incentives in the educational process.

Down go the grammar schools . . . and up come the independents

The continued growth and diversification of the economy dramatically widened the disparity between the content of traditional education and the needs of the commercial and professional classes. Together with the decline of the Church of England as an employer, this shift diminished whatever economic advantage the old syllabus might have conferred. Critics denounced the grammar schools as moribund and irrelevant, while parents increasingly sought more practical alternatives. As a result, the conservative endowed schools began to lose middle-class pupils to the few private academies that had sprung up in the late 1600s. Within a few decades this burgeoning change had solidified into a steep recession for traditional education, and a proliferation of new private schools.

In the eighteenth century, grammar schools continued their descent. Few new ones were created, some shut their doors, and the rest saw their enrollments drop significantly. When Nicholas Carlisle, Assistant Librarian to the Queen, conducted his multi-year investigation of hundreds of endowed grammar schools in the early nineteenth century, he found that many of them had lost touch with their prospective customers, and showed visible signs of decay. In Stourbridge, for example, he found that the grammar school had taught only a trifling number of students over the preceding forty years, "as Classical learning is in little estimation in a commercial town."[49] Despite the fact that Stourbridge's school sometimes had no pupils at all, both its head and assistant teachers continued to draw their full salaries. This was in fact not unusual, since teachers, once awarded tenure and assigned a fixed salary, were virtually impossible to remove—even in cases of serious neglect.[50]

Endowed grammar schools were not entirely beyond the reach of market forces, however. In the many cases where the endowment was low, schoolmasters generally took the financially expedient steps of recruiting private pupils or taking on outside employment to supplement their incomes, necessarily cutting into the time they had for their endowment students. Others, such as those in the towns of Donington and Cuckfield, taught only one or two endowment students, while conducting private lessons with scores of paying students on the schools' premises.[51] Finally, there were some teachers who simply converted the school buildings into private residences, took no pupils of any kind, and continued to draw their stipends.

Despite these systemic problems, there were schools, led by dedicated teachers, that continued to instruct pupils on the languages and literature of ancient times. To the extent that endowed schools modernized their curricula to attract students, however, it was due primarily to financial imperatives.

In direct proportion to the decline in health and popularity of endowed grammar schools, new tuition-charging institutions grew and flourished. Subjects long ignored by the grammar schools began to appear, and soon entirely new ones were added. Arithmetic and geography were among the first, and these were joined by anatomy, biology, bookkeeping, economics, surveying, naval studies, and many others. While sometimes maintaining vestiges of the traditional curriculum, independent institutions usually allotted them less time and importance than they devoted to the new subjects. At St. Domingo House School in Liverpool, for example, Latin instruction was given, but only after the children had received several years of training in French and German.[52]

Not only were the subjects new, but the methods were often innovative as well. In keeping with the applied scientific nature of many of the courses, experiments using telescopes, microscopes, and other devices complemented the familiar teaching methods. The teachers of Birmingham's Hill Top School conducted lessons with marbles to give children an intuitive grasp of arithmetic before introducing them to numbers and word problems. Physical surveying was used to teach trigonometry at the same institution.[53] One of the most concrete signs of the different attitude of the independent schools was that many catered to girls, while grammar schools did not. Though the curriculum for girls was sometimes less academically ambitious, and always included ample emphasis on morals, manners, and domestic skills, it was at least a step forward.

Schools for the poor

For the very poorest families, who usually had no interest in a classical education and who could not afford the tuition at the better private institutions, two options remained: religious charity schools and private "Dame" schools. Though charity schools generally taught basic reading skills, they suffered from the same conflict of goals as the grammar schools. Just as the wealthy donors who endowed grammar schools generally insisted on a traditional Latin curriculum, the middle-class religious societies that funded charity schools had ideas of their own as to what the poor should learn, and these only rarely took into account the interests of the poor themselves. The central purpose was always to inculcate the moral and religious views of the sponsors, frequently to the detriment of academic instruction.[54] A widely held view among religious societies was that "[r]eading will help to mend people's morals, but writing is not necessary."[55]

An additional problem with religious charity schools was that the teachers were appointed and supported by religious authorities, rather than by the students' parents. Since the people overseeing charity schools rarely had children attending them, there was little incentive for them to ensure the teachers' competency. Sometimes sound selections were made, but in the worst cases instructors were appointed who would never have been able to draw paying students. In Yorkshire, for instance, a "very deaf and ignorant" teacher was appointed by the parochial authorities "that he may not be burdensome to them for his support."[56] Not surprisingly, the appeal of these schools was limited. Despite the fact that private schools charged tuition, "the subsidized, endowed and charity schools of Manchester attracted only 8 percent of all those attending schools and there were empty places available."[57]

The ubiquitous Dame schools, usually located in the home of an elderly widow, also varied widely in quality based on the knowledge and skills of individual teachers. Competition generally kept the fees for such schools at a minimal level, however, and the freedom of families to choose among different teachers ensured that those who failed to meet their clients' expectations could remain in business for only a short time. Despite their many shortcomings, Dame schools taught far more students from even the poorest classes than did charity schools, throughout the early nineteenth century. This is not to say that, if poor parents had had more money to spend, they could not have obtained better schooling, but simply that the schooling they could afford accomplished their main aim: teaching literacy. What is particularly noteworthy is that private schools were more popular and at least as effective as their subsidized counterparts, while spending *less* money per pupil. Economist David Mitch has estimated that in the mid-1800s, subsidized schools spent roughly one-and-a-half times as much per student as tuition-charging private schools.[58]

Religious skirmish

The major religious denominations were not entirely beyond the reach of competitive incentives, as is evidenced by the rise of the monitorial system. Monitorial schools, in which the brightest students were trained to teach all the rest, drew enormous interest around the turn of the nineteenth century due to their ability to reach far greater numbers of children at a lesser cost. A single schoolmaster, after imparting the day's lessons to his core of "monitors," could simply sit back and supervise as they carried out the bulk of the teaching. Of course, the quality of instruction depended on the presence of sufficient numbers of bright and capable students, and in some cases it was probably only a small improvement over no education at all. Financially, however, the case was clear. The economy of having only one teacher for an entire school meant that formal education could reach every family that sought it.

This ability to reach a much wider audience quickly caught the attention of the Church of England, in large part because the first monitorial schools had been run by a Quaker, Joseph Lancaster, along nondenominational lines. The prospect of having so many children educated in what was a predominantly secular environment was anathema to the Church of England, and therefore it set about creating its own monitorial system with the elephantine title of "The National Society for Promoting the Education of the Poor in the Principles of the Established Church." Wherever Lancaster had founded a school, the National Society created one of its own in order to compete.

Soon the Church of England's network had grown vastly larger than that of its adversary. In keeping with its other educational efforts, the Church's monitorial schools were "instituted principally for Educating the Poor in the Doctrine and Discipline of the Established Church."[59] These schools were not intended to provide children with a stepping stone to higher studies, but rather to fit them to their positions at the bottom of the social and economic hierarchy. In strictly regimented lessons, the pupils were taught to be satisfied with their subservient role in life. Due to this doctrinaire style and the curricular limitations imposed by the Church, monitorial schools failed to transform English education, and eventually the monitorial approach was abandoned. Dame schools and other private ventures continued to reach a greater number of children than religious charitable institutions through the middle of the nineteenth century.[60]

The government intervenes

By the second half of the nineteenth century, the government's role in education had increased substantially. The main religious educational societies had been partially subsidized by Parliament since 1833 in an effort to improve the opportunities of the poor, and state inspectors visited their schools. Friction was high between clergy and state over the proper distribution of regulatory and funding powers, and many within the government felt there was insufficient emphasis in the schools on basic subjects and younger grades. In 1862 a "Revised Code" for education was passed into law with the well-intentioned goal of bringing competition and the profit motive into education. The "Payment by Results" program, as it came to be known, stipulated that schools should be paid based on a combination of attendance and student performance on tests administered by state inspectors. What the politicians failed to understand was that by placing the financial strings in the hands of state inspectors instead of families, they would pull the attention of teachers and administrators away from the pupils and toward the government. Failing to satisfy the inspector meant a significant loss in funding, perhaps even forcing a school out of business, while receiving a positive review increased an institution's income. Student learning, insofar as it was not measured by the inspector, was of little financial consequence. The results were tragic.

Even before the legislation was passed a few observers warned that payment based on a few simple tests would encourage teachers to curtail their instruction in other subjects. In the event, these fears were fully realized. Years after the system had been put into practice, scientist T. H. Huxley[61] observed: "[T]he Revised Code did not compel any schoolmaster to leave off teaching anything; but, by the very simple process of refusing to pay for many kinds of teaching, it has practically put an end to them."[62]

The testing system consisted of six separate levels, and since children could not be tested at the same level twice, or at a lower level from any previous attempt, schools held back older students so that they could be made to progress through all six levels, bringing in the maximum amount of cash over their educational lifetimes. To ensure top scores at inspection time, teachers adopted frequent testing and memorization sessions. Often the children were made to learn their entire reading texts by rote so that they would have the least chance of failing. While some inspectors attempted to subvert these ploys by supplying an altered text or by asking the student to read backwards, others simply passed them: "I consider it to be my duty according to the letter of the Code," one inspector said, "to *pass* every child who can read correctly and with tolerable fluency, whether he or she understand or not a single sentence or a single word of the lesson."[63] Reports from inspectors repeated the same criticism time and again, namely, that students were simply being made to memorize words without understanding their meaning. After years of experience with the system, the government-appointed Cross Commission confirmed these views in 1888, faulting the teaching of reading under the Revised Code for being "too mechanical and unintelligent."[64] The Commission's conclusions were very much in keeping with those of the government's own school inspectors. The most famous of the inspectors, poet and social critic Matthew Arnold, summed up the consensus among his colleagues:

> I find in [English schools], in general, if I compare them with their former selves, a deadness, a slackness, and a discouragement. . . . If I compare them with the schools of the continent I find in them a lack of intelligent life much more striking now than it was when I returned from the continent in 1859. This change is certainly to be attributed to the ["Payment by Results"] school legislation of 1862.[65]

Not only the education but even the welfare of many children was sacrificed under this system. If a child was absent on the day of the inspection, even if gravely ill, the school would lose his or her attendance allocation. As a result, it was not unheard of for schoolmasters to compel children stricken with serious, even infectious, diseases to attend. One inspector observed:

> To hear paroxysms of whooping-cough, to observe the pustules of small-pox, to see infants carefully wrapped up and held in their mothers' arms, or seated on a stool by the fire because too ill to take their proper places, are events not so rare in an inspector's experience as they ought to be. The risk of the infant's life, and the danger of infection to others, are preferred to the forfeiture of [the government] grant.[66]

Teachers, forced by financial necessity to provide only the narrowest education to their students, lost all spirit and enthusiasm for their work. Their vocation had been reduced to a game of cat and mouse between the school and the inspector, in which teachers had to learn how to manipulate the system in order to be successful.

Despite its significant impact on schooling, the Revised Code was not the government's most lasting foray into education. In 1870, the Forster Education Act added state provision of schooling to the government's existing roles in funding and inspection. Local school boards were created across the country to fill perceived gaps in the existing network of private and subsidized schools. Over the next several decades, state authority was progressively increased, attendance was made mandatory for children between the ages of five and thirteen, and tuition fees at state-run schools were gradually reduced to zero by 1918.

Outcomes

In the seventeenth through the nineteenth centuries, English literacy was transformed. Concentrated for so long among the wealthy, reading and writing finally became both valuable to and attainable by the public at large. Though there had not been a single newspaper published outside of Britain's urban centers prior to 1700, at least 130 village and county papers had gone into print by 1760. Many of these died out after a few years, but by the end of the century reading had become firmly established in country life.[67] In the cities, most notably London, the great demand for information, instruction, and entertainment was met by ever more and ever larger newspapers. Statistics which began to be recorded in the early to mid 1800s show that literacy climbed throughout that century, with only a few pauses and stumbles along the way. Looking at all this data, and at the rise of government involvement in education over the same period, many educators and historians have awarded much of the credit for the dissemination of reading skills to state intervention. A closer look at the evidence shows how undeserved this credit really was.

To begin with, government policy from earliest times to the nineteenth century was actually *hostile* to the spread of reading and writing. In 1662, the Licensing Act was passed by Parliament, renewing existing limits on the number of legal printers and appointing state and Church authorities as official censors to eliminate whatever books they found heretical or seditious. Publishers of unlicensed material were fined, imprisoned, or worse. For the "crime" of writing that "the execution of judgment and justice is as well the people's as the magistrate's duty," a printer by the name of Twyn was hanged in 1663, cut down before he was dead, then mutilated and beheaded.[68] It would be hard to construe this bit of government intervention as having a warming effect on the spread of printing and literacy.

Over the next two centuries the state's methods would become more refined, but the goals and results remained the same. As it became obvious to the Crown that prosecuting and martyring popular printers often increased rather than alleviated public discontent, it added a new tactic to its attacks on the press: taxation. After 1712, every newspaper was required to bear a government stamp, for which a tax payment was required. The stamp tax was not only enforced for just over a century, it was repeatedly increased to the point of heavily discouraging printing. Many other taxes and restrictions were heaped onto the printing industry in an effort to curtail free speech, particularly since that speech was often critical of the government. It was not until the mid nineteenth century that most of these taxes were repealed, but the price of printed matter fell in the 1830s and 1840s nonetheless, thanks to the invention of more-efficient printing presses.

Not only printing itself but also the reading and distribution of literature were subject to state suppression. The owners of pubs and other public places that allowed the distribution or discussion of the radically democratic papers of the early nineteenth century were subject to fines and prosecution.[69] Over a long period, the postal service was ordered by the Crown not to accept or deliver antigovernment materials. Overcoming all this opposition, Thomas Paine's "The Rights of Man" is thought to have sold over a million and a half copies in Britain at the turn of the nineteenth century, and the working classes bought up 200,000 copies of populist pundit William Cobbett's radical tract "Address to the Journeymen and Labourers," in just two months.[70]

Clearly the spread of literacy up to the 1830s was achieved in spite of, rather than thanks to, state intervention. But what of the government's school subsidies that began in 1833, and the introduction of state-run schools in 1870? To assess the effects of these policies, we can look at the historical literacy rates for the period, which come primarily from marriage records.[71] What the data show is that just over two thirds of newly married men were already literate by 1841, and that this figure increased to more than nine in ten by 1891.[72] Rates of literacy for women were somewhat lower early in the century, but the gap was gradually closed. In interpreting this evidence, the economist E. G. West has pointed out that two important facts must be kept in mind: the average age of marriage was twenty-eight, and the average age when a child left elementary school was eleven. So, if we want to know the effects that schools had on literacy in a given year, we have to look at the marriage records seventeen years later. Taking all this into account, it becomes clear that widespread literacy was already achieved *long before* there were any government education subsidies. What's more, almost universal literacy was achieved by individuals who had left school prior to 1874, at which time the implementation of the Forster Education Act was just getting under way, and could have had only a limited effect.

The early trend in school enrollment was substantially similar to that in literacy. According to official statistics, the number of children in schools rose from less than half a million in 1818 to 1.3 million in 1834 "without any interposition of the government or public authorities."[73] Remarkably, these figures actually underestimate both total enrollment and enrollment growth. Philip Gardner, an expert on schooling among the working classes in nineteenth-century Britain, has found that most education statistics of the time were collected by education reformers who had a direct interest in downplaying the breadth and effectiveness of private school efforts. Because these reformers wanted to erect a government-run school system, they had to demonstrate that private schooling was not performing adequately. Whether deliberately or not, the figures that they presented grossly underestimated the extent of private schooling, particularly in working-class districts. When he compared the total school enrollment figures collected by the education reformers in 1851 with the figures reported in the general population census of the same year, he found that the reformers' figures fell 135,893 students short.[74] He then investigated the city of Bristol in great detail, to determine which students had fallen through the cracks. His conclusion was that the education census commissioned by reformers reported as few as one half of the existing private schools serving the poor in and around that city, and that it underestimated the number of students attending each school.[75]

In light of Gardner's findings, the reports of education reformers are all the more impressive. Their statistics show that three times as many private as subsidized schools were created between 1841 and 1851, and that the pace of private school expansion was increasing. In 1850 alone, 3,754 new private schools were established, compared to only 616 new subsidized schools.[76] Just as in the years following the German Reformation, however, the increase in government funding to subsidized schools cut into the growth of independent educational efforts. Though a majority of students still attended private schools as late as the 1850s,[77] the tide had clearly begun to turn. Between 1833 and 1870, state funding increased from less than one third to more than two thirds of the tuition cost at subsidized schools. Even though parents had a strong allegiance to their independent schools, the difference in costs became so great that subsidized schools began to draw students away from the private sector. By 1870, private schools enrolled only about a quarter of all students, and by the 1880s, when public school tuition was almost nil, fee-charging private schools had all but disappeared.[78] The net effect of state intervention on enrollment was insignificant compared to its effect on private schools. Even before the Forster Education Act, virtually all children were receiving some schooling.[79] In essence, government intervention in education served primarily to extinguish private schools, rather than to increase the percentage of children receiving an education.

These figures, particularly for the early years of the nineteenth century, bear witness to the willingness of even the poorest and least-educated parents to see to the education of their children without state compulsion or supervision. The relative failure of subsidized schools to attract parents until their fees became much cheaper than those of private schools, indicates that parents were not only able to choose, but were willing to shoulder a financial burden in order to do so. This burden was made heavier by the regressive tax system in place at the time, which forced the poor to pay a proportionately greater share of the nation's taxes than the wealthy. Had these taxes been reduced, and had the subsidies funneled to charity schools been given directly to parents, they could have secured an even better education for their children.

Many historians, particularly those who favor government-run schools, have been at pains to show that the choices made by poor parents were bad ones, based on factors other than educational merit. Echoing the early nineteenth-century advocates of government education, they have claimed that private schools were dirty, disorganized, and ineffectual, that their teachers were mostly backward (having had little formal pedagogical training), and that parents who chose them were more concerned with day care than with education. In his book *Literacy and Popular Culture,* David Vincent acknowledges that conditions in independent schools serving the poor were not ideal, but provides evidence to show that parents were "willing to make full use of such purchasing power as they possessed, shopping around and transferring their patronage from one establishment to another,"[80] based on the effectiveness and cost of the instruction offered.

David Mitch has attempted to sort out these claims by comparing nineteenth-century literacy rates among private versus public school graduates in several areas of the country. In his first statistical analysis of the question, he found that private-school enrollment tended to increase literacy rates among both men and women, whereas public (i.e., state subsidized) school enrollment actually had a *negative* effect on male literacy, and a negligible one on female literacy. He suggested, however, that this result could have been due to other factors, such as differences between the clientele of the two kinds of schools. He then tried to control for these external factors in a second analysis, and found that, overall, private schools still had a significant positive impact on literacy, while the impact of public schools was insignificant.[81] In other words, what little evidence is available on the comparative effectiveness of subsidized versus entirely private schools tends to favor the private schools, not the other way around. This is entirely in keeping with the marginalization of literacy instruction in Church-run public schools.[82]

Economically speaking, the private schools of Britain were among the most successful in the world. Graduates of independent secondary schools, thanks to their practical training in mathematics, engineering, economics, surveying, navigation, and other disciplines, were well prepared to take advantage of contemporary scientific and technological developments, and to succeed in commerce and international trade. By the early nineteenth century, this wealth of technical expertise had helped to make Britain the world's leading manufacturing nation, responsible, according to some economists, for one quarter of the world's total industrial production. Britain also accounted for more than twice the volume of international commerce of its nearest rivals.[83] Of course, many other factors played important roles in these accomplishments. Apprenticeships, for instance, continued to be more common than secondary schooling throughout most of the nineteenth century, and the government's relative abstention from interference in the economy encouraged rapid growth. Still, the contribution of private technical schooling should not be underestimated.

The contribution of the nation's endowed grammar schools and traditional universities *cannot possibly* be underestimated, since it was so minuscule. These institutions played virtually no role in economic growth, buried as they were in the subjects and methods of the past. Still more revealing is the fact that, after 1870—the year in which Britain introduced government schooling— the country's industrial leadership began to wane, being overtaken by the United States and Germany in the late nineteenth and early twentieth centuries. It is too simplistic to suggest that state schooling was the only or even the primary cause of Britain's economic slowdown, particularly since students taught in state schools would not have had much of an effect on the economy for several years after their graduation. Over the ensuing decades, however, the government's increasing role in education was contemporaneous with a decline in Britain's place at the head of economic progress.

France: Educational Roulette during and after the Revolution

The French military leader and statesman Charles de Gaulle once asked, "How can you govern a nation that has 246 kinds of cheese?" In retrospect, the century following the revolution of 1789 appears to have been an attempt to answer that question by trial and error. After the revolutionary overthrow of its absolute monarchy, France was ruled, successively, as a republic, an empire, a constitutional monarchy, a second constitutional monarchy, another republic, a second empire, and a third republic. Countless variations existed within each of these governmental categories, making attempts at understanding the political history of nineteenth-century France at least as complex (and dangerous) as choosing the right morsel off the cheese cart in a Parisian restaurant.

Fortunately, the essential features of French education can be grasped without a detailed knowledge of the period's political organization. For the purposes of this section, it is enough to know that France had been ruled for generations by a succession of kings, and that this hereditary monarchy had been dismantled in 1789 by an uprising of the middle and lower classes. In its place, an effort was made to establish a democratic republican form of government, but the task proved far more difficult than expected. Over the ensuing decades, a variety of factions battled for control of the government. Most notable among these were republican revolutionaries and Catholic royalists. The republicans aimed to eradicate every vestige of the *ancien régime* (old order), including the Catholic Church, and this put them into a bitter power struggle with conservatives and the clergy. Caught in the middle of this epic battle were the schools and children of France.

Educational Conditions in France

In his December edict of 1666, King Louis XIV forbade "any establishment of colleges, monasteries, religious or secular communities . . . in any city or region of the kingdom . . . without [his] express permission by official letter well and duly registered in [his] parliamentary courts."[84] Demonstrating an excellent grasp of the arsenal of bureaucracy, he further stipulated that each application for royal approval be preceded by an extensive investigation of the pros and cons, containing the views of all interested parties including a long list of municipal and state functionaries and clergymen.[85] This arduous and time-consuming application, if and when it was completed, was then subjected to a royal review of indefinite length.

Efforts were made to circumvent the King's mountain of red tape, but since institutions that violated the procedure were subject to the confiscation of all their property, the creation of major new educational institutions was greatly slowed. Many small schools already existed and continued to do so, however. Somewhat more than half of the schools that existed in the late 1600s and early 1700s were affiliated with churches or monasteries, while the rest were operated as private ventures—usually by individual teachers. The distribution of these little schools was uneven, being fairly dense in northeastern towns, and more scattered in the rural southwest of the country. Exact figures for enrollment during this period are difficult to come by.

While Louis was regulating education to strengthen central government, his provincial officials saw the schools as an ideal means for extinguishing Protestantism. A particularly zealous example is that of M. de Bâville, administrator of the Languedoc region, who ordered mandatory attendance at Catholic schools until the age of fourteen, and mandatory catechetical instruction beyond that. To enforce this policy, a series of increasingly severe penalties were meted out to families that refused to comply. If fines and similar punishments failed to persuade recalcitrant parents, they risked having their children taken from them and given to Catholic families. In extreme cases, provision was even made for executing such conscientious objectors.[86]

It seems natural to suppose that the French Revolution, with its emphasis on human rights and freedoms, would have put an end to the manipulation of education for partisan political and religious ends. That, however, was not the case. From monarchy to republic and back again, both royalists and revolutionaries strove to use the schools to shore up their positions.

The government that eventually emerged from the bloodbath of 1789, while revolutionary in many respects, continued the age-old tradition of using schools as a tool. In order to undermine the power of its primary opponent, the Catholic clergy, the national assembly severed all ties between education and religion. Nuns and priests were ordered to sign a declaration restricting their freedom to teach their faith. Since compliance with this order was difficult to achieve, the government soon resorted to a more direct approach: outlawing the clergy entirely. In one of history's more remarkable contradictions, the revolutionaries argued that a truly free nation could suffer no religious or secular organizations among its citizens, and so abolished them.[87] Simply wearing religious garb became a crime.[88]

Without a well-organized transitional strategy, schooling quickly began to collapse. Like Emperor Nero fiddling as Rome burned, the French assembly continued to debate exactly what the new system should look like as the old one crumbled around them. A genuinely revolutionary minority defended the right of families to choose their schools, whether sectarian or otherwise, but their voices were lost amid a majority who believed the only choice was between moderate and absolute state control over education. So fervent was the belief in the power of the state and of the value of forced equality, that proposals for a totalitarian system much like Sparta's were put forward, in which children were to be taken away from their parents and educated in government communes. According to the delegate Le Pelletier, "The totality of the child's existence belongs to us [the state]; the clay, if I may express myself thus, never leaves the mold."[89]

Eventually a school law was passed, making attendance at state-run schools mandatory and requiring instructors to sign a "civic certificate" restricting their right to provide sectarian religious instruction. In place of the old Catholic teachings, a new "natural religion" was imposed on the youth of France. Students were issued catechisms which admonished them to "worship Reason and the Supreme Being," in the deistic republican fashion.[90] But having stripped away the traditional religious aspects of schooling, the assembly had made teaching decidedly unattractive to the priests and nuns who comprised the majority of educators. The supply of willing teachers was thus reduced to a trickle. Even where teachers were to be found, many families resented both the intrusion of the state into their lives, and the ouster of Catholicism, and therefore kept their children at home. As a result, the school system of the revolutionaries was implemented sporadically at best.

Government policy against religious schools did interrupt the supply of education, but in the absence of anything to take their place they began to reappear. Unsurprisingly, religious schools continued to be viewed by the republican political majority as strongholds of fanatics and royalists, to be struck down and annihilated. The continued affinity of many citizens for traditional institutions was itself viewed as a sign of ignorance.

The success of independent schools

Two decades after the revolution, the French education scene looked like precisely what it was: a battlefield. The general consensus of local officials and national observers was that an already weak system had been made worse. Report after report flowed into Paris, each lamenting the sad condition or complete absence of elementary schools. In the midst of this bleak educational landscape, a small group of philanthropists perceived what they thought might be an oasis. Having encountered and been impressed by English monitorial schools on a number of occasions, these men believed the system could help to circumvent the teacher shortage from which their country was suffering, while also replacing the outdated individual instructional technique with more effective group teaching. So, in June 1815, the first French monitorial school was opened in Paris.

From its original handful of students, the new school rapidly grew to an enrollment in the hundreds. Its success was widely praised, and by the fall several other monitorial schools had appeared. Beyond the cost-effectiveness of the method, several of its pedagogical innovations attracted significant attention. Monitorial schools cast aside the existing practice of teaching reading and writing as entirely distinct skills, with excellent results. They grouped students by aptitude in each particular subject, allowing them to progress through the curriculum at their own pace and simplifying the task of teachers. Finally, in what seems an obvious move to modern readers, Jesuit instructors taught the entire class together, rather than spending time individually with each child in succession. The one-on-one method, wherein most of the class would devolve into chaos as the teacher focused his or her attention on a single student at a time, had persisted in most subsidized schools until the advent of the monitorial system. Critics aptly pointed out that the monitorial system tended toward excessive regimentation, but this problem at least appears to have been less severe than in the monitorial schools of England's National Society, since the French schools were not part of a rigid, hierarchical organization, and the inculcation of a particular dogma was not their primary mission. While their quality must have varied dramatically, they were clearly an improvement over the status quo.

In practice, the advantages of monitorial teaching seem to have outweighed its weaknesses, for this approach, which became known as "mutual instruction" in France, soon spread throughout the country. By January 1819, there were already 602 monitorial schools. Later that same year the number had increased by an astounding 50 percent, to 912, and it continued growing at that rate, reaching 1,300 schools by February 1820.[91] Not only did the system succeed in opening more schools faster than any previous approach, it was in such great demand that many existing schools were forced to adopt its techniques in order to compete. "Instructors following the old method, seeing their pupils desert in order to run to the new one, are hurrying to adopt it themselves," observed a speaker at the general assembly in Paris.[92]

Unprecedented in their popularity with the citizenry, monitorial schools were nonetheless resented by the state and loathed by the Church. Managed and funded as they were by either secular private charities or municipal authorities, they enjoyed a significant measure of independence, making them difficult for the established powers to manipulate. The two most invidious characteristics of the system, as seen by Church and state, were its secularism and its meritocratic nature. Supporters of mutual education lauded the fact that it taught children "to obey merit . . . no matter who its repository may be,"[93] that is, to disregard notions of social class; but the clergy argued that this would subvert the social order.[94]

The vested interests fight back

The final nail in the coffin of independent schools was the resurgence of Catholic political power after the restoration of the monarchy in 1815. In the early 1820s the Church won an important victory, having Bishop Frayssinous appointed Minister of Ecclesiastical Affairs and Public Education and Grand Master of the Imperial University. Napoleon had created the Imperial University in 1806 as "a vehicle for the control of all public and private education,"[95] and it had remained a thorn in the side of the Church ever since. Having gained control of the top position within the University, the Church was subsequently able to push through legislation granting it wide-ranging powers over teachers and schools. By law, classes began and ended with prayers, the Catholic Church's catechism was learned in daily lessons, and teachers were made increasingly answerable to local priests. Due to their generally secular nature, and the fact that their origins lay in English Protestantism, monitorial schools were singled out for the fiercest attacks. Priests leveraged their pulpits, demonizing mutual teaching and its supporters in sermon after sermon. Where calumny and persuasion failed, resort was sometimes made to blackmail—with priests withholding the sacraments and even charitable grants for the poor in the community if they persisted in sending their children to monitorial schools.[96] After only a few years of this new regime, monitorial schools were all but extinguished: their numbers were reduced from 1,500 in 1821, to 258 by 1827.[97]

Despite the effort by Catholic royalists to take control of the Imperial University (under the Grand Mastership of Bishop Frayssinous), the institution eventually began to reassert its autonomy. By the early 1830s it was once again able to challenge the Church's power over French schooling, and an opportunity to advance its independence came in 1833 when new education legislation was put forward in the national assembly. Most of the ministers drafting the legislation were prominent members of the University, committed to its control of the educational system. The Church lobbied hard for concessions, however, and in the end won several compromises in the final law. The legislative Frankenstein monster thus created had limbs to suit *almost* everyone. The University won a monopoly for granting newly required teacher certifications; Catholic priests were selected to chair the thousands of regional supervisory committees; and municipalities, due to their limited political influence, ended up with the modest role of nominating a few local members to sit on the Church's committees. Parents, bereft of any political power, were granted few rights or freedoms under the law.

Though nominally meant to ensure the competence of both government and nongovernment teachers, the certification process was entirely divorced from instructional practice. The examiners, typically local college professors selected by the Imperial University, had little knowledge of a primary-school environment they had neither experienced themselves nor perhaps even observed.[98] Usually too easy and sometimes too difficult, the uneven certification process was of little help in improving the quality of instruction.

More damaging than haphazard teacher certification was the requirement for regional public school committees. Though headed up by local priests, these committees officially reported to the University, putting the Church in a subservient role. The clergy chafed at this limitation of its authority, and fought it with a variety of techniques. In a vast number of cases, priests simply refused to convene meetings, preferring to assume personal control over their local schools and schoolmasters. In those cases when the members did meet, internal squabbles were the norm, with the Catholic traditionalists and republican defenders of mutual education locked in unswerving opposition to one another. Thanks to their organization and influence, the priests usually emerged victorious, picking whichever instructor best suited their needs. It was common for pious and acquiescent schoolmasters to receive favorable treatment, being freed from any legal requirements which might disqualify them from teaching, while those educators with strong individual wills, or with more republican views, were persecuted and criticized in the priests' reports.

Committee members drawn from the local community were generally of little help in improving the process. Virtually all were otherwise employed and were neither willing nor able to spend a significant amount of time on the unsalaried position. With neither the necessary expertise nor the incentive to spur them on, their motivation quickly ebbed. Even proponents of the original education law admitted its failure. Addressing the assembly years after the law's passage, its chief proponent, minister François Guizot, declared:

There are 2,846 cantons [in France]. . . . For many years we have expended considerable effort organizing cantonal committees, but we have managed to create only 1,031; moreover, these still exist only on paper, there are hardly 200 that have taken any real action.[99]

For the rest of the nineteenth century, the battle for control of education waged on. Though primary schooling reached an ever-larger segment of the population, its nature at any given time continued to be decided by the faction with the greatest political clout. The degree of politicization and centralization of French schooling was well captured by the attitude of Hippolyte Fortoul, Minister of Ecclesiastical Affairs and Public Education from 1851 to 1856. Drawing a watch from his pocket he boasted: "At this moment, all the students of the *lycées* [secondary schools] are explaining the same passage from Virgil."[100] Under Fortoul, the hours, methods, and content of teaching were all codified. Teachers were forced to swear an oath of loyalty, support official candidates, and were even prohibited from growing beards or mustaches.[101]

Though the regimes of the 1880s and 1890s sought to make state education accessible to the entire nation, they stopped short of letting citizens decide what kind of education was appropriate. Jules Ferry, nominated Minister of Public Instruction in 1880, believed that all French children had the right to an education, but that the awarding of degrees must remain the prerogative of the state. This tool, coupled with the government inspection of all schools, was necessary in his eyes to maintain national unity and a common morality, and to regulate access to public office. Two national teachers' colleges, founded in 1883, insured a new generation of educators free from the conservative royalist views of the clergy.[102]

Outcomes

Nineteenth-century French education history is commonly viewed as a period in which increased state intervention led to the wider dispersion of literacy and culture.[103] Certainly it is true that both state schooling and literacy grew during the 1800s, but, just as in England, the role of government was neither as positive nor as decisive as it has often been portrayed. Literacy was already on the rise in the eighteenth century, and was widespread in some northern and eastern districts of France well before the appearance of state elementary schools. Also as in England, the government placed strict limits on the right to print and read books and newspapers.

In the summer of 1792, the revolutionaries suppressed all royalist newspapers, arrested their writers, and confiscated their presses. The journalist Durosoy, having vigorously defended the King's cause in the *Gazette de Paris,* was peremptorily executed.[104] Over the next several years, a host of laws were passed banning whatever newspapers most irritated the revolutionaries, and deporting their print-ers, managers, and pundits. As if to demonstrate that governments of all political stripes can use the tools of state coercion, the French revolutionaries imposed a stamp tax on monarchist newspapers, just as the English monarchy had imposed one in order to thwart revolutionaries. With few exceptions, the emperors and the republicans who ruled the French people from the Revolution until the 1880s en-deavored to keep tight control over the dissemination of printed material. Need-less to say, this climate did nothing to encourage the spread of reading.

A close examination of literacy statistics and figures for state school enroll-ment also casts doubt on the importance of government intervention. The most revealing fact is that areas which had high levels of state school enrollment al-ready enjoyed high levels of literacy before that enrollment could have pro-duced any effect. Enrollment of eight to twelve year olds in 1850, for example, was already strongly correlated with *adult* literacy in 1854. This makes it hard to argue that state schooling played a decisive role in raising literacy rates, be-cause communities with high school-enrollment already had more literate par-ents to begin with.

François Furet and Jacques Ozouf, the researchers who first observed this fact, concluded that the relationship between literacy and schooling was essen-tially circular; literate parents were more likely to seek education for their chil-dren, and educated children were more likely to become literate. The entire process stemmed from a growing demand on the part of the public for literacy, spawned by the spread of written material (despite government restrictions) and the increasing economic value of reading and writing. Furet and Ozouf wrote:

> In the long term, [schooling] is nothing but a product of the demand for educa-tion. Of course, a school founded purely out of individual generosity or at a bishop's initiative may produce a temporary improvement in education in a parish; but its chances of enduring and of generating far-reaching changes in cul-tural patterns are slim, unless it is not only accepted but actively wanted by the inhabitants.[105]

The truth of this assessment is attested to by the success of the independent monitorial schools, which not only flourished in response to popular demand, but led existing institutions to emulate their innovations. Far from encouraging such effective, free-enterprise schools, French governments impeded their growth by offering subsidized government schooling, which made tuition-charging institutions financially less appealing. Countless laws and regulations were also heaped on independent schools, limiting their freedom to innovate or outlawing them entirely.

The battles for control of French schooling did have a significant impact on the society at large, however. Though many educators argue that government schooling is better than a free market in education at fostering understanding and social harmony, this was no more true in France than it was in the United States. Whether controlled by republicans or monarchists, the state schools were used as a weapon with which to bludgeon their opponents. In their time in office, the revolutionaries cut the clergy's ties to education in order to weaken their influence on the people. As the Church rose once again to power, Catholic teachings were legally forced on the state schools, and private secular institutions came under heated attack. In contrast to this state compulsion, the independent monitorial schools placed no religious restrictions on their pupils or teachers. They were also the first to integrate children of upper and lower classes, but far from being supported by the education bureaucracies of clergy and government, they were fiercely opposed.

Between the early 1700s and the late 1800s, French economic output was lower than that of Britain, both in absolute terms and in its rate of growth. Population growth was significantly slower in France, however, and thus when the figures are looked at on a per-capita basis, they are more favorable. Still, some economists have argued that the French population grew more slowly precisely *because* its agricultural productivity lagged behind that of more rapidly developing nations. In any event, the French economy can be said to have made a decent, though not stellar, showing during the eighteenth and nineteenth centuries. Some industries, particularly rail transportation, were retarded by the French government's interventionist stance, which impeded the development of private markets. France also trailed Britain in widespread mechanical know-how. Though the French can be proud of their brilliant scientists and inventors of the period, they did not have the same quantity of engineers and technically trained laborers to capitalize on their discoveries. Unlike their neighbor across the Channel, the French lacked a broad base of practically oriented secondary schools. A few specialized technical universities were created within the state-run school system, but they reached too few students to have a significant impact on the national economy. For most students, state schools provided little training in the modern sciences and engineering disciplines, and private schools had been all but squeezed out of existence by the ever-expanding government system.

*Myth*conceptions

At the beginning of this chapter, I noted that the public's support for public schooling rests largely on two beliefs: that government education has helped to unite people of diverse backgrounds, and that it has brought literacy and learning to a greater part of the population than would otherwise have been possible. When held up to the light of history, these beliefs dissipate like the morning fog, revealing a very different reality beneath. Few institutions have caused as much strife and conflict as public schools. They have been used to beat down minorities of every color and creed, setting family against family and community against community. Protestants in both France and the United States used them to attack Catholicism, and Catholics, when they achieved the upper hand in French politics, turned them against Protestantism. U.S. whites used the public schools to segregate African Americans. Instead of welcoming immigrants in a spirit of mutual respect, government schools often sought to extinguish their cultures and beliefs. Far from promoting social harmony, government schools in the U.S. undermined it, forcing Catholics to set up their own schools in order to avoid the discrimination they suffered at the hands of the state system, and breeding resentment among many other immigrant groups who felt that their traditions were derided in the public schools. Blood was shed and property destroyed in disputes precipitated by the "common schools."

The assumption that public schooling was necessary to bring education to the masses is equally unsupported by the historical evidence. England and the United States had already achieved widespread literacy before government-run schools were introduced, as had parts of France. Furthermore, the arrival of state schools generally failed to speed up the diffusion of reading and writing, mainly because the growing demand for schooling was already being met by the private sector. When public schools finally appeared, they rarely caused an increase in the percentage of the population receiving an education. Instead, they redistributed students, enticing them away from existing private schools by offering free or subsidized tuition. Taken as a whole, nineteenth-century governments simply annexed the already thriving private school industry — jumping, in economist E. G. West's phrase, into the saddle of an already galloping horse. The following chapters reveal the path that government schools followed once they held the reins.

4

Coup d'École:
The War for Control of American Education

> *"Education is a weapon whose effects depend on who holds it in his hands and at whom it is aimed."* — *Joseph Stalin[1]*
>
> *"Each child belongs to the state,"* and the purpose of education is *"the training of citizens for the state so the state may be perpetuated."* —William H. Seawell, Professor of Education, University of Virginia[2]

School reformers of the 1800s got what they wanted. Since the turn of the century, public schools have been the sole purveyors of educational services to the vast majority of children, and the resources at their disposal have grown enormously. So how has our experiment with government-run schooling unfolded? Most noticeably, control over and responsibility for the education of children has been gradually withdrawn from families and bestowed upon elected and appointed officials at ever-higher levels of government. Instead of directing the course of their children's schooling, as they once did, parents are now principally spectators, their views and aspirations given far less weight than those of professional educators.

The reformers who argued for this transfer of power stressed that the stability and harmony of society would surely be improved by a strong public school system. Not only has the successful government takeover of education failed to live up to this promise, it has created a new social battlefront on which well-organized interest groups from across the political spectrum have regularly clashed, trampling the rights of their neighbors in their attempts to seize control of the state schools. Ironically, the group most frequently caught in the crossfire is one that education reformers have specifically dedicated themselves to helping: minority students.

In keeping with the authoritarian tradition of government-run schooling, citizens of all political stripes have tried to use the public schools as a tool for advancing their aims. Generally, the people who built up the public-education establishment and who have tried to harness it from within have been left-leaning, espousing a less rigid, less academically oriented curriculum, a larger role for government in the lives of the people, and a distaste for the competitive free-enterprise system. Conversely, the people who have attempted to influence or take over the system from the outside have chiefly been right-leaning, identifying themselves with conservatism, limited government, capitalism, and frequently with (Christian) religion. There are, of course, exceptions, but these generalizations accurately describe most of the players involved. The purpose of this chapter is not to champion one side or the other, but simply to chronicle the destructive power struggles between them that have plagued U.S. public schooling since its inception.

Educational Dictators, Part I: The Left

Continuing down the path trod by their nineteenth-century precursors, many reformist educators of the early 1900s saw families not as clients whose needs were to be catered to, but as opponents on the path to better schools. Sociologist and education pundit Edward A. Ross was among the most popular figures in the education community at the turn of the century, successfully promoting the use of public schools as a means of actively controlling and shaping the minds of children. Parents, Ross felt, were too unreliable to be left with the responsibility for their children's education, since they were not subject to any government selection or certification process. In his 1901 book *Social Control,* he wrote:

> Another gain lies in the partial substitution of the teacher for the parent as the model upon which the child forms itself. Copy the child will, and the advantage of giving him his teacher instead of his father to imitate, is that the former is a picked person, while the latter is not. Childhood is, in fact, the heyday of personal influence. The position of the teacher gives him prestige, and the lad will take from him suggestions that the adult will accept only from rare and splendid personalities.[3]

Seven years later, another familiar idea resurfaced among public school advocates: the active sorting of children into different study programs at the discretion of school personnel. Charles Elliot, a leading official of the National Education Association (NEA) and onetime president of Harvard University, proclaimed that "the teachers in elementary schools ought to sort the pupils and sort them by their evident or probable destinies."[4] The sense of *déjà vu* conjured up by these words is powerful indeed when one thinks back to the social-engineering projects envisioned by education theorists in revolutionary France.

The disparity between the goals of parents and those of professional educators grew most dramatically in the years following the creation of the Progressive Education Association. Founded in 1919 by a group of eighty-five prominent educators, the PEA had as its key principles the freedom of children to learn what they wanted, when they wanted; the redefinition of teachers as guides rather than instructors; and the fostering of cooperation between home and school. Unfortunately for families, the last of these principles received far less attention, in practice, than the other two.

George S. Counts, arguably the most influential of the association's members, soon drifted away from the idea of the home as a positive influence on children's lives and education. In his writings, he celebrated what he perceived to be the emancipation of the child from "the coercive influence of the small family or community group."[5] Over the years, his aspirations for public schooling diverged ever more sharply from the traditional role of conveying basic knowledge and skills. "Focus more on society, less on the child," he urged the other members of the PEA.[6] Counts did not hide his goal of using the public schools to transform American society, titling his 1932 manifesto *Dare the School Build a New Social Order?* In this tract, he sought to rally his peers to his cause, encouraging teachers to reach for power:

> To the extent that they [teachers] are permitted to fashion the curriculum and procedures of the school, they will definitely and positively influence the social attitudes, ideals and behavior of the coming generation. . . . It is my observation that the men and women who have affected the course of human events are those who have not hesitated to use the power that has come to them.[7]

Nor was Counts satisfied with using the schools as a tool of indoctrination — a word he used with approbation on more than one occasion.[8] The entire economic and political makeup of the nation, he believed, was in need of an overhaul. "If democracy is to survive," he wrote, "natural resources and all important forms of capital will have to be collectively owned."[9]

Counts found a warm reception for his ideas and, within a few years, like-minded professors from the Teachers' College of Columbia University had wrested control of the PEA away from those of its founders who advocated a more limited and child-centered view of schooling. So infectious was the reformist philosophy that it soon took hold of the NEA as well. Mundane aspects of schooling, such as the teaching of academic subjects, were crowded out of education discussions by plans for a social revolution. A report produced by the NEA's Department of Superintendents, titled "Education for the New America," called for government takeovers of the "credit agencies, [and] the basic industries and utilities," adding that a "dying *laissez-faire* must be completely destroyed, and all of us, including the owners, must be subjected to a large degree of social control."[10]

The official organ for disseminating progressive views to the educational community was the *Social Frontier.* Directed by Counts, John Dewey, Harold Rugg, and a handful of other idealists, this journal advocated dumping capitalism into the wastebasket of history and bringing in a collectivist society reminiscent of ancient Sparta or the early USSR. Indeed, the siren song of Russian socialism utterly beguiled these educators of the 1920s and 1930s, leading them to make inexplicable statements such as: "Russia is moving toward greater democracy and away from dogmatism in art and in education while in most democratic countries the trend toward authoritarianism is in the ascendant." Without noticing the irony, they claimed that "there can be no freedom of thought and expression . . . [in] an economy based on private property," while also urging the president to "harness the press, the radio, the cinema, the public educational system to the star of a new, economically secure and culturally free, social order."[11] As education historian Diane Ravitch has observed, this bespeaks a curious idea of freedom. Like Dorothy in *The Wizard of Oz,* these educators were swept up in the whirlwind of progressivism and carried a long way from traditional educational ideas. Unlike Dorothy, Counts and his colleagues rather liked Oz, and hoped that they would never have to go home again.

To make that wish a reality, leading educators lobbied hard for the elimination of local school boards, and for the centralization of the country's numerous small school districts into larger and more easily controlled conglomerations. In an article titled "School Boards as an Obstruction to Good Administration," the progressive educator Charles H. Judd demanded that school boards be abolished, and their responsibilities handed over to state-certified professional educators.[12] Grassroots opposition to these programs was fierce. Rural residents, those most likely to see their one- or two-room schoolhouses replaced by comprehensive central schools, organized themselves to oppose the forced consolidations pushed by state education officials and district administrators. When 1,000 small school districts across the state of New York convened meetings to discuss a pro-consolidation school bill in 1923, 980 voted to reject it. Far from being dissuaded by this massive show of opposition, backers of the bill became more determined than ever to press on with their agenda. One state official was reported to have said: "The farmers of New York State reminded us of a sick child who refuses to take its medicine! We intended to force the bill right down the throats of these farmers!"[13] Though this particular bill eventually died in the state assembly, the Senate Education Committee introduced a raft of similar bills in 1925. No public hearings were held on the new bills, and despite their wholesale rejection by the Rural School Improvement Society, an organization with widespread support among the state's small communities, they were passed into law. In combination with an existing centralization law, the new legislation "spelled the beginning of the end for the one-room rural school."[14]

Between 1929–30 and 1993–94, the number of one-room schoolhouses fell from roughly 150,000 to 442.[15] But the elimination of one-room schools was only the first element in a much grander progressive vision. After a preliminary round of school consolidations, the newly formed districts were perceived as still being unsatisfactorily small. As the years passed, adjacent districts continued to be thrust together, often in spite of resistance from their constituents. The success of this part of the progressive agenda was complete. In 1932, after years of consolidation, there were still 127,531 school districts nationwide.[16] By 1962, the number had dropped to 35,676, and it continued to decline until, in the 1993–94 school year, only 14,881 districts remained.[17] In *Tinkering toward Utopia,* David Tyack and Larry Cuban point out that this process decimated the number of school officials drawn from the general public, shifting control into the hands of public school professionals. As for increasing efficiency—the putative reason for the consolidations given by education reformers—the opposite has proven to be true in practice: smaller districts achieve more with less.[18]

A Thoroughly Modern Curriculum

As the progressives consolidated their power over government schooling, they began to experiment more and more with new curricula. The traditional disciplines, such as history and mathematics, were increasingly displaced by vaguely defined courses intended to prepare students for everyday life. In districts where these new courses were introduced, it was not uncommon for parents to object, calling for the elimination of frills from the curriculum and a return to basic academic subjects. This did not sit well with the reformers, many of whom apparently saw parents as backward and ill-informed interlopers in their domain. One prominent school principal remarked that "if the tax payer insists on paring the curriculum down to the essentials, it is the educators who must determine what the essentials are."[19]

And what, you might ask, did educators consider essential? Certainly not the traditional academic subjects. When the NEA's Commission on the Reorganization of Secondary Education released its "Cardinal Principles" report in 1918, it called for a curriculum teaching: "1. Health. 2. Command of fundamental processes. 3. Worthy home-membership. 4. Vocation. 5. Citizenship. 6. Worthy use of leisure. 7. Ethical character."[20] Remarkably, many progressives believed the report did not go far enough in burying traditional subjects, with one complaining that it was "almost hopelessly academic."[21]

The effects of this and other efforts at curriculum reform were considerable.

In the two decades prior to 1910, when the progressives' hold on public school curricula had still been relatively weak, enrollment in traditional courses such as algebra, geometry, history, Latin, French, and German had increased substantially. Among academic subjects, only physics and chemistry enrollment declined. Once progressive public school officials began to flex their administrative muscles, however, the challenging academic course became an endangered species. Between 1910 and 1949, the percentage of secondary-school students taking algebra was cut in half, from 56.9 percent to 26.8 percent. Enrollment in the living foreign languages went from 34.3 percent to only 13.7 percent of the student body. U.S. and English history were studied by more than half of all students in 1910, but by fewer than a quarter in 1949.[22]

Of course, the activities of progressive educators may not have been the only cause of the loss of emphasis on academic subjects. The proportion of high-school-aged children enrolled in school was five times higher in 1949 than it had been in 1910, and it is at least possible that some of these children were unable to cope with the difficult courses taken by the smaller and possibly more select group that had preceded them. But this explanation is called into question by the fact that the rapid growth in high-school attendance had begun long before the decline in academic subjects. Between 1890 and 1910—a period during which participation in challenging academic courses *increased*—the percentage of high-school-aged children enrolled in school tripled.[23]

The progressive war on traditional subjects was not confined to highly visible efforts to eradicate them from the curriculum. As curriculum historian Herbert Kliebard explains, "even when the name of a subject like history remained intact, the subject itself frequently took on a new character" consistent with the recommendations of the NEA.

In the mid-1940s, the scions of the progressive movement threw their support behind a new curriculum titled "Life Adjustment Education." Backed by colleagues at the United States Bureau of Education and the National Association of Secondary School Principals, advocates of the new plan of studies announced that children's lives should be adjusted to the putative needs of society. These needs, as it turned out, bore a distinct resemblance to those espoused in the NEA's 1918 "Cardinal Principles" report. The Life Adjustment curriculum stipulated that students be taught:

> Tools of communication; Strong body, sound attitude toward it; Satisfactory Social Relationships; Competence in and appreciation of improved family living; Knowledge of, practice in, and zeal for democratic processes; Sensitiveness to importance of group action; Effectiveness as consumers; Adjustment to occupation; and Development of meaning for life.[24]

In the avant-garde schools that adopted the new curriculum, traditional subjects such as mathematics, English, and history were replaced with lessons on "Personal living, Immediate Personal-Social Relationships, Social-Civic Relationships, and Economic Relationships."[25] One seventh-grade class dedicated an entire year to the question "How Can the Family Spend Their [sic] Leisure Time?"

Supporters of the new curriculum were often loath to exempt students from their vision of an ideal education, and families seeking a solid grounding in the academic subjects were sometimes penalized. In one school, an alternative "Scholarship Plan" was offered to those regressive parents and children who rejected Life Adjustment, but a 97 percent attendance rate was required in order for students to stay in the program. The school's prospectus was quite clear:

> The Scholarship Plan on the third cover page is a misnomer. It is better named a plan for recalcitrants. This is merely a protective device. Students and parents who have not accepted the Life Adjustment plan may graduate under the conditions of our old plan with the more stringent requirements to offset failure to do the work, develop the habits, and improve the attitudes inherent in the present [Life Adjustment] program. Our reasoning is as follows: If students and their parents believe that the only value of the high-school is in learning subject matter then the school will insist that they do more than a minimum standard. Our counseling is definitely pointed to the Life Adjustment method of graduation for all students.[26]

The extremes to which educators sometimes carried their ideas were truly incredible. In Ann Arbor, Michigan, the district administration banished textbooks from the schools and baldly informed teachers that they "were free to do what they wanted in the classroom, but they were not free to use a textbook."[27] Students attending one middle school in Tulsa, Oklahoma found all their traditional courses crammed into a single period, leaving them free to "spend the rest of the day in shop, playground, or laboratory."[28]

What did parents have to say about the new educational journey upon which progressive educators were taking their children? In Minneapolis, they had a great deal to say. Coming together to form the Parents' Council, they requested that the district make its progressive "Common Learnings" program optional, and reintroduce academic subjects. Resistant at first, school officials finally gave in to parents' demands, criticizing them nonetheless as "enemies of the public schools."[29]

The events in Minnesota foreshadowed a growing rebellion against progressivism. From 1949 through the early fifties, a deluge of books and articles condemning public schools flooded the educational landscape. With titles such as *And Madly Teach, Quackery in the Public Schools,* and *Educational Wastelands,* they were anything but equivocal. Progressive educators were denounced as charlatans who had utterly abandoned their responsibility for imparting knowledge and skills, contenting themselves with being "wet nurses, instructors in sex education, medical advisors, consultants to the lovelorn, umpires in the battle of the vertical versus the horizontal stroke in tooth-brushing, and professors of motor-vehicle operation."[30]

Far from addressing the concerns of these critics, the NEA's Defense Commission chose simply to vilify them as:

> Confirmed subversives who want to destroy free public education in order to undermine our democratic way of life; disgruntled teachers who have not kept abreast of the latest educational methods and attempt to justify their own shortcomings; unreasonable parents who try to blame all of their children's shortcomings on the schools; racketeers who capitalize on the nation's legitimate concern over the education of our children and milk unsuspecting citizens for their own gain.[31]

As the NEA's position statement implied, there were still many teachers who remained skeptical of progressive methods. It is difficult to say precisely what percentage of teachers had truly embraced progressivism by the mid-1950s, but it seems likely that they comprised a sizable minority of the educational workforce.

Distaste for progressivism among some segments of the public hit a new high in 1957, when the Soviet Union launched Sputnik I, the first artificial satellite. More than ever, Life Adjustment and similar programs were seen as an intellectual gutting of the school curriculum, and even a threat to national security. The USSR had won the first battle in the space race, so the thinking went, and an immediate improvement in mathematics and science teaching was necessary to prevent the U.S. from falling hopelessly behind. This seemed to be the last nail in the coffin of the progressive education movement. The Progressive Education Association had disbanded in 1955, and its journal, *Progressive Education,* had already gone out of print. The people had spoken, and what they wanted was a return to the teaching of detailed knowledge and skills.

Given the resistance that Life Adjustment education had encountered from parents for more than a decade, and those same parents' calls for strong academic training for their children, it would not be unreasonable to expect that the move away from progressive education would have been a boon to local control of the schools. It wasn't. Instead, power over the curriculum shifted from school officials and teachers' organizations to leaders in the universities. Thanks to the National Defense Education Act of 1958, cartloads of federal tax dollars were made available to government-appointed scholars, with the express intention of having them design new physical science, social science, and mathematics curricula and retrain teachers.

The impact of federally promoted school reform was slight. Academic subjects received renewed attention for a few years and some science materials designed at federal expense eventually made it into the schools, but teachers were slow to adopt the methodological recommendations of the government-sponsored curriculum reformers. At the same time, the very purpose for which government grants had been awarded—the reintroduction of rigorous, direct academic instruction—was undermined from the inside. Many of the scientists chosen to draft new curricula were partial to the progressive idea that students were best left to discover knowledge for themselves, at their leisure, rather than being explicitly taught by the teacher. One such scientist, David Hawkins, freely acknowledged his affinity for progressive educational ideas, making a pilgrimage to England to observe progressive schools in action. Rather than cut off funding on the grounds that Hawkins's program ran counter to the purpose of the National Defense Education Act, government officials saw fit to award his organization an additional grant in the mid-sixties.[32]

Also traveling to England in the mid-sixties in search of progressive insights was Lillian Weber, of the City College of New York's department of education. Having been delighted by the informal and relatively unstructured classrooms she saw, she returned to New York to apply those same techniques in a school in Harlem. Soon, teachers from around the state began asking for the lively and seemingly carefree approach to education that had come to be known as "open schooling." By 1970, the open schooling movement had gathered enough momentum for the State Department of Education to call a meeting embracing it. A few hundred teachers were expected to attend the December 7 gathering. Two thousand showed up. Hosting progressivism's return from the pedagogical grave was Ewald Nyquist, New York state commissioner of education. Addressing the crowd assembled in Albany that day, and in a later written report, Nyquist described open schooling in glowing terms:

> This kind of education refers to an approach to teaching that discards the familiar elementary classroom setup and the traditional stylized roles of teacher and pupils for a much freer, more informal, highly individualized, child-centered learning experience. . . .
>
> There is little uniformity in an open education classroom. Children move about freely, talk with each other, make choices, work alone or in small groups, and peruse materials relevant to them. There is no sign of mere busywork, meaningless drill, or conformist activities. . . .
>
> Students' feelings, interests, and needs are given priority over lesson plans, organizational patterns, rigid time schedules, and no-option structures. It must be noted that part of feeling good about oneself is being able to do, to exercise control over your own life.[33]

Open education was brought before a still wider audience by journalist Charles Silberman in his 1970 book *Crisis in the Classroom: The Remaking of American Education.* Silberman, like some of the British advocates of open classrooms who inspired him, believed that the abolition of formal instruction could coexist with, even advance, student achievement in reading, writing, mathematics, and the sciences. Within a few years his hopes were dashed. Other popularizers of the method were less interested in traditional subjects, and simply concentrated on convincing the public that open classrooms were good and that structured, teacher-led instruction was bad.

While laboratory and classroom research on the subject were all but nonexistent, there was an ample supply of exaggeration and outright fancy. Beatrice and Ronald Gross, for example, took the developmental theories of Swiss psychologist Jean Piaget and the British infant-school reformers and misrepresented them with abandon. The Grosses claimed, for example, that it was clear from Piaget's findings that "traditional teaching techniques are ineffectual."[34]

Few American teachers were sufficiently familiar with Piaget's work to realize that his studies shed no light on the relative effectiveness of different classroom teaching methods.[35] They had heard what they wanted to hear, and that was enough. Open schools sprouted up all over the country during the early seventies because teachers wanted to believe that this agreeable alternative to traditional instruction could work on a broad scale. At John Adams High School in Portland, Oregon, the staff "took it as a matter of faith that all students learn best in a free, unstructured setting where comparative evaluation and other extrinsic pressures are kept to a minimum."[36] They would soon discover the price of their wistful credulity.

For a few very intelligent and self-motivated students, those who no doubt would have continued their education whether or not they were in school, the vast amounts of unscheduled time and the virtual absence of curriculum requirements allowed rapid progress. For the rest of the student body, who still needed structure and guidance, the system was a failure. Average students felt lost and frustrated, while "alienated students . . . cut classes, roamed the halls," and were left totally unprepared for the world of work.[37] Parents were infuriated by what they saw as the abandonment of their children, forming an action committee called Citizens for a Better Adams. In the words of one parent: "Adams High does not teach respect for authority, discipline, basic scholarship, or orderly use of time. The school teaches gross egotism, extreme self-centeredness, myopic self-delusion, and general anarchy."[38]

Elsewhere, in a small inner-city school, open educator Roland Barth was shocked to discover that "the children did not welcome the opportunity to explore freely and make their own decisions; instead, they became disruptive and 'ganged up by tens and twenties outside the bathrooms and at the water fountains.'" According to Barth, the students were "merciless in their demands for teacher-imposed order." Many parents, particularly those of a conservative or traditional bent, were opposed to the reforms, complaining "about the permissiveness of the teachers and the noisiness of the classrooms."[39] By 1974, rumors of the death of open schools began to circulate, and no one contended that they were exaggerated.

Right around the time that open schools were petering out, one of the biggest news stories in twentieth-century American education grabbed the headlines: SAT scores were falling, and had been for over a decade. Though taken by only about a third of high-school seniors, the Scholastic Aptitude Test was widely seen as an indicator of overall school performance, and the indication wasn't good. The cries for a return to rigorous academic instruction that had first appeared during the 1950s returned with a vengeance, and the Back to Basics movement was born.

State departments of education around the country reacted to public outcries with a pair of ill-fated reforms. The first, minimum competency testing, aimed to ensure that all students mastered certain basic skills. As it turned out, however, the emphasis of the tests was much more on "minimum" than on "competency," and they failed to noticeably improve student achievement. The second approach was to require that students take a specific set of courses in order to graduate, equipping them, so it was supposed, with the necessary grounding in a common core of knowledge. This reform was equally ineffectual, due to the variation in what was actually taught under a given course title. While one "Junior English" classroom studied and learned from challenging works of literature, another—often in the same school—whiled away its time reading Superman and Batman comics.[40]

For a time, the Rube Goldberg-like machinations of state school bureaucracies diffused public criticism as parents waited to see how the reforms would play out. But as the hollowness of minimum competency testing and new graduation requirements became widely known, educators once again found themselves in a difficult situation. Elected state representatives, pundits, and much of the citizenry were calling ever more loudly for evidence of real accomplishment among high-school students, while tests such as the National Assessment of Educational Progress showed that students were performing well below expectations for their grade level. It was in this context that Outcomes Based Education, or OBE, was born.

In essence, educators accepted the popular idea of setting goals against which student performance could be measured, but chose to use vague criteria reminiscent of Life Adjustment education rather than the detailed academic goals that most critics had envisaged. Instead of focusing on requirements that students demonstrate a knowledge of key events in history, solve problems in algebra and physics, and write essays analyzing works of literature or defending positions on some topic of interest, the OBE movement became more and more steeped in children's attitudes, emotions, and social views. Typical "outcomes" asked the student to "function as a responsible family member," "maintain physical, emotional and social well-being," "demonstrate positive strategies for achieving and *maintaining mental and emotional wellness,*" or "demonstrate *positive* growth in *self-concept*" (emphases in the original).[41]

This is not to say that academic outcomes were avoided entirely, but they were generally couched in such broad terms as to make reasoned evaluation impossible. So, rather than expect a student to offer an intelligent interpretation of a challenging text, supporting her conclusions with references and plausible arguments, OBE asked her to "construct meaning from a variety of print materials for a variety of purposes through reading."[42] Even the most precise of all fields, mathematics, was not proof against the encroaching fog of OBE. The preschooler happily counting his toy blocks might just as easily have satisfied the requirement to "demonstrate understanding of concepts related to mathematical procedures"[43] as the high-school senior solving quadratic equations.

OBE's honeymoon was brief. Once parents realized that the latest education fad was more concerned with attitudes than with academic achievement, many of them fought it tooth and nail. Seven California school boards "voted against administering the state's new OBE-influenced assessment system"[44] for that very reason. All across Pennsylvania, parent groups expressed their opposition to an OBE proposal. Voicing some of those parents' concerns, Peg Luksik (a onetime candidate for the Republican gubernatorial nomination) asked state officials: "How do you measure someone's self-worth? How much is enough?"[45] In Virginia and Ohio, the public outcry was so fierce that both state governments withdrew their plans to introduce OBE into their schools.[46]

Though much of the opposition to OBE was led by religious and conservative groups such as the Eagle Forum, there were middle-of-the-road and left-leaning critics as well. Albert Shanker, head of the American Federation of Teachers, objected to "OBE's vaguely worded outcomes," claiming that they "encourage business as usual . . . and do nothing to raise student achievement."[47] Many parents critical of OBE saw the identification of their position with the "religious right" as a means of dismissing them out of hand. "I am not the radical right," said Linda McKeen, cofounder of the Parent Education Network, "and I do not want to be linked to [it]. . . . [P]eople use that to immobilize the opposition." Both Democratic Governor Roy Romer of Colorado and Democratic Congressman Peter Daly of Pennsylvania felt that their constituents were sufficiently opposed to OBE to warrant making public statements against it.[48]

Despite the absence of any public demand for OBE-style reforms, and despite the concerted opposition of many parents, OBE initiatives were introduced during the late 1980s and early 1990s in Alabama, Connecticut, Kentucky, Minnesota, North Carolina, Oklahoma, Pennsylvania, Virginia, and Washington, among other states. The actual outcomes of these cases have varied considerably. According to its critics, OBE seemed on its way out of Virginia in the mid-1990s, while it was believed to have set down roots in Oklahoma.[49] In many states and districts the battle continues, though the term OBE has generally been dropped by its advocates due to the negative associations it has developed.

Home-Schoolers Under Siege

The imposition of OBE against the will of many parents continues a long tradition of disregard for the family by influential figures in public education. In the scheme of things, however, it is a distinctly mild transgression. A much more brutal and authoritarian side of the government school system can be seen in its dealings with home-schoolers.

In most states, mountains of paperwork must be completed and regulations followed by anyone attempting to offer an education outside the public school system, whether in a private school or in the home. In the fall of 1982, three families decided to pull their children out of the New Plymouth, Idaho public schools in order to teach them at home, on the grounds that the government schools were undermining their children's religious faith. Local school district officials balked and took the families to court, arguing that they were not following all of the state's educational requirements. Siding with the district, the judge ordered the children returned to public schools, calling for the parents to be jailed if they failed to comply.[50]

After acquiescing in 1982, the three families decided to home-school once again in 1984, and this time refused to follow a court order to return their children to public schools. The parents were thrown behind bars and the children placed in foster care. Once again the children were returned to public schools as the families were released and attempted to satisfy the state's home-school requirements. In addition to bringing their homes into line with public building codes, the families would have been required to provide an hourly instruction schedule and a host of other details. Since they were unable to fulfill all the state's requirements, but unwilling to return their children to public schools, the court ordered that their children be placed indefinitely in foster homes. On January 10, 1985, armed sheriff's deputies "seized four boys and two girls, ages 7 to 15. Kicking and screaming, . . . the children were stuffed into cars and driven off. . . . The parents' visiting rights were limited to two hours each Sunday."[51] Similar cases in which families have been torn apart, children sent to foster homes, or parents imprisoned occurred during the 1970s and 1980s in Iowa, Michigan, Massachusetts, Missouri, and Rhode Island.[52]

The United States has a long and distinguished history of home-schooling. Many of its founders, presidents, industrialists, and inventors received most of their elementary education at home. The list includes such figures as Jefferson, Franklin, Adams, Madison, Washington, both Roosevelts, Wilson, Edison, and

Carnegie, among others. Despite this fact, the practice was rarely protected by law until quite recently. According to a popular legal reference on education published in 1984:

> Home instruction is not, generally, considered to fulfill the requirements of compulsory school attendance. Statutes which provide for private school instruction as fulfillment of compulsory attendance requirements . . . are not to be construed as permitting home instruction. Authority to exempt home instruction from compulsory attendance laws must be permitted by express statutory provision.[53]

In 1980, only three states had such statutory provisions expressly permitting home-schooling.[54] Not only has the right of parents to educate their own children not generally been protected by law, it has been actively assailed by virtually every union and professional association related to public schooling. In its 1991–92 resolutions, the National Education Association declared that home-schoolers should be placed tightly under the thumb of the public schools:

> If parental preference home schooling occurs . . . [i]nstruction should be by persons who are licensed by the appropriate state education licensure agency, and a curriculum approved by the state department of education should be used.[55]

Given the demonstrated hollowness of state teacher certification, and the poor quality of many of the methods and materials used by public schools (see Chapter 5), the NEA's stance seems difficult to justify, and would put an almost insurmountable burden on most home-schoolers. This, however, is only the union's official stance. Its members sometimes go further. According to Annette Cootes of the NEA-affiliated Texas State Teachers Association: "My own personal opinion is that home schooling is a form of child abuse because you are isolating children from human interaction. I think home schoolers are doing a great discredit [sic] to their children." The National Association of Elementary School Principals seems to agree, promoting laws that "enforce compulsory school attendance and prohibit at-home schooling as a substitute for compulsory school attendance."[56]

Even when parents are extraordinarily well-qualified for the task of teaching their children, public school officials have often fought vehemently to prevent them from doing so. Having already successfully taught one of their children at home, Massachusetts residents Susan and Peter Perchemlides decided to prepare a home-school curriculum for their eight-year-old son Richard in 1977. Though both parents were highly educated, and despite the fact that Richard was learning "music, art, math, cooking, earth sciences, gardening, ecology, astronomy, reading, writing, spelling, and yoga,"[57] local school officials filed complaints against the child's parents in the district court of Hampshire

County. An entire chapter in Stephen Arons's book *Compelling Belief* is dedicated to the conflict that ensued.

The Perchemlides' detailed and comprehensive study plan was assessed by an expert in private and public school instruction and found to be "the equivalent of a first-rate private academy both in its tutorial system and in . . . the curriculum." Disregarding this judgment, the local superintendent of the public schools vetoed the parents' plan and insisted Richard attend a public school. After a Kafka-esque nightmare in which Peter and Susan were ordered to comply with a set of rules that the school district refused to make explicit, their case was heard in the Hampshire County Superior Court. The judge's ruling was similar in many ways to the armistice between North and South Korea. The parties were still technically at war, but hostilities were halted for the time being. While the Perchemlides family was allowed to resume its home-schooling program, the right of public school authorities to supervise and approve the program was also upheld. The parents were thus forced to continually glance Northward toward the office of the superintendent, wondering when he would next choose to violate the peace.[58]

Fortunately for home-schoolers, times are changing. Between 1982 and 1992, thirty-two states changed their compulsory attendance laws, and four state boards of education "amended their regulations to specifically allow for home schooling,"[59] under certain conditions. States without explicit legislation concerning home-schooling now generally allow home-schoolers to operate as private schools, with some added stipulations. The conditions imposed by the states vary, but typically require home-schooled students to be tested on a periodic basis and to achieve results which are better than those of a specified percentage (usually 15 to 40 percent) of the public school population. Christopher Klicka, Senior Counsel of the Home School Legal Defense Association, reports that legislative amendments have reduced the number of conflicts between home-schoolers and their local public school districts, but have not eliminated them. Some districts and boards of education continue to overstep the laws of their states, adding restrictions on home-schooling and thereby precipitating court cases. In 1991, a state appellate court struck down the Michigan Department of Education's "Home School Compliance Procedures" on the grounds that they illegally enforced requirements which did not exist in the state's law.[60]

Clearly, some public school officials are not overly fond of those who seek to escape the public schools. A few even appear dead set against any action that might loosen their grip on the bodies and minds of their students—however commendable the action might be. When Pittsburgh resident Charles Hayden discovered in 1995 that his seventh-grade son Chris was at risk of flunking, he decided to pull him out of his last period study hall and tutor him at home. After spending at least two hours a day for eleven weeks with his father, Chris managed to bring his overall average up to 85.8 percent. Just the sort of story, you might imagine, that would warm the hearts of teachers and administrators who lament the lack of parental participation in education. What really happened is that officials in the Hempfield Area School District decided to take Hayden to court. He was accused of illegally withdrawing his son from school thirty-four times for their home tutoring sessions. Somehow, District Superintendent C. Richard Nichols believed that Hayden's extraordinarily successful tutoring was "similar to a student saying 'Home room is not real [sic] valuable, so I'll just sleep in.' "[61] The possibility that Hayden had a right to direct his son's education as he saw fit does not appear to have occurred to Superintendent Nichols.

Educational Dictators, Part II: The Right

> We are opposed to control of American public affairs by aliens or by so-called Americans whose primary allegiance is to some foreign power. . . . The allegiance of Catholics is to a foreign power, the pope, [and] their clannish attempts to extend the temporal power of the pope over the offices of this country is opposed to the best interests of America. . . . No child should be permitted to be educated in the primary grades in any private school. . . . We are just as much opposed to private schools of the so-called "select" kind as we are to denominational private schools.[62]

So declared Fred L. Gifford, Exalted Cyclops of the Oregon Ku Klux Klan, in March 1922. Not an unusual statement for a clan rally, you might think, but no doubt well outside the mainstream of Oregon public opinion. In fact, Gifford's comment was made to a reporter for the *Oregon Voter* newspaper, shortly before the Oregon Compulsory Education Bill was to appear on the ballot of that state. The OCEB, supported most vocally by the Ku Klux Klan and the Oregon Scottish Rite Masons, was a measure designed to ban private schooling. It stated that the parents or guardians of children between the ages of eight and sixteen must send them to public schools or be guilty of a misdemeanor. There was no question as to the motivation for this bill. In Klan pamphlets and speeches supporting the OCEB, Catholics were demonized and their schools condemned as subversive of traditional American values. George Estes, a prominent Klansman, wrote:

> Secretly and insidiously Rome controls the politics, the press, legislation, administration of law courts, and does not pay a cent to our civil government. It takes our property, rules us and spits in our faces; it licks the syrup off our bread and calls us nigger.[63]

Catholics, foreign language speakers, and immigrants were widely viewed as corrupting influences on the purity of America's culture and institutions, allegedly bearing foreign allegiances and holding socialist political and economic ideals. The obvious solution to this perceived problem was to impose a homogenizing, Americanizing, government-approved education on all residents of the state. Though the expression of these views was always most pointed when coming directly from KKK spokesmen, the views were clearly shared, in essence, by a majority of Oregonians. Not only was the OCEB put on the ballot through a grassroots initiative signature drive, but it received a majority of the votes cast and was passed into law. The same xenophobic thinking that had helped to bring government schooling into existence in the United States led Oregon voters to make it compulsory.

On the heels of the law's passage, a suit was filed by a Catholic school and a private military academy, arguing that the law was unconstitutional. After a district court ruling in favor of the private schools, the state appealed the case to the U.S. Supreme Court. Representatives for the state argued that it was the government's duty to ensure a properly trained and civic-minded population, to "safeguard its citizens from the 'moral pestilence of paupers, vagabonds, [and] convicts,'" and to "prevent the ignorant from being seduced by 'certain economic doctrines entirely destructive of the fundamentals of our government,' as advocated by 'bolshevists, syndicalists and communists.'"[64] These arguments were apparently not persuasive enough, and the Supreme Court eventually struck down Oregon's compulsory public schooling law in June 1925.

Evolution and Creation in the Schools

Nineteen twenty-five was a busy year for education activists. On March 13, Tennessee legislators decided that it was about time they clamped down on the ostensibly ungodly theory of evolution. The product of their efforts was a simple, concise bill that read as follows:

> Section 1. Be it enacted by the General Assembly of the State of Tennessee, That it shall be unlawful for any teacher in any of the universities, normals [teachers' colleges], and all other public schools of the state, to teach any theory that denies the story of the divine creation of man as taught in the Bible, and to teach instead that man has descended from a lower order of animals.

> Section 2. Be it further enacted, That any teacher found guilty of the violation of this act, shall be guilty of a misdemeanor and upon conviction, shall be fined not less than one hundred dollars ($100.00), nor more than five hundred dollars ($500.00) for each offense.[65]

Any suspicion that this bill was the work of a small group of radicals is easily dispelled. When asked to explain his campaign stance on evolution, representative John Washington Butler—the bill's author—replied: "I put in my circ'lars that I believed in the literal Bible, and that I was opposed to the teaching of evolution in the schools."[66] Butler's position on the issue helped him to defeat his more liberal opponent by a margin of ten to one. When introduced in the Tennessee legislature his bill evoked little discussion, passing in the House by a margin of seventy-one to five, and in the Senate by twenty-four to six.

The events that followed the bill's passage are well known, and have even been dramatized (and fictionalized) in the film *Inherit the Wind*. A young biology teacher by the name of John Scopes agreed to act as a test case for a constitutional challenge to the law by the American Civil Liberties Union. After teaching a class on evolution, Scopes was arrested and brought to trial. Ridiculed by journalists from the major northern and eastern papers, Tennessee became the butt of frequent jokes, and the town of Dayton, which was home to the trial, took on a carnival atmosphere as reporters and hucksters crowded the streets around the courthouse. According to a contemporary account, 165,000 words per day, on average, were sent out from the Dayton telegraph office to newspapers around the country.[67] Expressing a reaction typical of many Tennessee residents of the time, a letter to the *Knoxville News* declared:

> I notice you are trying to give our governor a black eye for signing the anti-evolution bill. Any thoughtful man should be against this awful theory of evolution. It should be legislated, routed, run and kicked out of existence back to its place of origin which is in hell, because its teachings are against the word of God.[68]

Though Clarence Darrow and Scopes's other attorneys had assembled a long list of leading scientists to explain the evidence supporting evolution, the prosecution argued that their testimony was irrelevant to the case at hand, which was simply to decide whether or not the existing law had been broken. Judge Raulston, himself a fundamentalist evangelist, agreed, allowing the scientists only to submit written depositions which were not made available to the jury. Eleven days after the trial began, Scopes was found guilty and fined $100.[69] The case was appealed to the Supreme Court of Tennessee, and the law's constitutionality was upheld in 1927. The teaching of evolution was illegal in Tennessee and would remain so for almost half a century. For reasons which are not entirely clear, the case was never appealed to the U.S. Supreme Court.

Thirty-six other states brought anti-evolution bills before their legislatures during the 1920s, with Arkansas, Mississippi, and Oklahoma joining Tennessee in passing them into law.[70] Though evolution was legally banned from the public schools in only a handful of states, public sentiment against it was far more widespread—and the publishing industry knew it. In order to make their products more palatable to biblical literalists on school boards and textbook selection committees around the country, publishers took hatchets to their science texts. School biology books published from the late 1920s onward ignored the theory of evolution, with later editions excising the words "evolution" and "Darwin" from their indices. More than thirty years after the Scopes case, public school science texts continued to avoid the topic of evolution.[71]

The battle over evolution finally took a sharp turn in 1965, when Arkansas's anti-evolution law was challenged by a tenth-grade biology teacher named Susan Epperson. In that year, Epperson's County School Board selected a textbook setting out the evolution of man from earlier apelike species. Since the state's 1928 statute forbidding the teaching of evolution was still on the books, Epperson would have been subject to dismissal for using it in her class. Three years after her initial court challenge was brought, it was heard by the U.S. Supreme Court. In their ruling, the justices declared:

> The law must be stricken because of its conflict with the constitutional prohibition of state laws respecting an establishment of religion or prohibiting the free exercise thereof. The overriding fact is that Arkansas' law selects from the body of knowledge a particular segment which it proscribes for the sole reason that it is deemed to conflict with a particular religious doctrine; that is, with a particular interpretation of the Book of Genesis by a particular religious group.[72]

Darwin was legally back in the classroom, but would he have to learn to share the limelight?

Given this ruling against the outright prohibition of evolution for religious reasons, evangelical Christians changed their tactics. If evolution was going to be taught, they reasoned, then the biblical creation story should be taught alongside it. In order to make this position as defensible as possible, its religious basis had to be minimized. So, with a stroke of the pen, the Genesis account of human origins went from being religious doctrine to "creation science." The pen, in this instance, was wielded by an attorney at the California-based Institute for Creation Research. Dubbed the "Balanced Treatment for Creation-Science and Evolution-Science Act," the ICR's model bill was promoted in state legislatures across the country, finding a receptive audience in both Louisiana and Arkansas.[73]

In 1981, an almost identical copy of ICR's model bill was presented before the lawmakers of Arkansas. After five minutes of debate in the Senate and no hearings of any kind, the measure was passed. According to Marcel La Follette, a researcher in the Science, Technology, and Society program at Massachusetts Institute of Technology, Governor White admitted signing the bill without reading it.[74] In the inevitable legal challenge that ensued, the state argued in a federal district court that "[creation science], while perhaps controversial, is well supported by competent scientific evidence."[75] Had the defense been able to prove this claim to the court's satisfaction, their prospects would have been reasonably good. That, however, was not the case.

Explicitly included in the bill's definition of "creation science" were the belief in a "sudden creation of the universe, energy, and life from nothing" and the belief in "the occurrence of a worldwide flood." In his written opinion, Judge Overton observed: "Among the many creation epics in human history, the account of sudden creation from nothing . . . and subsequent destruction of the world by flood is unique to Genesis." Strictly speaking, this statement is inaccurate. It is a matter of historical record that the ancient Sumerians, who lived in flood-prone southern Mesopotamia, were the originators of the creation and flood story at least as early as four or five thousand B.C., complete with "Shamash-napishtim" (who became known as "Noah" in the Judeo-Christian adaptation of the story), an ark, a "reconnoitering dove," and an eventual mountain roost for the ark.[76] Still, Judge Overton showed that leading proponents of "scientific creationism" openly believed that the sudden creation described in the bill was performed by God, and that the beliefs described as "creation science" do not satisfy any of the fundamental characteristics of science, such as empiricism, testability, and falsifiability. It was thus demonstrated that creationism was a religious belief rather than a scientific theory.[77]

After Overton struck down Arkansas's "Balanced Treatment" law, the state was entreated by ICR and the Moral Majority of Arkansas not to appeal the case, since a similar and potentially more legally defensible law had been passed in Louisiana. The state assented and the battle over evolution moved to a new address. Louisiana lost a summary judgment, an appeal, and finally a U.S. Supreme Court case based on its "Balanced Treatment" law. The nation's highest court ruled in *Edwards v. Aguillard* that "[t]he Louisiana Creationism Act advances a religious doctrine," and hence "violates the Establishment Clause of the First Amendment."[78] This 1987 decision did not put an end to evangelical Christian opposition to the teaching of evolution in the public schools.

In early March 1996, a bill prohibiting the teaching of evolution as fact was debated and approved by both House and Senate education committees of Tennessee. Teachers violating the law were to be automatically dismissed according to the original wording of the bill, but it was later changed to read "may be dismissed." One proposed amendment to the bill would have reintroduced creationism into the classroom, along the lines of the "Balanced Treatment" laws previously struck down by the courts. As a protest against the entire undertaking, the Democratic chairman of the Senate education committee "offered an amendment that would let educators be fired for teaching that the planets revolve around the sun."[79] After the bill was bounced back and forth between committees and the full legislatures, support for it began to wane—apparently on financial grounds. The $2,000,000 price tag of writing new biology textbooks that would adhere to the bill's various provisions was sufficiently distasteful, according to an *Education Week* reporter, to sink the legislation.[80]

Learning to Burn: Censorship in the Classroom

Though legislative attempts to keep ideas out of public school classrooms on religious grounds were initially successful, their effectiveness has been in decline for decades. It was only a matter of time, however, before evangelical Christians sought a new means of bringing public schools into line with their deeply held beliefs. Abandoning their efforts to realign the public school curriculum in its entirety, many conservative Christians began taking issue with individual books, courses, and even teachers they found to be offensive.

This new form of evangelical public-school activism made one of its first appearances in the town of Warsaw, Indiana. The year was 1977, and the spark that set off a chain reaction of animosity throughout the entire community was a little book titled *Values Clarification*. Used as the primary textbook in the course "Values for Everyone," and recommended as a supplementary book for teachers of various subjects, *Values Clarification* begins by dismissing the approach to teaching values practiced by many evangelical parents. In their introduction, the authors describe "moralizing," or the direct "inculcation of the adults' values upon the young," as "increasingly less effective"; they express the belief that it "frequently influences only people's words and little else in their lives"; and they argue that it leaves children unprepared to "make their own responsible choices."[81] Some Warsaw residents agreed with these views, while numerous others did not. When the book's discussions of a range of subjects objectionable to evangelical parents (including premarital sex, the question of whether sexual technique should be taught in schools, homosexuality, and abortion)[82] were thrown into the mixture, an explosive reaction was inevitable.

In fairly rapid succession, both the book and the course were banned by the mostly conservative Christian school board, a group of senior citizens doused forty copies with gasoline and set them ablaze in a parking lot, and a half-dozen other courses were eliminated from the curriculum, including "Gothic Literature," "Science-Fiction," and "Black Literature."[83] The board then passed a resolution dictating that "books and materials that could be construed as objectionable in this community shall not be used."[84]

In practice, one of the "materials" deemed objectionable was a young teacher by the name of Teresa Burnau. After reviewing the texts she had chosen for her course on "Women in Literature," Burnau's principal ordered her not to use several of them. The banned books, which included Sylvia Plath's *The Bell Jar* and Ira Levin's *The Stepford Wives,* contained either sexual references, liberated female characters, or a combination of both which proved objectionable to some "patrons of the school." Despite the fact that Burnau offered to provide alternative readings for students who requested them, she was ordered to drop the books. Even more telling is the fact that Burnau's class, like the "Values for Everyone" course mentioned above, was an elective—one curriculum option among many. Though she eventually complied with the principal's orders, Burnau was fired for her "inability to handle professional direction in a positive manner."[85] Ten other teachers were also asked to resign, two of whom refused and were fired along with Burnau.

Other cases have been more extreme. In Charleston, West Virginia, a 1974 battle over school books precipitated strikes at the local coal mines, a strike by parents in which eight thousand students were kept home, angry public confrontations, several shootings, severe beatings, sniper fire on a school bus full of children, and the dynamiting of at least one school building. The atmosphere was often vicious, the community fiercely divided. One Reverend Charles Quigley "asked for prayers for the death of three school board members who supported the adoption of the textbooks," saying: "I am asking Christian people to pray that God will kill the giants that have mocked and made fun of dumb fundamentalists." This was the result of one school district's use of textbooks deemed by a sizable portion of the local population to be "disrespectful to authority and religion, pornographic, [and] unpatriotic" and to contain passages painting "Christianity in a bad or hypocritical light."[86]

According to legal scholar Stephen Arons, "up to 30 percent of the nation's school districts have experienced book and curriculum conflicts [during the early 1980s], and these battles are becoming more widespread." In 1983, Arons's list of book burnings and bannings was already long:

> Solzhenitsyn is banned in Maine as well as Moscow; Malamud is viewed as anti-Semitic in Levittown, New York, and is trashed along with Langston Hughes who is alleged by white school board members to be "anti-Negro"; Maurice Sendak's four-year-old character Mickey must wear Magic Marker shorts in *In the Night Kitchen* lest the kindergartners of Springfield, Missouri, be corrupted. The texts of Oregon must not cast aspersions on the Founding Fathers, and those of Louisiana must teach the benefits of free-enterprise economics. . . .[87]

According to the American Library Association, book and curriculum challenges have "skyrocketed since 1980." In her book *What Johnny Shouldn't Read,* Joan Delfattore describes how the superintendent of schools for Bay County, California banned sixty-four classic books in 1987. The books in question were by such authors as Sophocles, Chaucer, Shakespeare, Benjamin Franklin, Mark Twain, Charles Dickens, Emily Brontë, William Faulkner, F. Scott Fitzgerald, and Ernest Hemingway.[88] The *Newsletter on Intellectual Free-*

dom reports that the following were just a few of the books challenged or banned from various public school libraries or curricula during the twelve-month period ending in March 1997 (reasons for the bannings are given in parentheses):

- *I Know Why the Caged Bird Sings*, Maya Angelou. (Too sexually explicit; doesn't represent traditional values.)
- *The Scarlet Letter*, Nathaniel Hawthorne. (Conflicts with values of the community.)
- *To Kill a Mockingbird*, Harper Lee. (Conflicts with values of the community.)
- *Moby Dick*, Herman Melville. (Conflicts with values of the community.)
- *Beloved*, Toni Morrison. (Too violent.)
- *Catcher in the Rye*, J. D. Salinger. (Use of profanity.)
- *Twelfth Night*, William Shakespeare. (Encourages homosexuality.)
- *A Light in the Attic*, Shel Silverstein. (Too dreary and negative.)
- *Of Mice and Men*, John Steinbeck. (Use of profanity.)
- *The Joy Luck Club*, Amy Tan. (Conflicts with values of the community.)[89]

The list goes on (and on). It is understandable that parents wish to protect their children from works they consider morally objectionable, but banning books from the public schools creates a problem of its own. Few communities, after all, are homogeneous in their values. Many books regarded as classics by one segment of the population are deemed trash by another; many ideas that are subject to debate among some Americans are sacrosanct to others. Books and ideas viewed as harmful by a majority of voters in a given school district are very often banned to the dismay of a minority of parents who wish their children could study them.

The reason that activist parents—through their representatives on school boards—have been able to eliminate such a large and varied list of books from their public schools is because the courts have upheld their right to do so. Though particular cases on the issue have gone one way or the other, the thrust of the Supreme Court's rulings has been that school boards have considerable authority to make decisions regarding curricula and textbooks, so long as they do not promote a specific ideology or become entangled in clearly religious matters in doing so.

In the 1982 case *Board of Education v. Pico*,[90] a group of parents objected when their predominantly conservative local board banned several books from their children's schools. Though the Supreme Court eventually ruled in favor of the parents, the divisions within the Court and the specific reasoning behind the ruling served to bolster the power of school boards to act as censors. The majority opinion stated that the school board had acted in an overtly partisan manner, and that it was this characteristic of the board's actions, not the banning of the books itself, that decided the case. The way was thus left open for other school boards to ban books so long as they avoided the appearance of partisanship or religious bias. A significant minority of the justices—four out of the nine—dissented, arguing that school boards should have no limits set on their selection or rejection of books. This was very much in keeping with the views of the board, whose legal representatives in the case had declared that "[a] principal function of all elementary and secondary education is indoctrination" and that "in secondary school a prescriptive, inculcative or indoctrinative process applies."[91]

Judge Danny Boggs put it more colloquially in his 1987 opinion in *Mozert v. Hawkins County Board of Education,*[92] concluding that "on the present state of constitutional law, the school board is indeed entitled to say 'my way or the highway.'"[93]

African-American Education: Caught in the Crossfire

It is difficult to find a group of people that has been dealt a worse hand by modern government schooling than African Americans. Sometimes as a direct result of racism, and sometimes as an unintended consequence of well-intentioned reforms, the effect of public schools on black education has frequently been disastrous.

The long years during which it was illegal to teach slaves to read created an enormous pent-up demand for education among southern blacks. There is evidence of a scattering of underground black schools in the antebellum South and a corresponding number of literate slaves, but the majority of African Americans who suffered under the "peculiar institution" were afforded no educational opportunities. When the pall of slavery was finally lifted after the Civil War, former slaves emerged with an almost universal thirst for learning. Booker T. Washington wrote:

> Few people who were not right in the midst of the scenes can form any exact idea of the intense desire which the people of my race showed for education. It was a whole race trying to go to school. Few were too young, and none too old, to make the attempt to learn. As fast as any kind of teachers could be secured, not only were day-schools filled, but night-schools as well.[94]

The truth of Washington's words is most compellingly brought home by private correspondences of the time. A great many poignant letters reveal that schooling was a priority for even the most destitute newly freed blacks. The following note—to an African-American Union soldier from his wife—is but one example:

My Dear Husband, . . . I and the children are all well—but I am in a great deal of trouble as Master John Humphries has come home from the Rebel army and taken charge of the place and says he is going to turn us all out on the Levee unless we pay him (8.00) Eight Dollars a month for house rent— Now I have no money of any account and I am not able to get enough to pay so much rent, and I want you to get a furlough as soon as you can and come home and find a place for us to live in. . . .

[Our] children are going to school, but I find it very hard to feed them all, and if you can not come I hope you will send me something to help me get along.

Come home as soon as you can, and cherish me as ever.[95]

With the help of northern philanthropists, black schools were opened even before the war was concluded, spreading across the South as city after city fell to Union forces. In Port Royal, South Carolina, thirty schools enrolling three thousand students were opened between January and December 1862, thanks to the provision of teachers by New England based Freedmen's Aid Societies.[96] A similar influx of teachers from the North occurred in most southern states.

But though the role of Yankee benefactors was important in many cases, the driving force behind the establishment and maintenance of black schools was the black community itself. In many cases, black Union soldiers were beseeched by the men and women they had only recently emancipated to help them establish schools. In Okolona, Mississippi, for example, Sergeant Eli Helen and Corporal Joseph Ingram were given leave by their commanding officer to collect funds for the creation of a school, after having been selected to do so by the city's black community.[97] Georgia's Black Educational Association was founded with the goal that "the freedmen shall establish schools in their own counties and neighborhoods, to be supported entirely by the colored people." The great majority of Georgia's black schools were financed in whole or in part by the freedmen themselves, and they owned almost half of the school buildings they used. This situation was sufficiently common for missionary William Channing Gannett to observe that most blacks showed "a natural praiseworthy pride in keeping their educational institutions in their own hands. There is jealousy of the superintendence of the white man in this matter. What they desire is assistance without control."[98]

Some white southerners, either secretly or openly glad to be rid of slavery, encouraged the spread of schools for freedmen, but their voices were drowned out by a tide of ignorance and racial hatred. According to W. E. B. DuBois, a common view in the South was that "[s]chooling ruins a nigger." The American Freedmen's Commission reported that blacks' "attempts at education provoked the most intense and bitter hostilities, as evincing a desire to render themselves equal to whites. Their churches and schoolhouses in many places were destroyed by mobs."[99] So fierce was the opposition to black education that anyone who taught the children of freedmen, regardless of race, was heaped with scorn. Though unsurprising to black teachers, this reaction often shocked and dismayed the white volunteers who had come down from points North with a sense of noble mission.

Overcoming the bitter and sometimes bloody resistance of militant racists, black schools established a foothold below the Mason-Dixon line. But there have been no easy steps in the educational ascent of black Americans, and the simple presence of schools was no guarantee that they would effectively serve the needs of freedmen and their children. Too often, former slaves were prevented from retaining control of their educational destinies by the very groups that purported to aid them.

During the late 1890s, a clearly defined consensus developed among northern school reformers dedicated to educating the southern black population. It was much the same consensus that had united landholders in Tsarist Russia, and religious educational societies in England during the first part of the nineteenth century: education for peasantry. Just as schooling had been construed by those groups as a means of preparing the poor for their preordained low position on the socioeconomic ladder, so it was for the former slaves of American plantation owners. Blacks, it was decided, were congenitally suited to menial tasks, unthinking, back-breaking labor, and conditioned obedience to their "betters"—i.e., whites. Speaking at an education convention in 1899, white would-be philanthropist William H. Baldwin summed up this position for his West Virginian audience:

> Time has proven that [the Negro] is best fitted to perform the heavy labor in the Southern States. "The Negro and the mule is the only combination, so far, to grow cotton." The South needs him; but the South needs him educated to be a suitable citizen. Properly directed he is the best possible laborer to meet the climatic conditions of the South. He will willingly fill the more menial positions, and do the heavy work, at less wages, than the American white man or any foreign race which has yet come to our shores. This will permit the southern white laborer to perform the more expert labor, and to leave the fields, the mines and the simpler trades for the Negro.[100]

As a result of this mind-set, the largest educational endowments provided by white school reformers came with strings firmly attached, and the strings pulled uniformly in the direction of unskilled labor. The most influential example of this education for peasantry was the Hampton Institute, founded in Virginia in 1868 by northerner Samuel Armstrong. Though Hampton was a teacher-training institution, its emphasis was not on pedagogy or even on children; instead, it stressed manual labor. Student teachers worked long and hard in the field, and toiled in industrial shop classes.

At first glance, and second, this seems a strange sort of preparation for future elementary school instructors, but the confusion is quickly dispelled when

Armstrong's social philosophy is taken into account. Historian James Anderson has made a strong case that Armstrong saw himself as a missionary among a people suited only to menial tasks. By ensuring that African-American schoolteachers became accustomed to manual labor—even favorable toward it—Armstrong felt that they would be more likely to steer their students in that direction. What he wanted was a perpetual stasis machine: a system of teacher training that would lock blacks into unskilled jobs indefinitely, keeping them in their "proper" place while placating southern whites.[101]

Though it took almost half a century, ex-slaves eventually brought Hampton into line with their own educational goals, pulling it into the mainstream of higher-education institutions. A similar fate awaited the Tuskegee Institute, a college modeled after Hampton and founded by one of its most famous alumni, Booker T. Washington. Despite the efforts of men like Armstrong and Washington, the great majority of African Americans expected more from their institutions of learning than the sort of manual training that could be picked up on the job. They wanted an intellectually challenging academic curriculum that would help them to move beyond the toil that had been their lot for generations.

Excellence Achieved

Without question, the greatest progress toward this end was achieved at Dunbar High School in Washington, D.C. Hardly a generation after Lincoln signed the Emancipation Proclamation, Dunbar students were ranking first on city-wide tests given at both African-American and white schools, and the majority were going on to college, unlike most of their contemporaries of either race.[102] Beginning in 1870 and carrying on into the mid-1950s, Dunbar graduated more famously successful young African Americans than any other school in the nation. Its alumni included, among many others:

> The first black general (Benjamin O. Davis), the first black federal judge (William H. Hastie), the first black Cabinet member (Robert C. Weaver), the discoverer of blood plasma (Charles Drew), and the first black Senator since Reconstruction (Edward W. Brook).[103]

How was all this accomplished? The key factors contributing to the school's achievements, according to a study by economist Thomas Sowell, were significant independence in management decisions, a student body drawn from families who had freely chosen the school, a rigorous academic curriculum, and a core of dedicated and able teachers. Though Dunbar was officially a part of the D.C. public school system, the city's white school officials seldom took an interest in the goings-on at Dunbar, leaving its principals significant discretion.

On the rare occasions when school bureaucrats did turn their attention to Dunbar, their efforts were harmful rather than helpful, generally seeking to bend the school into a vocational institution against the wishes of parents. Requests by parents for better science facilities and more advanced mathematics courses were resisted by public school officials.[104]

Despite their demands for challenging courses, Dunbar parents were not highly educated themselves. Apart from the 6 to 12 percent who were classed as "professionals," most worked in unskilled, semiskilled, and clerical jobs. What did distinguish them was their choice to send their children to Dunbar, since it was, in modern parlance, a magnet or charter school, accepting students on a voluntary rather than mandatory assignment basis.

The final ingredient in Dunbar's success was its long line of excellent teachers. Because Dunbar's principals had the freedom to make their own staffing decisions, they were able to select only those applicants who shared an interest in academic excellence. The rampant racism of the time kept so many avenues of employment closed to intelligent, well-educated African Americans that there was a positive surfeit of well-qualified and even overqualified candidates. Men and women who today would be university professors or engineers frequently ended up teaching at Dunbar in the early part of this century.

What Dunbar did not have were most of the things currently believed to be crucial to success by public school educators. It did not have small classes—forty students was a common size. It was not racially integrated. It was not adequately funded. Its principals rarely had any sort of formal training in pedagogy, and few if any had seen the inside of a teacher's college. Instead, they were graduates of liberal arts institutions such as Harvard and Oberlin.

In recent years, Dunbar's funding has been higher than ever before, its classes smaller, its staff more thoroughly steeped in the lore of schools of education. It has also died as an institution of learning, becoming instead a typical ghetto school, barely able to keep its students safe and in class, let alone offer them the kind of elite preparation received by former generations of Dunbar youth. The cause of this Pyrrhic victory was the flawed implementation of the Supreme Court's landmark school-desegregation ruling of 1954.

Excellence Lost

In the storm that accompanied Washington's public school desegregation program, in which African Americans generally favored complete integration, and whites the maintenance of some neighborhood boundaries, the pearl that was Dunbar was lost. Forced to become a neighborhood school, Dunbar was no longer free to accept academically oriented students from around the city; it was required instead to serve a student body drawn from its immediate vicinity. This change had a dramatic effect on the school's educational environment. Though no screening of applicants had been carried out by Dunbar during its open-enrollment heyday, its reputation ensured that few students who wished to coast through school and avoid work would have chosen to attend. Once students began to be assigned to the school based only on their place of residence, the intensity and fast pace of Dunbar's entire curriculum had to be downgraded. Enrollment in advanced classes dwindled rapidly, leading to their elimination. At the same time that the changing student body was undermining the demand for a traditional Dunbar education, the managerial autonomy that had made Dunbar unique was lost to increasing district control.[105]

Within only a few short years, according to Sowell, Dunbar was unrecognizable. Rather than acknowledging the school's strengths and attempting to reproduce them throughout the city, the district's desegregation reorganization plan eliminated the very features that had made Dunbar a success. Instead of raising other schools up to Dunbar's level, Dunbar was shackled and pulled down to theirs. Adding a shot of quinine to an already bitter educational cocktail is the fact that Dunbar is no more racially integrated at the end of the twentieth century than it was at the beginning. To quote the eponymous king Pyrrhus, "One more such victory and we are lost."[106]

The disastrous impact of D.C.'s mandatory desegregation policy on Dunbar High School was a side-effect of some very noble intentions. Six cruel decades after the "separate but equal" doctrine was first set down by the Supreme Court, all of the Supreme Court justices ruled in *Brown v. Board of Education* that legally imposed racial segregation denied "to Negro children the equal protection of the laws guaranteed by the Fourteenth Amendment."[107] In the implementing decree that followed a year after its 1954 *Brown* verdict, the Court indicated that public schools must admit children "on a racially non-discriminatory basis with all deliberate speed."[108] Sadly, not everyone agreed. In fact, resistance to the ruling in the predominantly segregationist South was fierce, and, for at least a decade, relentless. Governor Orval Faubus of Arkansas went to the surreal length of calling out armed troops to prevent a handful of African-American children from entering an all-white Little Rock public high school. (The reaction against the desegregation movement is further discussed in Chapter 8.)

Desegregation advocates were frustrated by the slow pace of change, and there was a concerted effort to find new ways of advancing the cause. The method that was eventually settled upon, first by a lower court and then by the Supreme Court, was to shift the criterion for adherence to the *Brown* decision from educational opportunities to educational results. Up until the mid-sixties, any school district that assigned students to schools in a race-blind fashion, or allowed students to freely choose their schools, was considered to be in compliance with the law. Even the NAACP, for a time, advocated freedom of

choice plans around the nation.[109] So long as students were treated equally under the law, and an avenue of desegregation was provided, neither the courts
nor most civil rights advocates deemed there to be any violation of the Fourteenth Amendment. This held true even if predominantly black or predominantly white schools continued to exist due to voluntary actions of families.

By 1968, simple constitutionality was no longer enough. In that year, an appellate court ruled that the de facto racial separation existing in a Virginia district was legal because students were allowed a free choice of schools, and
transportation was provided, even though few African-American families (15
percent) and no white families chose to attend other-race schools. This lower-
court ruling was overturned by the Supreme Court, which declared that a lack
of racial mixing in the schools, whether or not it was the result of legal compulsion, was unacceptable. There was an "affirmative duty," the Court decided,
"to eliminate 'dual' school systems 'root and branch.'"[110] The Court's decision
to require active, race-conscious student assignment programs in order to eliminate de facto segregation ran precisely contrary to its own *Brown* precedent,
which ruled such policies unconstitutional, and the NAACP lawyers who had
advocated this outcome admitted as much during oral arguments.[111]

So it was that compulsory integration became the legal tool by which civil
rights advocates hoped to improve the educational lot of black Americans, and
undo the effects of compulsory segregation. Was it an effective tool? Did
mandatory busing provide African-American children with a high-quality education and help them to reach their full academic potential? Did it at least bring
the educational opportunities of African-American children into line with those
of whites? These questions have been asked hundreds of times over the last
thirty years by educational researchers, and the answers are in.

Still the major study on the subject after more than a decade is the integration report of the National Institute of Education.[112] In 1984, the NIE commissioned papers from a disparate group of researchers to determine the effects of
school integration on black student achievement. After a careful analysis of the
research in the field, the panel concluded that desegregation generally had no
effect on students' mathematics achievement, and only a small effect on reading achievement. The distribution of the results was also telling: mandatory
programs had no effect on achievement; the few positive effects were found to
come from voluntary desegregation programs—the same kind of free choice
plans that the courts and the NAACP had initially advocated and then abandoned. The positive results were also concentrated among a small fraction of
the schools studied, with the rest showing negligible benefits, lending support
to the idea that institutional characteristics, rather than racial mixing itself, were
principally responsible for the students' improvements.

In the years since the NIE panel released its findings, corroborating evidence
has continued to accumulate. A search of ERIC (Educational Resources Infor-

mation Center), the most comprehensive computer database of education research, reveals that six statistical studies measuring academic effects of desegregation programs were carried out between 1984 and 1994.[113] Four found no academic benefits from desegregation plans.[114] The most recent of these, ordered by a U.S. district court in St. Louis, Missouri, was completed in 1992 by Robert Lissitz, Chairman of the Department of Measurement, Statistics, and Evaluation of the University of Maryland's College of Education. After a one-and-a-half year investigation, Professor Lissitz concluded that "the correlation of . . . achievement to months in the transfer [busing] program is essentially zero."[115]

Of the two studies which did find benefits from desegregation, the first noticed "only a few positive statistically significant differences" among the students of the school district studied,[116] and these were concentrated in two of the district's voluntary desegregation plans. The final study involved a controlled school choice plan in Cambridge, Massachusetts, in which families listed their first, second, and third choices of school and the district attempted to maximize first-choice placements while still maintaining racial balance. In only 9 percent of cases were families assigned to schools that did not appear among their choices.[117] The students in this program showed moderate academic improvements, similar to those produced by racially blind choice programs.[118]

The evidence of the past three decades leaves little doubt that mandatory busing, in and of itself, does not improve the academic achievement of African-American students. A more surprising result is that mandatory busing has failed even to achieve a mixing of the races within schools and classrooms. It has long been known that integration programs led to "white flight" from the urban school districts usually subject to such programs to the suburbs. Forced integration, furthermore, caused a much greater emigration than did voluntary programs.[119] What is not so well known is the fact that the "white" in "white flight" refers more accurately to the color of people's collars than to the color of their skin. That is to say, money, not race, is the best predictor of who fled forced-busing districts and who did not. Researchers Margaret Fleming and James Zafirau have demonstrated that "those students from higher income families (of all racial groups) tended to outmigrate in much greater proportion than did students from lower family income [groups]," and that this was a more significant predictor of outmigration than race.[120] Those most able to flee poor-quality urban schools have done so, while the rest are condemned by the present system to remain in them. This fact is not presented in order to gloss over the riots staged by unabashed racists to protest desegregation, but simply to show that racism was not the only or even necessarily the primary reason for the urban exodus that occurred during the seventies, eighties, and early nineties.

Given the income distribution among Americans, whites have more often had the option of fleeing to the suburbs, and a great many have chosen that option. So many, in fact, that *Time* magazine reported school segregation to be almost as extreme in 1996 as it was before the first mandatory busing policy was enacted in the early 1970s. Detroit's public school system, for instance, is presently 94 percent minority.[121] Across the country, 80 to 95 percent of the students languishing in the most troubled urban districts are members of racial or ethnic minorities.[122]

One goal of mandatory integration advocates on which progress has been made is the equalization of educational funding between blacks and whites. In the days of legal separation, white-run public school districts typically funded black schools at a fraction of the rate of their white counterparts. Though it is difficult to disaggregate modern per-pupil spending along strictly racial lines, a good approximation can be obtained by comparing the spending of large urban public school districts with state and national averages, due to the relatively high concentration of the African-American (and other minority) population in such districts. For example, public schools across the state of Massachusetts are 79.1 percent white, 9 percent Hispanic, and 8 percent black, while the Boston public schools are 47.9 percent black, 23.9 percent Hispanic, and 18.5 percent white. Comparing Boston to the state as a whole thus gives a good indication of the relative spending on minorities versus whites. In practice, Boston spent $6,397 per pupil in 1994, while Massachusetts schools as a whole spent $5,234.[123]

Numerous other major cities spend more per pupil in their public schools than the average for their states or for the nation. During the 1992–93 school year, the average per-pupil expenditures of all U.S. public schools was $5,170, not including interest payments or depreciation on buildings and equipment.[124] In that same year, the 90 percent minority Newark school district spent $9,501 per pupil, while New Jersey averaged $8,770.[125] By 1995, Newark's spending had risen to $10,564 per pupil.[126] Spending is generally lower in the South than in the Northeast, but the relative relationship between urban centers and state averages is similar. Tennessee spent $3,674 per pupil in 1992–93, while the 82 percent minority public schools of Memphis spent $3,945.[127] Many other urban areas, such as the 99.6 percent minority district of Compton, California, spend only fractionally more than their state average. Still others spend somewhat less. The City of New York, for instance, spent $350 dollars less per student in 1992–93 than the $7,770 average for New York state. Taking the big picture, the average per-pupil expenditure of three hundred major urban centers differs from the national average for all school districts by less than 1 percent.[128]

Contrary to expectations, closing the racial spending gap has not bridged the enormous gulf in educational opportunities between blacks and whites. The urban schools that now serve the majority of African-American children are, from virtually any angle, the nation's worst. Crime rates are higher, achievement is lower, and the buildings themselves are on the verge of ruin. Is this what newly emancipated African Americans hoped for and dreamed of at the close of the nineteenth century? Is this what civil rights activists fought for?

5

Teachers and Teaching in
the Government Schools

> *Along with the state's takeover of schooling came its regulation of the teaching profession. This step was promised to secure a more qualified and knowledgeable educational workforce, and to improve pedagogical methods. Did it?*

The Making and Breaking of Public School Teachers

Attitudes and Aptitudes

Many, perhaps most, women and men who go into teaching do so because they enjoy working with children, and want to have a positive impact on their lives. A study of Californian teacher candidates between 1946 and 1979 found that this was not only the number-one answer every year during that period, but that more teachers gave this reason in 1979 than ever before.[1] In his 1990 book *Teachers for Our Nation's Schools,* professor of education John Goodlad reported that "having a satisfying job" and "liking and wanting to help children" were the primary reasons education students had for deciding to become teachers.[2] To these goals, prospective teachers often bring a level of passion and dedication which is genuinely inspiring. Admittedly, there are also those who simply drift into the education department in their college or university, unsure of what they want to do in life, but it is uncommon to find a young teacher who is not imbued with a sense of mission.

A fact that might be greeted with less enthusiasm is that most teacher candidates "view the nurturing and interpersonal aspects of a teacher's role as more important than the academic aspects."[3] This was the recent conclusion of a research team that examined dozens of studies on the attitudes and characteristics of future teachers. They found that young men and women majoring in education not only minimized the importance of academics, but were also less likely to have enjoyed high-school academic subjects than noneducation majors. The Public Agenda foundation explored this issue further in a recent nationwide poll, asking teachers what they thought was the most important factor leading to career success.[4] Of the four options provided (persistence/drive, academic education, social skills, and connections), only one teacher in ten cited "academic education." Parents gave this answer three times as often.

Part of the anti-academic attitude of many teachers may be explained by the fact that education majors are less academically able, on average, than most other college students, usually scoring lower on standardized tests of mathematics, reading comprehension, and vocabulary. When high-school seniors take the Scholastic Assessment Test, they are asked to specify the field they plan to study in college, with the option of choosing "undecided." This allows their test scores to be tabulated according to intended field of study. The results of these tabulations show that prospective education majors received the lowest mathematics scores out of all ten discipline choices—including "undecided"—every year between 1978 and the present. They fared only slightly better on the verbal portion of the test, sometimes rising from last to next-to-last place.[5] It is possible, of course, that the SAT scores of actual education majors were higher than those of the high-school students who planned to enter that program. Not every college-bound high-school senior, after all, knows for sure what major he or she will eventually pursue. There is, in fact, some evidence of such a difference prior to the mid-1970s. By 1975, however, there was no significant difference between the scores of education freshmen and those of the high-school students who had intended to major in education the year before.[6]

Unfortunately, this is not the end of the story. A decade-long study that followed more than a thousand college education students through the first part of their careers found that those with the least academic aptitude were the most likely to enter the teaching profession immediately after graduating from college, and to stay in it once there. The brightest candidates were more apt to delay entry into the profession, to quit early, or never to practice as teachers at all, even though they became certified to do so. Many other studies have corroborated these findings, revealing that the vast majority of the brightest teachers leave the profession after brief careers.[7]

In an effort to raise academic standards within the teaching profession, the state of Massachusetts began requiring would-be teachers to pass a basic test of literacy and communication skills in 1998. The level of achievement expected from teaching candidates was not high. John Silber, head of the State Board of Education, admitted, "It wouldn't surprise me if it [the test] were at about the eighth-grade level."[8] State Education Commissioner Frank Haydu characterized the test as easier than the one taken by tenth-graders.[9]

Remarkably, the results were still disappointing. Fifty-nine percent of all test-takers failed, and thus failed to qualify for teaching licenses, under the test-score cutoff recommended by a panel of educators. According to Associated Press reporter Leslie Miller, "the samples showed some test-takers, when trying to rewrite sentences, misspelled words a 9-year-old could spell—although the words were right in front of them. Some wrote at a fifth- or sixth-grade level. Many wrote sentences lacking both nouns and verbs."[10] Commissioner Haydu called the outcome "painful," and said it "exposed a literacy problem at every level of society."

Because of this abysmal performance, and because the candidates had not been given sufficient warning that a passing grade would be a condition of employment, Silber and Haydu feared a lawsuit. To protect against this eventuality, the State Board of Education voted to temporarily lower the passing grade on the test, allowing several hundred more teachers to pass. The possibility that parents might wish to sue over having their children instructed by functional illiterates was apparently not discussed.

The board's decision to lower its already modest standards for teachers produced an inevitable political and public backlash. Within days, Commissioner Haydu resigned and the board took another vote rescinding its earlier decision to lower the passing grade.[11]

Not all government school teachers are low achievers with no interest in academics. Indeed, there are many intellectually gifted and scholarly educators scattered among U.S. public schools, but the poor academic skills of many of their peers are simply too important an influence on the nation's children to be ignored.

The Ed. School Experience

When teachers are asked to evaluate their own college education, their responses are split sharply between the practical and theoretical aspects. On the practical side, which is to say student-teaching assignments in actual elementary and high-school classrooms, there is broad approval. Most teachers feel that their practice teaching assignments were important learning experiences that increased their skill and confidence in the classroom. The few exceptions tend to be older individuals who come to teaching as a second or third profession, having already spent years managing or teaching others. Practical training, however, makes up only a part of most college education programs, with the rest being filled up with classes on the current views on proper teaching methods, and the history and philosophy of education. Questions on the value of these classes often elicit responses such as "what a waste of time," "useless," and "they don't translate well into the classroom." When asked to elaborate, teachers routinely give answers such as:

> No, I don't think teacher training on the college campus is necessary. I only had three education courses, just to get my credential. The education courses I had were irrelevant. Internship is important. You learn the ways to approach things. [Secondary Science Teacher]

> Student teaching experience alone is sufficient. Hands-on experience is important. But courses in college (philosophy, principles, etc.) are no use. I do not remember anything from them. Plus many college professors have no public school experience. [Secondary Language Arts Teacher][12]

It is hard to say how much of this negative perception is due to real shortcomings in teacher education, and how much is due to a lack of interest in the academic underpinnings of teaching on the part of education majors. Some European investigators, who have also run into dissatisfaction among student-teachers about their college training, have suggested that the students see theory and practice as totally separate, and since they cannot bridge the gap between college lectures and classroom experience, they do not see the value of academic studies.[13] On the other hand, the overall quality of college teacher-training courses has been broadly criticized for years, both by academics and by outside observers.[14] No doubt both of these causes are involved.

Does all this mean that the effect of teacher-training programs is limited to the practical know-how that students pick up during their in-school assignments? Not entirely. Attitudes about education are also shaped by the college of education environment. A study of U.S. ed. school freshmen conducted in the late 1980s found that they began their studies with traditional educational views (i.e., the teacher's role is to actively convey a body of knowledge and skills to students)—more traditional, in fact, than the views of liberal-arts majors as a whole. By the time they had completed their degree, however, education majors had not only caught up with but passed their liberal-arts peers in the direction of progressive educational thinking (i.e., the teacher's role is to facilitate the child's self-directed educational experiences).[15] Many other researchers, from as early as the 1930s all the way to the present, have observed the same trend. Their findings, moreover, have held true in both the United States and the United Kingdom.[16] Author Rita Kramer, who spent a year observing U.S. ed. schools in the late 1980s, was taken aback by the uniformity with which progressive educational views were espoused.[17]

Given that education majors begin their studies with fairly conventional ideas about education, and end up with much more progressive views, it should not come as a surprise that the faculty in departments of education have the most progressive views of all.[18] This was the conclusion of "What Schools Are For"—a 1992 study of several thousand students and faculty in colleges of education across the United States. The ideological supremacy of progressivism was also evident in the results of Public Agenda's 1997 survey titled *Different Drummers: How Teachers of Teachers View Public Education.* Public Agenda asked education professors which of the following two statements was closest to their personal philosophy: (1) "Teachers should see themselves as facilitators of learning who enable their students to learn on their own"; or (2) "Teachers should see themselves as conveyors of knowledge who enlighten their students with what they know." Ninety-two percent gave the more progressive answer (number one), while only 7 percent gave the second, more traditionalist answer.[19] Though espoused by a comparatively small core of "Frontier Thinkers" at the turn of the century, progressivism has grown into the dominant philosophy among education professors—a philosophy which is generally passed along to successive generations of public school teachers.

The fact that schools of education tend to produce a progressive consensus among their graduates is, in itself, no cause for concern. In theory, progressive-minded parents could request that their children be taught by these graduates, while parents wanting a more structured and teacher-directed learning experience could request teachers trained by other means. In reality, teachers' colleges have a monopoly on public school teacher training, and parents have virtually no say in the selection of government school teachers.

The public school teaching profession is very much like a medieval walled city, heavily fortified, and with only one main entrance. Guarding that entrance are the schools of education, which provide the only legal entry into the profession for the vast majority of candidates. Occasionally, the child population jumps unexpectedly and more candidates must quickly be admitted to the profession, but since the teachers' colleges can process only so many individuals at a time, alternative means of ingress must be provided. In such cases, small and relatively unpublicized doors are opened in the wall protecting the city, and a few likely prospects are ushered in. Teacher candidates brought into the profession in this way bypass some or all of the academic coursework doled out by schools of education, receiving a primarily practical course of training through apprenticeships with working teachers.

In the U.S., roughly four fifths of the states have some kind of alternative certification program.[20] Access to these programs is so strictly limited, however, that 99 percent of all teachers still must pass into the profession under the auspices of government-approved programs at schools of education. Speaking of an alternative certification program in one state, a government education official told researcher Emily Feistritzer: "If we hadn't designed this program, the state legislature would have, and we didn't want that to happen."[21] What is the effect of this strict gatekeeping? In their book *Who Will Teach?*, Richard Murnane and his colleagues report that

> [e]xtensive preservice training requirements deter many talented college students who would like to teach from ever doing so. Some never teach because they attend colleges that do not offer accredited teacher training programs, a lack that prevents students from pursuing a late-developing interest in teaching. Others, who do attend schools with approved programs, never teach because the required preservice courses appear dull and unrelated to the job of teaching and because completing the requirements reduces opportunities to take courses in other fields, including the liberal arts and business.[22]

John Silber, former president of Boston University, is somewhat less charitable, writing that "[t]he willingness to endure four years in a typical school of education often constitutes an effective negative intelligence test."[23]

If schools of education are indeed as intellectually bankrupt as critics allege, teachers certified by other means should perform at least as well as ed. school graduates both in the classroom and on tests of general and specific knowledge. As it happens, they do. In a recent survey of the research on teacher training, investigators concluded that though many attempts have been made to discredit alternative teacher certification programs, they "have not been shown to be inferior to traditional programs."[24] New Jersey was one of the first states to allow uncertified individuals to instruct public school students on an experimental basis. After four years of experience with the program, they found that the uncertified teachers scored in the top fourth of those taking the National Teacher Examinations (NTE, a series of standardized tests that many states require prospective public school teachers to pass). "Their scores in English, social studies, math, and science were higher than those of the traditional-route teachers, those with degrees in education."[25] Students taught by this group performed as well on standardized tests as those taught by the regular teachers. Similar results have been found in Georgia[26] and North Carolina.[27]

Malaise in the Classroom

Whatever their experiences in colleges of education, teacher candidates generally graduate enjoying the same sense of dedication and optimism with which they began. For some, this initial passion for teaching lasts throughout their entire career, but too often it is replaced over the years by fatigue, frustration, and burnout. I recall reading, some years back, about a teachers' conference at which the two most heavily subscribed sessions dealt with stress management and retirement planning. The mood of the profession as a whole seems to have grown more somber in the last twenty years. While three quarters of U.S. teachers polled in the 1960s would have stuck with their career choice if they'd had their lives to live over, the percentage dropped to less than half in the early 1980s, and hovered at just under six in ten in 1991.[28] When asked if they would like a daughter of theirs to take up teaching in the public schools, more teachers said no than said yes. Asked the same question regarding a son, teachers opposed the idea by a two-to-one margin. This was a significantly more negative response than that given by the general public, who favored both their sons and daughters becoming public school teachers.[29] Primary school head-teachers (i.e., principals) in England and Wales are no more upbeat than their counterparts across the Atlantic, with nearly half saying they would not encourage young people to take up teaching, and another quarter unsure.[30]

For anyone concerned with the health of education, the problem of low teacher morale is critically important. Every time a teacher loses his energy and excitement for teaching, he and the many students for whom he is responsible suffer a great loss. Educators who no longer find their jobs rewarding are naturally less likely to expend as much effort as those who continue to draw personal satisfaction from teaching. Any attempt to reduce the level of frustration and burnout in the teaching profession must, of course, begin by identifying its causes. The four most important factors appear to be working conditions, level of professional freedom, parental and administrative support, and career growth prospects.

A great variety of factors help to create a positive teaching environment. Most notable is the existence of a strong sense of community among the school staff. Research into teacher effectiveness and attitude has confirmed the obvious: schools that foster cooperation, a sense of shared purpose, and mutual support make teachers happier and more effective than those that do not.[31] Unfortunately, the same research shows that most teachers feel their schools are wanting in some or all of these areas. A recent survey in Chicago concluded that "[m]any high school teachers appear alienated from their colleagues and only weakly tied to the school and its improvement." Nearly all the secondary school teachers felt isolated from their colleagues,[32] but elementary teachers were noticeably more positive. Also very important to a teacher's morale is her ability to maintain discipline in the classroom. Three quarters of all teachers surveyed by the National Education Association (the largest teachers' union in the United States) find that discipline problems impair their effectiveness to some extent. Nearly half believe that their schools have not done nearly enough to help them deal with these problems.[33]

Salaries: One Size Fits All

One of the most frequently reported thorns in the side of teachers is their perception that they are underpaid. In the mid-1980s, 90 percent of U.S. teachers felt that their salaries were too low, and almost the same percentage believed that this was the primary reason many teachers were leaving the profession.[34] Of course, everyone wants a raise when it comes down to it, and the average teacher's salary did increase measurably between 1980 and 1990.[35] As of 1995, the average public school teacher's salary was $36,933, for working just over nine months of the year.[36] Perhaps reflecting this increase, a Metropolitan Life survey released in 1995 found that dissatisfaction with pay had noticeably decreased.[37] Still, teachers are faced with a frustrating situation, rare in most other professions: their salaries have little or nothing to do with how well they perform their jobs. Gifted educators, those who enthrall their students and help them to learn especially deeply and quickly, are paid no more than those who simply show up for work. Salaries in the public education system are almost universally determined by the number of years a teacher has served, and the number of college education credits she has accumulated. Longevity, rather than ability, determines a teacher's worth in this system, and no one, including teachers, believes that the two are equivalent. Experience, of course, is a source of improvement for many, but most teachers have worked with at least a few excellent new recruits and many burned-out veterans.

Though performance-based pay is the rule in virtually every nongovernmental enterprise, its application to public education has been increasingly rare. Generally proposed by people outside the teaching profession, either on school boards or in state legislatures, it has been resisted tooth and nail by teachers and administrators. In the 1950s, roughly one school district in ten had a merit-based pay scheme, but the percentage dropped steadily to only 4 percent in the late 1970s. By the mid-1980s, "more than 99 percent of teachers were paid on a uniform salary schedule."[38]

The failure of the public school system to recognize good performance with appropriate financial compensation and career growth opportunities takes a heavy toll on its teachers. One veteran teacher, who had decided to stick it out in the public system despite the fact that his hard work was rarely acknowledged, described the system's effects on a colleague:

> I had a friend, Allen, who was the finest teacher I ever knew. He left teaching after seven years to sell ladies' clothing because it troubled him so much that the system didn't distinguish between minimum competency and real talent and energy. He was a man of great pride; he's since become very successful.[39]

An additional problem with the existing pay system is that it is common for teachers to reach the top of the salary scale by their late thirties or early forties, a time at which people in other professions are often seeing significant growth in their earnings. Of course, teachers' salaries may continue to increase if the entire pay scale is adjusted upward, as has happened periodically over the past several decades, but such increases are never certain. Some researchers have concluded that this "concrete ceiling" encourages the ablest teachers to look for other jobs, either in school administration or outside the field entirely.[40]

Given all the drawbacks of fixed salary scales, one might expect to find teachers solidly behind performance-based pay systems, as both parents and the general public have been for more than twenty years.[41] In practice, however, teachers oppose such systems, often called "merit pay," by a two-to-one margin.[42] The main reason for this overwhelming rejection is the fear that evaluations of merit would not be done fairly. Administrators, teachers worry, might be biased in their assessments of teachers, favoring those with whom they were friendly and penalizing the others, independently of the teachers' classroom performance. Even if such a program were to start out in a fair and objective manner, most teachers expect it would eventually be undermined by favoritism and politics. A significant number of educators go so far as to say that it is not possible to objectively assess teaching performance at all, making the idea untenable even in principle.[43] Others, when pressed to explain why they believe this to be the case, moderate their position by saying that an objective assessment would be possible, but would require much knowledge and effort on the part of the evaluator. One educator I interviewed, who was teaching a language course to two groups of students in the same school and of the same age, noted that one of her classes was learning far more quickly than the other, because of their greater interest and aptitude. She worried that in a year in which neither of her classes was motivated to learn, she would receive a bad review even though her teaching performance was as good as ever.

Another oft-heard criticism of merit pay is that it would fail to produce the desired effect in teachers. Professional educators, so the theory goes, are above the push and pull of mere financial incentives, being motivated to become teachers and to strive for excellence only by such humanitarian goals as the success of their students. In reality, teachers and teacher-candidates are just as susceptible to economic imperatives as the rest of us. In surveying the evidence on salaries and teacher behavior, Richard Murnane and several other researchers found that "teaching salaries have a marked effect on the *size* of the pool of college graduates who enter teaching: the higher the salaries, the larger the pool."[44] They also found that teachers who are highly paid are more likely to stay in the profession than those who receive comparatively lower salaries, writing that "[a] teacher in the below-average salary stream was approximately one and a half times more likely to leave at the end of the first year than a teacher in the above-average salary stream." The same effect was evident over longer periods as well, with a $2,000 difference in salary resulting in a change in the median period of employment of one to two years.[45] The more teachers make, the longer they keep teaching.

Educators also express the apprehension that differences between their salaries might prove divisive, possibly arousing animosity between those who receive significant pay increases and those who don't. This presumes, of course, that compensation packages would be made public, a practice uncommon in the private sector. Even if salaries were kept private, however, many teachers are convinced that they would become more competitive with one another, not wishing to cooperate for fear of bolstering their peers' evaluations at their own expense, as if competing in a zero-sum game. Here again, their attitude rests on a false assumption, namely, that administrators would not value cooperation. In a private business, where a manager's own livelihood depends on the overall achievements of the employees under her, she has a strong incentive to encourage cooperation and camaraderie among them. This is not to say that all private-sector employers heed these incentives at all times, but rather that, on the whole, they are likely to, for to do otherwise is to commit professional and financial suicide.

It is here that we find the root of many teachers' objections to performance-based pay programs: classroom educators would have their performance evaluated by administrators whose own performance would not itself be subject to evaluation. Principals who consistently gave raises and bonuses to their friends among the teaching staff, while neglecting the rest, would not face pay cuts. Those principals who made excellent decisions based solely on merit would see no professional or financial compensation for their sound judgment. There would, in short, be no consistent incentive for principals to carefully and objectively evaluate their teachers. This last observation leads naturally to the idea of a performance-based pay system that includes not only teachers but principals as well, but this in turn begs the question of how to ensure that principals are themselves objectively evaluated. The task of sorting through these and other difficulties, and attempting to find solutions, is taken up in Part III of this book.

Working Conditions That Don't Work

One of the most visible trends in the working conditions of teachers over the past forty years has been the steadily falling pupil-teacher ratio. In 1955, there were 26.9 students for every teacher in the public schools. By 1995, the number had fallen to 17.1.[46] This remarkable drop is due to reductions in the average class size, the explosive growth in the number of small "special education" classes, and the hiring of more and more "resource teachers" who provide support to their counterparts in the classroom without actually teaching classes themselves. The percentage of teachers assigned to "special education" classes grew by a factor of thirteen between 1966 and 1991, and by all indications has continued to grow since that time.[47] Between 1961 and 1986, the size of the average elementary classroom dropped from 29 students to 24 students, where it has remained for the last decade. The number of students taught per day by the average high-school teacher fell from 138 to 93 between 1961 and 1991.[48]

These changes represent a drop in the workload of teachers. The typical teacher now has fewer assignments to grade, and fewer students to control and teach, than was the case three decades ago. Not surprisingly, there is a great deal of research showing that smaller classes mean happier teachers.[49] What may surprise some parents is that this extraordinarily expensive change in the way schools do business, which adds tens of thousands of dollars to the cost of each and every classroom, produces few measurable academic benefits. Surveying the field in 1990, researcher Allen Odden reached the conclusion that "class size reduction even down to 15 or 20 [shows] essentially little or no impact."[50] The few studies that do show a link between smaller classes and higher student achievement tend to involve only the early elementary grades.[51] Odden's conclusions were echoed in 1998 by University of Rochester professor Eric Hanushek, who wrote:

> Existing evidence indicates that achievement for the typical student will be unaffected by instituting the types of class size reductions that have been recently proposed or undertaken. The most noticeable feature of policies to reduce overall class sizes will be a dramatic increase in the costs of schooling, an increase unaccompanied by achievement gains.[52]

Shrinking class sizes are one of the few bright spots for America's public school teachers. In order for teachers to feel confident and at ease in the classroom, they need to feel they have the support not only of their peers, but of parents and administrators as well. The perceived absence of this support takes a heavy toll, and many teachers who leave the profession do so because of it. Surveys of teacher opinion regularly place lack of parental involvement among the top problems facing the public schools.[53] But parental involvement is a two-edged sword. Parents who are dissatisfied with their children's grades, or with a teacher's performance, are often viewed as meddlers. Problems also exist between classroom educators and their school and district administrators. A study of more than 7,000 public school teachers found that they generally had negative views of their principals' leadership and responsiveness. One of the major causes of concern is that principals fail to imbue their schools with a clear mission, leaving teachers feeling directionless and ineffective. The perception on the part of so many teachers that administrators have not established unifying goals for their schools should be cause for serious concern. Schools without well-defined goals not only make teachers feel less effective, they significantly lower student achievement.[54]

Another area in which teachers feel let down by their administrators is in the handling of violent and disruptive students. More than one in ten teachers was assaulted at school in the year 1993 alone. Some cases stagger the imagination. In May 1998, four sixth-grade girls beat their teacher for refusing to switch the classroom television to the Jerry Springer Show, a notoriously crude and (pardon the candor) moronic talk-show. The teacher, Ms. Aishah Ahmad, eventually overcame the onslaught, and the children were subsequently suspended. Unfortunately, she was not able to overcome the bitter disappointment of having been attacked by her own students, stating, "I don't ever want to go back to that kind of environment again."[55]

In a great many cases, teachers who have been attacked by students are dissatisfied with the actions taken by the school administration to deal with the matter. The experience of Deborah Sanville is a case in point. Attacked by a burly eighteen-year-old who pinned her to a wall, Ms. Sanville narrowly escaped a beating thanks to the intervention of another teacher. Expecting the student to be severely punished, she was dismayed when he was given only a five-day in-school suspension. Ms. Sanville was, unsurprisingly, unsatisfied. In pursuit of justice, she took her attacker to court. The student was charged with assault, but pled guilty to the lesser charge of disorderly conduct. According to teachers' union representatives from across the country, the number of cases in which teachers have had to take their violent students to court has doubled or even quadrupled in recent years.[56]

To some extent, teachers do not blame their principals for the increasingly mild punishments meted out to increasingly violent students. Fully two thirds of teachers feel that the courts, and hence the legislature, have "made school administrators so cautious they don't deal severely with student misbehavior."[57] The fear that a school will be sued by a child's parents discourages many principals from taking any action. The problem is most severe in cases where the child is considered disabled under the federal Individuals with Disabilities Education Act (IDEA, originally passed in 1975 as the Education of All Handicapped Children Act). A 1988 Supreme Court ruling based on this act makes it illegal for schools to remove disruptive disabled children from their regular classes unless the schools obtain parental consent. Though well-intentioned, this restriction creates grave difficulties in cases where the disabled children have trouble socializing peacefully with their classmates. One "communicatively impaired" child, whose one-hundred pounds made him a towering figure among his six-year-old peers, threw chairs, hit and bit his teacher, and kicked and punched other children and staff members. Jimmy P., as he was known, could not be suspended because the IDEA also makes it illegal to suspend children with disabilities for more than ten days. Jimmy's teacher and her assistant, caught between a whirling dervish and a hard place, both suffered severe stress and took medical leaves of absence by the end of the year.

In addition to the legal causes for growing restraint in dealing with school discipline problems, some have argued that personal motives are also involved. Most notably, teachers' unions contend that some principals suppress information about violent incidents and discourage teachers from pursuing offenders in court in order to avoid damaging their schools' reputations.[58]

Responsibility without Power

Another great frustration for many teachers is their lack of control over curriculum planning and school decision making. They feel, oftentimes, like the fictional leader of Great Britain in the BBC television series *Yes Prime Minister,* whose position was colorfully summed up as "responsibility without power, the prerogative of the eunuch throughout the ages." Teachers from all over the United States believe they have little influence on school policy. In a survey of 53,000 teachers, only one in three reported having a significant role in setting the curriculum or discipline policy, or in making student grouping decisions.[59] A poll of British head-teachers came up with similar results. Great Britain's national curriculum, of which few teachers feel a sense of ownership, has left the mood particularly gloomy. One head-teacher summed up the prevailing opinion by saying that "[t]he pace of change has been much too fast [and] consultation with practicing teachers negligible."[60] It isn't that teachers want to take on all the duties of their administrators, or to choose what and how they will teach entirely by themselves. What they do seek is the right to be consulted before new programs are thrust upon them and the right to push ahead with innovations they have found successful in their own classrooms.

As new educational fads and reform programs are foisted upon public schools year after year, many teachers begin to feel disenfranchised and profoundly cynical. Given this frame of mind, it is not surprising that few such top-down, mandated reforms have a noticeable impact on the classroom. In the words of one teacher:

> My own personal resistance to reform comes from discouragement. I have taught ten years in an inner city, multicultural high school. I work very hard and have tried all of the trendy programs and ideas that have been handed to me at district sponsored workshops, etc. I have been handed vision after vision in district and school workshops and been told to develop a plan whereby my colleagues [sic] and I will implement the current vision. Before we can get that vision off the ground, along comes another vision from a slightly different source and we go through the whole exercise again.[61]

In the U.S., the U.K., and France, the public generally agrees that local schools and school teachers should have more control than federal, state, or district bodies over such things as how children should be taught, and the allocation of the school budget.[62] This feeling is most pronounced in the United States, where three quarters of those polled are in favor of more say for local principals and teachers.[63] Where teachers and the public part ways is on their attitudes toward parental control over education. As we have already seen, a majority of both parents and the general public favor more control for parents over their children's education. Teachers, however, are uniformly and adamantly opposed to any changes in this direction, opposing school vouchers, for example, by a margin of more than three to one.[64] When asked "who should have the greatest influence in deciding what is taught in the public schools of your community," only 2 percent of teachers answered that it should be parents. In another question asking who should have the most control over textbook selection, so few teachers said "parents" that the "parents" column in the printed survey results simply shows an asterisk, indicating, according to the fine print, that less than one half of 1 percent of teachers gave this answer.[65] The number-one answer to both of these questions was "teachers."

While interviewing a young, obviously very intelligent teacher at a well-to-do suburban high school, I asked her for her thoughts on the movement toward increased parental control embodied by charter schools and vouchers. She responded as follows:

> Well, the problem with reforms like charter schools is that if parents are really involved in choosing or helping to found their school, they'll think that they have as much right to shape what goes on in it as the school staff. That's our job. That's what we spend years in college studying.

She went on to say, essentially, that deciding what and how to teach was almost entirely the educators' responsibility, and that parents should stand back and let them get on with it.

It must be said, however, that many teachers are opposed to increased parental involvement due to their own unpleasant experiences with some parents. Most members of the teaching profession have at one time or another encountered belligerent parents with excessive and entirely unrealistic demands. Telephone calls at home in the evenings and on weekends are not unheard of, and many are the teachers who have been reduced to tears after a meeting with a particularly rude parent. In thinking about increased parental control over education, teachers often worry that such incidents might become more frequent. Ironically, a lot of these problems stem from the fact that parents have too little, rather than too much, control in the government system. Home/school relations in the private sector, according to Harvard professor Susan Moore Johnson, tend to be more agreeable and supportive primarily because parents are free to choose schools that conform to their preferences, and because they know that their children can be asked to leave if they fail to follow a school's rules of conduct. It is also true that parents sometimes serve on the governing boards of independent schools, and this direct participation tends to make them "ready to listen, and in turn, the school staff [are] obliged to respond."[66]

The Principal's Plight

While principals share many of the attitudes, aspirations, and complaints of classroom educators, they also encounter difficulties of their own. Perhaps the greatest bane of principals in the public school system is their lack of control over staffing. Studies of effective schools show that one of the key ways in which principals can affect student achievement is the judicious hiring, retaining, and firing of teachers,[67] but due to school district policies and the provisions of teachers' union contracts, public school principals lack this fundamental ability taken for granted by managers in most other professions. Though teacher tenure laws have been opposed by the public for years,[68] they have flourished in the United States and elsewhere. These laws, together with the legal might of the teachers' unions, make it extremely difficult and expensive to fire teachers, even when there is significant evidence of misconduct or poor performance. During his visits to schools around the country, author Jonathan Kozol frequently heard complaints about the barriers principals face in trying to maintain a competent staff. One Chicago elementary school principal told Kozol:

> Teachers are being dumped from high school jobs because of low enrollment. But if they've got tenure they cannot be fired so we get them here. I've got two of them as subs right now and one as a permanent teacher. He's not used to children of this age and can't control them. But I have no choice.[69]

Another principal explained to Kozol that a number of his teachers should not even be in the field of education, but resignedly admitted: "I can't do anything with them but I'm not allowed to fire them."[70]

To make matters worse, teachers in many districts can be easily "bumped" out of their positions in a given school any time another teacher with more years of seniority decides to take their place. This can and does happen against the wishes of both principals and the "bumped" teachers themselves. Ironically, teachers and their unions strongly support tenure provisions, but nonetheless regret the resulting difficulty of dismissing bad teachers. In Metropolitan Life's 1995 survey of teachers,[71] fully 87 percent thought that making it easier to remove incompetent teachers would have a positive effect on the quality of teaching. More than half were "strongly positive." One principal voiced his frustration with the problem, known among some educators as the "parade of the lemons," in his own school:

> I have no control anymore. We have had five weeks of school, and already fifteen new teachers have come in—and fifteen have left because of "bumpings." . . . In addition, each year, mostly through inheritance from somewhere else, I get three to five inept teachers.[72]

The difficulty in firing and even giving low evaluations to bad teachers helps to perpetuate the lemon parade. Of the 62,000 teachers reviewed in New York City during the 1989–90 school year, "only 606—fewer than 1 percent—were rated Unsatisfactory by their principals." Emily Sachar, a journalist who spent a year teaching in the system, traces the problem to its root: "The greatest impediment to giving U [Unsatisfactory] ratings," she writes "is the fact that the principal who gives one may not transfer a U-rated teacher out of his school for three years." As a result, "there are principals who say to teachers 'You should be getting a U but I'll give you an S [Satisfactory] if you'll agree to get out of here.' "[73]

Public School Pedagogy: The Deficiency to Which It Is Susceptible

More than a hundred and fifty years ago, Horace Mann promised that if public schooling were "expanded to its capabilities," and "worked with the efficiency of which it is susceptible," the results would prove astonishing. Well it has been, and they did, only not quite in the way that Mann predicted. Far from bringing about a new era in educational productivity, the public schools have sidelined several of the most effective pedagogical methods ever invented, including some that predated its introduction by thousands of years. In their place, public schools have introduced a succession of flawed educational practices that were not developed through careful research and testing, but spawned in the ideologically charged imaginations of leading ed. school professors.

Madness in Their Methods

One of the most flagrant examples of public schools' pedagogical malfeasance is the complete disregard they have shown for the Follow Through study of the 1970s. Follow Through was a federally funded, large-scale experiment designed in the late 1960s and continuing on into the late 1970s, to identify effective instructional methods.[74] To achieve that goal, proponents of twenty-two different approaches to elementary-school teaching were allowed to introduce their methods into public schools around the country, and the effects of their methods on student achievement were measured on a wide range of outcomes.

A comprehensive analysis of the results was carried out in 1977 by Abt Associates, an independent research firm. Formal, structured teaching models "that emphasize basic skills," stated the report, "succeeded better than other models in helping children gain these skills."[75] One such program, called Direct Instruction or Distar, stood out. The most structured, most skill-oriented approach of the lot, Distar systematically broke new topics down into understandable parts, and then had students practice those component skills, eventually putting them back together to master the complete task. This Direct Instruction method emerged on top in virtually every category. It not only placed first in teaching basic skills as a whole, but came out first in all four subcategories (reading, arithmetic, spelling, and language) individually. Students taught by Direct Instruction placed a close second in advanced conceptual skills (behind the University of Georgia's Mathemagenic Activities Program), and even scored highest on tests of self-esteem and responsibility toward their work.[76]

To put these accomplishments in perspective, poor/disadvantaged students who had gone through several years of Direct Instruction performed at the national average of all students. This is not particularly remarkable unless you realize that students from this demographic group normally performed at the 20th percentile, which is to say, worse than 80 percent of their peers around the country. Non-disadvantaged children in the program performed even better, and the success of Distar was just as evident with non-native English speakers as with native English speakers.[77] What's more, the benefits that accrued to students from participation in the program continued even after they had returned to regular classrooms. Two, three, and even six years after they had left the Distar Follow Through program, disadvantaged former-participants still performed at a level above the control group of disadvantaged students who had not participated in Follow Through.[78]

While basic skills approaches in general, and Direct Instruction in particular, were coming out at the top of the heap in raising student performance, progressive methods that allowed children to guide their own learning and that focused on self-esteem or higher-order thinking skills received an embarrassing wake-up call. Not only did almost all of these methods fail to improve student performance, they actually caused it to drop relative to the performance of students not participating in Follow Through. Moreover—and this is where the embarrassment comes in—their failure was not restricted to children's academic skills, but extended into the very areas of self-esteem, conceptual skills, and attitude toward learning that they were intended to foster. Of the methods that deemphasized both basic skills and highly structured lessons, *none* produced a positive effect on students' reading and arithmetic performance:[79] one had no effect, and all the rest made students worse off than if they had been left in regular public-school classrooms. On tests of conceptual thinking skills, one such method produced a positive effect, one produced a negligible effect, and the rest once again made students worse off than they otherwise would have been. Finally, on measures of attitude and self-concept, *none* of the progressive methods produced a positive effect: one had no effect, and the remainder were detrimental to students.[80]

In any industry subject to the demands of its customers, the clear superiority of a method like Direct Instruction would soon have caused it to displace competing practices. Public schooling, however, is not one of those industries. Not only did Distar fail to catch on, many school systems that had used the method so successfully during Follow Through abandoned it shortly after the Abt study was released. Predictably, their students' scores began to fall off. Though disadvantaged former Distar students continued to outperform the disadvantaged non-Distar control group after the program was terminated, their gains with respect to the national average began to erode as soon as they were returned to regular classrooms.[81]

Now, twenty years later, Follow Through has been almost totally forgotten, and future teachers are taught in schools of education that instructional method really doesn't have much of an impact on student performance. According to professor John Stone, who has spent years observing the relationship between education research findings and the actual practices in public schools and teachers' colleges, the vast majority of textbooks on teaching methods "give little weight to experimentally demonstrated results." "Instead," he writes, "they present an eclectic assortment of approaches colored by a distinct distaste for methods that are structured, teacher-directed, and result-oriented."[82] The treatment in the popular college text *Curriculum and Instructional Methods for the Elementary and Middle School,* by Johanna Lemlech, is typical. Lemlech writes:

> In classrooms where students are given little opportunity to choose what they will learn, how they will learn, and the way in which they will be evaluated for learning, there is a greater likelihood that the classroom is structured through intrinsic rewards, incentive programs, and normative evaluation. As a consequence, learning will become joyless. There is also a tendency in these classrooms to overemphasize repetition, drill, and commercially produced dittos for practice materials. Some believe this . . . may be the cause of negative motivation patterns.[83]

In spite of the fact that the most effective pedagogical approach tested in Follow Through was also the one to make the most intensive use of drills and practice materials—and in spite of the fact that it produced the most motivated, most self-confident learners—structured teaching is portrayed in a negative light with respect to student attitudes, and its superior effectiveness in teaching reading, language, arithmetic, and spelling goes unmentioned. Other ed. school textbooks, such as Allan Ornstein's *Secondary and Middle School Teaching Methods,* suggest that research findings should be considered, but only as one in a long list of ingredients making up a complex pedagogical soufflé:

> In considering what is best for you, you must consider your teaching style, your students' needs and abilities, and your school policies. As you narrow your choices, remember that approaches overlap and are not mutually exclusive. Also remember that more than one approach may work for you. You may borrow ideas from various approaches and construct your own hybrid. The approach you finally arrive at should make sense to you on an *intuitive* basis. Don't let someone impose his or her teaching style or disciplinary approach on you.[84]

Rather than recommending that a teaching style be based on demonstrably successful methods, Ornstein suggests that methods should be chosen based on the teacher's personal style. Intuition, not reason or the use of hard evidence, is promoted as the right way to select instructional techniques. As the following section shows, this anti-empirical philosophy is not restricted to the teaching of reading.

The emperor's new math

In the early 1960s, a movement arose to redress perceived problems in the teaching of mathematics. Until that point, elementary mathematics instruction had consisted chiefly of memorizing the multiplication tables and the rules of arithmetic, while secondary schools taught algebra and geometry in a similarly mechanical fashion. It is generally conceded that some schools and some teachers conveyed a deeper understanding of and love for mathematics, but the overall verdict of contemporary experts was that mathematics instruction was "a disaster."[85]

In an effort to provide students with a genuine understanding of mathematical concepts, and to make the subject more interesting, university education departments around the country began developing new curricula. These soon became known, collectively, as the New Math. The defining characteristics of the New Math were a greatly reduced emphasis on memorization and repetitive drills, the introduction of many topics not previously taught in elementary or secondary school (such as set theory and numbering systems other than base 10), and increasing use of deduction to prove abstract mathematical theorems (such as the commutative and associative axioms of arithmetic).[86]

Given the centrality of proof in mathematics, and its prominence in the New Math in particular, it is remarkable that developers of the new curricula did not feel the need to prove that their innovations would lead to greater student understanding. Mathematician Morris Kline criticized his peers on precisely these grounds. In his 1973 book *Why Johnny Can't Add,* Kline wrote:

> One would think that the framers of the modern mathematics curriculum would have experimented with many groups of children and teachers and thus produced some evidence in favor of their programs before urging them upon the country. The sad fact is that most of the groups undertook almost no experimental work. The sole significant exception was the University of Illinois Committee on School Mathematics headed by Professor Max Beberman. And even this group never offered any evidence for the superiority of its curriculum.[87]

Despite the absence of any experimental evidence favoring the New Math, it was soon in use by the teachers of millions of public school students.[88] This should come as no surprise given that the instructional methods and materials it replaced had also never been formally evaluated against alternative approaches. Throughout history, public school curriculum decisions have almost always been reached without the benefit of rigorous classroom trials.

When the National Council of Teachers of Mathematics (NCTM) published a set of curriculum standards in 1989, they vowed to reverse this trend. "Schools, teachers, students and the public at large currently enjoy no protection from shoddy products," they wrote, adding that "anyone developing products for use in mathematics classrooms should . . . present evidence about their effectiveness."[89] Ironically, this tenet was violated by the very standards document in which it appeared. Nowhere in the 258-page document was there any reference to experiments comparing the relative merits of the NCTM's preferred methods versus alternative instructional approaches. In fact, the concluding "Next Steps" section of the report pointed to an entirely different basis for the NCTM's recommendations: they were said to be "based on a set of values, or philosophical positions, about mathematics for students and the way instruction should proceed."[90]

As it happens, the values and philosophy of the NCTM's leaders fell neatly into the progressive pedagogical tradition (John Dewey being one of the first authorities cited).[91] As a result, the organization's standards document laid out a series of recommendations similar in most respects to the (no longer new) New Math. The New Math's sidelining of memory and drill work was preserved, with the standards document specifically stating:

> Programs that . . . emphasize symbol manipulation and computational rules, and that rely heavily on paper-and-pencil worksheets do not fit the natural learning patterns of children and do not contribute to important aspects of children's mathematical development.[92]

The NCTM even introduced innovative new ways of minimizing the role of paper-and-pencil drills, and the memorization of the multiplication tables, by calling for calculators to be used by "all students at all times."[93]

Not only were the NCTM's claims for the superiority of its methods unsupported by research, they were in direct conflict with the results of the Follow Through experiment, which found that highly structured lessons using worksheets were among the most effective approaches for teaching the mathematical basics. More recent comparisons of these methods are also available. In a 1992 investigation conducted by Bonnie Grossen and others at the University of Oregon, two groups of sixth-graders were matched for ability, and then one group was taught using techniques favored by the NCTM while the other was taught using a drill-intensive direct instruction program developed by Siegfried Engelmann, the principal author of Distar. Apart from method, there were two key differences between the classes: the NCTM teacher spent many hours each evening preparing for her classes, and assigned a significant amount of homework, while the direct instruction teacher taught her students using a prerecorded video-disc produced by Engelmann, had virtually no preparation time, and assigned very little homework. The results? The *lower* half of the direct instruction class outperformed the *upper* half of the NCTM class on *every* measure. Even on specific topics that were covered in the NCTM class but not in the direct instruction class, the NCTM students performed significantly worse.[94]

Year after year, similar results continue to pour in. One of the most recent installments was published in the Winter 1995 issue of the journal *Effective School Practices*. The study in question compared the mathematics achievement of two groups of first- and second-graders, the first taught using a direct instruction curriculum known as "Connecting Mathematics Concepts" (CMC) and the second taught using a progressive "discovery learning" curriculum called "Math Their Way" (MTW/CGI). The authors, Sara Tarver and Jane Jung, found that

> [a]t the end of second grade, CMC students had significantly higher scores than MTW/CGI students on both the computation and the concepts/applications components of mathematics achievement. In addition, the CMC students had significantly higher scores on a survey of student attitudes towards mathematics. Comparisons of grade equivalents suggest that the Direct Instruction CMC curriculum benefited high-performing as well as low-performing students.[95]

This outcome was of course predictable given the well-known evidence from Follow Through, but it failed to dissuade proponents of less formal approaches to math instruction. Though the standards laid out by the NCTM have not received blanket acceptance, they have influenced practices in thousands of schools—perhaps one in your neighborhood. In California, a state as frequently beset by disastrous educational fads as by natural disasters, the official mathematics curriculum is closely modeled on the NCTM's recommendations. As students' math scores sank on the state's own California Learning Assessment System tests, parents and elected officials began to balk. In 1995, the governor's chief education advisor denounced the state's standards as "'fuzzy' learning espoused by 'radicals [who] are convinced that basic skills are not important.'" Parents in Palo Alto formed a group to oppose the curriculum, dubbing it the "new 'new math.'"[96]

Across the curriculum there is damning evidence against many of the instructional methods advocated for and used in public schools—a smoking gun of pedagogical malpractice covered with the fingerprints of the education establishment. In the face of this overwhelming evidence, the profession has but one line of defense: it means well. The educators who have championed the use of "progressive" methods have done so because they have genuinely believed in those methods. As study after study shows their approach to be inferior in the classroom, these educators persist because they believe that the studies are somehow flawed and that a progressive approach holds some as-yet-unmeasured benefits for students. They could, of course, be right. The question that parents and citizens must ask themselves is: Do we really want to leave the decisions about how children are taught entirely up to this group of public school educators, or do we want a choice?

Look, Say, Fail: The Story of Reading Instruction

For most of the nineteenth century, U.S. early reading instruction generally revolved around the alphabet and the sounds of its letters. The traditional practice was to begin with the sounds of the letters individually, then to combine them into syllables, and finally, into words. Variations on this ordering existed, but they all emphasized recognizing (or "decoding") written words by sounding them out, a method broadly known as phonics. One popular variation was to teach children the letters not simply by showing them the alphabet, but by presenting them with a small number of common words. Once the students had understood that words were made up of letters, and had been exposed to all of the letters, conventional phonics teaching was begun. Despite its widespread use in one or another form, phonics was not without its critics.

Advocates of a new approach to teaching children to read claimed that phonics had two key flaws: the names of letters only rarely corresponded to their pronunciations in words, and the structured approach of building words up from their components did not correspond to the way children learned to speak (i.e., by saying whole words). Public school crusader Horace Mann was the most eloquent spokesman for these views, writing in his 1843 Report to the Massachusetts Board of Education:

I am satisfied that our greatest error in teaching children to read, lies in the beginning with the alphabet,—in giving them what are called the "Names of the Letters." . . . The "Names of the Letters" are not elements in the sounds of words; or are so, only in a comparatively small number of cases. To the twenty-six letters of the alphabet, the child is taught to give twenty-six sounds, and no more. . . . It would be difficult, and would not compensate the trouble, to compute the number of different sounds which a good speaker gives to the different letters and combinations of letters in our language . . . but if analysed, they would be found to amount to hundreds. Now how can twenty-six sounds be the elements of hundreds of sounds as elementary as themselves?[97]

An obvious problem with Mann's criticism is that it misrepresented phonics. It is clear from both the instruction manuals of the time and from the statements of contemporary educators that popular phonics approaches made a clear distinction between the names of letters and the sounds associated with them, including the fact that individual letters could have multiple sounds. *The Teaching of Reading by the Phonic Method,* a manual for teachers published in the early nineteenth century, used different diacritical marks over the vowels to indicate their various pronunciations.[98] How anyone could have concluded otherwise was a mystery to the teachers Mann criticized in his reports.[99]

Mann also championed the idea that children could and should learn to read in the same way they learned to speak—beginning with whole words. For Mann, the letters of the alphabet were "skeleton-shaped, bloodless, ghostly apparitions," while syllables were "cadaverous particles."[100] Essentially, he held that by exposure to printed matter, children would automatically learn to recognize whole words without having been taught to recognize the letters of the alphabet, and without being aware that word spellings were in any way related to pronunciations. Gradually, students would be introduced to more and more words, perhaps a thousand or two thousand, and only then, after months or even years of guessing, would they begin to study phonics and spelling.

After a brief experiment with this new "word" or "look-say" method, which local teachers believed to have a negative effect on achievement, Boston schools returned to predominantly phonics-based approaches to teaching reading. For fifty-odd years, look-say teaching lay dormant, stirring occasionally but never rising to prominence in the nation's schools. Then, toward the end of the century, it came awake, and this time it was unstoppable. Though phonics was still emphasized by public school teachers as late as 1908,[101] its days were numbered. In the early 1930s, historian of reading Nila Smith wrote: "In general, phonetics is taught much more moderately than formerly and is subordinated to other phases of reading instruction. . . . There is a decided tendency to delay the teaching of phonetics much longer than has previously been the case."[102]

Leaders of the new progressive movement in education, such as Francis

Parker, G. Stanley Hall, and the still famous John Dewey, identified with the spirit of the look-say method, rejecting, as it did, the highly structured teaching common to phonics classes. Progressive education was meant to release the child from what was perceived as the straitjacket of traditional schooling, set him free to explore learning in his own way and, perhaps most importantly, to enjoy his time in the classroom. An organized and teacher-directed class in letter-sound correspondences simply didn't fit the bill. So the most influential figures in education came down squarely in favor of the look-say method, and public schools soon fell into line behind them.

The emphasis among early leaders of the movement was clearly not on the development of competence in the traditional elementary disciplines of reading, writing, and arithmetic. The look-say method was not preferred over phonics because it was believed to teach reading more quickly or effectively, but because it allowed the child to be pleasantly exposed to a wide range of ideas. For Stanley Hall, who advocated that reading and writing "should be neglected in our system before [age] eight,"[103] literacy was greatly overrated:

> Very many men have lived and died and been great, even the leaders of their age, without any acquaintance with letters. The knowledge which illiterates acquire is probably on the whole more personal, direct, environmental and probably a much larger proportion of it practical. Moreover, they escape much eyestrain and mental excitement.[104]

Hall won over many of his contemporaries with these arguments, citing examples such as Charlemagne to highlight the achievements of illiterates. He was, it seems, unaware of the fact that Charlemagne was one of history's most aggressive literacy campaigners, encouraging the establishment of schools for the unlettered masses. The emperor himself tried desperately to learn to read and write, by some accounts sleeping with a writing tablet under his pillow so that he could practice in his few free moments.

Though reading had been knocked off its pedestal, it was by no means forgotten, and debate over the best way to teach children to read spawned numerous studies. These early studies have been analyzed and reanalyzed over the years, and the consensus among modern researchers is that phonics instruction was shown to be superior to the look-say method. The advantages were greatest when children were asked to read words they had not specifically been taught, because look-say children lacked the ability to readily break words down into their component parts and sound them out. Though the look-say method led to higher levels of comprehension in the first grade, because students were able to recognize by sight much of the limited vocabulary on which they were tested, phonics emerged as the better method by the time students were in second grade. Several studies found that students taught by the phonics method read more slowly than their look-say counterparts, but this deficit disappeared when accuracy, along with speed, was taken into account.[105]

This first round of studies was sufficiently conclusive to lead many researchers beyond the question of which method was best, to ask how phonics could most effectively be applied. Between the 1940s and the 1970s, two main approaches to phonics were compared: synthetic and analytic. The primary difference between these approaches was that the first built up from letters to syllables and finally to words, whereas the second began with words, and then broke them down into their constituent sounds. Synthetic phonics also tended to be more intensive and systematic than the analytic method. Though the results of this series of investigations was not as decisive as the one that came before, most studies gave the nod to the synthetic approach.

A funny thing happened as a result of all these research findings on the advantages of phonics over look-say, and of synthetic phonics over analytic phonics: Nothing. The story of reading instruction from the turn of the century to the 1950s was one of the increasing entrenchment of the look-say method. By the late fifties, phonics was almost entirely absent from reading instruction texts. What's more, the defense of illiteracy by some progressive educators continued. In 1951, a school principal by the name of A. H. Lauchner wrote:

> When we come to the realization that not every child has to read, figure, write and spell . . . that many of them either cannot or will not master these chores . . . then we shall be on the road to improving the junior high curriculum.
>
> Between this day and that a lot of selling must take place. But it's coming. We shall some day accept the thought that it is just as illogical to assume that every boy must be able to read as it is that each one must be able to perform on a violin, that it is no more reasonable to require that each girl shall spell well than it is that each one shall bake a good cherry pie. . . .
>
> If and when we are able to convince a few folks that mastery of reading, writing, and arithmetic is not the one road leading to happy successful living, the next step is to cut down the amount of time and attention devoted to these areas in general junior high-school courses. . . .
>
> One junior high in the East has . . . accepted the fact that some twenty per cent of their students will not be up to standard in reading. . . . That's straight thinking.[106]

Lauchner's confidence that educators could sell the public on the benefits of illiteracy seems to have been unjustified. Tests of functional literacy conducted during the forties and early fifties showed that anywhere from a quarter to a half of all Americans were unable to read and understand simple documents, and public worry and discontent began to build. The public's apprehensions finally erupted in the mid-fifties with the publication of Rudolf Flesch's book *Why Johnny Can't Read,* which advocated a return to early phonics instruction.

In response to the outcry, some phonics instruction was reintroduced into public schools over the next several decades, but the change was insubstantial. When Flesch wrote *Why Johnny Still Can't Read* in 1981, he estimated that only one school in six was using the sort of intensive synthetic phonics approach supported by research on reading instruction methods.[107] Most schools used an ad hoc combination of look-say and occasional unstructured phonics, which was neither empirically grounded nor particularly appealing to most teachers. Still, explicit, systematic phonics did have a foot in the door in some places, and given its demonstrated superiority over other methods an optimist might expect it to have spread like wildfire. Alas, there is little room for optimism in the history of U.S. public schooling.

Progressive educators continued to abhor any instructional strategy that called for drills, worksheets, or highly structured, teacher-directed lessons. In fact, they rejected the whole idea that complex skills could be broken down into clearly defined units, taught separately, and then recombined to achieve mastery—a concept at the heart of all explicit phonics instruction. In opposition to systematic, skills-based approaches, they argued that learning to read was as natural as learning to speak, and that children would therefore become literate on their own if exposed to rich works of literature in a supportive environment. This view came to be known as the "whole language" philosophy of reading.

Because whole-language advocates generally reject the systematization of pedagogical methods, fully detailed and elaborated instructional plans are hard to find. After studying a wide range of whole-language publications, teacher and researcher Dorothy Watson concluded that it is "not a program, package, set of materials, method, practice, or technique; rather, it is a perspective on language and learning that leads to the acceptance of certain strategies, methods, materials, and techniques."[108]

In practice, whole-language teachers often (but not always):

- Read predictable, illustrated stories to students over and over until the students have essentially memorized them.
- Encourage children to guess words they do not recognize by looking at the pictures which accompany the text or by inferring their meaning from the context of the story.
- Periodically introduce a letter sound and suggest that children guess unknown words by looking at first and sometimes last letters. (Sounding out entire words is not encouraged.)
- Do not correct children when they guess the wrong word, particularly if the meaning of the children's guess is similar to the meaning of the correct word.
- Encourage students to invent their own spellings when they write, rather than teaching them the accepted spellings, and do not correct spelling errors once they have been made.

These practices, and opposition to intensive systematic phonics, proved eminently popular within a public-education establishment dominated by progressive thinking. In the late 1980s, "a survey of 43 texts used to train reading teachers found that none advocated systematic phonics instruction—and only nine even mentioned that there was a debate on the issue."[109]

In the early 1990s, schools in Alexandria, Virginia embraced the whole-language approach. According to the *Washington Post,* at least one principal confiscated his school's entire collection of spelling and phonics workbooks. Fearful that their students would fall behind, "some teachers ended up doing spelling and phonics on the sly. In other schools nobody knew what they were supposed to do." Looking back on the fiasco in late 1995, one well-respected teacher told the *Post* reporter:

> We were supposed to read nice stories and then do cutsie [sic] activities—an art project, some "critical thinking"—centered around the stories. The impression was given that phonics is dead. Now . . . the handwriting, the spelling, the reading comprehension is worse than ever. The administrators who pushed whole language are trying to cover themselves and say they never told us not to teach phonics.[110]

No state threw itself so slavishly at the feet of whole language as California. In 1987, a reading program was introduced that focused on teaching children to read simply by exposing them to literature. Phonics, and structured, direct teaching in general, fell by the wayside. Here too, elementary school officials often seized phonics and spelling texts to ensure the widest possible adoption of the approved methods.[111] Textbook publishers were warned by the state education department that only instructional materials taking a whole-language approach would be considered. Despite their objections to the omission of phonics, publishers were forced to fall into line in order to have any hope of penetrating the lucrative California textbook market. The only series of kindergarten through eighth-grade materials eventually approved by the state was pure whole language.

What happened next? Reading achievement in California began to decline. The only test for which state-level data are available both before and after the adoption of whole-language is the California Assessment Program (CAP). In the three years prior to the introduction of the whole-language curriculum, the CAP reading scores of third-graders had risen steadily from 268 to 282. After the introduction of whole language in 1987, the scores stagnated for one year and then began to fall off, hitting 275 by 1990. Perhaps coincidentally, the CAP was discontinued in that year.[112]

By 1994, fourth-graders in California were tied for last place on the National Assessment of Educational Progress's reading report card. Only a third of California's fourth-graders reached even the "Basic" (lowest) level of proficiency identified by the test. The other two thirds did so badly as to literally be off the charts. In theory, these results could simply have been a reflection of California's disproportionately high ethnic and immigrant populations, but the evidence indicates otherwise. A breakdown of the results by ethnicity[113] reveals that:

- Californian whites had the worst scores, on average, of whites anywhere in the nation.
- Hispanic Californians had the worst scores, on average, of Hispanic students anywhere in the nation.
- Californian blacks had the second lowest scores, on average, of blacks anywhere in the nation.

The collapse of reading did not go entirely unnoticed. Numerous parents and some teachers complained that children were not being taught to sound out new words, or to use any other specific reading skills. Unfortunately for the students, parents who sought a clear explanation of how simple exposure to words would allow their children to become literate, and who requested explicit phonics instruction, were ignored. When one former school-board member toured the state, interviewing teachers, parents, and current board members, "most told her the new instructional methods weren't working."[114] Despite this fact, her and others' attempts to change the state's reading program were blocked by the department of education. In the process, she was labeled a "phonics nut" by some state officials.

Following their children's poor showing on the 1994 NAEP reading test, Californian parents and citizens' groups publicly demanded a return to systematic phonics instruction. Rather than acknowledge the disastrous results of the pure whole-language approach, many advocates of the method refused to face reality. Professor Kenneth Goodman, one of the best-known popularizers of whole language, dismissed the poor performance of students taught by that method, saying: "The test scores—that simply is political fodder. . . . I think what you have to look at is the [conservative] political agenda [of phonics advocates]."[115] Meanwhile, journals sponsored by the National Council of Teachers of English published articles on how to defend whole language, rather than how to fix it.

Bill Honig, who was state superintendent of schools when California enshrined whole language, is somewhat more candid, concluding from his experiences that phonics is a necessary part of any reading instruction program. In an interview with *Education Week,* Honig went on to imply that the abandonment of structured phonics teaching was an honest mistake, stating that "breakthrough research about how children learn to read was unavailable" in 1987.[116] As described above, however, a mountain of evidence favoring systematic phonics had already been accumulated by the 1970s. That research was made available in a single comprehensive survey of the field conducted by professor Jeanne Chall in 1967 and updated in 1983. Her conclusion? Reading instruction that begins with structured phonics lessons

> [p]roduces better results, at least up to the point where sufficient evidence seems to be available. . . . The results are better, not only in terms of the mechanical aspects of literacy alone, as was once supposed, but also in terms of the ultimate goal of reading instruction—comprehension and possibly even speed of reading.[117]

Nor was Chall's an isolated voice. Numerous other researchers had come to the same conclusions prior to California's leap into pedagogical oblivion in 1987.[118] The consensus was summed up in 1984 in the *Handbook of Reading Research,* which stated that "phonics instruction is necessary and essential for many children; consequently, it should be an integral part of all beginning reading programs."[119] Surely someone in the state department of education must have been familiar with these findings, if not superintendent Honig himself.

As additional evidence favoring phonics continued to accumulate in the late eighties and nineties,[120] much of the elementary education community remained locked in the deathly embrace of a pure whole-language approach. In her recent book *Reading Process and Practice: From Socio-Psycholinguistics to Whole Language,* Constance Weaver remarks that "whole language educators . . . assume that an emphasis on skills detracts from the process of learning to read."[121] Weaver even harks back to the days of Stanley Hall, when progressive educators were blunt about their emphasis being on children's enjoyment rather than their academic achievements, concluding one section of her book with the following statement:

> The moral of the story is that we should not expect whole language classrooms to immediately succeed in producing entire classrooms of chldren [sic] who can read, write, compute, and reason perfectly; but we can and do expect that whole language classrooms will generate continued learning and enhanced self-esteem and pleasure in learning. And if some learners still need more support or more time than one classroom teacher can provide, we should not be surprised.[122]

Whole-language philosophy is not entirely without merit. Its emphases, at least in principle, on understanding the meaning of texts and on using original literature rather than the processed cheese of modern textbooks are commendable. These worthy goals are undermined, however, by the means whole-language practitioners choose to apply. It is well known that children taught by the whole-language method make more mistakes when they read. Their ability to recognize words is inferior to that of children instructed in phonics.[123] As if this were not sufficiently damning, whole-language teachers often oppose the idea of correcting their students' errors—or fail to acknowledge them as errors at all. More than twenty years ago, whole-language guru Kenneth Goodman shocked the readers of the *New York Times* with his idea of "reading miscues" (what you or I would call mistakes). Goodman was asked the following question by a *Times* reporter: "A student learning to read comes upon the sentence 'The boy jumped on the horse and rode off.' But instead of saying 'horse,' the student substitutes 'pony.' Should the teacher correct him?" Remarkably, Goodman's answer was an unambiguous no.[124]

Lest the reader think this comment outdated or exceptional, consider the section on "miscues" from Weaver's 1994 book on teaching children to read. After observing a student named Erica's attempt to read a passage of text out loud, Weaver described many of the child's mistakes with evident approbation. When Erica read the sentence " 'I ain't nasty,' I said, properly holding my temper in check," but said "proudly" instead of "properly," Weaver was full of praise, pointing out that the character in the story "was indeed a proud young girl."[125] So long as the error makes sense in the context of the passage, whole-language proponents are loath to correct it—even if it does not have the same sense as the correct word. In their book *Evaluation: Whole Language, Whole Child,* authors Jane Baskwill and Paulette Whitman exhort teachers to distinguish between "[m]iscues resulting in loss of meaning ('house' for 'horse')" and "[m]iscues resulting in *no loss of meaning* ('home' for 'house')."[126] And yet, would it really be quite the same if Dorothy made the journey from Oz back to Kansas by repeating: "There's no place like house, there's no place like house . . ."?

Children who are taught to casually substitute words they know for ones they do not recognize, and who learn by their teachers' example that any more-or-less meaningful word will do, are doomed to have a stunted, inaccurate understanding of the texts they read. English is not a guessing game and close is not good enough. All horses are not ponies, and "properly" does not mean "proudly." If a child manages to reach adulthood without having learned to accurately read the exact words on a printed page, that child will be sorely handicapped.

The Lobotomization of Textbooks

The reading texts of the 1800s and early 1900s were challenging and often profound books. Their authors sought not only to teach basic literacy skills, but also to raise students to the highest possible levels of understanding—to imbue them with a love of wisdom and an appreciation for the graceful and subtle use of language. Even reading texts meant for twelve- and thirteen-year-old children were comprised of "selections of prose and poetry from the best American and English writers"[127]—not simplified or paraphrased, but in their original forms. Take, for example, the work of British essayist and dramatist Joseph

Addison. The following passage from Addison's "Reflections in Westminster Abbey" appeared in William McGuffey's *Fourth Reader for Advanced Students*. First published in 1836, the book was intended for the equivalent of today's eighth- to tenth-graders:

> When I am in a serious humor, I very often walk by myself in Westminster Abbey, where the gloominess of the place and the use to which it is applied, with the solemnity of the building and the condition of the people who lie in it, are apt to fill the mind with a kind of melancholy, or rather thoughtfulness, that is not disagreeable. I yesterday passed a whole afternoon in the churchyard, the cloisters, and the church amusing myself with the tombstones and inscriptions which I met with in those several regions of the dead.
>
> Most of them recorded nothing else of the buried person, but that he was born upon one day and died upon another. The whole history of his life being comprehended in these two circumstances that are common to all mankind. I could not but look upon those registers of existence, whether of brass or marble, as a kind of satire upon the departed persons, who had left no other memorial of themselves, but that they were born, and that they died.[128]

Remarkably, Addison's passage was not an aberration. McGuffey's whole series of readers, of which roughly 120 million sets were sold between 1836 and 1920, was filled with rich and elegant language. Other textbook publishers shared similar views on what children could and should read. Consider this excerpt from Edgar Allan Poe's "Island of the Fay," which was included in William Elson's *Grammar School Reader, Book Three* (1910), intended for seventh-graders:

> It was during one of my lonely journeyings, amid a far distant region of mountain locked within mountain, and sad rivers and melancholy tarns writhing or sleeping within all—that I chanced upon a certain rivulet and island. I came upon them suddenly in the leafy June, and threw myself upon the turf, beneath the branches of an unknown odorous shrub, that I might doze as I contemplated the scene. I felt that thus only should I look upon it—such was the character of phantasm which it wore.
>
> On all sides—save to the west, where the sun was about sinking—arose the verdant walls of the forest. The little river, which turned sharply in its course, and was thus immediately lost to sight, seemed to have no exit from its prison, but to be absorbed by the deep green foliage of the trees to the east—while in the opposite quarter (so it appeared to me as I lay at length and glanced upward), there poured down noiselessly and continuously into the valley a rich golden and crimson waterfall from the sunset fountains of the sky.[129]

While it is possible to find easier passages in the readers of the period, the ones presented here are not atypical. Middle-school-aged children routinely read authors such as Jefferson, Tennyson, Keats, Emerson, Longfellow, and many others. Of course, not every child of a given age was expected to master the same text. In the 1800s, students progressed through the successively more difficult readers more or less at their own pace, for classrooms had not yet become rigidly divided into grades. If a bright twelve-year-old was hard at work on McGuffey's fourth reader while her older brother studied the third, nothing was considered particularly amiss. Still, expectations were high, and even the brightest students were afforded challenging and enlightening reading experiences.

Two factors combined in the 1920s and 1930s to change all that. First of all, the look-say method of reading instruction began to supplant the traditional phonics-first approach, making it necessary to greatly reduce the written vocabulary to which children were exposed. Children generally enter school with large spoken vocabularies, but very small written ones. When they are taught how to decode new written words into the spoken words they already know, their written vocabularies can grow quite quickly. But, since students in the 1920s and 1930s were no longer being taught to identify words by sounding them out, they simply could not cope with the rapid introduction of new words common to earlier reading texts. Each new word had to be memorized as a whole, rather than decoded by putting together the sounds represented by its letters, so the task of reading works of great literature became all but impossible. Though a student acquainted with the alphabet and its sounds would have had a good chance of pronouncing, and thereby recognizing, the long but familiar word "immediately," a child taught only by the look-say method might well have seen it as a mass of unintelligible letters, even though he would have recognized the word if it had been spoken or if he could have sounded it out.[130]

The second factor that pushed reading textbooks into a tailspin was a well-meaning but overzealous attempt to cater to children experiencing difficulty with the existing texts. As public schools adopted a formal age-based grading system, it became more apparent than ever that all children did not learn at the same pace. Some progressed through the assigned readers without undue problems, while others struggled to keep up or fell behind. A number of solutions to this problem could have been adopted, such as grouping students by achievement-level rather than age, or by offering textbooks tailored to the abilities of different students in a given class, but neither of these alternatives was chosen. Instead, *all textbooks* were simplified to the level of the slowest students.

By the end of the 1930s, reading texts had already been made easier than some researchers suggested was appropriate, but the lobotomization of books continued.[131] Many school officials and educational theorists maintained that easier was always better, and used newly developed "readability" formulas to reject all but the simplest texts. Publishers competed with one another to excise new words and truncate sentences in their efforts to meet the demand for high "readability." After a forty-year race for the basement of literacy, educators finally struck bottom during the 1960s and 1970s. Since that time, reading texts have remained at an abysmally low level of depth and complexity in comparison to their nineteenth-century precursors.

To understand the extent of the damage done during this intellectual purge, you have only to read the following excerpt from the eighth-grade reader *Worlds Beyond,* published in 1989 by Silver Burdett & Ginn:

> It was a typical wagon train of the 1840s. The swaying wagons, plodding animals, and walking people stretched out along the trail for almost a mile.
>
> Near the end of the train, a boy holding a hickory stick moved slowly through the dust. He used the stick to poke and prod the cows that trudged beside him, mooing and complaining.
>
> "Get along!" he shouted. "Hey! Hey! Get along!"
>
> Dust floated in the air. It clogged the boy's nose, parched his throat, and coated his face. His cheeks were smeared where he had brushed away the big mosquitoes that buzzed about everywhere.
>
> Up ahead, his family's wagon bounced down the trail. He could hear the *crack* of his father's whip above the heads of the oxen that pulled the wagon. The animals coughed and snorted. The chains on their yokes rattled with every step they took.[132]

This story, "The Long Road West," is neither the most challenging nor the most trivial one to be found in today's eighth-grade readers. Its short, choppy sentences, simple vocabulary, and lack of intellectual profundity are fairly representative of what publishers such as Macmillan,[133] Harcourt Brace Jovanovich,[134] and D.C. Heath and Company[135] have to offer. Unlike the passages from earlier textbooks cited above, which score at the college level on modern readability scales, this one is barely at the seventh-grade level, despite being targeted at eighth-graders.[136]

In some cases, contemporary reading textbooks such as the one quoted above are restricted to low-achieving students, with their more advanced fellows being assigned literature anthologies, but there is little difference to be found between the two. Though literature anthologies are more likely to include passages from well-known authors, the particular tracts chosen are still vastly simpler than those used prior to 1910 or even 1920. Take, for example, Nathaniel Hawthorne's "Theseus," reproduced in the popular eighth-grade anthology *Enjoying Literature* (1989):

> In the old city of Troezene, at the foot of a lofty mountain, there lived long ago a boy named Theseus. His grandfather, King Pitheus, was the sovereign of that country. His mother's name was Aethra. As for his father, the boy had never seen

> him. But from his earliest remembrance, Aethra used to go with Theseus into a wood and sit upon a moss-grown rock which was deeply sunken into the earth. Here she often talked with her son about his father. She said that he was called Aegeus and that he was a great king and ruled over Attica and dwelt at Athens, which was as famous a city as any in the world.
>
> "Mother," asked the boy, "why cannot I go to Athens and tell King Aegeus that I am his son?"
>
> "That may happen by and by," said Aethra. "You are not yet big and strong enough to set out on such an errand."
>
> "And how soon shall I be strong enough?"
>
> "You are but a boy," replied his mother. "When you can lift this rock and show me what is hidden beneath it, I promise you my permission to depart."[137]

Neither this passage in particular, nor the anthology in which it is found, is noticeably more challenging in its use of language than the modern eighth-grade reader discussed above. The mid-sixth-grade readability score received by "Theseus"[138] is actually below that of many excerpts offered in *Worlds Beyond* and other readers. Overall, the passages in eighth-grade literature anthologies such as Scribner Laidlaw's *Enjoying Literature* and Scott, Foresman's *Explorations in Literature*[139] seem to hover between sixth- and ninth-grade readability levels—not even approaching the level of passages in older readers (like Elson's and McGuffey's) intended for seventh- to ninth-graders.

For some children, today's textbooks are no doubt sufficiently challenging, if dry and uninspiring; but for many others they are painfully oversimplified. Those students in the top quarter or third of ability, who, in bygone years, would have been reading unedited versions of Poe's "Island of the Fay" or Addison's "Reflections in Westminster Abbey" by the seventh or eighth grade, are being cheated each time they are assigned passages from "dumbed-down" modern compilations. For these students, current "language arts" assignments fall far short of the eclectic readers used more than one hundred and fifty years ago.

Does this mean that textbook publishers are incompetent? Not at all. In order to stay in business, publishers have to produce the kind of books that public schools will buy. In the words of one textbook publishing executive: "If the customer wants a pink stretch Cadillac, I may think it's tacky and wasteful, but I would be a fool to produce a fuel-efficient black compact if nobody is going to buy it."[140] Publishers have "dumbed-down" textbooks because dumb sells.

Textbook Selection: They Choose, You Lose

In principle, the deterioration in textbooks could be reversed in an instant if more-challenging reading materials, suited to the varied interests and abilities of students, were consistently demanded by the public schools. To understand how unlikely it would be for this to happen, you have to know how textbooks are chosen.

Up until the nineteenth century, most schools had no control over the selection of textbooks—they were chosen and supplied by families themselves, and teachers simply had to make do. The demise of this somewhat impractical arrangement was hastened by the introduction of government schooling. As the public school system grew in size and power, its officials subsumed many of the responsibilities formerly vested in parents, including the provision of textbooks. First teachers, then principals, and eventually local school districts set the curriculum and selected appropriate reading matter. But for public schooling's staunchest advocates, this was not enough. The perceived benefits of statewide textbook adoption proved irresistibly seductive.

The two key arguments put forward by education reformers were that great economies of scale would be reaped, and that leaps in quality would be achieved, if a state-level committee of "experts" were appointed to choose the books that all schoolchildren would read. Problems with this idea, such as the differences in aptitude and interest among children, and the lack of consensus on many issues among parents, were glossed over with precious little ado, and the wheels of educational "progress" rolled on. Since the 1920s, almost half the states have had some form of state-level textbook-adoption process in place.

With the exception of New York, the states that delegate textbook selection to their localities are smaller than the state-level adoption states, but the key difference is not size, it is power. Like any customer who buys in enormous quantities, an adoption state wields tremendous influence over textbook publishers. Losing an adoption-state contract can mean a multimillion dollar hit to a publisher's bottom line. A state with decentralized textbook purchasing is impotent by comparison, since it cannot promise publishers such large orders.

Adoption states have thus come to dominate the textbook publishing industry over the years, with California, Texas, and Florida carrying the greatest weight. Together, these states comprise one quarter of the entire public school student population of the United States.[141] When the textbook-adoption committee of one of these states demands an addition to or deletion from a publisher's offerings, it is a good bet that the change will be made. But the costs of printing multiple versions of, say, a tenth-grade biology text, are significant—the more different versions, the lower the publisher's profit margin. As a result, publishers try to produce a single book that will meet the specifications of all the adoption states, and then offer that book to every state and district in the land. To do so, controversy must be scrupulously avoided, reducing the stew of life to a thin broth—palatable to everyone, though not necessarily appetizing to anyone. In 1967, textbook scholar Hillel Black wrote: "Censorship of any controversial issue or literary work in an attempt to avoid alienating a potential segment of the market is standard practice. Examples include the systematic exclusion of a play like Shakespeare's Othello."[142] The trouble with Othello is that publishers feared his relationship with a white woman might not meet with the approval of some southerners. Thus, his story was lost to open-minded students in both the North and the South.

But aside from cultural and ideological pasteurization, what is the effect of statewide textbook adoption? What do the committees look for in a submission? Based on trends in the content of textbooks, the primary answer appears to be "pictures." Year by year, the pages of school books, whether elementary or secondary, history or social studies, are filled with more and glossier pictures. Each successive edition, furthermore, tends to introduce a dazzling new array of pictures to replace the old, while the text and organization remain relatively unchanged. This kind of superficial change would doubtless be detected upon close inspection, but investigators such as Harriet Tyson-Bernstein and Arthur Woodward have shown that textbook committees rarely have the time, the training, or the incentive to make a thorough evaluation.[143] No particular expertise is required to sit on most states' selection committees, and members can be appointed by any number of different political bodies for any number of reasons.[144] Very often, committee members take a quick glance at the book, verify that the topics listed in their state's curriculum guidelines are at least mentioned in its table of contents or index, and if so, approve it. Not exactly the sort of expert review promised by progressive school reformers in days of yore.

Among the other factors weighed at adoption time is a book's inclusion of references to or pictures of women and minorities—the more, the better. But this rough heuristic, and the fact that publishers realize it is a rough heuristic, creates a problem. To win approval, publishers take the expedient step of adding in plenty of photographs of women, minorities, and minority women which do not necessarily have any educational bearing on the text they accompany.[145] Everyone who matters in the selection process—that is, everyone except the teachers and students who actually use the disjointed texts thus produced—seems to find this solution acceptable.

One of the most common measures used by textbook-adoption committees in evaluating submissions is also one of the most damaging. It is the belief that for books, newer is invariably better. But apart from advanced science texts covering leading-edge developments in their fields, there is no sound reason for preferring a recent copyright date to an old one. As shown in the previous section, the content of nineteenth- and early-twentieth-century readers was generally far superior to that of contemporary "language arts" texts. For elementary classes in history, literature, mathematics, philosophy, art, and many other subjects, newness confers little or no advantage. Furthermore, a recent publication date does not guarantee up-to-date content. There is overwhelming evidence, according to Tyson-Bernstein, that brand-new textbooks often contain outdated information.[146] Despite these facts, there is a widespread policy among state and district adoption committees to eliminate from consideration any textbook more than three years old.[147] This essentially pointless requirement is one of the key factors contributing to high textbook prices and the superficial nature of changes from one edition to the next. The cost of printing a new edition is substantial. In fact, manufacturing costs are the single most expensive item in the production of textbooks.[148] The more frequently publishers are forced to release new editions, the greater their incentive to minimize editorial expenditures by altering only the appearance rather than the content of the book.

In addition to the frequent use of misguided selection criteria, some committee members appear to use no discernible criteria whatever. In the 1980s, the late Richard Feynman was asked to sit on California's selection committee to review mathematics textbooks. A Nobel laureate in physics known for his ability to give straightforward and interesting explanations of complex concepts, Feynman was eminently qualified for the job. Nonetheless, he proved ill-suited to the state textbook-adoption process. He refused, for instance, to provide a rating for a book he had not received. When asked for his opinion on the missing book, one of a three-book series, Feynman informed the other committee members that he had none, since he had not read it. Despite his sensible answer, Feynman was asked the same question again, and with some dismay gave the same answer. As it turned out, the book in question had been withheld from the reviewers because the publisher had been unable to complete it before the submission deadline, and had sent a book of blank pages in its stead. Amazingly, several people on the committee *had* provided ratings for the non-book. More shocking still, the average rating received by the collection of blank pages was slightly higher than that of the books containing actual words. Feynman eventually concluded that some committee members were too busy to read the books and offered ratings anyway so as not to appear derelict.[149]

Though the blank book episode was perhaps the most amusing of Feynman's experiences on the committee, it was by no means the most ominous for California's families. He also described how the selection process, by stifling direct price competition between publishers, regularly cost taxpayers substantial amounts of money. As the adoption procedure was structured, the cost of books was often not taken into account until very late in the game. This prevented price competition between publishing houses, removing the incentive to set low prices. In one exceptional case, however, the committee was unable to decide between two texts, and recommended both to the state school board, asking them to choose between the two. Since one of the two texts was slightly cheaper than the other, it was the initial choice, and the representative for that book's publishing firm stood up and announced that the book could be ready early, by the next term. A representative of the competing publisher, who was also present, responded that his firm should be allowed to enter another bid, since the date had been changed. What ensued was an accidental bidding war that slashed $2,000,000 from the amount the state had been planning to pay for a single textbook order.[150] This aberration aside, it seems that the normal operation of California's statewide textbook-adoption process generated economies of scale for the publishing industry, rather than the schools.

Of course, the fact that publishers did not typically have to compete with each other on price did not mean that they failed to seek competitive advantage; they were just able to do so more cheaply. "The way they competed," said Feynman, "was to impress the members of the curriculum commission." This they accomplished by providing gifts of dried fruit, monogrammed briefcases, "free" lunches, and seminars explaining the texts to the committee members — seminars which, of course, would not be given to the actual teachers or students using the texts.

Ironically, publishers themselves occasionally complain about these gift-giving practices. In February 1998, twelve textbook publishing companies filed protests against the Louisiana selection process on the grounds that a competing firm had gained an unfair advantage by flying one of the selection committee members to an out-of-town seminar. The accused publisher, Scott Foresman–Addison Wesley, had this explanation for its actions: "The facts are that all major companies do these sorts of things all the time."[151]

The pedagogical and curricular flaws outlined above have had a grave effect on the achievement of public school students. That effect is described in painful detail in the following chapter.

6

The Performance Crisis in Public Schooling

Myth? . . .

"In 1983, the Reagan White House began to make sweeping claims attacking the conduct and achievements of America's public schools—claims that were contradicted by evidence we knew about. . . . Slowly, then, we began to suspect that something was not quite right, that organized malevolence might actually be underway. . . . The more we poked into our story, the more nasty lies about [public] education we unearthed; the more we learned about how government officials and their allies were ignoring, suppressing, and distorting evidence."—David Berliner and Bruce Biddle, The Manufactured Crisis: Myths, Fraud, and the Attack on America's Public Schools

. . . Or Reality?

Math class at Walt Whitman Intermediate School in Flatbush, Brooklyn. Photo courtesy of Emily Sachar.[1]

This chapter presents a guided tour of U.S. public school performance, touching on all of the most contentious issues: Is student achievement really low and declining? Has spending really skyrocketed? Are mismanagement and corruption as rampant as critics allege? The answers to these questions (unfortunate *Yes*'s, all) are presented in the following two sections.

Despite its overall weakness, government schooling is not without the occasional bright spot; some public schools do manage to meet most of the public's needs, and the roots of their success are explored in the third section of this chapter. The fourth and final section adds something that is typically lacking in evaluations of public schooling: perspective. It is only by comparing the lack of overall progress in government-run schools to trends in other industries and fields of human endeavor that we can fully appreciate the magnitude of the public schooling crisis.

Stagnation and Decline in Academic Achievement

What the Tests Reveal: The Eclectic Slide

How do today's public school students compare, on average, to those of two, four, or eight decades ago?[2] Are they academically better or worse off? That question is answered in the following subsections, which draw together the results of a broad range of national and international studies.

Overall achievement before 1970

As far back as 1906,[3] researchers began conducting "then and now" studies that analyzed changes in student achievement over time, particularly in reading proficiency. Several attempts have been made to piece together the results of these studies in order to obtain a coherent long-term picture. The best such effort[4] was conducted by Professors Lawrence Stedman and Carl Kaestle in 1991. As a caveat to their conclusions, Stedman and Kaestle observed that many "then and now" comparisons were not nationally representative and failed to control for demographic changes[5] in the test groups over time, undermining the validity of their results. These problems were especially severe in the older studies, and thus the evidence for the early to mid-1900s is somewhat sketchy.

With that proviso in mind, Stedman and Kaestle found that average reading achievement for students in school at any given age stagnated for the first seventy years of the twentieth century.[6] Their reference to age level was meant to account for the increasingly popular practice of social promotion. Students in the earlier part of this century were not generally promoted to the next grade unless they had mastered the previous grade's material, whereas modern students are frequently pushed through the system regardless of their level of achievement. This means that the students in any given grade today are younger, on average, than students who were in that same grade fifty or eighty years ago. Age (rather than grade) is thus a more reliable indicator of how long a student has been in school, and provides a fairer basis for comparing the effectiveness of historical and modern schools.

Though the original Stedman/Kaestle analysis was careful to consider many of the significant influences on student achievement (such as the age factor just described), the analysis did overlook one relevant aspect of pre-1970s schooling: the ever-lengthening school year. In 1909–10, pupils attended school for an average of 113 days.[7] By 1969–70, the figure had jumped to 161.7 (where it has remained, roughly speaking, ever since).[8] Because classes were in session five days a week, this amounts to a difference of almost two and a half months of schooling per year. Students in the sixth grade in 1969–70 had thus attended school for fifteen more months than 1909–10 students.[9] The difference for tenth-grade pupils was twenty-five months—about three additional school years. Taking these variations into account is just as important as comparing students by age rather than grade, since it provides a more accurate picture of how much time students actually spent in the classroom. Students in the late sixties received much more schooling but scored no higher on reading achievement tests, indicating a probable decline in the efficiency of public school instruction during the first two thirds of the twentieth century.

Overall achievement after 1970

Student achievement has stagnated or fallen in most subjects since 1970, with the largest and most thoroughly established decline occurring in basic literacy. That is the verdict of the five most reliable sources of evidence: the National Assessment of Educational Progress (NAEP), the International Evaluation of Education Achievement (IEA), the Young Adult Literacy Survey (YALS), the National Adult Literacy Survey (NALS), and the International Adult Literacy Survey (IALS). Together, these five groups of tests cover the gamut of ages from 9 to 25, and a full range of academic subjects. A great many other measures of student achievement are available, predominantly norm-referenced[10] tests such as the Iowa Test of Basic Skills, but these are properly regarded by the majority of analysts as unreliable indicators of national trends,[11] and thus they are not considered here.

The NAEP covers the most curricular ground, measuring the knowledge and skills of U.S. students in reading, writing, mathematics, science, geography, literature, and U.S. history. Tests in some subjects date back to 1969, while most of the others were introduced during the seventies. Every few years, the NAEPs are administered to nationally representative samples of fourth-, eighth-, and twelfth-graders. Taken as a whole, their results have remained essentially flat, with a slight, but statistically significant, downturn between 1992 and 1994 in reading.[12] NAEP writing scores for eleventh-graders also show a slight decline since the late 1980s. Those who stress self-esteem over academic achievement can console themselves, however, with the fact that students' perceptions of their writing ability improved noticeably despite the drop in their actual performance.[13] The key NAEP results are graphed in Figures 1 and 2.

Figure 1. NAEP Mathematics and Writing Score Trends

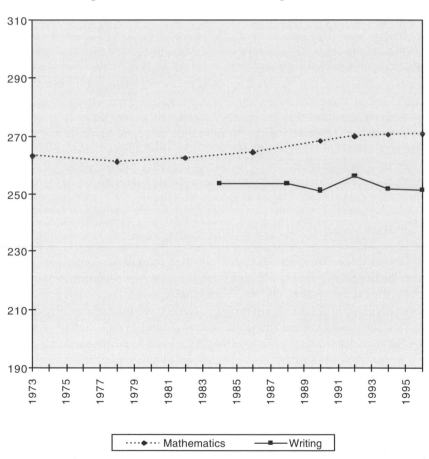

Data sources: Jay R. Campbell, Clyde M. Reese, Christine O'Sullivan, and John A. Dossey, *NAEP 1994 Trends in Academic Progress* (Washington, DC: NCES, 1996), v; and Jay R. Campbell, Kristin E. Voelkl, and Patricia L. Donahue, *NAEP 1996 Trends in Academic Progress* (Washington, DC: NCES, 1997), v.

Figure 2. NAEP Reading and Science Score Trends

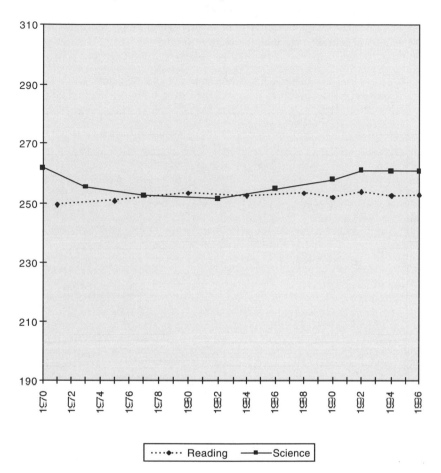

Data sources: Jay R. Campbell, Clyde M. Reese, Christine O'Sullivan, and John A. Dossey, *NAEP 1994 Trends in Academic Progress* (Washington, DC: NCES, 1996), v; and Jay R. Campbell, Kristin E. Voelkl, and Patricia L. Donahue, *NAEP 1996 Trends in Academic Progress* (Washington, DC: NCES, 1997), v.

The next set of trend results comes from the IEA, and encompasses reading, mathematics, and science achievement. The IEA tested the reading abilities of students from numerous countries in both 1970 and 1990. The two tests were not entirely identical, but the recent doctoral dissertation of Petra Lietz has made score comparisons possible by looking at how students performed on items that were common to both tests.[14] The results, charted in Figure 3, reveal that reading achievement of U.S. fourteen-year-olds dropped from 602 to 541 during the twenty years leading up to 1990—a decrease of about 8 percent on the 800-point scale. Only one of the other seven participating countries suffered a worse drop in achievement than the United States.

Figure 3. IEA Reading Score Trends of U.S. Students

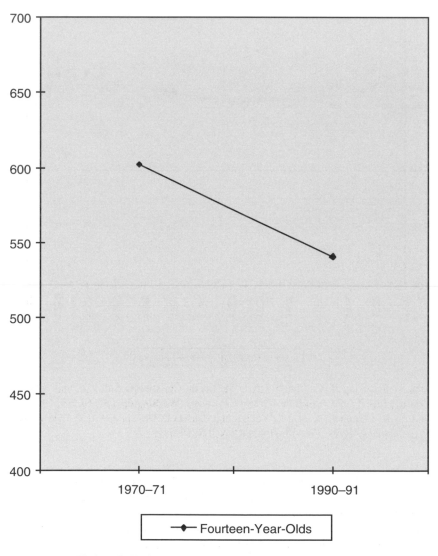

Data source: Herbert J. Walberg, "U.S. Schools Teach Reading Least Productively," *Research in the Teaching of English* 30, no. 3 (1996): 333.

The IEA's First and Second International Mathematics Studies (FIMS and SIMS) were conducted in the mid-1960s and the mid-1980s, respectively, and tested both thirteen- and seventeen-year-olds. Taken as a whole, scores were essentially constant, with younger students losing ground, while the older students

Figure 4. Trends in IEA Mathematics Scores of U.S. Students

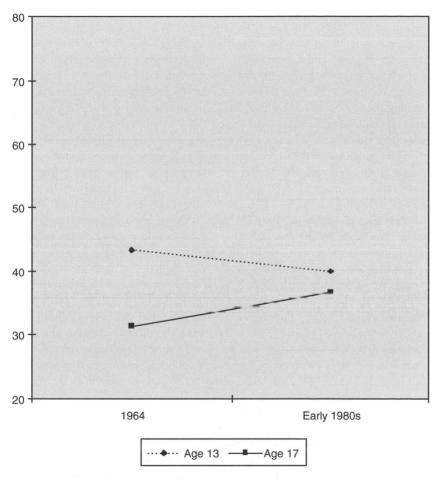

Data source: David F. Robitaille, "Achievement Comparisons between the First and Second IEA Studies of Mathematics," *Educational Studies in Mathematics* 21 (1990): 395–414. Note that the data for seventeen-year-olds is based on only eighteen questions which were common to senior levels of the first and second international mathematics tests. The accuracy of the trend line for that age group is thus in some doubt, and is included here only for completeness. (Note also that thirteen-year-olds and seventeen-year-olds were given different tests.)

gained somewhat. As depicted in Figure 4, the gain recorded by seventeen-year-olds was slightly larger than the drop of their younger counterparts, but the reliability of the data for seventeen-year-olds is in doubt. David Robitaille, author of the study comparing FIMS and SIMS results, acknowledged that "[o]nly 18 of the 136 items used in the second study at the Senior Level had also been used in the first. This limits the drawing of achievement comparisons between the two studies [at the Senior, i.e., seventeen-year-old, Level]."[15]

Science knowledge was tested by the IEA in 1970–71 and 1983–84, and was scored on an 800-point scale. Both ten-year-olds and fourteen-year-olds participated, with the raw U.S. score results indicating a marginal improvement for the younger group and a more significant drop among older students.[16] Taking the two age groups together, the raw scores pointed to a decline in U.S. science achievement over time, but this was not the whole story. The researchers conducting the tests noticed that U.S. students participating in 1983–84 were, on average, eight months older than their 1970–71 counterparts, giving them an advantage on the test. When this age advantage was statistically adjusted away, the IEA found that scores for both groups of U.S. students had dropped—by 16 points among ten-year-olds, and by a whopping 47 points among fourteen-year-olds (see Figure 5).[17] These were by far the worst performance trends of any participating nation. In 1997, the results of the IEA's Third International Mathematics and Science Study (TIMSS) were released, but unfortunately no effort was made by the researchers involved to allow comparisons between TIMSS results and those of earlier IEA math or science studies.

Reading tests of older students and recent high-school graduates echo the disappointing findings of the IEA. Several sophisticated investigations of literacy skills have been conducted since the mid-1980s.[18] Two of these studies, the National Adult Literacy Survey (NALS) of 1992 and the Young Adult Literacy Survey (YALS) of 1985, were designed to be directly comparable, using the same 0 to 500 score range, and the same five levels of achievement.[19] As shown in Figure 6, the average score of twenty-one- to twenty-five-year-olds fell from 293 to 280 over the intervening seven-year period (from the middle of level 3 to the bottom).[20]

In 1994, an International Adult Literacy Survey (IALS) was conducted in seven nations, including the United States. Its overall structure and scoring system were identical to those of its U.S.-only precursors, and the specific kinds of tasks required to score at each of the five levels of achievement were essentially the same.[21] Unfortunately, the lead researcher for both the IALS and the NALS cautions that the results of the tests might not be entirely comparable due to differences in some details of the testing procedures.[22] Keeping this caution in mind, the verdict of the IALS is still grim. One out of every four U.S. sixteen- to twenty-five-year-olds scored at the lowest level of literacy achievement in 1994, a larger percentage than ever before and the second worst showing among the nations tested.[23] These results, along with those of the NALS, are charted in Figure 7.

Figure 5. Trends in IEA Science Scores of U.S. Students

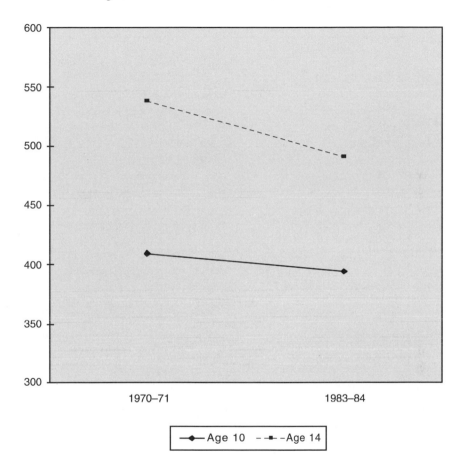

Data source: John P. Keeves and A. Schleicher, "Changes in Science Achievement: 1970–84," *The IEA Study of Science III: Changes in Science Education and Achievement: 1970 to 1984* (New York: Pergamon Press, 1991), 278. Note that the IEA statistically adjusted scores to account for slight age differences between the 1970–71 and 1983–84 test groups.

Figure 6. Trend in Literacy among Twenty-one- to
Twenty-five-year-olds on the YALS and NALS

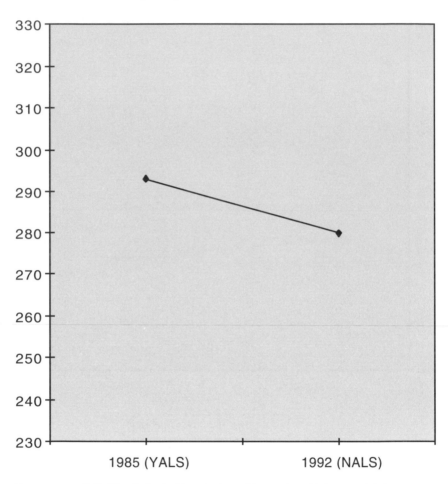

Data source: I. S. Kirsch, L. Jenkins, A. Jungeblut, and A. Kolstad, *Adult Literacy in America* (Washington, DC: NCES, U.S. Department of Education, 1993), 23.

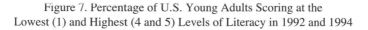

Figure 7. Percentage of U.S. Young Adults Scoring at the
Lowest (1) and Highest (4 and 5) Levels of Literacy in 1992 and 1994

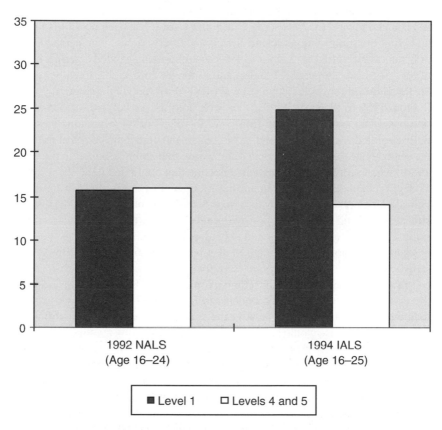

Data sources: National Center for Education Statistics, *Digest of Education Statistics 1995* (Washington, DC: U.S. Department of Education, 1995), 415; and Organization for Economic Cooperation and Development and Statistics Canada, *Literacy, Economy, and Society* (Paris: OECD Publications 1995), 152–54.

The atrophy of excellence

Previous sections have shown that the academic skills of the average American young person have been flat or slipping for at least three decades, but what about high achievers? How have the top third of U.S. students, those presumably most likely to play key roles in industry and public life, been doing? To find out, we can look at the Scholastic Assessment Test (SAT, formerly the Scholastic Aptitude Test). The SAT is well suited for use as a measure of advanced achievement. In addition to attracting most of the brightest high-school seniors, the SAT had, until it was "recentered"[24] in 1994, done an effective job of discriminating between good and excellent performance. Prior to 1994, every question on the test counted toward the final score. Since that year, it has been possible to miss up to four questions without losing any points. Every student who earned a 730 or better on the verbal SAT prior to 1994 would now be handed a perfect score of 800. So, while current SAT scores are no longer comparable to earlier ones, the test is useful for evaluating historical trends prior to the mid-nineties.

From 1950 to the early 1960s, scores on both the verbal and mathematical portions of the SAT fluctuated from year to year, but these variations essentially canceled each other out and scores began and ended the period at roughly the same level. As many Americans are aware, that stability ended in the mid-1960s, when scores began a sustained decline that continued until about 1980. Today, mathematics scores remain below their all-time highs, but have regained much of the ground they lost. Scores on the verbal portion of the test are still near their all-time lows, however, and therefore they have received the most scrutiny from both critics and defenders of public schooling.

Many educators have attempted to dismiss the verbal SAT score trend as a statistical illusion. Their arguments have focused on the increasing diversity of test takers along two main lines: ethnicity and academic ability. According to the first theory, more minority students (who generally receive lower scores than whites) began taking the test in the sixties and seventies, thus bringing down what otherwise would have been a stable or increasing average score. The second theory (sometimes called the "democratization" theory) suggests that increasing participation of low-achieving students, independently of race or ethnicity, caused the decline in average scores. In their 1992 article "What's Really Behind the SAT-Score Decline?" Charles Murray and Richard Herrnstein demonstrated that these factors failed to explain the bulk of the drop.[25]

In order for the ethnicity theory to hold water, it must be shown that the verbal scores of whites remained stable or rose during the period in question, so Murray and Herrnstein focused on the trend in the scores of white students. Using both published and unpublished ethnicity breakdowns supplied by the Educational Testing Service, they were able to chart white verbal scores independent of changes in the participation of other ethnic groups. This allowed them to control for the increasing percentage of minority students taking the test in the seventies. Taking all of this into account, as well as the little-known fact that the verbal portion of the SAT actually became eight to thirteen points *easier* between 1963 and 1973,[26] Herrnstein and Murray determined that white students' scores dropped by somewhere between thirty-four and forty-four points between 1963 and 1980. The overall SAT score drop of the late sixties through the late seventies was thus caused as much by the falling scores of white students as by the increasing participation of minority students.

The fall in white students' average verbal scores could, however, have been caused by growth in the test-taking population, if many of the new white participants turned out to be low-achievers. The evidence does not support this theory. To begin with, the proportion of the white high-school senior population taking the test actually dropped from one third to roughly one quarter between 1963 and 1972, continuing to fall until 1976. This trend is reflected in the overall figures as well, which show an absolute drop in the number of students taking the SAT during the early seventies, despite a significant rise in the number of high-school graduates.[27] By looking at college admissions trends and other evidence from the period, Herrnstein and Murray came to the conclusion that this shrinking SAT-taking population was more likely the result of increased rather than decreased selectivity—that the students taking the test in the mid to late seventies were, on the whole, an even more elite subset of the senior population than the test takers of the 1960s. Despite this fact, their scores were substantially lower than the scores of their predecessors.

Earlier SAT trends also discredited the "democratization" theory. As many researchers have pointed out, the SAT-taking population grew considerably between the early fifties and early sixties, rising from about one student in fourteen to almost one in three. Rather than dropping during this period, scores went up marginally.[28]

Thus, the verbal abilities of the top third of high-school seniors appear to have dipped during the sixties and seventies, and they have yet to regain their lost ground. But what about the best of the best? Changes in the performance of top SAT takers over time yield yet another clue in the investigation of advanced skills. The results are still more disappointing.

The earliest published figures show that between 1972 and 1979, the proportion of SAT takers scoring above 600 on the verbal portion of the test dropped by roughly 36 percent, from 11 percent of the test-taking population (or 112,530 students) to only 7 percent (or 69,440 students).[29] And, as we have seen, this drop at the top occurred after several years of decline in the overall average had already taken place. Since 1979, the percentage of students scoring over 600 has remained at this low level. In 1994, only 7.58 percent of test takers scored over 600.[30]

Are today's kids just dumber, or are schools less effective?

Declining test scores could mean that students are getting less intelligent or less well prepared to learn, that schools are getting less effective, or a combination of both. Many educators have favored the first explanation, arguing that deteriorating family and social conditions have left children less well prepared for intellectual, academic work. By the time they start school, the theory goes, today's kids are already behind those of two or three generations ago. As it happens, a host of nationwide measures indicate that young children have consistently been getting brighter and better prepared to learn over the course of the twentieth century, and that the younger U.S. students are, the better they do on international tests.

The data on IQ trends are a prime example of this history of improvement. Between 1932 and 1978, *every*[31] major IQ study showed an increase in the average IQ of Americans. This trend has continued to the present day, with average IQ scores of all age groups relentlessly rising by roughly three points per decade. Writing in *American Scientist* magazine in 1997, Ulric Neisser observed that among children

> [t]he pattern of score increases for different types of tests is somewhat surprising. Because children attend school longer now and have become much more familiar with the testing of school-related material, one might expect the greatest gains to occur on such content-related tests as vocabulary, arithmetic or general information. Just the opposite is the case: "Crystallized" abilities such as these have experienced relatively small gains and even occasional declines over the years. The largest Flynn effects [IQ gains] appear instead on highly g-loaded [general intelligence] tests.[32]

The Metropolitan Readiness Tests, which are designed to measure how well-prepared students are to acquire basic reading and mathematical skills, also show a considerable increase.[33] According to a study published in 1976, "eighty percent of preschool children in 1974 scored above the average established by preschool children in 1964."[34] The combination of improving educational potential and stagnant or falling educational performance points to serious deficiencies in U.S. schools. Though kids are capable of more and more, they are being taught less and less.

The ineffectiveness of U.S. schools is also apparent in students' scores on international tests. Essentially, these tests show that the more time Americans spend in school, the worse they do compared to children of the same age in other countries.

As we have seen, American children are starting school better prepared than ever. By the fourth grade, after only a few years of schooling, they are still doing well, placing second out of eighteen industrialized countries in the 1990–91 IEA reading test. On the Third International Mathematics and Science Study (TIMSS) of 1994–95, U.S. fourth-graders placed third in science and seventh in mathematics. By the time they reach fourteen, however, their scores begin to drop. U.S. students fall to sixth place in reading, twelfth place in science, and eighteenth place in mathematics by the eighth grade, among the same groups of countries.[35] The worst performance is to be found among high-school seniors, however. U.S. seniors placed eighteenth (fourth from last) in mathematics and science literacy, fifteenth (second-to-last) in advanced mathematics, and sixteenth (dead last) in physics.[36] Finally, sixteen- to twenty-five-year-old Americans placed second-to-last among the eight countries participating in the 1994 International Adult Literacy Survey.[37]

The academic performance of American students really does get worse, with respect to that of their foreign peers, the longer they stay in school. Looked at another way, U.S. public schools are among the least efficient in the world. American students learn less mathematics between the fourth and eighth grades than students from any other country participating in the TIMSS. U.S. students learned the second least amount of science between fourth and eighth grades.[38]

Back to the past?

People who present evidence of declining academic achievement are widely assumed to be nostalgic old conservatives who hearken back to the halcyon days of their youth when everything was bright and gay. In this case, the assumption would be inaccurate. Ample evidence has been presented in previous chapters to show that public schools have been dysfunctional for generations. Schools may have been better in some ways in the 1920s or the 1950s, but that does not mean they were as good as they could have been, and it definitely does not mean that they were better than schools could be made today.

Abnormal Distributions: Corruption in High-Stakes Testing

The tests described in the previous section are taken by small but representative samples of students and recent high-school graduates. That means they speak volumes on national trends, but are mute when it comes to the performance of individuals. If you want to know how much your child has learned, the IEA, YALS, etc. won't help you. Most students don't take these tests, and even if they did, scores are not reported for particular students, schools, districts, or (with some exceptions)[39] states.

There are a great many other tests, however, that are meant to provide just that missing information. Most states administer their own tests to all or virtually all of the students within their borders, and while they rarely reveal to parents how well their children performed, they do make the data available by district and sometimes by school. If this were the end of the story, it would already be obvious that state-level testing programs put more pressure on public school personnel than do national and international studies. When students at a given school do particularly badly on an IEA examination, that fact goes unreported and the negative publicity it would generate does not materialize. The same cannot be said for highly publicized state test results, which have been blessing or cursing the employees of public school districts for years.

Press coverage is the least of the pressures generated by state-level testing programs such as the (now defunct) California Assessment Program or the Connecticut Mastery Test. Over the past two decades, results of these sorts of tests have increasingly been used to reward high-performing schools (and sometimes teachers) and penalize low performers—so much so that they are now known collectively as high-stakes tests.

The incentive to raise student scores on these tests has been significant and its effects profound: in 1987, New Mexico physician John Cannell shocked the public with the revelation that all fifty states claimed their students scored above average.[40] Though Cannell was heavily criticized by educators, his conclusion was eventually confirmed by researchers appointed by the U.S. Department of Education.[41]

This "Lake Wobegon" effect was caused by the way in which state-level tests are administered and evaluated. Instead of comparing students between states on a yearly basis, high-stakes test results are generally compared to the scores of a "norm" group of students tested as many as seven years earlier. When all the states were claiming to be above average, they were really saying that current students were scoring better than the earlier norm group.

There are two ways to explain these remarkably consistent score gains: (a) kids were learning more, or (b) their test results were artificially inflated. The correct answer is most likely (b). A great body of evidence has been amassed over the last ten years pointing to widespread corruption of state testing programs. High-stakes test results are referred to in the scholarly literature as "polluted" and "contaminated" by fraud and are considered to be virtually useless as measures of actual student achievement. This, in fact, is the chief reason that such tests were not considered in the previous section on academic performance trends.

Forging ahead: Outright cheating in the schools

The most flagrant but probably least common form of cheating is a backroom affair in which teachers or principals go through their students' completed test forms one by one, changing some of the incorrect answers to correct ones. Test doctoring is relatively uncommon for two reasons: it is easy to detect (at least in theory), and it requires a complete absence of conscience and professional ethics on the part of the individuals involved. Still, it happens.

A recent and particularly notorious case took place in Fairfield, Connecticut in 1996. In the spring of that year, district officials decided to take a closer look at the high-scoring Stratfield School, in the hope of learning valuable lessons that might translate into improved performance at other schools. What they found surprised them: an uncommonly high rate of erasures on standardized tests. After retesting Stratfield and two other schools on the widely used Iowa Test of Basic Skills, the district sent the completed forms to Riverside Publishing Company, the test's publisher. In their official reply, Riverside stated: "The evidence clearly and conclusively indicates that tampering occurred with the Stratfield School answer documents." A separate review by the state department of education also revealed suspiciously high rates of erasures on the Connecticut Mastery Test (CMT), with an improbably high percentage of those changes making wrong answers into right ones. Harcourt Brace Educational Measurement, which publishes the CMT, wrote: "It is very unlikely that this occurred by chance."[42] The final nail in Stratfield's coffin was hammered home when its students were retested under tighter security: students' scores fell to a level below the district average, from their earlier height of as much as 40 percent above it.[43]

Cheating in Fairfield was stumbled onto by accident, even though it was easy for the test publishers to recognize the irregularities in Stratfield School's test forms once they were asked to examine them. This is typical. It is a well-established fact that statistical methods can be used to identify probable cheating on standardized tests. It is equally well-established that only a tiny fraction of public schools bother to apply them.[44] California is one of the only states that systematically examines answer sheets for signs of tampering, and its approach only scrutinizes roughly 5 percent of the tests submitted. Some schools are automatically flagged by computer for having unusually high erasure rates on their test forms, while others draw attention if their scores jump dramatically from one year to the next.[45] Of the forty schools identified as having suspiciously high erasure rates on the 1985–86 California Assessment Program (CAP) test, only one denied cheating. Though these schools represented just under 1 percent of the 5,000 schools participating in the CAP, they were almost certainly the tip of the iceberg. A separate local investigation by the Los Angeles Unified School District found an additional eleven schools under its jurisdiction guilty of cheating in the same year, none of which had been turned up by the state-level audit.[46]

In short, few states have organized programs for detecting cheating, and those that do seem to miss a fair number of cheaters. But how many slip through the cracks? John Cannell amassed a considerable amount of anecdotal evidence in the late 1980s from teachers and administrators around the country. One of the most interesting cases he brought to light was an investigation carried out in Chicago, in which allegations of cheating had been leveled at twenty-three schools. To further their investigation, Chicago testing officials decided to compare the suspect schools with a control group of seventeen other schools that were deemed above suspicion. As it turned out, enough evidence was amassed to confirm cheating in sixteen of the twenty-three suspect schools and in two of the control schools as well! In fact, officials of the district acknowledged that they "may have underestimated the extent of cheating at some schools."[47]

By far the most telling evidence of cheating comes from public school educators themselves. In the summer of 1992, a national survey report was published in the scholarly journal *Educational Measurement: Issues and Practice.* The report's authors, Janie Hall and Paul Kleine, asked 2,256 teachers, principals, testing coordinators, and superintendents from around the country if their colleagues engaged in blatant cheating. Forty-four percent said yes.[48] The responsibility for administering standardized achievement tests normally falls to teachers alone, however, and thus it is to be expected that they would have the most accurate information on the prevalence of cheating. It is troubling, therefore, that 55 percent of the teachers surveyed were aware of flagrantly unethical testing practices such as changing students' answers, teaching specific test items in advance of the test, and giving hints during the test. A third of teachers reported that between 5 and 10 percent of their colleagues cheated in these ways, and an additional one out of five teachers reported that more than 10 percent of their colleagues engaged in such practices.

Emily Sachar, a journalist who took a year-long sabbatical to teach in the New York City public schools, gives a first-hand account of the grading practices on the city's mandatory Preliminary Competency Test in Writing:

> Many of the language arts [English] teachers at Whitman feared that giving failing marks might be interpreted as a damning reflection on the quality of their teaching. And several administrators worried that poor scores on the writing test would also reflect negatively on the school, since these marks . . . were used to judge a school's success.
>
> It was easy enough to pass the students. We—not some objective strangers—would be marking them. We would work in pairs using a grading approach called "the holistic method," passing any student who turned in a "reasonably coherent" paper. We were to disregard structure, and ignore grammar, spelling, and punctuation entirely. "If you can basically get through it, that's good enough," a language arts teacher told us. "Pass the kid."[49]

Before delving into even more common forms of testing corruption, it is worth looking into the fate of teachers and principals when their schools are caught cheating. Of the cases described in the preceding paragraphs, only one has resulted in disciplinary action. The principal of Connecticut's Stratfield School was suspended by an eight-to-one vote of the school board in February 1997, pending termination hearings.[50] Officials in Chicago took no action against any of their suspect school employees, and Los Angeles school district officials "decided not to punish teachers who changed answers or gave students 'inappropriate assistance' during the test because the district had not adequately informed them of proper testing procedures."[51]

The rarity of disciplinary action against teachers and principals who are caught does little to discourage would-be cheaters from "going over to the Dark Side." In some cases, they do not even feel the need to conceal their actions. In the fall of 1996, years after the investigation described by Cannell, a Chicago elementary school principal and a curriculum coordinator openly gave teachers "copies of the Iowa Tests of Basic Skills so they could prepare their students for the [upcoming] examination."[52]

Teaching to the test

In the Hall/Kleine survey mentioned above, more than three quarters of all respondents said that they were aware of teachers who taught certain material solely because they knew it to be on a standardized test. In fact, half of all teachers reported that more than 10 percent of their colleagues "taught to the tests," as this form of cheating is called. Only one teacher in five was unaware of any such test fraud by her peers.[53]

Teaching to the test happens not only on the level of individual teachers, but even across entire school districts. An amazing 92 percent of all educators polled by Hall and Kleine indicated that their school district changed its curriculum "to better match the skills and knowledge measured by" standardized tests. Seventy-one percent went so far as to state that the curriculum had been altered to "match particular questions" on the tests. Detailed local surveys from various parts of the country have also shown the prevalence of fraudulent test procedures. In two separate studies, professors Nancy Haas and Susan Nolen found that "unethical practices which inflate test scores without concurrently raising students' achievement level were common."[54] Only 15 percent of teachers surveyed in Maryland and Kentucky believed that the test scores in their schools were higher because students were learning more. "Most said their school's scores had improved because teachers and students were more familiar with the test, students had worked with practice tests and other test-preparation materials in class, and students' test-taking skills had improved."[55]

Teaching to the test gives an artificially inflated impression of what students know, since tests can only ever measure a fraction of the coursework children are supposed to have learned. Students who are taught the specific topics on which they will be tested may well receive high scores even though they have no real understanding of the subject outside the handful of areas in which they were carefully drilled.

The ubiquity of teaching to the test might be partially explained by the way in which it is perceived by teachers. There is probably little doubt in anyone's mind that forging students' answers on completed test forms is a crooked, unscrupulous act. Tailoring classroom instruction so that it coincides with a particular test is not seen in a similarly negative light. One poll asked teachers if they considered it cheating to teach students actual test items. More than one in ten said no.[56] If such a flagrant breach of test security is not considered cheating by one teacher in ten, the number who believe that more subtle forms of teaching to the test are ethical is certainly higher.

Unnatural selection: Weeding out low achievers
from the test-taking population

Most people who have school-aged children or who follow press coverage of education are aware that there has been a boom in the number of students classified as disabled by public schools over the past twenty years. Three things they might not know are the chief reason for the boom, the way it is regarded by researchers outside the public-education establishment, and its impact on standardized test scores.

In addition to the worthy practice of attempting to accommodate physical impairments such as blindness and mental retardation, public schools have embraced a legal construct known as Specific Learning Disabilities (SLDs). According to the federal Education of All Handicapped Children Act of 1975 (EAHCA), a child suffers from a Specific Learning Disability if two conditions hold true: his basic language or mathematics skills are behind those of his agemates, and these skills are noticeably below the expected level for someone of his intelligence. The law does stipulate that the child must also have been receiving "appropriate learning experiences" prior to his diagnosis, but these are not defined, leaving their interpretation up to educators themselves.[57] Since no teacher has ever defined his chosen methods of instruction as inappropriate, this is a toothless clause, and is entirely ignored. In the world of public schooling, SLD diagnosis is often reduced to a devastatingly simple formula: if a child is smart but cannot read or do math, he is disabled.

There are so very many things wrong with this proposition that it would take a book to do them all justice. Only a brief summary is possible here. To begin with, dubbing such poorly defined disabilities "Specific" goes beyond simple irony and into the realm of Orwellian doublespeak. But more important than Congress's heavy-handed attempt at linguistic legerdemain is its flouting of common sense. The notion that disability is the necessary cause of all reading failure among children of normal intelligence is patently nonsensical. It completely ignores the possibility—indeed probability[58]—that a child might not have been properly taught to read in the first place.

Given public schools' frequent use of defective reading instruction techniques (see Chapter 5), it should come as no surprise that the number of SLD cases is large and growing. How many children have been diagnosed as disabled under the Individuals with Disabilities Education Act (IDEA, the new name of the amended EAHCA)? During the 1994–95 academic year, roughly two and a half million school-aged children[59] were classified as learning disabled under federal law: one out of every eighteen public school students nationwide. That number is up from one in fifty-six students in 1976–77.[60] By the early 1990s, one out of every eight New York City public school students was classified as disabled in some (usually nonphysical) way.[61] In the states of Massachusetts and New Jersey it was one in six.[62]

As Figure 8 makes clear, the percentage of children participating in federal programs for the speech or language impaired, the mentally retarded, the hearing impaired, the orthopedically impaired, and the visually impaired, has been dropping since 1977, and the percentage of seriously emotionally disturbed children remains low at 0.95 percent, but there has been a frightening growth in the diagnosis of Specific Learning Disabilities. Over the last twenty years, the percentage of all children who are claimed to be afflicted with SLDs has more than tripled, from 1.8 percent to 5.75 percent.[63]

Of course, it is possible that a few such children really do suffer from a disability, rather than simply from a dysfunctional school system, but several caveats to the SLD diagnosis make this possibility remote. Namely, the IDEA states that students who are achieving below expected levels cannot be classed as learning disabled if their deficit is due to "a visual, hearing, or motor handicap; mental retardation; emotional disturbance; or environmental, cultural, or economic disadvantage."[64] Still, there is the chance that some brain defect, different from mental retardation, afflicts these children. In fact, proponents of disability explanations for educational failure have been attempting to find such physical causes for most of this century. Thus far, they appear to have failed. In his book *The Learning Mystique,* professor of clinical psychiatry Gerald Coles chronicles the evidence that there are no demonstrable neurological differences between learning-disabled children and non-learning-disabled children, and that learning-disabled children cannot even be reliably differentiated from low-ability students who are not believed to suffer from a learning disability.[65] A recent investigation of the learning disability (LD) field by noted psychologist Robert J. Sternberg and special education professor Louise Spear-Swerling supports Cole's central findings.[66] Professor Wade Roush summarizes the state of the field as follows:

> The definition, diagnosis, and basic scientific understanding of LD has remained remarkably elusive. There's no agreed-upon psychological test, no biomedically discernible problem, that characterizes LD. As a result, children are usually diagnosed as learning disabled when their reading or math competency lags sig-

Figure 8. Enrollment in Federal Disability Programs as
a Percentage of All U.S. Public School Students

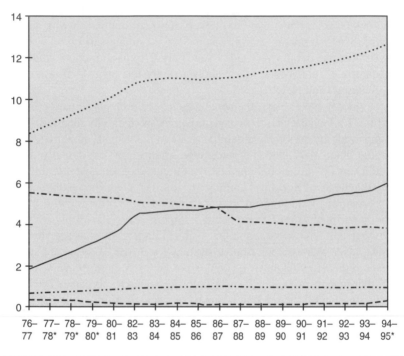

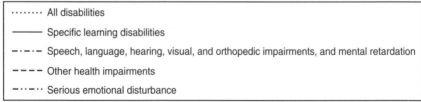

········ All disabilities

———— Specific learning disabilities

—·—·— Speech, language, hearing, visual, and orthopedic impairments, and mental retardation

— — — — Other health impairments

—··—··· Serious emotional disturbance

Data sources: National Center for Education Statistics, *Digest of Education Statistics, 1996* (Washington, DC: U.S. Department of Education, 1996), Table 51; and U.S. Department of Education, Office of Special Education Programs (OSEP), *Eighteenth Annual Report to Congress on the Implementation of the Individuals with Disabilities Education Act* (Washington, DC: U.S. Department of Education, 1996). Values for the years marked by asterisks are estimates. Note that the data for the school year 1981–82 are not provided in the source tables.

nificantly behind the level predicted by their IQ scores. . . . Yet the size of the discrepancy between performance and IQ scores that merits the label varies from state to state—indeed, one "cure" for LD can be to move across state lines.[67]

Despite the lack of evidence, many advocates of physical disability explanations for reading failure continue to defend their besieged positions—with no greater success than their predecessors.[68]

The raging epidemic of SLDs is so conspicuous that pressure to do something about it is mounting. Rather than admit to years of probable misdiagnoses, however, the public-education establishment appears to have branched out into previously untapped disability designations. The reader may have noticed in Figure 8 that the "Other health impairments" classification registered an up-tick between 1992–93 and 1994–95, after being mostly flat for a decade. According to the U.S. Department of Education, the number of students in this category grew by 89 percent (or 50,160 students) in the four years leading up to 1994–95—many times faster than any other category of disability. "Much of this increase," Department researchers state, "may be related to an increased number of students diagnosed with Attention Deficit Disorder."[69] This was to be expected given that the Department of Education notified the states in 1991 that children diagnosed with ADD would thenceforth be eligible for funding under certain existing disability categories.[70]

Research actually linking ADD to health impairments is just as scarce as evidence linking SLDs to brain defects. Psychologists Gay Goodman and Mary Jo Poillon point out that "the characteristics for ADD have been subjectively defined by a committee rather than having been developed on the basis of empirical evidence."[71] The diagnostic manual of the American Psychiatric Association concedes that there are "no laboratory tests that have been established as diagnostic" for ADD or ADHD (Attention Deficit Hyperactivity Disorder). The criteria offered for identifying these purported ailments include such vagaries as "is often forgetful in daily activities," and "often talks excessively." There is even a catchall "ADHD Not Otherwise Specified" category which gives the mental health profession a virtual carte blanche for labeling children.[72] Educators on the front line are more aware of this fact than anyone. A team comprising a school psychologist, a special education teacher, a school nurse, a principal, and a social worker observed in *Phi Delta Kappan* magazine that

> [n]ot every human action (or lack of action) that is not identical to the actions of the majority can be attributed to some affliction. Such different behavior might just be the product of human choice. We must, therefore, be somewhat skeptical about ADD-classified children who, when removed from the classroom setting, magically lose their ADD symptoms. . . . We need to continually point out the facts that there is no concrete proof that the condition known as Attention Deficit Disorder even exists and that diagnosing the affliction remains more an art than a science.[73]

If so, it is no doubt the only art permitted to dispense psychoactive prescription drugs to children.

Where does the apparently excessive diagnosis of innate learning disabilities and ADD fit in with U.S. academic achievement? Children classified as learning disabled are generally exempted from taking standardized tests. Though the evidence seems to indicate that few such children actually suffer from neurological disabilities, learning-disabled students do score below average for their age and grade on most tests of academic ability, so when they are eliminated from the test-taking pool, average scores go up. Deliberately labeling students disabled solely to raise test-score averages has not been the only or even the primary reason for the growth in learning disability and ADD classifications, but it has nonetheless had an effect on those averages.

Remarkable though it may seem, there actually are cases in which students are stamped as learning-disabled or ADD just to improve a school's test results. In their article "Flunk 'Em or Get Them Classified," researchers Anne McGill-Franzen and Richard Allington write that "we found evidence, albeit typically indirect, that some decisions to classify children as handicapped were motivated by a desire to remove low-achieving students from the high-stakes assessment stream (and, ultimately, the public accountability reports)."[74] Not all their evidence was indirect. One principal described his school's practice of flunking or classifying as learning disabled, children who were expected to fail a high-stakes third-grade test. He then complained that teachers sometimes suggested that low-achieving students might be able to take the test, adding, "They don't realize that my neck is on the block if the students take the test and fail it. So I want them exempted."[75]

Under the IDEA, all children deemed disabled are entitled to special educational services (funded jointly by state and federal governments). Given the dubious nature of the "learning disabled" classification, it is reasonable to ask whether the special educational services prescribed to learning-disabled children actually help them to learn more. Overall, the research shows "little evidence of positive effects, especially academic effects, of special education placements"[76] resulting from learning disability diagnoses. Children branded as learning disabled can and do make considerable progress in reading when taught using proven, systematic instructional methods, but these are precisely the methods most often dispensed with (rather than dispensed) in public schools.[77]

Keeping parents in the dark

One might expect, given the artificially inflated nature of high-stakes test scores, that schools would be extremely anxious to broadcast these scores to parents and the public. Not so. As it turns out, for all their rosy discoloration, standardized test scores are not nearly as flattering to students as good old-fashioned school grades. After all, it is far easier to simply assign pleasingly positive grades regardless of student achievement than it is to contrive to influence standardized test results. So long as parents can be kept happily ignorant of their children's actual accomplishments with a string of A's and B's, what need is there to resort to even moderately accurate measures?

Just how distorted grades are depends on the school in question. If its students really are above average, teachers have little incentive to bestow excessively generous grades, since they are secure in the knowledge that most parents will be satisfied with the marks their children actually earn. It is in average and below-average schools that grades come into their own as a means of massaging the truth. (This is in contrast to institutions of higher education, where grade inflation is also common but is generally ascribed to the influence of student course evaluations, and the corollary pressure on professors to award pleasing grades.)

Wherever it is concentrated, grade embellishment is clearly on the rise. In 1966, a third of college freshmen had received an average high-school grade of C or worse, while about 16 percent had gotten A's. Those proportions were reversed by 1996, when one third of freshmen had received A's in high school and only 14 percent had been graded C or lower.[78] The surge in grades is even more remarkable if college enrollment trends are taken into account, since a considerably higher percentage of high-school graduates are now attending college than in 1966.[79] As already described, reliable measures of academic trends do not coincide with this tremendous rise in average grades.

The following example from the mid-1990s illustrates how the ignorance of parents can be the bliss of educators. The parents of Zavala Elementary in East Austin, Texas had accepted their children's grades (A's and B's for the most part) at face value for years when a newly appointed principal decided to have the students' scores on state-mandated standardized tests read aloud at a PTA meeting. As it turned out, Zavala was among the lowest achieving schools not just in Austin, but in the whole state. Teachers at the school had refrained from informing parents of the poor scores, avoiding, as a result, any pressure to raise them. Naturally, parents were outraged. A fierce discussion ensued and some families pulled their children from the school. Those who remained put extreme pressure on the school's staff to improve their children's performance—which, it seems, was the principal's intention. If such an unusually forthright and dedicated principal had not been appointed at Zavala, there is no reason to expect that parents would ever have been disabused of their misapprehensions.[80]

The Wages of Bureaucracy: Mismanagement, Corruption, and Neglect

In his novel *The Trial,* Franz Kafka conjures up a vast, terrifying bureaucracy known as the Court. No matter where the protagonist of the story turns, he finds himself at the mercy of its legions of functionaries, a pawn to their incomprehensible aims. The typical state education establishment makes Kafka's Court look like a neighborhood ice-cream shop.

After touring the sprawling offices of Chicago's Board of Education in the late 1980s, two visiting Japanese education officials asked if they were viewing the U.S. Department of Education. Flabbergasted to discover they were in the midst of a single city's public school bureaucracy, they remarked that it was larger than the office complex of the Japanese National Ministry of Education.

The difference in bureaucratic bloat between government-run and independent schools within the United States is also striking. In major cities, central public school offices regularly employ five, ten, or even fifty times the number of administrators per pupil as corresponding private Catholic schools.[81] In his book *Libertarianism: A Primer,* David Boaz writes: "The New York city public school system has 6,000 central office bureaucrats, while the Catholic school system of New York serves one-fourth as many students with just 30 central administrative staff."[82]

Like all unchecked bureaucracies—remember the late Roman empire?—government schooling has been marked by vigorous spending growth, declining efficiency, and a noticeable lack of regard for the public it is meant to serve. This litany of ills is the subject of the following sections.

Insatiable U.: Public Schooling's Voracious Appetite for Money

Public schooling is expensive. Public schooling is inefficient. Critics frequently make these charges and educators usually deny them. The facts, however, are clear. Public school spending per pupil, adjusted for inflation, has skyrocketed over the course of the twentieth century while student achievement has not only failed to improve overall, it has declined in several areas.

As can be seen in Figure 9, public schools spent fourteen times as much per pupil in 1996 as they did in 1920. Even if student performance had increased somewhat over the years, this spending rise would be excessive. Given that performance has either stagnated or deteriorated, the rise in inflation-adjusted expenditures is difficult to justify.

Public schooling's unseemly appetite for tax dollars is an embarrassment to advocates of government-run education. Naturally, there have been attempts to excuse or rationalize away the system's profligacy, and these have fallen into two categories: arguments based on how the money is spent, and efforts to make the spending growth appear smaller.

One possible reason why today's schools are vastly more expensive than those of the 1920s and 1930s, is that modern schools cost more to build and maintain. It is true that some students today enjoy more elegant and well-appointed school buildings than did their grandparents, and higher costs for

Figure 9. Total U.S. Public School Expenditures per Pupil in
Average Daily Attendance (Adjusted for Inflation)

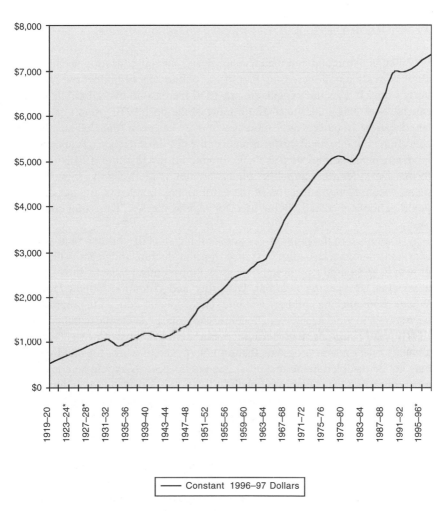

Constant 1996–97 Dollars

Data source: National Center for Education Statistics, *Digest of Education Statistics, 1997*
(Washington, DC: U.S. Department of Education, 1997), Table 169. Data for the periods
1920–21 to 1928–29 and 1994–95 to 1996–97 are estimates.

these buildings are to be expected; but construction and maintenance costs were negligible factors in the growth of per-pupil spending.[83] And, as will be explained in a later section, many schools across the nation are in worse repair now than they have ever been—despite the current high level of spending.

A costly IDEA: The rise and rise of special-education spending

Unlike construction and maintenance costs, special-education spending really has made up an increasing part of the public school budget over the last thirty years. It does not explain the pre-1970 increase in overall public school expenditures, but it does account for more of the post-1970 growth than regular education. In other words, more new money has been funneled into special education than into regular education over the last three decades. Proponents of government schooling, such as the Economic Policy Institute (EPI),[84] hold up this fact as evidence that public schools are not as inefficient as they initially seem, because only a fraction of the extra money taxpayers are spending on public schools is actually being used for regular classes. This is an odd thing to say.

As explained in the previous section, real physical disabilities such as deafness and mental retardation have been on the decline for years. The recent growth in special-education rolls has been almost entirely due to dubious diagnoses such as Specific Learning Disability and Attention Deficit Disorder. What's more, placing children in public school special-education programs has been shown to yield a paucity of benefits, particularly academic benefits. So the EPI is really arguing that because public schools have thrown enormous amounts of money at programs that do not appear to work, for children who may not be disabled in the first place, the public schools should be considered more efficient. On the contrary, special education is a particularly poignant example of the gross mismanagement and inefficiency endemic to government schooling. If students were taught to read using proven instructional methods, and if public schools were able to maintain the more studious atmospheres common in independent schools (see Chapter 8), it seems likely that diagnoses of (and hence spending on) learning disabilities and ADD would be drastically reduced.

It should be noted, however, that even though the percentage of children suffering from mental retardation and other genuine disabilities has declined, the cost of educating them has increased enormously. After the passage of the Individuals with Disabilities Education Act (IDEA)[85] in 1975, special-education placements costing twenty, thirty, or even one-hundred thousand dollars per year have gradually become commonplace. This is because the IDEA, and the legal precedents based on it, specifically prohibit the consideration of cost in the design of special-education instruction programs. Based on public opinion data discussed in Chapter 1, it is unlikely that this unlimited spending policy would win the support of most citizens (were they informed of it). While the financial effects of the IDEA cannot be blamed on public school mismanagement, they are nonetheless the direct results of government intervention in education. In passing the "blank check" IDEA, Congress seems to have bowed to pressure from a vocal minority (the persuasive disability lobby), giving little heed to the interests and preferences of the general public.

Calculating inflation

A more subtle attempt to make public schooling seem less financially corpulent relies on the calculation of inflation. According to this view, inflation should be estimated differently for schooling than for the average industry. Richard Rothstein and Karen Miles, the theory's main proponents, argue that public schooling is very labor-intensive, and that labor costs sometimes rise faster than the average rate of inflation represented by the Consumer Price Index (CPI). As a result, they suggest that schooling should only be compared to other labor-intensive industries for the purposes of calculating its real spending growth.[86]

The federal Bureau of Labor Statistics provides a special inflation index for the service sector, which Rothstein and Miles modified to create their own education index, titling it the Net Services Index (NSI). The most remarkable thing about the NSI, given its authors' intentions, is that it has not differed appreciably from the CPI over the past ten or fifteen years. According to economist Eric Hanushek, the difference between the two indices amounts to only two tenths of a percentage point in annual spending growth, over the period from 1982 to 1991.[87] How much of a difference does this make? Over the nine-year period in question, the NSI explains less than 2 percent of the growth in public school spending.[88]

Rather than making public schools look better, a careful inspection of the inflation issue suggests that costs may have skyrocketed even more rapidly than is indicated by Figure 9. Figure 9 attempts to show real spending growth by adjusting for the effects of inflation using the CPI, and the CPI is now widely believed to be inaccurate. Both the Bureau of Labor Statistics (which calculates the CPI) and the chairman of the Federal Reserve Board consider the Consumer Price Index to overstate inflation by somewhere between 0.5 and 1.5 percent annually.[89] That means that Figure 9 may understate the actual growth in public school spending. Compounded over the seventy-six years covered by the graph, the aforementioned CPI error would lead to an understatement of real growth of anywhere from one-and-a-half to three times. In other words, public school spending might not just have increased by a factor of fourteen, it might be twenty-one to forty-two times larger in real terms than it was in 1919–20. This is assuming, of course, that the CPI error exists, and has remained at roughly the same magnitude over the entire period in question, an admittedly gross and speculative assumption. It is safe to say, however, that there is considerable evidence indicating that the CPI figures understate the historical growth in real education spending.

Since the Net Services Index calculated by Rothstein and Miles is based on price information published by the Bureau of Labor Statistics,[90] it too would understate the growth in public school expenditures if the CPI is skewed as suspected.

Explaining the rise in public school spending

Clearly there has been a significant real increase in public school spending over the past seventy years. Much of this increase is accounted for by a combination of two factors: declining student/staff ratios and increasing teachers' salaries. In 1949–50, the average number of pupils per staff member in elementary and secondary schools was 19.3. By 1990, that number was cut in half to 9.1, and it has remained at that level to the present.[91] Even if average teachers' salaries had remained constant over that period (relative to inflation), this would have led to an enormous increase in the cost of schooling, since the salaries of instructional staff make up the bulk of school budgets. In fact, the average inflation-adjusted income of teachers doubled between 1949–50 and 1989–90, from about $19,000 per year to $38,000 per year.[92] By 1995, the average public school teacher's salary was one-and-a-half times that of the average private school teacher (see Chapter 8). Together, these factors account for a quadrupling in public school instructional costs over the stated period.

The growth of special education, and the demand for additional teachers and teaching assistants that it has precipitated, is often cited as the main reason for the decline in student/staff ratios. This does not appear to be the case. The expansion of special education services only began in the mid-1970s (following the passage of the IDEA), but the student/staff ratio had already fallen from 19.3 to 13.8 by 1970. Special education accounts for much of the growth in the public school workforce over the past two decades, but was irrelevant to the earlier and much larger increase in public school staffing.

Many other factors have been involved in the increasing per-pupil cost of public schooling, most of them implying a decline in efficiency. In 1992–93, for example, school districts around the nation spent a total of $9.2 billion on student transportation. This figure, while large, might seem forgivable were it not for the fact that the real per-pupil cost of busing has been rising steadily for fifty years. In 1949–50, the annual cost of transportation was $184 per student (in 1992–93 dollars). By 1977–78, the figure had risen to $285, going on to peak at $420 in 1990–91, and subsequently dropping back to $394 in 1992–93.[93] Some of this increase might be due to higher oil prices and the need to bus students over longer distances, but these factors would be at least partially mitigated by the higher fuel-efficiencies and lower maintenance costs of modern engines. If public schools were currently able to transport students at the same per-pupil cost as they did in the late seventies, they would save taxpayers roughly $2.5 billion dollars every year.

Money can't buy them learning

The data presented thus far show that when all U.S. public schools are lumped together they appear to be grossly, and increasingly, inefficient. Evidence at the level of individual schools and school districts reveals the same thing.

During the 1980s, several investigators compared public school spending with student achievement to see if more money led to higher test scores. The best known of these was economist Eric Hanushek, who collected and analyzed sixty-five case studies of school efficiency. What Hanushek found was that 80 percent of the case studies showed either no significant relationship between spending and achievement or, in a few cases, a negative relationship (more spending was associated with worse scores).[94] He concluded that higher per-pupil spending in the public school system had little effect on student performance. Because of the damning nature of this evidence, and the fact that it was brought to political prominence by the Republican U.S. secretary of education, it was roundly attacked by supporters of public schools. Both Hanushek's raw data and his conclusions were called into question.

One of the most frequently heard criticisms was that the studies Hanushek analyzed were of varying quality and that some were out of date, coming from as far back as the 1920s. Both of these criticisms were addressed, however, in a separate investigation conducted by professors Stephen Childs and Charol Shakeshaft. Their analysis was expressly concerned with the quality of the data involved, and of the 467 efficiency studies they examined, only forty-five met their stringent criteria. With some disappointment, Childs and Shakeshaft also conceded that "the relationship between student achievement and level of educational expenditures is minimal."[95] The Childs and Shakeshaft paper was an even more compelling refutation of the "out-of-date data" criticism leveled at Hanushek's work. In observing the trend in public school efficiency over time, they found that it had actually been decreasing. They saw the largest (but still very small) correlation between spending and achievement prior to the 1960s;

they found an even smaller one during that decade; and they actually noted a negative (though insignificant) correlation thereafter.

The second line of attack mounted against these findings was typified by a 1991 article that appeared in the *Phi Delta Kappan* education journal, written by education consultant Keith Baker. In his article reassessing the inefficiency evidence, Baker made the claim that "the important feature of the literature is not the significance but the direction of all studies."[96] By this unique process of thought, it would be reasonable to pay your mechanic hundreds of dollars so long as he made some improvement in your vehicle, however insignificant. In other words, you could bring in a car which was leaking gasoline and had brake trouble, and you would be told to feel satisfied even if the mechanic did nothing more than fix the cigarette lighter—a positive, though insignificant, change.

One of the most recent studies on the subject of increased spending on public schools was released in April 1994 by Harvard professor Gary Orfield. Based on an examination of districts in Maryland, Arkansas, Texas, and Detroit, he concluded that despite two decades of additional court-ordered spending on students in predominantly black public schools, there was no indication that the education of these students had improved.[97] In Orfield's words, "Just putting money into schools is not likely to produce benefits." This is precisely the same conclusion reached by yet another study of public school cost-effectiveness, published several months later in the *New England Journal of Public Policy*.[98] The obvious question that comes to mind is: Why not? How is it that increased spending on public education, unlike increased spending on houses, food, or pretty much anything else, does not lead to better quality? The answer is twofold: the public education system does not always spend the public's money on education, and when it does, it often spends the money unwisely.[99]

Kansas City: A case in point

Since 1985, Kansas City, Missouri has been among the highest-spending school districts in the United States, particularly among urban centers. It was in that year that federal district judge Russell Clark ordered the state to pay for a wholesale revamping of the existing system with the goal of enticing the white middle class back into Kansas City's public schools and thus, somehow, increasing overall student performance. By the spring of 1998, the bill had run to nearly $2 billion over and above the regular district budget.

This dramatic spending increase produced fifty-six magnet schools,[100] a business and technology high school, an agribusiness high school with two greenhouses and myriad laboratories, an engineering and technology high school, and an "advanced-technology" high school featuring some sixteen fields of specialization. A vast array of computers graced the new $32 million Central High

School. Teaching methods and curricula spanned the globe, with eleven schools concentrating on international studies, and two elementary schools using the methods of Maria Montessori. In the athletics department, the school system enjoyed fencing instruction by the former head coach of the Soviet Olympic fencing team, and an Olympic-size pool with an underwater viewing room.[101] Teachers' salaries were raised by 40 percent, and the student/teacher ratio was reduced to 12 or 13 to 1. In other words, Kansas City did virtually everything that advocates of public schooling claimed would result in increased integration, increased overall achievement, and a smaller "achievement gap" between the races.

None of it worked. Though the plan has had more than a decade to show results, white enrollment has actually decreased from 27 percent to 20 percent of the student population, average test scores have not gone up, and the black/white achievement gap remains as large as ever.[102] According to University of Missouri professor John Alspaugh:

> Some key statistics suggest that things have gotten worse since the spending binge began. Pupils in elementary schools which have not been turned into magnet schools regularly outperform pupils in generously funded magnet schools. The rise in expenditure has coincided with a fall in the maths scores of middle school pupils and a surge in the drop-out rate . . . which has risen every year, without fail, since the decree was handed down, and now stands at a disgraceful 60%.[103]

In 1997, Judge Clark acknowledged that his plan to spend the city's public school problems away had failed, and ruled that the desegregation funding program be terminated in 1999.

Education writer Paul Ciotti produced a detailed report on the Kansas City experiment, and attributed its failure to a variety of factors such as the district's inability to systematically fire incompetent teachers and administrators and hire more able ones, the fracturing of communities that followed the replacement of neighborhood schools with district-wide magnet schools, and the program's focus on attracting suburban whites instead of meeting the academic needs of urban blacks.[104]

How the school crumbles

Pedagogy is a complicated matter. Citizens with forgiving natures might be willing to accept a certain amount of waste from their public schools on the grounds that it is difficult to determine how to spend education money effectively. To avoid such ambiguities, this subsection concentrates on one very simple area of expenditure: building maintenance. Keeping floors clean and facilities operational is not rocket-science. Organizations that routinely fail to manage these tasks are dysfunctional in the extreme: none more so than public schools.

The public schools of Hartford, Connecticut spend more than $9,000 per pupil every year. Despite this considerable expenditure, school buildings there are literally falling apart. The *Hartford Courant* reports that numerous schools are unable to even supply their bathroom stalls with doors due to mismanagement and bureaucratic red tape. Regular building maintenance in the district is almost unheard of, precipitating expensive calamities. In the middle of the 1994–95 academic year, one school had to be suddenly evacuated so that its roof could be replaced, which meant that students had to be doubled up in other schools for months. Leaking urinals are left unfixed, causing thousands of dollars in water damage. Private contractor Johnson Controls found so many public school building-code violations, and so few safety procedures in place for maintenance workers, that it refused to sign a state-mandated certificate of safety compliance.[105]

Conditions in Orange County, Florida are no better. Thanks to an inability to accurately forecast student-enrollment changes—an inability which is common to public school systems—the district has purchased thousands of modular, prefabricated classrooms (read "mobile homes"). Design flaws in these structures have led to waterlogged floors, leaking doors and windows, and the mold and rot that naturally ensue. Though internal memos show that administrators were aware of the problem for years, the fiasco only became public after a story in the *Orlando Sentinel*.[106] One administrator discounted the problems, quipping that "everything molds in Florida."

Sadly, schools in the nation's capital are among the worst. Though they spent about $9,200 per pupil in 1994, the majority of Washington, D.C. schools are falling apart, according to a congressional report prepared by the U.S. General Accounting Office.[107] Rather than keeping up their schools with regular maintenance, D.C. officials have cut capital spending in order to support a bloated, disorganized bureaucracy that consumes one of the largest shares of the total budget of any district in the country. The story is equally grim in Saint Louis City, Missouri. Though it spends one-and-a-half times the state average, and more than a thousand dollars above the national per-pupil average, many of its schools can only be called disasters. Walk into the city's schools and "you can smell the urinals a hundred feet away,"[108] states a member of the board of education. According to a teacher interviewed by author Jonathan Kozol, each passing year means "one more toilet that doesn't flush, one more drinking fountain that doesn't work, one more classroom without texts." "Certain classrooms are so cold in winter," the teacher added, "that the students have to wear their coats to class, while children in other classrooms swelter in a suffocating heat that cannot be turned down."[109] It is hard to imagine that members of the overwhelmingly minority student population of Saint Louis City public schools enjoy noticeably better learning conditions and educational opportunities in the 1990s than they did in the dark days of legal segregation.

The public school maintenance catastrophe stretches from sea to shining sea. A 1996 report by the General Accounting Office stated that one out of every three U.S. public schools needs extensive repairs or outright replacement. Inner-city facilities are in the worst shape of all: two thirds of the schools serving the nation's ten million inner-city students have defective plumbing, heating, and/or foundations.[110]

Jonathan Kozol and numerous other public school advocates suggest that further infusions of money would solve the problems listed above, but many districts spending less than the national average are able to keep their toilets from overflowing and their heating systems from putting children through a freeze-thaw cycle. It's not the size of your budget, it's how you use it, and public schools use their budgets abysmally. Given that public schools cannot even keep their own facilities from falling apart, is it any wonder that they fail at the more complex task of teaching our children?

Pulp *Non*fiction: True-Crime in the Classroom

A staple criticism aimed at market-oriented school reforms is that for-profit education would be subject to corruption and fraud—the implication being that public schools are less liable to suffer from these failings. In reality, government school personnel are no less apt to engage in criminal activity than members of any other industry. This section airs some of public education's dirty laundry to show that susceptibility to corruption is not a valid reason for preferring public to private schooling.

Two cities, New York and Chicago, top the list of reported public school crimes, but this is most likely due to better reporting than to genuinely higher rates of crime than other large urban districts. For years, New York City's school district was perhaps the only one in the country with a high-profile, full-time investigator.[111] Chicago's school district joined New York's in 1995, hiring author and investigative reporter Maribeth Vander Weele away from the *Sun-Times* and appointing her chief of school investigations. While such investigators do not uncover all the illicit acts of public school employees, they certainly increase the percentage of perpetrators who are caught.

In districts enjoying either education investigators or top-notch reporters, felonious activities have been traced to everyone from custodians, to school board members, to state superintendents of public instruction. The criminal escapades of New York City school custodians have been so outlandish as to land them on CBS's *60 Minutes* television program.[112] In 1992, the city's special commissioner of investigation found numerous cases of payroll fraud, violations of the district's anti-nepotism rule, theft, use of the district's own auditing system to hide theft and budget misuse, and embezzlement of user fees. Time-clock abuse was found to be standard practice.[113] Reporters at *60 Minutes* concentrated on the more colorful cases, such as the janitor who spent a considerable part of his work-day sailing and maintaining his thirty-four-foot yacht, while bringing down a salary of $83,000. Not all of his colleagues were so fun-loving. Two custodians allegedly traded in semiautomatic weapons, sometimes at school. One of them was even gracious enough to offer his services to an undercover police officer for a contract killing.[114]

Though a variety of recommendations were made by the commissioner's office, the situation does not appear to have greatly improved. The city's comptroller launched another investigation into apparent fraud by 337 custodial helpers in 1996, noting claims of between eighteen and fifty-seven hours of overtime work per week in addition to the regular forty-hour shift. *Education Week* reported that "[s]ome workers said they put in 100 hours a week, and several submitted timecards for work performed at the same time in different locations."[115]

New York City's 1993 community school board elections were also rife with corruption, according to a report from the special commissioner's office. The investigation "found fraud and corruption as well as administrative mismanagement in many areas of the election process." Parent-voter registration was entirely compromised:

> In some areas, anyone could vote, often multiple times, and many parents were not allowed to vote at all. . . . Many absentee ballots were cast under false names, without the knowledge and consent of the unsuspecting "voters." In some districts, teachers and staff were pressured into supporting a candidate. Election guidelines were also found to be ineffective and frequently broken.[116]

This report, at least, produced a few concrete results. In May 1996, five Bronx school officials were arrested for vote fraud amid charges of widespread corruption, while a former Brooklyn principal pleaded guilty to stealing public funds and pressuring teachers to join a political club. In the ballot-fraud case, "prosecutors charged that administrators in District 10 in the Bronx induced homeless people, nursing home residents, and college students to apply for absentee ballots that were then cast by others." The Special Commissioner of Investigations also accused "the school board chief in District 9 . . . of repeatedly using school staff members, equipment, and funds for personal gain."[117]

The range of criminal activity in the city's public schools is so broad that it strains the imagination. On one day the *New York Times* reports that a student has worn a wiretap to catch his teacher attempting to extort money from him for a passing grade,[118] while on another, school busing contracts are linked to organized crime.[119] School construction projects were so infested with graft in the 1980s that a special School Construction Authority was created in 1989 to eliminate the problem. Just four years later, administrators at the new Authority were found to have accepted $140,000 in bribes to rig contracts worth $6 million.[120] A year after that, yet another multimillion-dollar scandal at the School Construction Authority made the headlines,[121] and no end to the corruption is in sight.

Meanwhile, in Chicago, a teacher by the name of Stephen Levine reported hearing rumors in 1992 of colleagues "receiving brown envelopes for 'doing a good job.'" After being given such a package—containing $225 for work he had not performed—Levine contacted authorities. Auditors eventually discovered that the transactions of "brown envelope days" were common knowledge among school staff, who had profited illegally to the tune of $45,000 over an eighteen-month period chiefly by billing for work on nonexistent vocational education programs.[122] Student records relating to those programs were conveniently disposed of by the school immediately prior to the audit.

The staff of another Chicago school, Henderson Elementary, saw fit to spend $27,380 on a resort trip for local school council members and guests, repairs to the principal's car, numerous dinners, and a $50 casino ticket. According to Vander Weele, Chicago school district records show that half a million dollars was misappropriated by district employees between 1985 and 1992. Teachers and principals embezzled thousands by siphoning off concession sales, writing illicit school checks, raiding student accounts, pocketing graduation fees, and sundry other ploys. What came of this financial free-for-all? In one case, a principal whose school bank accounts were mysteriously overdrawn by tens of thousands of dollars, who resigned under pressure, and who was repaying a fraction of the missing money, was later rehired by the Chicago public school system. In other cases, such principals were never fired in the first place. No principal was ever prosecuted as a result of the audits; only about 3 percent of the money was ever repaid; and the public would never even have known about the incidents if the *Chicago Sun-Times* had not successfully sued the school system in 1992, demanding the release of internal school audits.[123]

The audit findings discussed above are only the tip of the iceberg. Fewer than 20 percent of Chicago schools are audited each year, but of those that are, a considerable percentage are found to have budget shortfalls. In her book *Reclaiming Our Schools,* Vander Weele writes: "From 1985 to 1992, for example, 17 to 30 percent of the schools audited had shortages in concession money, 3 to 20 percent in bank deposits, and 8 to 19 percent in student fees."[124] At many schools, furthermore, records are in disarray or are not up-to-date, preventing auditors from even assessing balances, let alone determining if money is missing.

The previous paragraphs might make it look as though Chicago and New

York possess a monopoly on public school crime. Not so. Payroll fraud seems to be just as much of a problem in Dallas as in the Big Apple,[125] and some of the most dramatic criminal escapades are to be found in less well-known public school districts. Take, for example, Stephen A. Wagner, the former chief fiscal officer of California's Newport-Mesa district. Wagner, it seems, liked jewels. He liked them so much that he apparently stole children's lunch money in order to buy them. Initially, Wagner was alleged to have diverted about $800,000 from food-services accounts into his secret slush fund, but just a week after his arrest, prosecutors raised their estimate of how much the chief fiscal officer had stolen to a cool $3 million.[126]

Public school corruption can be found almost anywhere there are public schools, and it reaches all the way to the top echelons of the establishment. California's state superintendent of public instruction, Bill Honig, was convicted on four counts of felony conflict of interest in 1993. Honig, who presided over the state's embrace of whole-language instruction, was found guilty of directing $337,509 worth of state contracts to his wife's nonprofit education company during the late eighties. Thanks to these contracts, Honig's wife was able to pay herself a salary of $100,000 in 1989, a fact which Honig illegally omitted from state financial disclosure forms. While Honig never admitted that his actions were criminal, he did eventually accept responsibility for them during a court appeal, and the charges were downgraded to misdemeanors.[127]

None of this is to say that schools operating for profit in a competitive market would be free of corruption. On the contrary, it can be said with certainty that there would be some level of criminal abuse among private schools. The purpose of this section has simply been to point out that government schools already suffer from these same problems, and that their consumers lack the recourse they would have in an educational market. Private schools found guilty or even simply suspected of fraud can be immediately abandoned by cautious parents—giving those schools, incidentally, a strong incentive not to commit fraud in the first place. With public schools, parents' options are far more limited, as are the incentives for school employees to keep on the straight and narrow path.

As Rare as Pearls: Public Schools that Succeed in Spite of the System

So far, this chapter has been unrelentingly critical of public schooling. That is because government schools, for the most part, are very bad at doing the things people expect of an educational system. But there are exceptions. Some public schools overcome the institutional hurdles before them and deliver a satisfactory or even a good educational experience. How do they do it?

Education researchers have been attempting to answer this question for years, and have identified certain attributes of successful schools. These include such things as "clearly defined goals," "a focus on academics," "an emphasis on outcomes," "strong leadership from the principal," "limited interference from central office bureaucrats," and "effective instruction." Apart from being painfully obvious, the results of "effective schools" research invite the rather important question: How do you bring about these desirable characteristics, and why are they so rare in public schools? After all, it doesn't do much good to identify the features of good schools if you can't figure out how to reproduce them.

Two fellows of the Brookings Institution—John Chubb and Terry Moe—made a commendable effort to answer that question in 1990, with their book *Politics, Markets, and America's Schools*. According to the authors, who carefully analyzed an enormous amount of data from five hundred schools nationwide, freedom from outside interference in decision making is key. Autonomy from meddling central-office bureaucrats and school board members is not just one important aspect of effective schools, they claimed, it actually fosters several of the other desirable organizational features mentioned above, such as principal leadership and clearly defined goals. When principals and teachers are left alone, Chubb and Moe argued, they tend to take the initiative, focus on what is important, and improve their school's organization and effectiveness. When constantly poked and prodded by outsiders, however, they are more likely to feel disenfranchised and to let things slide, resulting in schools without a sense of mission or a coherent strategy for improvement.

The virtue of Chubb and Moe's argument is that it does explain why so few public schools perform well: they are rarely free from the kind of interference that the authors associate with poor organization. Public schools are continually pulled to and fro by district administrators and school board members, in addition to being constrained by reams of state regulations. In a separate ten-year study of school effectiveness, researchers Charles Teddlie and Sam Stringfield discovered that "[a]cross all [phases of the project], we were struck by the lack of meaningful influence from the district offices on school effectiveness. In fact, the only influences we saw were negative and were of little import to overall school effectiveness." They added: "Central office behavior toward school improvement was either benign neglect or interference."[128] Public school principals typically have vastly less control over their schools than their private-sector counterparts and are thus less able to create and maintain effective organizations.

Chubb and Moe's view does have a problem, however, in that it fails to explain why many successful public schools begin as poor performers, and then improve noticeably without any increase in their autonomy. The research on effective schools is filled with comments from teachers to the effect that student achievement at their schools had ranked poorly in state- or district-wide tests up until the arrival of a new principal or curriculum coordinator who, without any change in the district's policy or behavior, had managed to turn things around. Another common example that does not fit the Chubb and Moe view is the case of similar schools in a given district that enroll comparable students and have the same level of autonomy, but produce very different educational outcomes.

To be fair, Chubb and Moe realize that autonomy does not explain all the variation between effective and ineffective schools. Their model of school effectiveness includes several other variables,[129] and their policy proposal—the creation of a competitive educational market—goes well beyond what would be necessary if autonomy were the only factor involved. In fact, Chubb and Moe describe some other features of competitive markets (besides increased autonomy) that lead to the superior effectiveness of private schools.[130] Those features are not present in public education systems, however, so they are not relevant to the question at hand: What causes the remaining differences between good and bad public schools, once autonomy has been taken into account?

The answer can most often be traced to the arrival of a highly motivated new teacher or principal, as was the case at Zavala Elementary School (discussed earlier in this chapter). This is the underlying theme of a great many qualitative investigations into good public schools. In study after study, teachers at top-rated schools attribute their institutions' successes to the exceptional efforts of one or a few remarkable individuals.

Twin Peaks Middle School is representative. During the 1970s, the school had languished under "something less than excellent administrative leadership. . . . Things were not meshing well. . . . [P]arent participation was at a low ebb. . . . [M]any key staff members felt programs were premature, and the result of insufficient planning." The principal who had presided over Twin Peaks during its unhappy days left in 1979, and Judy Endeman took over the position. From the start, the staff was happy with the school's new leader, and was "particularly pleased with her drive, enthusiasm and creative bent." Endeman immediately began holding open houses at the school, interviewing parents and teachers, and designing an improvement plan. A decade later, Twin Peaks was ranked one of the best middle schools in the nation, and students volunteered such comments as: "[W]e . . . are fortunate to have such active, caring administrators."[131]

The "effective schools" research is extremely consistent. Teachers at effective schools regularly eulogize their principals with statements such as: "In essence, the man is a visionary"; and "His vision and foresight is truly phenomenal. I've never seen anyone who has it as he does." Teachers, too, are frequently regarded as outstanding at high-performing schools. One language arts consultant declared that the staff at her current school "had ambitious academic expectations for every child. I mean they really are dedicated and I've serviced many schools in town and I feel this staff is unusually academically ambitious for children."[132]

In short, public schools succeed on those rare occasions when all the planets are aligned. Outside bureaucratic interference must be at a minimum, the principal must be exceptionally dedicated, attentive, and focused on academic achievement, and the staff must be willing and able to take on the demanding task of fulfilling the school's academic mission. All this must happen, moreover, despite the absence of systemic incentives that generally exist in the private sector, such as professional and financial compensation in line with the extraordinary efforts of the staff. In other words, none of the dedicated and talented individuals who help to create truly effective public schools are likely to receive more recognition, responsibility, or money than their peers who just plod along doing the minimum amount of work required by their contracts. Is it any wonder that good public schools are so few and far between?

A Relatively Bad Performance

While this chapter has been generally funereal in tone, it is conceivable that someone might read it and still retain a grain of hope for public schooling. Spending has risen explosively, yes, but the states and their citizens are not yet bankrupt. Achievement has declined in several subjects, but scores have not yet hit bottom and a few have even remained constant. A small number of public schools, scattered here and there across the country, do manage to provide a reasonable education. Things could be worse! As a matter of fact, they are.

Isolated public school successes can only keep hope afloat if we restrict our consideration to the field of education. Once we compare these rare successes to the tremendous progress in other areas of human activity, it becomes clear that they are nothing more than a few remaining bits of flotsam from an institution that sank years ago.

In virtually every industry and field of endeavor, the last seventy-five years have produced astonishing improvements. Services are more numerous, of better quality, and more easily accessible. Athletes are faster, stronger, and more skillful. Machines are more efficient, lighter, cheaper, and safer, and so many new inventions have enhanced our working lives that modern jobs, from secretary to auto mechanic, would be almost unrecognizable to a person from the 1920s.

Imagine how different things would be if these fields had been afflicted with the stagnation and decline experienced by public schools. Instead of having a huge range of transportation choices, you would be left to decide between a horse and a Model T Ford, both of which would cost far more today than they did seventy-five years ago, despite a lack of improvement in either. Of faxes and photocopiers, microwaves and televisions, there would be none. If by some remarkable chance the computer had been invented, it would continue to occupy the space of a large building and have only a fraction of the capacity of a modern hand-held calculator.

Readers may wonder how all these innovations and improvements were achieved given the poor performance of U.S. public schools. The answer is that a host of favorable social and economic conditions and incentives have existed in America since well before the turn of the century, despite the expansion of government schooling. The combination of industrialization, the division of labor, the profit motive, one of the most flexible labor markets in history, and the expansion of national and international trade has had an enormous beneficial effect on productivity. None of these factors depended on the existence of state schooling, though U.S. technological and cultural achievements would no doubt have reached even greater heights had they been bolstered by a truly effective educational system. A detailed explanation of the causes of the "Western economic miracle" can be found in the book *How the West Grew Rich: The Economic Transformation of the Industrial World,* by economists Nathan Rosenberg and Larry Birdzell.[133]

The point of these observations is that the benchmark against which public schooling must be measured is not stagnation but constant progress. The norm in free societies is continuous innovation and improvement in technologies, methods, and performance, not the static or deteriorating condition of public education. Apart from cultures and institutions that have willfully renounced progress, government schooling stagnates alone, a fossilized legacy of central planning and good intentions gone awry.

The problem, moreover, is not a uniquely American one. Public school systems all over the world share many of the same problems as the U.S. system. Even government-education success stories are more complex than they are often portrayed to be. These observations are documented in detail in the following chapter.

7

Common School Problems:
The World Tour

To date, people around the world have treated their own nations' public school woes as though they were unique. It is time that we realized we are all in this boat together, and that the letters neatly etched into the bulkhead spell T-I-T-A-N-I-C.

To that end, this chapter takes the reader on a guided tour of government education monopolies in three modern nations, revealing the common problems that flow so generously from that common source.

Most of the problems highlighted in the chapters on U.S. public schooling afflict state-run school systems around the globe. Public opinion of public schools is often poor; familiar groups of antagonists regularly wage battles over the content and delivery of government education; and, with some exceptions, academic achievement in several key areas is low and/or declining. The following sections explore these general patterns, along with a few surprises, in Japan, England, and Canada.

Japan: A Tale of Two Systems

Japanese public school students match or outscore their peers around the world on international tests of mathematics, and are at or near the top in most other subjects as well. For this reason, many observers believe Japanese public schooling should be used as a model for other countries. They are mistaken. Several of the most important reasons for Japan's academic success lie outside its government school system, and even though its public schools outshine those of other countries in certain respects, they nonetheless suffer from the crippling flaws endemic to state-run education. Ironically, Japan does have a thriving private market for educational services which *is* worthy of emulation.

Academic Achievement

A great deal has been written on the causes of Japan's academic success. The consensus among experts in the field points to a combination of four factors: the motivating effects of high-stakes entrance exams; considerable parental involvement (usually by mothers); sound pedagogy in the public schools; and perhaps most importantly, the widespread patronage of private, for-profit supplementary schools.

Most Japanese employers place enormous importance on the university from which job applicants graduate. After they are hired, new employees are frequently grouped according to the accepted ranking of their alma mater.[1] Graduates of the most reputable institutions, the universities of Tokyo and Kyoto, for example, are groomed for management, while those from less prestigious universities are directed into less prestigious (and lower-paying) jobs. This rigid credentialism has placed a premium on degrees from "A-level" universities, and since entrance to such universities is based solely on exam results, high-school seniors have only two choices: study until they cannot study any more, or resign themselves to second-rate jobs for the rest of their lives. Competition for the limited number of freshman places at the most prestigious institutions is brutally intense, and the entire process is referred to not-so-affectionately as "examination hell."

From the later elementary grades to the end of high school, the university exams loom large in the lives of Japanese children. The examination process consists of an initial nationwide test taken by all university-bound students, called the Joint First Stage Achievement Test, followed by an admission test unique to each university. These exams have a powerful trickle-down effect on lower levels of schooling. It is generally believed that some senior high schools offer better preparation for the exams than others, making them highly sought-after. Since entrance to senior high school is also governed by a competitive examination, junior high school students face similarly intense pressure to study and perform well academically. Not even elementary school students are entirely spared from this pressure.

While examination hell is given considerable credit for students' high scores on international tests, it is also denounced by parents, the media, and even the

Ministry of Education. Criticism of the examination process revolves around the stress it introduces into the lives of children, and the obvious fact that locking-in all students' futures based on a pair of written tests may not be the best way of serving their varied educational and career aspirations. Leaders of Japan's Ministry of Education, as well as its critics, lament the stifling conformity produced by the present system, and worry that it impedes the development of creative, independent thinkers.[2] To the extent that other countries mimic Japan's competitive testing program, they can expect to improve their scores on whatever material they happen to test, but the intense pressure these tests exert on children, and the narrowing effect they have on those children's education, could be considered a disincentive to doing so.

Parental involvement is another key to Japan's comparatively good educational performance. Since Japanese mothers stay at home with their children more often than women in many other industrialized countries, it should not be surprising that they are better able to supervise their children's education. Combined with the already described importance of academic success, this has led to very active participation by mothers in students' schoolwork. A phrase, "education mama," has even been coined to refer to the many mothers who spend a great deal of time looking for ways of improving their children's educational performance. There are even "mama *juku*"—private schools that prepare mothers in the subjects their children are studying.[3] The help and encouragement of mothers no doubt has a beneficial effect on student test scores, but since the career preferences of men and women differ appreciably from country to country, this factor in Japanese educational success is not liable to be widely emulated.

Far easier to reproduce would be the Japanese public schools' effective pedagogical methods and materials. Japanese teachers tend to introduce topics once, cover them with great thoroughness, and then move on. U.S. (and Canadian) government schools, by contrast, generally use a "spiral" curriculum, in which the same topics are repeatedly introduced in successive grades, rarely if ever being explained in depth. According to Harold Stevenson, who has spent decades comparing Asian and American education, the Japanese approach leads to greater understanding, and allows new topics to be introduced at a younger age, since class time in higher grades is not spent reviewing elementary topics.[4]

The differences between textbooks in the two countries are also stark. Japanese texts (particularly in math) introduce only as many topics per semester as students can reasonably be expected to learn. They are generally thin, inexpensive paperback books bought by, rather than loaned to, the students. U.S. textbooks are enormous and costly by comparison, stuffed with much more information (and more colorful charts) than can possibly be covered in the time allotted to them.[5] "Overwhelmed by the length of the texts and aware that the concepts will be encountered by students again at a later grade," write Stevenson and his colleague Karen Bartsch, "many teachers may exert little effort to cover the material contained in the elementary and secondary textbooks."[6] Stevenson and Bartsch conclude that "American textbooks may form an obstacle to the learning of mathematics by American students."

The curricula and textbooks of Japanese public schools thus seem to be better than those of many other government school systems.[7] Given the dismal performance of government school systems throughout history, however, this is not saying much—it is akin to being the fastest sprinter in professional sumo wrestling. Still, many education pundits have been quick to suggest the adoption of Japan's methods and curricula as a solution to their own countries' educational woes. Even if the Japanese approach were ideally suited to present conditions, however, simple mimicry would be dangerously shortsighted. Educational demands change over time, and it might not be long before the present practices of the Japanese are hopelessly out of date. Much more valuable than copying existing practices is the development of an educational system that can be depended upon to constantly search out and deliver the best methods over the long term. It would be much better, in other words, to teach our schools how to fish than to simply hand them a few pieces of sushi, however tasty they may be.

The question thus becomes: Can Japan's government-run educational system teach other nations how to run effective, efficient schools that will respond to families' changing needs in the years to come? Alas, no. The Japanese education establishment is not an especially reliable fisherman; it is a lucky one. The relatively effective pedagogy currently in place in the nation's public schools is not the result of an open and competitive process of research, development, and field-testing. It is a rigid mass of regulations handed down by central government bureaucrats at the Ministry of Education. It is revised only infrequently, and its revisions are not based on the avowed concerns of families, but rather on the opinions and predispositions of whichever officials happen to be in power. The fact that Japan's government school system currently employs many effective educational methods and textbooks is no guarantee that it will continue to do so in the future, that it will be able to adapt to changing demands, or that it will avoid the many other flaws inherent in state-run education.

Japan's centralized approach to school governance is reminiscent of Russia's during the cold war, and the comparison is illustrative. At that time, Russian pedagogy was in some ways far superior to that of the United States. Russian schools offered the intensive early instruction in phonics generally missing from American institutions. Russian reading texts were endowed with vocabularies many times larger than their U.S. equivalents, and were filled with unedited excerpts from the works of such brilliant writers as Tolstoy and Chekhov.[8] Though nineteenth-century U.S. textbooks enjoyed similar characteristics, the public school reading material of the mid-to-late twentieth century has been grossly simplified by comparison. But the strong literacy programs of Soviet Russian education were not brought about through reliable and responsive market forces. Instead, they were put in place at the whim of government officials. Not all officials were so wise. The Russian government's official rejection of modern genetics, in favor of the grossly misguided views of T. D. Lysenko,[9] retarded the study of the life sciences in that country by many decades. Reliance on bureaucrats to make consistently correct decisions is simply not a viable educational strategy.

Like Russian schools of the 1950s and 1960s, Japanese public schools are currently superior in certain respects to those of other state-run systems. Nevertheless, they suffer all the pitfalls inherent in government schooling. Though Japanese texts are not pervaded with pro-government propaganda as Russian textbooks were,[10] they have been repeatedly faulted (both domestically and abroad) for their distorted and sanitized depictions of the causes and events of the Second World War.[11] Japanese education bureaucrats, insulated as they are from consumer demand and the incentives of the marketplace, are unresponsive to (and even unaware of) variation in consumer demand and are ill-equipped for change and innovation. These and other problems are described in more detail below.

Anatomy of a Power Struggle

> No Japanese institution in the postwar period has experienced more political conflict than public education. The machinery of educational policy making has witnessed intense and persistent conflict between the Japan Teachers' Union (JTU) and government authorities, especially at the national level. Fist fights in the national legislature, teachers' strikes and sit-ins, mass arrests, and legal suits have occurred regularly. Hostility, distrust, and acrimony have often divided faculties and paralyzed schools.[12]

Thus writes Thomas Rohlen, one of the most respected foreign experts on Japanese education. As in so many other countries, public schooling is an ideological battlefield in Japan. The dominant JTU, while representing teachers with wide-ranging political affiliations, is generally led by socialists or communists. The government education bureaucracy, on the other hand, has been staunchly conservative for generations. Each of these antagonists tries desperately and continuously to make public schools conform to its own agenda, with three undesirable (but inevitable) results: an endless succession of highly publicized clashes, an extreme case of educational rigor mortis, and a disregard for the needs and preferences of students and their parents.

The present structure of Japanese public schooling dates back to the American Occupation that followed World War II. Before the war, government education officials had ruled supreme, writing nationalistic textbooks to suit their military ambitions, and ensuring that teachers followed the mandated curriculum meticulously. By encouraging unionism and decentralizing the governance of public schools, the occupying U.S. forces curtailed the government's authority and helped to lay the groundwork for the JTU. Predictably, irascible relations between the JTU and the Ministry of Education began as soon as Japan regained its sovereignty in 1952, as the Ministry of Education sought to regain some of its lost powers, and the union fought to retain the foothold it had been given.

School boards were the first bone of contention. Locally elected school boards had been put in place during the Occupation, but the Ministry of Education alleged that they introduced an undesirable degree of politicization into education. Like their counterparts in U.S. education bureaucracies of the early 1900s, central government officials in Japan also claimed that decentralization of educational authority would inevitably lead to inefficiency. According to the Ministry, these problems could be alleviated by making school board membership an appointed rather than elective office. A more plausible explanation for the Ministry's opposition to locally elected school boards is that it feared they would be dominated by the teachers' union, seriously undermining the Ministry's own power. This appears to have been the interpretation of the JTU, which organized a series of national demonstrations to halt the Ministry's plan to eliminate school board elections. Twenty-nine other organizations joined the union in its battle, but with a majority in the federal parliament, the conservative Liberal-Democratic Party (LDP) government carried the day.[13]

The last half-century has been filled with similar skirmishes. A major attempt at reforming the nation's school system took place in the late sixties and early seventies, but "efforts to bring about more flexibility in Japan's schools," and to reform the entrance examination system, "completely failed."[14] Mutual distrust and gross differences of opinion between the union and the LDP's Ministry of Education were key causes of the deadlock. The next major reform effort, again promoted by the ruling LDP party, was the creation of an ad hoc council on school reform during the 1980s. It lasted for three years, produced three reports full of vagaries, and led to little or no change in the status quo. According to one scholar, "the general public [believes] that the National Council on Educational Reform was a failure."[15]

Observers of the Japanese educational scene are unanimous in their views of the intractable antagonism between the JTU and the Ministry of Education: "Although the postwar political and ideological struggles for control of Japanese education have significantly affected the administration of schools and the quality of faculty relations," notes Thomas Rohlen, "they have not transformed either instruction or the routines of high school education."[16] Haruo Ota, of Soai University, goes one step further:

In the course of the all-out battles between Nikkyoso [the JTU] and the Ministry of Education, little consideration has been given to the education of children; educational questions have been subordinated to the issue of control. Consequently, Japanese education has developed the testing system, under which high priority is put on the selective function of education rather than on the educational function itself.[17]

Antipathy between the teachers' union and Ministry bureaucrats certainly deserves much of the blame for the excessive rigidity of Japanese public schooling, but it is an insufficient explanation. The Ministry has far more power over the schools than the JTU, and could push through a great many changes if it so chose, yet it has not done so. In the conclusion to his book on Japanese education reform, British researcher Leonard Schoppa traces part of the stagnation problem to the Ministry itself. Regarding its bureaucrats and politicians, he observes:

> Their influence depends on strengthening and expanding the present system rather than reducing the governmental role and allowing greater diversity and choice. Most are interested primarily in obtaining a larger share of the budget. Particularly in the latest round of reform, these tendencies made [them] one of the leading forces opposed to change. . . . They are unable to criticize the existing system without criticizing themselves.[18]

A bureaucracy is a bureaucracy is a bureaucracy, whether in Tokyo, Ottawa, or Washington, D.C. And just as the ill effects of bureaucracy know no national boundaries, they are as freely distributed at the local level as at the national. After more than a year of investigations into the workings of Japanese high schools, Rohlen concluded that local (prefectural) offices of education "do not generate significant innovation" in curriculum, textbooks, or any of the other areas in which the Ministry of Education has primary authority.[19] Just as in the United States, Canada, and most other countries, public school principals in Japan lack the basic "control mechanisms common to most modern organizations. Tenure is automatic from the first day. Teachers cannot be fired for anything short of gross or illegal misconduct. There is almost no discretion in the wage system, and there are no promotions to manipulate."[20]

The combination of political gridlock with a highly regulated, centralized, bureaucratic governance structure has meant that Japanese public schools have not even attempted to discover, let alone act upon, the needs of individual families.[21] Schoppa, who spent little time discussing public opinion in his study, explains his omission by stating that the public's influence is so indirect and informal that it has not played a discernible role in the shaping of Japanese schooling.[22] The public, in Japan as elsewhere, is a bystander in its own public education system.

Athens Redux: Japan's Booming Education Market

> Taro is a typical fifth grader of *Nishishiroyama* Elementary School. His typical
> school day begins at 8:30 a.m. and ends at 3:30 p.m. He arrives home at 4:00.
> Coming home at 4:00, however, does not mean that he can enjoy the rest of the
> day. At 4:30 p.m. he leaves home for a *Shingaku-Juku*. He studies arithmetic there
> until 7:45 p.m. and then comes back home. After supper he begins to do his home-
> work assignments.[23]

Though it receives little attention in the foreign press, Japan has a thriving,
multibillion dollar a year private education industry. By the fifth grade, one
child in three is enrolled in a *juku*, a private "after-school school" operated for
profit. *Juku* attendance begins as early as the first grade, becoming more and
more common as children approach senior high school. Over half of eighth-
graders were found to be enrolled in *juku* in 1991, and estimates for ninth-
graders are as high as 70 percent. A Tokyo survey found that nine out of ten
students had attended a *juku* by the time they reached the ninth grade.[24]

The key role *juku* play in raising Japan to international academic preeminence is widely recognized among researchers who have studied them. The following views are typical:

> The quality of the Japanese primary and secondary educational system cannot be
> maintained without the support of a [supplemental] educational system, such as
> *juku*, which compensates for the inflexibility of the formal system.[25]

> Without [*juku*], the success of Japan in the area of education would be unthink-
> able.[26]

Reasons for attending private supplemental schools vary from family to family, but three in particular stand out: improving students' chances on high-
stakes entrance exams, obtaining remedial help for students falling behind in
the public schools, and obtaining advanced instruction for students not challenged by the pace in public schools.

The Ministry of Education is hostile to *juku*, as government school systems
have nearly always been to independent schools. But, while the Ministry tells
parents they should not send their children to *juku*, parents counter that curricular changes introduced by the government "are not reflected in university entrance exams, thus placing increased pressures on parents and students to learn
material outside the regular school setting."[27] Few people, it seems, argue that
the knee-jerk credentialism of Japanese business is sensible or desirable, but
parents are keenly aware that it exists, and thus feel obliged to give their children the best possible chance of being accepted at an "elite" university.

Juku also sell flexibility. Because Japanese public schools are designed to offer a homogeneous educational experience, they inevitably lead to problems for students who deviate too far from the average. If all children were identical little learning machines, the government's policy of educational conformity might have merit, but since they are not, both slow and bright students find themselves marginalized in the public schools. Fortunately for those children, there are alternatives.

Rather than foisting an arbitrary curriculum on students, *juku* ask what it is children need and parents want. They test students to ascertain their level of competence and then group them accordingly, so that instruction can be specifically tailored to the areas of greatest need. Contrary to the beliefs of doom-saying American educators, the practice of ability grouping does not lead to warehousing students in slow educational tracks—that, after all, would be bad for business. Instead, *juku* administer frequent tests to follow each student's progress in the subjects in which he is enrolled, and then reform their classes based on the test results so that children are always receiving the precise kind and level of instruction they require.[28] Students also tend to enjoy more personal attention in *juku* than in public schools.[29]

The selection, compensation, and work practices of teachers differ appreciably between *juku* and public schools. Hiring restrictions imposed on government schools are absent from *juku,* and thus private school teachers come from a multitude of backgrounds. Some are traditionally trained educators, but many are scientists, economists, college professors, other professionals, and university students who are interested in teaching. "Free market competition," explains professor Delwyn Harnisch, "provides a strong incentive for improving instructional effectiveness in *juku,*"[30] forcing managers to employ and retain only those teachers who are consistently able to deliver instructional services that parents and students are willing to pay for. He goes on to say:

> Instruction in a *juku* is usually more work- and time-intensive than in the public schools. This is due to the many homework assignments and exams in *juku,* and the necessity to meet certain specific requirements and to eliminate individual learning deficits and difficulties. Finally the strong parental expectations and pressure of testing also play a role.[31]

But the job has its perks. The opportunity to offer personalized instruction to truly motivated students is appealing to teachers disheartened by the disengaged, disinterested attitudes commonly found among students in compulsory schools.[32] Salaries are generally good, and since they are based on performance rather than the fixed scale common to public schools, top *juku* instructors can and do earn as much as professional Japanese baseball players.[33] Like ancient Athenian sophists, these highly popular teachers sometimes travel about the country as free agents.

While a few *juku* are so popular that they cannot accept all comers, this is not a widespread problem. Successful private schools rarely limit their enrollment to a fixed number of pupils, being spurred by the profit motive to continually hire more teachers and expand to new locations in an effort to keep up with demand. Many *juku* are still one-room, one-teacher operations, but the largest chains enroll up to a million children nationwide.[34]

Another reason that students are generally able to gain admission to a private school of their choosing is that different *juku* cater to different audiences, thus spreading out the demand. Some *juku*, called *yobiko*, are focused solely on helping senior-high-school students and recent high-school graduates to pass the university entrance examinations. Even among these there is great variation, however, since individual *yobiko* often prepare students for the specific exams of only one or two institutions. Students thus seek out the *yobiko* which are geared to the universities they wish to attend. Since a sizable percentage of students fail to pass the admission test of their preferred university on their first attempt, a great many high-school graduates enroll in full-time, year-long *yobiko* training programs in preparation for taking the test a second time.

In addition to preparing students for university and high-school entrance exams, *juku* also offer general academic training (such as the remedial and advanced instruction described above) and also nonacademic training. There are *juku* offering education in music, art, calligraphy, physical fitness, and sundry other disciplines.

In spite of their many excellent qualities, *juku* have their detractors. Some feel they are mindless cram schools that focus excessively on rote memorization, and there is at least a kernel of truth in this criticism, but it is the market, not the *juku*, that is ultimately responsible. By placing their emphasis on students' pedagogical pedigree rather than on their abilities, the Japanese have created a market for education degrees rather than for education. As market-driven enterprises, *juku* are forced to provide what their customers demand. The demand for high test scores on entrance exams forces private schools to take whatever steps are most effective in raising those scores, and intensive memory work is one of those steps. The problem is often overstated, however, since the university-specific exams also require considerable reasoning and writing skills, which are not (and cannot be) taught by simple memorization. To teach more sophisticated skills, *juku* apply more sophisticated methods.

Juku are also chastised for contributing to educational inequality, since parents do not all purchase equal amounts of their services. In reality, the issue is less clear. Children do not learn all subjects at the same pace, so the rigidly uniform instruction of public schools is itself inherently unequal in its ability to meet students' needs. Children who are brighter or slower than average are placed at a disadvantage, since the National Curriculum is either too simple or too advanced for their abilities. By responding to this natural variation in ability, *juku* are actually more equitable than the state system, unless one believes that bright children should be deliberately held back, or slow children left behind.

Even students with comparable levels of innate ability may receive different amounts of supplemental schooling, however—thus putting some at a relative advantage in the workforce over others. What critics seem to ignore, though, is that this is what parents clearly want. While many Japanese publicly avow a desire for a uniform, equal system of education, most seek precisely the opposite in practice. Parents, after all, want what is best for their own children, and most other considerations, including equality, take a back seat in their pursuit of that goal. If the Japanese truly wanted an egalitarian system of education, they would outlaw *juku* and all direct spending on education by parents. Instead, they have an enormous and rapidly growing private industry that effectively caters to the desires of parents to provide their own sons and daughters the best possible education. Transactions speak louder than words.

Conclusion

Japan's public school system is very much like the Jesuit schools of the early seventeenth century. It is uniform, governed by a detailed plan of studies, administered by a vast bureaucratic empire, and, for the time being at least, superior to many other government school systems. Unfortunately, the similarity does not end there. Like Jesuit schooling on the eve of the Enlightenment, Japan's state-run education bureaucracy is fiercely resistant to change, all but incapable of innovation, and out of touch with the families it is meant to serve. This inability to respond to evolving conditions doomed the Jesuit system to eventual moribundity and irrelevance. Nothing appears to be preventing the Japanese government school system from following the same course.

In contrast to the bleak prospects of Japan's state schools, its dynamic for-profit education industry seems poised for dramatic growth. *Yobiko* already offer full-time classes for high-school graduates, and have begun to expand their services to younger students. The difference between supplemental schools and regular schools is blurring, and it is easy to foresee a time when *juku* will no longer be restricted to the after-school niche they presently occupy. For those seeking a way to increase responsiveness, accountability, efficiency, and innovation in education, *juku* have a lesson to teach, and they will even teach this one for free: markets deliver.

The *Dis*United Kingdom

Over the last half-century, English education policy has been just as contentious as that of the United States or Japan. As in those nations, progressives and traditionalists have continuously fought for control over the organization, methods, and curriculum of the state school system. More specifically, the issues at the heart of England's educational debate have been:

- Progressive versus traditionalist teaching methods
- Academically selective versus one-size-fits-all comprehensive schools
- Local control over lesson plans versus the mandatory National Curriculum
- The existence of semi-autonomous "grant maintained" schools (essentially what are known in North America as charter schools—see Chapter 10)

These issues, and their effects on the education of English children, are discussed in the following sections.

The Rise of Progressivism

Until recently, pedagogical methods in the U.K. were not laid down at the national level. Teachers' instructional practices have thus been shaped primarily by their training in colleges of education. College education professors, in turn, have been influenced by a succession of prominent education philosophers.

In the early 1900s, the reigning philosophy of education was still very traditional. The teacher was expected to convey man's accumulated knowledge and wisdom to her students in a structured fashion, deciding what was worthy of study and what was not. That began to change as a result of such influential figures as Edmond Holmes, a onetime head of the government's official school inspection organization. In his 1911 book *What Is and What Might Be*, Holmes argued for a progressive vision of schooling that placed control of the educational experience firmly in the hands of the child. Holmes's book had little if any immediate effect on English classrooms, but was extremely popular and well received in the academic education community, where professors began to propound the same progressive views to their students. This, in turn, fostered a new generation of teachers whose pedagogical methods diverged from those of their older, more experienced counterparts. Though some of these new teachers discarded their progressive methods when placed in emphatically traditionalist schools, each successive graduating class turned out by the schools of education spread progressivism a little further. Since some of these same graduates went on to become professors of education themselves, a self-reinforcing cycle was created that eventually led to the dominance of progressive methods and philosophy in colleges of education and in the nation's schools.

Though progressivism's rise was gradual, certain milestones do stand out. The most famous of these was the Plowden report of 1967. Produced by the government-appointed Central Advisory Council for Education, the Plowden report aimed to assess "primary schooling in all its aspects" and to make policy recommendations. In retrospect, its most controversial and widely implemented suggestions were the elimination of student groupings based on ability (i.e., "streaming"), and an emphasis on progressive, child-directed, discovery learning.

In the wake of the Plowden report, champions of progressive methods advocated special training programs to promote their views both in colleges of education and among practicing educators. According to S. R. Dennison, a professor of economics and former vice-chancellor of the University of Hull, one

> senior lecturer at a College of Education, and a leading advocate of comprehensive education, called in 1970 for "a fundamental change in teacher attitudes," with, in the colleges of education, "a process of de-indoctrination of students who were themselves still mostly the products of [traditional] grammar schools" and presumably possessing all their vices of "élitism," narrow academic standards, etc.[35]

Many teacher candidates, in other words, had ostensibly been brainwashed by their own educational experiences and needed to be deprogrammed by colleges of education, and then reprogrammed with the correct, progressive views. Another advocate went further, proposing in-service training that would encourage all teachers to embrace the elimination of streaming and of academically selective schools.[36]

Though only a fraction of the nation's schools became completely Plowdenized in succeeding years, virtually all felt progressivism's influence. By the late 1970s, ability grouping was all but extinct and discovery learning had largely displaced structured, teacher-led instruction. In the early 1970s, an investigation of teachers' attitudes toward academics and job preparation revealed the same pattern that has been found in the United States. Teachers in the U.K. are "more 'people-oriented' in their values than most other occupational groups, placing emphasis on personal relationships, 'helping other people' and 'working with people'," and putting "correspondingly less value on what is seen as useful, efficient, economic."[37] For English children and their families, by contrast, "career prospects come first by a long way."[38]

Reading instruction has also been transformed by the rise of progressivism. A 1990 study of elementary reading teachers found that most preferred a loosely defined mix of whole language and phonics, while few favored the sort of intensive, systematic phonics instruction most strongly supported by reading research. Of those expressing a clear methodological preference, eight times as many declared themselves whole-language teachers as declared themselves phonics teachers.[39] According to a 1989 government inquiry, the textbooks from which teachers-in-training are expected to learn how to teach reading are now dominated by a whole-language approach that eschews explicit systematic phonics. The National

Foundation for Educational Research (NFER) announced two years later that 60 percent of recent teachers' college graduates said "they had been taught little or nothing about phonics" and "did not feel confident about teaching children to read." According to the NFER report, this was due to the fact that schools of education made little or no distinction between the process of learning how to decode printed text (i.e., how to read) and learning to enjoy literature.[40]

In a 1995 study comparing Swiss and English approaches to mathematics and science instruction, researchers observed that "most of the time [English] pupils are left to their own resources. The teacher's role is mainly to help individual pupils when there are difficulties and to check their work." In science classes, English "teachers tended to refrain from instructing pupils in the scientific principles at issue" and encouraged them to "pursue their own lines of inquiry." These practices contrasted sharply with those of Swiss teachers, who spent far more time directly instructing their entire classes in the subjects at hand.[41]

Traditionalist instructional methods have not been entirely displaced, however. Since progressive philosophy is based on a set of beliefs about the development of young children, higher levels of education have been somewhat less affected by it. A 1997 survey conducted by Bernard Lamb revealed that only 6 percent of secondary school English teachers had been discouraged from using traditional whole-class instruction, while 28 percent had been encouraged to use it (the rest were left to themselves). Progressivism's effects are felt even in secondary schools, however. When asked about grammar, 69 percent of teachers responded that it should be taught "as it arose from pupils' work," a view consistent with progressive discovery learning. Only 28 percent of respondents believed that grammar should be taught explicitly.[42]

In promoting progressive pedagogy, supporters rarely argued that it would improve academic achievement. In fact, few even bothered to collect evidence on this question. Whether intentional or not, this omission can only have helped their cause, for the evidence that has been collected is not generally favorable.

The broadest English comparison of progressive and traditional methods was carried out by Neville Bennett in the 1970s, at roughly the same time as the U.S. Follow Through experiment (see Chapter 5). Bennett's results were substantially similar to those of Follow Through—students in informal progressive classrooms fell behind those in formal, teacher-directed classes in all academic areas tested: reading, mathematics, and English. Explaining his findings, Bennett wrote:

> Informal teachers wish to foster self-expression in their pupils, but it should be recognised that this seems to lead to more behaviour which tends to work against effective learning—such as general social gossip, gazing into space or out of the window and various negative behaviours. . . . Pupils in formal classrooms engaged in work related activity much more frequently, the differences being most marked

among pupils whose initial achievement level was high. . . . The same general pattern was also true of low achievers in informal classrooms, who engaged in significantly less work than pupils of a similar level in formal situations.[43]

The concordance between Bennett's findings and those of Follow Through is not unusual. Education professor Maurice Galton, himself an adherent of many of the ideas at the heart of progressive pedagogy, wrote in 1995: "Looking back on this era . . . it is now possible to conclude that . . . the main findings of Bennett's studies have been frequently replicated both in the United Kingdom and in the United States."[44]

One particularly notorious replication took place in the city of Leeds. Between 1985 and 1990, the Leeds Local Education Authority (the equivalent of a U.S. school district) spent 13.75 million pounds on a special program called the Primary Needs Project (PNP). This project increased the size of the teaching staff and promoted the use of progressive methods such as mixed ability grouping, fragmenting classes into groups focused on a variety of different curriculum areas, and child-directed, rather than teacher-directed, learning. Robin Alexander, head of the independent evaluation project studying the PNP, wrote in his 1991 report:

> Reading scores at 7+ and 9+ [i.e., the scores of seven-year-olds and nine-year-olds] from 1983–91 showed no evidence that the injection of extra staff and money into Leeds Primary Schools, especially those in the inner city, had a positive impact on children's reading ability. . . . On the contrary, scores showed a decline towards the end of the evaluation period, especially in the inner city schools where PNP resources were concentrated.[45]

The verdict on mixed-ability grouping (placing children of different ability levels in the same classroom) has been similarly negative. By the mid-1970s it had become the default practice in government schools, but a reaction was soon to follow. In 1980, mixed-ability classes were condemned by the government school inspectors of the Inner-London Education Authority (ILEA). Their conclusion was that "mixed-ability grouping for the large majority of subjects after the 2nd or 3rd year [grade] was 'barely suitable' for the middle range of ability and left the 'least able unheeded and the most able unchallenged.'" Lumping together bright, average, and slow children in the same classrooms fell under sustained criticism in the 1980s, and the practice was already becoming less common as early as 1981.[46]

As in other nations, public school progressivism has been a lightning rod for educational conflict. Some parents and educators have been attracted to its child-centered ideology, while others have resented it for displacing the teacher as the source of instruction and classroom organization, and many have also criticized it for undermining academic achievement. Battles on these grounds have taken place all over England. At a school in Sunderland, for example, "six years of parental protests and a petition from 35 of the 55 teachers . . . [in response to] the breakdown of discipline and the collapse of standards" forced a progressive principal "to accept a radical reform plan, including the introduction of 'streaming' and the abandonment of mixed-ability teaching, 'directly counter to his progressive educational convictions.'"[47] The costs of such fierce confrontations in terms of lower staff morale, lost parental and community support, etc., are clearly high.

From the 1980s onward, the tide of public opinion has shifted against progressivism. While it remains popular in many colleges of education, whatever public support it once had has eroded considerably. The evidence that progressive methods are academically inferior to more traditional ones has proven sufficiently compelling in some quarters that the Labour party — historically allied to the progressive cause — has performed a radical about-face on education policy. In June 1996, a year before his election as prime minister, Tony Blair declared that he "would abolish mixed-ability teaching" in favor of grouping students of similar ability in the same classes — to the considerable consternation of teachers' organizations and some members of his own party.[48] An article appearing just a few weeks earlier in the *Daily Mail* made Labour's shift even more explicit:

> [Labour Party] education spokesman David Blunkett admits schools were wrong to discard proven methods of teaching reading, writing, and mathematics.
>
> In the most fundamental reversal of Labour attitudes to primary education for 30 years, he pledges to scrap the failed progressive experiments of the Sixties and Seventies if the Party is elected. . . . Mr. Blunkett declares: "Teachers must use teaching methods which work, not simply the latest fashion."[49]

Since taking power, Blair and Blunkett have been quick to reassert their commitment to reversing the progressive tide. Not only will phonics and direct instruction be reintroduced into classrooms, declared Blunkett after the 1997 Labour victory, but "teacher training colleges which persist in using progressive methods and refuse to 'go back to basics' will lose their government funding and could eventually face closure."[50]

To implement its back-to-basics policy, the Blair government has designed a National Literacy Strategy (NLS) with guidelines for the teaching of reading. Despite the government's avowed intentions, however, the strategy does not recommend the use of any of the better-known intensive systematic phonics programs (e.g., Open Court, Jolly Phonics, or Reading Mastery, the successor to Distar), nor does it lay out a detailed, empirically tested phonics program of its own. Instead, the NLS suggests a vague mix of phonics and whole-language ideas which is only slightly different from the methods already being practiced in much of England and the United States today (with unimpressive results). In direct opposition to most traditional phonics programs, for instance, the NLS exhorts teachers to have children memorize approximately two hundred common words by sight, rather than sounding them out phonetically. It also encourages the use of word guessing based on the context of the story "to predict or confirm information [derived] from other [reading] strategies."[51] In traditional phonics programs, word guessing is actively discouraged.

Whatever the particular methods imposed by the Labour government, it is clear that the rights and preferences of individual families are not considered important. Prime Minister Blair has declared: "If we want to get [education policy] right, it has to be driven through from the top, no holds barred."[52] Government authorities are firmly grasping the nettle of school reform, but in doing so they are as likely to injure families as to aide them.

What is a parent to do, for example, if she prefers open classrooms, discovery learning, and other progressive practices for her children, despite the evidence against them? What if she believes the National Literacy Strategy is not the return to traditional methods that she had hoped for? What if she favors a pedagogical approach that is neither progressive nor traditional? She, due to the actions of her own government, has little say. Her views and the reasons for which she holds them are irrelevant. A single pedagogical vision is being imposed by the central government, leaving little room for the diverse marketplace of ideas that obtains in most other areas of modern life. Even citizens currently in accord with the government's strategy have no guarantee that their views will remain *en vogue* after the next election.

Student Grouping: A Comprehensive Problem

During the 1920s and 1930s, it became increasingly common for students in the U.K. to sit for an exam called the "eleven-plus," which derived its name from the age at which it was given. Children securing high marks on this test were eligible to attend selective grammar schools which prepared them for college, while those receiving lower marks were directed into "secondary modern" schools which were intended to provide them with a general education and to prepare them for joining the workforce. Opposition to this selection policy grew after the end of World War II, most notably among progressive and socialist educators who perceived the test as not only inaccurate but inherently unjust. Translating these criticisms into policy, the Labour government of Harold Wilson issued "Circular 10/65" in 1965, stating: "It is the Government's declared objective to end selection at eleven-plus and to eliminate separatism in secondary education."[53] In place of the dual system of grammar and secondary modern schools, Circular 10/65 advocated uniform, "comprehensive" secondary schools for all children regardless of ability. Viewed as anti-merito-cratic by traditionalists, this policy was reversed by a Conservative government in 1970. It was reinstated in 1974, however, after the Labour party returned to power. In an attempt to make "comprehensivisation" more difficult to reverse, Labour then passed the Education Act of 1976, which required Local Educa-tion Authorities (LEAs, the equivalent of U.S. school districts) to submit plans for eliminating selection and grouping by ability and introducing comprehen-sive schools. Not surprisingly, this act was itself repealed (by the Education Act of 1979) when the Conservatives regained control of the government.[54]

Despite having fired the last major salvo in this fourteen-year battle, the Con-servative party was less than triumphant. In 1965, there were only 221 com-prehensive schools and 1,180 selective grammar schools. In 1979, the numbers were 3,203 and 254, respectively.[55] Though the Conservatives held power throughout the eighties and most of the nineties, the trend away from selective schools continued. A 1997 Labour government White Paper put the number of grammar schools at 161, and vowed that no other selective schools would be added.[56]

Though the practice of sorting students into two groups on the basis of their eleven-plus scores served some students well, it was open to criticism on sev-eral fronts. Children do not, after all, fall neatly into two well-defined groups at the age of eleven, nor do their capacities and interests develop along one of only two preordained lines thereafter. It could also be argued that the eleven-plus exam usurped the right of parents to decide the kind of education best suited to their children. A related objection, often voiced by the progressive op-ponents of selective schooling, was that government-sponsored streaming of students could be abused to favor certain socioeconomic groups at the expense of others.

One educator, who had been obliged as a child to attend a secondary mod-ern school due to his poor showing on the eleven-plus, wrote in the *Times Ed-ucational Supplement* that "children wept openly when they failed the [eleven-plus] test," and admitted: "I wanted to be [in a grammar school] too and felt condemned. Failing the eleven-plus has haunted me to this day."[57] Writing in the same issue, another former secondary modern student summarized his ex-perience this way: "[M]y overall impression was that it was a quiet, orderly school, where nothing of any real importance was going to be learned in the four years after which most of us would be expected to find factory work."

Progressive educators and the Labour party consistently attacked the eleven-plus selection policy, but rather than freeing up the system by providing fami-lies with more varied choices and allowing students to move more easily among a greater variety of educational environments, they advocated herding all stu-dents into uniform comprehensive schools. Their goal was not so much to en-sure that each child received the kind of education appropriate to him, but rather to guarantee that all children were treated equally by the school system. The fact that all children do not have identical educational needs and aspirations was forgotten or ignored.

The ideological fervor with which comprehensivisation was promoted is noteworthy in and of itself. While the House of Commons produced a calm, measured resolution on the subject, stating the need to "preserve all that is valuable in grammar school education . . . and make it available to more children,"[58] emotions ran rather higher behind the scenes. Anthony Crosland, then Labour's Minister of Education, privately declared: "If it's the last thing I do, I'm going to destroy every fucking grammar school in England and Wales. And Northern Ireland."[59]

Providing all students with a uniform, comprehensive education is difficult to reconcile with parental liberty. To the extent that parents are free to choose their schools, there is always the possibility that they will sort themselves out according to their personal values or their children's interests and abilities, thus spoiling the prospects for truly heterogeneous school populations. This conflict was not overlooked by advocates of comprehensivisation. In 1970, the National Union of Teachers asserted that "parental choice should not be exercised contrary to public [i.e., government] policy," referring to the union goal of randomly assigning students to schools to avoid any incidental grouping by ability that might occur if parents had a say.[60] Barbara Bullivant, onetime national secretary of the Campaign for the Advancement of State Education, warned in 1978 of "grave dangers in unrestricted right of choice," which could "operate against a particular school in favour of a particular school."[61] Her goal, it seems, was to ensure the survival of all state schools, both good and bad, rather than to deliver to families the sort of education they sought.

The pursuit of educational equality even extended beyond the state schools. The very existence of private schools, and the right of parents to send their children to them, was a source of intense frustration for many supporters of comprehensive schooling. What, after all, was the point of randomly mixing up state school populations if higher-income families could escape the government sector entirely, opting for independent schools? To redress this perceived problem, the Labour party endorsed for many years a platform of abolishing private schools—placing the party in the illustrious company of the Ku Klux Klan, which championed a similar policy in Oregon in the 1920s.[62] A vote on this issue was held during a 1981 Labour party conference and was approved by the overwhelming majority of members, but with a Conservative government in power, it could not be acted upon.[63]

Tony Blair's more centrist Labour government, elected in 1997, has eschewed the radical step of shutting down England's private schools, but resistance to parental choice and support for the complete comprehensivisation of state schooling persist within the party. Significantly, the "worst internal row of Tony Blair's leadership"[64] erupted a year before the election, when it became publicly known that Harriet Harman, Labour's Shadow Health Secretary, chose to send her own son to a selective grammar school rather than to one of the comprehensives so vigorously championed by her own party. According to *The Times,* Harman defended herself and her husband against "an avalanche of hypocrisy charges," protesting that:

> Our choice that we are having to make here and now makes no difference to our education policy. I support our education policy, but I think most parents in the country will understand that we had to make the right decision for our child and that we would have been less than human if we had done anything else.[65]

So while Harman felt it would be "less than human" for her to relinquish her own right to educational choice, she had no problem at all denying that same right to every other parent. "To choose" appears to be one of those irregularly conjugated verbs: I have the right to choose, you have no business choosing, they shouldn't even dream about choice.[66] To be fair, not all Labour party members suffer such gross inconsistency between their personal actions and their public stances. Gerry Steinberg resigned his position as Labour's education committee chairman, saying, "I believe the action taken by Harriet Harman is in direct contradiction to Labour's policy on comprehensive education and somebody had to make a stand."[67] Tony Blair, however, supported Harman's right to choose, and if that support was perhaps in conflict with Labour policy, it was at least consistent with his own personal actions: he had already come under fire himself for sending his son Euan to an "opted-out" school (the equivalent of an American "charter school" or "public school of choice") rather than to the school to which he would have been automatically assigned by the state.

Though some advocates of comprehensivisation professed the belief that phasing out selective schools would lead to high achievement levels for all students,[68] the academic effects of the policy were never seriously evaluated until the comprehensive revolution was essentially complete.[69] Now that the verdict has finally come in, it is not comforting. According to John Marks and Maciej Pomian-Srzednicki of the National Council for Educational Standards (NCES), selective school systems comprising both grammar and secondary modern schools produce "substantially higher" examination results, on average, than systems that include only comprehensive schools.[70] What is perhaps more remarkable is that this finding applies not only to students as a whole, but also to specific socioeconomic subgroups. No matter what a student's social class, the NCES report implies, chances are that he would be academically better off in a selective Local Education Authority (LEA) than in a fully comprehensive one.

It must be acknowledged, however, that the chief argument put forth in favor of comprehensive schooling was not that it would raise achievement for all students. Much more commonly voiced was the assumption that a nonselective school system would level the educational playing field, eliminating or at least dramatically reducing the disparities in student achievement which existed between grammar and secondary modern institutions. It is thus ironic that great disparities in student achievement continue to exist despite the overwhelming dominance of comprehensive schools. In fact, Marks and Pomian-Srzednicki found that "[e]xamination results per pupil differ even more substantially from school to school *within the same (all comprehensive) LEA* than they do from LEA to LEA."[71]

The Government Curriculum and Parental Choice

Disregard for parental freedom is by no means a Labour party innovation, for it was the Conservative Thatcher government that set down in 1988 a National Curriculum which all state-funded schools are obliged to follow. Serious sacrifices are demanded by any universally imposed lesson-plan, and England's National Curriculum is no exception. Parents whose educational priorities differ from those of the reigning party are ignored; students whose abilities are considerably behind or in advance of the average for their age are swamped or bored; children who develop a fascination with a particular subject at the "wrong" time (i.e., any time other than the one decided by the state) cannot readily have their interests accommodated; subjects not included in the official curriculum are marginalized or dropped entirely; alternate pedagogical theories about the best ages at which to begin certain kinds of instruction cannot be put to the test, etc.

The National Curriculum suffers from all of these ills. According to the Department for Education and Employment, parents "cannot withdraw [their children] from any part of the National Curriculum."[72] A corollary of this regulation is that state schools have little time left in their schedules to offer intensive instruction in areas not included in the government syllabus. The National Association of Head Teachers has said that "obsession with passing tests in English, mathematics and science meant other subjects were being overlooked."[73] Readers may recall that the very same problem arose 125 years ago under the "Payment-by-Results" scheme, described in Chapter 3. It would appear, however, that the memory of the English parliament does not reach back to the nineteenth century.

Since state schools continue to group students by age rather than ability, and since the National Curriculum specifies not only the subjects to be taught but also the order in which topics are introduced, slow and bright children are marginalized just as in Japanese public schools. Unlike Japan, however, England lacks a well-developed private education market to compensate for the increasing uniformity of its public sector, making the prospects for exceptional children grimmer still. The best ages at which to introduce particular subjects, such as foreign languages, are also hotly debated, making the government's stipulations extremely controversial among pedagogical experts.[74] While the National Curriculum requires foreign language classes to begin at age eleven, the National Association of Head Teachers has advocated starting them at age seven.[75]

Even those delighted with the National Curriculum as it currently stands have reason to be apprehensive: if one government can introduce such a program, a subsequent one can just as easily change it. The flip-flopping of government policy on comprehensivisation during the 1960s and 1970s is ample evidence of this. According to Maurice Galton, one of the principal aims of the National Curriculum was to drag teachers away from progressive methods and toward direct, whole-class instruction.[76] But if Labour and Conservative governments continue to alternate as they have in the past, it seems exceedingly likely that the National Curriculum will be pulled all over the pedagogical map in the years to come. Historical precedents also provide cause for worry about government control of the curriculum. Such powers have frequently been used to promote state religions, to distort the teaching of history, to denigrate poorly regarded cultures and minority groups, etc.

Grant-Maintained Schools

Though the Conservative government's imposition of an official curriculum was a step backward for educational liberty, its introduction of "grant-maintained" status was a step forward. Under the 1988 Education Act, any English state school can "opt out" of LEA control and choose to be funded directly by the central government, assuming this is the wish of its board of governors and of the majority of parents. Virtually all administrative, budgetary, and staffing decisions then rest in the hands of the individual school. As with North American charter schools, no students are automatically assigned to an "opted-out" institution. Instead, parents voluntarily apply to have their children admitted. Up to 15 percent of a grant-maintained school's student body can be selected based on aptitude in a particular subject or subjects, and interviews with parents can also play a role in the admissions process.

Those most keenly in favor of the grant-maintained school policy no doubt expected it to release a torrent of market forces on the educational landscape. What has emerged is more of a light drizzle. Test scores are indeed higher at schools that have opted out of LEA control, with eight of the top ten schools in the government's 1997 performance tables turning out to be grant maintained, but these results do not account for any differences that might exist in the students' initial aptitude. It is at least possible, therefore, that the students now attending grant-maintained schools would have been above average no matter what institution they attended. Still, other findings are also impressive. The government Office for Standards in Education (OFSTED) reports that schools which have opted out rate "higher than the LEA sector in areas such as extra-curricular provision, the school as a community and management and cost-effectiveness."[77]

An obvious downside of the legislation governing grant-maintained schools is that it provides them with neither the incentives nor the wherewithal to expand in order to meet pent-up demand. In 1994–95, there were 54,427 appeals lodged by parents to get their children into the state school of their choosing after having received an initial rejection, a 160 percent rise from six years earlier. Fewer than two parents in five were successful on appeal, and that does not take into account the many parents who did not bother fighting the system. Shortages of places in popular schools prevent countless families from winning the placements they seek.[78]

The problem is that there is no way for the governors of grant-maintained schools to finance a major expansion or to justify the risks of undertaking such an expansion. While some start-up funding is available to ease the transition from LEA to opted-out status, this is a onetime only affair, after which grant-maintained schools receive only per-pupil operating expenses.

In the private sector, the range of funding sources is far greater. Consider the Japanese market for private, after-school schools. While this market is not perfect, and some applicants are rejected, the profit motive has encouraged the most successful school chains to expand to staggering proportions (up to one million students!), allowing them to serve a vastly greater clientele than any public school. A similar pattern can be observed in other for-profit industries: How often do popular bookstores or supermarkets turn away hundreds of desperate customers year after year rather than expanding their operations to meet the growing demand? Failure to expand to meet demand is a shocking anomaly in every business but schooling, where government and nonprofit private providers dominate the field. This issue is discussed further in subsequent chapters.

Another problem with grant-maintained schools is that they cannot "opt out" of the National Curriculum. While parents now have a larger number of schools from which to choose, the diversity of those choices is more constrained than ever. There is no possibility of grant-maintained schools offering language-immersion programs, for instance, or focusing class time on one area of specialization such as music or science. Whatever the intentions of the Education Act of 1988, it is clear that its National Curriculum and grant-maintained schools sections are mutually contradictory with regard to educational freedom.

Having briefly discussed the merits and demerits of grant-maintained schools, it is only fair to point out that the discussion may have been academic, for these schools may not long retain the modest degree of autonomy and discretion they currently enjoy. During its 1996–97 election campaign, the Labour party had vowed to abolish the right of schools to opt out of LEA authority, and promised to merge existing grant-maintained schools back into the LEA fold. The government of Tony Blair has thus far refrained from directly fulfilling that pledge, but it has laid the groundwork for doing so by placing the responsibility of funding grant-maintained schools once more in the hands of the LEAs.[79] Since they are no longer to be maintained by a direct government grant, opted-out schools have been renamed "foundation schools." Since control over the purse-strings of education has generally been followed by control over the content, it seems likely that LEAs will eventually regain much of their authority over opted-out schools.

Trends in English Educational Performance

Finding out how English children are performing academically is not easy. The editors of the *Times Educational Supplement* complained in September 1996 that "the sparsity of the available evidence about standards is itself a cause for concern."[80] Despite the difficulties, it is possible to piece together a rough picture of students' educational performance, and the picture is not especially flattering.

The first round of results from the National Curriculum testing program, released in January 1996, proved disappointing. While seven-year-olds scored fairly well, student performance appeared to drop off in the higher age groups, just as in the United States. More than half of all eleven-year-olds failed to reach level 4, the target level for their age group, in either mathematics or English, though 70 percent did manage to meet the science target. At age fourteen, half of all students were expected to score at or above level 6. As it turned out, only 20 percent succeeded in English, 25 percent in science, and 33 percent in mathematics.[81] The following year's results showed improvement among eleven-year-olds in English and mathematics, but still only slightly over half of students were reaching the levels expected for all. Science scores declined somewhat, in part due to an adjustment of the standard, but they remained better than those in English and math.[82]

Internationally, English fourth-graders ranked an uninspiring seventeenth out of twenty-six countries participating in the Third International Mathematics and Science Study (TIMSS), while eighth-graders ranked sixteenth.[83] In science, English students fared better, placing eighth among fourth-graders and ninth among eighth-graders.[84] Of the countries outscoring England in science, only three or four showed significantly better results.[85]

Both the National Curriculum and international test results are subject to criticism. It is possible, after all, that the government's curriculum standards have been set too high, and that students' performance only appears weak. International comparisons could also be misleading. As described in the case of Japan, a ranking of public school systems from around the world says nothing of how well students could be doing if education were a competitive, for-profit industry. The best way to sidestep these concerns is to look at changes in student performance over time, to see if English state schooling has been able to keep up with the rapid progress in other fields that has taken place in the last fifty to one hundred years. Once again, the data fail to instill confidence. In the summer of 1996, after six years of the National Curriculum, professor Jim Campbell concluded that there were "no detectable signs of any improvements in primary pupils' basic skills. . . . In fact, the evidence suggests the reforms failed to halt a longer standing slide in numeracy."[86] The gains in reading and mathematics on the National Curriculum tests that occurred between 1996 and 1997 do offer some hope, but that hope is undermined by evidence of an earlier, long-term decline. Education researchers Tom Gorman and Cres Fernandes investigated changes in the reading ability of English and Welsh students between 1987 and 1991, concluding that overall performance had declined during the period in question, and pointing to other evidence suggesting that the decline had already been underway before 1987.[87]

Professor David Robitaille's analysis of changes in international mathematics achievement between the 1960s and the 1980s also showed a drop for English students, from 71 percent of answers correct to 64.3 percent correct.[88] Evidence of the deterioration in math skills over the past twenty years has also been assembled by education professor David Reynolds, who attributes the decline, in part, to faulty classroom practices in state schools.[89] Science, with the exception of the recent drop on the National Curriculum test, is the one bright spot in academic trends. Between 1970 and 1984, English fourteen-year-olds made modest gains in science, while ten-year-olds made larger gains. Though English students still placed at or near the bottom in 1984 even after these gains,[90] the already-mentioned TIMSS results show that they have since risen to the middle of the international pack.

In the face of all this evidence pointing to stagnation or decline in academic achievement, officials from the Department for Education and Employment are quick to point out that students' grades have been going up on a series of subject-area tests called the General Certificate of Secondary Education (GCSE). The percentage of sixteen- and eighteen-year-old students passing these tests has risen consistently since the mid-1980s.[91] Among its other uses, the GCSE serves as a criterion for college admission.

Unfortunately, the GCSE seems to have fallen victim to grade inflation. Marking schemes have apparently been altered, difficult categories of questions stricken, and the contents of the tests otherwise simplified, thereby producing the appearance, but not the actuality, of improving performance. University professors from fields as disparate as mathematics and German have fiercely criticized the degradation of GCSE standards. According to author Melanie Phillips, who researched the issue in preparation for writing her book *All Must Have Prizes,* examiners are put under considerable pressure to show constant or increasing grades from year to year, in part because low grades would mean fewer students eligible to attend university (thus injuring the universities' bottom lines).[92]

Just as interesting as the changes in student performance over time is the distribution of high and low achievers among the nation's schools. In 1997, the government published the first ever primary school "league tables," a ranking of 14,500 schools across the country based on their pupils' success on the National Curriculum tests. The two most dramatic and widely reported facts about the rankings were the remarkable success of church schools, and the great variation in scores among schools enrolling children from similar neighborhoods.

Thirty-seven percent of English state schools are run by churches (usually Anglican or Catholic), and thus enjoy greater freedom from government management than their secular counterparts. Despite comprising just over one third of the total number of state schools, church schools won two thirds of the top 100 places in the 1997 ranking—a finding consistent with the U.S. research on religious schools conducted by James Coleman and the team of Bryk, Lee, and Holland (see Chapter 8).[93]

Also remarkable were the wide differences in rankings of schools serving similar student bodies. A 1997 article in *The Times* reported that "although there is some correlation between test results and [socioeconomic] deprivation, there is still a huge variation between schools with a similar social intake. So, for instance, primary schools with the most deprived pupils range from a 70 percent success rate at 11-year-old English tests [well above the national average] to 0 percent."[94]

While its overall performance is mediocre to poor, and though it has generally gotten worse over time, English government schooling does enjoy one area of undisputed growth: spending. Inflation-adjusted per-pupil expenditures at the primary level rose from $2,336 (U.S. dollars) in 1985 to $3,120 in 1992. Secondary schools increased spending from $3,864 to $4,390 over the same period.[95] This growth follows on the heels of a 60 percent rise in primary school spending, and a 44 percent rise in secondary school spending, between 1960 and 1980.[96] Ironically, an analysis by the National Council for Educational Standards revealed in 1985 that student test scores tended to be lower in LEAs with higher expenditures per pupil.[97]

Canadian Discontent

The Condition of Canadian Education

Canadians are apprehensive about the quality of their public schools. A 1993 Gallup poll asked citizens if they thought that "students in Canada are receiving the education they need in order to compete in the future." Only 39 percent said "Yes"—53 percent said "No."[98] In the same year, the government of British Columbia surveyed that province's residents and found that 96 percent felt their public schools were in need of improvement. Two thirds of respondents viewed the need for improvement as "great."[99] The London (Ontario) Council of Home and School Associations polled parents in 1991 and found them "clearly concerned about the quality of their child's education; and about the education system generally." Journalist and author Andrew Nikiforuk reports that the 1,261 written comments collected along with the survey painted an even sharper picture, with three quarters showing strong disapproval of the local school board and only 8 percent showing approval.[100]

As in other nations, confidence in government-run schooling is not only low, it is declining. The following question was put to Canadians three times over the past twenty-five years: "On the whole, would you say that you are satisfied or dissatisfied with the education children are getting today?" Dissatisfaction was expressed by 41 percent of respondents in 1973, 53 percent in 1978, and reached 56 percent in 1992.[101] Polls conducted by the Canadian Education Association, a major teachers' union, show a significant decline in the grades that Canadians assign to the public schools in their area: 18.9 percent of the public gave their schools an A rating in 1979, but only a third as many (6.2 percent) gave the same rating in 1990.[102] When asked in a 1993 Angus Reid poll how the quality of education had changed over the past twenty-five years, 46 percent of Canadians felt it had gotten worse, while only 30 percent felt it had improved.[103]

Though it is easy to see that most Canadians feel their government schools are performing poorly, it is more difficult to ascertain precisely how students are doing academically. Canada's failure to participate in many of the international education studies that have been carried out over the past three decades has made it hard to assess test score trends in reading, mathematics, and science. Provincial education ministries have typically spent little effort evaluating the results of their programs. A report released in 1998 by British Columbia's Ministry of Education (covering the academic year 1995–96) is candid about the ministry's own performance on the issue: "Despite the education system's efforts to improve students' preparation for employment, little is known about the effectiveness of these efforts." The report goes on to say that the effects of the ministry's programs for "at risk" students, "special-needs" students, and aboriginal students are all unknown because it has not bothered to measure their results.[104]

What little evidence is available is anything but comforting. The only reliable measure of student achievement that has been around long enough to offer useful trend information is the Canadian Test of Basic Skills (CTBS), which assesses reading, other language skills, and mathematics performance at the fourth and eighth grades. In analyzing the results of the CTBS, former Economic Council of Canada senior economist Thomas Schweitzer found that there was

> a substantial deterioration between 1967 and 1973. This was followed by a minor improvement between 1973 and 1980, but almost all of this gain was again lost between 1980 and 1991. In consequence, the 1991 performance was well below that of 1967.[105]

Young adult literacy levels are also worrisome. Joint research by Statistics Canada and the Economic Council revealed that in 1992, more than a quarter of sixteen- to twenty-four-year-olds were unable to read a typical newspaper article and 44 percent were unable to do the sort of simple arithmetic necessary to calculate a restaurant bill or a series of catalogue purchases.[106] An OECD (Organization for Economic Cooperation and Development) study conducted in the same year yielded better, but nonetheless disappointing, results: Ten percent of Canadian sixteen- to twenty-five-year-olds were found to perform at or below the lowest level measured by the tests. They were found to be incapable, in other words, of completing a job application or writing a coherent resume. Another quarter of sixteen- to twenty-five-year-olds performed only slightly better.[107] Students in British Columbia registered test-score declines of between 1.7 and 3 percent in mathematics and science between 1991 and 1995.[108] Interestingly, Canada is one of the only nations where immigrants are more likely than native-born citizens to achieve at the highest two literacy levels.[109]

As in the United States, declines in achievement have not necessarily been reflected in students' classroom grades. Between 1989–90 and 1993–94, the percentage of students whose scores warranted an A or B on British Columbia's provincial English examinations dropped from 42.8 percent to 29.4 percent. The actual percentage of A's and B's awarded in schools, by contrast, rose from 40 percent to 50 percent over the same period.[110]

Canadians are not especially happy with their government education systems; student academic achievement appears to have declined in some areas over the past three decades; and there is certainly room for improvement in literacy. Given this unsatisfactory situation, it is disheartening to note the ever-rising cost of Canada's government schools. Statistics published by the Canadian Teachers' Federation show that, after adjusting for inflation, per-pupil public school spending in Canada nearly doubled between 1970–71 and 1990–91, from $3,543 to $6,273 (in constant 1991 Canadian dollars).[111] Over roughly the same period, expenditures on administration rose ten times faster than expenditures on instructional supplies. Canada now enjoys the distinction of having among the highest public school teachers' salaries in the industrialized world.[112] This growth in spending unaccompanied by improvements in student performance has been widely criticized—sometimes by the system's own leadership. In 1995, Newfoundland's associate deputy minister of education, Robert Crocker, admitted that "it is doubtful if the high cost of education in Canada is justified by the results."[113] University of British Columbia professor David Robitaille concurs: "It's true that there's a lot of money spent without any testing to see how well it's spent, and that's not healthy."[114]

The Roots of Failure

To understand why Canada finds itself in its current educational predicament, it is helpful to know how government-run schooling took hold within its borders. As in the vast majority of nations, public schools were not introduced in response to a groundswell of demand on the part of the public, but rather were pushed along by the relentless urgings of well-intentioned, paternalistic ideologues. The undisputed leader among these promulgators of state schooling was Egerton Ryerson. In 1858, he wrote:

> The State, therefore, so far from having nothing to do with the children, constitutes their collective parent, and is bound to . . . secure them all that will qualify them to become useful citizens to the state.[115]

Ryerson became assistant superintendent of schools for what is now the province of Ontario in 1844, and was promoted to superintendent two years later. He held the office for three decades, and in that time did more to advance the government takeover of education than any other Canadian. Most of his ideas on tax funding and government operation of schools, compulsory attendance, training and regulation of teachers, and even textbook selection and censorship were passed into law during his tenure.

The motivation behind this flurry of activity was Ryerson's profound belief that his fellow citizens, like so many errant sheep, were incapable of looking after themselves and needed to be herded and watched over by a vigilant government. Ryerson saw himself not as a public servant, bound to ascertain and meet the avowed demands of the people, but as a philosopher-king charged with shaping public attitudes along whatever lines he considered best. His contemporary, John Carroll, wrote that his ambition had run "in the direction of influencing public opinion on those questions and measures the carrying of which he deemed to be for the good of the church and the country."[116] Writing to the British governor of the province, Ryerson explained that "the youthful mind of Canada" must be "instructed and moulded in the way I have had the honour of stating to your Excellency, if this country is long to remain an appendage to the British Crown."[117]

While studying the educational systems of Europe, Ryerson was greatly in-spired by the extent of the royalty's power to manipulate schools in its efforts to produce a docile and supportive citizenry. According to education historian Neil McDonald, Ryerson concluded that the French king ruled with more ab-solute power than his English counterpart, and that this was only possible thanks to total government control "of the French system of education, from the university down to the primary school." Ryerson's confidence in the ability of the French monarchy to use this power effectively was exaggerated, given that the royalists were ousted from power repeatedly during the nineteenth century, but it is useful to know where his sympathies lay. Thoughts of monarchical power over education clearly gave him much cheer, and he happily concluded that "democracy, popular opinion to the contrary, was on the wane in Europe and constitutional monarchy was in the ascendancy."[118]

Ryerson's authoritarian, centralizing agenda was not without its critics. One particularly prophetic objection was voiced in 1847 by Robert Spence, who

> was certain that the granting of free schools would undermine parental responsi-bility in educational matters. Once the parent ceased to pay for the schooling of his children, the crucial link between himself and the teachers was severed, and a gradual decline in family interest in the schools would take place.[119]

As noted elsewhere in this book, Spence's fears have been fully realized in the currently low levels of parental participation in public schools, as compared with the significantly higher level of parental involvement in fee-charging schools. Three years after Spence's warning, the editor of the *Huron Signal* wrote:

> When we consider the influence which education exerts on the opinion and char-acter of mankind and consider the influence which the Chief Superintendent is to exercise over the education of the youth of Canada, we feel bound to declare such a power should not be entrusted to Egerton Ryerson nor to any other man. The truth is, that the office of Chief Superintendent should be abolished.[120]

Such criticisms, along with complaints that Ryerson was a particularly dic-tatorial and confrontational figure, were raised periodically throughout his su-perintendency, but their effects were limited.

Part of Ryerson's success can be attributed to three characteristics that he shared with other effective state-schooling advocates: he was an eloquent speaker; he had ample free time and resources with which to indulge his elo-quence; and the promises he made on behalf of government education were grand, wonderful, and wide in their appeal. Like Horace Mann, Ryerson had a potent combination of intelligence and rhetorical ability. Also like Mann, he enjoyed a high-profile government position from which to propound his views. He acknowledged that his official duties placed few demands on his time, leaving him free to

> prepare publications calculated to teach the people at large to appreciate . . . the institutions established amongst them; and to furnish, from time to time, such expositions of great principles and measures of the administration as would secure the proper appreciation and support of them on the part of the people at large.[121]

Rather than trying to convince politicians to follow the will of the people, Ryerson aimed to convince members of the public that their views should reflect those of the government. Since there was no preexisting public outcry for increasing state control of education, Ryerson had a considerable task ahead of him, but he prevailed by exercising the prerogative of politicians throughout the ages: the art of the promise. A universal system of state schooling, vowed Ryerson, would prevent a "pestilence of social insubordination and disorder" from being spread by "untaught and idle pauper immigration,"[122] and would also eliminate illiteracy, economic and class disparities, political corruption, and, indeed, crime as a whole.[123] The similarity of these grand promises to those of Mann and other U.S. reformers is truly remarkable.

Far from perpetrating a deliberate subterfuge, however, Ryerson sincerely believed his own extravagant claims. He apparently convinced himself of the miraculous powers of state-run education as easily as he convinced much of the public: by relying on wishful thinking, leaps of faith, and the occasional selective use of statistics. As education historian Alison Prentice has shown, Ryerson and other public school promoters "cited the 'laws of nature' or 'divine providence' as justification for much that they wished to promote," including "particular approaches to school management."[124] No careful, comprehensive study of the relative benefits of different forms of school governance was conducted. Instead, Ryerson built his arguments on his unquestioning belief in the power of government. "Government operates on mind," he wrote with Orwellian fervor, as "a minister of God" showering blessings on its subjects.[125]

Now and then, Ryerson did seek out the odd piece of evidence to lend credence to his beliefs, as is revealed by his periodic references to statistics purporting to show a correlation between illiteracy and both immorality and crime. A careful study of the data by history professor Harvey J. Graff reveals, however, that the superintendent's selective use of the facts led him to false conclusions. Contrary to Ryerson's claims, for example, alcohol abuse was actually more widespread among the literate than the illiterate, according to official arrest records.[126] This is not to argue against the merits of literacy, of course, but rather to highlight Ryerson's less than rigorous treatment of the evidence.

Though the data are sketchy, it seems that a majority of the public was already literate before public schools were firmly established in Ontario, and well before attendance was made compulsory.[127] As in other nations, school enrollment depended more on economics than on legislative dictates. On the early nineteenth-century frontier, where there was little division of labor and a commensurately low standard of living, older children were needed on family farms and in family shops. It was chiefly for this reason that attendance was not a universal affair.[128] As the economy grew more diverse and sophisticated, income levels rose and children's labor could more and more easily be spared. This, along with the increasing economic value of education, led to rising attendance rates. Attendance in Toronto had climbed above 80 percent of school-aged children by 1863, and was higher still in most other cities in the province.[129] Ontario's compulsory attendance law, though the first in the nation, was not enacted until 1871. Quebec did not introduce mandatory attendance until 1942, but, according to the national census of 1900, it had the country's highest rate of average daily attendance proportional to students enrolled. Based on these and other statistics, York University professor Paul Axelrod concludes that compulsory school legislation not only did not cause large-scale participation in education, but actually occurred after high enrollment rates had already been achieved — a pattern consistent with the experiences of England and the United States.[130]

The Paternalism of Government Schools

Two key points emerge from the previous section: First, literacy and school enrollment were widespread and growing before provincial governments took over the education industry. Second, the campaign for an expansive system of government schools was not based on a desire to meet the avowed educational needs of families, but rather was intended to mold the attitudes of citizens in accordance with the ideas of bureaucrats and politicians. It should come as no surprise, given this paternalistic origin, that modern Canadian public schools are not renowned for their responsiveness to the demands of parents.

In Canada, as elsewhere, the educational priorities of public school leaders differ substantially from those of the public. While Canadians generally evaluate schools in terms of results, most educators prefer to emphasize progressive educational processes. A study conducted in Ontario in the early 1990s asked the public and educators to rank six different ways of looking at education. The general public placed the greatest emphasis on developing career skills and intellectual capacities. Educators, by contrast, ranked the importance of open-ended, child-directed learning experiences well above intellectual and career outcomes. This disparity is even more clearly visible in the answers to the question: "Are regular standardized assessments of student achievement important?" Only 15 percent of educators answered yes—compared to 94 percent of the general public.[131] Geraldine Gilliss, Director of Research and Information Services for the Canadian Teachers' Federation, asserts that teachers do value intellectual development, but that preparing children to earn "a living, if it appeared in teachers' goals at all, would assume a very secondary importance."[132] Teachers, writes Gilliss without further comment, have their own objectives. Implicit in her statement is the fact that these objectives need not correspond to those of parents.

The ability of public school educators and bureaucrats to independently determine the kind of education received by Canadian children has grown perceptibly over the past century. As the management of public schools has passed to ever higher and more remote levels of government, the power of individual parents to influence the course of their children's education has diminished. The U.S. pattern of consolidating small schools and boards into larger and larger conglomerations has been replicated in Canada. As in the United States, this move was based more on ideology and wishful thinking than on any consistent body of evidence that the larger conglomerations would operate with greater efficiency. The once considerable power of local boards to staff and run their schools has been eroded by numerous restrictions imposed on their operations by provincial governments.[133]

The most dramatic (and successful) recent attempt by a provincial government to consolidate its control over public schools played itself out in the fall of 1997 in Ontario. The legislation, known as "Bill 160," gave the minister of education the power to set class sizes, control the amount of time teachers spend in the classroom and preparing for classes, lengthen the school year, reduce the number of "professional development" days for teachers, and even set education property taxes.[134] Needless to say, the teachers' unions were not amused. Their response to Bill 160 was the largest teachers' strike in North American history, involving 126,000 teachers and more than two million students. Phyllis Benedict, president of the Ontario Teachers' Federation, which represents the members of the province's five teachers' unions, called the education minister "a liar," "a slick huckster," and "a snake oil salesman," during a massive teacher rally at Toronto's Maple Leaf Gardens.[135] Despite the illegal two-week strike, the final version of Bill 160 differed in few respects from the original draft.

Most other provincial governments are moving in the same direction, shrinking the number of school boards (or eliminating them entirely, as in New Brunswick) and taking over their financial responsibilities.[136] Only Quebec is flouting the trend, devolving some powers from school boards and provincial bureaucrats and placing them in the hands of parent/teacher school committees. In a sense, Quebec is in the process of creating a very weak form of charter schools. Some staffing, budgeting, and limited curriculum powers will be bestowed on the new committees, but these must be exercised within a strict regulatory and legal framework. The committees must follow the core provincial curriculum, and they can neither create new schools nor close existing ones (those powers remain with school boards). Most remarkably, half of a committee's members must be teachers at the school in question.[137]

Obviously, the professional expertise of teachers must be brought into play in the operation of schools, but the peculiarity of this particular arrangement becomes clear when it is hypothetically carried to other fields. Consider auto repair. In Quebec, it is customary to allow each individual car-owner the right to contract with any auto shop he chooses when his car is in need of repair. He is free to get the recommendations of mechanics from different shops, and has sole authority when it comes time to decide who will do what to his automobile. How would the public react if the provincial assembly passed a law stating that auto repair decisions would henceforth be made by committees comprised equally of customers and mechanics from each individual shop, and that car-owners would be automatically assigned to a given shop? The only expert opinion available to car-owners would come from the mechanics who would be doing the work, and they would have far more say, collectively, about what would be done to the automobile than the individual owner himself. Would this be considered an improvement over the current arrangement? It is erroneous to claim, incidentally, that education has a broad social impact whereas auto repair does not. A set of defective brakes can precipitate a very dramatic impact on one's fellow citizens.

One reason for Quebecers to support the new committees is that they would constitute an increase in parental authority when compared to the status quo. But before this baby-step toward parent empowerment is lauded excessively, it is best to remember that what the province giveth, the province may taketh away. Ultimate authority over the public schools will continue to reside with the provincial government, and if political winds shift (and they do tend to shift, now and again, in *La Belle Province*) it is easy to imagine a return to a more centralized system of school governance. It was the Quebec legislature, after all, that passed a pair of education laws (the *Régimes Pédagogiques*) in 1981, reminiscent of the Jesuits' *Ratio Studiorum* in their level of detail and centralization of power. "All textbooks and other teaching material," stated the *Régimes,* "must be approved by the Minister [of Education]. Unauthorized textbooks and materials are not permitted." "All programs and courses," the *Régimes* continued, "are prescribed or approved by the Minister of Education. . . . School boards may design special programs for their own needs but these must first be approved by the Minister."[138]

The ruling party, moreover, was not above using its power over the curriculum to further its own ideological and political agenda. The *Parti Québecois* (PQ) government was elected in 1976 on a platform of French cultural and political sovereignty, which was to be achieved through secession of the province from the rest of Canada.[139] As an elementary student in Montreal in the late 1970s, even before the passage of the *Régimes,* I remember with great clarity being assigned a new, hastily-put-together paperback geography textbook. This textbook was memorable because it was conspicuously graced with a map of Canada that referred to that country's western-most province as *"Colombie Canadienne,"* rather than the customary *Colombie Britannique* (British Columbia). The notion that some part of Canada was named after Great Britain was, apparently, so unpleasant to the educators of the time that the province was simply rechristened. When I pointed out this error in the textbook, an uneasy young teacher maintained that *Colombie Canadienne* was indeed the correct, "official" term for that chunk of the Canadian landscape. Much embarrassment was saved when this revisionist naming was abandoned some years later.

Apparently using George Orwell's *1984* as their legislative blueprint, the PQ went on to set the grades at which French and English would be taught as second languages to the province's residents. French was taught to non-Francophones starting in the first grade. English instruction for non-Anglophones was deferred until the fourth grade.[140] Foreign immigrants to the province, furthermore, are obliged by law to send their children to French-language schools.

The public schools of "Canadian"—or rather British—Columbia also have a history of paying less heed to their customers than to the special interests who staff and control them. In 1986, a Royal Commission was appointed to "examine all aspects of British Columbia's school system"[141] and make recommendations for reform. In staffing the project, commission director Barry Sullivan "asked the various education special-interest groups to nominate" their preferred candidates. The commission was thus manned by professors of education, public school superintendents, and district administrators. Enormous weight was given to their final report, written in 1989 by lead researcher Tom Fleming, and an ambitious program known as "Year 2000" was initiated to translate its mostly progressive recommendations into public policy.

The single most remarkable aspect of the ensuing four-year endeavor was that parents and the public at large played almost no role in shaping what or how children would be taught. From start to finish, the plan was developed by the education establishment for the education establishment. Year 2000's designers "ignored the public," Fleming later acknowledged. Aggravating this situation, the project's public relations director, Janet Mort, apparently failed to take her job title literally, deciding to sell the program to teachers rather than to the people. "We really missed the boat on the public and parents," she eventually told author Mike Crawley.[142] Though the program was officially killed by the new NDP (New Democratic Party) government in 1993, its legacy lives on in the form of curriculum guidelines which are discussed in the following section.

The behavior of the British Columbia public school establishment toward parents and the public has not been limited to malign neglect. On occasion, the establishment has taken an active role in resisting their educational efforts. So-called "traditional schools" are a case in point. Unhappy with the progressive pedagogy practiced in their public schools (see the following section), a group of parents from the town of Surrey requested that their local board establish a "traditional school," which would apply time-tested and/or research-based methods such as direct instruction, would have more structured, academically oriented classes, and would "leave instruction in life skills to parents."[143] Though the district superintendent opposed the plan, the board's elected trustees gave their approval.

The proposed school's fate was put in jeopardy, however, when the British Columbia Teachers' Federation (BCTF) attempted to block its opening using an obscure contractual clause. The clause in question required all teaching positions "in new schools to be posted by the end of April," while the traditional school plan was not approved until the end of May 1994. The motivation behind the BCTF's opposition is not entirely clear, though the local Surrey union leader, Kelly Shields, apparently felt that the parent group requesting the new school was "motivated by an intolerant right-wing agenda."[144] Shields and BCTF president Ray Worley seemed to believe that it was up to them to decide which parents should be heeded and which should be rebuffed. To give weight to their views, they threatened to "blacklist teachers who applied,"[145] to work in the school if and when it did open.

The BCTF eventually relented, however, and Surrey Traditional opened its doors in September of 1994. Two months later, the *Vancouver Sun* reported that "parents in more than a dozen other B.C. communities" were demanding similar schools for their children.[146] Not all of them were as lucky as the Surrey group. A parent organization called the Burnaby Academic School Committee, which requested the establishment of a traditional school in their community, received rejections from both their school board and an official District Parents' Advisory Committee.[147] The government school system thus makes it possible for one group of parents to sanction or suppress the educational aspirations of other groups of parents — not a situation especially conducive to happy, harmonious community life.

The March of Progressivism

The nineteenth-century campaign to adopt government schooling in Canada was not based on rigorous factual comparisons of alternative educational systems. Instead, it stemmed from an almost religious belief in the power, benevolence, and efficiency of government. This triumph of ideology over empiricism set a precedent that has been followed ever since, manifesting itself at present in the dramatically unscientific educational decisions of Canadian education bureaucracies.

The area in which provincial government educators depart most noticeably from sound pedagogical practice is in the teaching of reading. As has already been pointed out in earlier chapters, the overwhelming preponderance of evidence points to the superiority of explicit, carefully structured, synthetic phonics lessons over other approaches to early reading instruction. The reader will also recall that, despite its proven effectiveness, this method is frequently sidelined in the United States because it does not integrate well with the prevailing doctrine in ed. schools. The same is true in Canada.

British Columbia's Ministry of Education currently stipulates student outcome requirements for each subject and grade level. In the case of kindergarten and first-grade reading, one requirement is that "students will predict unknown words by using picture clues, their knowledge of language patterns, and letter-sound relationships."[148] In fact, this is not an outcome at all, but rather a description of a process. Though the description is vague, it is entirely consistent with progressive whole-language reading instruction in which children are taught to "predict" (guess) the meaning of an unfamiliar word by looking at nearby pictures, inferring from the context of the story (which may have been read to them several times), and using the sound of the initial (and sometimes also the final) letter.

The Ministry's intent to promote whole-language reading instruction need not be inferred from its "outcome" requirements. In addition to stipulating these requirements, the Ministry also provides a set of recommended pedagogical methods and measures of achievement which are clear embodiments of whole-language philosophy, and which run counter to the evidence on the best way of teaching children to decode written English. The chief instructional strategy recommended to teachers of kindergarten and first-grade students reads as follows:

> Choose an illustrated story that can be readily understood by looking at pictures without reading the words. Show the class only the illustrations, stopping frequently to encourage students to ask questions, participate in discussions, and make predictions based on the illustrations. Ask questions such as:
>
> - What do you think this story is about?
> - What do you think will happen next?
> - What do you think life is like for this character?
>
> Read the story to the class, asking students to identify initial and final consonants in key words. As they listen, encourage students to read and predict new words

by using the illustrations as clues. Invite students to follow as the teacher's hand traces the sentences, modelling left-to-right progression as the words are read.[149]

This is pure whole-language doctrine and has nothing whatever to do with teaching children how to systematically decode written English into the oral language with which they are already familiar. The remaining three "strategies" recommended by the Ministry consist of group activities that are equally irrelevant to direct, synthetic phonics.

The Ministry of Education's second- and third-grade requirements and recommendations are equally unflagging in their promotion of whole-language methodology. "Outcomes" for these students include the expectations that students will:

> Use an expanding range of strategies—including pictorial, graphic, structural, and phonics clues—to derive meaning.

> Use picture clues to predict content and make connections between illustrations and written text.[150]

Though phonics receives a token mention in the above list, it is clearly meant to be used in the ad hoc fashion popular among whole-language teachers, rather than in the structured, intensive manner supported by reading research. Evidence of this fact comes from the title of the book chosen by the Ministry for teaching the subject: *Learning Phonics and Spelling in a Whole-Language Classroom.*

Alas, British Columbia is not alone in its antiscientific approach to early reading instruction. Seven provinces (British Columbia, Manitoba, New Brunswick, Newfoundland/Labrador, Ontario, Prince Edward Island, Quebec) include only whole-language works on their lists of textbooks approved for use in public school classrooms. Whole-language books account for roughly three quarters of the approved texts in the remaining provinces.[151] Even in cases where phonics texts are included on the reading lists, they tend to be marginalized by an official policy de-emphasizing the role of phonetic decoding skills. In Saskatchewan, for example, the Department of Education's elementary *Curriculum Guide* states: "*Phonics is not the foundation for beginning or remedial reading.*"[152] It propounds the notion that "[r]eaders work from the meaning of the printed message to identification of individual words, word structures or parts and letters." How, the confused parent might well ask, is a child supposed to obtain meaning from a printed message until he or she can identify the meanings of the words which make it up? Saskatchewan's government educators have an answer, though it may not please everyone: "Have students predict story contents using the title and cover illustration or information."[153] Not only *can* a book be judged by its cover in Saskatchewan, it actually *should* be so judged according to the province's curriculum guide. Naturally, other whole-language suggestions are offered besides looking at the cover, such as looking at the interior pictures and guessing the meaning of unknown words from known ones. Nothing that could be confused for a systematic, synthetic course in the sound/letter correspondences and blending rules of the English language is advocated.

The document's authors, whose views shape the way that hundreds of thousands of children are taught to read, do not cite a single empirical study comparing different methods of reading instruction to support their views. They ignore everything from broad-scale experiments such as Follow Through, to research syntheses such as Marilyn Jager Adams's 1990 book *Beginning to Read,* choosing instead to base their beliefs on the predominantly anecdotal and philosophical writings of whole-language devotees.

Dismayed by the de-emphasis of early systematic phonics, the Canadian Psychological Association (CPA) sent a position paper, written by Dr. Marvin Simner, to all the provincial Ministries of Education and to several professional organizations in 1993. This paper explained the need to train children in phoneme awareness and phonetic decoding techniques, and urged the provinces to revise their reading policies accordingly. Seven of the eight ministries that replied to the association's recommendations claimed that they already had balanced reading programs in place which included some phonics training, and that their instructional policies were not in need of revision. In its response to the ministries' replies, the CPA attempted to explain that the token use of phonics commonly adopted in whole-language classrooms was not, in fact, consistent with the research findings on beginning reading, and was in need of significant improvement. Unfortunately for public school students across the country, the Canadian Psychological Association's pleas have fallen on deaf ears.[154]

We Are Not Alone

No nation has a monopoly on educational problems. Conflicts over the content of government schooling are a truly international affair, and most state educational systems have adopted dubious pedagogical methods at one time or another. The reason these woes are so ubiquitous is that they are encouraged by the system itself. By its very nature, government schooling tends to produce a much more limited range of educational services than free markets. When diverse populations are squeezed into comparatively uniform schools, friction is the inevitable result. Ineffective instructional techniques have also cropped up in most corners of the world, and there is even cause for concern in high-ranking public school systems such as Japan's. While Japanese public schools have avoided the more harmful recent fads, this is not because they enjoy a reliable mechanism for choosing empirically proven instructional techniques. Instead, Japanese schools and families have simply been fortunate that their monolithic Ministry of Education has made comparatively sound instructional decisions over the past few decades. There is no guarantee that this sensible decision-making will continue under the next generation of bureaucrats. And if ineffective methods were adopted, parents would not be able to avoid them given the centralized nature of the Japanese public school curriculum.

Japan's for-profit market for supplemental schooling does have a mechanism for promoting consistently sound pedagogical planning, however. By virtue of intense competition and the complete freedom of parents to take their money elsewhere, *juku* are forced to continually evaluate their instructional programs and strive to improve them. *Juku* that fail to keep ahead of (or at least keep up with) the competition risk going out of business, while those that succeed reap greater rewards than are common in the public sector.

But are the private schools of most nations really dramatically superior to government-run schools? Do they hold the key to greater responsiveness, lessened social conflict, and improved performance? Do they have failings of their own? These questions are taken up in the following chapter.

8

The Class Really Is Keener on the Other Side: The Case of Independent Schools

> *In late October 1995, officials of the Pepsi company announced at Jersey City Hall that their corporation would donate thousands of dollars in scholarships to help low-income children attend the private school of their choice. The immediate response of the local public school teachers' union was to threaten that a statewide boycott of all Pepsi products could not be ruled out. Pepsi vending machines around the city were vandalized and jammed. Three weeks later, company officials regretfully withdrew their offer.[1]*
> *What are government school teachers' unions so afraid of?*

A Matter of Choice

Why Parents Choose Independent Schools

Private schooling does not come cheap. Nor is it easy to fall into accidentally, given the time and effort involved in selecting schools, completing application forms, interviewing principals and teachers, etc. Roughly one out of every ten American families nonetheless assumes the added financial and personal responsibility of enrolling its children in an independent school.[2] Why?

Three answers to this question are repeated in survey after survey of independent-school parents: superior academic quality, religious or moral considerations, and a more disciplined atmosphere. Convenience issues, such as school location, rarely play a dominant role in the choices of independent-school families.[3]

Topping the list of responses in virtually all polls of independent-school parents is academic quality. The 1993 National Household Survey conducted by the U.S. Department of Education, for instance, reported that the lure of "a better academic environment" was the number-one reason parents gave for choosing independent schools.[4] What's more, this emphasis on learning cuts across the entire range of independent schools from high-profile academies like Exeter or Andover to inner-city parochial schools serving low-income families. When 11,000 Catholic-school parents in Washington, D.C. were asked to specify their most important reason for choosing a Catholic school, the majority gave "academic program" as their reply. Religion, the second most frequent response, was cited as the primary consideration by only a quarter of respondents. Even more remarkably, the survey revealed that almost one out of every five families sending their children to D.C.'s Catholic schools was not Catholic.[5] Clearly, the belief that independent schools offer better instruction in knowledge and skills is the prime motivating factor drawing parents into independent schools.

Religious and moral considerations generally come next on the list of priorities, and the role they play in school choice is eminently understandable. Government-run schools in the United States were originally steeped in religion and made frequent use of the Protestant Bible. Over the course of this century, however, they were gradually secularized, and the Supreme Court formally erected a wall separating church and school in the 1960s. As a result, public schools lost much of their appeal to Protestant parents seeking to have their children taught in a religious environment. Families of other faiths had, of course, never been able to turn to government schools for religious instruction. It has thus fallen on independent schools to satisfy this demand. Across the U.S., just under one third of independent-school parents mention religion as the primary motivating factor in their choice—a somewhat higher figure than the one already mentioned for D.C. Catholic-school parents.[6] Among families opting to teach their children at home, of whom roughly two thirds are evangelical Protestants, religion is a still more prominent factor.[7]

Finally, public worry over government-school discipline problems, which has been growing since the seventies, rounds out the list of factors driving parents into the private sector. After noticing that thousands of families had left the public system of Montgomery County, Maryland, for independent schools, district officials surveyed the fleeing parents to determine the cause of their exodus. More parents mentioned discipline than any other reason, though it was not generally cited as the most important factor in their decisions ("religion/values" was most often cited as the number-one reason for moving to the private sector).[8]

Low-Income and Minority Parents: Choosing to Refute Their Critics

Whenever it is proposed that the responsibility for choosing schools should be returned to parents, government-school educators convinced of the public's backwardness quickly float a raft of objections. Since calling the entire citizenry incompetent to choose its schools is not apt to rally widespread support, and since it casts a pall on the public schools themselves for having produced such a great number of intellectually deficient graduates, criticism is most often focused on subsets of the population. An especially popular target is the poor, inner-city minority parent. These parents, educators charge, would be unable to choose good schools for their children.[9]

Whether earnest or otherwise, this paternalistic belief is firmly grounded in nothing at all. Study after study has shown that it is not only possible for low-income parents to make wise school choices, but that they have actually been doing so for years. The same three factors that motivate the average independent-school parent also motivate those with lower than average incomes. Like their wealthy counterparts, poor Catholic-school parents in Washington, D.C. named "academic program" as their key reason for choosing independent schools.[10] A broader study of inner-city Catholic-school parents found that the poorest families were even more likely to rate academics "very important" than the wealthiest.[11] Given the often chaotic and violent conditions in urban public schools, it is not surprising that parents in these communities also seek out independent schools for their more-disciplined environments.[12]

Nationwide, poor and middle-class parents are almost equally likely to actively choose their children's schools (as opposed to having them automatically assigned).[13] Of course, the options open to low-income families are far more limited, and most schools chosen by them are within the public system. Thanks to private and public voucher programs, however, some low-income parents are afforded access to independent schools. Milwaukee, Wisconsin has had a government-run school voucher program since 1990, open only to families with earnings close to or below the national poverty line.[14] Parents participating in the program, whose household incomes averaged $11,340 in 1994, overwhelmingly cited academic reasons for choosing their children's private schools. The most popular answer was educational quality, which was described as a very important factor by 88.6 percent of participants. "Teaching approach or style" was a close second.[15]

The motivations of low-income parents are even more clearly visible in the several dozen privately run voucher programs scattered across the U.S. By including religious schools, something the publicly funded Milwaukee program is currently prohibited from doing,[16] and by serving many more families, private voucher efforts present a fuller and more accurate picture. The motivations of parents have been studied in three of these programs,[17] and in each case roughly 90 percent of respondents cited educational quality as their primary reason for choosing an independent school.[18] Participants in all three programs also cited school atmosphere and discipline, while convenience issues were generally given the least importance. Parents in Indianapolis's Educational Choice Charitable Trust (ECCT) voucher program placed school location tenth in importance out of twelve factors influencing their choice of school.[19]

Poverty, then, does not prevent parents from making rational decisions about schooling. The case of minority status is still more conclusive. Not only are minority families more likely to actively choose their children's schools than whites, their decisions also tend to be more strongly driven by academic considerations. Across the United States, almost one out of every four African-American families chooses its children's schools. The figure for whites is less than one in five.[20] And while the Washington, D.C. study referred to above found that both African Americans and whites gave "academic program" as their chief reason for choosing Catholic schools, the percentage of African Americans giving that reason was significantly higher: 55.8 percent versus 47.0 percent.[21] None of the voucher studies cited above broke down parents' priorities by race or ethnicity, but the overall racial and ethnic composition of the programs does shed some light on the subject. As already stated, about nine out of every ten participants in each of the voucher programs named academic quality as their number-one basis for choosing independent schools. But while their priorities were very similar, their racial and ethnic makeup varied significantly: of the four programs referred to above (including Milwaukees's public program), one was predominantly African American, another predominantly Hispanic, and the two remaining programs enrolled a fairly even mix of races and ethnic backgrounds.

The belief that parents with limited formal schooling are unable to choose wisely finds little more support than the income and racial criticisms dispensed with above. Across U.S. voucher programs, the average parent is generally somewhat less schooled than the public at large,[22] but still manages to make intelligent choices. It is true that voucher program participants tend to have had more years of schooling than is typical among low-income individuals, but there is no evidence that a set number of years of schooling is required before a parent can make a rational school choice for her own child. Wisconsin state legislator Polly Williams sums up the attacks on the ability of low-income minorities to choose their children's schools in this way:

> I am one of those people who is supposed to be very stupid because I am black, I live in the inner city, I am poor, and I raised my children in a single parent home. Well, those are lies. The only thing different about us is that we have been deprived of resources and access. When you empower parents like me, there is a major difference. We become responsible for our own lives. . . . We want to be empowered, and that is what the [Milwaukee] choice program has done.[23]

The Independent-School Experience

Battles over books, tests, activities, and curriculum are so common in the public system that they are taken for granted. Sometimes the sources of conflict change with the seasons: Should the school celebrate Halloween? How about Christmas? Others crop up in response to new state or local policies: Is the new testing system a brilliant innovation or a complete disaster? And then there are old favorites such as evolution versus the biblical account of creation.

Whatever the cause of contention, the scene is all too familiar. School board officials sit behind folding tables on the stage of the school auditorium or in a corner of the gymnasium. One after another, agitated, sometimes angry parents take the floor and give voice to their convictions on one side or the other of the issue. When a decision is handed down, there are winners and losers, but rarely does anyone go home feeling entirely unscathed.

Contrast this often hostile environment with that of independent institutions. It is simply unheard of for a group of irate parents to stage a protest over a book in the library of their local private school, or for community leaders to demand that their independent parochial schools stop holding religious services. The reason that such conflicts are conspicuously rare in the private sector is twofold: independent schools cannot legally force themselves on their communities, and families can choose the school best suited to their needs.

In the nineteenth century, state supreme courts could and did rule that all public school children must read the Protestant Bible, and in our own time these courts can and do order students to perform public service against their will, and to use or not to use particular books. No independent school has the power to coerce and control a child's education in this way. If a private school begins to tread on the wishes of its patrons, they are free to leave it for another at any time, providing it with a strong incentive to be accommodating.

No single school or approach to schooling can satisfy the needs of all families or prevent all educational conflicts. This is a lesson that government-run schooling has taught time and time again. But by providing parents with a choice, and permitting them to engage in educational comparison-shopping, free educational markets have brought this goal closer to reality than any other system of schooling.

Strength in Diversity

There is no such thing as a typical independent school. Private institutions are free to set their own curricula, to hire and fire their teachers, to choose their own philosophy, and to affiliate themselves—or not—with a particular religion. All that freedom leads to considerable diversity in the kind of education offered by independent schools.

Catholic schools make up one of the largest subgroups in the U.S. private education sector, and tend to be thought of as more or less interchangeable, but just among these schools there is considerable variation. In addition to parochial schools, organized at the level of a single parish and overseen by the local pastor, there are also diocesan and academy-style Catholic schools. Diocesan schools tend to be larger than their parochial counterparts, enroll students from a wider area, and offer a broader range of courses. Academies, also called "private" Catholic schools, usually reflect the priorities of the particular religious orders that run them, while nonetheless sharing a common resemblance to secular private academies—for instance, in their emphasis on institutional traditions. Along with these organizational differences, Catholic schools can be coed or single-sex, can emphasize English or a foreign language, and can be more or less infused with religious teaching and activities.

San Francisco provides a wonderful example of the diversity within Catholic schooling. Of the city's nine Catholic elementary schools, several are primarily extensions of their parish communities, enrolling Catholic children almost exclusively and requiring all students to attend religious services. Others, such as St. Thomas More school, are not affiliated with a specific parish, seeking instead to serve both Catholic and non-Catholic students from around the city. Though most of San Francisco's Catholic elementary schools offer foreign language courses, two in particular place a special emphasis on language. St. Mary Chinese Day School requires all students to study Cantonese from kindergarten through sixth grade, and Mandarin in grades seven and eight, a popular program with Chinese-American parents seeking to keep their linguistic heritage alive. The school associated with San Francisco's French parish, Ecole Notre Dame des Victoires, offers an enrichment program in the language of Molière. For the convenience of single-parent households and those with both parents working, virtually all of the city's independent elementary schools offer some form of after-school care. Catholic schools are no exception in this, and most provide indoor and outdoor activities, games, study periods, and sometimes additional classes to keep students engaged until their parents are able to pick them up.[24]

To this already diverse mix of institutions, secular independent schools add an even wider range of options. Though Britain's independent education sector enrolls only 4 percent of the student population—and hence was omitted from the previous chapter's discussion—it exhibits surprising variety. Many people think first of elite private academies when British independent schooling is discussed, but this handful of venerable institutions—somewhat confusingly called "public schools" in the U.K.—are in fact outnumbered by much less expensive private schools.

According to journalist and teacher Janis Griffith, who interviewed the staffs at a dozen low-cost independent schools in South Wales, the attitude of head-masters (principals) ranged from a "bend over backward to accommodate all potential clients" mentality, to the belief that their school offered a unique experience that like-minded parents would seek out. Even more telling than the differences between schools, however, were the adaptations that individual schools made over time in an effort to maintain the largest and most loyal possible client base. "Some single-sex schools became co-educational," wrote Griffith, "while some of those that catered [to] secondary-age children have opened primary departments or even added nurseries." In one case, a boys' school and a girls' school initiated a joint venture in which they offered a complementary set of advanced classes to each others' students, which neither could have made available on its own.[25]

Another of Britain's seldom-mentioned independent-school options is the black voluntary school. One of the chief advocates of such schools, University of Birmingham professor Máirtín Mac an Ghaill, believes they are a response by members of the black community to their experience of racism in the government-run system. Another motivating factor behind the spread of voluntary schools is the perception on the part of many inner-city blacks that the state-run institutions are not accountable to them and are not responsive to their needs.

Because they serve mostly poor communities, black voluntary schools are often staffed and managed entirely by volunteers, allowing them to minimize or even forgo charging tuition. The teachers nonetheless have to earn a living, of course, so classes tend to be held on weekends, in the evenings, and during vacations. Educational policies vary among voluntary schools, with some advocating that children of Caribbean descent make greater use of their native Creole dialects in the classroom, while others believe that the state system does not concentrate enough on the basics in English and mathematics, shunting poorly taught black students into watered-down academic programs in later years.

In talking with parents to understand what leads them to establish and attend these schools, Mac an Ghaill was repeatedly told that teachers at state institutions often made them feel unwelcome. "The teachers see you as a trouble-maker if you ask questions," said one mother. A frequent complaint of both parents and students was that government schools were staffed and run by people from outside the local community, robbing students and parents of any sense of ownership of the school. "You feel better when it's your own place," said one student, "like our church. You feel proud. You can be yourself, the pressure is off, you can learn."[26]

Independent schools exist to serve all kinds of communities. Some seek to tailor themselves to the needs of particular religious, ethnic, linguistic, or racial groups, while others attempt to embrace all comers. Many schools in the latter category try to distinguish themselves through their pedagogical methods. Of these, the best known are Montessori and Waldorf schools. Montessori schools follow the educational methods laid out by Italian teacher, physician, and educational researcher Maria Montessori. For younger children, roughly those under seven years of age, Montessori advised the use of concrete objects to teach fundamental ideas and skills. Classrooms modeled after her recommendations tend to be filled with blocks, pyramids, spheres, cylinders, beads, and many other objects, the manipulation of which conveys ideas such as size and color, physical relationships, as well as pre-mathematical skills. In early reading instruction, Montessori schools adopt a structured phonics-based approach. Classes combine individual activities where each child sets his own pace, with cooperative, responsibility-building activities such as having the children clean and organize their classrooms.[27]

The Waldorf school experience emphasizes teaching the "whole child," and gives added attention to the sometimes neglected fields of art and music. As the traditional subjects are introduced, they are presented first at a low level of detail, and then revisited more completely in later months and years, as the children's knowledge and skills allow a deeper understanding. Grades are not generally given at the elementary level, but instead the teacher writes a comprehensive assessment of each student's performance. Like Montessori schools, those following the Waldorf model can be found around the world, and though they operate as distinct enterprises, they usually belong to associations that allow them to share information and expertise.[28]

The Independent Advantage

While independent schools cater to an enormous variety of tastes, and vary their methods and environments accordingly, they nonetheless share a few key characteristics. In particular, independent schools generally have higher parental involvement, a more academic orientation, better teacher morale, a much stronger sense of community among students, staff, and parents, and far less managerial bureaucracy than government-run schools. There are exceptions, of course, but years of research have found these conditions to hold in the vast majority of cases.

Increased parental involvement

It has been known for some time that independent schools generally have a higher level of parental involvement than government-run schools. A national U.S. survey conducted by the Department of Education during the 1990–91 school year found that public school teachers were roughly six times more likely to complain about lack of parental involvement than private school teachers were.[29] Like most other advantages of independent schools, this has been dismissed by many critics as a simple reflection on the kinds of parents who opt for a private education: these same parents, it is argued, would be more active no matter which schools their children attended. The late sociologist James Coleman, together with Thomas Hoffer, investigated this claim in the 1980s by comparing the level of parental participation in independent versus state-run schools while taking into account family background. What they found was that families in the same income bracket, with the same level of education, whether single-parent or two-parent households, etc., were more likely to volunteer for school projects and attend parent-teacher conferences if their children attended private, particularly Catholic, schools.[30]

The same results have been found year after year in the official reports on the Milwaukee public voucher program. According to the fifth-year report by John Witte and others at the University of Wisconsin–Madison, parents' level of school involvement increased significantly once they were permitted to transfer their children from public to private schools, even when their level of commitment was already high.[31]

What accounts for this phenomenon? According to Coleman and Hoffer, the increased level of involvement could be traced directly to the parents' sense of the school being an integral part of their community. In the early 1970s, a researcher by the name of Otto Kraushaar surveyed thousands of independent-school parents across the United States and visited scores of schools, and came to essentially the same conclusion. But Kraushaar went one step further, explaining that the improved home-school relationship fostered by independent schools was a natural consequence of the "contract" between patrons and schools:

> The parents choose the school because they believe the environment to be right for the child, and the school chooses the pupil because he is believed to be suited to the school environment; both the patrons and the school have a stake in seeing that the contract is fulfilled satisfactorily.[32]

Greater sense of community

In addition to forging stronger bonds between parent and school, the private sector is also better at creating a closely knit community within the school itself. With 55 percent of independent U.S. schools enrolling fewer than 150 students, and an additional 25 percent enrolling between 150 and 299 students,[33] there is a real possibility for all the pupils and staff to know one another by name—a possibility that is quite often realized. The fact that the majority of public school students are enrolled in institutions with over 600 pupils makes the achievement of such a personalized atmosphere more difficult.[34]

But the community spirit of independent schools goes well beyond the effects of small school size. For years, independent schools have been more effective than their state-run counterparts at developing trust and understanding between students and teachers. According to teachers themselves, the private sector suffers only one fifth the rate of student absenteeism, half the rate of teacher absenteeism, and one sixth the rate of physical conflicts between students as the public sector. Vandalism, crime, drug abuse, student disrespect for teachers—all are vastly lower among independent schools. Student apathy, viewed as a serious problem by a fifth of all public school teachers, concerns only one out of every twenty-five private school teachers.[35] Once again, critics would claim that these advantages result from the kinds of families who opt for independent schooling, rather than from the schools themselves. Once again, they would be wrong. An extensive study of Catholic independent schools has revealed that even adjusting for a host of socioeconomic and demographic factors, the schools exert a significant positive effect on the behavior and morale of both students and teachers.[36]

Is all this achieved by a cavalier use of suspensions and expulsions, or by refusing to admit students likely to cause trouble? Apparently not. Statistics are most readily available for the much-studied Catholic schools, and they reveal that, on average, these schools suspend or dismiss only a handful of students per year. Nor is the tight screening of applicants widely practiced: the typical Catholic school accepts 88 percent of all who apply, and only one third of Catholic schools maintain waiting lists. What's more, the criteria for rejection vary from school to school, making it quite possible that a student who failed to gain acceptance to one Catholic school might be accepted at another. As noted above, some Catholic schools prefer to enroll the children of their own parishioners, while many others do not; virtually all have limits on the number of subsidized-tuition places available, but demand varies from school to school. Some, to be sure, are wary of highly disruptive students, or those far below the expected achievement level for their grade, but one Catholic school in five recently "reported having accepted students in the previous year who had been expelled from public schools for either disciplinary or academic reasons."[37] More than a quarter of inner-city parochial schools have no admissions criteria whatsoever.[38]

Having dismissed draconian expulsion and screening policies as Catholic schools' primary means of securing a studious and communal environment, we are left to conclude that, in the words of musician Adam Ant, "It must be something inside." Anthony Bryk, Valerie Lee, and Peter Holland studied the organizational roots of Catholic schools' inviting atmosphere in their 1993 book

Catholic Schools and the Common Good. In it, the authors show how a combination of sound school policies and voluntary action on the part of families makes possible a genuine sense of the school as a community. Enrollment in a Catholic school, or any other independent school, implies the acceptance on the part of parents and students of that school's norms of conduct, whatever the students' past behavior. There is an implicit agreement between family and school that each stands to gain from its association with the other, so long as both fulfill their parts of the bargain. The school must offer a valuable learning experience in a safe and nurturing environment, and the family must help to support that environment both through the student's conduct and the parents' financial support.[39] The fact that this agreement is actively entered into by both parties serves to strengthen the bond between home and school in a way that is rare in the public sector, where families and schools are little more than pawns thrust together by the stroke of an administrator's pen.

Higher teacher morale

The more communal atmosphere of independent schools is most clearly visible among the school staff. Teachers in independent schools are significantly happier about all aspects of their professional lives than their public school colleagues. In all nine measures of school organization studied by a group of researchers from the University of Michigan, from "overall sense of control" and "staff's influence in decision making" to the "school's sense of community," independent-school teachers had much more positive attitudes.[40] These results are charted in Figure 1.

A separate study conducted in New Jersey asked government-school teachers why they had chosen to work in a public rather than a private setting. The vast majority cited better pay as the primary reason.[41] Private school teachers answered differently:

> When teachers in independent schools were asked what they like most about teaching in that setting, they cited the professional ethos that pervades their schools: the freedom they have to choose textbooks, to construct curricula, and to "teach the way I want to within the structure." They also mentioned the "personalized atmosphere" and the "family-like environment" of their schools.[42]

The impact of this freer and more satisfying environment on educators is enormous. Independent-school teachers generally put in more hours in a wider range of areas than their public school colleagues, while being paid significantly less. On average, public school teachers are paid *one-and-a-half times* as much as teachers in independent schools.[43] Beginning public school teach-

Figure 1. Public and Independent Teacher Attitudes on a
Range of School-Related Issues

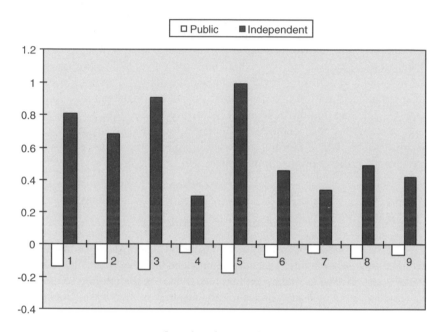

Issue, by column number:

1. Your overall sense of control
2. School's sense of community
3. Extent of good student behavior
4. Principal's leadership
5. Staff's influence in decision making
6. School's encouragement of innovation
7. Administrative responsiveness
8. Collaboration time allowed teachers
9. Your knowledge of other courses in your school

The combined average response of all public and independent teachers surveyed on each issue is 0. Positive numbers represent more positive attitudes, negative numbers, more negative attitudes (with a standard deviation equal to 1).

Data source: Valerie E. Lee, Robert F. Dedrick, and Julia B. Smith, "The Effect of the Social Organization of Schools on Teachers' Efficacy and Satisfaction," *Sociology of Education* 64 (1991): 196.

ers in the New Jersey study were found to be earning more, on average, than those who had been teaching in independent schools for seven years. These same independent-school teachers spent 50 percent more time preparing for classes than did those in the public sector. Roughly twice as many of them helped to organize school plays and clubs, while more than three times as many served as student advisors. Private school teachers were also more likely to monitor study halls, supervise computer labs, participate in faculty committees, and perform administrative duties. What's more, teachers in independent schools were twice as likely to emphasize their own desire to continue learning in explaining why they love teaching.[44]

In her national study titled *Teachers at Work,* Harvard professor Susan Moore Johnson found the same contrast. "Compared to their public-school counterparts," she wrote, independent-school teachers "expressed clearer notions of their schools' goals and purposes; they identified the values that they shared with others in their schools, they explained how these understandings were grounded in their schools' histories and were reinforced and expressed in their traditions."[45] Public school teachers were "often perplexed" when asked the same questions regarding their schools' mission and values; many failed to come up with an answer. Those who did offered statements that would not reassure a prospective student or parent. "It probably does have some unifying culture and I'm just not aware of it," observed one teacher of his public school.[46] Johnson's conclusions as to the causes of the disparity in the views of public and independent school teachers echoed those of other researchers:

> The prominence of cultural bonds in private schools and their virtual absence in most public schools can be explained by differences in their organizations. Because private schools are typically independent, small, stable, and homogeneous, those who work in them can better agree on goals, champion hardy values, celebrate successes, find direction in their history, and rekindle purpose with traditions. Public schools, by comparison, are . . . embedded in public bureaucracies . . . are subject to frequent and wholesale changes in membership and are responsible to diverse interests.[47]

Given the greater sense of mission, satisfaction, and shared purpose enjoyed by independent-school educators, it is not surprising that their views on formal tenure policies differ from those of government-school teachers. While public-sector teachers and their unions are overwhelmingly in favor of tenure, only a quarter of teachers in religious — and only a fifth in nonsectarian — independent schools agree. In general, independent-school teachers and principals "believe that there should be no permanent tenure, and that the school should be free to dismiss teachers if their work becomes unsatisfactory even after three or more years of service."[48] In keeping with this view, the granting of tenure is rare among private schools.

Less bureaucracy

One of the least publicized but most dramatic differences between independent and state-run schools is the enormous bureaucracy gap. In the private sector, control over virtually all decisions resides in the individual school. The public system, by contrast, is characterized by an all-encompassing centralization of power at the district and state levels.

With these contrasting organizational structures come contrasting levels of bureaucracy. In 1987, the Chicago school system employed 3,300 people in its central and district offices. The Catholic Archdiocese of Chicago managed to serve 40 percent as many students, distributed over a wider area, with only thirty-six central office administrators. An even greater disparity existed in New York City, where Catholic schools employed twenty-five administrators compared to 6,000 in the public system, though Catholic schools enrolled one fourth as many students.[49] In the spring of 1996, the *Baltimore Sun* compared Hartford County's public school system with that of the nearby Archdiocese of Baltimore, which serves virtually the same number of students. Even though the Archdiocese's students were spread out across twice as many schools, it required only one ninth the number of central administrators.[50]

Though the administrative hierarchies of Catholic schools may seem tiny in comparison to those of state schools, the non-Catholic majority of independent schools generally have no external bureaucracy whatever. There are two key reasons for the private sector's ability to dispense with sprawling central offices and endless layers of management: direct funding and freedom from regulation. Because the bulk of independent-school costs are covered directly by parents in the form of tuition, there are few of the funding application forms and reports that occupy so much administrative time in government schools. Minute regulations, which plague state schools by the thousands, are also less pervasive in the private sector, making it unnecessary for independent schools to hire scores of administrators whose chief responsibilities are to ensure, and demonstrate, compliance with government regulations.

Faced with the striking absence of administrative complexity in private schools, it is natural to ask if there is a downside. Are there any economies of scale enjoyed by centralized public systems that independent schools are forced to do without? Unfortunately for taxpayers, the answer is no. In fact, the reverse is true. Small rural school districts have the lowest per-pupil expenditures, and large city districts have the highest, with medium-sized districts falling in between. Each of the three largest districts in the United States—New York City, Los Angeles Unified, and Dade County, Florida—have yearly per-pupil expenditures between $700 and $1,000 dollars above the national average.[51] Schools in major inner-city Catholic dioceses also tend to spend more per pupil than the average Catholic school, but the difference in their case amounts to less than $100.[52]

Greater academic emphasis

Another factor that distinguishes independent schools from those in the public sector, which is very much in keeping with the reasons families opt for independent schooling, is their greater emphasis on academics. The average Catholic-high-school student graduates with a year more of mathematics and a half-year more of foreign-language instruction than her government-school counterpart. Across the subject areas, Catholic students end up with roughly 25 percent more academic curriculum credits than public school students.

A significant part of this difference, according to Bryk, Lee, and Holland, is due to the fact that Catholic-school pupils are twice as likely to be enrolled in a demanding academic program as pupils in public schools: 72 percent versus 38 percent (public school students are more likely to be enrolled in vocational or watered-down "general" programs). Conversely, only one Catholic high school student in ten follows a vocational program, compared to more than one student in four in public schools. Even within the same program, however, Catholic-school students take a heavier academic course-load than do public school students. Comparing pupils in the "academic," "general," and "vocational" tracks, Bryk and his colleagues found that those in private schools took, respectively, 12 percent, 38 percent, and 95 percent more academic courses.[53]

These data do much to dispel the notion that differences in academic emphasis between the two sectors are purely the result of different student backgrounds, but there is also evidence that track placement itself is affected by school sector. Specifically, academic-track students in Catholic schools were twice as likely to have been placed in that track (as opposed to choosing it) as public school academic-track students.[54] It is clear that in Catholic high schools the assumption is that all students should follow an academic program unless they actively seek to do otherwise. In public schools, there is far less of a push toward academics.

The greater academic emphasis of independent Catholic schools was also confirmed in another national U.S. study, conducted by James Coleman. Coleman found that "the Catholic school advantage in mathematics, English, and foreign-language course-work cannot be wholly or even largely attributed to the more advantaged family and academic backgrounds of Catholic students." In fact, in two out of the three subject areas (mathematics and English), student background characteristics had hardly any effect at all on the heavier course-load of Catholic-school students.[55]

A low fad diet

A quarter-century ago, education historian and scholar Otto Kraushaar wrote that "the 'market' of the avant-garde school is limited and precarious. Most parents do not wish their children to be the subjects of any 'far-out' experimentation which would imperil their acquisition of the three R's."[56] As the first chapter of this book demonstrated, Kraushaar's statement is as true today as it was then. Most, though not all, independent schools are forced to resist the temptation to jump from fad to fad as public school systems do,[57] for fear of alienating their clientele. The sense of history and tradition that pervades private institutions also creates educational inertia, forcing advocates of instructional innovations to weigh the possibilities of each new idea against the proven record of existing practice.

The careful scrutiny independent schools apply to prospective changes in curriculum and organization serve to block many but not all of the flawed schemes that appear so frequently on the educational scene. To their credit, however, private schools are much quicker to abandon detrimental and ineffective innovations than are government-run schools. In the 1970s, when many public schools were embracing open classrooms, some Catholic schools tried out the concept as well. Shortly thereafter, the Catholic schools returned to their traditional scheduling and curriculum patterns, which they have retained ever since. As open classrooms came under scrutiny, public schools simply moved on to watered-down "core" classes and new fads such as Values Clarification and Outcomes Based Education. Catholic schools, meanwhile, generally held to the more traditional methods their patrons sought.[58]

Sometimes, of course, an educational innovation has both good and bad features, and in this case independent schools are often impressively selective in their responses. Whole-language proponents, for instance, very sensibly advocate introducing children to rich literary works as soon as they are able to appreciate them, but often foolishly shun direct formal instruction in phonics. According to Robert Kealey, Executive Director for Elementary Schools of the National Catholic Education Association, private Catholic schools generally practice the sensible aspects of whole language (such as reading to young students on a daily basis from rich texts) while continuing to stress phonics. Teachers typically use systematic lessons from phonics workbooks in addition to the phonics tasks included in selected reading texts. In fact, the Modern Curriculum Press phonics textbook series was "developed by a group of Catholic educators from the Diocese of Cleveland."[59]

The instructional conservatism of independent schools does, of course, have its downside. While virtually every other field of human endeavor can boast of tremendous gains in efficiency and quality over the course of this century, independent schools, like their public counterparts, have been comparatively stagnant. The reasons for this lack of advancement are discussed at the end of this chapter.

Race, Integration, and Private Schools

When U.S. federal courts ordered the desegregation of public school districts in the 1960s and 1970s, some white parents fled to the private sector, and new private schools, dubbed "segregation academies," were opened for the chief purpose of preserving white-only classrooms.

In Louisiana, during the spring of 1961, the legislature introduced a series of bills meant to encourage the privatization of schooling as a way to circumvent public school desegregation orders. Any community in which a majority voted to close down the public schools could do so under these bills, and subsidies were to be made available so that families could more easily afford the tuition at private segregation academies. In an effort to appear unbiased, the bills did not mention race as a consideration or motivating factor. Nevertheless, the intent was clear. Fines were to be imposed "upon anyone caught inducing others to attend integrated schools," and financial rewards were to be paid to informers. All of these bills passed by overwhelming majorities, though most were immediately struck down by the courts.[60]

Despite the eventual failure of these and most similar legislative measures, segregation academies did attract many white parents opposed to integration. Nationwide, it was estimated that as many as half a million students were withdrawn from public schools between 1964 and 1975 in order to avoid mandatory integration.[61]

The role that private schools played in this early pattern of racial isolationism has led many civil rights advocates to be skeptical of policies, such as vouchers (see Chapter 10), that would increase private school enrollment. Two important facts should ease those concerns: private schools have been no more of a refuge for opponents of integration than have suburban public schools, and enrollment data indicate that private schools have become as well integrated as public schools over the past four decades—if not more so.

Though up to half a million students may have been placed in private schools to avoid integration, this accounts for only a tiny fraction of the white flight seen around the country between the late 1960s and the mid-1970s. Many more children were simply moved to predominantly white suburban public schools. In Los Angeles, 60 percent of all white students assigned to minority public schools failed to show up in the first year of that city's desegregation plan, and white no-show figures above 40 or 50 percent were common in other parts of the country.[62] But during the height of white flight, between 1970 and 1973, total private school enrollment actually decreased by 17 percent (public school enrollment also decreased, but only by 3 percent). The majority of families fleeing integration clearly did not seek refuge in the private sector.[63]

It must be reasserted, however, that racism was not the only factor in white flight, whether to private schools or to suburban public ones. Desegregation expert David Armor observes that Los Angeles's particularly high rate of white no-shows may have been partially attributable to the extreme length of the bus-rides required by desegregation plans (averaging fifty-five minutes each way).[64] And, as noted in Chapter 4, income is a better predictor of flight from urban schools than race.[65] The higher rate of white emigration to the suburbs is thus tied, in part, to the higher average incomes of whites.

None of this is meant to imply that racism was not also a factor, but whatever role it may initially have played appears to have declined in importance over the past three or four decades. In the 1968–69 school year, 93 percent of all independent-school students were non-Hispanic whites, 3.6 percent were African Americans, and 3.3 percent belonged to other racial or ethnic groups.[66] Thirty years later, the percentage of African Americans in independent schools has almost tripled to 9.1 percent, approaching the (12.6 percent) proportion of African Americans in the population at large. The overall percentage of minority students in independent schools has leapt from 6.9 percent to 22 percent during the same period.[67] Even after this rapid rise, the rate of growth in black independent-school enrollment continues to outpace that of total independent-school enrollment or white independent-school enrollment.[68]

These figures indicate a growing minority presence in the private sector as a whole, but they say nothing about the extent to which minority and white students share the same schools and classrooms. To supply that missing information, James Coleman compared the degree of segregation among public schools, Catholic schools, and non-Catholic private schools. He considered school systems to be highly segregated if nearly all the students of a given race or ethnicity were concentrated in a few schools, and he considered them integrated if the different races and ethnicities were evenly distributed among all the schools in a given system. What Coleman found was that by the early 1980s, non-Catholic independent schools had the least African-American/white segregation, followed by Catholic schools. Public schools were by far the most segregated along racial lines. In the case of Hispanic/non-Hispanic segregation, Catholic schools were the least segregated, public schools were next, and non-Catholic independent schools were the most segregated. Coleman also examined economic segregation, assessing the amount of mixing between mid-to-high-income families and low-income families. By this measure, both types of independent schools were well integrated, with public schools being somewhat less so.[69] Finally, Coleman examined the extent of religious integration in the public and private sectors. Not surprisingly, he found that private schools were more segregated by religion, because they are free to cater to families seeking religious instruction in particular faiths.

Coleman's method of assessing integration is admittedly somewhat coarse. It would be possible, for example, for an individual school to enroll equal numbers of African-American and white students, without those students engaging in meaningful interaction with one another. Political scientist Jay Greene and his colleague Nicole Mellow recently attempted to overcome this limitation by looking at the level of integration in school lunchrooms. Voluntary lunchroom seating patterns, they reasoned, are a much better indicator of true integration than are overall school-enrollment figures. What Greene and Mellow found is that private schools, particularly religious ones, produce much higher racial integration in their lunchrooms than do public schools.[70]

Public schools thus appear to be less effective at integrating students by race and socioeconomic status than private schools, and they appear to succeed at integrating students by religion chiefly because they are prohibited from offering religious instruction. This should not be too surprising. Public school districts, after all, are often demographically isolated, drawing their pupils from racially and economically homogeneous catchment areas. It may also be the case that race and economic status have far less influence on parents' private school choices than many public school advocates claim—an interpretation supported by the opinion poll data cited earlier in this chapter and also in Chapter 1. Parents now seem to be more concerned about the quality of their children's schools than the color of their children's classmates.

Cost

To this point, private schools have been shaping up fairly well. But aren't they exorbitantly expensive? The simple fact is that the average independent school costs half as much per pupil as the average public school: $3,116 versus $6,653 during the 1993–94 school year (the most recent year for which national private school data are available). These averages, however, hide significant variations within the private sector. Schools affiliated with religious organizations spend considerably less than nonsectarian schools. Independent Catholic schools charged an average tuition of $2,178 in 1993–94, while other religious schools averaged $2,915, and nonsectarian private schools averaged $6,631.[71]

This discrepancy has led many critics to suggest that religious schools are able to charge low tuitions solely because of parish subsidies and endowments. In reality, parish subsidies accounted for only about $700 per year per student in Catholic elementary schools during the 1992–93 school year. Endowments from alumni and community members were far smaller, accounting for only 2 percent of Catholic-school income in the same year.[72] Thus, even taking these funding sources into account, the cost of religious independent schools remains around half that of public schools.

In addition to being far cheaper on average, Catholic schools also enjoy economies of scale. As their enrollments increase, their per-pupil costs drop, from $2,147 in 1992–93 for schools with fewer than 200 students, to $1,889 for schools enrolling more than 500 students. As mentioned in Chapter 3, public school per-pupil expenditures actually *increase* as school size goes up.[73]

Clearly, Catholic and other religious schools deliver their educational services far more economically than the public system. The same cannot be said of nonsectarian private schools, which charge an average tuition virtually identical to the average per-pupil spending at government-run schools. Tracking down the cause of this cost differential is as easy as flipping through the photographs in a typical guide to private schools. Without even glancing at the tuition figures it is fairly easy to make a rough estimate of a school's cost by looking at its buildings and grounds. Any institution housed in an awe-inspiring gothic structure surrounded by manicured lawns and acres of land is not likely to be had for only two or three thousand dollars a year. Conversely, private schools with modest facilities, whether religious or otherwise, are generally much less expensive. As it happens, most of the independent schools enjoying spectacular buildings fall in the nonsectarian category, while most religious-school buildings are less opulent, a fact which is no doubt responsible for a significant part of the difference in average per-pupil expenditures. Differences in teacher costs also play a role, since some Catholic schools employ teachers who are members of the cloth and who receive a small stipend rather than a salary. In recent years, however, lay teachers have comprised the great majority of the Catholic-school teaching force, making differences in instructional costs less and less significant.

Another key factor in the greater cost of nonsectarian independent schools is their typically smaller class sizes, often less than fifteen or even a dozen students per class. Take, for example, the independent, nonsectarian Kiski secondary school for boys in Saltsburg, Pennsylvania. The description of its athletic facilities alone is staggering, including:

> The field house, an indoor swimming pool, three football fields, four soccer fields, three baseball fields, a nine-hole golf course, a 400-meter all-weather track, eight all-weather tennis courts, an outdoor basketball court, a ski slope with rope tow, and approximately 100 wooded acres. An outdoor swimming pool is used during the summer, and the campus pond is available for fishing in the summer and ice-skating and ice hockey in the winter.[74]

When these facilities are coupled with a student/teacher ratio of seven to one and an average class size of ten students, it is obvious that tuition at Kiski must be at least several thousand dollars a year higher than that among the more modestly appointed campuses of most religious independent schools. If anything,

Kiski's yearly tuition for day-students (as opposed to boarders) of $7,700 for the 1996–97 school year seems a positive bargain compared to public high schools, which generally offer far less impressive facilities and larger classes while spending nearly as much per pupil.

It should be noted that considerable spending variations exist within the public sector as well, with per-pupil spending ranging from lows of roughly $4,000 in some districts, to highs of over $12,000 in others.[75]

Outcomes of Independent Schooling

Academic Achievement

Academic achievement, as measured by standardized tests, is one of the most popular ways of comparing the outcomes of state-run and independent schools. On the face of it, the private sector's advantage on this score is impossible to deny. The results of the 1994 National Assessment of Educational Progress reading report card tell a well-known story. In the fourth grade, for example, independent-school students scored nineteen points higher, on average, than public school students (on the 500-point scale). The significance of these results is brought home by the fact that only thirty points separate the "basic" achievement level (208 or higher) from the "proficient" achievement level (238 or higher).[76]

For years, many educators have dismissed the higher scores of independent-school students as artifacts of elitist admissions policies, but research conducted during the eighties and nineties suggests otherwise. By 1987, James Coleman was able to write that "most critics have come to agree, on the basis of analyses already completed using the 1982 data . . . that there is a positive [private] Catholic sector effect on achievement in the areas of reading comprehension, vocabulary, mathematics and writing."[77] (Note that the academic effects of nonsectarian private schools, for which data are harder to come by, are discussed later in this section.)[78]

To move beyond the simple recognition of a difference and begin to estimate its size, Coleman conducted further research in the late 1980s. In particular, he compared the growth in student achievement between sophomore and senior years in Catholic high schools with that in government-run high schools, while controlling for the effects of family background. Once again, the results showed greater gains for Catholic-school students in both verbal and mathematical skills. "The magnitude of the differential effect," Coleman wrote, "is about one grade equivalent," with Catholic-school students acquiring an average of about three years of high-school learning compared to the two years of growth in the public sector.[79] (Though a typical year of high-school learning is perhaps not as great a quantity as one might hope or expect.)

Coleman's findings were echoed in the 1990s by Anthony Bryk and his colleagues, who studied the differences in mathematics achievement between private-sector (Catholic) and public-sector students. Mathematics performance was chosen as an ideal point of comparison, since it has been found to be the subject least affected by home-related factors and most dependent on classroom instruction.[80] Once again, the average achievement level of Catholic-school students exceeded that of government-school students even after family background, social class, and race/ethnicity were controlled for. Over the course of their high-school education, the difference was equivalent to 3.2 years of additional learning.[81]

Still more interestingly, the results showed that Catholic schools minimized the achievement disparity between pupils of high and low social class, as well as the disparity between white and minority students, while these disparities were actually exacerbated by public schools. The gap between white and minority public school students, for example, is already greater by sophomore year than it is in Catholic schools, and it widens toward senior year in the public schools while actually shrinking in the Catholic schools. Looked at another way, it can be said that in Catholic schools, minority students learn faster than white students during the last two years of high school, whereas they learn more slowly in state-run schools, falling further and further behind. Catholic schools, therefore, not only raise student achievement above the level of public schools, but they do so more equitably than public schools as well, helping disadvantaged and minority youths catch up to their more socially and economically advantaged peers.[82]

As noted above, data on the academic effects of nonsectarian private schools are much less readily available than those for Catholic schools. Several recent studies do point toward similar benefits among nonsectarian schools, however. The first such study compared the academic achievement of low-income students who participated in the government-run Milwaukee school voucher program with those who applied but were rejected due to a legal limit on the size of the program. Because the decision to accept or reject a given family was made on a random basis, this comparison provides the best possible indication of the relative effects of independent-school versus government-school attendance. Furthermore, since only nonsectarian independent schools have thus far been eligible to receive vouchers in Milwaukee's program, the results are useful for distinguishing their effects from those of religious schools.

According to Jay Greene of the University of Texas and Paul Peterson and Jiangtao Du of Harvard University, students attending private schools under the choice program began to show significant academic gains over the control group after three years in the program. On average, private school choice students had reading scores 3 percent higher after three years in the program and 5 percent higher after four years. The average mathematics gains were 5 and 12 percentage points for third and fourth year participants, respectively. While these gains may seem slight, they are nonetheless remarkable when one considers the modest size and vigor of the educational market created by Milwaukee's voucher program. Roughly 80 percent of the participating students were enrolled in just three schools during the years in which the achievement gains were accrued. Putting the results in perspective, the authors added that "if similar success could be achieved for all minority students nationwide, it could close the gap separating white and minority test scores by somewhere between one-third and more than one-half."[83]

In a separate assessment of the Milwaukee experiment, Princeton University professor Cecilia Elena Rouse also found that participation in the voucher program led to improved academic achievement. Rouse reported that students randomly selected to participate in the voucher program scored significantly higher in math than those randomly rejected from the program (due to limits on the number of participants), though by her calculations there was no significant difference in the students' reading scores.[84]

Three qualifications of these results are in order. With the overwhelming majority of choice students in the publicly run Milwaukee program concentrated in only three schools, the ability to generalize to schools in the rest of the nation is limited. The scope of the studies' findings is further restricted due to the small number of students involved, a legacy of the tight restrictions on the number of participants that only began to be eased in the fall of 1996. Most importantly, the very modest amount of competition and parental choice afforded by such a small-scale experiment concentrated in such a small number of schools can only offer the palest reflection of the possibilities that would exist in a full scale competitive educational market encompassing all of Milwaukee's schools and children.

The Milwaukee experiment is not alone, however. Two other voucher experiments contribute to the mounting body of modern evidence indicating a private-sector advantage in academic outcomes. The first of these is Indianapolis's privately funded voucher program, studied in 1996 by researchers David Weinschrott and Sally Kilgore. As in the Milwaukee experiment, Weinschrott and Kilgore compared the achievement of students receiving vouchers (and hence attending private schools) with those who applied to the program but were unable to participate due to funding constraints. Showing remarkable consistency with the Milwaukee findings, the Weinschrott and Kilgore results indicate an initial small dip in achievement immediately following the transfer from public to private schools, after which choice students began to outperform the control group that had remained in public schools. In Indianapolis, the improvement was found both in mathematics and in language skills.[85]

Preliminary findings are also available from the first year of Cleveland,

Ohio's government-run voucher program. Jay Greene, William Howell, and Paul Peterson compared test scores for students attending two private schools participating in the program with the scores of comparable students who did not receive vouchers. Students attending private schools were found to have outperformed their public school peers in both math and reading. This result is all the more interesting given that the two private schools in question had been newly established in response to the voucher program, and were perceived as particularly problematic by voucher critics.[86]

A subsequent study by Indiana University researchers failed to find any academic benefits arising from participation in Cleveland's voucher program after its first year of operation.[87] Peterson and Greene have pointed to serious flaws in the Indiana report, however. The problems they identified included arbitrary exclusion of some participating schools, dubious prior achievement data, biased analysis techniques, the selection of an above-average public school control group, and the selection of a tiny (5 percent) nonrandom sample of voucher students. The Indiana University researchers have disputed these claims, alleging in response that the study conducted by Peterson, Greene, and Howell was flawed and biased. Peterson and his colleagues have subsequently responded to these counter-charges.[88]

In their landmark 1990 book *Politics, Markets, and America's Schools*, authors John Chubb and Terry Moe carried the investigation of student achievement one step further, not only finding private schools superior to public schools, but identifying one of the main reasons for their superiority. "Private schools," they wrote, "are disproportionately likely to ... post large [student] achievement gains": private schools accounted for 38 percent of the schools they categorized as "high performance" with respect to increasing student achievement, but accounted for only 2 percent of their "low performance" category.[89] To trace the causes of this strength, the authors held constant such factors as average student performance, severity of behavior problems, parents' socioeconomic status and school contacts, and school size. What they discovered was that even after controlling for these variables, private schools still had far more effective organizations than public schools, enjoying stronger leadership and clearer goals.

Parental Satisfaction

According to a survey carried out by the U.S. National Center for Education Statistics (NCES), the parents of independent-school children are far more satisfied with every aspect of their schools than are government-school parents (see Figure 2). This is true, moreover, whether the government schools are automatically assigned to parents or chosen through an open-enrollment, magnet, or charter program.[90] Other surveys reveal somewhat lower public school parent satisfaction ratings than the NCES study. *Phi Delta Kappan* magazine's

Figure 2. Percentage of Parents Who Are "Very Satisfied"
with Aspects of Their Child's School, by School Type: 1993

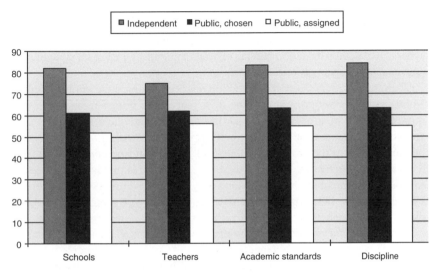

Data source: J. R. Campbell, P. L. Donahue, C. M. Reese, and G. W. Phillips, *NAEP 1994 Reading Report Card for the Nation and the States* (Washington, DC: National Center for Education Statistics, U.S. Department of Education, 1996), 33.

1997 annual Gallup poll, for example, found that only 15 percent of public school parents gave their local schools an A rating, while 43 percent rated them C, D, or Fail (41 percent gave them a B).[91] Nevertheless, the NCES data are useful for showing the considerable differences that exist in parental satisfaction between public and private sectors.

Those parents whose children have attended both public and private schools offer another perspective on parental satisfaction. This information is readily available from voucher programs that have compared parents' attitudes toward their schools before and after entering the program. Universally, these comparisons have favored independent schools. In Indianapolis, parents whose children transferred to a private school thanks to the voucher program reported being much more satisfied one year later on every one of thirteen measures, from teacher and principal performance to the amount their children learned. After two years in the private sector, once parents and children had become accustomed to the new environment, the level of parental satisfaction usually dropped slightly, but still remained above the level enjoyed in public schools.[92]

In only one of the thirteen measures did parental satisfaction eventually drop below the level at which it had been in public schools: the parents' evaluation of their own children's effort. One likely explanation for the drop, in light of the fact that parents still believed their children were learning significantly more in private schools, was that their expectations for what their children could accomplish had increased. Given the link between parental expectations and children's performance, this can only be seen as a good sign. Once private schools had demonstrated to parents all that their children were capable of, parents began to expect more from them.

The same jump in parental satisfaction has accompanied the publicly funded Milwaukee voucher program. In the fifth year of the program, as in the first, more than three quarters of choice parents gave their private school experience an overall rating of A or B. Barely half gave the same rating to their previous public schools. At the other end of the scale, fewer than 5 percent of choice parents rated their private schools a D or an F, while almost one in four gave such low ratings to the public schools which they had left.[93] Parents participating in Cleveland's voucher program are also more satisfied with their private schools than they had been with their public schools.[94]

Remarkably, the positive reactions of participants in government-run voucher programs seem restrained when compared to the attitudes of parents receiving vouchers from privately funded programs. Fully 90 percent of participants in Milwaukee's private Partners Advancing Values in Education (PAVE) voucher program rate their private schools an A or a B, and only 2 percent give them a D or an F. One obvious factor that could account for much of this difference is the freedom of PAVE parents to choose from among all of Milwaukee's independent schools, including religious institutions. Some of the effect no doubt derives from many parents' desire for a religious education, but the simple opportunity to choose from a much wider number of schools—102 in the private program versus twelve in the government-run program—must also play a role.[95]

The PAVE experience is not unique. In 1992–93, the most recent school year for which data are available, parents in San Antonio's private Children's Educational Opportunity (CEO) voucher program awarded their schools an A or a B 87 percent of the time, and a D or an F only 2 percent of the time.[96] Families in Indianapolis's private voucher program, while not as completely satisfied as those in PAVE or CEO, were nonetheless quite as happy with their independent schools as parents in the government-run Milwaukee program, and far more satisfied with their chosen independent schools than they had been with their public schools.[97]

High School and Beyond

The achievement gains and improvements in parental satisfaction to be had in independent schools cannot benefit the student who drops out. If, in response to their more demanding curricula, slow or undisciplined students were more likely to drop out of independent schools, the advantages of these schools would clearly be diminished. Fortunately, this does not appear to be the case. Coleman's 1987 study of Catholic independent schools showed that their dropout rates are much lower than those of public schools, irrespective of students' race, ethnicity, academic performance, discipline history, or socioeconomic status.[98] Coleman also suggested that the dropout rates of other independent schools were not substantially different from those of public schools, but since his sample data for nonsectarian schools were limited, no strong conclusions about them can be drawn.

According to Coleman, Catholic schools' advantage in retaining students derives from the more closely knit community they are part of and help to create. These schools are most often formed around a local parish, and parents, students, and staff often see one another at Sunday mass or simply come into contact with one another more frequently in moving about their neighborhood. Public schools, because of their greater size and their use of busing, draw students from a much wider area and thereby weaken their ties to any given neighborhood. Nonsectarian independent schools, while often sharing the communal atmosphere of their Catholic counterparts, are generally forced to seek out students from a large geographical area as well, due to their more direct competition with nonsectarian "free" government schools. Competing directly against a product that is given away free, even if that product is not of the highest quality, is a difficult task.

Once out of high school, the independent-school advantage persists. Children who attend Catholic schools are roughly 60 percent more likely to attend a four-year college than public school students, and those who attend other private schools are almost twice as likely to attend a four-year college. What's more, only about half of this gain is attributable to background characteristics of the children and their families.[99] Most of the remaining gain can be tied to the increased likelihood of students, regardless of their background, being directed into academic programs in independent schools. What is left of the difference is accounted for by heavier independent-school workloads, both in courses taken and homework done. Here, too, however, the results for nonsectarian schools are only tentative, given the small sample size used in Coleman's comparison.

Once they get to college, former private school students are also more likely to stick with it. If they do drop out of college, they are more likely to go back. These variations are correlated with good high-school achievement and good high-school work habits, which are themselves fostered by Catholic and other private schools, so Coleman concluded that differential college success "is related to the performance differences in high school between sectors."[100]

Coleman's results were dramatically reinforced in 1997 by University of

Chicago economics professor Derek Neal. Neal used a nationally representative sample of urban students to compare the effects of inner-city public and Catholic schools. After controlling for the background characteristics of students (e.g., parents' level of education, parents' occupation, family structure, reading materials at home), Neal discovered that private "Catholic schools succeed in communities where public schools fail miserably."[101] The typical inner-city minority student, Neal concluded, had a 62 percent chance of graduating if he attended a public school, but a remarkable 88 percent chance of graduating if he attended a Catholic school. In fact, Neal reports that among Catholic schools the graduation rate for urban minority children is higher than that of urban white children. Nonetheless, urban whites also benefit significantly from attending Catholic schools.

A Funny Thing Happened on the Way to the Market

Compared to government-run schools, independent schools enjoy better discipline, a stronger sense of community, a clearer focus on academics, higher teacher morale, less bureaucracy, greater parental involvement, superior student achievement, and improved college performance. This is not cause for celebration, however, for compared to anything *but* government-run institutions, the record of independent schools in the twentieth century is deserving of only the faintest praise. As described in the concluding section of Chapter 6, most human enterprises have undergone stunning advances in productivity, quality, and efficiency over the past hundred years, and have been transformed by radical new technologies. Most independent schools have done little better than to plod along at a constant pace, with perhaps a modest improvement here or there.

But why? Why has education, in the private as well as the public sector, stood still while the rest of the world has moved on? Two reasons stand out as particularly important: competition has been stifled by the 90 percent share of the educational market enjoyed by "free" government schools; and private schooling, unlike the rest of the private sector, is overwhelmingly dominated by non-profit institutions.

History has shown that the compulsory tax-support of public schools shrinks the market for independent schools. Since the mid nineteenth century, private institutions have been all but squeezed out of the education industry, and now represent just over 10 percent of U.S. schools. A tenth of the schools means a tenth of the competition and a tenth of the innovation that might be expected under a wide-open educational market.

The limited size of the private education sector is clearly part of the problem, but possibly a smaller part than the not-for-profit status of most independent schools. Nonprofit schools are prohibited from distributing any part of their net earnings to private shareholders or individuals. The operators of such schools can draw reasonable salaries, and there is some latitude in the determination of what is reasonable, but they are much more limited in the level of compensation they can receive than are the owners of for-profit schools. Because nonprofits are forbidden from distributing earnings to shareholders, they lack one of the principal means by which for-profit businesses raise funds. Nonprofits can and do receive donations from private individuals, but, as will be explained below, these donations often come with strings attached—strings that limit the uses to which the funds can be put.

The stultifying effects that nonprofit status has had on independent schooling are clearly laid out by William J. McMillan in his book *Private School Management*. Himself an independent-school headmaster, McMillan learned from years of experience and observation that

> [w]hereas in most other kinds of business a successful enterprise tends ultimately to branch out and multiply into other locations, in private schools neither academic quality nor financial success has been a cause of proliferation. The very best private elementary and secondary schools have been satisfied to perpetuate their own existence, with little inclination to expand their services into other geographic areas (or into an enlarged enrollment of "customers" in their existing campus).[102]

McMillan traces the number-one reason for this institutional calcification to the absence of the profit motive. Expanding a school's operations entails costs and risks, even for the most successful institutions. "In commercial businesses," he writes, "the risks are at least weighed against a profit opportunity, something utterly lacking among most private schools."[103] His other reasons, moreover, devolve almost immediately back to the lack of a profit motive. For instance, he indicates that donors to nonprofit schools, often alumni, want their money to go to the original school, not a new acquisition. They are motivated not by profit, but by a desire to perpetuate the specific tradition in which they themselves were educated. This is perfectly reasonable from their point of view, but it curtails the possibility that the successful school's operations will be extended to a wider clientele, by limiting the funds available for that purpose.

A look at the higher-education market confirms McMillan's analysis. While few elementary and secondary schools are run for profit, the practice is more common among career colleges. Several of the major players in post-secondary career training, such as DeVry, ITT, and the Apollo group, are profit-making businesses.[104] In contrast to their nonprofit counterparts at the K–12 (kindergarten through twelfth-grade) level, these institutions routinely grow and shrink in response to changes in demand. Successful for-profit colleges (also called "proprietary" colleges) sometimes run campuses in several countries and dozens of states. Poorly performing institutions either are forced out of business as their students are lured away by competitors,[105] or are acquired by new management able to turn their fortunes around.[106] The niche market which these institutions occupy is thus far more dynamic than the much larger market of nonprofit K–12 schools.

Several factors have conspired to squeeze profit-making institutions out of K–12 education. The most long-standing and pervasive of these is the attitude among educational theorists that education should not "be exploited for private gain."[107] Opposition among leading educators to for-profit schooling was already widespread by 1928, according to a University of Pennsylvania Ph.D. thesis published in that year. The thesis, which surveyed thousands of private educational institutions all across the United States, found that even the owners and operators of proprietary schools felt the need to defend their profit-making status. In response to the question "Is your school run for profit?" the following answers were typical:[108] "No profit beyond ordinary livelihood." "Run for a living." "Technically, yes, but I want a good school to deserve a profit." "Profits put [into] enlargement and betterment of school." One even wrote: "Yes, but look forward to being run not for profit under Board of Trustees."

Though opposition to proprietary schooling has been widespread among educators for more than a century, it has had no empirical basis. There do not appear to have been any rigorous studies comparing the outcomes of for-profit versus nonprofit schools prior to the latter half of the twentieth century, by which time most proprietary schools had already been converted to nonprofit status or had ceased to exist.

Ideology, not empiricism, seems to have been the source of educators' distaste for proprietary schools. Antipathy toward profit-making and capitalism generally have been defining traits of such influential educators as Horace Mann and John Dewey. Dewey's preference for central economic planning over free markets is well-documented,[109] and in 1847, Mann wrote:

> The day is sure to come when men will look back upon the prerogatives of Capital, at the present time, with as severe and as just a condemnation as we now look back upon the predatory Chieftains of the Dark Ages.[110]

This mind-set has continued to the present day. In recent years, the National Education Association has regularly advised its members on how to "Fight Privatization."[111]

The anti-profit bias of many educators has not only worked directly against proprietary schools, it has also shaped public opinion via the public schools. The operation of the free enterprise system has been a grossly neglected subject in most public schools for decades. Based on a survey reported in the *American Economic Review,* New Yorkers have no better understanding of the workings of competitive markets than do Muscovites, who have only recently been introduced to capitalism.[112] As generation after generation has been schooled by "free" government institutions, for-profit education has begun to seem not just abnormal but even reprehensible.

A second reason for the atrophy of for-profit education has been the relatively inhospitable environment created by tax laws. In 1928, virtually all the states exempted nonprofit private schools from paying property taxes, but twelve of those states denied this benefit to schools operated for profit[113] (though it was not demonstrated that the services provided by these schools contributed any less to the general welfare than those of their nonprofit counterparts). Today, nonprofit private schools are exempted from paying federal taxes under Section 501 (c) (3) of the Internal Revenue Code,[114] while for-profit schools are not. This places proprietary schools at a considerable financial disadvantage compared to their nonprofit counterparts.

Finally, the very existence of "free" government schools discourages parents from paying for private schooling—reducing the market for all private schools, and hence reducing the profit potential of proprietary educational institutions (at least those which would seek to expand their operations). Families are only willing to spend so much of their income on education, and with $279 billion already being funneled into the government-run system every year,[115] comparatively little is left over for private enterprise.

This combination of factors—the bias against profit-making schools, the tax benefits enjoyed by nonprofit schools, and the competition of "free" government schools—has not only created a considerable disincentive to the creation of new proprietary schools, but has led many established for-profit institutions to adopt nonprofit status. Many of today's most respected prep schools were founded and earned their reputations as proprietary institutions. The prestigious Taft School of Watertown, Connecticut, established in 1890 by the brother of President William Howard Taft, was operated for profit until 1926. The Lawrenceville school of Lawrenceville, New Jersey was operated as a profit-making academy from its inception in 1810 until it was endowed by the John C. Green Foundation in 1878 (and thereafter became a nonprofit). While these and similar institutions continue to enjoy excellent reputations since becoming nonprofits, they have not expanded to new locations as would be normal for successful profit-making businesses.

The entrepreneurial spirit has left the educational body not just in the United States, but all over the world. With the exception of Japan, there does not appear to be a single industrialized nation in which for-profit institutions constitute a majority in the private education sector, let alone in the school industry at large. Three quarters of Holland's schools are "private," the largest percentage of any nation in modern times, but hardly any are operated for profit. What's more, they are so heavily regulated as to resemble government-run schools far more than independent ones. The reason? Virtually all of Holland's "private" schools are funded by the state, and with state funding has come state control. The Dutch government, for instance, defines teacher accreditation requirements, fixes salary scales, curtails the firing of teachers, sets curriculum standards, says how much can be spent, makes it illegal to charge consumers for education (with the exception of very small facilities fees), and prohibits profit-making in subsidized schools.[116]

Conclusion

In summary, existing private schools enjoy numerous advantages over government schools. They foster higher parental involvement and satisfaction, improve student performance, create more studious and welcoming environments, raise teacher morale and autonomy, limit bureaucracy, control costs, cater to the needs of religious families, and improve children's chances of graduating from high school and going on to college. They also integrate the races and socioeconomic classes at least as well as state schools. Despite all these advantages, they do not constitute a truly free and competitive market. Comprising only 10 percent of the K–12 schools in the U.S. (even less in Canada and England), and operated as nonprofits, they have not produced the kind of innovation seen in other sectors of the economy. Even the most successful nonprofit schools have generally failed to expand to new locations, preventing them from reaching out to a wider clientele.

Part III

What Works

9

What Makes Schools Work?

> *Looking back on the preceding chapters, one thing is eminently clear: All educational systems are not created equal. While some serve people's needs with admirable success, uniting families and communities, others marginalize parents, impose unpopular curricula, and cause animosity and social discord. Why? What makes some school systems so effective at doing the things we want them to do, while others languish between mediocrity and failure? The answer can be found in five interrelated traits that have characterized every consistently successful school system for the last two and a half thousand years: choice and financial responsibility for parents, and freedom, competition, and the profit motive for schools—in essence, a free market in education.*

Radical? Yes. Put succinctly, this prescription for educational excellence is the antithesis of virtually every state school system in existence today. Heresy? That too. Many people—good people—are simply not comfortable with the idea of profit-making schools, or the elimination of government oversight of education. These same people, however, generally share most if not all of the educational goals outlined in the first chapter of this book. And there's the rub: It just so happens that the way to reach those goals, to finally get what we want from our schools, is at odds with both our current approach to schooling and our most dearly held notions about how schools should work.

So, what to do? The first step is to recognize that just because an idea is radical or even heretical does not mean it should be rejected. The American Revolution was radical—treasonous in the eyes of the British monarchy—but was based on sound principles and led to the establishment of a great nation. The tossing out of Newtonian mechanics in favor of Einstein's relativistic model of the universe was equally revolutionary. In both cases, change came about because people recognized that it was necessary for the achievement of a desired end—liberty in the former case, scientific accuracy in the latter. As the first two sections of this chapter will show, the reintroduction of a free educational market is equally crucial to the achievement of educational excellence on a long-term, widespread basis.

But facts alone are not enough. Competition and profit making in education are such alien ideas to so many of us that they are likely to be resisted even though the weight of the evidence strongly favors them. This problem is tackled head-on in the third section, which explains why competition and the profit motive—along with the other three factors listed above—work as well as they do. Once the reasons behind their effectiveness are understood, they will no longer seem quite so heretical.

Finally, it is worth noting that while choice, responsibility, freedom, competition, and the profit motive have proven to be the best ways of organizing schooling, they do not constitute, by themselves, an ideal system. There are obvious areas, such as subsidizing the education of the poor, that need further attention—attention that is given in the concluding chapter of this book.

Parental Essentials

School Choice

The first element in successful school systems has always been the ability of parents to choose their children's schools and otherwise direct their education. Not only have parents generally made wise choices when given the chance, they have done a better job, by the measures described in Chapter 1, than the officials of government-run school systems.

Enjoying complete freedom over their children's instruction, classical Athenian parents ensured that they acquired the rudiments of reading, mathematics, athletics, and music, after which the typical student went on to become an apprentice to a trade. Keeping in mind that few jobs in early Athens required any sort of advanced schooling, this combination of academic and practical training was perfectly suited to the times, and not so very different from what parents seek today. But scholars were continually adding to and enriching the body of human knowledge, eventually outpacing the ability of traditional elementary schooling to keep up. When that happened it was Athenian families, not government officials or education experts, who demanded a secondary level of education. To meet that demand, wandering teachers flocked to the city from all over the Mediterranean. The results of this unregulated, customer-driven system were the most literate society in existence at the time, the most sophisticated economy, and an intellectual and artistic flowering that has put to shame almost every other place and period in history.

Educational choice was also the norm during the golden age of Islam, bringing with it similar heights of achievement. Left entirely free of regulation and compulsion, parents obtained for their children an education that made the Muslim empire perhaps the richest, most diverse culture of the middle ages. Its engineers, scholars, and poets became the primary channels through which both new and ancient learning flowed into Europe, stoking the fires of the Renaissance.

When reading and writing began to gain a foothold among the common people of Germany on the eve of the Reformation, it was due to the voluntary actions of parents who saw and understood the benefits of literacy. The same forces were responsible for the spread of technology, science, and the English language in the independent schools of eighteenth- and nineteenth-century Britain—disciplines that fueled Britain's economic growth.

Today, study after study has confirmed that parents who have the opportunity to choose their children's schools base their decisions on sound academic, discipline-related, and moral grounds. Their ability to choose wisely is demonstrated by the superior academic achievement and stronger community environment they and their children generally enjoy in independent schools. Parents who take the initiative and opt for independent schooling are more satisfied, on average, with virtually every aspect of their children's education than parents whose children are assigned to an institution by a public school bureaucracy.

Despite the protestations of some educators, there is no evidence that poor or otherwise disadvantaged parents make worse educational choices than government pedagogues. Poverty-stricken English families during the early 1800s frequently scrimped and saved in order to send their children to private schools, rather than settle for what they considered to be inferior subsidized schooling—a difficult but rational choice given that charity schools generally placed a greater emphasis on inculcating dogma than on imparting academic skills. The same trend is on the rise in modern America, where low-income inner-city families increasingly make an extra financial effort to pull their children out of a public school system they believe to be a failure, placing them instead in private schools. Pilar Gonzales, a working-class Milwaukee mother, lights "candles a lot of the time instead of using electricity," and cooks "one huge meal for the week to avoid using the stove very often," so that she can save enough money to send her children to private Catholic schools rather than to the city's free public schools.[1]

The available evidence overwhelmingly indicates that the decisions of these low-income families are based on essentially the same criteria that motivate their wealthier counterparts. As public and private school voucher programs have expanded, more and more poor families have been afforded the opportunity to direct their children's education, and the net result has been undeniably positive.

Educational systems in which schools are automatically assigned and curricula are set by "experts" have a far worse record of keeping pace with the needs of families. Ancient Spartan parents were entirely robbed of their educational responsibilities, and the content of their children's schooling was narrowly and unwaveringly focused on military training. Families in post-Reformation Europe could opt for Jesuit schooling, but by doing so relinquished all control over what was to be taught. As families' needs changed along with the world around them, Jesuit schools remained frozen in time, failing to modify their increasingly outdated curriculum. Eighteenth- and nineteenth-century English grammar schools suffered the same fate, refusing to add modern languages and sciences to their syllabi until the march of progress (and most of their prospective customers) had passed them by.

Parental choice has also proven to be the best way of dealing with the differences in values and priorities that have always existed among families. Rather than trying to stamp out this natural diversity as many government-run systems have done, educational choice has allowed it to flourish, permitting families of different creeds and views to coexist without conflict. The patrons of today's private Catholic schools, Montessori schools, and Muslim academies do not demonstrate on each other's doorsteps. They do not attempt to force their own textbooks or methods on each other. They generally do not precipitate any kind of animosity whatever. Furthermore, there is no evidence that graduates of these schools are any less tolerant or civic-minded than public school graduates.

The record of government schools is appalling by comparison. Since its inception, U.S. public schooling has been a battle zone, as left-wing and right-wing activists have sought to wrest control of the system and bend it to their will. Public schools have, in the past, practiced racial apartheid and forced sectarian religious practices on students, both with the approval of the courts. In the process, they have fomented anger and dissension among parents, trampled the rights of countless families, caused riots and book-burnings, and generally upset the communities they are meant to serve. Has this been an aberration? Has it only been the U.S.'s particular approach to government-run schooling that has spawned these problems? No and no. The U.S. educational system has done nothing more than inherit the woeful legacy of state schooling, just as so many other nations before it. In France, Protestant republicans and Catholic royalists treaded equally heavily on the prerogatives of families after the revolution, alternately foisting the Catholic Bible on students and tearing it from their hands. In the early sixteenth century, the German state schools championed by Luther and his fellow reformers trampled the people's growing interest in practical studies, imposing instead a classical Latin program. The list of similar abuses is long.

Taking away parents' control over their children's education also has subtler and more insidious effects. Bit by bit, public schools have taken over more and more of the educational decisions that were once left to parents. Parents are told when to send their children to school, where, and for how long; what they should be taught, by what means, and by whom. Modern public school parents are required to do little more toward their children's education than get them dressed in the morning and point them toward the school bus. They often feel powerless to affect the educational system, and know that their efforts to assert themselves are all too frequently rebuffed. The natural result of the negligible, passive educational role assigned to parents by public schooling is a growing apathy toward that schooling. Parental apathy is the number-one reason public school teachers give for leaving the profession, and one of the major complaints of those who stay on.

It was not always the case that schooling just happened to a child as soon as he reached a certain age. Prior to the advent of government-run educational systems and mandatory attendance laws, families were required to make a conscious decision as to whether, where, and for how long their children would be sent to school. In general, it was parents, not officials, who selected their children's schools, teachers, and even textbooks in colonial and early republican America, and these responsibilities compelled them to be more involved in education. This situation continues today among independent-school parents, who actively compare the schools available to them and take a greater interest in their children's education once they have chosen a school. Regardless of the background of these parents, educational participation is significantly higher among them than among those who rely on public school administrators to oversee their children's education. It is no coincidence that teachers in independent schools are much less likely to complain of parental apathy than their colleagues in government-run institutions.

Financial Responsibility

Educational choice and control do not grow on trees. They are not simply handed out whenever parents ask for them. The only way that parents have reliably been able to retain these essential freedoms has been by assuming responsibility for the cost of their children's education. Neither governments nor charitable organizations, however well-meaning, have typically allowed parents discretion over their children's education unless the parents themselves have been footing at least part of the bill.

People want to see their money spent in accordance with their values, so when charities gather funds to offer a subsidized education to low-income families, they generally prescribe the kind of instruction that the recipients of their philanthropy will receive. England's Anglican National Society schools did not ask nineteenth-century parents what sort of education they were looking for. They taught those things, and only those things, that were deemed appropriate by the Society's leaders and members. Endowed grammar schools instructed students not according to their wishes or the wishes of their families, but according to the curriculum that the schools' founders had stipulated when the endowments were made. This problem is at least mitigated when there are multiple institutions to choose from, and parents can pick the one whose agenda is the least objectionable.

There is no question, however, that the attenuated competition between non-fee-charging schools affords parents far less power and choice than does a vigorous for-profit educational market. Even under competitive conditions, most charitable and endowed institutions have agendas from which they cannot or will not deviate significantly. This contrasts sharply with fee-charging, particularly for-profit, enterprises, which must attract and retain customers in order to remain in business. While England's National Society schools and endowed grammar schools were slow to alter their curricula in response to public demand, fee-charging dame schools provided precisely the sort of lessons they were paid to provide—without an alternate source of funding, they had no alternative.

Government financing of education is even worse, since the citizens from whom taxes are collected are rarely of one mind on educational issues in the way that the members of charitable organizations might be. At best, the majority, but very often an organized minority, sets the educational agenda for the entire state. This means that the regulations applied to government schools frequently fail to satisfy many taxpayers, let alone the parents whose children are being educated.

Even private schools are not immune to the effects of outside financing. In the Netherlands, in an effort to ensure that taxpayers' money is not misspent, both state-run and "independent" schools accepting government subsidies must follow a long list of regulations, governing everything from teacher salary scales to the curriculum. Thus, while parents are nominally offered a choice of schools, their power to determine how their children are taught in state-subsidized institutions, whether public or private, is limited.

The extent to which parental control is curtailed is proportional to the scope of the subsidy. Many private nonprofit schools, which raise money from alumni and other donors, heed parents' demands in some areas, but defer to their donors in others. A donor, for instance, might decide to award a grant to his alma mater for the construction of an indoor pool, though the parents might prefer that the money be spent on a computer lab. Needless to say, the decision would rest entirely with the donor. Donors can also band together to demand changes in a school's staff or policies, in which case the school's board of directors would have to carefully weigh the potential loss of donations (if it should refuse the demand) against any repercussions from parents. The decision, in all likelihood, would be based on an assessment of who spoke for the largest portion of the school's budget: the donors, or the parents who might leave.

Some parents, of course, cannot afford to pay for all or even a part of their children's schooling. In this case, subsidization is a necessity, and the question becomes from whom and how much. The first question is the easier one to answer: Low-income parents are best served when they have a choice of funding sources to help them finance their children's education, since both governmental and private donors tend to place restrictions on parents' educational options. The more sources of educational funding that families have available to them, the more likely it is that they will be able to obtain the kind of schooling they want for their children.

The question of how much funding low-income parents should receive is more complex. Obviously, low-income parents can use all the money they can get, so a "free" education is in that sense ideal. As noted above, however, the more a child's education is subsidized by someone else, the less control the parents have over that education. With a loss of control comes the marginalization of the parents' role in their children's education, along with the possibility that their children will not be taught in accordance with their own ideals. Frustration and feelings of powerlessness are widespread among low-income public school parents, particularly in inner-city districts, for just this reason.

For parents who are truly destitute and have no option but to accept considerable or full subsidization of their children's education, there is still hope. In many cases, parents receiving subsidies of one kind or another have become enfranchised in their children's education by committing their time and effort to the running of their schools. Sometimes on a voluntary basis and sometimes as a requirement of their contract with the school, low-income parents have assumed the duties of fund-raisers, secretaries, maintenance workers, teachers' aides, and in some cases even teachers. This gives the parents an increased stake in their children's educational success and increases their level of control, while helping the school to reduce its costs and thereby stay in business. England's black voluntary schools are the clearest example of this practice, sometimes being staffed and run almost entirely by parents.

School Organization

Freedom

Parental choice is meaningless unless there are a variety of options from which to choose, and thus a necessary next feature of excellent school systems is the freedom of teachers and principals to vary their services according to their own judgment.

No one told the ancient Greek sophists what to teach and what not to teach.[2] Anyone was free to offer lessons in any field he chose. The variety of instructional options that flourished under this system, and the success that flowed from it, were unprecedented at the time and even compare favorably with modern school systems. Prior to the introduction of government schooling in the United States, prospective students could browse through newspaper advertisements for a wide range of lessons. No law stipulated what must or even should be taught, and yet a whole gamut of offerings from mathematics to foreign languages was available. Age restrictions were all but unheard of, so children and youths could study any subject which they were capable of understanding. For adults and teenagers who worked during the day, classes were available at night and on weekends.

Conversely, it has ever been a sign of ill-health among educational systems for the curriculum to be prescribed by outside authorities. English grammar schools, whose teachers were generally required by their contracts to follow a classical Latin course of studies, were observed to be in an advanced state of decay by the early 1800s, having lost touch with the needs of the public. Nineteenth-century French and Russian politicians gloated that all students of a given age studied precisely the same material at precisely the same time of day in their government schools, failing entirely to sense the irony of their satisfaction: namely, that the wide range of aptitudes commonly found in children of the same age made such indiscriminate homogenization of studies a hopelessly misguided rather than ideal state of affairs.

Allowing teachers to make their own choice of methods is also critical. Not forced to abide by the latest fads, independent-school educators have been able to preserve time-tested approaches to teaching while those in government schools have suffered at the mercy of bureaucrats and politicians. The dismal results of California's sidelining of phonics and structured direct teaching after 1987, during which phonics workbooks were sometimes confiscated from classrooms so that teachers would be forced to toe the party line, is just one example. The "New Math," and its more recent variant the "New New Math," are further examples of how the imposition of methods espoused by experts is not a reliable way to ensure effective teaching.

Innovation, too, requires that teachers have the freedom to choose their own methods and materials. To the extent that outside agencies and regulations discourage educators from trying out new ideas, they curtail the prospects for real improvement in instruction.

In order to thrive, schools must be free to control not only their curricula and methods but also their students. Fearful of lawsuits based on innumerable state and local education laws, public school teachers are all but prevented from disciplining their students, and from ejecting persistent troublemakers from their classrooms. Prior to the rise of public schooling, it was taken for granted that if a student was violent or constantly disruptive, and not interested in being in a given school, then that student should be allowed to leave voluntarily, or be expelled if he refused. The inability of today's public schools to exercise this kind of authority has reduced innumerable classrooms, in inner cities and elsewhere, to chaos, as one or a few belligerents have prevented all their fellow students from learning. Public school teachers today feel helpless in dealing with such situations given the limited range of options available to them.

Though private schools typically accept the vast majority of students who apply, and only rarely resort to suspensions or expulsions, they manage to maintain a much more studious climate not only in the classroom, but throughout their facilities. The fact that private schools have the power and willingness to expel students if necessary is such an effective deterrent that there is seldom a need to resort to actual expulsions. In the government system, students are well aware that they are placed there by law, and that public schools have little option but to retain them.

Does this mean that rebellious or otherwise difficult-to-educate students find themselves with no educational options when schools are free to refuse them? Not at all. A vast number of existing private schools are specifically geared toward serving these children, as a quick scan through any modern guide to private schools will attest. Though it is often claimed that the government system accepts every child, this is not in fact the case. Nationwide, U.S. public schools send more than one hundred thousand students to the private sector because they cannot cope with them themselves.[3] Many of the independent institutions enrolling these students are religiously affiliated or operated for profit, but government funds flow to them nonetheless. In practice, the same freedom that allows some private schools to reject such students allows others to cater to their special needs.[4]

The discussion thus far has concentrated on the need for teachers to have autonomy in their work, but the same requirement extends to principals. The two most important powers of the school principal are the ability to set the school's overall mission and to select and maintain a team of effective teachers. When principals enjoy these powers, as they do in independent schools, every aspect of teachers' attitudes is improved, as is the achievement of their students.[5] Principals whose hands are tied in these areas by bureaucratic red tape cannot effectively do their jobs, and both staff and students suffer as a result. Thanks to tenure laws and powerful unions, dismissing a public school teacher can take years and cost anywhere from one hundred thousand to just under a million dollars. Thus, rather than being fired, bad teachers are usually passed from school to school in the public system, perhaps to your child's school, until they reach retirement age. Good public school teachers, on the other hand, rarely receive the inspiration and direction that they need to excel, and excellent ones are the first to leave the profession. Salaries that have no relation to classroom performance serve only to aggravate the staffing problems of public schools.

Competition

Choice and responsibility for parents, and freedom for schools, make educational excellence a possibility, but by no means provide a guarantee. In the past, educational leaders who have sought the freedom to teach what and how they wished have sometimes disregarded the needs and preferences of parents, pursuing instead their own interests and ideas. Think, for instance, of progressive educator George Counts, who counseled his colleagues to take control of American schooling and use it to bring about a social revolution, or of the many evangelical Christian groups that have sought to outlaw the teaching of evolution in public schools. The government-run school systems of modern democracies have certainly been an improvement over those of monarchies and empires, but they have only abated the tyranny, not eliminated it.

Throughout history, these abuses of professional freedom on the part of educators have been most reliably avoided through competition. When school managers know that they have to compete for the opportunity to serve each and every one of their students, they are much more likely to deliver the services for which families ask. While monopolistic government-run school systems have produced an endless parade of pedagogical dictators, competition forces teachers and principals to offer the kinds of services people want.

But tyranny is not the only problem brought on by the absence of competition. Without the need to win-over its customers with superior services and results, public schooling has frequently adopted defective teaching methods and inferior materials. Independent schools have been more consistent (though by no means flawless) in choosing proven pedagogical approaches over passing fads, and in encouraging their students to take more (and more challenging) academic courses.

Another advantage conferred by competition is cost-effectiveness. Private schools manage to do a better job of educating children while spending roughly half as much per student as public schools. The public school monopoly, unconstrained by the threat of competition, has allowed its costs to rise out of all proportion with the quality of education it provides. In fact, the consensus among researchers in the field of education economics is that public schools spend taxpayer funds so poorly that there is no relationship, on average, between how much money they spend and how much students learn.

Competition also forces schools to do the best they can with each and every student. Schools working in a competitive market cannot and do not classify children as "learning disabled" simply because they have fallen behind the rest of their class. The explosive growth in the number of public school students dubiously diagnosed with such ailments as "Specific Learning Disabilities" has no parallel among independent schools. As explained in Chapter 6, there is considerable evidence that normal children are frequently labeled "learning disabled" by the government system, and that the rate of misdiagnosis has increased alarmingly in recent years. Furthermore, the teaching methods used to "treat" these putatively disabled learners are generally ineffective. "Learning-disabled" children who learn little in their special education classes have been shown to be capable of considerable advancement when taught using conventional direct instruction techniques, even when the teachers have been inexperienced college students. Students who have worn the "learning disabled" label throughout most of their twelve years of public schooling and emerged as illiterates have been taught to read in less than six months by independent tutors using the same systematic phonics techniques that work so well with non-learning-disabled students. In short, the need to compete has forced independent schools to take considerable responsibility for the performance of their students, while public schools have been free to point at external causes, safe in the knowledge that most parents have a great financial incentive to send their children to the public schools no matter how bad their services.

Even something as simple as proper building maintenance is commonly dispensed with when schools are not forced to compete to attract students. Inner-city government schools, though they spend considerably more than their comparatively clean and well-maintained private counterparts, are frequently allowed to fall into ruin, with flooding toilets, defective heating systems, and crumbling masonry. Because of mandatory attendance laws and the government monopoly on tax-supported schooling, low-income families are routinely forced to send their children into schools that no one with a choice would accept. Conditions in many modern public schools, schools that annually spend seven, eight, or even nine thousand dollars per pupil, are less conducive to learning than the rustic and far less expensive private venture schools of the early nineteenth century. It is no wonder that public school teachers in the inner city are twice as likely as their fellow citizens to send their own children to tuition-charging independent schools.

Finally, the public school monopoly leaves parents almost entirely in the dark on the subject of how well their children are performing relative to students in other schools, states, and countries. Parents are regularly lulled into a false sense of complacency by their children's deceptively high grades, while students' deficient scores on standardized tests are kept hidden from them by a system that has no incentive to admit to its own failures. The high-stakes tests themselves even give an inflated impression of achievement due to corruption in the testing process. This contrasts sharply with the highly competitive situation in the Japanese supplemental school industry and in classical Athens, where the sophists constantly blasted the flaws in each other's teachings, allowing current and prospective clients to make informed decisions as to the real value of their services.

The Profit Motive

The four requirements so far described, choice and responsibility for parents, and freedom and competition for schools, are generally able to prevent the worst abuses of educational systems. What they cannot do, by themselves, is bring about excellence or revolutionary advances on a broad scale. It is entirely possible for schools operating under these conditions to simply perpetuate their own existence without expanding or improving their services or developing creative new technologies or methods. Where there is no push to go one step further, to make an extra effort or take a calculated risk, stagnation is the natural result. The spark that can jump-start educational entrepreneurs out of this natural rut is the chance to earn a profit from their efforts.

The case of twentieth-century private nonprofit schools is both the most recent and most compelling argument for reintroducing the profit motive into schooling. Though it has done a better job than government schooling, the independent nonprofit education sector has performed very poorly when compared to industries dominated by for-profit enterprise. Consider, for example, the computer industry. Fifty years ago, the computer was an utterly new invention with only the most limited capabilities, taking up the space of a large room, and costing so much as to be affordable only to governments and international corporations. Today it is an incredibly useful, versatile machine which can fit on a desktop or even in a hand, and which is financially within reach of most families. For more than a decade, the power of computers has doubled every two years, while their prices have been cut in half with the same frequency (for an effective quadrupling of processing power per dollar). Successful computer hardware and software companies have been among the fastest-growing businesses in history, reinvesting a considerable portion of their profits to finance enormous expansions in production capacity and to continually add new products and services to their list of offerings. Conversely, high-tech companies whose products have not appealed to consumers have quickly failed or been forced to improve.

Education cannot be expected to progress with the speed of an industry based entirely on technology, but the paucity of growth and dynamism exhibited by public and private nonprofit schools is unusual in any field. The best and most successful among these schools have generally failed to expand their facilities, serving roughly the same number of students in the same locations year after year. Few can boast of educational innovations that have been empirically tied to improvements in student achievement. Instead, they have either been pedagogically stagnant or have been swept to and fro by ill-conceived educational fads. Poor and mediocre schools, those that would have been forced to improve or shut down in a competitive for-profit marketplace, have continued to limp along unchanged, to the great misfortune of their students.

Not only has the absence of the profit motive caused pedagogical progress to lag well behind that of other human endeavors, it has also caused schools to fail to make full use of new technologies that other industries have developed. Despite the tremendous potential for personal computers to revolutionize teaching, the great majority of modern classrooms do not look substantially different from those of three or four generations ago. Even when computers are introduced into schools, they are almost always treated as an appendix to existing instructional programs, rather than as a basis for new approaches to teaching.

Computers could, for example, greatly enhance education by tailoring lessons to the level of each individual pupil, rather than teaching every student in a class the same material at the same time. This would help to prevent the all too common failure of public schools to teach students to read. Once a student is "socially promoted" past the grades in which reading is typically taught, the system has few provisions for redressing the problem. Illiterate and barely literate children are consistently given textbooks and assigned materials well beyond their capacity. Instructional computer programs could administer diagnostic tests to determine students' present level of accomplishment in reading, and continue from there.

At the managerial level, the absence of profits has dissuaded entrepreneurs from turning their attention to schooling. When limited amounts of competition and choice have been introduced into schooling without also adding the possibility for profit making, as is the case with most public charter schools in the United States (see Chapter 10), entrepreneurs have shown little interest. But running a school efficiently and responsively, balancing research-and-development costs against the need to keep tuition down, keeping organized financial records, etc., are activities upon which entrepreneurs thrive. To most educators, they are alien. As a result, many of the most visible problems confronting charter schools have to do with management and financial decisions.

In those states with the most regulation-bound charter-school laws, where the difficulties of founding and operating charter schools are many, few if any charter schools are actually created. The red tape and managerial hoops that prospective school managers must endure discourage educators from even trying to open a school, and the lack of any chance of making a profit turns off businesspeople who might otherwise have taken a crack at it.

In addition to curtailing educational innovation among public and nonprofit private schools, the absence of the profit motive has discouraged efforts to deliver existing educational services more cheaply and efficiently. While competition has helped to keep costs under control in the private education sector, the lack of potential profits has dulled the quest for efficiency even there. Within the public schools the situation can only be described as pathological, as costs have gone higher and higher while student achievement has either stagnated or fallen off.

The ability of good schools to make a profit is also crucial in attracting and keeping top-quality teachers in the profession. While some public school teachers do not earn the salaries paid to them, others deserve far more. These women and men, the truly brilliant educators who can elicit from their students the greatest achievements, who understand their subjects thoroughly and can explain how those subjects relate to other branches of human knowledge, are the first to leave public schooling. Intelligent as they are, they know when their talents are going unnoticed and unrewarded, and sooner or later they become fed up and seek employment where their skills will be recognized.

The profit motive encourages schools to keep these teachers happy and well-paid. Teachers in the for-profit sector, from Isocrates in the fourth century B.C. to modern Japanese *juku* instructors, have earned comfortable incomes from their work when they have been allowed to charge a fee appropriate to the level of demand for their services. Thanks to modern technology, such high-quality teachers can now reach thousands of students, thus keeping their per-student fees low while making far more money than they could within the public school system. So long as most of the world's teachers and educational dollars are employed in government-run institutions, this option is likely to be open only to a few.

Why?

In a mystery novel, this would be the point where all the evidence has been laid on the table and the culprit has been caught, but most of the readers are still saying, "Why?" Why *did* the butler do it? It is not enough to know that the preponderance of evidence points toward choice, responsibility, freedom, competition, and the profit motive as the best ways to organize schooling. Until it all makes sense, until we understand the reasons why these factors work so much better than the alternatives, few people will be willing to bring about such a major change in the way their children are educated. An explanation of those reasons is provided in the following pages.

Parental Choice and Responsibility

The need for parental choice is one of the easiest to understand: if educational goals and priorities differ from family to family—and they do—no system that presents a single worldview or curriculum can possibly satisfy them all. The most notorious example is religion. When schools are not allowed to offer religious instruction, and parents want it, there is a conflict. When schools adopt a particular religious view to the exclusion of all others, parents of other faiths and nonreligious parents rightly object, and there is still conflict. Similar disputes arise over everything from teaching methods to school discipline policies. It is only by allowing each family to choose the kind of schooling it deems most appropriate that these clashes can be and are avoided.

The need for parents to take control of their children's education and to assume, as much as possible, the financial responsibility for it, can also be explained fairly succinctly: responsibilities breed responsibility, whereas things that take care of themselves are taken for granted. Parents have a virtually endless list of tasks to accomplish and fires to put out, so when the opportunity to unload some of their responsibilities comes along, it is almost impossible to resist. The siren song of government schooling says to parents: Don't worry, we're experts, we've got education covered, you go deal with something else. Worse yet, if parents somehow break the spell and do try to take responsibility for their children's education, they usually find themselves thwarted by the laws, regulations, and bureaucracy that maintain public schooling's status quo. After a few failed attempts at making a difference, the vast majority become frustrated and sink back into apathy.

This double-whammy can be avoided only by forcing parents to make the important educational decisions themselves, rather than allowing them to delegate those responsibilities to a system that has proven itself thoroughly unsound. Independent-school parents are more actively involved in their children's schooling because they are obliged to be. When there is no default public school to fall back on, parents have no choice but to compare the independent-school options open to them, and the choices they make are consistently better than those foisted upon them by putative experts.

While most public school teachers today quite reasonably lament the lack of involvement shown by parents, we must never forget that many prominent champions of government-run schooling have been trying to marginalize the role of parents since the days of ancient Sparta. Even in nineteenth- and twentieth-century America, public school superintendents, professors of education, and bureaucrats in state departments of education have repeatedly sought to eliminate local control of schools, to limit parental influence over the curriculum, and to essentially dislodge parents from their traditional role as primary educators. They have succeeded, and until their handiwork is undone, parents will continue to be disenfranchised from their own children's education.

Fortunately, there is a time-tested method for parents to break the cycle of apathy induced by public schooling: taking back the financial reins of education. Shouldering the cost of tuition has enabled parents to regain control of their children's education for two reasons. First, as Pliny the Younger observed almost two thousand years ago, "if the appointment of teachers is left entirely to the parents," they will be "conscientious about making a wise choice through their obligation to contribute to the cost. People who may be careless about another person's money are sure to be careful about their own." Not only does Pliny's observation hold as true today as it did in Roman times, it applies to virtually every aspect of schooling. The second reason is that the educator-ideologues who have actively sought to minimize parental control over education could not have succeeded without a guaranteed source of funding in the form of tax dollars. If asked directly, few parents would have voluntarily paid someone to wrest control of their children's education. This fact was brilliantly illustrated in 1886 by Californian Zach Montgomery, using the following analogy:

> Now, suppose . . . two model men and neighbors should some day come to your house and address you thus: . . . We are informed that you are the [parent] of a bright, beautiful, and intelligent little girl, now about seven years old—just the proper age to begin her education. We feel quite anxious that she should be properly educated, and, to tell you the plain truth, we are afraid that if we leave the matter entirely with you her education will be neglected. Now here is what we propose to do. We propose that we—your two best friends—together with yourself, shall all enter into a written contract, binding ourselves during your daughter's minority to contribute annually a certain percentage upon the assessed value of our property, which shall constitute a fund for the education of this, your little girl. But it must, at the same time, and in the same contract, be stipulated that it shall at all times be in the power of a majority of us three to select the teachers and the school books for your child. Should you, against the wishes and without the consent of a majority of us, take your child away and send her to some other school, you must agree to forfeit—should we choose to exact it—not exceeding twenty dollars for the first offense, and not less than twenty dollars for each subsequent repetition thereof. You must also agree and bind yourself in advance not to withhold your assessment, even should you withdraw your child from the school of our selection, because we should in that event need the money for the education of other children.[6]

This, it must be remembered, is a much more appealing agreement than the one parents enjoy with their local public school systems, in which they hold not a third of the responsibility for their children's education, but only an infinitesimal fraction.

Market Ability

The last three requirements for educational excellence—freedom, competition, and the profit motive for schools—can best be understood as a group, since it is only when taken together that they bring about the checks and balances of a free educational market. The power of such a market rests on a single, simple principle: its ability to unite the interests of families and schools. By establishing a set of incentives that make it advantageous for educators to ascertain and serve the needs of families, free educational markets reliably bring about the most effective and efficient schools. Not only do government-run systems fail to achieve this end, they actually set the interests of teachers against those of parents, precipitating the same host of problems in every nation where they are introduced.

There is no question that the great majority of educators, whether they work in the public or the private sector, are motivated by a desire to serve the needs of students and their families. But alongside this altruistic interest are numerous others: the desire to be in control, to maximize income, to enjoy leisure time, to limit tiring extra work, to avoid professional embarrassment, and so on. While government schooling throws these other interests into conflict with the central aim of serving families, free markets actually bring them together. The best way to demonstrate this idea is to examine the interests and incentives at play in a host of different schooling situations, in market versus government-run contexts.

Control

Take the issue of control. Everyone aspires to be in control of his or her own work. Being told how to do your job by an outsider can be a frustrating, even demeaning experience, one that most people would prefer to avoid. Teachers and principals are no exceptions to this rule; when parents complain to them about their policies or actions, they, like the rest of us, are naturally predisposed to want to carry on doing things as they have always done them. Parents, on the other hand, want their comments taken seriously and acted upon immediately. The interests of the two parties are thus often opposed to one another.

In public schooling, that is where the matter rests. Some teachers overcome the urge to ignore the complaints, particularly if a parent's case is ironclad, but many do not. The teacher has no compelling interest to heed the parent's wishes, and thus can disregard them at his or her own discretion.

Competitive markets are different. Parents who are unhappy with a private school's services can withdraw their children from it at any time. Doing so not only causes the school an immediate loss of income but also potentially damages its reputation, tainting its long-term business prospects. Since salaries and jobs in for-profit schooling are directly tied to a school's success, teachers and principals have a powerful vested interest in seeing that parents are kept happy. If they succeed, they thrive. If they fail, their careers and livelihoods are in jeopardy. The goals of educators and the goals of parents are thus brought together and harmonized.

Spending

A similar relationship holds with regard to school spending. In a competitive market, a school cannot maximize its profits by indefinitely hiking tuition fees. That would only drive its patrons to less expensive competitors, hurting rather than helping its bottom line. It is thus in the best interests of the school to offer educational services at least as good as those of its competitors while charging a slightly lower fee, or to make sure that it can justify a higher fee by demonstrating superior results. This not only ensures that tuition is kept under control, but also provides a stimulus for schools to become as efficient as possible. When educators in a for-profit school manage to maintain the quality of their services while spending less per pupil, they get to keep some or all of the difference. When they can improve quality significantly with only a modest increase in costs, their profits increase.

Government schooling provides no such positive incentives. In fact, it does the opposite. In the public sector, a manager's prestige and salary tend to be associated with the size of the budget under his or her control—the bigger, the better. Since public school bureaucrats who save money are more likely to see their budgets cut than increased, thrift is penalized rather than rewarded. Conversely, any additions to the budget, however irrelevant to educational achievement or parental satisfaction, are feathers in the education bureaucrat's cap, improving his or her standing within the system. Efficiency is discouraged, waste encouraged. It is no accident that public schooling costs considerably more than private schooling on average, or that inner-city school districts can spend eight or nine thousand dollars a year per pupil and still fail to supply their bathrooms with toilet paper or stall doors.

To make matters worse, the endless upward spiral in costs that this misguided incentive structure has precipitated only makes it more likely, not less, that parents will be forced to send their children to public schools. The regular increases in taxes that are needed to pay for government schooling's gluttony continually chip away at families' discretionary income, pushing the independent-school option further and further out of reach.

At the root of all spending-related differences between free-market and government-run schools is one simple fact: in the private sector, the money educators earn or forfeit is their own; in the public sector, it is not. Just as parents are more careful about the kind of schooling provided to their children when they themselves are footing the bill, so too are teachers and principals more attentive in spending that money when they stand personally to gain or lose by their decisions. In competitive markets, then, educators have a clear financial stake in the success of their schools, and that success is measured by the number and loyalty of the patrons who are willing to pay for their services.

Good and bad teachers

When it comes to taking on extra work and putting in extra effort, most new teachers are quite generous. Irrespective of the sector in which they work, recent college graduates entering the profession tend to be filled with idealism and energy. In for-profit schools, this behavior is generally encouraged. Teachers capable of meeting or exceeding parents' expectations are an asset to the school's bottom line, especially when they are able to pass along their skills and enthusiasm to their colleagues. Private school managers therefore have an incentive to compensate excellent performance with increased salaries and leadership opportunities—an incentive that is magnified by the knowledge that the most talented teachers are those who can most easily find work elsewhere if they become dissatisfied with their current school.

Given their fixed salary scales and rigid career ladders, public schools cannot and do not reward excellence. Mediocre and even incompetent teachers are treated no differently by government schools than those who come to class thoroughly prepared and who bring out the best in their students. The superior performance that can readily be acknowledged and compensated for in profit-making schools is ignored by the public system. Initially, this difference tends to have only a slight effect on teachers' actions, because idealism runs so high in youthful new recruits to the profession, but over the years the difference takes its toll. Low morale, a comparatively small problem in the private sector, is rampant in government-run schools because many public-sector teachers eventually come to feel that striving for excellence is literally a thankless job. This also helps to explain why the brightest and most motivated teachers are the first to leave public schooling for other lines of work.

The flip side of this coin is the bad teacher, who was either never suited to the profession, or became burned-out after years of service. Bad teachers cannot long survive in for-profit schools. Once parents begin asking to have their children moved to different classes and threaten to find another school if they are not accommodated, principals in the for-profit sector have only three choices: spur improvement in the teacher's performance, fire him, or risk losing business and jeopardizing the institution's future. Since the teacher's livelihood is also at stake, he too has a powerful incentive to either shape up or find work to which he is more suited.

The same situation plays itself out very differently in public schools. In the worst case, which also happens to be the typical case, parents have little or no choice of public schools. If they are not happy with their assigned school they cannot easily move their children to an alternative one. Occasionally, a limited amount of school choice does exist within the public sector, such as in open-enrollment districts or where charter schools are available. But this is almost irrelevant given the elaborate and inordinately expensive process required to fire poorly performing public school teachers. Except in the rarest and most flagrant cases of educational malpractice, teachers can rest assured that their jobs are protected by tenure laws and the legal might of their unions. The principal, too, is generally safe from serious repercussions even if he or she chooses to do nothing with regard to the bad teacher. In this context, one of two things generally happens: the bad teacher joins the "parade of the lemons" and is marched over to a different public school where parents are unaware of his or her short-comings—or absolutely nothing.

Professional growth

In competitive markets, the teachers who are in greatest demand command the highest salaries and enjoy the most job security. Teachers thus have incentives to improve their skills in those areas valued by their clients. Monopolistic government systems provide no such incentives. Teachers are paid chiefly on the basis of years worked rather than their ability to meet the needs of parents and students. Since no one really believes that this salary-scale approach spurs improvements in performance, a number of modifications have been cobbled onto it over the years. These efforts have amounted to lashing feathers to a brick in the hope of making it fly.

The most notable attempt to raise the skills of public school teachers has been the practice of bumping them up a rung or two on the income ladder when they complete a training course. School districts are typically responsible for deciding which courses are acceptable for this purpose, but in practice, virtually any class offered by a college of education can qualify. A delightful example of how far awry this practice can go is the whale-watching "course" offered for credit to public school teachers by a major west-coast university in the early 1990s. Teachers who paid a small fee for the whale-watching expedition and several hours of class time could expect to see "continuing-education" dividends on payday. To quote Dave Barry, "I am not making this up!"

Such flagrant abuses of in-service training programs are comparatively rare. Roughly two thirds of the classes taken by public school teachers can be reasonably construed as having some bearing on the subjects they are paid to teach.[7] But the simple fact that a course is related to a teacher's subject area does not mean that it will make him or her a better, more knowledgeable instructor, and therein lies the main problem with the system: teachers are paid for taking courses whether or not their teaching improves as a result. To make matters worse, teachers realize this fact, and are thus put in precisely the same predicament as their own students, who are frequently criticized for being more concerned about achieving a passing grade than learning the subject matter. Because their salary hikes are bestowed simply for passing the course, whether or not they master the material and subsequently apply it, there is no incentive for teachers to make the effort to do so.

The fact that public school teacher training programs do not work terribly well is well known and much talked about within the education research community. Every now and again a few new feathers are strapped to the brick and hopes are raised that it will take flight at any moment, but bricks do not fly, and an effective professional development program cannot be created within the incentive structure of government schooling.

Information

Parents need information. In order to choose the best school for their children, they need to know the pros and cons of each institution they are considering. Amassing this information can be difficult and time-consuming, so for practical reasons it is best if some third party has an incentive to digest all the relevant facts and present them to parents as clearly, concisely, and honestly as possible. This is precisely what is achieved through vigorous competition.

Each school in a competitive market is clearly interested in promoting its own strong points. In the late 1980s and early 1990s, after an element of competition was introduced into English education via grant-maintained schools, principals began printing up brochures and holding open-houses for parents on a regular basis. Needless to say, there is little impetus for a given school to tell parents of its own weaknesses, but there is every reason for its competitors to do just that. The wandering sophists of classical Athens had good reason to point out the faults in each other's teachings: any student who left the entourage of one sophist was a prospective customer for the rest. In Japan, bookstores are rife with guides to help students find the *juku* best suited to their needs. The advertising campaigns of U.S. long-distance telephone carriers also illustrate how businesses seek to explain the benefits of their offerings and identify the flaws in those of their competitors.

The same incentive that leads competitors to highlight each other's faults also discourages fraud and false advertising. Schools cannot easily pack up and move to a new location, so reputation is crucial. If one school begins peddling misinformation to prospective customers, it is in the interest of its competitors to identify and make public this deception as quickly as possible. The system is by no means perfect, but it provides checks and balances that do not exist in government-run school systems.

While public school educators of high moral fiber may be inclined to expose any corruption, deception, or pedagogical malpractice they come across, they are hardly encouraged to do so. Whistle-blowing is dangerous within any organization, frequently sparking the animosity of colleagues, and since all public schools in a state are part of the same monopoly, any criticism by one educator against another is whistle-blowing. If anything, the heavily unionized character of the profession makes the matter worse, since union lawyers can be counted upon to defend the job and reputation of virtually every teacher accused of incompetence or wrongdoing. By revealing the misconduct of a colleague, public school teachers thus ensure that they will be thrown into conflict with both the system in which they work and the union that represents them.

The impact of these disincentives to coming forward is enormous. It is almost unheard of for inept or criminal public school educators to be exposed by their fellow employees. Apart from journalists, who occasionally take an interest in the workings of their public school districts, there is no one with the time, expertise, and incentive to ferret out such cases. The result is that they fester for years, often decades, before being discovered, and even then are rarely remedied in any permanent way. The enormous amount of pedagogical malpractice that has been discovered in those few districts that *have* been investigated in any depth reveals the tip of what can only be an enormous iceberg: principals giving teachers copies of standardized tests in advance of the official test date so that they can prepare their students; mysteriously high rates of erasure and correction on students' test forms at certain schools; fraudulent overtime charges; graft; cronyism; and the list goes on.

Even schools which are free of criminal activity suffer from the absence of any systemic incentive for schools to inform parents of the bad news regarding the quality of their services along with the good. So long as parents can be happy seeing a nice distribution of grades on their children's report cards, there is no reason to incur their wrath by revealing that scores on standardized tests are considerably lower. At the state level, where standardized test scores are often made public, they are reported in such a way as to fool parents and citizens into thinking that every state is above average. Contrary to the old adage, the truth will not "out" unless it is to someone's advantage to "out" it. Free markets ensure that advantage; school monopolies do not.

Pedagogy

There are many different ways to structure classrooms and present material. In choosing between one set of practices and another, teachers have many competing interests. Most would obviously want a method that they believe to be effective, but also one that they enjoy, that keeps the children happy and engaged, that does not require too much preparation or grading time, and that agrees with their personal philosophy of education. So how do the free-market and public school environments affect these incentives?

In the case of schools competing for profit, the first incentive is slightly altered. It is not sufficient for teachers or principals to *feel* that a method is effective, they have to be able to prove it to parents. Assume, for instance, that the teachers of Holistic Elementary School believe children learn to read best when they are simply exposed to interesting books in a rich, unstructured environment, while the staff of a competing school, call it Aristotle Primary, begins with intensive organized instruction in phonics. If both of these schools serve the same neighborhoods, and one of them, say Aristotle Primary, consistently outperforms the other (for example, its students consistently earn higher scores on standardized tests, and its graduates go on to more demanding and more respected high schools), which will parents choose?

To prevent a mass exodus of its students, Holistic would almost certainly have to begin using phonics or some similarly effective means of teaching reading. Attempts to cover up or forge its results would have little chance of success, and would carry with them disastrous consequences. Genuinely successful schools such as Aristotle Primary would be eager to pay for the independent auditing and publication of their scores, knowing them to be a strong selling point, so if Holistic chose not to publish its test results, or to refuse to have them audited, many prospective customers would reject it, suspecting it had something to hide.

The above example assumes that since the students at both schools were drawn from the same neighborhoods, they would generally have similar socioeconomic backgrounds, making this factor irrelevant for the purpose of the comparison. It is nonetheless possible that a third school, say Rocky Balboa Elementary, could successfully carve a niche for itself even though its students earned lower test scores. If the principal and teachers of Rocky Balboa could demonstrate that their methods helped slow learners catch up to their peers, parents whose children had been having trouble reading might be persuaded to give the school a try. The fact that the school's overall average test scores were lower would be less important to parents if they were convinced that their children's progress would be faster at Rocky Balboa than at competing schools.

While teachers in a competitive market might want to adopt whichever methods they like the most on a personal level or whichever methods require the least amount of work, they can only do so when those methods do not conflict with the need to demonstrate concrete positive results. Furthermore, they are forced by competition to ascertain which methods actually do yield the best results, because if a competitor finds out first, they stand to lose customers for as long as they stick with their less effective techniques.

Another constraint that affects private-enterprise schools but is much less important to government-run schools is cost-effectiveness. There is no point in a private school adopting the best possible approach to teaching reading if it costs so much that no one can afford it. Because there are limits on how much parents are willing and able to spend on education, private schools must try to achieve an optimal balance between successful teaching practices and cost control. One-on-one tutoring, though often very effective, is inordinately expensive, and thus its use has to be limited. Some educational computer software, by contrast, can help children improve their skills in a range of areas at a considerably lower cost. Finding ways to give parents the biggest bang for their educational buck is in the interest of both parents and private schools.

The selection of pedagogical methods in public schools is quite different. Depending on the district and subject involved, the power to select methods may rest with the teacher himself, or with a committee at the district or state level. At whichever level decisions are made, the need to show concrete results is much weaker than in competitive markets. Most public school systems do not release any kind of standardized test results at the individual student level or even at the school level, allowing only district-wide or statewide averages to be published. As George Gallup wrote several decades ago: "Since [parents and the general public] have little or no basis for judging the quality of education in their local schools, pressures are obviously absent for improving the quality."[8]

To the extent that parents have some external means of assessment, such as comparing their own children's progress to that of friends' or relatives' children in other schools, they can and do criticize their public schools when they find them wanting. As explained above, however, parental criticism can be and is much more easily disregarded in government-run than in private-enterprise schools. In the absence of a compelling need to provide children with the kind and quality of education parents seek, the other incentives at work in the teaching profession take precedence. Whenever a method comes along that educators believe to be effective, and that coincides with their views of how children should be taught, there is a good chance that they will adopt it without first consulting the research available on the subject.

In many cases, the decision regarding what practices will be used to teach a particular subject are made not by the classroom teachers themselves, but by committees of public school bureaucrats. Throughout history, advocates of government-run schooling have promised that this reliance on "expert" opinion would ensure that only the best pedagogical methods were put into use in the schools. They have, of course, been wrong, and it is not difficult to see why: the incentives affecting the judgment of public school experts, and the conditions in which they work, are even worse than those influencing teachers.

Textbook selection committees, discussed in Chapter 5, are a case in point. Committee members are paid nothing or next to nothing for their services and generally have full-time jobs outside of choosing textbooks, so they have little incentive to exert themselves when evaluating textbooks, and have a strong incentive to direct their attention elsewhere. If they make poor decisions, they suffer virtually no personal consequences: their careers are not jeopardized; their salaries are not put at risk. If they repeatedly make excellent decisions, they enjoy no special compensation. Even if they had the time to survey the scholarly research on the subject and consult with a large body of parents and reputable teachers, they would have no vested interest in taking on such an arduous task.

Curriculum committees are no better. The criteria used for selecting curricula are typically drawn up by public school administrators who have nothing personally at stake in their decisions. They rarely bother to field-test their criteria under controlled conditions, because they have nothing to gain by conducting such elaborate assessments. Conversely, they have little to lose if their criteria are ill-informed, biased, and entirely unsupported by empirical evidence. Despite the fact that California's Department of Instruction did a terrible disservice to the state's children by phasing out systematic phonics in the late eighties, there were no significant repercussions for those responsible. Parents could not simply toss out the staff of the Department of Instruction in the way that they could have left a poorly performing school in a free educational market. They were stuck with the public school administrators' decision for roughly seven years; and contrary to the protestations of those administrators, there was a great mass of evidence already assembled *before* they made their decision which could have, if heeded, averted disaster.

A further problem with the pedagogical choices of public school administrators and textbook selection committee members is that they have no incentive to take the cost of their decisions into account. If presented with two comparable policies or materials, they have no compelling interest to use cost as the basis for choosing between them. None of the money they spend comes out of their own pockets, and none of the money they save goes into them, as happens in for-profit schooling. They are free, therefore, to choose based on whatever other criteria seem most important to them. They might fall back on entirely arbitrary criteria, or be swayed by free lunches and gifts offered by the marketers of one or the other option under consideration. In the case of the California textbook adoption committee on which physicist Richard Feynman served during the 1980s, the members were entirely unaware that they were wasting millions of dollars, because they had no incentive to discover that fact. It was, after all, the taxpayers' money, not their own.

One of the most glaring examples of inefficiency in the public schools has been their continuously shrinking class sizes and declining teacher workloads. As noted in Chapter 5, little or nothing is gained by reducing class sizes to twenty or even fifteen students, and yet elementary school classes have shrunk by 20 percent over the last three and a half decades, and the average number of students per day taught by high-school teachers has been cut by a third over the same period. This practice has added tens of thousands of dollars to the annual cost of each class, and hundreds of thousands to each school. Many pedagogically effective programs could have been implemented with these funds, but were not because it is clearly in the interests of educators to reduce their own workloads, while the incentives for them to keep costs under control and to spend money wisely are much less compelling.

Innovation and expansion

Developing and testing new pedagogical techniques and technologies is a risky, expensive business. If an innovation proves to be ineffective or too costly, a private school stands to lose either customers or money, or both. Expanding a school's services is an equally dangerous proposition, entailing as it does the purchase of new facilities and equipment and the hiring of additional employees. If demand were to fall suddenly, the school's owners would be left with a flood of bills and a trickle of income. The only way to entice educational entrepreneurs to take on these risks is to provide them with an incentive that makes the effort worthwhile. Nonprofit schools have no such incentive, and the result has been an almost total lack of innovation and expansion. In for-profit schools, however, any means of attracting more patrons or lowering costs without injuring quality can pay off financially for the school's staff, and thus the challenges of achieving those ends are more than offset by the prospective advantages. Japan's nationwide *juku* chains are a case in point.

While most modern educators insist that schooling is somehow fundamentally different from other forms of human enterprise, the evidence presented in the course of this book has shown otherwise. Teachers and school administrators respond to the same incentives as everyone else, and when a risk is not associated with a commensurate or greater gain, it is rejected. Suppressing or eliminating market risks and incentives, as public schools do, is therefore deeply problematic. Since no one is held responsible for any downside associated with the introduction of defective methods, public schools have been beset by an endless succession of pointless, ineffectual, and even harmful pedagogical fads. The only way to ensure that genuinely effective innovations are encouraged, while defective ones are discouraged, is for schools to be organized along competitive and for-profit lines.

The supermarket effect

There is no question that parents in free educational markets do not all take the same amount of care in choosing their children's schools. The typical family finds out the essential facts about each institution, perhaps visits one or two of them, and then makes its decision. There are also families who spend a great deal more or a great deal less time and effort researching their options. So the question arises: What about the parents who are neglectful of their responsibilities? Why don't their children do considerably worse in educational markets than in government monopoly systems? The answer is the "supermarket effect."

Not every shopper carefully compares grocery prices, and very few do so for every item they buy every time they go to the supermarket. Despite this fact, prices are held in check, and tend to be comparable from one grocery store to another. The reason is that *enough* people are price-conscious *enough* of the time for it to be in the store managers' interests to set reasonable prices. Over time, a supermarket that charges considerably higher prices than its competitors loses enough business due to the departure of savvy customers that it is forced to lower prices or to shut its doors. Thanks to those few price-conscious individuals, then, all of the store's customers benefit from the lower prices the store is forced to adopt. As a result, it is possible for someone to go into an unfamiliar grocery store, buy all the items on his or her list, and be fairly confident that the price charged will be reasonable.

This same effect holds in other free-market enterprises, including education. When parents have educational choice and schools must compete to attract their business, enough parents are cautious in making their selection for it to be in the interest of school managers to offer a quality service at a fair price. Those parents who are not careful are, essentially, free riders, benefiting from the informed decisions of their neighbors without having to expend any great effort themselves.

Community Concerns

When it comes to serving the needs of individual families, the case for the superiority of educational markets over government monopolies is a strong one. Even some diehard advocates of public schooling are willing to admit it. What prevents them from throwing their support behind choice is not the fear that parents will fail to get the kinds of schools they want, but that they will succeed. A great diversity of schools would spring up under a system of unhindered educational freedom, and supporters of government schooling worry that such diversity would lead to social discord and balkanization. While these concerns stem from the best intentions, it is difficult not to be shocked by their bald and bitter irony: not only do free educational markets have an excellent record at securing social harmony, but the government-run systems espoused by their critics have been the chief cause of school conflict throughout history.

It is not the patrons of private Atheist Academies and Evangelical Elementaries who tear into one another on the subject of evolution versus creation. It is not the private Afrocentric school, or Orthodox Jewish school, or Classical Western Culture school that sows dissension among the families in its neighborhood. It was not the private Catholic primary school of nineteenth-century

America that drove its community into a frenzy by foisting its version of the Bible on all the local children. It was, however, the state schools of post-revolutionary France that set citizen against citizen by favoring republican or royalist views according to the whim of despots; and it is the modern U.S. public school system that factionalizes the population on issues of curriculum and religion, eating away at the fabric of the nation year after year like the relentless action of waves eroding what could be a peaceful shore.

Not only is there an inexhaustible well of examples to prove the socially divisive effects of public schooling, but the reason behind them is also perfectly clear: when a country, state, or community has only one official provider of education, its people do battle with one another for the right to determine the substance of that education. By allowing parents to seek out the most suitable education for their children, and by refraining from identifying any one set of educational practices as "government-approved," free markets give families no reason to come to blows over each other's choices. The fact that their choices may be different, in some cases very different, does not lead to the sort of antagonism anticipated by critics. The wide range of views taught by ancient sophists, though stimulating public debate, did not breed resentment or hostility among the Athenian people. Quite to the contrary, the Athenians were renowned for their civic-mindedness and strong community spirit. Prior to the introduction of government-run schooling, education was rarely if ever a cause of civil strife in the United States; and after government schools began to cover the landscape, bringing with them the problems described above, independent schools continued to coexist peacefully with one another, despite their differences in philosophy.

Accepting the Exceptions

The preceding sections have attempted to explain why schools operating in free educational markets have done a better job of serving people's needs than those run by government officials. At the same time, they shed light on the reason why there are exceptions to that overall rule. The incentives that help to unite the goals of educators and parents in competitive markets, and those that throw them into conflict in government systems, are just that: incentives. While people generally follow the path of least resistance and heed these incentives, they are not forced to do so. It is entirely possible for private school teachers or principals to be rude and dismissive of parents, and to grossly raise tuition without commensurately improving the quality of their services. On the flip side of the coin, public school educators could consistently disregard their own interests, reject pay raises so as to keep expenditures down, and spend weeks and months of their own time pouring over educational research in an effort to learn the most effective techniques for teaching their subjects—all in the knowledge that their sacrifices will be neither acknowledged nor compensated in any way, and that their future career prospects will be little different from those of their less dedicated and competent colleagues.

These, of course, are extremes, but they serve to illustrate two points: no system involving human beings is ever perfect, educational markets being no exception to that rule; and while government-run schools can periodically approach excellence, they can do so only by relying on the Herculean labors of rare and exceptional individuals—a narrow and fragile base on which to rest the education of our children.

10

Can Government Schooling Be Fixed?

Countless attempts have been made over the years to fix government school systems. They have met with little success. The same problems encountered from the first century to the nineteenth century are still with us at the end of the twentieth. Is the present crop of proposed reforms likely to fare any better?

To answer that question, this chapter looks at four popular proposals: government scholarships (vouchers), charter schools, private management of public schools, and government-mandated curriculum standards. Each is evaluated in light of the evidence of earlier chapters, and on how well it would foster the conditions for educational excellence distilled in Chapter 9. The reforms are discussed in order from most promising to least promising. This ordering makes it possible to avoid repeating all the drawbacks which apply to more than one proposal. For example, many of the flaws of voucher programs also apply to charter schooling, but these are touched upon only briefly if at all in the charter school section.

Government Scholarships: Trick or Treat?

Governments could require a minimum level of schooling financed by giving parents vouchers redeemable for a specified maximum sum per child per year if spent on "approved" educational services. Parents would then be free to spend this sum

323

and any additional sum they themselves provided on purchasing educational services from an "approved" institution of their own choice. The educational services
could be rendered by private enterprises operated for profit, or by non-profit institutions.[1]

So wrote Milton Friedman in his 1962 classic *Capitalism and Freedom*. The
idea that governments could pay for education without actually running schools
has an impressive pedigree, from the Nobel prize winning Friedman back to
John Stuart Mill,[2] Thomas Paine,[3] and even Adam Smith.[4] After more than two
hundred years, it is finally being taken seriously.

Interest in publicly financed scholarship or "voucher" programs has risen
considerably since the 1980s, and two pilot programs are already in operation
in Milwaukee and Cleveland. These programs differ from the ideals of voucher
advocates in two important ways: size and eligibility. The Milwaukee and
Cleveland plans limit participation to a maximum of a few thousand children
whose parents must have incomes close to or below the poverty line. Most of
the voucher initiatives that have been put before voters (and rejected) in several U.S. states[5] have aimed to serve all families regardless of income level.

In order for the voucher agenda to be taken seriously, two questions must be
answered: Would universal government scholarships do a significantly better job
of meeting the public's educational needs? And would such a program have un-
wanted side-effects? The following sections attempt to answer these questions.

Where They're Strong, Where They Go Wrong

The move from government-run schooling to government-funded scholarships would undeniably bring modern educational systems several steps closer
to the model of excellence described in the previous chapter. Freedom, competition, and the profit motive for schools, as well as parental choice, would all be
enjoyed to a greater degree than they are today, though to a lesser extent than in
entirely private markets (see below). Of the five characteristics shared by successful school systems throughout history, only one would be almost completely
excluded under government scholarships: parental financial responsibility. On
the whole, then, we should expect the widespread adoption of government scholarships to improve the educational conditions and outcomes valued by families.

Given the limited scope of existing voucher programs, and the resulting circumscription of both competition and choice, they cannot be expected to produce much of an impact. In Milwaukee's program, just three schools enroll 80
percent of participating students.[6] Three schools do not a market make. Taking
that into account, their results are promising. As reported in Chapter 8, families participating in the Milwaukee voucher program are much more satisfied

with every aspect of their children's schools than they had been in the government-run system. According to both of the research teams which compared participants in the program with applicants who had been randomly rejected, students did better in mathematics as a result of their participation. One of the two teams found improvements in reading as well. Results from the private voucher program in Indianapolis, Indiana, and preliminary results from the Cleveland public program, also indicate some academic improvement.

Parents are more satisfied. Students are doing somewhat better academically. So what's the problem? Actually, there are five areas in which government scholarships either already have or eventually will run into trouble: fraud, over-regulation, church/state entanglement, escalating costs, and lack of parental financial responsibility. All of these are discussed below.

Before getting into the details, though, one general observation is in order. At present, voucher programs are tiny, new, radical, and carefully scrutinized. The parents who seek them out are likely to be the most motivated, and every school that participates is closely watched by critics and advocates alike. If government scholarships became the norm, this acute level of interest and excitement would inevitably wane. In the long term, vouchers would be taken for granted just as public schools are currently taken for granted by a great many people. Oversight of the programs, now a critical concern of policymakers and policy analysts around the nation, would settle into a "business as usual" mode. In other words, some problems are likely to manifest themselves later rather than sooner, once vouchers are no longer in the spotlight.

The Risk of Fraud and Mismanagement

Public spending demands public oversight. When voters decide to tax themselves to subsidize education, they usually want some assurance that the money is being spent wisely and efficiently. Part of the reason public school bond levies are so frequently rejected is that citizens are not convinced that the government education bureaucracy is doing a competent job with the money it already receives. People do not want to throw good money after bad. Government-funded vouchers will be no exception to this rule, and therein lies a terrible dilemma: unregulated vouchers are liable to suffer from fraud and waste, but regulations attempting to curtail such abuses will almost certainly undermine the essential virtues of the scholarship concept—not to mention failing to accomplish their intended aims.

As already mentioned, every facet of the two existing pilot voucher programs has been probed and prodded by countless observers. It is particularly worrisome, therefore, that two of the seventeen Milwaukee schools accepting scholarship students were shut down in 1996 due to apparent fraud. *Education Week*

staff writer Cheryl Gamble reported in February of that year that Exito Education Center and the Milwaukee Preparatory School "had misrepresented their
enrollment figures."[7]

The possibility of inflating enrollment figures in order to pilfer government
coffers is inherent in any funding mechanism that separates payment from consumption. Public bureaucrats do not have first-hand knowledge of every student and every school to which they must allocate tax money, and are thus subject both to errors and to deliberate attempts to mislead them, as the Milwaukee
cases attest. Parents, on the other hand, typically know how many children they
have, and are not easily duped into paying tuition for fictitious additional children. It is only the removal from parents of the responsibility of paying for their
children's education that makes this sort of fraud feasible.

Naturally, regulatory efforts might be made to reduce the likelihood of enrollment fraud. Schools receiving government scholarships might be required
to provide frequent and comprehensive documentation of their student rolls,
much as public schools are generally required to do. For the sake of argument,
let us assume that the same heavy burden of paperwork is forced on every private school that wishes to participate in a voucher program—a provision that
would almost certainly require most private schools to hire an additional employee. Surely that would offer considerable protection from enrollment fraud?
Alas, no. The biggest case of enrollment fraud of which I am aware was per-
petrated by the heavily regulated public schools of Washington, D.C. A 1995
investigation of that district found that it enrolled about 67,000 students, but
that it reported 81,000, a difference of 20 percent![8] This should come as no surprise in a government school bureaucracy that does not know how many employees it has, who they are, or where they work.[9] In April 1998, a Los Angeles public school administrator pleaded guilty to inventing enough phantom
students to bilk taxpayers of $700,000,[10] a scheme made possible by the fact
that districts receive funding from the state on a per-pupil basis.

There is nothing special about public schooling in this regard. The government-run Social Security program, which also severs the tie between payment
and consumption, is estimated to lose $23,000,000,000 (yes, $23 billion) of taxpayer money annually, due to a combination of fraud and mismanagement.[11]

The problem of fraud has not been overlooked by government scholarship
proponents. One suggested solution is to provide parents with education vouchers in the form of debit cards (or computerized "smart-cards"), which would
contain information about the card-holders and the value of the scholarships
their children were to receive. Unfortunately, similar attempts to curtail welfare fraud have already run into trouble.

In south Houston, police opened up their own convenience store to see if
debit-card-using welfare recipients would ask for illegal cash payments, rather
than purchasing groceries as intended by the Texas Department of Human Ser-

vices and the U.S. Department of Agriculture (which runs the federal food-stamp program). Within a few days they had their first such request, and ten weeks into the sting operation the number of people allegedly wanting in on the deal had grown to 225. According to the Associated Press, the fraudulent transactions proceeded as follows: "officers would agree to debit a welfare recipient's account for $100, give the person $70 and keep the remaining $30 for themselves."[12] Variations on this scheme could just as easily be orchestrated around government scholarship debit cards.

In addition to the illicit cash-for-benefits transactions just described, government scholarship programs (whether or not they used debit cards or smart-cards) could also be defrauded if program administrators issued cards in false names. Whenever the consumer is not also the payer, such abuse is difficult to avoid.

The Regulation Ratchet

One of the chief advantages of government scholarship programs over government-run schooling is that parents would have greater freedom to obtain the kind of education they value for their children, and schools would have the autonomy to teach what and how they thought best. But these freedoms would inevitably lead to friction, as some voucher-redeeming schools elected to teach things objectionable to a portion, perhaps even a majority, of the people within their communities. Imagine, for example, tax-funded schools expounding the virtues of laissez-faire capitalism, atheism, communism, witchcraft, alien visitation, astrology, racial supremacy, etc. While few U.S. citizens would wish to impose legal restraints on the freedom to profess such ideas, a considerable number might well object to paying for their dissemination. Opponents of state scholarships have put this fact to effective use in their efforts to turn public opinion against voucher initiatives. During the 1992 voucher campaign in California, the state's largest teachers' union drew attention to a self-proclaimed coven of witches that apparently planned to open a voucher-redeeming school if the law was enacted.[13]

The only way for a state-run scholarship program to assure voters that their taxes would not go to support teaching which they found objectionable would be to regulate the schools allowed to redeem the scholarships. Controls would have to be placed on the curricula of participating schools. As new cases were reported, new restrictions would likely be passed, adding to the regulatory burden imposed on private scholarship schools. While many people might be indifferent or even somewhat opposed to a particular regulation, they would be unlikely to make the effort necessary to stop a well-organized pro-regulation campaign. One only has to look at the enormous body of law to which public schools are presently subjected to see that the regulatory process is like a ratchet, working in only one direction: it is easy to add new regulations, but difficult to remove old ones, causing the total regulatory burden to inexorably increase over time. Think, too, about how "de-regulation" makes the headlines whenever it is proposed for one or another industry, whereas new regulations are added with such unrelenting frequency that only a tiny fraction ever receive media attention.

Regulatory bloat is only natural. When people choose to spend money on something, they like to know they are getting what they pay for. Doing that is comparatively straightforward when the money is their own. But government spending makes the relationship between buyer and seller an indirect one, since individuals can no longer monitor their own investments. To satisfy our desire for accountability, we thus impose regulations which, we hope, will do the job for us. But not everyone has the same educational preferences, as was made evident in Chapter 1. As a result, a panoply of regulations tends to arise, as countless different interest groups attempt to restrict the kinds of activities they find objectionable. In the end, the freedom of schools to innovate, and to tailor their services to particular audiences, is impeded.

As noted in Chapter 8, government-subsidized "private" schools in the Netherlands are forced to follow state curriculum guidelines, to follow government-determined teacher salary scales, to operate as nonprofit enterprises, and to abide by numerous other restrictions. The effect is to make the Dutch educational market only slightly more diverse than a typical government-run school system, and to remove some of the key factors, such as the profit motive, necessary to stimulate substantial innovation. The same trend can be observed throughout history. From imperial Rome, to the late medieval Muslim empire, to nineteenth-century England and America, government funding of children's education has invariably led to sweeping government controls over schools. Each additional dollar of state spending has resulted in another twist of the regulatory ratchet, moving schools further and further away from the kind of free and dynamic market that has shown itself to be most effective in meeting the needs of parents and societies at large. There is a real possibility that the widespread adoption of government-funded scholarships would eventually lead to the adoption of a government curriculum in all schools, not simply public ones, bringing on all the negative side-effects discussed later in this chapter.

This, perhaps, is the most dangerous aspect of government scholarships, for if the state assumes control over private schools, there will no longer be even the slightest extant reminder of how education could be. Already, most of the nonprofit schools that dominate the private education sector are a pale shadow of the flexible, customer-driven businesses that thrive in other industries. Adding an extra regulatory burden can only further choke off the potential for excellence in education.

Church/State Entanglement

> Congress shall make no law respecting an establishment of religion, or prohibit-
> ing the free exercise thereof. . . .
>
> —First Amendment, U.S. Constitution

Religious instruction in government schools has rightfully been deemed to violate the First Amendment. Numerous organizations, such as the American Civil Liberties Union (ACLU) and various state and national teachers' unions, have claimed that government scholarship programs involving religious schools are equally unconstitutional. Their arguments are based on Supreme Court precedents such as *Committee for Public Education & Religious Liberty v. Nyquist* (1973),[14] in which the majority ruled that a private school tuition reimbursement program for low-income parents was incompatible with the establishment clause of the First Amendment because most of the private schools that would benefit from the grants were sectarian.

Voucher supporters counter that more recent and favorable Supreme Court cases have supplanted *Nyquist*. In *Mueller v. Allen* (1983),[15] for example, the Court was asked to decide the constitutionality of a state law providing a tax deduction to parents to defray the costs of tuition, transportation, and textbooks for their children. Even though the prime beneficiaries of this deduction were families with children in parochial schools, the majority opinion was that

> [t]he historic purposes of the [establishment] clause simply do not encompass the
> sort of attenuated financial benefit, ultimately controlled by the private choices of
> individual parents, that eventually flows to parochial schools from the neutrally
> available tax benefit at issue in this case.[16]

The First Amendment, Chief Justice Rehnquist wrote in *Mueller,* was designed to prevent "that kind and degree of government involvement in religious life that, as history teaches us, is apt to lead to strife and frequently strain a political system to the breaking point." Tax deductions in support of unrestrained parental choice in education did not constitute such a harmful involvement in the view of the Court.

Even if government scholarship programs do not constitute an establishment of religion, however, another legal hurdle may stand in their way. Consider the arguments over the proposed expansion of Milwaukee's voucher program to include religious schools. In a brief presented to the Supreme Court of Wisconsin,[17] the ACLU drew attention to the second clause of Article I, section 18, of the Wisconsin constitution, which states that no person "shall . . . be compelled to attend, erect or support any place of worship, or to maintain any ministry, without consent. . . ." After deadlocking on the case, the Wisconsin Supreme Court sent it back to the circuit court in which it had originally been tried. Siding with the ACLU, circuit court judge Paul Higginbotham wrote in January 1997:

> Perhaps the most offensive part of the [law] is [that] it compels Wisconsin citizens of varying religious faiths to support schools with their tax dollars that proselytize students and attempt to inculcate them with beliefs contrary to their own.[18]

Higginbotham's ruling was subsequently appealed and, seven months later, was upheld by a Wisconsin appellate court.[19] This ruling was itself appealed, bringing the case before the state's Supreme Court for a second time. In a June 1998 decision seen as pivotal by both advocates and opponents of vouchers, the Supreme Court of Wisconsin reversed the lower courts, finding that state-funded vouchers redeemable at both religious and secular schools violated neither the U.S. Constitution nor the provision of the state constitution cited above. The U.S. Supreme Court has declined to hear an appeal of this case.

Interestingly, the Wisconsin Supreme Court did not directly consider the ACLU's assertion that the expanded Milwaukee voucher program coerced taxpayers into supporting religious institutions. Instead, the court interpreted the coerced-support clause to apply to the students, not the taxpayers. The expanded voucher program, Justice Steinmetz wrote, "does not require a single student to attend class at a sectarian private school. . . . Nor does the [program] force [student] participation in religious activities."[20] Based on these facts, the court ruled that the program did not violate the compelled-support clause.

Justice Steinmetz explained the court's decision not to consider the compelled-support clause from the point of view of taxpayers by stating that it had already considered essentially the same issue in dealing with the "benefits" clause of the Wisconsin constitution. The benefits clause of Article I, section 18, states that no money shall "be drawn from the treasury for the benefit of religious societies, or religious or theological seminaries." In rendering a decision on this clause, the court relied most heavily on its previous ruling in *Atwood v. Johnson*,[21] which stated:

> The contention that financial benefit accrues to religious schools from [this program] is equally untenable. Only actual increased cost to such schools occasioned by the attendance of beneficiaries is to be reimbursed. They are not enriched by the service they render. Mere reimbursement is not aid.[22]

This interpretation is supportable only if the term "benefit" is strictly defined to mean financial gain. If, on the other hand, benefit were construed to include helping religious schools to spread their message to a wider audience of students, then the expanded Milwaukee voucher program might indeed violate the benefits clause. Furthermore, the court's view on the redundancy of the benefits clause and the compelled-support clause is debatable. Such debates may be of more than academic interest, for at least twenty other states have similar constitutional clauses, known as Blaine amendments (a fuller discussion of this can be found in the Conclusion).

However federal and state constitutions are read on this issue, the importance of religious freedom in American life is paramount. Had government compulsion played as large a role in American religion as it has in American schooling, the nation may well have suffered perennial "Church Wars" just as it has suffered perennial "School Wars." If tax-funded vouchers redeemable at religious schools were widely adopted, it is at least possible that religious tensions in America would rise. Many people argue that this would not be the case, given the broad public acceptance of existing government subsidies to religious daycare providers and religious universities. Perhaps they are right. It seems prudent, however, to at least explore the possibility of variations on the voucher idea that leave the choice of subsidizing religious schools up to individual taxpayers (this, too, is discussed in the Conclusion).

Spending Growth: It's Raining Lobbyists!

U.S. public school spending (recall Chapter 6, Figure 9) has undergone a steep and unremitting rise for at least the past seventy years. Why? By now it should be obvious that the lack of competition, the profit motive, and parental choice naturally leads to inefficiency. But that simply means that public schools are likely to misspend the tax money they receive, not that they will necessarily receive larger and larger sums of money. Spending in government schools has risen because there have been well-organized interest groups who have had a vested interest in raising spending. Teachers' unions in particular have been very effective in looking after their members, ensuring a fairly consistent rise in teachers' salaries over the years. Taxpayers, on the other hand, are not well organized, and do not have enough information to know whether or not increased spending will really produce better educational results. On the whole, most people assume (mistakenly) that what they are told by self-interested lobbyists is true: that public schools are always underfunded and that more money will inevitably lead to improved student performance.

This phenomenon, once again, is the result of third-party payment—of having someone other than the consumer footing the bill. Lobbyists and the people they represent are far fewer in number than the total taxpaying population. That means that if they squeeze just a little more money out of every taxpayer, they can distribute a lot more money among themselves. In other words, their incentive to raise taxes by half a percent is much greater than the average citizen's incentive to prevent taxes from going up a half a percent. This imbalance has resulted, in the case of government schooling, in a dramatic rise in spending over the years, and the same imbalance would hold under a government scholarship scheme. In fact, it could be even worse. All the private schools that currently do not receive government subsidies would add their own lobbyists to the existing roll of public school lobbyists. Though private schools currently charge about half as much in tuition as public schools spend, that would be likely to change if they manage to plug into the lucrative tax system in the way that public schools have.

There is no effective remedy to this problem. If all education is paid for from the public purse, taxpayers should expect their purses to become lighter and lighter over time, as public and private schools discover new ways to spend their money — ways that may not have much to do with improved results.

No Parental Financial Responsibility

What we pay for, we pay attention to. What we get for free, we feel free to ignore. To the extent that government scholarships defray the cost of tuition, they dispense with parental financial responsibility. As argued in the previous chapter, the requirement to contribute to the cost of their children's education is one of the greatest incentives for parents to take the time and care necessary to make wise decisions. Without this incentive, it is easier for parents to be distracted by other important concerns, and thus to abdicate their educational obligations to their children.

Historically, state subsidization has had just as powerful (and deleterious) an effect on parental involvement in education as it has on the expansion of school regulations. In the nineteenth century, parents in the United States were, of necessity, deeply involved in almost every aspect of their children's schooling. In towns, they were obliged to choose from among the available schools, and in rural areas, where only one school could be supported, they were jointly responsible for the selection of teachers. Teachers who failed to satisfy a majority of families were commonly dismissed by them. In many cases, parents went so far as to select and purchase their own textbooks. Whether schools were entirely private or quasi-public institutions, parents were expected to pay for their own children's tuition, except in cases of dire poverty. This gave them a tremendous impetus to take their responsibilities seriously.

Parents today do not generally know how much is being spent on their children's education in government schools, and thus have no basis for determining whether or not they are getting their money's worth. Government scholarships would certainly give parents more options than they currently have, but they would not provide the compelling incentive of personal financial responsibility. Writing a monthly check for several hundred dollars does a lot to focus a person's attention on the quality and value of the services he or she is receiving.

Perhaps the most important argument for parental financial responsibility is the tired (but still accurate) old adage "He who pays the piper calls the tune." If parents were footing most or all of the bills for their children's education, the problems described in preceding sections would be far less pernicious. With little or no state spending, the need for state regulation would be largely obviated, the church/state imbroglio would be circumvented, lobbyists would have no one to lobby, and fraud would be more easily controlled and detected.

Refundable Tax Credits: Vouchers by Any Other Name . . .

The idea of subsidizing education through credits on existing tax forms, rather than by a special-purpose school voucher, has been around for a long time. Though these two mechanisms are frequently treated interchangeably, tax-credit advocates argue that their proposal offers distinct advantages. With vouchers, the government is clearly doling out cash for the express purpose of allowing parents to send their children to private (possibly religious) schools. Tax credits, on the other hand, would appear to marginalize the state's role in education, simply allowing parents to keep more of the money they earn, and thus indirectly making it easier for them to afford tuition payments if they choose to send their children to a nongovernment school. This distinction, to the extent that it holds true, means that tax credits categorically avoid church/state entanglement and most other problems having to do with government education subsidies. After all, the money is never even collected in taxes in the first place. The parents earn it, and they obviously have the right to spend it as they see fit.

But all tax credits are not created equal. While "nonrefundable" credits behave very much as the previous paragraph describes, there are also "refundable" tax credits which have the additional feature of paying out public funds to citizens who pay little or no taxes. Working families at or near the poverty line, and those on welfare, can claim a refundable tax credit just as easily as middle-class families. So, while the assessed tax of a middle-income household might be greater than the value of the credit, in which case the credit simply reduces the family's tax bill, the assessed tax of a low-income household could well be less than the value of the credit, meaning that such a household would receive a subsidy for the difference. Families who pay no taxes whatsoever would receive a government subsidy equivalent to the full value of the refundable credit. In other words, refundable tax credits—the kind most often championed by supporters of school choice—are extremely similar to vouchers or scholarships in the case of low-income families, and therefore share most of their flaws. (Nonrefundable tax credits, which are superior in some ways to vouchers, are discussed more fully in the Conclusion.)

Voucher Misconceptions

The problems just described are serious, and must be taken into account when the merits and demerits of government scholarships are added up. There are, however, a great many other objections to vouchers that simply do not stand up to scrutiny. What follows is a representative sample of the most common myths. To forestall accusations that these arguments are straw men, they are quoted directly from the myth makers themselves.

Myth #1: Scholarships will leave many children behind

> Vouchers would help the few at the expense of the many. . . . The ablest, easiest to educate students would use vouchers to attend private schools. More difficult and expensive to educate children would be left in public schools with even fewer advocates and resources.
> —National Education Association (NEA) Center
> for the Advancement of Public Education[23]

> Far from creating the positive qualities of healthy "competition," vouchers would build an uneven playing field and institutionalize a two-tier system of haves and have-nots. Harming public schools to improve private schools hurts individuals, as well as our society as a whole.
> —Minnesota Education Association (an NEA affiliate)[24]

An enormous body of evidence contradicts these claims. Far from being an intellectual elite, the students who currently leave public schools to participate in government scholarship programs are, as a whole, academically *below* average.[25] The allegation that students with special, and expensive, educational needs would be rejected by the private sector is mystifying, given the fact that public schools *already* send many of their most difficult-to-educate children to private schools. The *Washington Post* reports that D.C. public schools spend "$21 million annually to send 1,079 special education students to private schools because the District fails to provide services in its own schools."[26] There is no reason why vouchers would have to affect such arrangements, since the voucher amounts for children with special needs could be varied in size, or supplemented, using funding formulas similar to those currently used by state schools.

It is the bitterest irony that government-school advocates imagine vouchers would create a system of haves and have-nots, for while their idealistic rhetoric has always touted the ability of public schools to bring about educational equality, the reality has been tragically different. The great disparity between the public education provided to poor inner-city students and to wealthier suburban ones is absolutely stunning, and is denied by no one acquainted with the evidence. But the evidence also shows that this gap in educational quality would be *reduced* by voucher programs, not exacerbated as critics charge. In their book *Catholic Schools and the Common Good,* Anthony Bryk, Valerie Lee, and Peter Holland observed that the correlation between socioeconomic status and achievement is less significant in private Catholic schools than in public schools.[27] That is to say, the difference between the achievement of low-income and high-income students is smaller in Catholic schools than it is in government institutions. The level of economic integration is also greater in private schools. As James Coleman reported in the late 1980s, poor and higher-income students intermingle more in private-sector than in public-sector schools.[28]

Still further support for the ability of private schools to narrow the gap between rich and poor, black and white, is to be gleaned from existing scholarship programs. As mentioned earlier in this chapter, three out of four leading research teams investigating the academic effects of voucher programs have found that participation raises the scores of low-income students in one or more subject areas, helping to close the gap between their scores and the national averages.

But even when the above evidence is acknowledged and accepted, many people still wonder: What about "non-choosers," those families left behind in deteriorating public schools? This question, though well-meaning, is based upon a failure to grasp the essence of school choice programs, and upon an inability to imagine a world without state-run schools. In any cogently designed scholarship program, *there would be no "non-choosers."* All parents would be required to actively select their children's schools. While critics will claim that many (poor) parents are incapable of handling this responsibility, the facts presented in Chapters 3 and 8 confute them. Crushingly poor and minimally educated parents in nineteenth-century England could and did compare educational alternatives and make competent choices for their children, leading to a continuous rise in literacy from one generation to the next. Around the United States, low-income families regularly make sound school choices, sometimes with the help of private or public vouchers, but much more often thanks entirely to their own hard work and initiative. Yes, a considerable number of parents are unfamiliar with the relative merits of various pedagogical techniques, or with the requirements of the modern job market, but these parents can benefit tremendously from the supermarket effect described in Chapter 9, by which the choices of a discerning minority of consumers help to increase the quality of services received by all. What twenty-five hundred years of experience have shown is that the decisions made by families in the educational marketplace are consistently superior to the policies of state school systems. It is true that government scholarship programs will not entirely eliminate educational inequality, but they will considerably reduce the gap that exists in most government systems.

The issue of racial segregation and inequality has also been raised in conjunction with vouchers, but this has already been dealt with at some length in Chapter 8.

Myth #2: Schools, not parents, would do the choosing

> While vouchers give parents the illusion of school choice, the real choice remains with admissions officers of selective private schools.
> —National Education Association[29]

> Vouchers fail to offer the 'choice' that proponents claim. The 'choice' remains with the private schools that will continue to pick and choose the students they wish to accept and reject. Public schools open their doors to all students.
> —Minnesota Education Association[30]

In the real world, this is not what happens. Japan's free market in private supplemental schooling offers innumerable choices to the educational consumer. Rather than turning away large numbers of students, most successful schools simply expand to meet growing demand. It is true that the increased competition and choice a voucher system would bring about would still not guarantee that every family received precisely the educational experience it sought, but this is true of any system of school governance. In fact, it is much *more* true of public schools than it would be of voucher systems. In most U.S. public school districts, students are automatically assigned to schools by bureaucrats entirely ignorant of their needs and preferences. They have *no* choice. At best, parents can select from among a set of government-run schools that are all forced to abide by a comprehensive and restrictive education code which homogenizes their pedagogical offerings, teaching staffs, and extracurricular services.

There is no question, given the modern and historical evidence presented in this book, that competing markets of private schools consistently provide families with more options than government-run school systems. Nevertheless, it is worth repeating that nonprofit schools are much more likely than for-profit schools to have long waiting lists, and are apt to reject a larger percentage of their applicants. The absence of the profit motive, as noted in Chapter 8, robs nonprofits of the incentive to take on risky expansion projects. Still, even nonprofit Catholic private schools accept the vast majority of their applicants. While Bob Chase, head of the NEA, told the *Minneapolis Star* that "religious schools currently reject two of every three children who apply,"[31] the National Catholic Education Association reports that the typical Catholic school accepts 88 percent of all students who apply, and that only a third of Catholic schools have waiting lists.[32]

Myth #3: Government scholarships would raise taxes

> Voucher plans are costly. . . . Taxpayers would pay for the vouchers of the 4.8 million children already attending private schools, many of them from affluent homes, as well as for children newly enrolling in private schools. Low-cost vouchers of $1,000 for elementary and $1,500 for secondary students (which would not cover tuition at either private or religious schools) would cost $5.2 billion a year in additional tax spending just to provide vouchers for the students already in private schools. That's an enormous tax subsidy for upper-income families, paid for by every taxpayer.
>
> —National Education Association[33]

First, a few facts: On average, U.S. private schools cost roughly half of what public schools cost.[34] Even though private school spending is often a combination of tuition and funds raised through donations or foundations, the average private school still spends only a fraction of what the average public school spends. Some public school districts spend more per pupil than tuition at the nation's most elite private prep schools. New Jersey's Union County Regional School System, for instance, spent $16,504 per student in 1995. Tuition at the prestigious Exeter Academy in New Hampshire was $14,000 in the same year.[35] At present, far more wealthy families send their children to public than to private schools.[36]

Taken together, these facts indicate that: (1) Giving every school-aged child in the country, including the 11 percent already enrolled in private schools, vouchers for the full average tuition charged by private schools would save over one hundred billion dollars a year nationwide.[37] It would even be possible to offer vouchers worth more than the current average private school tuition and still spend only a fraction of the money consumed by the nation's public schools. (2) Upper-income families benefit considerably more from the largesse of taxpayers within the current public school system than they would under a system that only gave vouchers for the average tuition charged by private schools, because public schools in wealthy neighborhoods spend far more than most private schools. Moreover, if government scholarships continue to be means-tested, as they are in Milwaukee and Cleveland, then upper-income families will not be eligible (though they would save money at tax-time, given that a state-funded voucher system would be cheaper to maintain than state-funded public schools).

Myth #4: Vouchers would accelerate the rise in education spending

> A voucher system is likely to get more expensive over time as private schools
> raise tuition in response to government subsidies.
> —Connecticut Education Association (an NEA affiliate)[38]

True enough, but this is a conspicuous case of the pot calling the kettle black. Public schools have raised their expenditures by a factor of fourteen over the last seventy-odd years (even after adjusting for inflation), without demonstrating any substantial improvements in student achievement. In many respects, such as student safety and the teaching of reading, they have gotten noticeably worse.

Unbridled tuition hikes over and above the value of the vouchers are not likely to be a serious long-term problem. Private schools would still be forced to compete with one another to provide the best possible education for a given price, and in order to induce parents to supplement the voucher's value with their own money, they would have to demonstrate some kind of improvement in the outcomes parents value—a litmus test to which public schools are not subjected.

The real question is: Would the lobbying efforts of private, scholarship-redeeming schools be more effective in raising the value of the voucher than public-sector teachers' unions and other special-interest groups have been in lobbying for higher public education spending? This is a difficult question, and there is no obvious answer. To claim that vouchers would necessarily lead to an even more rampant growth in spending than public schools, without providing any supporting evidence, is specious.

Myth #5: Vouchers would undermine the goals of public schooling

> The fact is that America established public education to level the playing field, to
> provide equality of the most basic opportunity, the opportunity to learn. Every ef-
> fort to improve our schools must remain faithful to that commitment. At a time
> when America is fractured by race, religion, and income, we can't afford to re-
> place the one remaining unifying institution in the country with a system of pri-
> vate schools pursuing private agendas at taxpayer expense.
> —National Education Association[39]

Unlike the statement quoted above, this book has taken great care to distinguish between the educational ends sought by the public, and the means used to achieve those ends. What it has shown is that state-run schooling is inherently less able to bring about the ends that people actually seek than competitive educational markets. Government schools have always failed to live up to the utopian promises and prognostications of their advocates. State schools are not now and have never been "unifying institutions." Their frequent attempts to coerce conformity have resulted not in blissful community relations, but in confrontation and even violence. They have perpetuated racial, ethnic, and religious discrimination, and have unnecessarily forced citizens into conflict with one another over differing views of culture, history, and the origins of humanity. It is free educational choice, not government schooling, that has historically been associated with the harmonious coexistence of diverse populations. Independent Catholic schools and secular voucher-redeeming schools both do better jobs of narrowing the achievement gap between rich and poor than does the government-run educational system. Anyone who honestly champions the purported *goals* of public schooling has more cause to support a voucher system than to support the public schools themselves.

Charter Schools: Too Little of a Good Thing

Charter schools are publicly funded schools managed by parents, teachers, or private companies, and overseen by a local or state chartering agency (often a school board or university). They are freed from some of the regulations that apply to conventional public schools, but they must meet performance standards set down by their charter. Rather than having students automatically assigned to them, charter schools enroll students on a purely voluntary basis. The movement began in 1991, when Minnesota passed the nation's first charter school law, and by 1998 there were eight hundred charter schools in twenty-nine states (compared to a total of 108,000 schools nationwide).[40]

Charter schooling is inspired by a sound idea: since market forces help to raise efficiency and customer satisfaction in other areas of the economy, why not allow them to do the same for schooling? Given the historical superiority of free educational markets over centralized, monolithic school systems, charter school advocates are definitely on the right track, but they are playing with model trains when they could be harnessing diesel locomotives. Charter schools enjoy only three of the five market characteristics identified in the previous chapter, and even those are heavily compromised. Parental choice, school freedom, and inter-school competition are all greater under charter programs than under conventional government schooling, but they are still pale shadows of the conditions that exist in free and competitive markets. Of the remaining two ingredients, financial responsibility for parents and the profit motive for schools, the first is completely incompatible with charter school laws, and the second is either forbidden outright or severely hobbled.

Expect Modest Improvements

As explained below, charter schools suffer from many defects and constraints over and above those already listed for government scholarships. Still, they offer the hope of substantial improvement when compared to the status quo in public education.

There is little empirical evidence yet available by which to judge the academic performance of charter schools, but the early findings are at least promising. The state of Massachusetts has conducted a value-added comparison of charter schools and traditional public schools, and has found better-than-average academic gains in six out of eight charter schools tested, while the two remaining comparisons were inconclusive.[41]

While the nation waits for further academic results, it can certainly take note of the increases in satisfaction that have accompanied most families' moves from conventional public schools to charter schools. In the conclusion to their two-year investigation of charter schools, researchers at the Hudson Institute wrote that "three-fifths of students report that their charter school teachers are better than their previous schools' teachers." Over two thirds of parents, they add, say their charter schools are "better with respect to teaching quality, parental involvement, curriculum, extra help for students, academic standards, accessibility and openness, and discipline."[42]

The Inherent Flaws of Charter Schooling

Though charter schools should yield some improvements in the quality of public school services, their effects are likely to be miniscule when compared to those of free and competitive markets. Charter schooling also fails to solve some of the most pernicious social problems caused by state-run education. The paragraphs that follow give a general overview of the ways in which charter school laws interfere with the requirements for educational excellence, and subsequent subsections provide details and examples.

Parental choice is limited under charter school programs in the same way as it is under traditional public schooling, though admittedly to a lesser degree. The public is taxed to pay for a small subset of the educational options that would be available in a free market, making it comparatively expensive for parents to obtain educational services outside that subset. A system dominated by charter schools would thus loosen, but not remove, the straitjacket that has restrained the U.S. schooling industry since it was taken over by the state a century and a half ago. Educational services that do not fit neatly into the current conception of a school, or that cannot easily be funded by a government formula, cannot germinate under charter school laws.

The freedom of schools to conduct their operations as they think best is similarly constrained under charter school laws. Would-be charter schools must run a legal and political gauntlet. The fact that an institution does not qualify for charter status does not mean that families would not wish to patronize it. Some states, California for instance,[43] forbid existing private schools from becoming chartered. Furthermore, once a school does receive the state's blessing, it must follow whatever managerial and pedagogical policies are set out in that state's charter law, which can be burdensome, or conflict with the school's mission, or both.

Charter schools are substantially protected from private-sector competition by virtue of their ability to receive tax dollars rather than charging tuition at the door. Even competition with other public schools frequently lacks bite, as some contracts stipulate that the staff of failed charter schools must be given other jobs by the local public school district, rather than having to earn the right to be rehired on a case-by-case basis.

Inevitably, charter schools also dispense with parental financial responsibility, a problem already discussed in the section on vouchers.

One of the most critical flaws in the typical charter school law is the proscription against profit-making.[44] As earlier chapters have shown, nonprofit schools have stagnated for a hundred years in both their business practices (e.g., failure to expand to meet demand) and their pedagogical practices (failure to develop and apply new and substantially better instructional techniques). Given the additional regulations to which most charter schools are subjected, it is likely that nonprofit charter schools will do even worse in these respects than nonprofit private ones.

Note that the same caveat raised with respect to government vouchers also applies to charter schools: so long as they are a new concept, they will be subject to intense public scrutiny, making abuses of every kind more difficult to conceal and perpetuate. But if charter school programs become a public policy fixture, they are likely to suffer from the same degree of fraud, waste, and mismanagement that currently afflicts traditional public schools. To evaluate charter schools fairly it is necessary to consider how they will look once they, too, are taken for granted by the public and the media.

A Stillborn Reform?

For charter schools to have a significant impact on U.S. education as a whole, they must number in the tens of thousands. In 1998, there were roughly eight hundred charter schools nationwide. Clearly, a staggering amount of growth is required, but is it probable?

In his penetrating analysis of charter schooling, political scientist Bryan Hassel draws pessimistic conclusions about the potential for charter schools to replace traditional state schools, or even to become serious rivals. To secure a sizable share of the quasi-market for public education, and to have an impact on existing public schools, Hassel observes that at least the following three criteria must hold:

> Entities other than local school boards must be able to authorize charter schools.
> Laws must allow many charter schools to open.
> Full per-pupil operating funds must follow the child.

Of the twenty states Hassel has examined, only two (Arizona and Michigan) satisfy all of these criteria.[45]

Even in the unlikely event (see below) that the charter concept is "enacted fully and without compromise by a state legislature," Hassel reasons that charter school numbers are still unlikely to reach the level needed for their effects to be widely felt. As both Hassel and the team of Chester Finn, Bruno Manno, Louann Bierlein, and Gregg Vanourek have shown, new charter schools can only be created at tremendous effort and expense.[46] Facilities, advertising, pedagogical planning, budgeting, equipment purchase, custodial arrangements, adherence to complex legal codes, etc., all impose a heavy load on prospective charter school founders. None of these start-up costs are covered under present laws, forcing most charter schools to rely entirely on volunteerism and charitable gifts at this stage of their development.

There are partial exceptions, however. Private school-management businesses such as the Edison Project can shoulder the plant-management and curricular burdens, allowing founders to concentrate on raising local interest, recruiting students, the often elaborate application process, and ongoing relations with state and local authorities. But even Edison rarely if ever provides capital funding to construct or purchase school buildings. Avoiding these capital costs was, in fact, the decisive factor that led Edison's directors away from their original goal of starting private schools, and into the management of charter (and traditional) public schools.[47] Since charter schools enroll, on average, only half as many students as typical public schools, and since only a fraction of charter schools are conversions from existing public schools, the problem of capital funding is an enormous roadblock to charter school expansion.

This roadblock is an artifact of the public, nonprofit status of charter schools. Many sectors of the economy have even higher start-up costs, but still create vast numbers of new businesses. The source of that dynamism is the ability of entrepreneurs to attract investors with the lure of profits. Charter school founders, by contrast, are not permitted to distribute profits to their investors, and as a result they are cut off from the chief source of start-up funding used by entrepreneurs in other fields.

Even without the day-to-day responsibilities of managing the school, charter school founders/directors have to commit a great deal of time and effort to the project, and are ultimately responsible for the activities of the school. Expecting them to do this on a voluntary or part-time basis means that only a small number of highly motivated individuals will come forward to take on the task. In volunteer and part-time educational bodies throughout history (the case of nineteenth-century France comes to mind), participants have generally had many other personal and professional commitments which have undermined their ability to give the necessary attention to their educational duties.

The operation of charter schools can, of course, be contracted out to for-profit businesses once the schools have been conceived and organized by volunteers, but such after-the-fact participation does nothing to promote the creation of new charter schools in the first place. Entrepreneurs have to wait around for nonprofit grassroots networks to form, to resolve their differences, and to then come looking for help. Any attempt by a for-profit enterprise to deliberately throw together a "volunteer" front organization to circumvent the law would be frowned upon, to say the least, by state charter-approving bodies.

Charter Schooling's Priceless Flaw

The inability of for-profit businesses to found charter schools is not the only hurdle that stands between the charter school concept and the effective application of market forces. Unlike independent private schools, charter schools run by private contractors cannot set their own prices; their income is dictated purely by their state's charter law and their overseeing regulatory body. This often-ignored detail severs a crucial link in the chain of factors that are responsible for the efficiency and innovation of free economies.

First, consider the fact that no charter school can charge more than its per-pupil government allowance. With this one simple step, the process responsible for the most important technological developments of the twentieth century is switched off. How many people could afford computers when they first became commercially available? Or cellular telephones? Or televisions? Refrigerators? Washing machines? The answer, uniformly, is very few. Not long ago, subscription cards for *The Economist* newspaper featured a 1950s quote from the then-head of IBM stating: "I believe there is a world market for five computers." The reason for this abysmally erroneous forecast was that the computers of the time had a very limited range of uses, took up the space of small buildings, and cost more than all but a few nations and multinational corporations could afford. It is only because manufacturers were able to charge the full cost of these machines, plus a profit, that they were able (and had an incentive) to continue refining them and devising ways of building them more efficiently.

Since there was a market, however small, for these early and very expensive computers, manufacturers of computer components also had an incentive to build better and faster circuits. Just as the first HDTVs (High-Definition [digital] Televisions) will be priced beyond the means of the average family, so too were the first color televisions before them, and the first black-and-white televisions before them. And yet, by 1970, 95.3 percent of U.S. households were able to afford, and did in fact own, a television set. VCRs went from being a pricey plaything of the wealthy in 1970 (in only 1.1 percent of U.S. households) to being in four out of every five homes in America by 1994.[48] Cellular telephones, which were initially sold for hundreds, sometimes thousands, of dollars, are now being given away free, with users required only to pay monthly service charges.

Imagine what would have happened if the manufacturers of all these technological wonders had been told that they could not sell their new products unless they priced them at a level the average family could afford, and, furthermore, that the quality of the products had to be much greater than was the case with early models. The answer, obviously, is nothing. Nothing would have happened because manufacturers would have lost enormous sums of money in research and development without being able to recoup those costs in their selling prices. They would have taken one glance at their R&D budgets, another at the prices they would be allowed to charge for their new products, and would have quickly decided that pursuing their bright ideas would lead to a financial meltdown.

The very same situation applies to charter schools. If an entrepreneurial private contractor were to conceive of an expensive but potentially very effective pedagogical innovation, he would be discouraged from implementing it within a charter school system due to his inability to charge a higher tuition to cover his higher initial costs, let alone to make a profit. Faced with this reality, charter schools, whether run by nonprofit groups or contracted out to private for-profit enterprises, are unlikely to spend their fixed incomes developing pedagogical advances whose costs they will not be able to earn back. Pedagogical progress is thus apt to languish far behind the pace of market-driven industries, since the abortion of innovations in their early (and expensive) stages means that schools will never have the opportunity to find ways of delivering those innovations more cheaply and effectively, thus preventing them from ever reaching a broader population.

The free-market innovation process may offend the sensibilities of educational egalitarians, due to the fact that innovations are usually enjoyed first by the wealthy and only afterward by the general public. Nonetheless, it is the only process that has a proven record of stimulating valuable improvements in technology, and of eventually making those improvements available on a grand scale. The alternative, which we have already experienced for more than a hundred years, is for all schools to stagnate together.

So much for the proscription against raising prices. What about lowering prices? Here the issue is not about what is permissible (charter schools could clearly return some of their per-pupil allotment if they so chose), but rather about what is encouraged. In free markets, lowering prices is a key means of gaining a competitive edge. While lower prices cause profit margins to drop on a per-customer basis, potential increases in the number of customers can more than offset the loss, actually improving a company's bottom line.[49] Businesses thus have an incentive to find ways of serving more customers for less money, without lowering the quality of their products or services.[50]

Charter schools don't. A charter school that managed to offer an educational experience in line with that of its competitors, while returning some money to taxpayers, would not be any more appealing to potential customers as a result. It is not the customers, after all, who would be enjoying the savings. Charter schooling is thus unlikely to lead to the efficiency increases that are common in other industries. In fact, charter school managers and employees will constitute a special-interest group just as public school employees currently do, and if their lobbying efforts are as successful as those of the teachers' unions, it is safe to predict that charter schools will do their part in continuing the awesome rise in public-education spending of the past half-century.

As Flexible as Peanut-Brittle

Two obviously valuable educational options that are not provided by charter programs are flexible part-time instruction and out-of-state instruction. It is unreasonable to expect that any single school could offer the range and quality of services that could be obtained by picking and choosing among multiple providers in an open market. Parents may find that one school is exceptionally good in the arts and literature, but weak in mathematics, and yet may want their children to have a well-balanced education. In such situations they might seek out a specialty school known for its expertise in math. The Kumon private school chain, with 1,400 mathematics and reading specialty schools in the United States and Canada, is a current example.[51] A student could thus take her mathematics lessons from a specialist on a part-time basis, and enroll in a more traditional school for all her other classes, perhaps receiving a discount on her tuition for not enrolling in that school's math lessons.

Other parents might choose to assemble an educational program for their children by sending them only to specialty schools in a variety of different subject areas, or they might choose to combine home-schooling with professional instruction in one or two disciplines which they do not feel competent to teach, following Socrates' 2,500-year-old description of Athenian practice: "Parents teach [their children] whatever they themselves know that is likely to be useful to them; subjects which they think others better qualified to teach they send them to school to learn, spending money upon this object."[52]

Another option would be for students to alternate between attending school for a few months, and then learning the operations of a family business for a few months, along the lines of college-level work-study programs. Or, instead of business experience, children might have their part-time formal studies supplemented by the opportunity to live with friends or relatives in other parts of the country or the world for periods of time.

Specialty schools offering instruction in only a single subject could not qualify as charter schools in most states, since charter schools are usually expected to provide a complete course of studies. Similarly, charter funding formulas based on the average number of students in daily attendance presuppose that all students are enrolled in the same number of courses, making it difficult to account for any students who opt out of one or more courses to pursue them at other schools. There are funding formulas based on individual course units, but these have already proven incapable of handling the variety of educational approaches devised by charter school founders. Chester Finn, Bruno Manno, and Louann Bierlein have documented problems of this sort, pointing to charter schools that

> use banks of computers and file servers that enable students to learn at any time and virtually anywhere through cyberspace. Others use community-based projects and competency-based learning, one result being that their students spend little time in the school building. Funding formulae based on their physical presence clearly clash with such educational strategies.[53]

While some technology-based virtual schools have found ways to appease regulators for the time being, such as by requiring students to be on-line a certain number of hours a week, it is not clear that such difficult-to-verify arrangements will prove workable or acceptable in the long run and on a broad scale.

Virtual schools pose yet another problem for charter schooling: the tremendous prospects for long-distance learning that have been created by the expansion of the internet and the falling cost of personal computers are undermined by the need for charter schools to be located in a family's state of residence. Some citizens are likely to balk, after all, at sending their tax dollars out of state, and authorities from South Carolina to California would have a difficult time enforcing their charter school laws on educators in Montreal or Hong Kong. Parents who wished to hire foreign citizens to teach their children foreign-language writing skills via the World Wide Web could not readily do so as part of a charter school program, whether or not their fellow taxpayers approved.

The number and variety of such scenarios is truly endless, and trying to retrofit them to anachronistic charter school schemes would be an exercise in futility. The organization of charter schools has to remain fundamentally similar to that of traditional schools because of the accountability and funding mechanisms built into the legislation that governs them. The fact that the relative inflexibility of charter school laws (as compared to free markets) has not been more widely noted and criticized is a testament to the narrowing of vision that has taken place during the reign of public schooling, with regard to the educational possibilities of a highly computerized, networked society.

State versus Church

Unlike religious voucher-redeeming schools, which would receive government support only indirectly as a result of the independent decisions of individual families, religious charter schools would undeniably violate the constitutional prescription against the political establishment of religion. There are currently no religious charter schools, and even charter advocates have not suggested that any could or should be created. As experience has shown, however, the mandatory secular status of state schools is one of the prime causes of the public school wars that have rocked the United States for more than a century. The vast majority of families are religious, and many of those wish to have their religion integrated into their children's regular educational experiences. So long as that is impossible within the reigning school system, these families will be frustrated, and they will continue to try to influence the laws affecting all state schools in order to further their cause. Those efforts are unlikely to succeed, but they can be counted upon to keep alive the confrontational spirit that state schooling has created between many secular and religious groups.

Student Selectivity

Few people would argue that every school is well suited to every student. Even most critics of vouchers and markets admit that parents should have some choice of schools, in order to increase their chances of finding one that is right for their children. It is strange, therefore, that the equally true converse proposition does not enjoy equal support. The fact is that not every student (or family) is right for every school, and in order to ensure a good match between their clients and the programs they offer, schools must have considerable flexibility in their admissions policies. They must be able to accept students whose needs they anticipate being able to satisfy, and reject those who they feel are outside their areas of expertise.

As noted earlier, private schools typically reject only a small percentage of their applicants, largely because parents tend not to apply to schools that have educational missions obviously at odds with the needs of their children. But it is easy to imagine situations in which a school might wish to refuse admission to some applicants, especially if it targeted a particular audience of which the applicant was not a member. Schools aimed at recent immigrants, at a single sex, at budding scientists or musicians, at children with an affinity for art or acting, at particular ethnic groups, at children with a history of violent or disruptive behavior, etc. all may wish to limit their enrollments to students whom they deem capable of benefiting from their instruction, and who would not be likely to impede the progress of their fellow pupils. Interfering with a school's ability to make these decisions clearly undermines its chances of successfully serving its chosen clientele.

Though public schooling's staunchest advocates are adamant in their demand for randomized admission policies, some public schools are moving toward student selectivity. Starting in the 1998–99 academic year, Milwaukee's public high schools will be allowed to pick their pupils. "We want schools that have a focus to be able to set some standards,"[54] explained one board member. In California, the 1997–98 school year saw the opening of several all-girl and all-boy schools within the public system.[55]

Charter school laws explicitly prohibit this kind of selectivity. Typically, all charter schools in a given state are required by law to admit applicants on a random basis. In Massachusetts, for example, oversubscribed charter schools must follow a lottery process that gives preference to local residents.[56] Advocates of such provisions have the intention of preventing segregation within the chartered public school sector, but they fail to recognize two important points (which were presented in Chapter 8): first, such provisions have already failed to integrate existing public schools, and second, private schools which are not subject to such provisions are already better integrated than public schools.

After all, schools, particularly those operated privately and for profit, have an enormous incentive to accept every student they reasonably can: their financial well-being and institutional futures depend on securing a large and growing student body. The same incentives apply, though to a lesser extent, to public charter schools, which would be likely to have their charters revoked if their enrollments shrunk below a certain minimum level. Just as these economic incentives encouraged eighteenth-century English nonconformists to admit children of all religions to their schools, and just as they led nineteenth-century French monitorial schools to admit children of different social classes, so they can be expected to encourage diversity today. For people who are genuinely concerned with the ends rather than the means of achieving diverse student populations, it is a simple choice between a legislative approach that has proven to be a failure, and a market approach that has proven successful.

Manacled Management

Some states, such as Wisconsin, Minnesota, and Michigan, require their charter schools to hire only state-certified teachers. In other states, individual charter contracts sometimes demand teacher certification. This obligation is entirely unjustified, and greatly impedes the ability of parents and schools to choose teachers on their individual merits. As demonstrated in Chapter 5, government-certified teachers perform no better in the classroom than their uncertified counterparts, and actually receive lower average scores than uncertified teachers on the National Teacher Examination. Certification is almost always contingent on graduating from an approved college of education, but such programs tend to "deter many talented college students who would like to teach from ever doing so,"[57] and are widely regarded by both researchers and their own graduates as being of limited benefit (see Chapter 5). Mandatory teacher certification thus acts as a barricade, keeping many experienced, well-educated people out of the teaching profession.

Arizona and Massachusetts,[58] among other states, give preference to former public school teachers who join a charter school and then want to go back to the district, irrespective of the reason they left the charter school. So if a teacher is fired from a charter school, he or she will have little difficulty transferring back into the public schools. In its contracts with school districts, the Edison Project typically agrees to similar exit provisions for its teachers.

Roughly a quarter of states with charter laws on the books insist that charter schools abide by collective-bargaining agreements negotiated by public school teachers' unions.[59] Other states, such as Massachusetts, explicitly consider charter school employees to be public employees for collective-bargaining purposes, opening the way for the unionization of those charter school teachers who are not already unionized. With their tenure rules, salary scales, and curbs on dismissing poor performers, union agreements precipitate many of the problems highlighted in Chapter 5. Teachers who, thanks to union agreements, do not face the risk of losing their jobs for poor or lackadaisical performance have no systemic incentive to innovate or strive for excellence.

On the bright side, many fledgling charter programs exempt charter schools from both certification requirements and collective-bargaining agreements. As a result, charter schools have become havens for some of the most independent-minded, dedicated, and performance-oriented people in the profession. The single most important reason teachers give for leaving existing public schools to join charter schools, voiced by more than three quarters of all those surveyed, is the pursuit of a superior educational philosophy.[60] But the typical classroom educator, as earlier chapters have shown, is not especially interested in philosophy or the search for effective pedagogical methods. By their own admission, the majority are motivated primarily by a desire to work with children, and are turned off by education theory. What charter laws are currently doing, therefore, is pulling the most professional educators out of the existing system and concentrating them within charter schools. If this is all they succeed in doing, their net effect on teacher performance will be marginal at best. They will have redistributed, but not improved, the public school labor force.

In order for charter schools to significantly improve the educational workforce, they must do two things: retain long-term control over hiring, firing, compensation, and all other aspects of personnel management, and expand to the point where they are more than a token presence in the educational marketplace. The dismal prospects for the proliferation of charter schools have already been touched upon, but even if charter schools do defy the odds and become serious contenders in the quasi-market for public schooling, it is almost inevitable that they will become just as thoroughly unionized as traditional public schools.

Strong charter school laws, those which offer genuine independence, have been vigorously opposed by the teachers' unions wherever they have been proposed, and have usually been weakened by major concessions in the process. This opposition, it must be remembered, is directed at laws that almost always limit the number of charter schools allowed to open, so that they pose no threat, for now, to the status quo. Imagine the opposition that would arise if charter schools were suggested as a universal solution, to be expanded to the fullest extent possible, basically replacing traditional public schooling. Would teachers' unions sit idly by while their constituency was torn from them? Or would they fight back, trying to hobble the charter laws and unionize any nonunion charter school teachers, reestablishing their dominance? Few special-interest groups in any field have the funding or the organizational prowess of the teachers' unions, and none have as strong an incentive to defend charter school laws as the unions have to attack them.

So long as salary scales rather than performance determine teachers' compensation, and so long as teachers can retain their jobs due to seniority rather than because they are competent, the current disproportionately high rate of attrition among the best and brightest teachers will continue, as will the difficulty in dismissing poor performers.

Testing Requirements: Short Route to a State Curriculum

The freedom of charter schools is bestowed at a price: charter schools must demonstrate that they are improving student performance in order to remain in operation. Certainly this is a sound idea in principle, but in practice it raises two troublesome questions: To whom must charter schools demonstrate improvements? By what criteria must the improvements be measured?

In competitive educational markets, families decide for themselves whether or not a school's service is satisfactory, using whatever criteria are most meaningful to them—a mechanism, history has shown, that works better than any other. Charter schools, by contrast, are evaluated by bureaucrats who do not, in all probability, have children attending them, using government-chosen tests that may or may not reflect the educational goals of the schools' clients. This situation leads to a potential split in the focus of a charter school's management: should it concentrate on meeting the avowed needs of its client families, or on producing high scores on state tests? The payment-by-results program implemented in England in 1862 (see Chapter 3) led to a similar dilemma for educators, one that was eventually resolved in favor of producing the highest possible test scores to the exclusion of other considerations. In the end, the curriculum in government-funded schools was dictated by the content of government tests. The same fate could easily befall charter schools.

In essence, the performance-accountability clauses of state charter school laws are likely to accelerate the adoption of government curricula, if not by official decree then simply as a side-effect of the imposition of high-stakes tests. The demerits of government curricula are described in a later section.

Given the widespread testing fraud that has plagued high-stakes tests in public schools (see Chapter 6), it is also reasonable to doubt that these performance-accountability clauses will even ensure that charter schools are meeting government expectations.

The Approval Process: Corruption Made Easy

Charter schools would be subject to all the fraud concerns described in the section on government scholarships, and to one additional avenue of abuse: the charter approval and renewal process.

Under free markets and most voucher plans, there are few barriers to the entry of new schools. Any team of educators capable of attracting paying (or voucher-holding) customers can open up shop. Charter laws, by contrast, impose a significant barrier to entry, in the form of a state approval process. Would-be charter founders must win the endorsement of a state board of education, public school district, or selected university. This process creates a moral hazard: the officials responsible for approving and renewing charters could accept or reject applications, or revoke or renew existing charters, for personal reasons, or due to bribery, without necessarily suffering any personal hardship. The officials, after all, would probably not have children enrolled in the charter schools on which they pass judgment, or have children who might wish to enroll in a prospective new charter school. So long as their biases or illicit activities were not discovered, they could blithely continue to base their decisions on improper grounds.

The severity of this problem is inversely proportional to the number of different charter-approving bodies. Many states, however, allow only the local public school district to pass judgment on charter schools within a given area, a clear conflict of interest given the potentially competitive relationship between charter and traditional public schools.

Private Management of Public Schools: Putting a Contract Out on Education

Yet another high-profile reform of the 1990s is the contracting out of public school management to private, for-profit firms. Of the five necessary and interdependent conditions for educational excellence, private contracting guarantees only one: the profit motive. Parental financial responsibility is absent, school freedom is limited, and neither parental choice nor inter-school competition is generally increased above the levels existing in public schools. Worse yet, introducing the profit motive without adding competition and choice to keep it in check is a recipe for fiscal misconduct. There is thus little reason to expect that contracting out will produce a net long-term improvement in the quality or efficiency of public schooling.

Contracting Out: Please Sign Here, Dr. Faustus . . .

Private contracting suffers from virtually all of the flaws of charter and voucher programs, along with a few of its own. Of particular importance is the fact that private contracting does not guarantee parents a choice of schools. In the early 1990s, the public school districts of Baltimore, Maryland and Hartford, Connecticut contracted with Education Alternatives, Inc. (EAI) to run some of their schools. Neither of these contracts made attendance at the EAI schools voluntary. Instead, students were simply assigned to them as they would have been to any government school. The same was true of privately managed Turner Elementary School in the Wilkinsburg, Pennsylvania school district. To the extent that they do not offer parents a range of educational choices, contracting arrangements are no better than the unresponsive state-run school systems they are meant to reform.

A notable exception to the practice of automatically assigning students to privately run public schools is the Edison Project. In addition to its charter schools, Edison also runs several public schools on an individual contract basis, independent of charter laws. One of Edison's requirements before it will take over a school is that all of its students freely choose to attend. This stipulation does little to increase parental choice, however, unless parents have access to a variety of schools all run by different contractors, a situation which has yet to arise.

As with charter schools, the renewal of contracting arrangements is often dependent on test results. A typical requirement is that some portion (usually a large majority) of students score above certain benchmarks on academic tests. Such performance-based contracts are guaranteed to have a dramatic effect on what and how children are taught, an effect that can easily come into conflict with the goals of parents. Critics of educational privatization are quick to point to a 1969–70 public school contracting experience in Texarkana, a twin municipality straddling the Texas/Arkansas border. During the time when it was hired to manage the city's school district, the contractor, Dorsett Educational Systems, failed to provide

> instruction in science and social studies, as it had initially promised the district. Since the company's fees were tied to students' test gains in math and English, these two subjects became the focus of all Dorsett's efforts.[61]

Worse yet, this performance contract led Dorsett's employees to teach to the test,[62] just as high-stakes district-level and state-level tests have done in public schools (see Chapter 6), and as the payment-by-results program did in England during the 1860s (see Chapter 3). A detailed discussion of other education contracting experiences of the 1970s can be found in Myron Lieberman's *Privatization and Educational Choice*.[63]

A related problem is that contracts tying profits to test results encourage contractors to focus on average students at the expense of slower and brighter ones, since the brightest children will likely meet contract standards without much help from teachers, and the slowest ones might not make it even with extensive help. This may have been the case in Gary, Indiana, at the Bannecker Elementary School run by private contractor Behavioral Research Laboratories (BRL) during the early 1970s. A report published by the Twentieth Century Fund concluded that, "compared with a national sample of students, middle-range Bannecker students improved more, while high- and low-performing students improved less."[64] Similar incentives in public schools have led to the practice of exempting slow students from tests, or classifying them as disabled, so that they will not bring down the averages on high-stakes tests (see Chapter 6).

After more than a century of failed attempts to tie government expenditures to educational outcomes, we still have not learned a very simple lesson: the criteria by which parents evaluate the quality of their children's education are so broad and so varied that they cannot be codified in simple performance contracts. Most often, the contracts emphasize one or two outcomes above all the rest, giving schools an incentive to dispense with the less lucrative areas of study. Furthermore, even if a comprehensive measure of educational outcomes could be drafted, it could not simultaneously serve the many disparate and conflicting goals that citizens hold.

Contracts with private school-management firms are also breeding-grounds for corruption. As in charter programs, the individuals authorized to approve contracts generally have nothing personally to gain or lose as a result of their decisions. This makes them susceptible to bribery. In 1978, BRL was accused of giving kickbacks to a public official in order to secure a multimillion-dollar sale of reading materials to the Ocean Hill–Brownsville district in Brooklyn.[65] New York City's history of graft in its public school contracts stretches back for decades, and adds up to hundreds of millions of dollars. It is not alone (see Chapter 6). Extending contracting beyond peripheral services (such as transportation), to the actual management of schools, will certainly widen the scope for such abuses.

Contracting is also likely to have little or no positive effect on the educational workforce. Most contracts stipulate that privately run public schools must hire government-certified teachers and abide by collective-bargaining agreements negotiated by public school teachers' unions. In some cases, such as Baltimore's, teachers at the EAI-run schools were not even employees of EAI; they were considered public school district employees. Situations such as this do nothing to make teachers associate their own professional futures with the future of the school. Teachers know that they will retain their jobs whether or not the school succeeds, and may even be better off, in the long run, if the school fails. In fact, the Baltimore Teachers' Union (an affiliate of the American Federation of Teachers) fought long and hard to expel EAI from the city.

One exception to the union and certification requirements was the 1995 contract between Alternative Public Schools, Inc. (API) and the public school district of Wilkinsburg, Pennsylvania. API was empowered to dismiss any and all teachers previously employed at Turner Elementary School and replace them with its own nonunion employees. Inevitably, local and state teachers' unions were furious and immediately set about challenging the contract in court. Though the unions sought and received an injunction to prevent API from taking over the school, it was quickly overturned by the state supreme court. Two years passed, during which API appeared to be fairly successfully serving the needs of local families. Then, in September 1997, a state court ruled on the union suit, stating that there was no authority in Pennsylvania law "for districts to turn over schools to private, for-profit companies."[66] Since unions are sure to file similar challenges everywhere that contracting is undertaken, the legal hurdles to private management of public schools seem high.

Private contractors are not only at the mercy of the courts, but of capricious public school districts and city governments as well. During its contract with EAI, the city of Baltimore spent itself into insolvency and was forced to drastically cut its budget. Despite having agreed to pay the company $44 million a year to manage nine public schools, it decided in 1995 to renege on the contract and pay only $37 million instead. When EAI objected and demanded to be paid what it was owed, city officials invoked a clause which allowed them to uni-laterally cancel the contract.

A similar fiasco brought down EAI's operations in Hartford, Connecticut. The Hartford school district contracted with EAI in 1994 to run all of its thirty-two schools, but later amended the contract, limiting the company's role to con-trolling the district budget and improving only six schools. According to a front-page article in *Education Week,* EAI was to keep in profits any savings it managed to eke out of the budget. EAI then spent $11 million dollars on tech-nology and capital improvements for Hartford schools, but was only reim-bursed $343,000 by the district. John Golle, EAI's chief executive officer, claimed that the company's purchases were budgeted operating expenses that should have been fully reimbursed and not counted against the savings/profits portion of the contract. Board members disagreed, and refused to pay. As in Baltimore, district officials decided to terminate their agreement with EAI rather than resolve the dispute, and promptly locked the company out of dis-trict schools so that it could not retrieve the computers it had purchased and in-stalled, and for which it had not been reimbursed.[67]

Fearful that the district's actions would precipitate a lawsuit, city officials ex-tended a tentative olive branch, suggesting that the company could continue in some form of budget-management role. This was not to be, however, given the stalwart resistance of the school board, and so the dispute dragged on. In July 1996, the Reuters news service reported that Hartford officials had agreed to pay EAI $2.73 million for computers and capital improvements, but the com-pany maintained that it was still owed several million dollars.[68] EAI's financial statement for the fiscal year ending in June 1997 reflected a $650,000 payment by the city toward settling the broken contract.[69]

Reflecting on his company's tortuous experiences managing public schools, John Golle had this to say in February 1996:

> As we go about the task of rebuilding our revenue base, our criteria is [sic] crys-tal clear—we will only accept contracts that allow us to use our own employees and curriculum, the contracts must be granted directly by a state agency with full funding over an extended period of time, and attendance is by choice. . . . Our past experiences with managing public schools without the proper control has been a good lesson for our company.[70]

Based on EAI's actions since Golle's statement, such contracts do not appear easy to come by. Apart from a single contract to manage a dozen charter schools in Arizona—the state affording by far the most freedom to its charter schools—the company refocused itself in the summer of 1997 toward operating entirely private schools.[71]

As a final observation on private contracting, it is worth noting the distinction between contracts to operate individual schools and contracts to operate multiple schools or entire districts. While single-school arrangements offer at least the possibility (if not generally the reality) of parental choice, the same cannot be said of district-wide arrangements. When a school district contracts out its entire operations, as the one in Chelsea, Massachusetts has done, it succeeds only in passing control over its tax-funded education monopoly from one entity to another. This is not an education reform, but rather a superficial change in management, and as such it is likely to produce the same deleterious effects as our existing public school systems.

Government-Imposed Curricula: Double-Edged Cookie-Cutters

The most common claim made in support of government curricula is that "[s]tandards can improve academic achievement by clearly defining what is to be taught and what kind of performance is expected."[72] Unless readers are willing to accept this claim on faith, they can safely ignore it, because there is no compelling evidence that it is true. In her book *National Standards in American Education,* respected education historian and government standards advocate Diane Ravitch discusses many arguments pro and con, but does not demonstrate that government curriculum guidelines raise student achievement.

Dismayed by the lack of evidence mustered by supporters of government curriculum guidelines, Columbia University researcher Richard M. Wolf decided to compare the results of the nations participating in the Third International Mathematics and Science Study to determine whether or not national standards were correlated with higher achievement. They weren't. Though most of the participating countries did "have a national curriculum or syllabus," Wolf wrote, there was "virtually no relationship between student performance and having a national curriculum or syllabus."[73]

Upon reflection, Wolf's findings should come as no surprise. Having clear goals is a requirement for success in almost any undertaking, but goals are meaningless when the incentives and infrastructure needed to reach them are not in place. Tacking national curriculum standards onto government-run schools could not possibly bring about a major improvement in educational outcomes because the lack of such standards is not the reason government schools are currently failing. Is school violence caused by differences in the course of studies between schools? Are bright teachers the first to leave the public schools because they pine unrequitedly for a national curriculum? Do their incompetent colleagues linger almost indefinitely within the system because there is no standard curriculum? Can the rampant spending growth of state school bureaucracies be traced to the absence of a government-decreed lesson plan? No. Even supporters like Ravitch acknowledge that government standards "are unlikely to make much difference in schools where adults have not established an orderly climate conducive to learning."[74]

Another argument made in favor of a national curriculum is that citizens must share a common core of knowledge and values, and that the way to achieve that ideological unity is to inject it into youngsters with the help of federal government controls on the content of schooling. This is an intoxicating vision for some, but it is quickly dispelled by a steaming cup of hot reality. As history has repeatedly shown, government control over curricula has almost invariably balkanized rather than unified citizens. Except among the most homogeneous populations, national standards serve only to aggravate the conflicts created by state-run schooling. Even in Japan there has been a continuing battle between progressive and conservative forces over the content and direction of the government education system. The impact on more culturally diverse nations is naturally much worse.

State-mandated curricula do nothing to correct the misguided incentives that distort the government-schooling industry. Without the proper incentive structure, there is no reason to expect that sound pedagogical methods will be used, that schools will be safe and studious places, that excellent teachers will be properly compensated and weak ones helped to improve or dismissed, or that budgets will be carefully controlled. Without choice for parents and freedom for schools, conflict between families over the content of education becomes inevitable. In fact, history reveals a frightful list of consequences that have befallen nations with state curricula. The most grievous of these consequences are summarized below.

A Note on "Voluntary" Standards

Standards advocates who worry about government control of the curriculum frequently suggest that their standards could be voluntary. But voluntary for whom? No one is suggesting that each individual family be given the right to opt in or out of national standards. Only state departments of education (or in some cases, school districts) are to be given the authority to adopt or reject government curriculum guidelines. In defense of his government testing proposal, President Clinton himself has pleaded that "the tests are voluntary. No state, no school district has to participate."[75] It is as though the president has forgotten the role of parents in deciding what their children will be taught and tested on.

Such token voluntarism does nothing to assuage the concerns about government compulsion in education raised in the following sections. The fact that a majority of education bureaucrats favors some particular set of standards is no guarantee that it will meet with uniform public approval. A significant number of families already object to the curriculum guidelines followed in the public schools of their states (see Chapter 4). Grassroots parent organizations have sprung up across California to oppose the standards set down by the National Council of Teachers of Mathematics (NCTM),[76] standards which have been "voluntarily" adopted by numerous public school districts around the country. Whether the source of government compulsion is at the federal, state, or district level is entirely irrelevant.

With Compulsion Comes Confrontation

As demonstrated in Chapter 1, families do agree on many of the educational basics, but this is not an argument for imposing a uniform national curriculum. To the extent that parental preferences overlap, there is no need to give their shared goals the force of law. What all value, all will seek, assuming they have the freedom to do so. Furthermore, there are a great many aspects of the curriculum on which parents do not see eye to eye, from knowledge, to skills, to values. Taking one group's conception of the ideal course of studies, and compelling every family to follow it, is a tactic that has been tried countless times over the centuries, and its results are well known: conflict, animosity, and confrontation.

Just five generations ago, U.S. public school children in many states were forced to study the Protestant Bible regardless of their faith, justifiably arousing the resentment of non-Protestant families. The entire nineteenth-century French experience was one of alternating government-curriculum mandates which were anathema to one part or another of the populace. In post-Reformation Germany, the many parents who sought instruction in modern languages and practical skills for their children were grossly impeded by Luther and Melanchthon's predilections for classical Latin studies.

More recently, school wars between liberal and conservative parents (and educators) have shredded the social fabric of communities across the United States. In addition to the examples presented in Chapter 4, many more are described by professor Stephen Arons in his book *Short Route to Chaos*. For example, a 1992 Florida statute ordained that public school children must be made to "understand that a specific culture is not intrinsically superior or inferior to another." This was not a self-evident principle with which all the state's residents agreed. In fact, it was so totally contrary to the views of some Floridian parents that the Lake County School Board passed its own requirement that the public schools teach "our republican form of government, capitalism, a free enterprise system, patriotism, strong family values, freedom of religion, and other basic values that are superior to other foreign or historic cultures." The result of this difference of opinion was not a harmonious negotiation in which common ground was established; it was an angry, vitriolic legal and verbal war that made headlines from the Florida Keys to the Pacific Northwest. In the end, the best-organized and best-funded group (the state department of education, backed by the teachers' unions) won, and its opponents lost.[77]

Gidget's Not a Widget

On several occasions in the preceding chapters it has been noted that all children do not progress through all subjects at the same rate. Some are keen to do math, others find it a chore. Poetry and literature are voraciously consumed by certain students, while causing indigestion in others. These observations are usually taken for granted by anyone who has raised children or attended school, and they provide a powerful argument against government-enforced, uniform, age-based curriculum standards. Who does not remember the pupils who were continually struggling to keep up with the rest of the class, or those whose academic appetites clearly outstripped those of their teachers? A good friend of mine, who had an interest in the World Wars, read *Mein Kampf* from cover to cover with only limited difficulty (but much dismay) while she was in the seventh grade!

The great variation in student learning rates across subjects has been ignored by many standards advocates, but in one notable case it has been flatly denied. E. D. Hirsch, author of such popular and generally laudable books as *Cultural Literacy* and the *What Your* [nth] *Grader Needs to Know* series, takes the following view:

> Policymakers should be particularly alert to the objection, unfounded in research, that such a system of grade-by-grade accountability would . . . prevent each child from "progressing at his or her own pace." The notions that children can progress through school at their own pace and that teachers are in any position to decide what a child's innate pace actually is are egregious fallacies unsupported by research. These naturalistic ideas cannot stand up to common sense, much less experimental investigation. There is no natural pace for gaining the nonnatural learnings of alphabetic literacy and base-ten mathematics. Moreover, it is impossible to conduct an effective classroom when there are attempts to accommodate twenty-five different "paces" of learning.[78]

Hirsch's main point in this passage, that children do not progress at different rates and that teachers could not gauge those rates even if they existed, is false. His secondary point about the impossibility of accommodating twenty-five widely different learning rates in a single class is an irrelevant straw man.

The disparities in aptitude among children of the same age, and the differences in the speed at which they learn, are well known and well documented.

In England, after six years of a universally adopted national curriculum that has been criticized as excessively detailed and constraining, tests nonetheless show great disparities in the performance of students. Even among children as young as seven years old, there is already an achievement spread in basic literacy and numeracy skills equivalent to three years of study, according to research conducted by the Social Market Foundation, a leading economic policy institute, that compared schools in similar neighborhoods.[79]

This, it must be repeated, is under a system which attempts to offer a uniform educational experience to all children of a given age. The variation is greater still when students are grouped together based on their aptitude in particular subjects, and then taught at a rate that is appropriate to their capacities. Such tailored, ability-grouped classrooms typically produce, according to professor James Kulik, gains of between two and three months of additional learning per year no matter which group students happen to fall into (e.g., slow, average, or bright). Programs aimed at high-achievers produce even more startling results, allowing their participants to cover a typical curriculum in half the time normally allotted, or, alternately, to study five to six months worth of additional material per school year.[80] The fact that all levels of students learn more when they are grouped by aptitude rather than age leaves little doubt that teachers are able to do a competent job of gauging learning rates. The fact that the brightest students progress far more rapidly than their average and below-average peers demonstrates that children can and do progress at different paces.

Similar examples can be found around the world and throughout history. Japan's flourishing private education market routinely tests students, groups them by ability, and then teaches them at the appropriate level, much to the satisfaction of both students and parents. Four hundred years ago, Jesuit colleges all over the globe were allowing students to progress through their graded curriculum based on mastery of the material rather than age, sometimes promoting students in mid-year to insure that they were in the class best suited to their level of understanding and rate of progress.

Finally, Hirsch's observation on the difficulty of teaching students of widely varying ability in the same classes is entirely beside the point. In the absence of rigid age-based grading there is no need to teach students of vastly divergent abilities in the same classes. Grouping children by age rather than by their mastery of the subject matter is a recent and misguided innovation adopted by regimentation-prone government schools. Once this artificial and harmful practice is dispensed with, teachers will find out what the Jesuits discovered centuries ago, that teaching children of roughly the same ability, regardless of slight age differences, is more effective, easier, and more pleasant for all concerned.

This brings us to a related concern of standards advocates: How would educational markets deal with the high rate of student mobility common to many countries? Wouldn't the lack of a nationwide curriculum create chaos when students moved from one school to another? This worry is an artifact of the arbitrary age-based grouping practices of most contemporary schools. Once these practices are replaced with a more natural grouping by student performance level, mobility is no longer a problem. Students who transferred to a new school would simply be placed in the class appropriate to their level of understanding. A student who had just mastered arithmetic and was about to begin learning algebra would be placed in an algebra class. The child who was learning the finer points of expository writing in her previous school would be placed in an advanced writing class in her new school. Age, up to a point, need not be a factor. This approach was used without noticeable difficulty in most nations prior to the introduction of state schooling, and is used today in Japanese *juku* and in North American for-profit schools such as the Kumon chain (mentioned earlier in this chapter).

A Ticket to Moribundity

While necessary and virtuous in many ways, written law is not especially flexible. Unless actively revised by legislatures on a regular basis, laws do not easily adapt to changing circumstances. Legislatures, in turn, are not typically thought of as sources of rapid and timely action. These factors make curriculum legislation a bad idea in the long haul. After all, people change.

Much of what we regard as fact today was either unknown or widely disbelieved in generations past. The mores of modern society are undeniably different from those of just a few decades ago, and are likely to be different from those of a few decades hence. Whenever changes in knowledge and values collide with our legal and political systems, it is safe to expect a bounty of chaos, confusion, and error. Take the Internet. It has been around for over a decade, and yet on-line copyright and free-speech issues are far from resolved. When the U.S. Congress decided to pass a law attempting to protect minors from indecent material on the World Wide Web, it ran afoul of the Constitution and its legislation was struck down by the Supreme Court.

Such difficulties are inevitable when politicians and lawyers try to keep up with complex new technologies, practices, and ideas. What is not inevitable is that these difficulties should descend upon the schoolhouse. Before jumping on the national curriculum bandwagon, it is wise to remember the experience of the Jesuits. Governed by a Rule of Studies formally established in 1599, Jesuit schools enjoyed considerable popularity and success until the dawn of the Enlightenment in the eighteenth century. From that point on, their fixed curriculum became increasingly moribund in a world hungry for instruction in the burgeoning sciences. Putting educational progress in the hands of congresses and parliaments is apt to produce similar results.

Official Knowledge

Historically, one of two things has happened when governments have obtained control over the curriculum. Most commonly, ruling authorities have distorted the content of school lessons to favor their own agendas and to vilify their critics. This has happened in autocracies and in democracies that have had weak opposition parties. In a few cases, especially in democracies with many vigorous and competing political factions, the curriculum has been neutered— expunged of all material offensive to any of the combatants. U.S. public schools have, at different times, played out both of these scenarios, and a further centralization of the curriculum would only make matters worse.

We must not forget the depiction of immigrants (especially Catholics) by U.S. public schools in the nineteenth and early twentieth centuries. How must it have felt for newly settled Irish families to read in their children's government-school textbooks that America was becoming "the common sewer of Ireland"?[81] Neither must we forget the one-sided nature of many of the textbooks that have been used in public schools over the years. Harold Rugg's 1933 elementary social science textbook uncritically advocated that the textile, railroad, and agriculture industries be taken over by government collectives, and called for plans "to redistribute the national income among the people."[82]

If these examples seem dated, if it is hard to imagine such things happening nowadays, consider the following. The same interest groups who lobby Congress and thus shape the laws which govern us all are already getting educational materials favorable to their causes adopted in the public schools. Imagine how much easier their task would be if, instead of having to entice countless individual teachers, they could concentrate all their resources on lobbying a single agency: the federal Department of Education.

The variety of sales literature masquerading as lesson plans is stunning, and education professor Alex Molnar has collected many examples in his book *Giving Kids the Business*. "OPEN IMMEDIATELY," announces one packet from Lifetime Learning Systems addressed simply to "Third Grade Teacher." Inside this hefty envelope, which promises an "educational program" called Count Your Chips, is an ill-disguised and utterly ridiculous promotional campaign for potato chips. Students are given many "fun facts" about this snack food, and are asked to become Chip-e-maticians by calculating "how many one ounce bags of chips [an average person eats] in a year." Another pedagogical Trojan horse, promoting the General Mills "Gushers" candy, has the following instructions for teachers: "[D]istribute the samples of GUSHERS supplied with this program, and suggest that students each place a GUSHER in their mouths. Then discuss the process needed to make these fruit snacks 'gush' when you bite into them." What will children learn from this exercise? Ostensibly, they will gain knowledge of the Earth's "geothermic 'gushers': volcanoes, geysers and hot springs." Oddly, children are not asked to estimate the lesson plan's impact on the sales of Gushers candies or on General Mills' bottom line.

Similar campaigns purport to teach kids to count by adding up pepperoni slices on Domino's pizzas, or to improve their writing skills by making them form sentences out of company trademarks. "I had a hamburger and Pepsi at McDonald's,"[83] for instance. But why do teachers actually use these corporate curricula? The answer should not surprise this book's readers. Special-interest groups offer teachers incentives to make it worth their while, putting them, in a sense, on the payroll. In order to turn educators into travel agents, the Governor's office of Puerto Rico and the Puerto Rico Tourism Company jointly spent $400,000 on a tourism-promoting lesson plan which was distributed to 219,000 teachers across the United States. The carrot, in this case, was "an all-expense-paid vacation for two to the resort island for the 20 teachers who used the teaching materials most creatively and described it in an essay."[84] According to a spokeswoman for the Puerto Rican tourism office, the response was "very good."

If Puerto Rican authorities achieved a "very good" response by offering just a chance to win a resort trip, imagine how much more successful they would be if they could guarantee one. And if they had to lobby only a handful of state or federal bureaucrats, instead of 219,000 individual teachers, they could easily afford to make such a guarantee. If control over the curriculum is placed in the hands of Congress, how likely is it that the lobbyists who currently win vast federal subsidies from our lawmakers, who have built an empire of "corporate welfare" programs, will simply ignore a captive market including virtually all of the nation's children?

Many parents would object to their schools being turned into retail outlets, and in a free educational market they could demand that commercialized curricula be kept out of the classroom. Schools would have to oblige or lose their customers. At present, public schooling gives parents far less power and far fewer options. Public schools are already "giving kids the business," and there is very little that most parents can do about it. The imposition of a national curriculum would make escaping such propaganda more difficult than it already is.

Even if no single party or interest group is able to dominate the curriculum-setting process, it is likely that many disparate groups would succeed in eliminating material they find objectionable, reducing the content of schooling to a thin gruel. This already happens with existing state-level textbook-adoption procedures in the United States,[85] and the problem would be sure to worsen under a system of national standards, due to the narrowing and homogenizing effect such standards would have on the market for textbooks.

The Case of the Disappearing Disciplines

More than a century ago, English scientist T. H. Huxley made the observation that the government standards and testing program known as Payment by Results "did not compel any schoolmaster to leave off teaching anything; but, by the very simple process of refusing to pay for many kinds of teaching, it has practically put an end to them."[86] Though modern national curriculum proposals are not typically tied to school funding, they are nonetheless liable to have the same deleterious effect.

Evidence presented in Chapter 6 demonstrates that U.S. public schools already alter their curricula to fit the material they know to be on state-level or district-level tests. To the extent that a subject is not part of a mandatory state curriculum, it is likely to be marginalized. This trend is already evident in England under its national curriculum. According to the National Association of Head Teachers, the "obsession with passing tests in English, mathematics and science [means that] other subjects [are] being overlooked."[87]

But What about High Standards?

Having rigorous standards that encourage the pursuit of excellence is a wonderful idea, but there need not be a single standard for an entire nation. Ancient Athens did not achieve the highest level of literacy of its time by passing a law to that effect, and neither did the early medieval Muslim empire. They did so by allowing parents to seek out the best teachers for their children, thereby giving bad teachers an incentive to improve or leave the profession for lack of students. The standards and expectations of modern private schools, which are typically higher than those of public schools,[88] are not elevated by the pen of a lawmaker but by the private schools' sense of mission, their desire to excel, and their need to meet the demands of their customers. High standards are best achieved today as they have always been, through the need for individual schools to maximize their students' potentials or risk losing them to competitors.

Considering Our Options

While several of the reforms discussed in this chapter promise some improvement over the status quo, they do not fully enjoy the ingredients for educational excellence discussed in Chapter 9. Government curriculum standards can essentially be written off, and contracting-out generates as much trouble as it does benefits. Charter schools, if they became widely disseminated, would no doubt lead to an improvement in the quality of state schooling, but could not approach the level of choice, performance, innovation, or efficiency of competitive, for-profit educational markets. The most promising of the four reforms seems to be government scholarships, but even they are beset by several grave problems.

What to do, then? The first step is to stop asking how state schooling can be tweaked to minimize its faults, and start asking: What is the *best* we can do for our children? For decades, public schools in many nations have repeated a futile cycle of criticism, reform, failure to improve, criticism, and so on. Based on the inherent flaws in state schooling that are evident throughout its 2,500 year history, it seems likely that this cycle will continue indefinitely—a perpetual stagnation machine—unless we decide to stop it.

In the concluding chapter, this book steps off the public school reform merry-go-round, and suggests an approach to school governance based on the most successful systems of past and present.

Conclusion:
Achieving Educational Excellence

> *Free educational markets have consistently done a better job of serving the public's needs than have state-run school systems. But what would a modern competitive education industry actually look like? Could all families, regardless of income level, benefit from such a system? How could we bring an educational market into being?*

An Educational Vision

Imagine a competitive education industry driven by the needs and preferences of families. Educational service providers would be forced to choose pedagogical methods based on effectiveness rather than ideology. Practices that have until now been uncritically inherited from preceding generations would be regularly reexamined to determine whether or not they continued to serve the needs of contemporary students. Research-and-development spending would increase dramatically as competing providers sought to find better and more cost-effective ways of serving their clients. The impact of such changes would be enormous.

Public school systems in English-speaking nations have all but abandoned the most effective known approach to early reading instruction (synthetic phonics) for nearly a century, causing unnecessary reading problems in countless children. Such a widespread disaster would be all but impossible in a competitive, for-profit environment. Schools using synthetic phonics would be quick to demonstrate the superior achievement gains of their students, thus drawing away pupils from nonphonics schools.

The anachronistic eight-month school year would also be likely to change. In the agrarian economy of the mid nineteenth century it was often necessary for children to labor on family farms during the warm months. This is no longer the case in most of the industrialized world. Schools competing in an open market would offer a whole range of other scheduling options to suit the contemporary needs and preferences of families. As in the modern for-profit higher education sector, many schools would begin offering their services year-round. Home-schoolers and older students interested in independent study would be able to make use of as much or as little professional schooling as they desired, and could do so on whatever schedule was convenient for them.

Public schools and districts have grown ever larger over the last hundred years, often despite the demand for smaller, more personal institutions of learning. A competitive education industry would offer schools in all shapes and sizes. As in Japan's thriving supplemental school market, there would be small local service providers along with vast nationwide chains. Families would have the option of choosing large high schools with comprehensive course offerings, or more intimate educational environments with specific, well-defined goals. Rather than attending a single institution for all of their studies, mature students could take responsibility for their own education, picking and choosing courses from a variety of different service providers.

With the help of the Internet, even families in the most remote rural areas would be able to enjoy the benefits of a competitive educational market. While many rural communities are only able to support one or two physical schools, families in these regions would have access to all the same "virtual" schools as their urban counterparts. As communications and computer technology continue to improve, students and teachers will be able to interact in ever more meaningful ways via computer connections, and the barriers imposed by geography will be lowered ever further. Today, even though education is still dominated by monolithic state school systems, private educational services are already proliferating on the Internet. The variety and quality of these services will be greatly enhanced as a higher and higher percentage of educational spending is directed into the innovative private sector. Even in cities, where physical schools will be numerous and competition intense, the flexibility of Internet learning services will provide families with many new options. The traditional schoolhouse will increasingly be seen as just one educational choice among many.

This rediscovered flexibility in education would release enterprising students from the regimentation of public schooling. Instead of herding children along a beaten educational path from elementary school all the way through college, a competitive education industry would offer them many opportunities to take charge of their own studies. After a century of conformity-inducing state education, it is easy to forget the great intellectual and artistic heights which young adults can reach. At the age of nineteen, Benjamin Franklin was not delivering newspapers. He was editing them. Under a deregulated education industry, such precociousness would flourish.

Educators themselves would also enjoy the liberating effects of a free market. The most brilliant, effective, and inspirational teachers would rise to unprecedented heights within their profession. With the help of technology, they would be able to reach out to millions of students around the world, and train scores of other teachers to follow their successful methods. The elimination of mandatory government teacher certification would drastically reduce credentialism in the profession, and focus attention on educators' performance rather than their pedigree. Some families might wish to consider only teachers certified by a professional organization, while others would feel comfortable judging educators' skills for themselves, based on the success of their pupils, their reputation, word of mouth, and personal opinions. The teaching talent pool would thus be greatly expanded and enriched.

Instead of arbitrarily grouping all students by age, many schools would offer to place children in classes geared to their actual performance level in specific subject areas. This practice, already used with success in Japanese *juku,* would certainly appeal to students who learned at a faster or slower pace than typical children of their age. Fourteen-year-olds capable of reading Molière in the original French could be encouraged to do so, while seventeen-year olds still struggling with newspaper columns could receive the time and attention they required. Grouping students by performance instead of age would all but eliminate placement problems associated with transferring children between schools, since they could simply be placed in whichever classes were closest to their level of competence.

The current battles over school-to-work training that plague many public systems could be easily resolved, since children and their parents would be free to choose the kind of program they preferred. Co-op programs such as those which exist at the college level could be extended to upper secondary students, allowing them to gain experience in the workings of actual businesses. Students more interested in advanced academic training could receive college-level science, mathematics, and liberal arts courses in lieu of co-op experiences. Since the choice would be left up to families, no one would feel put-upon or moved to protest, as is so often the case in government systems.

The same principle applies to virtually every other area of community conflict precipitated by official state schooling. Battles over sex education, condom distribution, religious instruction, the celebration of religious holidays, the interpretation of history, public-service graduation requirements, outcomes-based education, etc. would all become unnecessary under a free market, as each family could choose the educational services most conducive to its own needs and beliefs. Far from balkanizing societies, history shows that such freedom would foster peaceful coexistence.

Caveat Lector

The preceding chapters should have encouraged a healthy skepticism toward the promises of education reformers. Cautious readers may reasonably ask what distinguishes the prognostications just described from the illusory visions of Horace Mann and Egerton Ryerson. The answer is that this chapter is the conclusion to an empirical investigation that Mann and Ryerson never thought to undertake. Rather than examining the historical record to determine the likelihood that their chosen approach to education would succeed, they allowed themselves to be blinded by their romanticized view of government. Our ancestors were swept along for the ride, persuaded more by the fervor of the reformers' rhetoric than by the weight of their evidence. After one hundred and fifty years of experience with state schooling, we should now have the wisdom to resist their siren song. When we are promised educational salvation, whether through privatization or yet another tweak to the government system, we should consider the evidence and arguments carefully.

The remainder of this chapter outlines a series of policies that would help to bring about a free educational market. These policies are offered only as suggestions, and are not meant to exclude other approaches from consideration. The reason for this tentative tone is that while government takeovers of private-sector education have occurred repeatedly over the centuries, there have been few if any cases where government school systems have been privatized. In other words, we are pretty much on our own when it comes to figuring out the best way of reintroducing competition and choice in education.

Many different education reforms have been suggested in recent years, and it is not yet clear which would provide effective transition paths from state schooling to free-enterprise education, and which would yield only cosmetic changes to the status quo. Thus, great care must be taken in the design of education reform policies. In particular, it must be remembered that the historical success of free markets has rested on five factors: choice and financial responsibility for parents; and freedom, competition, and the profit motive for schools. To the extent that any of these factors is compromised by a given policy, the benefits of that policy will be commensurately reduced. That is not to say that compromises should not be considered, but simply that their limitations must be recognized and weighed against any perceived advantages they may have.

The Price of Freedom

Free educational markets have numerous advantages over the status quo, but could families really afford to foot the bill for their own children's education? Clearly, many can and already do, but middle-income families have reason to be cautious. At present, they are entitled to "free" government schooling for all their children. That schooling is often deficient, inefficient, and unresponsive when compared to the services available in free markets, but at least other people help pay for it. If private schools replace government institutions, the educational expenses of middle-income parents would undoubtedly increase. How would they cover those costs without putting undue strain on their budgets? Assuaging that very reasonable concern is the purpose of the next section.

Without some sort of financial assistance, most low-income families would find it difficult or even impossible to provide their children with the kind of schooling necessary to succeed in the modern world. As Chapter 1 has shown, most citizens are aware of this fact, and are willing to dedicate a considerable amount of their own money toward ensuring that all families have access to a quality education. What has been lacking, throughout history, has been an effective and efficient mechanism for translating the public's philanthropic goals into reality. A proposal for just such a mechanism is presented below.

Finally, for citizens without children, or for those whose children have already finished school, the economics of educational markets undeniably make sense. Existing public schools are both expensive and ineffective, so taxpayers are currently spending a lot of money and getting very little to show for it. As this book has argued, the educational outcomes of competitive markets are far superior to those of government school systems, and their costs are lower. Thus, no matter which variation on the market theme is eventually adopted, it is almost certain to entail a smaller financial burden on the taxpaying public.

The Market and the Middle-Income Family

The average per-pupil expenditure of U.S. public schools was $7,371 in 1996–97. In 1993–94 (the most recent year for which comparable data are available), private school tuitions averaged less than half what public schools spent per pupil at the time. Even adding in the other sources of funding enjoyed by private schools, such as donations[1] and endowment interest, their average costs are still not much more than half those of schools in the public sector. This leads us to an important conclusion about financing education in a free market: the total cost is likely to be less than that of existing public school systems (and is likely to buy a better level of service).

Wonderful as that may seem, it disguises a potential difficulty: under state-run systems, the costs of elementary and secondary schooling are spread throughout an individual's entire taxpaying life,[2] whereas free-market schooling is a pay-as-you-go affair. Young families with school-aged children tend to have lower incomes than those whose children have grown up and are no longer living at home. As a result, they pay a considerably smaller share of the costs of public schooling than older taxpayers. A completely free educational market would eliminate this age-based redistribution of wealth, since each family would have to pay for its educational services as it consumed them.

How would this affect middle-income families? Under the private scholarship scheme described in the next section, the amount of money that would have to be collected to subsidize the education of low-income families would be very small when compared to the current expenditures on government-run schooling. That means that the tax burden on middle-income families would also be much less. The typical family, therefore, would have larger savings by the time their children entered school and a higher after-tax income once their children were in school, making it easier for them to pay for tuition. Another mitigating factor is that elementary school tuition is considerably cheaper than secondary school tuition. This coincides advantageously with the normal progression in salaries that comes with age. Families with young children would most likely have lower incomes, but also lower educational costs, than families with high-school-aged children. By the time children reach high-school age, their parents are better able to finance secondary schooling.

The Japanese situation is informative. Senior high school is not compulsory in Japan, and one out of every four senior high schools is a privately run, tuition-charging institution. Nonetheless, that nation's enrollment rate for seventeen-year-olds was 90.3 percent in 1992, compared to 72 percent in the United States where high school is "free" and in many states is compulsory for children up to age seventeen or even eighteen.[3]

Nonetheless, some large families, and those with incomes toward the low end of the middle bracket, might still find it difficult to fully cover the costs of their children's education. There are three obvious ways of dealing with this potential difficulty: loans, tax breaks, and participation in scholarship programs. Just as many parents borrow money to send their children to college, so too could they take out loans to help spread out the cost of K–12 schooling. The great drawback of this approach, from the standpoint of parents, is that interest rates for educational loans at the K–12 level are currently very high, on a par with the 17 to 20 percent rates charged by credit-card companies. Interest rates are high because, in the case of unsecured loans, lenders have little recourse if borrowers default. You can repossess a car but not a child. When defaulted loans cannot easily be recouped, interest rates have to be high enough to cover the inevitable losses. If a way could be found to reduce interest rates, educational loans might become a solution worth considering. Given the lower expense of private as compared to public schooling, paying off such a loan would likely be less expensive, in the long run, than paying education taxes for the rest of the parents' lives.

Apart from the lack of appeal that loans may have for parents already carrying sizable debt burdens, they have the added drawback that repayment must typically begin immediately. This option might become viable, however, if a loan program could be devised that deferred repayment for several years, or that at least allowed smaller payments to be made in the initial years.

A second way to ease the financial burden on parents, one that delays much of the payment until after high school, is to provide educational tax deductions or exemptions. For every school-aged child, parents could deduct a certain amount from their state and local taxes to help defray the cost of tuition. This would mean that older taxpayers would be shouldering a slightly higher percentage of the total tax burden, just as they do under the current government school system. Looked at from the perspective of a given taxpaying couple, however, this would simply amount to shifting a portion of the cost of their children's education from their low-earning years to their high-earning years, since they would eventually lose the tax break as their children grew older. Tax deductions or exemptions for education costs have already been approved in several states, such as Illinois, Arizona, and Minnesota, and have been proposed in many others (Michigan is a recent example).

In order to avoid most of the problems ascribed to vouchers in Chapter 10, these credits would have to be "nonrefundable," which is to say that taxpayers would end up keeping more of the money they themselves earned, but would receive no public funds from the government. Since they would not be the beneficiaries of public funding, there could be no concern with church/state entanglement in the use of tax credits. Nonrefundable tax credits also have the virtue that they would be somewhat less likely to perpetuate government regulation of education. It would be possible to issue credits based solely on the taxpayer's number of school-aged dependents, and leave the decisions regarding the education of those dependents to the individual.

Unfortunately, tax credits are not without their flaws. Critics, such as Marshall Fritz of the Separation of School and State Alliance, argue that they reduce parental financial responsibility and promote a welfare/entitlement mentality among parents.[4] Others point out that while tax credits are somewhat less susceptible to regulation than vouchers, they are nonetheless likely to precipitate considerable regulation of education in the long run—restricting both parental choice and the freedom of educators. Anyone who has filed a tax return will have to admit that restrictions, provisos, and limitations abound when it comes to most deductions and credits. Tax credits would also put educational funding at the mercy of politics, and their value would therefore be subject to unpredictable fluctuations. These concerns are certainly valid, and they must be taken into account when determining whether or not a given tax-credit program is likely to be of real, long-term benefit. For reasons described earlier in this book, the ideal situation would be for all families to be able to assume full financial responsibility for their own children's education. Whether tax credits would provide a bridge toward that end, or would, as some allege, actually undermine it, is a matter deserving much more attention than it has yet received.

As a third option, lower-middle income families who required financial assistance could turn to the private scholarship-granting organizations described in the following section.

A Private Scholarship Network

Ensuring that low-income families have access to a quality education for their children is not easy. The most common approach, having the government build, finance, and operate "free" schools, has consistently failed. Large-scale private efforts to run charity schools have fared only marginally better, because these efforts have much more closely resembled government schooling than free educational markets. In nineteenth-century England, for example, charity schools run by the major religious denominations were far more interested in inculcating their own dogma than in teaching the practical skills that low-income children needed to improve their lives. The schools belonging to a given organization did not compete among themselves and, naturally, were not operated for profit, so they had little incentive to innovate or to tailor their services to the demands of families.

Government-funded scholarships are an attempt to alleviate the problems of centralized, monopolistic school systems (both public and private), by severing the link between funding and management in education. Doing so allows low-income parents to receive the funds they need while leaving them free to use those funds at whichever schools best meet their children's needs. As the previous chapter demonstrated, however, government scholarships suffer from a variety of flaws: they perpetuate the church/state controversy and the regulation ratchet; they encourage lobbying for ever-higher scholarship amounts; and they set up an incentive structure conducive to fraud, corruption, and mismanagement.

But there is nothing inherent in the concept of scholarships that requires money to pass through the hands of bureaucrats. Before the proliferation of state agencies and programs that has characterized the twentieth century, it was commonplace for public projects of all kinds to be financed by private organizations. In the past decade, this tradition has reawakened in the form of privately funded scholarship-granting institutions. There are already roughly forty private scholarship-granting charities in the United States. They collect donations from businesses and individuals and then provide scholarships for low-income parents to send their children to private schools. The government is not involved in any way, and the satisfaction ratings of participating families are as high or higher than for any other group of parents with school-aged children (see Chapter 8). Currently, because public schools are still thought of as the official providers of education, these private scholarship-granting agencies raise relatively small amounts of money, and educate only a few hundred or a few thousand students each. This need not be the case. If government schools were phased out over time, and if citizens were encouraged to donate to these private agencies in lieu of paying education taxes, the agencies could, in theory, raise enough money to educate all low-income children.

Despite their advantages over state-funded scholarships, private scholarships still suffer from two drawbacks associated with third-party payment systems: potential loss of parental control, and lack of parental financial responsibility. Since all organizations, public and private, tend to attach strings to the funds they distribute, scholarship recipients may find their freedom curtailed. Existing private scholarship-granting charities place few if any restrictions on the choices of participating families (unlike government programs), but it would be naive to suppose that this hands-off attitude would prevail indefinitely and universally.

Ensuring that low-income families have access to more than one scholarship-granting institution could minimize the effects of any restrictions imposed by scholarship grantors. What is necessary, then, is competition between private scholarship-granting charities for the opportunity to subsidize the education of any given child: an open market for education scholarships. With private scholarship programs continuing to proliferate, it is only a matter of time before competition between those programs becomes a reality.

The advantages of competition among scholarship-granting charities would be considerable. The fact that citizens would have more than one option when making their educational donations would mean that they could avoid giving funds to organizations with reputations for mismanagement, or high overheads. It may be impossible to entirely eliminate fraud and corruption, but these ills would have a much more difficult time flourishing in a system where donors have control over who receives their money. At present, when taxpayers revolt against corrupt and defective public school districts, their only alternative is to withhold their money altogether by voting down school tax increases. This is no solution, given that the vast majority of citizens do want to contribute to the education of their neighbors so long as they know their money is actually making it into classrooms, and so long as those classrooms actually teach things which will be of value to children in later life. The existence of multiple scholarship-granting institutions would mean that citizens disgruntled with one institution could give their money to another.

Another tremendous advantage of raising money through private contributions rather than taxes is that it entirely avoids government involvement in the funding of religious schools. Private scholarship-granting institutions would be free to fund or not to fund religious schools depending on the preferences of their contributors. No citizen would be forced to subsidize a religious education that conflicted with his or her own beliefs, but all citizens would be free to support religious schools if they so chose.

As Chapter 9 argued, parental financial responsibility encourages parental involvement in education. It follows, therefore, that financial responsibility should be preserved to whatever extent possible within the structure of a scholarship program. Truly destitute parents could be given scholarships to cover the entire cost of their children's education, while those able to pay a portion of their children's tuition, however small, could be required to do so. For example, a particular scholarship-granting institution might decide that its elementary-school scholarships would vary in size from a minimum of $500 to a maximum of $4,000 (or 100 percent of a given school's tuition, whichever is lower). Families with no income to speak of could be issued scholarships for the full $4,000. Families able to pay only $50 a month toward tuition could be required to do so. Families experiencing only slight or temporary economic difficulties could be given scholarships for the minimum $500, and could be required to pay the remainder of their children's educational expenses. Such a graded scholarship system would be able to give parents at least some direct financial responsibility for their children's education, while still enabling all low-income families to obtain quality schooling for their children. It would allow low-income parents to feel that they were fulfilling their responsibility to provide their children with a sound education, and would provide them with an incentive to monitor the quality of their schools' services.

Parents receiving full scholarships for their children's tuition would not have these financial incentives. They could become just as easily disenfranchised from their children's private schools as so many of today's parents are from their children's public schools. There is, however, a potential solution to this problem. Money, after all, is only a proxy for a certain amount of labor or goods. We tend to be careful about how we spend our money because we have to work to earn it. It would thus be possible to require parents receiving full scholarships to contribute some of their own time and effort at their chosen school, in lieu of paying a portion of their children's tuition. Many private schools already require parents to help raise money, do secretarial tasks, keep school facilities clean and operational, or in some other way aid the school in its efforts to educate their children.

Two possible objections to school participation requirements for scholarship recipients are that they would place a burden on low-income parents that wealthier families would not face, and that they could conceivably interfere with parents' attempts to find gainful employment and thus earn enough money so that they would no longer need the scholarships. The first objection misses the point made in the previous paragraph: In a free educational market, all parents would have to work to send their children to school. Most families would work regular jobs to earn money to pay for tuition, while some low-income families would help out directly at the schools.

The second concern would pose little problem in practice, since private scholarship-granting organizations would not be forced to follow a rigid legal code in the way public schools are. If it was clear that a scholarship-receiving parent was busy interviewing for jobs, or studying for a degree, school participation requirements could be waived on an individual basis.

One of the greatest advantages of private scholarship organizations over state-administered programs is their potential for establishing long-term personal relationships with scholarship recipients. At present, low-income parents often feel disenfranchised from their public schools. They do not know whom to hold accountable, or from whom to seek assistance. School district offices tend to be bureaucratic and impersonal, while teachers and principals, particularly in inner cities, are frequently unresponsive to the concerns and questions of parents. This explains, in part, why support for scholarship programs is higher among low-income minority parents than any other group.

The lack of personal ties between low-income parents and their public schools is symptomatic of most state services. In his book *The Tragedy of American Compassion,* Marvin Olasky shows that private charities have historically been better than government welfare programs at developing bonds between those needing assistance and those providing it. This is not a new insight. In 1894, a comprehensive study of American charities found that government services were "necessarily more impersonal and mechanical than private charity or individual action."⁵ The chief cause of impersonal service on the part of government agencies is that they are bound to operate within a rigid regulatory framework. Though needs vary from family to family, government programs must treat everyone equally. Private philanthropic organizations are not constrained in the same way and are thus able to tailor their efforts to each individual.

While private philanthropic efforts have generally been better at fostering interpersonal bonds than government ones, not every private organization makes the effort to get to know the people it seeks to help. What is certain, however, is that those that do are more successful at getting people back on their feet and able to support themselves than those that do not. This is another case in which being able to choose among agencies would be crucial, since both donors and recipients could seek out scholarship-granting agencies known for their personal attention and their strong links to the local community.

A fringe benefit of the more personalized nature of private charities is that it makes them more difficult to defraud. Given their personal knowledge of their recipients, they are less easily fooled by those who would abuse their services. The importance of this benefit should not be underestimated. Another of

Olasky's key findings is that the public's generosity is directly related to its level of confidence in the effectiveness and efficiency of a given philanthropic program.[6] By discouraging fraud, private charities would remove a major impediment to public spending on education.

Potential Funding Problems

The idea of supporting the education of low-income families through voluntary contributions, as opposed to tax-funded public schools, is morally objectionable to many advocates of state-run schooling. They believe that the current legal compulsion to pay for public schools demonstrates society's commitment to educational justice, and that it would be unethical to do away with it. Their argument is not well-founded. It might make sense to discuss the morality of tax support for public schools if those schools could consistently and effectively serve the needs of low-income families, but they cannot. The record of government schooling in this area is abysmal, and forcing a defective educational system on the poor is clearly not an ethical thing to do.

The moral case for preferring government scholarships to voluntarily funded ones is also unconvincing. As noted in the previous chapter, government involvement in education, even when restricted to funding, has serious drawbacks that private contributions do not. It precipitates political lobbying by special interests, causes church/state conflicts, and frequently leads to state control of education. But even if there were no perceptible differences between tax-funded and privately funded scholarship programs, one could still argue that *non*government programs would be morally superior, since they would be based on voluntary action rather than state compulsion.

A more mundane but also more widespread concern regarding voluntary private funding of scholarship programs is whether or not they would raise enough money. Since the definition of "enough" varies from person to person, this concern is sure to be a major issue. The only way of guaranteeing that a minimum dollar amount is raised is to require it by law, perhaps through an education tax, but this once again raises the specter of state control, church/state conflicts, etc., and thus threatens to undermine the essential virtues of private scholarship programs.

Despite these risks, the public may deem some form of tax support for scholarship programs indispensable. If so, it is crucial that the tax laws be designed in such a way as to minimize their negative effects. One approach would be to tax only those citizens who do not already donate to scholarship-granting organizations. For example, consider a couple whose assessed education tax is $500. The couple would have two options: they could either pay the tax *or* donate $500 (or more) to a scholarship-granting charity of their own choosing. In the latter case, they would receive an exemption from the education tax.

This approach would at least abate the problems inherent in tax-funded vouchers. As explained in the previous chapter, the expansion of Milwaukee's government voucher program was challenged (albeit unsuccessfully) on the grounds that it forces taxpayers to subsidize religious institutions. Under the "opt-out" plan described above, taxpayers would have the option of donating their education funds to any scholarship-granting organization of their choosing, sectarian or nonsectarian. No one would be forced to support a program he found objectionable on religious or any other grounds, but all would be free to donate to religious institutions if they so chose.

That leaves us with the question of what to do with the funds collected from taxpayers who did not donate directly to a scholarship-granting organization. The obvious solution would be to operate a nonsectarian government scholarship program alongside the private programs. Given the already described disadvantages of that approach, it is worth considering alternatives. One promising mechanism for distributing the education taxes would be to mimic private-sector "matching-grants" programs, whereby corporations match some or all of the charitable donations made by their employees. The state could maintain a record of which private scholarship organizations attracted the most money in private donations, or the greatest number of private donations, or some function of the two, and then automatically distribute the tax money to the top one hundred organizations in proportion to their popularity with citizens.

Such a matching-grants program would alleviate the need for a massive government bureaucracy dedicated to distributing scholarships to students and regulating scholarship-accepting schools. Instead, the collective will of the people would determine how the money would be distributed, and any taxpayer who preferred donating to a lesser-known scholarship program would be free to do so.

The foregoing tax proposal is offered as a way of minimizing the damage caused by state involvement in education funding. It has not been established, however, that compulsory tax support for education is necessary or even advantageous. The key to generous giving, according to author Marvin Olasky, is twofold. Donors must recognize that the need in question is genuine, and they must be confident in the ability of a particular program to meet that need. If opinion polls are any indication, the public is not only willing but also eager to voluntarily support the education of low-income children. Clearly, they recognize the need. As for confidence in the effectiveness of a given scholarship program, this would be virtually guaranteed if the public were able to choose from among multiple programs all vying for the chance to help low-income families.

Having just argued that a network of private scholarship-granting charities is the most promising way of funding the education of children from poor families while preserving the greatest amount of parental freedom and responsibility, it must be acknowledged that this approach has its critics. Because the scholarships described above would be based on financial need, they would not be received by wealthier families, and it has been said that "any program limited to the poor is apt to be a poor program." The implication of this aphorism is that unless the upper and middle classes are beneficiaries of a given program, their support for it will be limited. Proponents of this line of reasoning tend to favor equal government vouchers for children at all income levels over either means-tested tax credits or a system of private scholarships like the one described above.

This is a grave criticism. Low-income families stand to be among the greatest beneficiaries of a free educational market, but the benefits they reap will depend to no small extent on the size of the scholarships available to them. There is not sufficient room here to fully explore this concern, but, on the surface at least, there are several reasons to suspect that it may not be justified. Horace Mann used a similar argument in the nineteenth century in support of government-run schooling, entreating wealthy and middle-class families to send their children to the state schools in order to enlist their resources and efforts in expanding the system to its fullest capabilities. After more than a century of public school attendance by roughly 90 percent of the citizenry, the disparity between the education of rich and poor is greater than ever. The participation of members of the upper and middle classes in government schooling has not, in fact, secured the equality or efficiency that was promised.

Another relevant observation is that the concern over means-testing seems less applicable to voluntary private programs than to mandatory government ones. Most taxpayers have no interaction whatsoever with the government programs they fund unless they happen to be beneficiaries of those programs. It is understandable, therefore, that their support might suffer to the extent that they are unaware of any good that a given program might be doing. Worries about government inefficiency (such as the $23 billion wasted every year by Social Security) also discourage taxpayers from favoring increased spending on government programs. Voluntary private programs, on the other hand, require more active participation by donors, and also tend to provide donors with positive feedback on the outcomes of the programs. Furthermore, having a choice of scholarship-granting charities would mean that citizens would not be forced to direct their donations to an institution they believed to be corrupt or mismanaged.

Easing the Transition

How can we most smoothly make the transition from a centralized, government-run educational system to a for-profit market of competing private schools? While a detailed answer to that question will no doubt be the work of many people over several years, one thing is clear: the more closely the process is linked to the free choices of individual families and citizens, the fewer problems will arise. In other words, allowing parents and taxpayers to opt out of government schooling on a voluntary, incremental basis will engender much less friction than obliging them to do so all at once.

A gradual transition to free-market schooling would be facilitated by the programs described above. Families opting to place their children in private schools would receive a tax exemption or scholarship to help defray the costs of tuition, and taxpayers without school-aged children could receive an exemption from their education taxes by donating money to the private scholarship-granting institution of their choice. As more and more parents and taxpayers shifted to the private sector, demand for public schooling would naturally fall. The first public schools to close would be those which could no longer attract students. Successful public schools, on the other hand, could continue to operate just as long as families continued to value their services. There is no reason why privately collected vouchers could not be redeemed at government schools, so even if the entire taxpaying population were to opt out of their education taxes by donating to scholarship-granting charities, publicly run schools could continue to function.

This transition strategy is not without its problems and complexities, however, and the following sections try to identify some of the major issues with which the public and its elected representatives would have to deal.

The Educational Provisions of State Constitutions

In 1875, a congressman and repeatedly unsuccessful presidential candidate by the name of James G. Blaine proposed an amendment to the U.S. Constitution requiring that

> [n]o money raised by taxation in any State for the support of public schools, or derived from any public fund therefor, nor any public lands devoted thereto, shall ever be under the control of any religious sect; nor shall any money so raised or lands so devoted be divided between religious sects or denominations.[7]

Though religiously neutral on its face, the bill was supported almost exclusively by Protestant Republicans fearful of the continued existence and expansion of Catholicism and Catholic schooling. Tellingly, the Republican-controlled Senate added the provision that the amendment should never be interpreted to exclude the Protestant Bible from public schools.[8] When it came to a vote, Congress split strictly along party lines, and the amendment failed to receive the necessary two-thirds majority.

Though it died in Congress, Blaine's idea was taken up with vigor around the country. According to a legal counsel for the ACLU, "twenty-one state constitutions specifically prohibit state aid, maintenance, or support of sectarian schools, in addition to other prohibitions on aiding religious institutions generally."[9] Article IX, section 4 of the Washington state constitution loudly proclaims: "SECTARIAN CONTROL OR INFLUENCE PROHIBITED. All schools maintained or supported wholly or in part by the public funds shall be forever free from sectarian control or influence." The California constitution (Article 9, section 8) concurs, stating that "[n]o public money shall ever be appropriated for the support of any sectarian or denominational school, or any school not under the exclusive control of the officers of the public schools."

In a completely free educational market these provisions would be irrelevant. Since no state funds would be raised to pay for schools, there could be no violation of the Blaine amendments. A problem could arise, however, if taxes were used to subsidize private scholarship-granting organizations serving low-income families. Even if all scholarship-granting charities that received state funds were secular, a case might be made that the Blaine amendments would prohibit such charities from allowing parents to use their scholarships at religious schools.[10]

Two solutions present themselves. Either the Blaine amendments would have to be repealed, or scholarships funded in whole or in part with tax money would not be useable at sectarian institutions. Privately funded scholarships could, of course, still be used at religious schools (another of their advantages).

A more direct roadblock to the disestablishment of government schooling is that its existence is explicitly required by the constitutions of many states. Florida's constitution (Article IX, section 1) states that "[a]dequate provision shall be made by law for a uniform system of free public schools." Subsequent sections call for the creation of school districts, a state school board, and the election of public school superintendents. Article 9, section 5 of California's constitution charges the legislature to "provide for a system of common schools by which a free school shall be kept up and supported in each district at least six months in every year, after the first year in which a school has been established." A similar clause can be found in Article IX, section 2 of the Washington state constitution.

Interestingly, Massachusetts, the state most responsible for the creation and popularization of government schooling in the U.S., is one of the few states whose constitution does not appear to require the existence of government schools. So while Massachusetts seems to have hedged its bets, most other states would have to amend their constitutions in order to return to free-market provision of education.

Educating Disabled Children

How would the education of disabled children under a free educational market in the U.S. compare with the existing special education practices of public schools? This question has to be answered in two parts, depending on whether or not existing federal special education law, the Individuals with Disabilities Education Act (IDEA), is left unchanged.

First, let us assume that the IDEA (also known as PL-142) is left as it is. In that case, it would still require that "all children with disabilities have available to them a free appropriate public education."[11] If the term "public education" is taken to mean government-run schooling, then it would be necessary to maintain special government-run schools to which disabled children would be assigned, while all other children would be free to attend whatever private schools they chose. This, however, is extremely unlikely, since many disabled children already attend private schools at public expense under PL-142. "Public education" would thus most probably be construed to mean government-funded schooling. In accordance with other provisions of the IDEA, and with the case history of special education litigation, children who were diagnosed as disabled would be assigned an Individualized Education Plan (IEP) by a committee comprised of state-appointed specialists and the children's parents, and then would be given the equivalent of an unlimited scholarship to purchase all the educational services provided for in the IEP. The only departure from current practice would be that all special education services would be purchased from private providers rather than from a mix of private and public providers.

The IDEA could thus continue to operate virtually unchanged under a free educational market. As explained in Chapters 1 and 6, however, there are many drawbacks to the law as it is currently written and interpreted. The "blank check" policy for funding IEPs bears little relationship to public opinion on special education spending, since nearly half of U.S. citizens advocate spending no more on disabled children than on nondisabled children. Even among the half of citizens who do support additional spending on disabled children, there is no evidence that annual expenditures above $20,000 per special education student are widely accepted (though such expenditures are not uncommon under the present system). Worse yet, the law's all-encompassing definition of "Specific" Learning Disabilities (SLDs) has led to an epidemic of healthy children being incorrectly classified as disabled because they read at below expected levels—even though their poor reading can very often be traced to defective instruction.[12] Whether or not citizens choose to replace government-run schooling with a free and competitive educational system, there is ample justification to completely overhaul the IDEA.

The Fate of Teachers

The greatest effect that privatization and deregulation would have on the educational workforce is in the abolition of barriers to entering the profession. While some parents might specifically request teachers who have graduated from colleges of education and who have been officially certified by a government body or professional organization, many would not. Private schools would be free to hire educators on the basis of ability and subject-matter knowledge rather than credentials. This would open up the profession to individuals from a variety of industries and backgrounds, enormously expanding the educational talent pool. Practicing economists and physicists, historians and writers, would once again be free to teach at the secondary level, so long as they could demonstrate the ability to convey their skills and understanding to students. Competition for teaching positions would be increased in the process, allowing schools to be more selective in staffing decisions.

Disestablishing government schools would probably have a less significant impact on the overall size of the teaching workforce, at least in the short term. Currently, class sizes are smaller in private schools than in public ones, and therefore it might be argued that the demand for teachers would increase. On the other hand, research shows little or no relationship between class size and student learning (except in the first grade), so a competitive market might encourage some private schools to spend less on keeping classes small and more on other, more effective educational strategies, thereby decreasing the demand for teachers. It is impossible to predict the net effect of such forces with any accuracy, particularly in the long term.

Given that U.S. public school teachers earn an average salary one-and-a-half times larger than that of their private-sector counterparts, it stands to reason that public school teachers would, on average, suffer a drop in pay under privatization. Part of the salary premium enjoyed by public school teachers can be attributed to the heavy unionization of the public school teaching profession. But it is unlikely that such high unionization levels would persist in a free educational market. It is well known that unions have thrived in government-operated sectors of the economy while they have atrophied in the private sector. Sheltered from competition, government enterprises are able to continually increase their consumption of resources in a way that would spell bankruptcy for private businesses. Unionization is a self-regulating affair in the private sector, since unions that demand too much undermine the viability of their companies and hence their own long-term interests. Public-sector unions have no such checks and balances—they know that public schools will not be allowed to go out of business, and thus can make far greater demands.

On the other hand, the comparatively low salaries currently paid to private school teachers may not hold at the same level in a completely privatized education industry (which would need about ten times as many teachers as are currently employed by private schools). In other words, it may be that there are only a limited number of teachers who are able and willing to work for the salaries currently paid to private school teachers, and that once all those individuals are employed, schools will be forced to pay higher salaries in order to fill their remaining positions. Teachers might otherwise opt to leave the profession for other, better-paying lines of work. As reported in Chapter 5, lower-paid public school teachers tend to leave the profession at a higher rate than their better-compensated peers.

One aspect of teacher compensation is sure to change under a free educational market: maximum income. At present, public school teachers' salaries are determined by length of service rather than performance, which limits variation. Under a competitive market, salaries would be based on how highly a given teacher's services were valued by families, and by how many families that teacher could serve. Teachers in high demand would command high salaries. Those reaching large numbers of students would also command premiums. One need only look at the private Japanese education labor market for a vision of the future. The most successful teachers, those who have considerable skill and knowledge and who make use of modern technology to broadcast their lessons to thousands if not millions of students, command salaries comparable to those of professional Japanese baseball players. Teachers who are less in demand and who teach only small numbers of students in traditional classrooms, would most likely have salaries more in line with current private school averages.

The teacher's work year is also likely to change. Summer vacations are a vestige of earlier times when children worked in the fields and farms during the warm months, and attended school only when the weather made their labor unnecessary. This is no longer the case, and a flexible educational market would naturally respond to modern demands.

There is no question that the move to a free educational market would result in much change and uncertainty for public school teachers. If government schools are gradually phased out in favor of a free educational market, the transition should be made as smooth as possible for current public school teachers. There are a number of things that might make this transition easier: small business training to help teachers form their own schools, job hotlines to assist teachers in finding places at new or existing private schools, well-considered severance packages, etc. The important thing is to do everything reasonably possible to ease the move for educators.

However comprehensive and well-designed such a transition strategy might be, it is certain that any move toward privatization would be vigorously opposed by the teachers' unions, which have consistently fought privatization in the past. The main point of a union is to improve the salaries, benefits, job security, and working conditions of its members, and, as noted above, the current level of job security and financial compensation enjoyed by public school teachers would be jeopardized by privatization.

Given the considerable size of the National Education Association and the American Federation of Teachers (which have a combined membership of approximately three million), and their remarkable achievements as lobbyists and campaigners (including class size reductions, teacher salary increases, ubiquitous tenure laws, the forced payment of union agency fees by nonunion teachers,[13] the creation of the federal Department of Education, the sinking of numerous school choice ballot initiatives, etc.), many observers suggest that the unions will have little difficulty in preventing the return of a competitive education industry. What these observers fail to consider is that the unions achieved many of their goals only because they convinced enough of the public that those goals would also benefit children. The unions themselves have not voted down a single voucher or charter-school ballot initiative. They have not cast a single vote in either a federal or a state legislature. They have only influenced the opinions of voters and legislators. If the public becomes convinced, on the evidence, that privatization is in the best interests of their children and their nation, they and their elected representatives will act accordingly. While there may be three million teachers' union members, there are roughly 150 million registered voters in the United States. Disseminating the evidence on school choice to these 150 million voters is, however, no small task.

Learning from Experience

Vast numbers of government-owned enterprises have been privatized around the world in the past two decades, providing invaluable lessons on the best ways to proceed. Based on their detailed survey of privatization in the Czech Republic, Hungary, and Poland, researchers at the Central European University (CEU) found several common factors that contributed to success. First and foremost, they concluded that privatized businesses were most likely to flourish when they "did not take over any movable assets from their [government-run] predecessors" or attempt to carry-over existing business structures or practices of their predecessors. This finding casts serious doubt on the merits of charter school programs and contracting-out arrangements that allow existing public schools to be handed over, intact, to new (private) managers. The CEU researchers explained their reasoning in this way:

> Considering the disadvantages of the organizational structure of the old state sector, its inefficient routines and, above all, the vested interests of its central *nomenklatura* management, the value contributed by the business assets other than real estate may well be negative . . . and this burden may seriously lessen the chances of genuine restructuring.[14]

The second most important finding in the CEU investigation was that the entry of entrepreneurs unconnected with the old government enterprises was the "most significant factor in increasing the levels of postprivatization investment."[15] Greater investment, the authors plausibly argued, implies a greater level of commitment on the part of owners to the success of their new businesses.

A separate privatization study conducted by the World Bank concluded that it is more cost-effective to sell off a government-run business as-is, rather than spending public money trying to make improvements before the sale (in the hope of raising the sale price). The consensus of privatization studies, according to the World Bank, is that

> [l]arge new investments for plant modernization or rehabilitation prior to sale should be avoided. Getting the private sector to finance investments and take the risk is a prime reason for privatization in the first place. There is also little evidence that governments recover the costs of physical restructuring in the form of higher sales prices.[16]

The government should therefore not undertake repairs to dilapidated public school buildings (see Chapter 6) immediately prior to selling them. Moreover, both teams of investigators concluded that public properties should be sold rather than leased, because

> [p]rivate ownership itself makes a difference. Some state-owned enterprises have been efficient and well managed for some periods, but government ownership seldom permits sustained good performance over more than a few years.[17]

Overall, the message of these and other studies is clear: "The process of privatization, although not simple, can work and has worked; this is true for a variety of enterprises in a variety of settings."[18]

Phasing Out Government Schools: Is It Necessary? Is It Wise?

Many reasons for wishing to hold on to government schooling have been discussed in previous chapters, and it would not be practical to repeat them all here. Two particular arguments resonate so strongly with so many people, however, that they deserve to be considered again: first, that public schooling's problems are really just an inner-city affair, and that suburban schools are not in need of major change; and second, that government-run educational institutions are necessary for the preservation of democracy.

Misplaced Complacency: Suburbs and Their Public Schools

Given the extreme nature of the crisis afflicting inner-city schools, suburban residents are often justified in believing that their own public schools are not so bad. This is not, however, a reason for complacency. Suburban government schools still suffer from virtually all of the failings described in the earlier chapters of this book. The following is a short list of those failings:

- Stagnation and decline in academic achievement
- Deterioration in the quality of textbooks during the course of the twentieth century
- Defective pedagogical methods
- An artificially constrained and poorly trained workforce
- Violence and lack of discipline
- Community conflicts over religion and the curriculum
- Inefficiency
- High cost
- Limited parental choice
- Low parental involvement (compared to private schools)
- Unnecessarily large and impersonal high schools
- Corruption and deception in student testing

The suburban public schools of today function along essentially the same lines as those of eighty or ninety years ago. This stagnation in the science and art of instruction has few parallels outside of the public/nonprofit sector, and it would not be tolerated in competitive for-profit industries. A for-profit enterprise that failed to improve its services and/or cut its costs over such a long span of time would long ago have succumbed to its competitors. It is only because profit-making educational institutions have been squeezed out of the education industry by the expansion of "free" state schools that this dramatic failure to innovate has not been more readily recognized. Who, today, would seriously consider buying a Model T Ford as a commuter vehicle? Or flying on an airline whose fleet consisted of wooden biplanes? Or going to a physician unfamiliar with the thousands of new drugs invented or discovered during the last hundred years? And yet this is essentially what is being done every time a child is sent off to public school—or, for that matter, to most nonprofit private schools. Constant improvement and innovation are the norm in human activities, and we should expect nothing less from our schools.

In their textbooks and pedagogical methods, suburban public schools are no more immune to the ill effects of state schooling than are their big-city counterparts. Due to the power of textbook-adoption states such as Florida, California, and Texas, textbooks are fairly homogeneous throughout the country, and all have been dumbed-down substantially in their vocabulary and sentence complexity over the past hundred years. Even the processes for choosing among these much-diminished works are flawed. Suburban teachers, moreover, receive essentially the same training as urban teachers. Both are typically inculcated with a passel of empirically discredited pedagogical views, and few graduates of teachers' colleges feel they benefited substantially from the academic training they received.

The belief that violence and discipline problems are confined to urban public schools was shattered by the rash of mass murders by rural and suburban public school students in 1997 and 1998. Moreover, when it comes to causing community strife, suburban public schools may be even worse than inner-city schools. The constant battles over the teaching of evolution versus creationism, sex education, the celebration of Christmas and Halloween, the spin given to the study of national history, and sundry other topics are generally suburban public school affairs, and are virtually unheard of in the private sector.

While not quite so egregiously inefficient as the public schools of Washington, D.C., or Hartford, Connecticut, suburban public schools spend roughly twice as much as the average private school without showing any superiority in outcomes. It is hard to justify paying this enormous price premium for a service that does not warrant it.

The most notorious case of test cheating by public school employees over the past several years did not take place in New York or Los Angeles, but in the Rockwellian suburban community of Fairfield, Connecticut. And the decline in reading ability of U.S. children has not been restricted to the big cities, but is truly national in scope.

We have been expecting far too little of our educational institutions for far too long, and we are paying an increasingly heavy price for that complacency, both financially and in terms of educational outcomes.

Can We Really Do Without Government Schools?

> Public education is more than a simple mechanism for delivering a commodity to consumers. Like other public institutions, it is a "vehicle for deliberation, debate and decision-making." Through these processes, education becomes a public service that contributes to the comparative well-being and strength of both local communities and the nation as a whole. . . . Public schools have also been mandated to actualize the American promise that every citizen is "created equal."[19]

These lovely sentiments, expressed in a study published by the Twentieth Century Fund, have little to do with the reality of government schooling. Far from bringing citizens together, the endless succession of confrontations precipitated by state-run schooling has consistently torn communities apart. Public schools,

by their very nature, attempt to force consensus on many issues where it is neither possible nor even desirable—issues such as the role of religion in education
or the interpretation of a nation's history. On issues where communities are already in agreement, there is no need to resort to force to achieve consensus, and
hence no need for the heavy hand of government in the educational process.

Certain fundamental values must indeed be shared in order for societies to
thrive, but these values are cultivated far more effectively by free educational
markets than by state school systems. It is the height of hypocrisy to attempt to
teach the value of liberty and respect for people of other creeds and ethnicities
in a school system that denies families the right and the dignity of choosing how
their children will be educated. It is equally hypocritical to teach the free-
exercise clause of the First Amendment in state schools that are barred from
teaching religion.

If our goal is to allow citizens of diverse backgrounds to live in harmony with
one another, then our model should not be that of ancient Sparta, which sought
to eradicate all variation among its citizens through a brutal and homogenizing
public school system. Far better examples were set by the school systems of classical Athens and the early medieval Muslim empire, which not only embraced
the diversity of their populations but built great achievements on it. The contributions of the immigrant philosophers and craftsmen of Athens, and of the Jewish and Christian translators, writers, and scientists of the early medieval Muslim empire, were enormous and far-reaching. Safe in the knowledge that their
governments were not actively trying to suppress their cultural and religious heritage, they had little reason to fear or resent their neighbors. Their differences
rarely put them into conflict with one another, and did not prevent them from
sharing many fundamental educational goals. The basic elementary curriculum
in both societies was in many respects remarkably homogeneous despite the absence of government-imposed standards or government-run schools.

Contrast this with the late Muslim or Roman empires, after the introduction of state funding and subsequent state control of education. Religious and
political differences could no longer coexist peacefully; instead, they became
entrenched and deeply divisive. The same has been true of U.S. education
since the introduction of state-run schooling. In fact, the campaign to establish public schools garnered much support from the Protestant majority on the
specific grounds that it would help to prevent the spread of Catholicism, and
would purify immigrants of their undesirable foreign ways. Today in the
United States it is private Catholic schools, not government ones, that do a
better job of minimizing the achievement differences of different racial
groups. And it is private schools, not public schools, that do a better job of
integrating the races.[20]

True equality of educational opportunity is extremely difficult to obtain. It has
only been approached once in human history, in ancient Sparta, and it was only
feasible then for two reasons: First, the Spartan government made it impossible

for citizens to accumulate wealth, and thus no one had the resources to subsidize his own children's education. Second, all children were forced to attend uniform government boarding schools. If we adopted similar collectivist policies, and separated children from their parents at the age of seven, we might be able to approach absolute equality too, but it is unlikely that this would prove desirable or popular.

Modern democracies are based on the right of citizens to retain most of the fruits of their labor, and some people's labor is more highly sought after than others'. Individuals thus have different amounts of personal wealth that they can commit to their children's education. Given these realities, the only way to guarantee equal financial resources for education would be to make it illegal for families to spend anything on their own children's education, requiring all educational spending to be done by the government. This too would prove unacceptable. So, if people have different amounts of wealth, and if they are allowed to spend that wealth on their own children's education, absolute equality of (financial) educational opportunity is *impossible*.

Thus, the real question is: What system of educational governance and funding will give low-income families the best educational opportunities, both in absolute terms and relative to the average family? On that score, the tax breaks and private scholarship network described above are clearly superior to both state-run and state-funded systems. With the exception of Spartan education, state-run systems have never lived up to their advocates' promises of equality, and contemporary public systems produce less equitable results than the private sector (see Chapter 8). Because of their direct local involvement with parents, private scholarship-granting organizations could also allow parents to spend their scholarships on any reasonable educational service or technology that comes along. Government bureaucracies are notoriously incapable of providing such open-ended flexibility.

Final Words

This book was conceived and written to answer a single question: What kind of school system can best fulfill the public's educational goals? Its recommendation, phasing out state schools in favor of a for-profit educational market, is admittedly radical by contemporary standards. Many people retain a certain fondness for public schooling, and so this prescription may seem worse than the ills it is meant to cure. But is that fondness really for the *institution* of public schooling, or for the *ideals* of public education? As the preceding pages have shown, they are far from identical. The modern and historical evidence points inexorably to the fact that government involvement in education tends to interfere with the very principles it is meant to advance. If the reader takes only one idea away from this book, let it be that.

Notes

Introduction

1. Pliny the Younger, *Letters and Panegyricus [of] Pliny*, with an English translation by Betty Radish (London: William Heinemann, 1969). See the section on Rome in Chapter 2 below for the full quotation and context.

Chapter 1. Getting Used to Disappointment

1. Charles L. Glenn, Jr., *The Myth of the Common School* (Amherst: University of Massachusetts Press, 1988), 80.
2. Duke Helfand, "Board Approves Shotguns for School Police," *Los Angeles Times,* February 24, 1998, A1.
3. Gallup International and the C. F. Kettering Foundation, "The Fourth Annual Gallup Poll of Public Attitudes toward Education," in Stanley M. Elam, ed., *A Decade of Gallup Polls of Attitudes toward Education, 1969–1978* (Bloomington: Phi Delta Kappa, 1978); Alec M. Gallup, "The 18th Annual Gallup Poll of the Public's Attitudes toward the Public Schools," *Phi Delta Kappan,* September 1986; and Stanley M. Elam and Alec M. Gallup, "The 21st Annual Gallup Poll of the Public's Attitudes toward the Public Schools," *Phi Delta Kappan,* September 1989.
4. Organization for Economic Cooperation and Development (OECD), *Public Expectations of the Final Stage of Compulsory Education* (Paris: OECD Publications, 1995), 131.
5. The percentages were 92 percent and 83 percent, respectively, ranking first and second out of a list of eight possible answers. They were reported in a 1990 Market and Opinion Research International poll, in E. H. Hastings and P. K. Hastings,

eds., *Index to International Public Opinion, 1990–1991* (New York: Greenwood Press, 1991), 87.

6. OECD, *Public Expectations,* 71; and Stanley M. Elam, Lowell C. Rose, and Alec M. Gallup, "The 26th Annual Phi Delta Kappa/Gallup Poll of the Public's Attitudes toward the Public Schools," *Phi Delta Kappan,* September 1994.

7. "Baffled," *The Economist,* December 9–15, 1995, 27.

8. The participants were Canada, Germany, the Netherlands, Poland, Switzerland (French), Switzerland (German), and the U.S. D. Viadero, "Americans Land in Middle of International Literacy Scale," *Education Week,* December 13, 1995, 6.

9. David Charter, "Exams Ban on Calculators after Maths' Standards Fall," *The (London) Times,* December 7, 1995.

10. Note that mathematics scores on the National Assessment of Educational Progress (NAEP) have increased since 1991, but only by a very small percentage. See Chapter 6.

11. OECD, *Public Expectations,* 70.

12. George H. Gallup, "The 15th Annual Gallup Poll of the Public's Attitudes toward the Public Schools," *Phi Delta Kappan,* September 1983.

13. Millicent Lawton, "Students Post Dismal Results on History Test," *Education Week,* November 8, 1995, 1.

14. Ibid., 12.

15. Millicent Lawton, "Students Fall Short in NAEP Geography Test," *Education Week,* October 25, 1995, 23.

16. Louis Harris and Associates poll (1992), in E. H. Hastings and P. K. Hastings, eds., *Index to International Public Opinion, 1992–1993* (New York: Greenwood Press, 1993), 73.

17. Jean Johnson and John Immerwahr, *First Things First: What Americans Expect from the Public Schools* (New York: Public Agenda, 1994).

18. "But Where's the Proof?" *Times Educational Supplement,* May 26, 1995, II.

19. Harold W. Stevenson and James W. Stigler, *The Learning Gap* (New York: Touchstone, 1994), 39–43.

20. Personal communication.

21. See the discussion of Spartan education in Chapter 2.

22. EMNID Institute (Germany) poll (1991), in Hastings and Hastings, *Index, 1992–1993,* 73.

23. OECD, *Public Expectations,* 131.

24. Maynard Shipley, *The War on Modern Science: A Short History of the Fundamentalist Attacks on Evolution and Modernism* (New York: Alfred A. Knopf, 1927), ix–x.

25. Stephen Arons, *Compelling Belief: The Culture of American Schooling* (New York: McGraw Hill, 1983), 18.

26. Microsoft Network (MSN) News, March 7, 1996.

27. Stanley M. Elam and Lowell C. Rose, "The 27th Annual Phi Delta Kappa/Gallup Poll of the Public's Attitudes toward the Public Schools," *Phi Delta Kappan,* September 1995, 41–56.

28. Elam, *A Decade of Gallup Polls*; and Various authors, Annual Education Polls, *Phi Delta Kappan,* September 1977 to 1994.

29. Elam, Rose, and Gallup, "26th Annual Poll."
30. Johnson and Immerwahr, *First Things First,* 10.
31. Ibid., 11.
32. "Five Die in Arkansas School Shooting: Two Boys Charged in Ambush that Leaves Eleven Wounded," *Florida Today,* March 25, 1998, Sebastian River/Palm Bay Editions, News Section; Geoff Becker, The Associated Press, "Fatal Shootings Stress Importance of Listening," *The State Journal-Register* (Springfield, IL), April 27, 1998, News Section; and "Parent: School Shootings Shared Traits; Urges Campaign to Stop Violence," *The Cincinnati Enquirer,* April 28, 1998, Metro Section.
33. Gillian Gaynair and Ashley Bach, "After Springfield, Schools Crack Down," *The Oregonian,* June 2, 1998.
34. U.S. Bureau of the Census, *Statistical Abstract of the United States: 1995* (Washington, DC: Bureau of the Census, 1995), Table 319, 205.
35. Gallup International and the C. F. Kettering Foundation, "The First Annual Gallup Poll of Public Attitudes toward Education," in Elam, *A Decade of Gallup Polls,* 12.
36. "Asking the Voters," *Education Week,* March 22, 1995, 4.
37. Alec M. Gallup and David L. Clark, "The 19th Annual Gallup Poll of the Public's Attitudes toward the Public Schools," *Phi Delta Kappan,* September 1987, 46. In a separate poll, 86 percent of those polled felt that stronger penalties would be very effective. See Elam, Rose, and Gallup, "26th Annual Poll," 44; and Johnson and Immerwahr, *First Things First,* 11.
38. John J. Convey, *Parental Choice of Catholic Schools as a Function of Religion, Race, and Family Income,* Research report presented at the annual meeting of the American Educational Research Association, San Francisco, April 16–20, 1986; and Sarah B. Edwards and William W. Richardson, *A Survey of MCPS Withdrawals to Attend Private School,* Research report, 1981, unpublished, ERIC (Educational Resources Information Center) document no. ED226096. See the ERIC website at: http://www.accesseric.org:81/index.html
39. Jessica Portner, "Juvenile Weapons Offenses Double in Decade, Report Says," *Education Week,* November 22, 1995, 3.
40. Kate Kelliher, "N.Y.C. Schools: Violence Persists," *Daily Report Card,* May 31, 1995.
41. Sara Sundberg, "Constitution State: Crackdown on Weapons in School," *Daily Report Card,* September 14, 1993.
42. U.S. Bureau of the Census, *Statistical Abstract of the United States: 1993* (Washington, DC: Bureau of the Census, 1993), Table 310, 197.
43. Tom R. Williams and Holly Millinoff, *Canada's Schools: Report Card for the 1990s, A CEA Opinion Poll* (Toronto: Canadian Education Association, 1990), 12.
44. "Two Teens Charged after Stabbing in High School," *The Montreal Gazette,* March 10, 1996, B6; "Teens Charged in Stabbing at Ottawa School," *The Montreal Gazette,* March 11, 1996.
45. National Center for Education Statistics, *Digest of Education Statistics, 1993* (Washington, DC: U.S. Department of Education, 1993), Table 94, 104.
46. Johnson and Immerwahr, *First Things First,* 42–43.

47. Barbara Kantrowitz and Pat Wingert, "A Dismal Report Card on the National Math Test," *Newsweek,* June 17, 1991, 65.
48. Karen Diegmueller and Jeanne Ponessa, "Teachers," *Education Week,* March 13, 1996, 8.
49. Gallup and Clark, "19th Annual Poll," 21.
50. David Ruenzel, "A Choice in the Matter," *Education Week,* September 27, 1995, 25.
51. Richard J. Behn and Douglas Muzzio, *Empire State Survey* (New York: Lehrman Institute, 1995).
52. Phil, telephone caller on the "School Reform" episode of the radio call-in show *Talk of the Nation,* National Public Radio, December 17, 1994.
53. The percentage of respondents saying that parents had very little or almost no control, by area: "Books placed in the school libraries," 66; "Curriculum (i.e., the courses offered)," 65; "Books and instructional materials," 72; "Teacher and administrator salaries," 75; "Selection and hiring of administrators," 76; "Selection and hiring of teachers," 81. See Stanley M. Elam, "The 22nd Annual Gallup Poll of the Public's Attitudes toward the Public Schools," *Phi Delta Kappan,* September 1990, 45. Note that the chart bars in Figure 1 do not necessarily add up to 100 percent, due to some responses of "Undecided."
54. Stanley M. Elam, Letter to the editor, *Education Week,* January 10, 1996, 34.
55. Various authors, *Phi Delta Kappan* polls, September 1983 to 1991; and National Catholic Educational Association (NCEA), *The People's Poll on Schools and School Choice: A New Gallup Survey* (Washington, DC: National Catholic Educational Association, 1992), 16.
56. The new question read: "A proposal has been made which would allow parents to send their school-age children to any public, private, or church-related school they choose. For those parents choosing nonpublic schools, the government would pay all or part of the tuition. Would you favor or oppose this proposal in your state?"
57. Elam, Rose, and Gallup, "26th Annual Poll," 49. The *Phi Delta Kappan* continues to play with the wording of its voucher question, making trend assessment difficult, but recent results are still interesting. Using the following curt formulation: "Do you favor or oppose allowing students and parents to choose a private school to attend at public expense?" the *Phi Delta Kappan* found in 1997 that 44 percent of the general public agreed, while 52 percent disagreed. When the term "public expense" was changed to "government expense," the general public was evenly split on the issue, 48 percent to 48 percent. With both phrasings, 4 percent of respondents were undecided. These results are in line with a steady increase in support for vouchers since 1993.
58. Behn and Muzzio, *Empire State Survey,* 39–40; Jean Johnson et al., *Assignment Incomplete: The Unfinished Business of Education Reform* (New York: Public Agenda, 1995), 13; Social Surveys (Gallup Poll) Limited survey (1990), in Hastings and Hastings, *Index, 1990–1991,* 87; and SOFRES (Metra International) survey (1984), in E. H. Hastings and P. K. Hastings, eds., *Index to International Public Opinion, 1984–1985* (New York: Greenwood Press, 1985), 112.
59. Gallup and Kettering, "First Annual Gallup Poll of Public Attitudes toward Education," 11–12, 20.

60. Stanley M. Elam and Lowell C. Rose, "The 27th Annual Phi Delta Kappa/Gallup Poll of the Public's Attitudes toward the Public Schools," *Phi Delta Kappan,* September 1995, 42–43.
61. Harold W. Stevenson, "Learning from Asian Schools," *Scientific American* 267, no. 6 (December 1992): 70–76; Harold W. Stevenson and James W. Stigler, *The Learning Gap: Why Our Schools Are Failing and What We Can Learn from Japanese and Chinese Education* (New York: Touchstone, 1992), 34, 113–29.
62. Gallup and Kettering, "First Annual Gallup Poll," 20.
63. Jonathan Kozol, *Savage Inequalities: Children in America's Schools* (New York: HarperPerennial, 1992), 46.
64. Richard J. Murnane, "Why Money Matters Sometimes, A Two-Part Management Lesson from East Austin, Texas," *Education Week,* September 11, 1996, 48.
65. Canadian Institute of Public Opinion poll (1986 and 1992), in Hastings and Hastings, *Index, 1992–1993,* 71.
66. Louis Harris and Associates poll (1992), in ibid., 72; and Stanley M. Elam, Lowell C. Rose, and Alec M. Gallup, "The 23rd Annual Phi Delta Kappa/Gallup Poll of the Public's Attitudes toward the Public Schools," *Phi Delta Kappan,* September 1991, 51.
67. National Center for Education Statistics (NCES), *Digest of Education Statistics, 1993* (Washington, DC: U.S. Department of Education, 1993), Table 398, 421.
68. See, for instance, the January 1996 CNN/USA Today/Gallup poll, *USA Today,* January 9, 1996; and Gerald F. Seib, "It's School Time: A Sleeper Issue Is Waking Up," *Wall Street Journal,* December 20, 1995, A16.
69. Elam, "22nd Annual Poll," 45.
70. In Great Britain: Social Surveys Limited (Gallup) poll (1993), in E. H. Hastings and P. K. Hastings, eds., *Index to International Public Opinion, 1993–1994* (New York: Greenwood Press, 1994), 87; in the United States: Elam, Rose, and Gallup, "26th Annual Poll," 51.
71. Elam, Rose, and Gallup, "23rd Annual Poll," 46.
72. Social Surveys Limited (Gallup) poll (1987), in E. H. Hastings and P. K. Hastings, eds., *Index to International Public Opinion, 1987–1988* (New York: Greenwood Press, 1988), 88.
73. Social Surveys Limited (Gallup) poll (1993), in Hastings and Hastings, *Index, 1993–1994,* 92–93.
74. Elam, Rose, and Gallup, "26th Annual Poll," 48.
75. Karen Diegmueller and Debra Viadero, "Playing Games with History," *Education Week,* November 15, 1995, 33.
76. Peter West, "The New 'New Math'," *Education Week,* May 10, 1995, 22–23.
77. Elam and Rose, "27th Annual Poll," 41–56.
78. Of those favoring standards, 24 percent thought they should be set by national authorities, 27 percent thought the state should set them, and 39 percent thought they should remain at the local level. Thomas Toch, Robin M. Bennefield, and Amy Bernstein, "The Case for Tough Standards," *U.S. News & World Report,* April 1, 1996, 54.
79. Diegmueller and Viadero, "Playing Games with History," 34.

80. Lowell C. Rose, Alec M. Gallup, and Stanley M. Elam, "The 29th Annual Phi Delta Kappa/Gallup Poll of the Public's Attitudes toward the Public Schools," *Phi Delta Kappan,* September 1997.

81. The National Center on the Educational Quality of the Workforce, *The EQW National Employer Survey: First Findings* (Philadelphia: EQW, 1995).

82. "Intel Struggling to Fill New Jobs," *Seattle Times,* March 4, 1996, B2.

83. Charles J. Sykes, *Dumbing Down Our Kids: Why American Children Feel Good about Themselves but Can't Read, Write, or Add* (New York: St. Martin's Press, 1995), 22–23.

84. Jerry, telephone caller on the "Educational Crisis?" episode of the radio call-in show *Talk of the Nation,* National Public Radio, September 27, 1995.

85. David C. Berliner and Bruce J. Biddle, *The Manufactured Crisis: Myths, Fraud, and the Attack on America's Public Schools* (New York: Addison-Wesley Publishing Company, 1995), 2–4, 9.

86. Mortimer J. Adler, *We Hold These Truths: Understanding the Ideas and Ideals of the Constitution* (New York: Macmillan, 1987), 22.

87. Asahi Shimbun poll (1984), in Hastings and Hastings, *Index, 1984–1985,* 105.

88. National Opinion Research Center poll (1993), in Hastings and Hastings, *Index, 1993–1994,* 480.

89. David J. Armor, *Forced Justice: School Desegregation and the Law* (New York: Oxford University Press, 1995), 203–4.

90. Peter Schmidt, "Second NAACP Official Questions Merits of Busing," *Education Week,* November 29, 1995, 3.

91. "Black Mayors Try to End Mandatory School Busing," *Seattle Times,* November 16, 1993, A5.

92. Peter Schmidt, "Policies Using Race to Assign Pupils Attacked," *Education Week,* September 27, 1995, 12.

93. Ibid.

94. Controversy over the mainstreaming of the physically handicapped tends to be restricted to the most extreme cases in which considerable amounts of medical equipment and constant medical attention are required for the child in question to participate in a regular class. The difficulty in such cases tends to be the determination of responsibility for paying for the necessary (and sometimes very expensive) medical care.

95. Elam and Rose, "27th Annual Poll," 41–56.

96. An on-line discussion group is comprised of individuals sending written messages to one another over a computer network such as America On Line, the Microsoft Network, or the Internet. These particular "posts," as they are called, were made in the fall of 1995. Some abbreviations have been expanded within the text.

97. Stanley M. Elam and Alec M. Gallup, "The 20th Annual Gallup Poll of the Public's Attitudes toward the Public Schools," *Phi Delta Kappan,* September 1988, 38.

98. Allan Odden, David Monk, Yasser Nakib, and Lawrence Picus, "The Story of the Education Dollar: No Academy Awards and No Fiscal Smoking Guns," *Phi Delta Kappan,* October 1995.

99. Larry Bartlett, "Economic Cost Factors in Providing a Free Appropriate Public Education for Handicapped Children: The Legal Perspective," *Journal of Law and Education* 22 (1993): 49.

100. Lynn Schnaiberg, "District Seeks to Pare $136,000 Spec.-Ed. Bill," *Education Week,* September 27, 1995, 5.

101. National Center for Education Statistics, *Digest of Education Statistics, 1993,* Table 164, 163.

102. Behn and Muzzio, *Empire State Survey,* 22.

103. Chester E. Finn, Jr., *We Must Take Charge* (New York: The Free Press, 1991), 35.

Chapter 2. Right from the Beginning: Classical Athens and Beyond

1. Because most of the research on the history of Asian schooling has not been translated into English or French (the languages I am able to read), the coverage of this book is limited to the Western, Middle Eastern, and Slavic traditions. From the limited data that is available, however, the key factors historically affecting educational outcomes in China, Japan, and other Eastern countries appear to overlap significantly with those at work in the areas covered herein.

2. Aristotle, *The Athenian Constitution* (London: Penguin Books, 1984), part 5, 46–47; and Bernard Knox, ed., *The Norton Book of Classical Literature* (New York: W. W. Norton & Company, 1993), 238–42.

3. There is some debate in the academic community over whether or not the Lycurgus of legend actually existed, and if so, which of the acts imputed to him were genuinely his. This book follows the current consensus in accepting the fact of his existence, and, for simplicity, treats all of the acts ascribed to him by Xenophon and Plutarch as his own—the task of sorting out the precise details of his life is left to the specialists.

4. In the past, some historians had argued that Athenian parents were legally responsible for teaching their children to read and write, but William Harris, in his book *Ancient Literacy* (Cambridge, MA: Harvard University Press, 1989), has shown that this was an informal tradition rather than a law.

5. Plato, "Protagoras," in *The Dialogues of Plato* (New York: Random House, 1937), vol. 1, 96.

6. Kenneth J. Freeman, *The Schools of Hellas* (New York: Teachers College Press, 1904), 81–82.

7. Ibid., 44.

8. Plato, "Protagoras," 86.

9. Freeman, *Schools of Hellas,* 88–90.

10. Plato, "Protagoras," 96.

11. Freeman, *Schools of Hellas,* 110, citing Aristophanes, *The Wasps,* 959.

12. H. I. Marrou, *Histoire de l'éducation dans l'antiquité* (Paris: Éditions du seuil, 1965), 205.

13. Freeman, *Schools of Hellas,* 165.

14. Edith Hamilton, *The Echo of Greece* (New York: W. W. Norton & Company, 1957), 55.

15. Adam Smith, *The Wealth of Nations* (New York: The Modern Library, 1995), 837.
16. Plato, "Menexenus," in *The Dialogues of Plato,* vol. 2, 776.
17. It has also been suggested that Plato might have written this to disparage Pericles, though there is no way to ascertain his true intention.
18. Will Durant, *The Life of Greece* (New York: Simon & Schuster, 1939), 253.
19. Xenophon, "Spartan Society," in *Plutarch on Sparta,* trans. R. J. A. Talbert (New York: Penguin Books, 1988), 167.
20. Plutarch, "Lycurgus," in *Plutarch on Sparta,* 26.
21. Ibid., 27.
22. Spartan girls were encouraged to train and compete in athletics, however.
23. Xenophon, "Spartan Society," 168–69; and Freeman, *Schools of Hellas,* 18.
24. Plutarch, "Lycurgus," 30.
25. Ibid., 28.
26. Sextus Empiricus, "Against the Professors," in *Sextus Empiricus,* with an English translation by the Rev. R. G. Bury, vol. 4 (London: William Heinemann, 1992), 199.
27. Isocrates, "Panathenaicus," in *Isocrates in Three Volumes,* with an English translation by George Norlin (London: William Heinemann, 1982), 2:503–5.
28. Only free, native-born males could be citizens in classical Athens, so this figure does not include women, resident aliens, or slaves. Literacy among women would have been much lower given their limited formal education. Among slaves it would have been somewhat lower, but since many slaves performed clerical and managerial services for their owners, they too were often required to be literate. Foreigners who settled in Athens were frequently involved in trade or commerce and thus would probably have had literacy rates similar to those of natives. Rural residents would have had a much lower literacy rate than their urban counterparts. See the following note for further details.
29. Until the late 1980s there was a general consensus among historians that the majority of ancient Athenians were literate to some degree. William Harris, one of the more influential recent writers on historical literacy, introduced a healthy dose of skepticism to the debate with his book *Ancient Literacy,* arguing that the evidence for any conclusion was comparatively thin, and that we should not be too confident in the accuracy of our estimates. Though he does not dispute Athens's preeminence in literacy, he suggests that all estimates of ancient literacy are inflated. His argument hinges on two assumptions. The first is that certain social and economic conditions are necessary to create a demand for widespread literacy and that these conditions did not exist in ancient Greece—including Athens—and the second is that an extensive network of schools cannot exist without considerable external funding, generally from the state or a religious organization. To some extent, there is merit in these arguments, but Harris pushes his case a bit too far. He gives an overly pessimistic view of the size and diversity of the Athenian economy, stating, for example, that Athens had no insurance business (*Ancient Literacy,* 19), when economic historian Rondo Cameron avows that it did (see Cameron, *A Concise Economic History of the World* [New York: Oxford University Press, 1993]). Harris's belief in the importance of state or religious educational subsidies in the growth of schooling is also exaggerated, as is demonstrated by the evidence from nineteenth-

century England and the U.S., as well as the enormous private market for supplemental schooling in modern Japan (all of which are discussed later in this book).

30. It has been suggested by an anonymous reviewer that the public spending undertaken by Pericles in the mid fifth century B.C. played a significant role in the cultural and economic flowering, and perhaps also the growth in literacy, that Athens enjoyed during that period. There is little evidence to support this view. Most of the public works carried out at Pericles' command were only possible because of the considerable wealth generated by the bustling Athenian economy, which in turn was fed by Athens's vigorous education market and an absence of hampering regulations. Pericles took no action to promote or regulate Athenian education and hence had no direct effect on literacy and little if any indirect effect on the city's economy and artistic splendor. Athenians supported the arts before and after his tenure. Furthermore, several of Pericles' projects were paid for with funds siphoned from a pan-Greek alliance known as the Delian League, and this action generated animosity among other Greeks toward Athens which contributed to its downfall (first to Sparta and later to Alexander the Great).

31. Durant, *The Life of Greece*, 275.

32. Cameron, *A Concise Economic History of the World*, 35.

33. Durant, *The Life of Greece*, 255.

34. Thucydides, *History of the Peloponnesian War* (New York: Penguin Books, 1979), 145–46.

35. Isocrates, "Panathenaicus," 501–3.

36. Many of France's republican revolutionaries advocated an all-encompassing role for the state in education. See Chapter 3 for details.

37. Several early nineteenth century U.S. advocates of government schooling, such as James G. Carter and Dr. Benjamin Rush, held up Sparta as a model of state control over education. See Chapter 3 for details.

38. Plutarch, "Lycurgus," 37.

39. Ibid., 17. Note too that the iron employed as money was treated in such a way as to be fragile and unusable, eliminating even its value for practical applications.

40. Durant, *The Life of Greece*, 85.

41. Miklós Haraszti, *The Velvet Prison: Artists under State Socialism* (New York: The Noonday Press, 1987).

42. Freeman, *The Schools of Hellas*, 12. Turtaios (also spelled "Tyrtaeus") was a militaristic state poet of Sparta.

43. Durant, *The Life of Greece*, 74.

44. To the Greeks, their country is known as Hellas, and thus the settlements and culture they established have come to be called Hellenistic.

45. J. Lempriere, *Lempriere's Classical Dictionary of Proper Names Mentioned in Ancient Authors* (New York: Routledge & Kegan Paul, 1987), 31.

46. Colin McEvedy, *Atlas of World History* (New York: Penguin Books, 1985), 58.

47. Pergamum was an ancient Greek city-state located in what is now the Izmir province of Turkey. It was best known for its library, and its cultural and artistic wealth. Its king, during Crates' service, was Eumenes II.

48. Suetonius, "On Grammarians," ii, iii, in *Suetonius*, vol. 2 (Cambridge: Harvard University Press, 1992), 397–99.

49. Cicero, "The Republic," iii, iv, in *Cicero* (London: William Heinemann, 1988), 16:233.

50. This is a snide reference to equestrian statues of lawyers, which were apparently popping up around Rome more rapidly than Martial would have liked.

51. Martial, *Epigrams,* Book 9, epigram 68 (London: G. Bell and Sons, 1926), 429.

52. Keith R. Bradley, *Discovering the Roman Family: Studies in Roman Social History* (New York: Oxford University Press, 1991), 107–12.

53. James Bowen, *A History of Western Education, Volume One, The Ancient World: Orient and Mediterranean* (New York: St. Martin's Press, 1972).

54. C. Pharr, T. S. Davidson, and M. B. Pharr, *The Theodosian Code and Novels and the Sirmondian Constitutions* (Princeton: Princeton University Press, 1952), #13.3.5, 388.

55. This exemption occurred in the year 425 A.D.; see ibid., #14.9.3, 414.

56. Ibid., #14.9.3, 414.

57. Suetonius, "Vespasian," 18, in *Suetonius,* 311.

58. Edict of Vespasian on Physicians' and Teachers' Privileges, 74 A.D., in A. C. Johnson et al., *Ancient Roman Statutes* (Austin: University of Texas Press, 1961), #185, 151.

59. Pacatus, in Edouard Galletier, trans., *Panégyriques Latins* (Paris: Belles Lettres, 1955), vol. 3, 73.

60. T. J. Haarhoff, *Schools of Gaul: A Study of Pagan and Christian in the Last Century of the Western Empire* (London: Oxford University Press, 1920), 141.

61. Galletier, *Panégyriques Latins,* 52.

62. Henry Hodges, *Technology in the Ancient World* (New York: Barnes & Noble, 1992), 222.

63. Ibid., 209.

64. Pliny the Younger, *Letters and Panegyricus [of] Pliny,* with an English translation by Betty Radish (London: William Heinemann, 1969), 277–83.

65. Bruce Bartlett, "How Excessive Government Killed Ancient Rome," *The Cato Journal* 14, no. 2 (1995): 287–303.

66. Haarhoff, *Schools of Gaul,* 153, footnote 1.

67. Ibid., 156–57.

68. Ibid., 170.

69. Ibid., 174.

70. *Encyclopedia Britannica,* 15th ed. (Chicago: University of Chicago Press, 1989), vol. 23, 889.

71. Will Durant, *The Age of Faith* (New York: Simon & Schuster, 1950), 123.

72. M. Nakosteen, *History of Islamic Origins of Western Education* (Boulder: University of Colorado Press, 1964), 15–17.

73. Ibid., vii.

74. Ahmad Shalaby, *History of Muslim Education* (Karachi: Indus Publications, 1979), 16–23.

75. Durant, *The Age of Faith,* 94, 304.

76. Nakosteen, *Islamic Origins,* 52.

77. Ibid., 45–46.

78. Munir-ud-Din Ahmed, *Muslim Education and the Scholars' Social Status* (Zürich: Verlag, 1968), 52.

79. Shalaby, *History of Muslim Education,* 56–57; Nakosteen, *Islamic Origins,* 38; and Durant, *The Age of Faith,* 308–9.

80. Durant, *The Age of Faith,* 244.

81. Nakosteen, *Islamic Origins,* 41.

82. Abraham Blinderman, "Medieval Correspondence Education: The Responsa of the Gaonate," *History of Education Quarterly* 9, no. 4 (1969): 471–74.

83. Nakosteen, *Islamic Origins,* 42.

84. Robert Schwickerath, *Jesuit Education* (St. Louis: B. Herder, 1904), 24.

85. Germany was not a unified nation during the sixteenth century, but rather a collection of essentially autonomous principalities.

86. Gerald Strauss, "Techniques of Indoctrination: The German Reformation," in *Literacy and Social Development in the West: A Reader* (Cambridge: Cambridge University Press, 1981), 97.

87. Roger Chartier, Dominique Julia, and Marie-Madeleine Compère, *L'Éducation en France du XVIe au XVIIIe Siècle* (Paris: Société D'Édition D'Enseignment Supérieur, 1976), 4.

88. Friedrich Paulsen, *German Education, Past and Present* (London: Adelphi Terrace, 1908), 78.

89. Luella Cole, *A History of Education: Socrates to Montessori* (New York: Holt, Rinehart and Winston, 1960), 439.

90. Strauss, "Techniques," 98.

91. Charlotte Methuen, "Securing the Reformation through Education: The Duke's Scholarship System of Sixteenth-Century Würtemberg," *Sixteenth-Century Journal* 25, no. 4 (1994): 841–51.

92. Susan C. Karant-Nunn, "Alas, a Lack: Trends in the Historiography of Pre-University Education in Early Modern Germany," *Renaissance Quarterly* 43, no. 4 (1990): 790.

93. Schwickerath, *Jesuit Education,* 144.

94. Edward A. Fitzpatrick, *St. Ignatius and the Ratio Studiorum* (New York: McGraw Hill, 1933), 181–82.

95. Ibid., 151.

96. Ibid., 130.

97. Ibid., 176.

98. Ibid., 126.

99. Cited in Karant-Nunn, "Trends," 796.

100. Paulsen, *German Education,* 87.

101. In Sparta, some political offices were elected by the citizenry, and some policy issues were put to popular vote.

Chapter 3. Revolutions: The More Things Change . . .

1. *The Boston Gazette,* March 21–22, 1720, in Sol Cohen, ed., *Education in the United States: A Documentary History* (New York: Random House, 1974), vol. 2, 439.

2. Early in its history, "United States" was still a plural term, revealing the extent to which the states viewed themselves as distinct and sovereign.

3. Carl F. Kaestle, *Pillars of the Republic: Common Schools and American Society, 1780–1860* (New York: Hill and Wang, 1983), x, 25.

4. Alexis de Tocqueville, *Democracy in America* (New York: Random House, 1990), vol. 1, 315, vol. 2, 55.

5. Francis Grund, *The Americans, in Their Moral, Social, and Political Relations,* in Cohen, *Education in the U.S.,* vol. 2, 941–45.

6. Kaestle, *Pillars of the Republic,* 37–38.

7. Stanley K. Schultz, *The Culture Factory: Boston Public Schools, 1789–1860* (New York: Oxford University Press, 1973), 160.

8. Majority Report to the Primary School Committee, *On the Petition of Sundry Colored Persons for the Abolition of the Schools for Colored Children* (1846), in Leonard W. Levy and Douglas L. Jones, eds., *Jim Crow in Boston: The Origin of the Separate but Equal Doctrine* (New York: Da Capo Press, 1974), viii, 17; Schultz, *The Culture Factory,* 160–61; and Carter G. Woodson, *The Education of the Negro Prior to 1861* (New York: The Knickerbocker Press, 1915), 95.

9. Kaestle, *Pillars of the Republic,* 39.

10. Schultz, *The Culture Factory,* 167, 171–72; and Majority Report, in Levy and Jones, *Jim Crow,* 18.

11. Majority Report, in Levy and Jones, *Jim Crow,* 20–22; and *Triumph of Equal School Rights, Proceedings of the Presentation Meeting* (1855), in Levy and Jones, *Jim Crow,* 5.

12. *Sarah C. Roberts v. The City of Boston,* 5 Cush. 198 (1849), reproduced from the original Court Record in Levy and Jones, *Jim Crow,* 206; and *Charles Sumner, His Complete Works,* in Levy and Jones, *Jim Crow,* 54.

13. *Homer Adolph Plessy v. John H. Ferguson,* 163 U.S. 537, 16 S.Ct. 1138 (1896), in *United States Supreme Court Reports, October Terms, 1895, 1896* (Rochester, NY: The Lawyers' Co-operative Publishing Company, 1897), 258.

14. Kaestle, *Pillars of the Republic,* 197.

15. Charles L. Glenn, Jr., *The Myth of the Common School* (Amherst: University of Massachusetts Press, 1988), 75.

16. Ibid.

17. Ibid., 91 (emphasis added).

18. See Chapter 4. Note that under current law, all fifty states require parents to secure an education for their children, but parents are free to choose public, private, or home-schooling options.

19. James G. Carter, "Influence of Early Education," in *American Education: Its Men, Ideas, and Institutions* (New York: Arno Press and The New York Times, 1969), 13, 16.

20. "Immigration," *The Massachusetts Teacher* (1851), in Cohen, *Education in the U.S.,* vol. 2, 995–97 (emphasis in original).

21. Ibid. (emphasis in original).

22. Glenn, *The Myth of the Common School,* 80.

23. Horace Mann, *Twelfth Annual Report of . . . the Secretary of the Board: 1848,* in Cohen, *Education in the U.S.,* vol. 2, 1100.

24. Schultz, *The Culture Factory*, 121–22.

25. Ibid., 120.

26. Kaestle, *Pillars of the Republic*, 163.

27. Ibid., 170–71.

28. Edwin S. Gausted, ed., *A Documentary History of Religion in America: Since 1865* (Grand Rapids: William B. Eerdmans Publishing Co., 1990), 49–54.

29. Zachary Montgomery, *The School Question from a Parental and Non-Sectarian Standpoint* (Washington, DC: Gibson Bros., 1886), 51.

30. Ibid.

31. Kaestle, *Pillars of the Republic*, 158.

32. O. Hosford, "The Relations of the National Government to Education" (1866), in *Proceedings of the National Teachers' Association, Afterward the National Education Association, From Its Foundation in 1857 to the Close of the Session of 1870*, ed. Henry Barnard (New York: C. W. Bardeen, 1870), 615.

33. Diane Ravitch, *The Great School Wars, New York City, 1805–1973: A History of the Public Schools as Battlefield of Social Change* (New York: Basic Books, 1974), 158.

34. Kaestle, *Pillars of the Republic*, 60–61; and Glenn, *The Myth of the Common School*, 210.

35. Edwin G. West, *Education and the State: A Study in Political Economy* (Indianapolis: Liberty Fund, 1994), 304.

36. Allan C. Ornstein, "School Size and Effectiveness: Policy Implications," *Urban Review* 22 (1990): 239–45.

37. Thomas J. Pugh, *Rural School Consolidation in New York State, 1795–1993: A Struggle for Control* (Ann Arbor: UMI Dissertation Services, 1994).

38. Michael Foot and Isaac Kramnick, eds., *The Thomas Paine Reader* (New York: Penguin Books, 1987), 10.

39. Kenneth A. Lockridge, "Literacy in Early America, 1650–1800," in *Literacy and Social Development in the West: A Reader,* ed. Harvey J. Graff (Cambridge: Cambridge University Press, 1981), 183–200.

40. Carl F. Kaestle, "Studying the History of Literacy," in Kaestle et al., *Literacy in the United States* (New Haven: Yale University Press, 1991), 24–25.

41. See the preceding note, the following three notes, and West, *Education and the State,* 302. West points out that in New York state, there were 380,000 children between five and sixteen years of age in 1821, and 342,479 of them (90 percent) were in school.

42. Edward A. Krug, *Salient Dates in American Education* (New York: Harper & Row, 1966).

43. The figures given are for five- to seventeen-year-olds. The increase was from 78.1 percent to 81.8 percent. See U.S. Bureau of the Census, *Historical Statistics of the United States: Colonial Times to 1970, Bicentennial Edition* (Washington, DC: U.S. Government Printing Office, 1975), H 419, 368.

44. The figures for whites are for children between the ages of five and nineteen. White enrollment in this age group dropped from 56.2 percent in 1850 to 53.6 percent in 1900. Note that these figures greatly understate the elementary school enrollment rates due to the fact that the customary school-leaving age for the mid-to-late nine-

teenth century was roughly eleven or twelve. This is apparent from the fact that in 1890, 98 percent of all children in school were enrolled at the elementary level. As a result, averaging-in all those children aged thirteen to nineteen who had already left school serves to grossly underestimate the percentage that attended elementary school. Also note that the figure given for blacks is actually an aggregate of nonwhite races, of which blacks comprised the overwhelming majority. See U.S. Bureau of the Census, *Historical Statistics of the United States,* H 433–35, 370.

45. Jeremy Atack and Peter Passell, *A New Economic View of American History from Colonial Times to 1940* (New York: W. W. Norton & Company, 1994), 4–12.

46. Kaestle, *Pillars of the Republic,* 65.

47. *Encyclopedia Britannica,* s.v. "United Kingdom: The Later Stuarts."

48. John Lawson and Harold Silver, *A Social History of Education in England* (London: Butler & Tanner Ltd., 1973), 172.

49. Nicholas Carlisle, *A Concise Description of the Endowed Grammar Schools in England and Wales* (London: Baldwin, Cradock, and Joy, 1818), vol. 2, 773.

50. Lawson and Silver, *Social History of Education,* 196.

51. Carlisle, *Endowed Grammar Schools,* vol. 2, 345, 597.

52. John Roach, *A History of Secondary Education in England, 1800–1870* (New York: Longman, 1986), 127.

53. Ibid., 124.

54. Roger S. Schofield, "Dimensions of Illiteracy in England," in *Literacy and Social Development in the West* (*supra* note 39), 202.

55. Frank Smith, *A History of English Elementary Education, 1760–1902* (London: University of London Press, 1931), 53.

56. Lawson and Silver, *Social History of Education,* 280.

57. Edward Royle, *Modern Britain: A Social History, 1750–1985* (Kent: Edward Arnold, 1990), 351.

58. David F. Mitch, *The Rise of Popular Literacy in Victorian England: The Influence of Private Choice and Public Policy* (Philadelphia: The University of Pennsylvania Press, 1992), 144.

59. National Society for Promoting the Education of the Poor in the Principles of the Established Church, "First Report, 1812," in J. M. Goldstrom, *Education: Elementary Education, 1780–1900* (New York: Barnes & Noble, 1972), 50.

60. Royle, *Modern Britain,* 351.

61. Huxley, a biologist and philosopher, is probably best known for his vigorous defense of Darwin's theory of evolution. After the passage of the Education Act of 1870, he sat on London's first school board.

62. Lawson and Silver, *Social History of Education,* 290.

63. Smith, *A History of English Elementary Education,* 268 (emphasis in original).

64. David Vincent, *Literacy and Popular Culture: England, 1750–1914* (Cambridge: Cambridge University Press, 1989), 88.

65. Matthew Arnold, "Report of the Committee of Council on Education, 1867–68," in *Education: Elementary Education, 1780–1900* (*supra* note 59), 132.

66. Smith, *A History of English Elementary Education,* 269.

67. G. A. Cranfield, *The Development of the Provincial Newspaper* (Oxford: Clarendon Press, 1962), v.

68. H. R. Fox Bourne, *English Newspapers: Chapters in the History of Journalism* (London: Chatto & Windus, 1887), 28.
69. A. Aspinall, *Politics and the Press: Circa 1780–1850* (London: Home & Van Thal, 1949), 42–45.
70. West, *Education and the State,* 158–59.
71. Various scholars have disputed the significance for literacy of being able to sign one's name in a marriage register. E. G. West has acknowledged the possibility that some illiterate individuals may have tried to learn to sign their names specifically for the occasion. He notes, though, that since the propensity for people to do this sort of thing probably didn't change much over the years, the changes in marriage signature rates are likely to give a good indication of progress in writing ability. Roger Schofield, on the other hand, asserts that people who had just learned to sign their name (though they otherwise were unable to write) would probably do so tentatively and poorly. Based on his own assessment of the signatures, he finds that this is not the case. He goes on to argue that, if anything, signature rates are likely to *underestimate* reading ability, because reading was taught separately from (and before) writing in nineteenth-century Britain: if someone had learned to sign his name in school, he would have already had to stay in school all through the reading instruction program.
72. Literacy among newly married men increased from about 67 percent in 1841 to 94 percent in 1891, reaching 97 percent by 1900. See West, *Education and the State,* 168.
73. Ibid., 172.
74. Philip W. Gardner, *The Lost Elementary Schools of Victorian England: The People's Education* (London: Croom Helm, 1984), 58.
75. Ibid., 72–76.
76. West, *Education and the State,* 175.
77. The official education census of 1851 reported that two thirds of students were already attending subsidized schools in that year, but due to Gardner's critique of the census, and to its inconsistency with some later figures, the percentage was probably much lower.
78. Gardner, *Lost Elementary Schools,* 188.
79. West, *Education and the State,* 177.
80. Vincent, *Literacy and Popular Culture,* 70.
81. Mitch, *Rise of Popular Literacy,* 147–49. Mitch adds that public schools do appear to have been better than their private counterparts in some counties, but given their overall inferiority, this observation is only of passing interest.
82. Vincent, *Literacy and Popular Culture,* 74.
83. Rondo Cameron, *A Concise Economic History of the World* (New York: Oxford University Press, 1993), 224.
84. Chartier, Julia, and Compère, *L'Éducation en France* (see note 87 of Chapter 2), 62–63.
85. Ibid. (Sound like something Sir Humphrey Appleby might say?)
86. Ibid., 13.
87. P. Chevallier, B. Grosperrin, and J. Maillet, *L'Enseignement Français de la Révolution à Nos Jours* (Paris: Editions Mouton, 1969), 32.

88. Maurice Gontard, *L'Enseignment Primaire en France, 1789–1833* (Paris: Belles Lettres, 1959), 94.

89. Felix Ponteil, *Histoire de L'Enseignment en France, Les Grandes Étapes, 1789–1964* (Paris: Sirey, 1966), 66–67.

90. Howard C. Barnard, *Education and the French Revolution* (Cambridge: Cambridge University Press, 1969), 133.

91. Gontard, *L'Enseignment Primaire,* 293.

92. Ibid., 294.

93. François Furet and Jacques Ozouf, *Reading and Writing: Literacy in France from Calvin to Jules Ferry* (Cambridge: Cambridge University Press, 1982), 134. (Like so many works published in French, the original version of this book did not include an index, making it much less valuable as a research tool. Resignedly, I therefore relied primarily on the English translation.)

94. Joseph N. Moody, *French Education Since Napoleon* (Syracuse: Syracuse University Press, 1978), 23.

95. Sandra Horvath-Peterson, *Victor Duruy and French Education* (Baton Rouge: Louisiana State University Press, 1984), 27.

96. Ponteil, *Histoire,* 192–94; and Gontard, *L'Enseignment Primaire,* 377.

97. Ponteil, *Histoire,* 194.

98. Ibid., 349. Note that University professors were usually graduates of elite government schools, called *lycées,* which included their own primary schools; thus, they would rarely have been familiar with the elementary schools of the common citizens.

99. Archives Parlementaires, *Archives Parlementaires de 1787 à 1860, Series* 2 (Paris: Librairie Administrative de Paul Dupont, 1879), vol. 83, 283. This passage was quoted in Gontard, *L'Enseignment Primaire,* 345, but because of differences in wording between the quotation and the original, the translation was made directly from the archives.

100. Moody, *French Education Since Napoleon,* 59.

101. Ibid.

102. Ibid., 286–90.

103. See, for instance, R. Grew and P. Harrigan, *School, State, and Society: The Growth of Elementary Schooling in Nineteenth-Century France — A Quantitative Analysis* (Ann Arbor: University of Michigan Press, 1991), 72.

104. Henri Avenel, *Histoire de la Press Française: Depuis 1789 Jusqu'à Nos Jours* (Paris: Ernest Flammarion, 1900), 120–21.

105. Furet and Ozouf, *Reading and Writing,* 66.

Chapter 4. Coup d'École: The War for Control of American Education

1. Quoted in Thomas P. Rohlen, *Japan's High Schools* (Berkeley: University of California Press, 1983), 210.

2. Quoted in Richard Mitchell, *The Leaning Tower of Babel and Other Affronts, by the Underground Grammarian* (New York: Simon & Schuster, 1987), 272.

3. Quoted in Herbert M. Kliebard, *The Struggle for the American Curriculum* (New York: Routledge, 1995), 80.

4. Quoted in Henry J. Perkinson, *The Imperfect Panacea* (New York: Random House, 1968), 145.
5. Kliebard, *Struggle,* 161.
6. Quoted in Perkinson, *Imperfect Panacea,* 205.
7. George S. Counts, *Dare the School Build a New Social Order?* (New York: John Day, 1932), 28–29.
8. See, for instance, ibid., 8.
9. Ibid., 45–46.
10. Gordon V. Drake, *Blackboard Power: NEA Threat to America* (Tulsa, OK: Christian Crusade Publications, 1968), 24.
11. Quoted in Diane Ravitch, *The Troubled Crusade: American Education, 1945–1980* (New York: Basic Books, 1983), 86.
12. David Tyack and Larry Cuban, *Tinkering toward Utopia* (Cambridge, MA: Harvard University Press, 1995), 18.
13. Thomas J. Pugh, *Rural School Consolidation in New York State, 1795–1993: A Struggle for Control* (Ann Arbor: UMI Dissertation Services, 1994), 413–15.
14. Ibid., 420.
15. National Center for Education Statistics, *Digest of Education Statistics, 1995* (Washington, DC: U.S. Department of Education, 1995), 96.
16. Tyack and Cuban, *Tinkering toward Utopia,* 19.
17. National Center for Education Statistics, *Digest, 1995,* 96.
18. Herbert J. Walberg and William J. Fowler, Jr., "Expenditure and Size Efficiencies of Public School Districts," research report, 1986, ERIC document no. ED274471.
19. Kliebard, *Struggle,* 185.
20. Commission on the Reorganization of Secondary Education of the NEA, "Cardinal Principles of Secondary Education," in *The American Curriculum: A Documentary History,* ed. George Willis et al. (Westport, CT: Praeger, 1994), 158.
21. Kliebard, *Struggle,* 98.
22. U.S. Bureau of the Census, *Historical Statistics of the United States: Colonial Times to 1970, Bicentennial Edition* (Washington, DC: U.S. Government Printing Office, 1975), 377.
23. National Center for Education Statistics, *Digest, 1995,* 68.
24. Kliebard, *Struggle,* 214.
25. Ibid., 186.
26. Ibid., 219.
27. Ravitch, *Troubled Crusade,* 57.
28. Ibid., 63.
29. Ibid., 71.
30. Ibid., 72–73.
31. Ibid., 74.
32. Ibid., 243–44.
33. Ewald B. Nyquist, "Open Education: Its Philosophy, Historical Perspectives, and Implications," in Ewald B. Nyquist and Gene R. Hawes, eds., *Open Education: A Sourcebook for Parents and Teachers* (New York: Bantam Books, 1972), 82–85.
34. Beatrice and Ronald Gross, "A Little Bit of Chaos," in Nyquist and Hawes, eds., *Open Education,* 15.

35. Piaget observed children at different ages and then made generalizations about natural stages of intellectual development. He also drew inferences from his observations regarding the ways that children learned when left to their own devices. He did not compare different approaches to teaching to examine their relative merits on academic outcomes. This fact is clear from his own writings. See Jean Piaget, *Science of Education and the Psychology of the Child* (New York: Orion Press, 1970), esp. ch. 4.
36. Tyack and Cuban, *Tinkering toward Utopia,* 104.
37. Ibid., 105.
38. Ibid.
39. Ravitch, *Troubled Crusade,* 250.
40. Arthur G. Powell, Eleanor Farrar, and David K. Cohen, *The Shopping Mall High School: Winners and Losers in the Educational Marketplace* (Boston: Houghton Mifflin, 1985), 24–27, 61, 183; and Robert Rothman, *Measuring Up: Standards, Assessment, and School Reform* (San Francisco: Jossey-Bass, 1995), 40–47.
41. The first two citations are for Ohio; they appear in Ramesh Ponnuru, "Revenge of the Blob," *National Review,* September 12, 1994, 48. The last two citations are for Kentucky; they appear in "Kentucky's Learning Goals and Learner Outcomes," publication of the Kentucky Department of Education, circa 1993, 8–9.
42. "Kentucky's Learning Goals," 5.
43. Ibid., 7.
44. Ponnuru, "Revenge of the Blob," 48.
45. Quoted in Rothman, *Measuring Up,* 145.
46. Bruno Manno, *Outcome-Based Education: Has It Become More Affliction than Cure?* (Minneapolis, MN: Center of the American Experiment, 1994), 7–9.
47. Shanker, quoted in Bruno Manno, "The New School Wars: Battles Over Outcome-Based Education," *Phi Delta Kappan,* May 1995, 721.
48. Manno, "New School Wars," 721; and Manno, *Outcome-Based Education,* 10, 18–19.
49. Robert Holland, *Not with My Child You Don't* (Richmond, VA: Chesapeake Capital Services, 1995).
50. Samuel L. Blumenfeld, *Is Public Education Necessary?* (Boise, ID: Paradigm, 1985), viii–ix.
51. Ibid., ix.
52. Stephen Arons, *Compelling Belief: The Culture of American Schooling* (New York: McGraw Hill, 1983), 88–89.
53. Kern Alexander and M. David Alexander, *The Law of Schools, Students, and Teachers in a Nutshell* (St. Paul, MN: West Publishing, 1984).
54. The states were Utah, Ohio, and Nevada. See Christopher J. Klicka and Gregg Harris, *The Right Choice: The Incredible Failure of Public Education and the Rising Hope of Home Schooling, An Academic, Historical, Practical, and Legal Perspective* (Gresham, OR: Noble Publishing Associates, 1992), 356.
55. Ibid., 231.
56. Ibid., 232.
57. Arons, *Compelling Belief,* 79.

58. Ibid., 77–86.

59. Klicka and Harris, *The Right Choice,* 357.

60. The case was *Clonalara v. State Board of Education,* 496 N.W.2d 66 (Mi.App.Ct. 1991), cited in Klicka and Harris, *The Right Choice,* 358.

61. Catherine Dressler, Associated Press, "Tutor Gets Lesson on Law," *Seattle Times,* June 15, 1995, A1.

62. From the *Oregon Voter* newspaper of March 25, 1922, quoted in Francis Paul Valenti, *The Portland Press, the Ku Klux Klan, and the Oregon Compulsory Education Bill: Editorial Treatment of Klan Themes in the Portland Press in 1922,* Master's thesis, University of Washington, 1993, 90.

63. From *The Roman Katholic Kingdom and the Ku Klux Klan,* quoted in ibid., 92.

64. E. Vance Randall, *Private Schools and Public Power: A Case for Pluralism* (New York: Teachers College, Columbia University, 1994), 60.

65. Maynard Shipley, *The War on Modern Science: A Short History of the Fundamentalist Attacks on Evolution and Modernism* (New York: Alfred A. Knopf, 1927), 194.

66. Ibid., 193.

67. Ibid., 210.

68. Ibid., 219.

69. Ibid., 204–11.

70. Joan Delfattore, *What Johnny Shouldn't Read: Textbook Censorship in America* (New Haven, CT: Yale University Press, 1992), 92.

71. Dorothy Nelkin, "From Dayton to Little Rock: Creationism Evolves," in Marcel C. La Follette, ed., *Creationism, Science, and the Law: The Arkansas Case* (Cambridge, MA: The MIT Press, 1983), 76; and William R. Overton, U.S. District Judge, Eastern District of Arkansas, Western Division, opinion on *McLean v. Arkansas,* in La Follette, ed., *Creationism, Science, and the Law,* 47.

72. *Epperson v. Arkansas,* 393 U.S. 97 (1968), section II.

73. Delfattore, *What Johnny Shouldn't Read,* 93–95.

74. Marcel C. La Follette, "Introduction," in La Follette, ed., *Creationism, Science, and the Law,* 1.

75. "Defendant's Outline of the Legal Issues and Proof," *McLean v. Arkansas,* in La Follette, ed., *Creationism, Science, and the Law,* 34.

76. Will Durant, *Our Oriental Heritage* (New York: Simon & Schuster, 1935); and J. M. Roberts, *History of the World* (New York: Penguin, 1990), 67.

77. Overton, opinion on *McLean v. Arkansas,* 56–68.

78. *Edwards v. Aguillard,* 482 U.S. 578 (1987), section V.

79. Robert C. Johnston, "Seventy Years after Scopes, Evolution Hot Topic Again," *Education Week,* March 13, 1996, 16.

80. Robert C. Johnston, "Tenn. Senate to Get New Chance to Vote on Evolution Measure," *Education Week,* March 27, 1996, 19; and "Tenn. Senate Kills Anti-Evolution Bill," *Education Week,* April 3, 1996, 11.

81. Sidney B. Simon, Leland W. Howe, and Howard Kirschenbaum, *Values Clarification: A Handbook of Practical Strategies for Teachers and Students* (New York: A & W Visual Library, 1978), 15–17.

82. Ibid., 49–52.

83. Edward B. Jenkinson, *Censors in the Classroom: The Mind Benders* (New York: Avon Books, 1982), 4–6.

84. Ibid., 11.

85. Ibid., 8.

86. Ibid., 17–23, 22, 18–19.

87. Arons, *Compelling Belief,* 14–15.

88. Delfattore, *What Johnny Shouldn't Read,* 119, 106–7.

89. Cited in Patrick Gustafson, "Books That Have Been Challenged," *The Christian Science Monitor,* May 19, 1998. Available on-line at: http://www.csmonitor.com/durable/1998/05/19/fp55s2-csm.htm

90. *Board of Education v. Pico,* 457 U.S. 853, 102 S.Ct. 2799 (1982).

91. Arons, *Compelling Belief,* 46.

92. *Mozert v. Hawkins County Board of Education,* 827 F.2d. 1058 (6th Cir. 1987).

93. Cited in Delfattore, *What Johnny Shouldn't Read,* 72.

94. Quoted in W. E. B. DuBois, *Black Reconstruction in America: 1860–1880* (New York: Atheneum, 1992), 641.

95. Ira Berlin, Barbara J. Fields, Steven F. Miller, Joseph P. Reidy, and Leslie S. Rowland, *Free at Last: A Documentary History of Slavery, Freedom, and the Civil War* (New York: The New Press, 1992), 525–26.

96. DuBois, *Black Reconstruction,* 642.

97. Berlin, Fields, Miller, Reidy, and Rowland, *Free at Last,* 519.

98. James D. Anderson, *The Education of Blacks in the South, 1860–1935* (Chapel Hill, NC: The University of North Carolina Press, 1988), 11, 5.

99. DuBois, *Black Reconstruction,* 645.

100. Quoted in Anderson, *Education of Blacks in the South,* 82.

101. Ibid., 33–78.

102. Thomas Sowell, "Black Excellence—The Case of Dunbar High School," in Nathan Glazer, ed., *The Public Interest on Education* (New York: University Press of America, 1984), 1.

103. Ibid., 2.

104. Ibid., 13–14.

105. The facts presented in the preceding paragraphs are drawn from ibid.

106. Born in 319 B.C., Pyrrhus was a king of the Molossi tribes of what is now northwestern Greece. His name is the origin of the term "Pyrrhic victory," due to a battle he won against the Romans at a terrible cost to his own army.

107. *Brown v. Board of Education,* 347 U.S. 483 (1954).

108. *Brown v. Board of Education,* 349 U.S. 294 (1955).

109. Dennis J. Hutchinson, "Green v. County School Board of New Kent County," in *The Oxford Companion to the Supreme Court of the United States* (New York: Oxford University Press, 1992), 347.

110. *Green v. County School Board of New Kent County,* 391 U.S. 430 (1968).

111. Hutchinson, "Green," 347.

112. Thomas Cook, David J. Armor, Robert L. Crain, Norman Miller, Michael Carlson, Walter G. Stephan, Herbert J. Walberg, and Paul M. Wortman, *School Desegregation and Black Achievement* (Washington, DC: National Institute of Education, 1984), ERIC document no. ED241671.

113. The query used was: "Subject = Desegregation-Effects, Keywords1 = academic OR test OR scholastic OR educational, Keywords2 = statistical OR research OR study OR analysis, Year = 1984 TO 1994". There were sixty-eight hits resulting from this search, and the NIE rejection criteria were then used as a guide to eliminate those studies that did not examine academic outcomes or failed in other ways to produce relevant and reliable results. The NIE's rejection criteria were as follows:

> 1) Type of study: a) non empirical, b) summary report. 2) Location: a) outside USA, b) geographically non-specific. 3) Comparisons: a) not a study of achievement of desegregated blacks (except in cases where we use a white comparison), b) multi-ethnic combined, c) comparisons across ethnics only, d) heterogeneous proportions minority in desegregated condition, e) no control data, f) no pre-desegregation data, g) control measures not contemporaneous, h) excessive attrition (review must provide specific justification for the inclusion of studies with excessive attrition, but amount was not specified), i) majority black in a segregated condition (unless the reviewer provides specific justification), j) varied exposure to desegregation (unless the reviewer provides a specific justification demonstrating that the variation in exposure time is not meaningful), k) groups are initially non-comparable (unless the reviewer provides a specific justification that the amount of divergence is not meaningful). 4) Study Desegregation: a) cross-sectional survey, b) sampling procedure unknown, c) separate non-comparable samples at each observation. 5) Measures: a) unreliable and/or unstandardized instruments, b) test content and/or instrument unknown, c) dates of administration unknown, d) different tests used in pretests and posttests, e) test of IQ or verbal ability. 6) Data Analysis: a) no pretest means, b) no posttest means, unless the author reported pretest scores and gains, c) no data presented, d) N's [numbers of subjects] not discernible.

114. Robert W. Lissitz, *Assessment of Student Performance and Attitude, St. Louis Metropolitan Area Court-Ordered Desegregation Effort,* report submitted to Voluntary Interdistrict Coordinating Council, January 1992, ERIC document no. ED342794; George A. Mitchell, *An Evaluation of State-Financed School Integration in Metropolitan Milwaukee, Volume 2, No. 5* (Milwaukee, WI: Wisconsin Policy Research Institute, 1989), ERIC document no. ED314515; Albert Bennett and John Q. Easton, *Voluntary Transfer and Student Achievement: Does It Help or Hurt?* Paper presented at the Annual Meeting of the American Education Research Association, New Orleans, LA, 1988, ERIC document no. ED294937; and John Q. Easton et al., *The Influences of School Type, Race, and Economic Background on Reading Achievement Gains,* Paper presented at the Annual Meeting of the American Education Research Association, Washington, DC, 1987, ERIC document no. ED283923.

115. Lissitz, *Assessment of Student Performance,* 41. The data were collected primarily from three sources: a writing achievement test used widely throughout the country; the Stanford Achievement Test; and a specially designed survey which included questions about the students' personal beliefs regarding school person-

nel, friends at school, personal work habits, and support from home. Remarkably, of the twenty-one conclusions arrived at in the study, the results in this avowed prime area of interest were relegated to the nineteenth position.

116. Marvin Alkin et al., *Integration Evaluation Report,* Los Angeles Unified School District, CA, Publication no. 548, ERIC document no. ED335362.

117. Christine H. Rossell and Charles L. Glenn, "The Cambridge Controlled Choice Plan," *Urban Review* 20, no. 2 (1988): 75–94.

118. See, for instance, M. V. Borland and R. M. Howsen, "On the Determination of the Critical Level of Market Concentration in Education," *Economics of Education Review* 12, no. 2 (1993): 165–69.

119. Finis Welch, "A Reconsideration of the Impact of School Desegregation Programs on Public School Enrollment of White Students, 1968–76," *Sociology of Education* 60 (October 1987): 215–21; and Christine H. Rossell, *The Carrot or the Stick for Desegregation Policy* (Philadelphia: Temple University Press, 1990).

120. S. James Zafirau and Margaret Fleming, *A Study of Discrepant Reading Achievement of Minority and White Students in a Desegregating School District: Phase IV* (Cleveland, OH: Cleveland Public Schools, Department of Research and Analysis, 1982).

121. James S. Kunen, "The End of Integration," *Time,* April 29, 1996, 39, 41.

122. National Center for Education Statistics, *Digest, 1995,* 98–102.

123. Massachusetts Department of Education, *1993–1994 Per Pupil Expenditures,* December 1995, available on-line at: http://info.doe.mass.edu/doedocs/ppe.html

124. National Center for Education Statistics, *Revenues and Expenditures for Public Elementary and Secondary Education: School Year 1992–93, Statistics in Brief* (Washington, DC: U.S. Department of Education, 1995), 7; ERIC document no. ED381896.

125. National Center for Education Statistics, *Digest, 1995,* Table 91, 100.

126. Paul Mulshine, "If You Can't Pass This Quiz, Thank the Teachers' Union," *The (Newark, NJ) Sunday Star-Ledger,* December 10, 1995; reprinted in the Educational Excellence Network's *Network News & Views,* January/February 1996.

127. National Center for Education Statistics, *Revenues and Expenditures, 1992–93,* 7; and National Center for Education Statistics, *Digest, 1995,* Table 91, 101.

128. The figures are: $5,096 per pupil for city school districts enrolling more than 20,000 students, versus $5,170 for the nation as a whole. Figures are drawn from (respectively) National Center for Education Statistics, *Digest, 1995,* Table 91, 98; and National Center for Education Statistics, *Revenues and Expenditures, 1992–93,* 7.

Chapter 5. Teachers and Teaching in the Government Schools

1. Susan M. Brookhart and Donald J. Freeman, "Characteristics of Entering Teacher Candidates," *Review of Educational Research* 62, no. 1 (1992): 37–60.

2. John I. Goodlad, *Teachers for Our Nation's Schools* (San Francisco: Jossey-Bass, 1990), 212.

3. Brookhart and Freeman, "Characteristics," 37–60.

4. Jean Johnson et al., *Assignment Incomplete: The Unfinished Business of Education Reform* (New York: Public Agenda, 1995), 43.
5. National Center for Education Statistics, *Digest of Education Statistics, 1995* (Washington, DC: U.S. Department of Education, 1995), 129.
6. Timothy W. Weaver, *America's Teacher Quality Problem: Alternatives for Reform* (New York: Praeger, 1983), 49, 164–65, 42–46; and Ernest L. Boyer, *High School* (New York: Harper & Row, 1983), 171–72.
7. Anne Hafner and Jeffrey Owings, *Careers in Teaching: Following Members of the High School Class of 1972 in and out of Teaching* (Washington, DC: National Center for Education Statistics, 1991); Weaver, *America's Teacher Quality Problem*, 49, 61–63; Geraldine J. Clifford and James W. Guthrie, *Ed School: A Brief for Professional Education* (Chicago: University of Chicago Press, 1988), 32; and Richard J. Murnane et al., *Who Will Teach? Policies That Matter* (Cambridge, MA: Harvard University Press, 1991), 69.
8. Leslie Miller, Associated Press, "More Than Half of Would-Be Teachers Make the Grade," *The Boston Globe Online,* June 22, 1998.
9. Leslie Miller, Associated Press, "One Third Fail Statewide Teachers Test," *The Standard Times* (online), June 20, 1998.
10. Ibid.
11. Editorial, "The Higher Standard for Teachers," *The Boston Globe,* July 2, 1998, A18.
12. Z. Justine and X. Su, "What Schools Are For: An Analysis of Findings from a U.S. National Study," *International Review of Education* 38, no. 2 (1992): 133–53.
13. J. H. C. Vonk, "The Professional Preparation of Primary School Teachers in Europe," in *Teacher Education 6: Research and Developments on Teacher Education in the Netherlands* (Bruxelles, Belgique: Association for Teacher Education in Europe, 1990), 157–70.
14. Thomas Sowell, *Inside American Education: The Decline, the Deception, and the Dogmas* (New York: The Free Press, 1993), 23–24.
15. Brookhart and Freeman, "Characteristics," 37–60.
16. H. J. Butcher, "The Attitudes of Student Teachers to Education: A Comparison with the Attitudes of Experienced Teachers and a Study of Changes During the Training Course," *British Journal of Social and Clinical Psychology* 4 (1965): 17–24; D. McIntyre and A. Morrison, "The Educational Opinions of Teachers in Training," *British Journal of Social and Clinical Psychology* 6 (1967): 32–37; Justine and Su, "What Schools Are For," 133–53; and Sowell, *Inside American Education,* 31–33.
17. Rita Kramer, *Ed School Follies: The Miseducation of America's Teachers* (New York: The Free Press, 1991), esp. 173–74, 209.
18. Justine and Su, "What Schools Are For," 133–53.
19. Steve Farkas and Jean Johnson, with Ann Duffett, *Different Drummers: How Teachers of Teachers View Public Education* (Washington, DC: Public Agenda, 1997), 11.
20. Susan P. Choy, Sharon A. Bobbitt, Robin R. Henke, Elliott A. Medrich, Laura J. Horn, and Joanne Lieberman, *America's Teachers: Profile of a Profession* (Washington, DC: U.S. Department of Education, 1993), 62.

21. Chester Finn, *We Must Take Charge: Our Schools and Our Future* (New York: The Free Press, 1991), 195–96.

22. Murnane et al., *Who Will Teach?*, 89.

23. Finn, *We Must Take Charge*, 44.

24. P. T. Sindelar and L. J. Marks, "Alternative Route Training: Implications for Elementary Education and Special Education," *Teacher Education and Special Education* 16, no. 2 (1993): 146.

25. Kramer, *Ed School Follies*, 204.

26. E. Guyton, "Comparison of Teaching Attitudes, Teacher Efficacy, and Teacher Performance of First Year Teachers Prepared by Alternative and Traditional Teacher Education Programs," *Action in Teacher Education* 13, no. 2 (1991): 1–9.

27. P. P. Hawk and M. W. Schmidt, "Teacher Preparation: A Comparison of Traditional and Alternative Programs," *Journal of Teacher Education* 40, no. 5 (1989): 53.

28. National Center for Education Statistics, *Digest, 1995*, 79; and Catherine Collins and Douglas Frantz, *Teachers Talking out of School* (New York: Little, Brown and Company, 1993), 16.

29. Alec M. Gallup, *Gallup Poll of Teachers' Attitudes toward the Public Schools* (Bloomington, IN: Phi Delta Kappa, 1985), 15.

30. Clare Dean, "Students Warned Off Teaching by Heads," *Times Educational Supplement*, May 11, 1994, 1.

31. Valerie E. Lee, Robert F. Dedrick, and Julia B. Smith, "The Effect of the Social Organization of Schools on Teachers' Efficacy and Satisfaction," *Sociology of Education* 64 (1991): 190–208.

32. Ann Bradley, "Survey of Chicago Teachers Paints Uneven Portrait of Reform," *Education Week*, September 6, 1995, 10–11.

33. National Education Association (NEA), *Nationwide Teacher Opinion Poll* (Washington, DC: NEA, 1979).

34. Gallup, *Gallup Poll of Teachers' Attitudes*, 10.

35. National Center for Education Statistics, *Digest of Education Statistics, 1993* (Washington, DC: U.S. Department of Education, 1993), 84.

36. As of 1991, the average total number of days worked by public school teachers was 185, which is equivalent to thirty-seven weeks or nine and a quarter months. See National Center for Education Statistics, *Digest, 1995*, 79.

37. Ann Bradley, "Nation's Teachers Feeling Better about Jobs, Salaries, Survey Finds," *Education Week*, December 6, 1995, 13.

38. David Tyack and Larry Cuban, *Tinkering toward Utopia* (Cambridge, MA: Harvard University Press, 1995), 130.

39. Emily Sachar, *Shut Up and Let the Lady Teach: A Teacher's Year in a Public School* (New York: Poseidon Press, 1991), 230.

40. Clifford and Guthrie, *Ed School: A Brief for Professional Education*, 30.

41. Gallup International and the C. F. Kettering Foundation, "The Second Annual Gallup Poll of Public Attitudes toward Education," in Stanley M. Elam, *A Decade of Gallup Polls of Attitudes toward Education, 1969–1978* (Bloomington, IN: Phi Delta Kappa, 1978), 56–57; George H. Gallup, "The 16th Annual Gallup Poll of the Public's Attitudes toward the Public Schools," *Phi Delta Kappan*, September

1984, 33–34; and Stanley M. Elam and Alec M. Gallup, "The 20th Annual Gallup Poll of the Public's Attitudes toward the Public Schools," *Phi Delta Kappan,* September 1988, 44.

42. Gallup, *Gallup Poll of Teachers' Attitudes,* 11.
43. Earl J. Ogletree, *Teachers' and Administrators' Opinion of Merit Pay,* Research report, unpublished, 1985.
44. Murnane et al., *Who Will Teach?,* 37, 46 (emphasis in original).
45. Ibid., 71–72.
46. National Center for Education Statistics, *Digest, 1995,* 78.
47. Ibid., 80.
48. Ibid., 79.
49. Allen Odden, "Class Size and Student Achievement: Research-Based Policy Alternatives," *Educational Evaluation and Policy Analysis* 12, no. 2 (1990): 224.
50. Ibid., 216.
51. See, for example, Frederick Mosteller, "The Tennessee Study of Class Size in the Early School Grades," *Future of Children* 5, no. 2 (1995): 113–27.
52. Eric A. Hanushek, "The Evidence on Class Size," Occasional Paper Number 98–1, W. Allen Wallis Institute of Political Economy, University of Rochester, February 1998.
53. Gallup, *Gallup Poll of Teachers' Attitudes,* 10; and Stanley M. Elam, "Differences between Educators and the Public on Questions of Education Policy," *Phi Delta Kappan,* December 1987, 294–96.
54. Lee, Dedrick, and Smith, "Effect of the Social Organization of Schools," 190–208; and Dominic J. Brewer, "Principals and Student Outcomes: Evidence from U.S. High Schools," *Economics of Education Review* 12, no. 4 (1993): 281–92.
55. Seattle Times News Services, "Students Beat Teacher for Refusing to Show 'Jerry Springer' on Class TV," *Seattle Times,* May 31, 1998.
56. Jessica Portner, "The Target of Attacks by Students, Teachers Turn to Courts for Relief," *Education Week,* July 12, 1995, 1, 9; and National Education Association, *Nationwide Teacher Opinion Poll.*
57. Gallup, *Gallup Poll of Teachers' Attitudes,* 14.
58. Lynn Schnaiberg, "Disciplining Special-Education Students: A Conundrum," *Education Week,* November 30, 1994, 1, 14–15; and Portner, "Teachers Turn to Courts for Relief," 1, 9.
59. Judith Anderson, *Who's in Charge? Teachers' Views on Control over School Policy and Classroom Practices* (Washington, DC: Office of Educational Research and Improvement, 1994); and Lee, Dedrick, and Smith, "Effect of the Social Organization of Schools," 190–208.
60. Dean, "Students Warned Off," 1.
61. Posted to an on-line discussion group in the fall of 1995.
62. Organization for Economic Cooperation and Development (OECD), *Education at a Glance, OECD Indicators* (Paris: OECD, 1995).
63. Stanley M. Elam, Lowell C. Rose, and Alec M. Gallup, "The 23rd Annual Phi Delta Kappa/ Gallup Poll of the Public's Attitudes toward the Public Schools," *Phi Delta Kappan,* September 1991, 52.
64. Elam, "Differences between Educators and the Public," 294–96.

65. Gallup, *Gallup Poll of Teachers' Attitudes,* 19.
66. Susan Moore Johnson, *Teachers at Work: Achieving Success in Our Schools* (New York: Basic Books, 1990), 98–99.
67. Brewer, "Principals and Student Outcomes," 281–82.
68. Gallup International and the C. F. Kettering Foundation, "The Second Annual Poll," in Elam, *A Decade of Gallup Polls,* 57. Note that this appears to be the last time the teacher tenure issue was put before the public, but it seems likely that sentiment is substantially unchanged on this issue, just as it has been on teacher accountability and performance-based pay.
69. Jonathan Kozol, *Savage Inequalities: Children in America's Schools* (New York, HarperPerennial, 1992), 46–47; and Sowell, *Inside American Education,* 29–31.
70. Kozol, *Savage Inequalities,* 69.
71. Robert Leitman, Katherine Binns, and Ann Duffett, *The Metropolitan Life Survey of the American Teacher, 1984–1995: Old Problems, New Challenges* (New York: Louis Harris and Associates, 1995), 44.
72. Ernest L. Boyer, *High School* (New York: Harper & Row, 1983), 226.
73. Sachar, *Shut Up and Let the Lady Teach,* 248, 250.
74. Follow Through was originally designed specifically to study poor/disadvantaged children, but a sufficient number of typical and even wealthy schools eventually participated in the program to allow the results to be generalized.
75. Linda B. Stebbins, Robert G. St. Pierre, Elizabeth C. Proper, Richard B. Anderson, Thomas R. Cerva, and Mary M. Kennedy, *Education as Experimentation: A Planned Variation Model, Volume IV-A, An Evaluation of Follow Through* (Cambridge, MA: Abt Associates, 1977), 143.
76. Ibid., 136.
77. Siegfried Engelmann, *War against the Schools' Academic Child Abuse* (Portland, OR: Halcyon House, 1992), 5.
78. Wesley C. Becker and Russell Gersten, "A Follow-up of Follow Through: The Later Effects of the Direct Instruction Model on Children in Fifth and Sixth Grades," *American Educational Research Journal* 19, no. 1 (1982): 88.
79. Note that one of the other methods studied—the Parent Education program—did produce a small positive effect in basic skills; but it did not specify a particular stance on structure in lesson plans or the classroom experience generally, so it is omitted from this discussion.
80. Stebbins et al., *Education as Experimentation,* 25, 136.
81. Engelmann, *War against the Schools' Academic Child Abuse,* 5–6.
82. John E. Stone, "Developmentalism: An Obscure but Pervasive Restriction on Educational Improvement," *Education Policy Analysis Archives* 4, no. 8 (1996); available at: http://olam.ed.asu.edu/epaa/v4n8.html
83. Cited in ibid.
84. Cited in ibid. (emphasis added).
85. Edwin E. Moise, untitled article in *Five Views of the "New Math"* (Washington, DC: Council for Basic Education, 1965), 1.
86. For an explanation of these terms, see any general work of mathematics or the book by Morris Kline cited in the next note.

87. Morris Kline, *Why Johnny Can't Add: The Failure of the New Math* (New York: St. Martin's Press, 1973), 103.

88. Ibid., preface.

89. National Council of Teachers of Mathematics (NCTM), *Curriculum and Evaluation Standards for School Mathematics* (Reston, VA: NCTM, 1989), 2.

90. Ibid., 254. The document subsequently states that "these values . . . are consistent with current research findings," but provides no citations in support of this vague claim.

91. Ibid., 7.

92. Ibid., 16.

93. Ibid., 8.

94. Engelmann, *War against the Schools' Academic Child Abuse,* 90.

95. Sara G. Tarver and Jane S. Jung, "A Comparison of Mathematics Achievement and Mathematics Attitudes of First and Second Graders Instructed with Either a Discovery Learning Mathematics Curriculum or a Direct Instruction Curriculum," *Effective School Practices* 14, no. 1 (1995): 49–56.

96. Peter West, "The New 'New Math'?" *Education Week,* May 10, 1995, 23.

97. Horace Mann, "Report for 1843," in *Annual Reports on Education by Horace Mann* (Boston: Horace B. Fuller, 1868), 310–12.

98. John Mason, *The Teaching of Reading by the Phonic Method* (Edinburgh and London: Oliver and Boyd, circa 1830s). Note that while this book was published in Great Britain, it is fairly typical of the phonic method as used in the United States in the early nineteenth century.

99. Mitford Mathews, *Teaching to Read, Historically Considered* (Chicago: The University of Chicago Press, 1966), 89.

100. Ibid., 77–78.

101. Thomas H. Briggs and Lotus D. Coffman, *Reading in Public Schools* (Chicago: Row, Peterson & Co., 1908).

102. Nila B. Smith, *American Reading Instruction: Its Development and Its Significance in Gaining a Perspective on Current Practices in Reading* (New York: Silver, Burdett and Company, 1934), 222.

103. Quoted in Herbert M. Kliebard, *The Struggle for the American Curriculum* (New York: Routledge, 1995), 41.

104. Quoted in Mathews, *Teaching to Read,* 136.

105. Jeanne S. Chall, *Learning to Read: The Great Debate* (New York: McGraw-Hill, 1983); and Dale D. Johnson and James F. Baumann, "Word Identification," in P. David Pearson, ed., *The Handbook of Reading Research* (New York: Longman, 1984), 583–608.

106. Quoted in Arthur E. Bestor, *Educational Wastelands: The Retreat from Learning in Our Public Schools* (Urbana, IL: The University of Illinois Press, 1953), 55–56.

107. Rudolf Flesch, *Why Johnny Still Can't Read* (1981; New York: Harper Colophon Books, 1983), 1.

108. Dorothy J. Watson, "Defining and Describing Whole Language," *Elementary School Journal* 90, no. 2 (1989).

109. Elizabeth McPike, "Learning to Read: Schooling's First Mission," *American Educator* 19, no. 2 (1995): 6.

110. Patrick Welsh, "Why a Twelfth-Grader Can't Read: Blame Fads, Fear of Phonics, and Frenzied Schedules," *Washington Post,* November 26, 1995; reprinted in the Educational Excellence Network's *Network News & Views,* January/February, 1996, 159–61.

111. Karen Diegmueller, "California Plotting New Tack on Language Arts," *Education Week,* June 14, 1995, 12.

112. Statistics cited in Jeff McQuillan, *The Literacy Crisis* (Portsmouth, NH: Heinemann, 1998), ch. 1.

113. J. R. Campbell, P. L. Donahue, C. M. Reese, and G. W. Phillips, *NAEP 1994 Reading Report Card for the Nation and the States* (Washington, DC: National Center for Education Statistics, U.S. Department of Education, 1996), 129.

114. Karen Diegmueller, "A War of Words: Whole Language Under Siege," *Education Week,* March 20, 1996, 15.

115. Ibid.

116. Diegmueller, "California Plotting New Tack," 14.

117. Chall, *Learning to Read,* 307.

118. See, for instance, Robert Dykstra, "Research in Reading," in Charles C. Walcutt et al., *Teaching Reading: A Phonic/Linguistic Approach to Developmental Reading* (New York: Macmillan, 1974); R. Anderson, E. Hiebert, J. Scott, and I. Wilkinson, *Becoming a Nation of Readers: The Report of the Commission on Reading* (Champaign, IL: Center for the Study of Reading, 1985); and Keith E. Stanovich, "Matthew Effects in Reading: Some Consequences of Individual Differences in the Acquisition of Literacy," *Reading Research Quarterly* 21 (1986): 360–406.

119. Dale D. Johnson and James F. Baumann, "Word Identification," in Pearson, ed., *The Handbook of Reading Research,* 595.

120. See, for example, M. J. Adams, *Beginning to Read: Thinking and Learning about Print* (Cambridge, MA: MIT Press, 1990); and Isabel L. Beck and Connie Juel, "The Role of Decoding in Learning to Read," *American Educator* 19, no. 2 (1995): 8, 21–25, 39–42.

121. Constance Weaver, *Reading Process and Practice: From Socio-Psycholinguistics to Whole Language* (Portsmouth, NH: Heinemann, 1994), 307–8 (emphasis added).

122. Ibid., 325.

123. See Chall, *Learning to Read*; and Johnson and Baumann, "Word Identification."

124. Cited in Flesch, *Why Johnny Still Can't Read,* 25–26.

125. Weaver, *Reading Process and Practice,* 273.

126. A "Miscue Recording Checklist," cited with approbation in Jane Baskwill and Paulette Whitman, *Evaluation: Whole Language, Whole Child* (New York: Scholastic Inc., 1988), 20 (emphasis added).

127. From the cover of William H. McGuffey, *The Eclectic Third Reader* (Cincinnati: Truman and Smith, 1837).

128. William H. McGuffey, *Fourth Reader for Advanced Students* (1836; Washougal, WA: Moore Learning Systems, 1983), 247.

129. William H. Elson and Christine Keck, *Elson Grammar School Reader, Book Three* (Chicago: Scott, Foresman and Company, 1910), 389.

130. Things would have been different, of course, if the child had learned phonetic rules on his or her own initiative, in spite of the teacher's efforts to keep them secret.

131. Jeanne S. Chall and Sue S. Conard, with Susan Harris-Sharples, *Should Textbooks Challenge Students? The Case for Easier or Harder Textbooks* (New York: Teachers College, Columbia University, 1991).

132. Russell Freedman, "The Long Road West," in *Worlds Beyond* (Needham, MA: Silver Burdett & Ginn, 1989), 169.

133. For example: Virginia A. Arnold and Carl B. Smith, *Doorways* (New York: Macmillan, 1987).

134. For example: Margaret Early, Bernice E. Cullinan, Roger C. Farr, W. Dorsey Hammond, Nancy Santeusanio, and Dorothy S. Strickland, *Reflections* (Orlando: Harcourt Brace Jovanovich, 1987).

135. For example: Donna Alvermann, Connie A. Bridge, Barbara A. Schmidt, Lyndon W. Searfoss, and Peter Winograd, *Roads Go Ever Ever On* (Lexington, MA: D.C. Heath and Company, 1989).

136. The quotation from Elson's book receives the following scores: Flesch-Kincaid Grade Level, 12.2; Bormuth Grade Level, 11.5; and Coleman-Liau Grade Level, 18.2. The McGuffey excerpt receives grade scores of 11.8, 11.6, and 19.3, respectively. "The Long Road West," by contrast, is rated at grades 4, 7.7, and 8.2, respectively.

The values generated by these formulas are intended to be rough approximations of the grade at which students could comprehend the given texts, and values above 12 correspond to college-level material. Flesch-Kincaid Grade Level is a function of the number of syllables per word and the number of words per sentence. Both Bormuth and Coleman-Liau Grade Levels are functions of the number of characters per word and the number of words per sentence.

137. Nathaniel Hawthorne, "Theseus," in *Enjoying Literature,* ed. J. Cassidy, E. Cooper, R. DiYanni, and R. Loxley (New York: Scribner Laidlaw, 1989), T=441.

138. The readability scores for the "Theseus" excerpt are: Flesch-Kincaid Grade Level, 6.1; Bormuth Grade Level, 5.3; and Coleman-Liau Grade Level, 8.2.

139. R. S. Cohen, N. C. Millett, and R. J. Rodrigues, *Explorations in Literature* (Glenview, IL: Scott, Foresman and Company, 1985).

140. Harriet Tyson-Bernstein, *A Conspiracy of Good Intentions: America's Textbook Fiasco* (Washington, DC: The Council for Basic Education, 1988), 2.

141. National Center for Education Statistics, *Digest of Education Statistics, 1995* (Washington, DC: U.S. Department of Education, 1995), 53.

142. Black is quoted in Sherry Keith, "The Determinants of Textbook Content," in Philip G. Altbach, ed., *Textbooks in American Society: Politics, Policy, and Pedagogy* (Albany, NY: State University of New York Press, 1991), 49.

143. Harriet Tyson-Bernstein and Arthur Woodward, "Nineteenth Century Policies for Twenty-First Century Practice: The Textbook Reform Dilemma," in Altbach, ed., *Textbooks in American Society,* 95.

144. In 1998, the sitting members of California's curriculum committee, which selects kindergarten through eighth-grade textbooks for the entire state, had been variously appointed by the governor, the state board of education, the state assembly, the state senate rules committee, and the state senate. Virtually all had full-time jobs outside of their textbook-selection duties.

145. Tyson-Bernstein and Woodward, "Ninteenth Century Policies," 96.
146. Tyson-Bernstein, *Conspiracy of Good Intentions,* 101.
147. Tyson-Bernstein and Woodward, "Nineteenth Century Policies," 94.
148. Tyson-Bernstein, *Conspiracy of Good Intentions,* 101–2.
149. Richard P. Feynman, *Surely You're Joking, Mr. Feynman! Adventures of a Curious Character* (New York: Bantam Books, 1985), 268.
150. Ibid., 273–74.
151. Paul L. McFall, president for sales, Addison Wesley; quoted in Kathleen Kennedy Manzo, "Publishers Claim Competitor Gained Unfair Edge," *Education Week,* February 25, 1998, 3.

Chapter 6. The Performance Crisis in Public Schooling

1. This photo originally appeared in Emily Sachar, *Shut Up and Let the Lady Teach* (New York: Poseidon Press, 1991), opposite page 160.
2. About nine out of every ten American students attend public schools, so the performance of students in nationwide studies would be a fair reflection of the performance of public schools even if private school students participated in those studies. In many cases, however, private schools do not participate, making the results of national tests an even more accurate measure of public school effectiveness.
3. Lawrence C. Stedman, "An Assessment of Literacy Trends, Past and Present," *Research in the Teaching of English* 30, no. 3 (1996): 283-302.
4. That is, the most comprehensive, most detailed, and most well reasoned.
5. Such as changes in the makeup of groups in terms of race or ethnic origin.
6. The precise quotation from Stedman and Kaestle is: "[R]eading achievement for students in school at any given age level has been stable throughout most of the twentieth century." It appears in Lawrence C. Stedman and Carl F. Kaestle, "Literacy and Reading Performance in the United States from 1880 to the Present," in Carl F. Kaestle et al., *Literacy in the United States: Readers and Reading since 1880* (New Haven: Yale University Press, 1991), 127. A considerable amount of new evidence on post-1970 student achievement only became available after the 1991 publication of their article, so Stedman and Kaestle's original treatment of that period is no longer current.
7. Note that the figures given here (for both 1909–10 and 1969–70) do not represent the official length of the school year (which was somewhat longer in each case), but rather the number of days actually attended by the average child.
8. National Center for Education Statistics (NCES), *Digest of Education Statistics, 1995* (Washington, DC: U.S. Department of Education, 1995), 50.
9. Kindergarten is excluded from these calculations because its duration in hours per day has varied considerably over the period in question, and because its purpose has ranged from predominantly custodial to predominantly instructional and back again, with no easily definable patterns.
10. A norm-referenced test is scored based on the relative performance of current students and an earlier "norm" group of students. This contrasts with criterion-

referenced tests, which are scored solely on the basis of the number of correct answers given by students.

11. This discussion will omit the trends in renorming studies for two reasons. First, as Lawrence Stedman rightly points out in "An Assessment of Literacy Trends": "[S]tandardized test renormings are not reliable measures of national trends" in educational achievement. This is due primarily to the fact that the samples of students used in renorming studies are frequently not nationally representative— sometimes they are taken from only one or two school districts. Numerous other researchers, including those at the U.S. Department of Education, have pointed to the frequent nonrepresentativeness of so-called "national" norms. Secondly, results on high-stakes norm-referenced tests such as the Comprehensive Test of Basic Skills (CTBS), the Iowa Test of Basic Skills (ITBS), etc. are widely acknowledged to be compromised by overt and subtle cheating by public school personnel, due to the pressures on school officials to demonstrate improving scores. The issue of cheating is taken up later in this chapter.

12. NCES, *Digest, 1995,* 113–26; and J. R. Campbell et al., *NAEP 1994 Reading Report Card for the Nation and the States* (Washington, DC: National Center for Education Statistics, U.S. Department of Education, 1996), 23.

13. NCES, *Digest, 1995,* 118–19.

14. Petra Lietz, *Changes in Reading Comprehension Across Cultures and Over Time* (Münster: Waxmann, 1996). Thanks are due to professor Herbert Walberg for making me and others aware of the Lietz (and related) findings in his article "U.S. Schools Teach Reading Least Productively," *Research in the Teaching of English* 30, no. 3 (1996): 328–43.

15. David F. Robitaille, "Achievement Comparisons between the First and Second IEA Studies of Mathematics," *Educational Studies in Mathematics* 21 (1990): 395–414.

16. The raw scores of American ten-year-olds increased from 410 to 416—the least progress of any nation. Fourteen-year-olds did worse, dropping 25 points, from 538 to 513.

17. John P. Keeves and A. Schleicher, "Changes in Science Achievement: 1970–1984," in *The IEA Study of Science III: Changes in Science Education and Achievement, 1970 to 1984* (New York: Pergamon Press, 1991), 278.

18. These tests measure literacy on three scales: prose reading; competence in handling printed quantitative information such as simple charts; and the understanding of common documents such as bus schedules and drug labels.

19. Level 1: 0 to 225; level 2: 226 to 275; level 3: 276 to 325; level 4: 326–375; level 5: 376 to 500. The tests also used the same three scales described in the previous note.

20. I. S. Kirsch, L. Jenkins, A. Jungeblut, and A. Kolstad, *Adult Literacy in America* (Washington, DC: National Center for Education Statistics, U.S. Department of Education, 1993).

Though the racial/ethnic composition of the test-taking population changed somewhat in the intervening years, a breakdown of the data shows that both white and Hispanic scores suffered real declines on all three subtests (prose, document, and quantitative), while the scores of blacks were mixed. White scores declined by 9 points on all three subtests. Hispanic scores declined by 20, 10, and 14 points, respectively. And scores for blacks rose by 8 points and 6 points, respectively, on the first two tests, while dropping by 7 points on the last test. The racial/ethnic breakdown of test takers was 76 percent white, 7 percent Hispanic, and 13 percent black in 1985; and 70 percent white, 15 percent Hispanic, and 11 percent black in 1992. No other racial/ethnic breakdowns were provided.

21. Take, for example, the definitions of Prose Level 1 from the NALS and the IALS. In the NALS of 1992, this definition reads: "Most of the tasks in this level require the reader to read relatively short text to locate a single piece of information which is identical to or synonymous with the information given in the question or directive. If plausible but incorrect information is present in the text, it tends not to be located near the correct information." Compare this to the definition from the 1994 IALS: "Most of the tasks at this level require the reader to locate one piece of information in the text that is identical or synonymous to the information given in the directive. If a plausible incorrect answer is present in the text, it tends not to be near the correct information."

22. Personal communication with Irwin Kirsch of the Educational Testing Service, May 6, 1996.

23. Organization for Economic Cooperation and Development (OECD) and Statistics Canada, *Literacy, Economy, and Society* (Paris: OECD Publications, 1995), 152–54.

24. In 1994, the College Board arbitrarily redefined the average SAT scores of 1990 students as the new norm. By 1990, students had fallen well below the old norm of 500 set in the 1940s, reaching 475 on the mathematics portion of the test and only 424 on the verbal portion. The recentering of the test simply remapped these lower scores to be 500, meaning that average mathematics scores were inflated by 25 points, and that average verbal scores were inflated by 76 points. Because students can now miss questions and still get perfect scores, the new SAT scores are not comparable to the old ones.

25. Charles Murray and Richard J. Herrnstein, "What's Really Behind the SAT-Score Decline?" *Public Interest* 106 (1992): 32–36.

26. Renorming studies conducted by the Educational Testing Service (ETS) in 1975 and 1977 concluded that the same student would score 8 to 13 points higher on the SATs of the early 1970s than he or she would have on the SATs of the early 1960s. The change can be attributed to somewhat easier questions being asked on the SATs of the early 1970s.

27. National Center for Education Statistics (NCES), *The Condition of Education, 1993* (Washington, DC: U.S. Department of Education, 1993), 243. It is not clear why fewer students were taking the test during this period.

28. See Paul Copperman, *The Literacy Hoax: The Decline of Reading, Writing, and Learning in the Public Schools and What We Can Do about It* (New York: Morrow Quill, 1980), 39; and Richard J. Herrnstein and Charles Murray, *The Bell Curve: Intelligence and Class Structure in American Life* (New York: The Free Press, 1994), 429–30.

29. NCES, *Condition, 1993*, 243.

30. NCES, *Digest, 1995,* 128.

31. The particular studies involved were the Stanford-Binet and Wechsler nationally

representative standardization samples. See James R. Flynn, "The Mean IQ of Americans: Massive Gains, 1932 to 1978," *Psychological Bulletin* 95 (1984): 29, 34. Thanks once again to professor Herbert Walberg for pointing me toward this study.

32. Ulric Neisser, "Rising Scores on Intelligence Tests," *American Scientist,* September–October, 1997, 440–48.

33. Over the years, considerable experimentation has gone into identifying the determinants of success in learning to read (such as phonological awareness and familiarity with the letters of the alphabet), and the Metropolitan Readiness Tests have drawn on and benefited from this research.

34. Copperman, *Literacy Hoax,* 55–56.

35. OECD, *Education at a Glance,* 208. In terms of reading test scores, U.S. fourteen-year-olds placed behind those of Finland, France, Sweden, New Zealand, and Switzerland.

36. IEA Third International Mathematics and Science Study (TIMSS), various reports available online at: http://www.csteep.bc.edu/timss

37. OECD, *Literacy, Economy, and Society,* 152. The astute reader might ask: Which eight countries participated in the IALS study of young adults? The answer: Canada, Germany, the Netherlands, Poland, Sweden, Switzerland (French), Switzerland (German), and the United States. Were they the top eight countries from the earlier IEA test of fourteen-year-olds? If so, then American fourteen-year-olds and young adults ranked about the same. This is not the case. Three of the top-scoring IEA countries (Finland, New Zealand, and France) were not represented in the IALS, and three of the countries that U.S. fourteen-year-olds had outperformed on the IEA (Canada [British Columbia], Germany, and the Netherlands) surpassed Americans on the IALS test of sixteen- to twenty-five-year-olds.

38. See the Mathematics and Science "Achievement in the Primary School Years" reports at: http://www.csteep.bc.edu/timss

39. The NAEP only began reporting partial state-level information in the early 1990s. Some international tests, such as the TIMSS, have also recently made state-by-state comparisons possible.

40. See John J. Cannell, *How Public Educators Cheat on Standardized Achievement Tests* (Albuquerque, NM: Friends for Education, 1989).

41. Robert L. Linn, M. Elizabeth Graue, and Nancy M. Sanders, "Comparing State and District Test Results to National Norms: The Validity of Claims That 'Everyone Is Above Average,'" *Educational Measurement: Issues and Practice* 9, no. 3 (1990).

42. Drew Lindsay, "Whodunit: Someone Cheated on Standardized Tests at a Connecticut School. And It Wasn't the Students," *Education Week*, October 2, 1996, 27, 28.

43. Helen O'Neill and Denise Lavoie, Associated Press, "A Winning School Loses Its Magic," *Seattle Times,* April 6, 1997, A6.

44. Robert B. Frary, "Statistical Detection of Multiple-Choice Answer Copying: Review and Commentary," *Applied Measurement in Education* 6, no. 2 (1993): 153–65; and Cannell, *How Public Educators Cheat,* 17.

45. Answer booklets that are identified by computer as has having more than two standard deviations above the normal number of corrections are flagged and then re-

examined by state officials to determine if tampering took place. See Cannell, *How Public Educators Cheat*, 15.

46. Elaine Woo, "Forty Grade Schools Cheated on Skill Tests, State Finds," *Los Angeles Times*, September 1, 1988, 1.

47. Cannell, *How Public Educators Cheat*, 14.

48. Janie L. Hall and Paul F. Klein, "Educators' Perceptions of NRT Misuse," *Educational Measurement: Issues and Practice* 11, no. 2 (1992): 20.

49. Sachar, *Shut Up and Let the Lady Teach*, 264.

50. Associated Press, "Prestigious School's Principal Suspended in Test-Score Scandal," *Seattle Times*, February 20, 1997, A8.

51. Woo, "Forty Grade Schools Cheated," 24.

52. David Hill, "Chicago Hope," *Education Week*, October 23, 1996, 30.

53. Hall and Klein, "Educators' Perceptions," 20.

54. Thomas M. Haladyna, Susan B. Nolen, and Nancy S. Haas, "Raising Standardized Achievement Test Scores and the Origins of Test Score Pollution," *Educational Researcher* 20, no. 5 (1991): 5.

55. Debra Viadero, "Teachers Found Skeptical about Revamped Tests," *Education Week*, April 17, 1996, 1.

56. Gonzales, 1985, cited in Haladyna, Nolen, and Haas, "Raising Test Scores," 5.

57. The exact definition is as follows: An SLD exists if "(1) The child does not achieve commensurate with his or her age and ability levels in one or more of the areas listed . . . when provided with learning experiences appropriate for the child's age and ability levels; and (2) The team finds that a child has a severe discrepancy between achievement and intellectual ability in one or more of the following areas: (i) Oral expression; (ii) Listening comprehension; (iii) Written expression; (iv) Basic reading skill; (v) Reading comprehension; (vi) Mathematics calculation; (vii) Mathematic reasoning." (The definition is quoted from H. Rutherford Turnbull III, *Free Appropriate Public Education: The Law and Children with Disabilities* [Denver: Love Publishing Company, 1990], 88.)

Note that while the definition mentions appropriateness of "learning experiences," these are not defined, and the actual effectiveness of the instruction received by the child is not mentioned. However well-intentioned this clause may have been, it has proven to be an inadequate barrier to the rampant and wanton growth in SLD classifications.

58. See Diane McGuiness, *Why Our Children Can't Read—And What We Can Do about It: A Scientific Revolution in Reading* (New York: The Free Press, 1997); and Wade Roush, "Arguing Over Why Johnny Can't Read," *Science*, March 31, 1995, 1896–99.

59. The figure for six- to twenty-one-year-olds was 2,513,977 in 1994–95. Since eighteen- to twenty-one-year-olds make up a tiny fraction (about 5 percent) of the federally classified disabled population, it is fair to say that roughly 2.5 million six- to seventeen-year-olds are diagnosed as learning disabled.

60. National Center for Education Statistics, *Digest of Education Statistics, 1996* (Washington, DC: U.S. Department of Education, 1996), Table 51; and U.S. Department of Education, Office of Special Education Programs (OSEP), *Eighteenth*

Annual Report to Congress on the Implementation of the Individuals with Disabilities Education Act (Washington, DC: U.S. Department of Education, 1996).

61. Charles J. Sykes, *Dumbing Down Our Kids: Why American Children Feel Good about Themselves but Can't Read, Write, or Add* (New York: St. Martin's Press, 1995), 187.

62. Chester Finn, "How Special Is Special Education?" *Network News & Views*, April 1996, 3.

63. National Center for Education Statistics (NCES), *Digest of Education Statistics, 1997* (Washington, DC: U.S. Department of Education, 1997), 65.

64. Turnbull, *Free Appropriate Public Education*, 88.

65. Gerald Coles, *The Learning Mystique: A Critical Look at "Learning Disabilities"* (New York: Fawcett Columbine, 1987).

66. Louise Spear-Swerling and Robert J. Sternberg, *Off Track: When Poor Readers Become "Learning Disabled"* (Boulder, CO: Westview Press, 1996).

67. Roush, "Arguing Over Why Johnny Can't Read," 1896.

68. See Sally E. Shaywitz, "Dyslexia," *Scientific American*, November 1996, 98–105. In this article, Shaywitz provides an excellent summary of the phonological decoding problems that prevent many children and adults from becoming proficient readers. She also assumes a biological cause for this deficit, but provides no supporting evidence for her assumption. To date, she has only found that good and bad letter-sound decoders demonstrate different patterns of brain activity during reading exercises. Differences in brain activity patterns can and do exist between normal individuals as well, and need not have inherent physical causes. For example, native speakers of a given language (and multilingual speakers who learn it fluently as young children) have different brain activation patterns when reading text in that language than people who learn it as adults. This does not imply that non-native speakers all have inherent mental defects.

Even if Shaywitz were to identify actual differences in the underlying neurobiology of poor letter-sound decoders and good ones, which she has apparently not done, this would not prove that the source of the differences was biological (or intrinsic to the children in any way). It has been reported that the brains of violinists are physiologically different depending on the age at which they begin to study the instrument. The regions of the brain controlling finger movement are significantly more developed among those who begin as young children than among those who begin as older children or adolescents. Nonbiological causes can thus lead to differences in brain structure.

Wade Roush reports that "Marcus Raichle, a neurologist at Washington University in St. Louis and a pioneer in the use of magnetic resonance imaging to study brain functioning, agrees that such techniques tell little about the practical significance of brain differences between normal and LD readers." Paula Tallal of Rutgers University goes so far as to liken many neuro-imaging studies to "modern-day phrenology." See Roush, "Arguing Over Why Johnny Can't Read" (*supra* note 58).

Despite a century of research there is no evidence to link learning disability diagnoses with inherent neurological deficits.

69. U.S. Department of Education, *Eighteenth Annual Report*; available at: http://www.ed.gov/pubs/OSEP96AnlRpt/

70. Thomas Armstrong, *The Myth of the ADD Child* (New York: Dutton, 1995), 9.
71. Ibid.
72. Richard E. Vatz and Lee S. Weinberg, "Overreacting to Attention Deficit Disorder," *USA Today* 123, no. 2596 (1995): 84–86.
73. Richard W. Smelter, Bradley W. Rasch, Jan Fleming, Pat Nazos, and Sharon Baranowski, "Is Attention Deficit Disorder Becoming a Desired Diagnosis?" *Phi Delta Kappan,* February 1996, 429–33.
74. Anne McGill-Franzen and Richard L. Allington, "Flunk 'Em or Get Them Classified: The Contamination of Primary Grade Accountability Data," *Educational Researcher* 22, no. 1 (1993): 19–22.
75. Ibid., 22.
76. Ibid., 21.
77. Coles, *The Learning Mystique,* 47.
78. Jeanne Ponessa, "College Freshmen Report Higher High School Grades," *Education Week*, January 22, 1997, 4.
79. Sixty-two percent of high-school graduates attended college in 1996, versus 50 percent in 1966. See NCES, *Digest, 1995,* 187.
80. Richard J. Murnane and Frank Levy, "Why Money Matters Sometimes," *Education Week,* September 11, 1996, 36, 48.
81. David Boaz, "The Public School Monopoly: America's Berlin Wall," in Boaz, ed., *Liberating Schools: Education in the Inner City* (Washington, DC: Cato Institute, 1991), 17; and David Boaz and R. Morris Barrett, "What Would a School Voucher Buy? The Real Cost of Private Schools," *Cato Briefing Papers,* no. 25, March 26, 1996, 6.
82. David Boaz, *Libertarianism: A Primer* (New York: Free Press, 1997), 245.
83. Capital outlay as a portion of total spending fell from 14.8 percent in 1919–20 to 9.3 percent in 1992–93. See NCES, *Digest, 1995,* 154.
84. Richard Rothstein and Karen Miles, *Where's the Money Gone?* (Washington, DC: Economic Policy Institute, 1995).
85. Originally passed under the title Education of All Handicapped Children Act.
86. Rothstein and Miles, *Where's the Money Gone?,* 6.
87. For the period from 1982 to 1991, the average annual growth in the CPI was 3.9 percent, while that of Rothstein and Mile's NSI was 4.1 percent. See Eric A. Hanushek, "The Productivity Collapse in Schools," Working Paper No. 8, December 1996, University of Rochester.
88. As Hanushek also points out, public schooling has become more labor-intensive than it needs to be. The teacher-student ratio doubled over the last forty years for no justifiable reason. While most industries learn to do more with less, public schooling is doing less with more. Given the tremendous advances in personal computers and educational software of recent years, and the evidence that smaller classes do not raise student achievement (see Chapter 5), public schools should be operating with *fewer* employees than they used to, not more. It is therefore misleading to compare public schooling, with its artificially inflated employee rolls, with labor-intensive private companies that must compete in the marketplace. No private company could afford to arbitrarily double its workforce without being able to translate this hiring bonanza into considerably higher output. The inflation

theorists have their argument backward: ballooning labor costs in public schooling are an indication of mismanagement, not a reason to claim public schools are more efficient (however marginally) than they seem.

89. Alan Greenspan, "Testimony of Chairman Alan Greenspan before the Committee on Finance, United States Senate," Federal Reserve Board, January 30, 1997.

90. The NSI is based on the CPI-services, the variant of the CPI which is meant to calculate inflation in the service sector. During the 1980s, the CPI-services did not differ appreciably from the CPI. In his testimony before the Senate Finance Committee, moreover, Fed chairman Alan Greenspan singled out the service sector as a culprit in the inflated inflation figures published by the Bureau of Labor Statistics.

91. NCES, *Digest, 1995,* Table 81.

92. Ibid., Table 80.

93. Ibid., Table 50.

94. Eric A. Hanushek, "The Economics of Schooling: Production and Efficiency in the Public Schools," *Journal of Economic Literature* 24, no. 3 (1986): 1141–77. See also Eric A. Hanushek, "Impact of Differential Expenditures on School Performance," *Educational Researcher* 18, no. 4 (1989): 45–51.

95. Stephen Childs and Charol Shakeshaft, "A Meta-Analysis of Research on the Relationship between Educational Expenditures and Student Achievement," *Journal of Education Finance* 12, no. 3 (1986): 260.

96. Keith Baker, "Yes, Throw Money at Schools," *Phi Delta Kappan* 72, no. 8 (1991): 630.

97. Gary Orfield, "Study Finds Separate Still Unequal," *Seattle Times*, April 7, 1994, A6.

98. Robert D. Gaudet, "The Impact of School Spending on Student Achievement: Results of MEAP Statewide Tests," *New England Journal of Public Policy* 10, no. 1 (1994): 9–28.

99. The latter point is even made by educators themselves, who have been at pains to point out that in the rare cases when public schools do spend money wisely, they show noticeable improvement. What these educators fail to acknowledge is that public schools do not, and indeed cannot, systematically spend money wisely: if they could, it would show up in the national and statewide efficiency studies, which it does not.

100. A magnet school is essentially a charter school specializing in one or more curricular areas. It may or may not be exempt from some state education regulations.

101. "The Cash Street Kids," *The Economist,* August 28, 1993, 23; and Paul Ciotti, "Money and School Performance: Lessons from the Kansas City Desegregation Experiment," *Cato Policy Analysis,* No. 298, March 16, 1998.

102. Ciotti, "Money and School Performance," 17–18.

103. "The Cash Street Kids," 23.

104. Ciotti, "Money and School Performance," 25–26.

105. Rick Green and Robert A. Frahm, "Paying a High Price for School Mismanagement," *Hartford Courant,* May 19, 1996.

106. Kerry A. White, "Resignation Follows Portable-Classroom Flap," *Education Week*, November 27, 1996, 8.

107. Jeffrey C. Steinhoff, *District of Columbia: Weaknesses in Personnel Records and Public Schools' Management Information and Controls. Testimony before the Subcommittee on the District of Columbia, Committee on Appropriations, House of Representatives* (Washington, DC: U.S. General Accounting Office, 1995); ERIC document no. ED387550.

108. Quoted in Jonathan Kozol, *Savage Inequalities: Children in America's Schools* (New York: HarperPerennial, 1992), 36–37.

109. Ibid., 37.

110. General Accounting Office, *School Facilities: America's Schools Report Differing Conditions,* Report no. GAO/HEHS-96-103 (Washington, DC: General Accounting Office, 1996); and Deb Riechmann, Associated Press, "Many U.S. Schools in Disrepair," *Seattle Times*, June 25, 1996.

111. This, at least, is the impression of Maribeth Vander Weele, former Chicago journalist and current chief of investigations for that city's public schools. See Hill, "Chicago Hope," 30. For Vander Weele's book, see note 114 below.

112. Sixty Minutes, "Cleaning Up," originally broadcast on November 15, 1992.

113. Suzan R. Flamm, "A System Like No Other: Fraud and Misconduct by New York City School Custodians," investigation report, New York City Office of the Special Commissioner of Investigation, 1992; ERIC Document no. ED352729.

114. Maribeth Vander Weele, *Reclaiming Our Schools: The Struggle for Chicago School Reform* (Chicago: Loyola University Press, 1994), 216.

115. "Overtime Pay Questioned," *Education Week,* March 27, 1996, 4.

116. Robert M. Brenner et al., "From Chaos to Corruption: An Investigation into the 1993 Community School Board Election," investigation report, New York City Office of the Special Commissioner of Investigation, 1993; ERIC document no. ED367054.

117. Caroline Hendrie, "Five Arrested, Fraud Alleged in Probe of N.Y.C. Elections," *Education Week,* May 1, 1996, 6.

118. "Alleged Extortion by Teacher Is Taped," *New York Times,* June 24, 1995, A15.

119. Selwyn Raab, "School Bus Pacts Go to Companies with Ties to Mob," *New York Times*, December 26, 1990, A1.

120. Selwyn Raab, "Bids Allowed by Contractor in Plea Accord," *New York Times*, November 5, 1993, B1.

121. Sam Dillon, "School Board's Maze a Factor in Scandal," *New York Times*, May 22, 1994, 31.

122. Vander Weele, *Reclaiming Our Schools,* 207–8.

123. Ibid., 212, 209–11.

124. Ibid., 213.

125. Bess Keller, "FBI Joins Probe of Alleged Employee Fraud in Dallas," *Education Week*, April 23, 1997, 3.

126. Gregory Crouch, "Embezzling of U.S. School Lunch Funds Suspected," *Los Angeles Times,* November 27, 1992, A3; and Gregory Crouch and Kristina Lindgren, "Ex-School Official Accused of Theft Faces More Charges," *Los Angeles Times*, December 3, 1992, A3.

127. John Hurst and Jean Merl, "Honig Found Guilty, Suspended from Job," *Los Angeles Times,* January 30, 1993, A1; and Richard Lee Colvin, "Ex-Schools Chief Honig's Sentence Reduced," *Los Angeles Times*, December 20, 1996, A3.

128. Charles Teddlie and Sam Stringfield, *Schools Make a Difference* (New York: Teachers College, 1993), 220, 223.

129. Their model included the following variables: school size, student tenth-grade achievement (and its effect on senior-year achievement), student behavior problems, parent socioeconomic status, and parent contacts with school. (For Chubb and Moe's book, see note 89 of Chapter 8.)

130. These include: complete parental choice of schools, the freedom of schools to set their own tuitions, and the freedom of schools to control their own admission/expulsion policies.

131. Robert Gilchrist, *Effective Schools: Three Case Studies of Excellence* (Bloomington, IN: National Educational Service, 1989), 47, 50.

132. Kathleen Binkowski et al., "A Qualitative Study of Higher and Lower Performing Elementary Schools," paper presented at the Annual Conference of the American Educational Research Association, San Francisco, CA, April 18–22, 1995, 19, 24; available as ERIC document no. ED386311.

133. Nathan Rosenberg and Larry Birdzell, *How the West Grew Rich: The Economic Transformation of the Industrial World* (New York: Basic Books, 1987).

Chapter 7. Common School Problems: The World Tour

1. Robert L. August, "*Yobiko*: Prep Schools for College Entrance in Japan," in Robert Leestma and Herbert J. Walberg, eds., *Japanese Educational Productivity* (Ann Arbor: Center for Japanese Studies of the University of Michigan, 1992), 267; and Satoshi Nakajima, personal communication.

2. Catherine C. Lewis, "Creativity in Japanese Education," in Leestma and Walberg, eds., *Japanese Educational Productivity,* 243–44.

3. John P. Dolly, "*Juku* and the Performance of Japanese Students: An American Perspective," paper presented at the Annual Meeting of the Japan/United States Teacher Education Consortium, Tokyo, Japan, June 1992; ERIC document no. ED355175.

4. Harold W. Stevenson and Karen Bartsch, "An Analysis of Japanese and American Textbooks in Mathematics," in Leestma and Walberg, eds., *Japanese Educational Productivity,* 103–33. See also Alice Gill and Liz McPike, "What We Can Learn from Japanese Teachers' Manuals," *American Educator,* Spring 1995.

5. Stevenson and Bartsch, "Analysis of Textbooks in Mathematics."

6. Ibid., 132.

7. Various other aspects of their classroom environments, such as greater time spent on instructional activities and more direct instruction by teachers, also play a role. See, for instance, Harold W. Stevenson and James W. Stigler, *The Learning Gap: Why Our Schools Are Failing and What We Can Learn from Japanese and Chinese Education* (New York: Touchstone, 1992).

8. Arther S. Trace, Jr., *What Ivan Knows That Johnny Doesn't* (New York: Random House, 1961), 9–29.

9. T. D. Lysenko was a Russian "scientist" whose ideas about genetics were grossly inaccurate but consistent with Marxist philosophy. Among his many counterfactual beliefs was the notion that traits or skills acquired during the life of an animal

could be genetically passed on to its offspring. His views were embraced by Stalin, and he was elevated to the top of the Soviet scientific hierarchy. His rise and fall are chronicled in Valery Soyfer, *Lysenko and the Tragedy of Soviet Science* (Piscataway, NJ: Rutgers University Press, 1994).

10. Trace, *What Ivan Knows,* 9–29.
11. Thomas P. Rohlen, *Japan's High Schools* (Berkeley: University of California Press, 1983), 255. See also the interesting articles on this subject written in 1996 by students of Chuo University, available on-line at: http://www.brokering.com/adv96/html/textbook.html. The students' articles reveal the high profile that Japanese government textbook censorship has had in the Asian media, remarking that 2,439 stories were written on the subject between July and September of 1982 in the major newspapers of nineteen Asian countries.
12. Rohlen, *Japan's High Schools,* 210.
13. Haruo Ota, "Political Teacher Unionism in Japan," in James J. Shields, Jr., ed., *Japanese Schooling: Patterns of Socialization, Equality, and Political Control* (University Park, PA: The Pennsylvania State University Press, 1993), 251.
14. Lucien Ellington, *Education in the Japanese Life-Cycle: Implications for the United States* (Lampeter, Wales: The Edwin Mellen Press, 1992), 207.
15. Ibid., 211.
16. Rohlen, *Japan's High Schools,* 237.
17. Ota, "Political Teacher Unionism," 258.
18. Leonard J. Schoppa, *Education Reform in Japan* (London and New York: Routledge, 1991), 252–53.
19. Rohlen, *Japan's High Schools,* 216.
20. Ibid., 218.
21. See, for instance, T. Sasamori, "Educational Reform in Japan since 1984," in H. Beare and W. Lowe Boyd, eds., *Restructuring Schools: An International Perspective on the Movement to Transform the Control and Performance of Schools* (Washington, DC: The Falmer Press, 1993), 154.
22. Schoppa, *Education Reform in Japan,* 255.
23. Delwyn L. Harnisch, "Supplemental Education in Japan: *Juku* Schooling and Its Implication," *Journal of Curriculum Studies* 26, no. 3 (1994): 323.
24. Ibid., 325, 332–33. Similar figures can be found in Dolly, "*Juku* and Performance," 2.
25. K. Kitamura, paraphrased in Harnisch, "Supplemental Education," 323.
26. T. Sawada and S. Kobayashi, paraphrased in ibid., 330. See also Dolly, "*Juku* and Performance," 18.
27. Dolly, "*Juku* and Performance," 3.
28. August, "*Yobiko,*" 281-82.
29. Harnisch, "Supplemental Education," 327.
30. Ibid., 326–27.
31. Ibid., 327.
32. This is especially true in a kind of *juku* known as a *yobiko* (described below in the text), where students are attending with a specific goal in mind (college entrance exams), and are highly motivated to study.
33. August, "*Yobiko,*" 290.

34. Harnisch, "Supplemental Education," 325.
35. S. R. Dennison, *Choice in Education* (London: The Institute for Economic Affairs, 1984), 45.
36. Ibid.
37. A. Morrison and D. McIntyre, *Teachers and Teaching,* quoted in Adam Hopkins, *The School Debate* (Harmondsworth, England: Penguin, 1978), 157.
38. Hopkins, *The School Debate,* 157.
39. Janet A. Miller, "Theoretical Orientation of British Infant School Teachers," unpublished research report, ERIC document no. ED327823.
40. Melanie Phillips, *All Must Have Prizes* (London: Warner Books, 1997), 91–92.
41. Ibid., 52–53.
42. Bernard C. Lamb, *The Opinions and Practices of Teachers of English: A National Survey of Teachers of English to 11 to 18-year-olds* (London: The Queen's English Society, 1997), 1, 3.
43. Neville Bennett, with Joyce Jordan, George Long, and Barbara Wade, *Teaching Styles and Pupil Progress* (Cambridge, MA: Harvard University Press, 1976), 152, 158.
44. Maurice Galton, *Crisis in the Primary Classroom* (London: David Fulton Publishers, 1995), 7.
45. Robin Alexander, *Primary Education in Leeds* (Leeds: University of Leeds, 1991), 136, quoted in Galton, *Crisis,* 74.
46. Dennison, *Choice in Education,* 42.
47. Ibid., 44.
48. Quoted in Jill Sherman and David Charter, "Teachers and MPs attack Blair's School Reforms," *The (London) Times,* June 8, 1996.
49. Tony Halpin, "We Failed Schools, Admits Blunkett," *Daily Mail,* May 30, 1996.
50. Andrew Grice, "Blunkett to Push Teaching Back to Basics," *The Sunday Times,* June 22, 1997.
51. Department for Education and Employment, *National Literacy Strategy: Framework for Teaching* (London: Department for Education and Employment, 1998).
52. Quoted in Jill Sherman, "Blair Sets Sights on New Deal for Schools," *The (London) Times,* January 13, 1997.
53. Department of Education and Science (of the United Kingdom), "Circular 10/65: The Organisation of Secondary Education," July 12, 1965, in J. Stuart Maclure, ed., *Educational Documents: England and Wales, 1816–1968* (London: Methuen Educational Ltd., 1971), 301.
54. Donald Mackinnon, June Statham, with Margaret Hales, *Education in the U.K.: Facts and Figures* (London: Hodder & Stoughton, in association with Open University, 1996), 53–58.
55. Dennison, *Choice in Education,* 4.
56. "Hot News," *Times Educational Supplement* (on-line version), July 7, 1997. Archived on-line at: http://www.tes.co.uk
57. John Wilson, "Let's Not Hear It for the Sec Mod [Secondary Modern School]," *Times Educational Supplement,* August 2, 1996.
58. Quoted in Antony Flew, *Power to the Parents: Reversing Educational Decline* (London: Sherwood Press, 1987), 27.

59. Quoted in ibid.

60. Dennison, *Choice in Education,* 21.

61. Quoted in ibid.

62. See Chapter 4.

63. Dennison, *Choice in Education,* 23.

64. Philip Webster and Jill Sherman, "Harman Will Not Quit Over Son's School," *The (London) Times,* January 23, 1996, Britain section.

65. Ibid.

66. This is a crude paraphrastic plagiarism of the following statement (made by the character Bernard Woolley in the BBC series *Yes Prime Minister*): "It's one of those irregular verbs, isn't it? 'I have an independent mind, you are eccentric, he is round the twist'?" See Jonathan Lynn and Antony Jay, *The Complete Yes Prime Minister* (London: BBC Books, 1992), 233.

67. Webster and Sherman, "Harman Will Not Quit."

68. See Phillips, *All Must Have Prizes,* 208.

69. See Flew, *Power to the Parents,* quotation at bottom of page 29.

70. John Marks and Maciej Pomian-Srzednicki, *Standards in English Schools: Second Report* (London: National Council for Educational Standards, 1985), 67–70, 113.

71. Ibid., 86–90, 114 (emphasis in the original).

72. Department for Education and Employment, "The School Curriculum: A Brief Guide," 1995. Available online at: http://www.open.gov.uk/dfee/schurric.htm

73. "Teach Pupils French from Age of Seven," *The (London) Times,* May 29, 1997, General News section.

74. Under the National Curriculum, foreign language instruction does not begin before the age of eleven, while there is considerable evidence (e.g., from the Canadian province of Quebec) that an earlier start leads to a greater degree of mastery.

75. "Teach Pupils French from Age of Seven."

76. Galton, *Crisis,* 37–40, 43, 48.

77. Gillian Shephard, "Department for Education and Employment: The Excellence of Grant Maintained Schools," M2 Communications (wire service), March 11, 1997.

78. David Charter, "School Admission Appeals Increase 160 Percent in Six Years," *The (London) Times,* August 7, 1996, General British News.

79. Part II, Chapter 1, section 22, paragraph 4 of the Schools and Standards Bill states: "In the case of a foundation, voluntary controlled or foundation special school, the local education authority's duty to maintain the school includes—(a) the duty of defraying all the expenses of maintaining it. . . ." See the Schools and Standards Bill, passed by the House of Commons and introduced to the House of Lords on March 26, 1998; available on-line at: http://www.parliament.the-stationery-office.co.uk/pa/ld199798/ldbills/094/1998094.htm#aofs

80. "Basics Again," *Times Educational Supplement,* September 13, 1996, A22.

81. Diane Hofkins, "Making Sense of the Results," *Times Educational Supplement,* February 2, 1996, 13.

82. "National Results," *The (London) Times,* featured education section, March 10, 1997.

83. A. E. Beaton et al., *Mathematics Achievement in the Primary School Years: The IEA's Third International Mathematics and Science Study (TIMSS)* (Chestnut Hill, MA: Boston College, 1996), 41 (Figure 1.3).

84. A. E. Beaton et al., *Science Achievement in the Primary School Years: The IEA's Third International Mathematics and Science Study (TIMSS)* (Chestnut Hill, MA: Boston College, 1996), 39 (Figure 1.3).

85. At the fourth-grade level, students in Korea, Japan, and the United States had significantly higher scores than those in England. At the eighth-grade level, students in Singapore, the Czech Republic, Japan, and Korea significantly outscored those in England. See Beaton et al., *Science Achievement in the Primary School Years,* 23 (Figure 1.1); and A. E. Beaton et al., *Science Achievement in the Middle School Years: The IEA's Third International Mathematics and Science Study (TIMSS)* (Chestnut Hill, MA: Boston College, 1996), 23 (Figure 1.1).

86. "Basics Again."

87. Tom Gorman and Cres Fernandes, "Reading in Recession: A Report on the 'Comparative Reading Survey' from the National Foundation for Educational Research," Research report, National Foundation for Educational Research, Slough (England); ERIC document no. ED350575.

88. David F. Robitaille, "Achievement Comparisons between the First and Second IEA Studies of Mathematics," *Educational Studies in Mathematics* 21 (1990): 406.

89. Geraldine Hackett, "Primary Maths in Trouble: New Research Suggests 'Trendy' Teaching Methods Do Not Add Up," *Times Educational Supplement,* May 17, 1996, A1.

90. Science trend scores were available for ten countries. See John P. Keeves and A. Schleicher, "Changes in Science Achievement, 1970–84," in *The IEA Study of Science III: Changes in Science Education and Achievement: 1970–1984* (New York: Pergamon Press, 1991), 278.

91. Toby Linden (Interview), "The British Are Coming . . . and Bringing School Reform Lessons," *School Reform News,* May 1998, 16.

92. Phillips, *All Must Have Prizes,* 18–23.

93. John O'Leary, "Church Primaries Are Top of the Class," *The (London) Times,* March 11, 1997, Britain section; and *Times Educational Supplement,* February 14, 1997, A18. See also the works by Coleman and by Bryk, Lee, and Holland cited in notes 30, 36, and 69 of Chapter 8.

94. "Righting Reading: British Children Could and Should Be More Literate," *The (London) Times,* June 4, 1997, leading article.

95. National Center for Education Statistics, *Digest of Education Statistics, 1996* (Washington, DC: U.S. Department of Education, 1996), Table 406.

96. Dennison, *Choice in Education,* 18.

97. Marks and Pomian-Srzednicki, *Standards in English Schools,* 112.

98. CIPO (Gallup Canada) Poll (1993), in E. H. Hastings and P. K. Hastings, *Index to International Public Opinion, 1993–1994* (New York: Greenwood Press, 1994), 90.

99. Mike Crawley, *Schoolyard Bullies: Messing with British Columbia's Education System* (Victoria, BC: Orca Book Publishers, 1995), 118.

100. Andrew Nikiforuk, *School's Out* (Toronto: Macfarlane Walter & Ross, 1993), 79.

101. CIPO (Gallup Canada) Poll (1992), in E. H. Hastings and P. K. Hastings, *Index to International Public Opinion, 1992–1993* (New York: Greenwood Press, 1993), 76.

102. Thomas T. Schweitzer et al., *The State of Education in Canada* (Montreal: The Institute for Research on Public Policy, 1995), 31.

103. Crawley, *Schoolyard Bullies,* 84–85.

104. Shafer Parker, Jr., "Mom and Dad vs. the System," *British Columbia Report,* January 26, 1998.

105. Schweitzer, *State of Education,* 46–47.

106. Bruce W. Wilkinson, *Educational Choice* (Montreal: The Institute for Research on Public Policy, 1994), 19.

107. Organization for Economic Cooperation and Development (OECD), *Literacy, Economy, and Society* (Paris: OECD Publications, 1995), 152–53.

108. Parker, "Mom and Dad."

109. The OECD defined the literacy scales as follows: prose literacy—the knowledge and skills needed to understand and use information from texts, including editorials, news stories, poems, and fiction; document literacy—the knowledge and skills required to locate and use information contained in various formats, including job applications, payroll forms, transportation schedules, maps, tables, and graphics. On the prose scale, 26 percent of immigrants achieved level 4 or 5, while only 21.8 percent of native-born Canadians did the same. On the document scale, the percentages were 28.3 and 24.2, respectively. Note that Canadian immigrants were also more than twice as likely to be found in the very lowest level of literacy, as was the case in every other nation for which the OECD had data. See OECD, *Literacy, Economy, and Society,* 155.

110. Parker, "Mom and Dad."

111. Calculated from the rate of spending growth (presented in constant 1981 dollars) and the figure for 1990–1991 spending shown in Stephen B. Lawton, *Busting Bureaucracy to Reclaim Our Schools* (Montreal: The Institute for Research on Public Policy, 1995), 109, 111.

112. Ibid., 28.

113. Robert K. Crocker, "Thomas Schweitzer's Report Card on the State of Education in Canada: A Commentary on Making the Grade," in Schweitzer et al., *The State of Education in Canada* (*supra* note 102), 111.

114. Quoted in Parker, "Mom and Dad."

115. Quoted in Alison Prentice, *The School Promoters: Education and Social Class in Mid-Nineteenth Century Upper Canada* (Toronto: McClelland and Stewart, 1988), 170.

116. Quoted in Neil McDonald, "Egerton Ryerson and the School as an Agent of Political Socialization," in Neil McDonald and Alf Chaiton, eds., *Egerton Ryerson and His Times* (Toronto: Macmillan Company of Canada, 1978), 84.

117. Quoted in ibid.

118. Ibid., 89.

119. Prentice, *The School Promoters,* 178.

120. Quoted in McDonald, "Egerton Ryerson," 94.

121. Quoted in ibid., 85.

122. Prentice, *The School Promoters*, 56.

123. Harvey J. Graff, "The Reality behind the Rhetoric: The Social and Economic Meanings of Literacy in the Mid-Nineteenth Century: The Example of Literacy and Criminality," in McDonald and Chaiton, eds., *Egerton Ryerson and His Times*.

124. Prentice, *The School Promoters*, 171.

125. Alison Prentice, "The Public Instructor: Ryerson and the Role of Public School Administrator," in McDonald and Chaiton, eds., *Egerton Ryerson and His Times*, 132.

126. Graff, "Reality behind the Rhetoric," 215.

127. Prentice, *The School Promoters*, 16.

128. Ibid., 159.

129. Ibid., 158, 164.

130. Paul Axelrod, *The Promise of Schooling: Education in Canada, 1800–1914* (Toronto: University of Toronto, 1997), 36. Note that I have cited Axelrod's attendance figures because I was unable to find enrollment figures for the given period.

131. Nikiforuk, *School's Out*, 62–63.

132. Geraldine Gilliss, "The Grade Is Made If One Looks at the Data Carefully," in Schweitzer et al., *The State of Education in Canada*, 120.

133. Prentice, *The School Promoters*, 156; and Lawton, *Busting Bureaucracy*, 16–17, 32.

134. Bill 160, second reading, available on-line at: http://www.ontla.on.ca/journals/bills/b160rp_e.htm; and Wendy McCann, "Voting Begins on Massive Changes to Education," *The Calgary Herald Online*, National News, November 16, 1997; available on-line at: http://www.southam.com/calgaryherald

135. Peter Small and Donovan Vincent, "Show of Strength before Talks with Snobclen," *The Toronto Star*, Greater Toronto section, October 7, 1997.

136. Editorial, "The Failed Promise of Schoolboard Democracy," *The Globe and Mail*, November 8, 1997; available on-line at: http://www.theglobeandmail.com/docs/news/19971108/Editorial/EBOARD.html

137. Rhéal Séguin, "Quebec Shifts School Powers: Parents, Teachers Get Greater Say," *The Globe and Mail*, November 14, 1997.

138. Norman Henchey and Donald A. Burgess, *Between Past and Future: Quebec Education in Transition* (Calgary, Alberta: Detselig Enterprises Ltd., 1987), 80.

139. This is a necessary simplification of twenty-five years worth of complex, festering political and public debate.

140. Henchey and Burgess, *Between Past and Future*, 81–82.

141. Crawley, *Schoolyard Bullies*, 19.

142. Ibid., 92.

143. Susan Balcom, "Teacher Union Challenges Trustees over Plans for 'Traditional' School," *The Vancouver Sun*, June 3, 1994, A1; and Crawley, *Schoolyard Bullies*, 141.

144. Balcom, "Teacher Union Challenges Trustees," A1.

145. Crawley, *Schoolyard Bullies*, 141.

146. Susan Balcom, "Surrey's 'Traditional School' Stirs Demands in Other Cities," *The Vancouver Sun,* November 22, 1994, B1.
147. Petti Fong, "Burnaby Split on Merits of 'Traditional School'," *The Vancouver Sun,* December 16, 1994, B1.
148. British Columbia Ministry of Education, "Prescribed Learning Outcomes," in *Instructional Resource Package for English Language Arts, Grades K to 1*; available on-line at: http://www.est.gov.bc.ca/curriculum/irps/elak7/k1comstr.htm
149. British Columbia Ministry of Education, "Comprehend and Respond (Strategies and Skills)," in *Instructional Resource Package for English Language Arts, Grades K to 1*; available on-line at: http://www.est.gov.bc.ca/curriculum/irps/elak7/k1comstr.htm
150. British Columbia Ministry of Education, "Comprehend and Respond (Strategies and Skills)," in *Instructional Resource Package for English Language Arts, Grades 2 to 3*; available on-line at: http://www.est.gov.bc.ca/curriculum/irps/elak7/23comstr.htm
151. Marvin L. Simner, *Beginning Reading Instruction: A Position Paper on Beginning Reading Instruction in Canadian Schools* (Ottawa: Canadian Psychological Association, 1993).
152. Saskatchewan Department of Education, "Instructional Guidelines: Spelling and Phonics in Context," in *English Language Arts: A Curriculum Guide for the Elementary Level,* 1992, emphasis in the original; available on-line at: http://www.sasked.gov.sk.ca/docs/ela/ela_onic.html
153. Saskatchewan Department of Education, "Instruction: Guided Reading and Thinking," in ibid.; available on-line at: http://www.sasked.gov.sk.ca/docs/ela/ela_guid.html
154. Marvin L. Simner, Canadian Psychological Association, personal communication, 1998.

Chapter 8. The Class Really Is Keener on the Other Side: The Case of Independent Schools

1. Drew Lindsay, "PepsiCo Backs Off Voucher Plan in Jersey City," *Education Week*, November 15, 1995, 3.
2. National Center for Education Statistics (NCES), *Digest of Education Statistics, 1995* (Washington, DC: U.S. Department of Education, 1995), 11. This table lists the ratio of private versus public school students, which is about 1 out of 9.
3. See Edith McArthur, Kelly W. Colopy, and Beth Schlaline, "Use of School Choice Educational Policy Issues, Statistical Perspectives [Revised]," National Center for Education Statistics, 1995; ERIC document no. ED387859.
4. Ibid.
5. John J. Convey, "Parental Choice of Catholic Schools as a Function of Religion, Race, and Family Income," Research report presented at the Annual Meeting of the American Educational Research Association, San Francisco, CA, April 16–20, 1986, 5; ERIC document no. ED269542.

6. McArthur, Colopy, and Schlaline, "Use of School Choice."

7. Richard Whitmire, "Number of Home-Schooled Kids Growing Rapidly," *Gannett News Service,* July 24, 1996, S12.

8. Sarah B. Edwards and William M. Richardson, "A Survey of MCPS Withdrawals to Attend Private School," Research report, 1981; available in the ERIC microfiche archives, E-2; ERIC document no. ED226096.

9. See, for example, Carnegie Foundation for the Advancement of Teaching, *School Choice: A Special Report* (Princeton, NJ: Carnegie Foundation for the Advancement of Teaching, 1992); Jonathan Kozol, "Flaming Folly," *The Executive Educator* 14, no. 6 (1992): 14–19; Henry M. Levin, "The Economics of Educational Choice," *Economics of Education Review* 10, no. 2 (1991): 137–58; and Rebecca S. Payne, "Poverty Limits School Choice in Urban Settings," *Urban Education* 28, no. 3 (1993): 281–99.

10. Convey, "Parental Choice," 5.

11. Patricia A. Bauch, "Can Poor Parents Make Wise Educational Choices?" in William Lowe Boyd and James G. Cibulka, eds., *Private Schools and Public Policy: International Perspectives* (New York: Falmer Press, 1989), 298.

12. Virgil C. Blum, "Why Inner-City Families Send Their Children to Private Schools: An Empirical Study," in Edward M. Gaffney, Jr., ed., *Private Schools and the Public Good* (Notre Dame, IN: University of Notre Dame Press, 1981), 19.

13. Seventeen percent of families earning less than $15,000 already choose their children's schools, as compared to 19 percent of families earning between $30,001 and $50,000. See McArthur, Colopy, and Schlaline, "Use of School Choice."

14. The program was open to families earning less than 1.75 times the national poverty line, to be exact.

15. John F. Witte and Christopher A. Thorn, *The Milwaukee Parental Choice Program, 1995* [computer file] (Madison, WI: Data and Program Library Service [distributor], 1995), Tables 4 and 5.

16. This prohibition is in place pending a U.S. Supreme Court ruling on the constitutionality of a proposed expansion of the program that would permit the participation of religious schools.

17. The three programs studied were Partners Advancing Values in Education (PAVE), operating alongside the public voucher program in Milwaukee; the Children's Educational Opportunity (CEO) Foundation in San Antonio, Texas; and the Educational Choice Charitable Trust (ECCT) program in Indianapolis, Indiana.

18. Janet R. Beales and Maureen Wahl, "Private Vouchers in Milwaukee: The PAVE Program," in Terry Moe, ed., *Private Vouchers* (Stanford, CA: Hoover Institution Press, 1995), 56; Valerie Martinez, Kenneth Godwin, and Frank R. Kemerer, "Private Vouchers in San Antonio: The CEO Program," in ibid., 90; and Michael Heise, Kenneth D. Colburn, Jr., and Joseph F. Lamberti, "Private Vouchers in Indianapolis: The Golden Rule Program," in ibid., 111.

19. David J. Weinschrott and Sally B. Kilgore, "Educational Choice Charitable Trust: An Experiment in School Choice," *Hudson Briefing Paper* no. 189, Special Report on School Choice, 1996, 9–10.

20. McArthur, Colopy, and Schlaline, "Use of School Choice." Note that school choices of African-American families tend to be concentrated within the public

sector rather than the private sector, while the reverse is true of whites. This difference can be attributed chiefly to demographics and income disparities between the races. Because the African-American population is more strongly concentrated in urban districts, which offer more public school choice opportunities, choosing a public school is a more commonly available option for African-American families, and since African-American household incomes are lower on average than those of whites, the financial burden of independent school tuition can only be carried by a smaller percentage of African-American families.

21. Convey, "Parental Choice," 5.
22. In 1994, the breakdown of U.S. educational attainment of persons twenty-five years old and over was as follows: Not a high-school graduate, 19.1 percent; High-school graduate, 34.4 percent; Some college but no degree, 17.4 percent; Some kind of college degree, 29.2 percent. (Does not add up to exactly 100 percent due to rounding error.) These figures were adapted from U.S. Bureau of the Census, *Statistical Abstract of the United States, 1995* (Washington, DC: U.S. Bureau of the Census, 1995), Table 240, 158.

    In the Milwaukee public voucher program, the average educational attainment of parents of applicants over the years 1990 to 1994 was as follows: Not a high-school graduate, 29.7 percent; High-school graduate, 22.4 percent; Some college but no degree, 39.8 percent; Some kind of college degree, 8.1 percent. (Does not add up to exactly 100 percent due to rounding error.) These overall figures were obtained by calculating a weighted average from the male and female head-of-household data reported in Witte and Thorn, *Milwaukee Parental Choice Program,* Table 5e.

    For the Milwaukee private voucher program, the 1992–93 figures were: Not a high-school graduate, 20 percent; High-school graduate, 25 percent; Some college but no degree, 46 percent; Some kind of college degree, 10 percent. See Beales and Wahl, "Private Vouchers in Milwaukee," 53.

    In the San Antonio program, the percentages for 1992 were: Not a high-school graduate, 13.5; High-school graduate, 32.5; Some college but no degree, 45; Some kind of college degree, 9.5. (These are averages of the separate figures given for men and women.) See Martinez et al., "Private Vouchers in San Antonio," 85.

    For the Indianapolis program, the figures for 1992–93 were: Not a high-school graduate, 9 percent; High-school graduate or General Equivalency Diploma, 35.5 percent; Some college but no degree, 45 percent; Some kind of college degree, 10.5 percent. See Heise et al., "Private Vouchers in Indianapolis," 107.

    Also note that among college graduates, a much higher percentage of the general public attained an advanced degree than was the case with voucher program participants.

23. Nina Shokraii, "Free at Last, Black America Signs up for School Choice," *Policy Review,* November/December 1996, 26.
24. Susan Vogel, *Working Parents' Guide to San Francisco Private Elementary Schools* (San Francisco, CA: Pince Nez Press, 1996).
25. Janis Griffith, "Small Private Schools in South Wales," in Geoffrey Walford, ed., *Private Schooling: Tradition, Change, and Diversity* (London: Paul Chapman Publishing, 1991), 85, 95–96, 93.

26. Máirtín Mac an Ghaill, "Black Voluntary Schools: The 'Invisible' Private Sector," in ibid., 133–36.

27. See, for example, Maria Montessori, *The Advanced Montessori Method*, 2 volumes (New York: Schocken Books, 1989).

28. David Schlesinger, "Frequently Asked Questions about Waldorf Education," The Waldorf Education mailing list, on-line at: http://www.io.com/~lefty/Waldorf_ FAQ.html

29. National Center for Education Statistics (NCES), *Digest of Education Statistics, 1995* (Washington, DC: U.S. Department of Education, 1995), Table 26, 31.

30. James Coleman and Thomas Hoffer, *Public and Private High Schools: The Impact of Communities* (New York: Basic Books, 1987), 54–55. As noted elsewhere, Coleman's figures on "high-profile" private schools are omitted from consideration due to the small data set available.

31. Witte and Thorn, *The Milwaukee Parental Choice Program*, Table 6, scales A2, A3, and A4.

32. Otto F. Kraushaar, *American Non-Public Schools: Patterns of Diversity* (Baltimore, MD: Johns Hopkins University Press, 1972), 93.

33. Stephen Broughman, *Private School Universe Survey, 1993–94* (Washington, DC: National Center for Education Statistics, 1996), Table 12 (NCES publication no. 96-143).

34. NCES, *Digest, 1995*, Table 94, 104.

35. Ibid., Table 26, 31.

36. Anthony S. Bryk, Valerie E. Lee, and Peter B. Holland, *Catholic Schools and the Common Good* (Cambridge, MA: Harvard University Press, 1993), 286.

37. Ibid., 128–29.

38. James G. Cibulka, Timothy J. O'Brien, and Donald Zewe, S.J., *Inner-City Private Elementary Schools: A Study* (Milwaukee, WI: Marquette University Press, 1982), 137.

39. Bryk, Lee, and Holland, *Catholic Schools*, 130.

40. Valerie E. Lee, Robert F. Dedrick, and Julia B. Smith, "The Effect of the Social Organization of Schools on Teachers' Efficacy and Satisfaction," *Sociology of Education* 64 (1991): 190–208.

41. Pearl R. Kane, "Public or Independent Schools: Does Where You Teach Make a Difference?" *Phi Delta Kappan*, December 1987, 289.

42. Ibid., 288.

43. National Center for Education Statistics (NCES), *Digest of Education Statistics, 1997* (Washington, DC: U.S. Department of Education, 1997), 82.

44. Kane, "Public or Independent Schools," 287–88.

45. Susan Moore Johnson, *Teachers at Work: Achieving Success in Our Schools* (New York: Basic Books, 1990), 219.

46. Ibid., 221.

47. Ibid., 220.

48. Kraushaar, *American Non-Public Schools*, 163.

49. David Boaz, "The Public School Monopoly: America's Berlin Wall," in Boaz, ed., *Liberating Schools: Education in the Inner City* (Washington, DC: Cato Institute, 1991), 17.

50. The Baltimore Archdiocese served 34,000 students in 101 schools in 1996, as compared to 36,000 students in 51 schools in the Hartford County public system. Cited in David Boaz and Morris Barrett, "What Would a School Voucher Buy? The Real Cost of Private Schools," *Cato Institute Briefing Papers*, no. 25 (March 26, 1996), 6.

51. NCES, *Digest, 1995*, Tables 87 and 91, 95–101.

52. Robert J. Kealey, *Balance Sheet for Catholic Elementary Schools: 1993 Income and Expenses* (Washington, DC, National Catholic Education Association, 1994), 18.

53. Bryk, Lee, and Holland, *Catholic Schools*, 103.

54. Ibid., 116.

55. Coleman and Hoffer, *Public and Private High Schools*, 49.

56. Kraushaar, *American Non-Public Schools*, 281.

57. Consider fads discussed in earlier chapters, such as look-say reading instruction, open classrooms, the "New Math," outcomes-based education, the "new New Math," whole language, etc.

58. Bryk, Lee, and Holland, *Catholic Schools*, 124.

59. Letter from Robert J. Kealey sent to the author on May 16, 1996.

60. Liva Baker, *The Second Battle of New Orleans* (New York: Harper Collins, 1996), 449–50.

61. Gary Orfield, *Must We Bus?* (Washington, DC: The Brookings Institution, 1978), 59.

62. David J. Armor, *Forced Justice: School Desegregation and the Law* (New York: Oxford University Press, 1995), 174–94.

63. Orfield, *Must We Bus?*, 60.

64. Armor, *Forced Justice*, 179.

65. James Zafirau and Margaret Fleming, *A Study of Discrepant Reading Achievement of Minority and White Students in a Desegregating School District: Phase IV* (Cleveland, OH: Cleveland Public Schools, Department of Research and Analysis, 1982).

66. Kraushaar, *American Non-Public Schools*, 238.

67. Broughman, *Private School Universe Survey*, 3.

68. David J. Dent, "African-Americans Turning to Christian Academies," *New York Times Education Life*, August 4, 1996.

69. James Coleman, "Predicting the Consequences of Policy Changes: The Case of Public and Private Schools," in Coleman, *Equality and Achievement in Education* (Boulder, CO: Westview Press, 1990), 255–56.

70. Jay P. Greene, "Integration Where It Counts: A Study of Racial Integration in Public and Private School Lunchrooms," paper presented to the American Political Science Association, Boston, September 1998.

71. NCES, *Digest, 1995*, Tables 60 and 163.

72. Kealey, *Balance Sheet for Catholic Elementary Schools*, 15–17.

73. On Catholic-school per-pupil costs, see ibid., 18; on the relationship between school size and costs, see Allan C. Ornstein, "School Size and Effectiveness: Policy Implications," *Urban Review* 22 (1990): 239–45.

74. *Peterson's Private Secondary Schools: 1996–97* (Princeton, NJ: Peterson's, 1996), 754–55.

75. See, for example, Jonathan Kozol, *Savage Inequalities: Children in America's Schools* (New York: HarperPerennial, 1992).
76. J. R. Campbell et al., *NAEP 1994 Reading Report Card for the Nation and the States* (Washington, DC: NCES, U.S. Department of Education, 1996), 33.
77. Coleman and Hoffer, *Public and Private High Schools,* 59–60.
78. While Coleman (in ibid.) reported results for non-Catholic private schools, he made it clear from the beginning of his study that "[w]ith respect to the effect of other private schools, we agree with the critics' point that the High School and Beyond (HSB) sample was sufficiently flawed (because of small size, possible bias due to some school refusals to participate in the research, and the heterogeneity of the population of non-Catholic private schools) that no strong inferences could be made about achievement effects of this sector" (ibid., 60).
79. Ibid., 92.
80. Bryk, Lee, and Holland, *Catholic Schools,* 245.
81. Ibid., 262–63.
82. Ibid., 246–47.
83. Jay P. Greene, Paul E. Peterson, and Jiangtao Du, with Leesa Boeger and Curtis L. Frazier, "The Effectiveness of School Choice in Milwaukee: A Secondary Analysis of Data from the Program's Evaluation," Harvard University Occasional Paper 96-3, August 1996, 4.

    Note that earlier studies conducted by John Witte and his colleagues (see note 15 above), the researchers appointed by the public school system to assess the effects of private school choice, did not find any academic gains due to participation. Unfortunately, Witte did not compare accepted choice applicants with rejected ones, as did the study by Greene et al. Instead, Witte compared accepted choice applicants with a subset of the local public school population who had not applied for participation. This has been described as comparing apples to oranges by several commentators, and clearly does not represent as sound a control group as the one used by Greene et al. Witte's results are thus suspect and are therefore not treated here.
84. Cecilia Elena Rouse, "Private School Vouchers and Student Achievement: An Evaluation of the Milwaukee Parental Choice Program," working paper, May 1997.
85. Weinschrott and Kilgore, "Educational Choice Charitable Trust," 15.
86. Jay P. Greene, William G. Howell, Paul E. Peterson, "An Evaluation of the Cleveland Scholarship Program," Research report, Harvard Program on Education Policy and Governance, September 1997, 43–44.
87. "IU Study Shows No First-Year Difference in Achievement between Voucher and Public School Third-Graders in Cleveland Schools," *Indiana University News,* available on-line at: http://www.iuinfo.indiana.edu/ocm/releases/metcalf.htm
88. Paul E. Peterson and Jay P. Greene, "Assessing the Cleveland Scholarship Program: A Guide to the Indiana University School of Education Evaluation," Research report, Harvard Program on Education Policy and Governance, March 31, 1998; available on-line at: http://data.fas.harvard.edu/pepg

    Peterson et al. allege that the Indiana University study improperly excluded most students from consideration, relied on initial test scores that were not credible, applied a statistical technique known to be biased toward underestimating program effects, compared voucher students to above-average public school students, studied too small a sample of students (5 percent), and did not adjust test scores for age or control for key background characteristics of students.

The Indiana University researchers replied to these charges in Kim K. Metcalf, "Advocacy in the Guise of Science," *Education Week,* September 23, 1998, 34. In this reply, lead researcher Metcalf contended that student exclusions were justified on the grounds that the excluded students took different tests, and that the Indiana University researchers did indeed properly consider background characteristics (and that the Harvard study conducted by Peterson et al. did not). Metcalf further argued that the Harvard study used an inappropriate measure of statistical significance which overstated voucher student score gains, and that the selection of this inappropriate measure might imply deliberate bias on the part of the Harvard researchers.

Most recently, the Harvard researchers have published a rebuttal to Metcalf's charges, defending their work and their criticisms of the Indiana University study. This rebuttal appeared as Paul E. Peterson, Jay P. Greene, and William G. Howell, "Good Motives Aren't Sufficient," *Education Week,* October 21, 1998, 37.

89. John E. Chubb and Terry M. Moe, *Politics, Markets, and America's Schools* (Washington, DC: The Brookings Institution, 1990), 259.

90. McArthur, Colopy, and Schlaline, "Use of School Choice," 2.

91. Lowell C. Rose, Alec M. Gallup, and Stanley M. Elam, "The 29th Annual Phi Delta Kappa/Gallup Poll of the Public's Attitudes toward the Public Schools," *Phi Delta Kappan,* September 1997.

92. Weinschrott and Kilgore, "Educational Choice Charitable Trust," 11.

93. Witte and Thorn, *Milwaukee Parental Choice Program,* Table 7; and John F. Witte and Christopher A. Thorn, "Fourth-Year Report: Milwaukee Parental Choice Program," Department of Political Science and the Robert La Follette Institute of Public Affairs, University of Wisconsin–Madison, December 1994, Table 7.

94. Greene, Howell, and Peterson, "Cleveland Scholarship Program," 42–43.

95. Beales and Wahl, "Private Vouchers in Milwaukee," 59; and Witte and Thorn, *Milwaukee Parental Choice Program,* part III.

96. Martinez, Godwin, and Kemerer, "Private Vouchers in San Antonio," 87.

97. Heise, Colburn, and Lamberti, "Private Vouchers in Indianapolis," 115.

98. Coleman and Hoffer, *Public and Private High Schools,* 116–17, 126–29.

99. Ibid., 154, 175.

100. Ibid., 185, 189, 210.

101. Derek Neal, "Measuring Catholic School Performance," *The Public Interest,* Spring 1997, 83.

102. William J. McMillan, *Private School Management* (Fort Lauderdale, FL: Ferguson E. Peters Company, 1979), 119.

103. Ibid., 121.

104. For-profit career training institutions such as these were criticized in the past for preparing students to enter fields already glutted with qualified workers. What these criticisms fail to consider is that the government provided loans to career-

college students freely and indiscriminately. This easily available money eliminated a key incentive for students to determine whether or not there was actually work available in their field of interest. Had students been forced to spend their own money, they no doubt would have been more careful, and had they been obliged to secure loans from private lenders, those lenders would have considered the employment prospects of graduates in various fields in order to assess the likelihood of repayment.

105. An example of this occurred when West Coast University of Los Angeles was forced out of business, in part because of the entry into its market of the highly successful University of Phoenix. See Kim Strosnider, "An Aggressive, For-Profit University Challenges Traditional Colleges Nationwide," *The Chronicle of Higher Education*, June 6, 1997, A32.

106. This occurred when sixteen proprietary schools belonging to National Education Centers were taken over by the thriving new Corinthian Schools corporation. See Alan L. Dessoff, "Private Lessons," *Techniques*, October 1996, 29.

107. Robert Danforth Cole, *Private Secondary Education for Boys in the United States* (Philadelphia: University of Pennsylvania, 1928), 24.

108. Ibid., 93.

109. Merle Curti, *The Social Ideas of American Educators* (Totowa, NJ: Littlefield, Adams, & Co., 1974), 510.

110. Quoted in ibid., 116.

111. For example: National Education Association, "Fighting Privatization: Advice from Athol," *NEA Today*, September 1997, 19. See also Myron Lieberman, *The Teacher Unions* (New York: The Free Press, 1997).

112. Cited in Myron Lieberman, "Public Education: No Risks, No Profits," *Insight on the News*, November 18, 1996, 28.

113. Cole, *Private Secondary Education*, 244.

114. Available on-line at: http://www.fourmilab.ch/ustax/www/t26-A-1-F-I-501.html

115. The $279 billion figure represents total expenditures for public elementary and secondary education for 1994–95. See National Center for Education Statistics, *Digest of Education Statistics, 1997* (Washington, DC: U.S. Department of Education, 1997), Table 163.

116. Estelle James, "The Netherlands: Benefits and Costs of Privatized Public Services—Lessons from the Dutch Educational System," in *Private Education in Ten Countries: Policy and Practice* (London: Routledge, 1989).

Chapter 9. What Makes Schools Work?

1. John Allen, "Church Is at the Center of Voucher Debate," *National Catholic Reporter*, March 28, 1997, 11–12.

2. The case of Socrates (though he was not, strictly speaking, a sophist) provides a famous exception to this generalization. Socrates was tried and sentenced to exile or death for his teachings (and he chose the latter option)—an episode which throws the otherwise free educational practices of the day into sharp relief.

3. Janet R. Beales and Thomas F. Bertonneau, "Do Private Schools Serve Difficult-to-Educate Students?" Research report, Mackinac Center for Public Policy, October 1997; available on-line at: http://www.mackinac.org/studies/s97-03.htm

4. Janet R. Beales, "Educating the Uneducatable," *Wall Street Journal*, August 21, 1996.

5. See Chapter 8, and Dominic J. Brewer, "Principals and Student Outcomes: Evidence from U.S. High Schools," *Economics of Education Review* 12, no. 4 (1993): 281–92.

6. Zachary Montgomery, *The School Question from a Parental and Non-Sectarian Standpoint* (Washington, DC: Gibson Bros., 1886), 56–57.

7. Susan P. Choy et al., *America's Teachers: Profile of a Profession* (Washington, DC: U.S. Department of Education, 1993), 52–53.

8. Gallup and Kettering, "First Annual Gallup Poll," in Stanley M. Elam, *A Decade of Gallup Polls of Attitudes toward Education, 1969–1978* (Bloomington, IN: Phi Delta Kappa, 1978), 20.

Chapter 10. Can Government Schooling Be Fixed?

1. Milton Friedman, *Capitalism and Freedom* (Chicago: The University of Chicago Press, 1982), 89.

2. John Stuart Mill, *On Liberty, and Other Writings* (Cambridge: Cambridge University Press, 1992), 105–8.

3. Thomas Paine, "The Rights of Man," in *The Thomas Paine Reader* (New York: Penguin, 1987), 338.

4. Adam Smith, *An Inquiry into the Nature and Causes of the Wealth of Nations* (New York: The Modern Library, 1994), 877–78. Note that the full text of Smith's section titled "Of the Expense of the Institutions for the Education of Youth" is available on my website (http://www.schoolchoices.org). Simply click on the "Classics" button.

5. Colorado voters rejected a voucher initiative in 1992, as did Californians in 1993, and Washington state voters in 1996. Several other states have also voted down voucher proposals.

6. See Chapter 8.

7. Cheryl Gamble, "Two Schools in Milwaukee Choice Program Close," *Education Week*, February 21, 1996, 3.

8. Peter Schmidt, "Council Moving to Gain More Say over D.C. Schools," *Education Week*, May 3, 1995, 1.

9. District of Columbia Financial Responsibility and Management Assistance Authority, *Children in Crisis* (Washington, DC: The Financial Control Board, 1996).

10. Editorial, "Phantom Students," *Wall Street Journal*, April 8, 1998.

11. "Fraudulent Behavior," *The Economist*, July 26, 1997, 25.

12. Michael Graczyk, Associated Press, "Sting Operation Finds Loophole in New Plan for Welfare Debit Cards," *Seattle Times*, March 27, 1997, A7.

13. California Teachers' Association, "Proposition 174 Is Bad News for Children and

Taxpayers," The CTA's official statement on Proposition 174, reprinted in *Voices on Choice* (San Francisco: Pacific Research Institute for Public Policy, 1994), 50.

14. 413 U.S. 756 (1973).
15. 463 U.S. 388 (1983).
16. Frederick Mark Gedicks, "Religion," in Kermit L. Hall, ed., *The Oxford Companion to the Supreme Court of the United States* (New York: Oxford University Press, 1992), 720–21.
17. Jeffrey J. Kassel, Melanie E. Cohen, Peter Koneazny, Steven R. Shapiro, Steven K. Green, "Brief of Respondents Warner Jackson et al.," No. 95-2153-Oa, January 16, 1996.
18. ACLU, "What He Said: Dane County Circuit Judge Paul Higginbotham's Ruling on the Milwaukee Religious School Voucher Program," January 16, 1997; available on-line at: http://www.aclu.org
19. ACLU, "Wisconsin Appeals Court Strikes School Voucher Plan," August 22, 1997; available on-line at: http://www.aclu.org
20. *Jackson et al. v. Benson et al.,* filed under 213 Wis.2d 1 (1998).
21. 170 Wis. 218, 175 N.W.2d 589 (1919).
22. Quoted in *Jackson et al. v. Benson et al.,* 213 Wis.2d 1 (1998).
23. NEA Center for the Advancement of Public Education, "Vouchers," *In Brief,* November 1996; available on-line at: http://www.nea.org
24. Minnesota Education Association (MNEA), "Private and Religious School Vouchers"; available on-line at: http://www.mnea.org
25. John F. Witte, "Who Benefits from the Milwaukee Choice Program?" in *Who Chooses? Who Loses? Culture, Institutions, and the Unequal Effects of School Choice* (New York: Teachers College Press, 1996), 124.
26. Sari Horwitz and Valerie Strauss, "A Well-Financed Failure," *Washington Post,* February 16, 1997, A1.
27. Anthony S. Bryk, Valerie E. Lee, and Peter B. Holland, *Catholic Schools and the Common Good* (Cambridge, MA: Harvard University Press, 1993).
28. James Coleman, "Predicting the Consequences of Policy Changes: The Case of Public and Private Schools," in Coleman, *Equality and Achievement in Education* (Boulder, CO: Westview Press, 1990), 250–68.
29. NEA Center for the Advancement of Public Education, "Vouchers."
30. MNEA, "Private and Religious School Vouchers."
31. Bob Chase, "Voucher System Would Hurt Schools, Not Help," Statement by the NEA President published in the September 30 [no year given] issue of the *Minneapolis Star*; available on-line at: http://www.nea.org
32. Bryk, Lee, and Holland, *Catholic Schools,* 128.
33. NEA Center for the Advancement of Public Education, "Vouchers."
34. National Center for Education Statistics, *Digest of Education Statistics, 1995* (Washington, DC: U.S. Department of Education, 1995), Tables 60 and 163.
35. Paul Mulshine, "If You Can't Pass This Quiz, Thank the Teachers' Union," *The Sunday Star-Ledger,* December 10, 1995.
36. Edith McArthur et al., "Use of School Choice Educational Policy Issues, Statistical Perspectives [Revised]," National Center for Education Statistics, 1995, ERIC document no. ED387859.

37. U.S. expenditures on public elementary and high-school education totaled $339 billion in 1996–97. Cutting this spending in half would leave a $169 billion savings, less $18 billion for the five million students already attending private school. Net savings would thus be on the order of $150 billion. Based on data from: National Center for Education Statistics, *Digest of Education Statistics, 1997* (Washington, DC: U.S. Department of Education, 1997), Tables 31, 59, and 169.

38. This is a quotation from a document on the CEA website (www.cea.org/ index.html) which has since been removed.

39. NEA Center for the Advancement of Public Education, "Vouchers" (*supra* note 23).

40. Data from the website of the National Conference of State Legislatures, updated June 3, 1998; available on-line at: http://www.ncsl.org/programs/educ/c1schls.htm

41. Bruno V. Manno, Chester E. Finn, Jr., Louann A. Bierlein, and Gregg Vanourek, "Charter School Accountability: Problems and Prospects," in *Charter Schools in Action (A Hudson Institute Project) Final Report* (Indianapolis, IN: Hudson Institute, July 1997), Part IV, 3.

42. Gregg Vanourek, Bruno V. Manno, Chester E. Finn, Jr., Louann A. Bierlein, "Charter Schools as Seen by Those Who Know Them Best: Students, Teachers, and Parents," in ibid., Part I, 1.

43. Section 47602, subdivision (c), of the California Education Code.

44. See, for example, Section 59-40-40, paragraph (1), of the South Carolina Code: "A 'charter school' means a public, nonsectarian, nonreligious, nonhome-based, nonprofit corporation. . . ."

45. Bryan Hassel, "Beyond the Schools: The Charter Idea's Potential for Impact on Public Education," Draft research report, presented at the Harvard Conference on Rethinking School Governance, June 1997.

46. See ibid., and Vanourek et al., "Charter Schools." The quotation at the beginning of the paragraph is from Hassel, "Beyond the Schools."

47. John E. Chubb, "Lessons in School Reform from the Edison Project," paper presented at the Harvard Conference on Rethinking School Governance, June 1997, 26.

48. U.S. Bureau of the Census, *Statistical Abstract of the United States, 1995* (Washington, DC: Bureau of the Census, 1995), Table 897.

49. Other factors, such as a long-term bid for increased market share (even at the cost of near-term losses), are also at play. Consult the economist or businessperson nearest you for further details.

50. If quality did drop, then the likelihood of successfully attracting additional customers would be greatly reduced.

51. Information on Kumon's approach can be found on its website (www.kumon.com).

52. Kenneth J. Freeman, *The Schools of Hellas* (New York: Teachers College Press, 1904), 58–59.

53. Chester Finn, Bruno Manno, and Louann Bierlein, *Charter Schools in Action: What Have We Learned?* (Indianapolis, IN: Hudson Institute, 1996), section 3.

54. Caroline Hendrie, "Milwaukee Will Let High Schools Pick Their Students," *Education Week,* September 3, 1997, 3.

55. Beth Reinhard, "California Opens Single Sex Academies," *Education Week,* September 10, 1997, 1.

56. Massachusetts Education Reform Act of 1993 (Charter School Section), Chapter 71, Section 89, part (h), paragraph 3.

57. Richard J. Murnane et al., *Who Will Teach?* (Cambridge, MA: Harvard University Press, 1991), 89.

58. Massachusetts Education Reform Act of 1993 (Charter School Section), Chapter 71, Section 89, part (h), paragraphs 10–11; Arizona Revised Statutes, Chapter 1, Article 8, Section 15-187.

59. Blanket provisions to this effect exist in Alaska, Arkansas, and Rhode Island. Wisconsin requires all its charter schools, except those in Milwaukee, to abide by union contracts. Georgia enforces collective bargaining agreements on charter schools unless this requirement is expressly waived in the particular charter contract. New Jersey and South Carolina require all public schools which convert to charter schools to continue to follow union contracts, whereas these states do not impose this requirement on charter schools started from scratch. See Paul Berman and Karen Seashore Louis, *A Study of Charter Schools: First Year Report* (Washington, DC: U.S. Department of Education, 1997); available on-line at: http://www.ed.gov/pubs/studies.html

60. Vanourek et al., "Charter Schools as Seen by Those Who Know Them Best," 1.

61. Carol Ascher, Norm Fruchter, and Robert Berne, *Hard Lessons: Public Schools and Privatization* (New York: Twentieth Century Fund, 1996), 26.

62. David Tyack and Larry Cuban, *Tinkering toward Utopia* (Cambridge, MA: Harvard University Press, 1995), 120.

63. Myron Lieberman, *Privatization and Educational Choice* (New York: St. Martin's Press, 1989), ch. 4.

64. Ascher, Fruchter, and Berne, *Hard Lessons,* 33.

65. Ibid., 34.

66. Mark Walsh, "Judge's Ruling Could End School-Privatization Venture," *Education Week,* September 3, 1997, 15.

67. Mark Walsh, "Hartford Ousts EAI in Dispute over Finances," *Education Week,* January 31, 1996, 1, 9.

68. Reuters Chicago newsdesk, "Education Alternatives <EAIN.O> Reach . . . ," July 1, 1996.

69. Reuters News Service, June 17, 1997.

70. Reuters Chicago newsdesk, "Education Alternatives <EAIN.O> Sets Contract Rules," February 6, 1996.

71. Reuters News Service, June 17, 1997.

72. Diane Ravitch, *National Standards in American Education: A Citizen's Guide* (Washington, DC: The Brookings Institution, 1995), 25.

73. Richard M. Wolf, "National Standards: Do We Need Them?" (forthcoming).

74. Ravitch, *National Standards,* 5.

75. Quoted in Walter R. Mears, "Politics Hit the Schoolhouse Door," *AP Analysis & News in Review,* September 30, 1997.

76. See, for instance, the Internet website of the group "Mathematically Correct" (http://ourworld.compuserve.com/homepages/mathman/). See also the website of "Where's the Math?" (http://206.86.183.194/math/default.htm).

77. Stephen Arons, *Short Route to Chaos* (Amherst, MA: University of Massachusetts Press, 1997), 15–20.
78. E. D. Hirsch, *The Schools We Need and Why We Don't Have Them* (New York: Doubleday, 1996), 229.
79. David Charter, "Tests at Seven Show Gap between Schools," *The (London) Times,* January 27, 1997, General News section.
80. James A. Kulik, *An Analysis of the Research on Ability Grouping: Historical and Contemporary Perspectives* (Storrs, CT: National Research Center on the Gifted and Talented, The University of Connecticut, 1992); available in the ERIC microfiche archives; ERIC document no. ED350777.
81. Carl F. Kaestle, *Pillars of the Republic* (New York: Hill and Wang, 1983), 163.
82. Harold Rugg, *An Introduction to Problems of American Culture* (Boston: Ginn and Company, 1933), 217.
83. Quoted in David France, "This Lesson Is Brought to You By . . ." *Good Housekeeping,* February 1996, 82.
84. Ibid., 80.
85. See Chapter 5, and Frances Fitzgerald, *America Revised* (New York: Vintage Books, 1980).
86. John Lawson and Harold Silver, *A Social History of Education in England* (London: Butler & Tanner Ltd., 1973), 290.
87. "Teach Pupils French from Age of Seven," *The (London) Times,* May 29, 1997, General News section.
88. A rigorous course of academic studies, for example, is more strongly encouraged in the private sector. See Chapter 8.

Conclusion: Achieving Educational Excellence

1. It is important to realize that public schools and school districts also receive private donations of both cash and goods (such as computers) on a regular basis. The figure for per-pupil spending in public schools is from National Center for Education Statistics, *Digest of Education Statistics, 1997* (Washington, DC: U.S. Department of Education, 1997), Table 169.
2. Since individuals who never have children make up a comparatively small percentage of the population, they are omitted from the present brief discussion of the issues. A more in-depth analysis should factor-in this group.
3. Of the 5,496 senior high schools that existed in Japan in 1997, 1,315 were privately owned and operated. See Research and Statistics Planning Division, Minister's Secretariat, Ministry of Education, Science, and Culture, "School Basic Survey," December 22, 1997. Available on-line at: http://www.jinjapan.org/stat/stats/16EDU24.html. For data on enrollment of seventeen-year-olds, see Organization for Economic Cooperation and Development (OECD), *Education at a Glance* (Paris: OECD Publications, 1995), 135.
4. Personal communication.
5. Marvin Olasky, *The Tragedy of American Compassion* (Washington, DC: Regnery Publishing, Inc., 1992), 111.

6. Ibid., 107.

7. Lloyd P. Jorgenson, *The State and the Non-Public School, 1825–1925* (Columbia, MO: University of Missouri Press, 1987), 139.

8. Ibid.

9. Memo from Robert S. Peck, ACLU Legal Counsel, regarding a proposed Private School Choice Demonstration Amendment, January 22, 1992. Available on-line at the ACLU's website (www.aclu.org).

10. Of course, if taxpayers could receive exemptions by donating to scholarship organizations of their choosing, then no citizen would be forced to contribute to a religious school or charity, so the Wisconsin-style prohibition against forced subsidization of sectarian institutions (discussed in Chapter 10) would not apply.

11. Part A—General Provisions, Section 601 (d) 1 (A), Individuals with Disabilities Education Act Amendments of 1997. Available on-line at: http://www.ed.gov/offices/OSERS/IDEA/the_law.html

12. See Chapter 6, and Diane McGuiness, *Why Our Children Can't Read—And What We Can Do about It: A Scientific Revolution in Reading* (New York: The Free Press, 1997).

13. Agency fees are "fees that nonmembers of a union must pay to the union as a condition of employment. Refusal to pay requires the employer to fire the employee. Nineteen states either mandate agency fees or allow teacher unions to bargain over the issue." Myron Lieberman, *The Teacher Unions* (New York: The Free Press, 1997), 172.

14. John S. Earle, Roman Frydman, Andrzej Rapaczynski, and Joel Turkewitz, *Small Privatization* (Budapest: Central European University Press, 1994), xxvii.

15. Ibid., xxviii.

16. Sunita Kikeri, John Nellis, and Mary Shirley, *Privatization: The Lessons of Experience* (Washington, DC: The World Bank, 1992), 8.

17. Ibid., 1.

18. Ibid.

19. Carol Ascher, Norm Fructer, and Robert Berne, *Hard Lessons: Public Schools and Privatization* (New York: Twentieth Century Fund, 1996), 9.

20. See Chapter 8.

Index

About the Author

Andrew J. Coulson, a Seattle-based writer and editor, is a Senior Research Associate of the Social Philosophy and Policy Center. He has written a variety of articles on school governance and the history of education, and is currently the editor of *School Choices,* an Internet website (www.schoolchoices.org) intended to foster informed public debate on education reform. He is a member of the editorial board of the *Education Policy Analysis Archives,* which is edited and published at Arizona State University. Prior to dedicating himself to the study of education policy, he was a computer software engineer with Microsoft Corporation.